THE POWER
OF THE PURSE

Appropriations Politics
in Congress

THE POWER
OF THE PURSE

Appropriations Politics
in Congress

RICHARD F. FENNO, JR., University of Rochester

Little, Brown and Company BOSTON AND TORONTO

To Mark and Craig

Acknowledgments

During my six years of research and writing on appropriations politics in Congress, I have accumulated nearly as many debts as I have data. Anyone doing a sizeable amount of interviewing in Washington becomes uniquely dependent upon other people for the quality of his product. He needs legislators and executives to talk with. He needs friends to make the Washington environment congenial and comprehensible. He needs experienced hands to help him gain access and avoid mistakes. He needs academic colleagues in and out of Washington to help him maintain perspective. He needs university and/or foundation support to help solve problems of time and travel. I have been particularly fortunate in every respect. And I want to take this opportunity to acknowledge my indebtedness to a number of benefactors — for their good will, good advice, interest, patience, hospitality, and support. There might have been a *Power of the Purse* without them; but few readers, I am sure, would have judged it worth the effort. None of these people can be held responsible for the deficiencies of the book, but they deserve considerable credit for such merits as it may possess.

Since the bulk of my 170-odd interviews were held under conditions of promised anonymity, the people who did most to help me write this book — members of the House and Senate Appropriations Committees, committee and personal staff members, other Representatives, other Senators, and officials of the executive branch — will have to accept my deepest thanks in an equally anonymous fashion. Two members of the House Committee will not, I hope, mind if I acknowledge an especially large debt to them. Representative Edward P. Boland and former Representative Harold C. Ostertag encouraged, supported, and assisted me in every phase of my research — to an extent that they may not themselves have appreciated. The help received from them was equalled, in spirit if not in authority, by the members of their respective staffs — most particularly, by two good friends, Joseph Donoghue and Harry Nicholas, who helped me to understand and to savor life on Capitol Hill. I want to thank, also, Joan Campbell, Ann Creighton, Agnes Anilian, Jane Borth, Helen Demory, Lois Romjue, and Sharon Wells for the countless times they gave me their cheerful welcome and their cheerful assistance. And I am much indebted to Martin Sweig for his sympathetic and valuable support.

Charles Clapp has been a source of advice and aid from the beginning to the end of the project. He has endured my impositions on his time and hospitality with inexhaustible kindness; and I remain greatly in his debt. Among my other academic colleagues, Donald Matthews and James Robinson were especially helpful in sharing their interviewing experiences with me at the outset of my research, and they have responded thoughtfully to my inquiries ever since.

I am indebted, generally, to Ralph Huitt whose writing on Congress has been both model and inspiration for me. And I owe a more particular debt to three knowledgeable and generous friends — Robert Peabody, Nelson Polsby, and H. Douglas Price. Each has given the entire manuscript a careful reading; and, collectively, they have saved me from many embarrassments of interpretation, fact and style. I acknowledge a special debt to my colleague Gerald Kramer for his expert counsel concerning the materials in Chapter Eight. Others who have helped with various parts of the manuscript include Lewis Froman, Harold Kaplan, Seymour Scher, and Aaron Wildavsky. Three of my students, Janice Plotkin, Alan Stern, and James Murphy, have assisted me, too, in a variety of ways.

For their crucial financial support I gratefully acknowledge the generosity of the Social Science Research Council, the Rockefeller Foundation, and the Committee on Grants-in-aid of the University of Rochester.

The lion's share of the manuscript typing was done, expertly and cheerfully, by Marguerite Gross — with assistance from Loretta Forbes, Mildred Verblaw, and Ellen Foxman. The editorial staff at Little, Brown and Company, especially Donald Hammonds, has been a constant source of good judgment. My thanks, also, to David Giele, Mary Louise Morse, Freda Alexander and Josephine Emerson for their expert editing of the manuscript.

Not only has my wife helped to carry the author's burdens, but she has buoyantly borne the burden of the author himself. But for her support, there would have been no book.

Contents

Introduction

The power of the purse is the historic bulwark of legislative authority. The exercise of that power constitutes the core legislative process — underpinning all other legislative decisions and regulating the balance of influence between the legislative and executive branches of government. In the United States, Congress wields the power of the purse under the constitutional provision which states that "no money shall be drawn from the treasury but in consequence of appropriations made by law." The sixteen-word injunction is strikingly straightforward and simple. But its brevity belies the complexity of the process by which money is taken from the Treasury and allocated among the agencies and activities of government — state and local as well as national — by the House of Representatives and the Senate. Scarcely a political relationship exists, inside Congress or between Congress and the executive branch, for which a prototype cannot be found somewhere in the labyrinth of appropriations activity. This is a book about that critical and complicated process.

The aims of the book are threefold. In order of their likely relevance and persuasiveness for the reader they are: first, to provide an empirical description of the contemporary appropriations process in Congress: second, to demonstrate the importance of committee-centered analysis for increasing an understanding of Congress; and third, to suggest the usefulness of certain bits of theory for students of Congress and its committees. Taken together, these three aims have dictated the book's organizational structure, its conceptual apparatus, and its research techniques. By way of introduction to the study, therefore, it seems appropriate to discuss these aims and some of their more basic consequences.

APPROPRIATIONS DESCRIPTION

The stated goal of producing an empirical description of the contemporary appropriations process underlines the fact that the primary purpose of the book is a substantive one. The interests of the author, that is to say, are dominantly subject-matter interests rather than theoretical or methodological ones. The book seeks, above all, to increase knowledge and understanding of all those relationships affecting congressional decisions to allocate federal revenues among the multiplicity of official claimants. Generalizations emphasizing the importance of such decisions have become textbook staples, and they need no belaboring here. But the fact of their significance serves to remind us that, good, bad, or indifferent, this is a book about an important political subject.

The Power of the Purse is certainly not the first description of appropriations politics in Congress. It is a successor, and hence a beneficiary, of numerous empirical studies. Especially helpful among these have been the seminal articles of Arthur Macmahon,[1] the general analyses of Dwaine Marvick[2] and Robert Ash Wallace,[3] the more specialized studies of Elias Huzar[4] and Earle Wallace,[5] and the executive-oriented work of Aaron Wildavsky.[6] Two features, however, distinguish the present book from those which have so plentifully nourished it. It is more comprehensive than its predecessors — in the time span covered or in the range of relationships examined, or both. It places a heavier reliance on interview materials and on dollars-and-cents appropriations data than those studies which have gone before.[7] And it utilizes different elements of theory from earlier studies. Only the reader can judge whether these differences in scope, data, and theory justify an addition to the descriptive literature. The hope is, however, that such departures have yielded a more inclusive and a more dependable set of empirical generalizations than has heretofore been possible.

[1] Arthur W. Macmahon, "Congressional Oversight of Administration: The Power of the Purse," *Political Science Quarterly* (March, 1943 and June, 1943), pp. 161–190, 380–414.

[2] Dwaine Marvick, "Congressional Appropriations Politics," unpublished manuscript (Columbia University, 1952).

[3] Robert Ash Wallace, *Congressional Control of Federal Spending* (Detroit: Wayne State University Press, 1960).

[4] Elias Huzar, *The Purse and the Sword: Control of the Army by Congress Through Military Appropriations* (Ithaca: Cornell University Press, 1950).

[5] Earle Wallace, "The Politics of River Basin Appropriations: A Case Study of the Roanoke River Basin," unpublished manuscript (University of North Carolina, 1959).

[6] Aaron Wildavsky, *The Politics of the Budgetary Process* (Boston: Little, Brown and Company, 1964).

[7] An exception, in terms of the use of quantitative data is: Otto Davis, M.A.H. Dempster, and Aaron Wildavsky, "On the Process of Budgeting: An Empirical Study of Congressional Appropriation," unpublished manuscript (Carnegie Institute of Technology, 1965).

To a large degree, a descriptive study of appropriations activity in Congress organizes itself. The process of appropriating money from the Treasury follows a fixed sequence. And, as we shall see, this traditional sequence, whereby every appropriation bill originates in the House of Representatives, is itself a key variable in appropriations decision-making. No matter what one's organizational preferences might be, the inexorable logic of the sequence cannot be sidestepped. The book does not cover the budget-making process as it proceeds in the executive branch prior to the submission of the President's budget. Nor does it consider the spending activity of the President and the executive-branch agencies once an appropriation bill has become law. (It does, however, discuss executive agency interaction with Congress during the appropriating process.) What the book does is to take the President's budget as given and analyze the flow of congressional decision-making from the House Committee on Appropriations (Chapters One through Eight), to the House floor (Chapter Nine), to the Senate Committee on Appropriations (Chapters Ten and Eleven), to the Senate floor (Chapter Eleven), to the conference committee (Chapter Twelve). In broadest sweep, therefore, the appropriations sequence gives a structural backbone to a descriptive sequence of twelve chapters.

COMMITTEE DESCRIPTION

The distribution of chapters reveals, however, that a policy of equal treatment for all decision-making stages has not been observed. The lopsided emphasis on the activity of the House Appropriations Committee reflects the author's judgment that this group is, by a substantial margin, the single most influential appropriations decision-maker in Congress. The exact magnitude of that margin (whether the House Committee deserves, as it seems to get, four times as much space as that given to the Senate Committee) will not be argued. The only point being asserted here is relative dominance of the House Committee.

The appropriations sequence gives the House Committee the decision-making initiative in Congress. And, using that initiative, the Committee sets the direction and magnitude of most congressional appropriations decisions. On behalf of the House and on behalf of its own members, the Committee cherishes the appropriations function more dearly and defends it more strenuously than does any other group. It examines the President's budget more comprehensively, more diligently, and more thoroughly than any other congressional body. In these judgments, executive branch officials concur. And so, too, do most senatorial participants. Not all of the first eight chapters focus directly on the activity of the House Appropriations Committee, but each contributes to the explanation of that activity. Ultimately, of course, the reader must judge whether such a concentration of attention is either warranted or worthwhile in terms of the avowed aim of describing congressional appropriations activity.

It may well be that appropriations politics is unique and that in other areas of congressional decision-making the impact of committee action is negligible. But if that is so, the propositions of political science have yet to reflect the evidence. No generalizations about Congress are voiced more frequently or held more firmly than those which proclaim the dominance of committee influence in congressional decision-making. Despite the time-tested unanimity of such generalizations, however, we probably know less about committees than we do about most other determinants of congressional behavior — about ideological groupings, political parties, constituency relations, and interest groups, for instance. It seems likely that our generalizations are correct and that the subject matter of committee activity remains a major underdeveloped area of research in American government. Such, at least, is the supposition which lies behind the second goal of this book — to demonstrate the value (if not the absolute necessity) of committee-centered research for an understanding of Congress.

To call attention to the relative paucity of committee-oriented research is not to imply that there has been none. *The Power of the Purse* surely owes some debts in this direction, too. Foremost among them is the debt which every student of Congress owes, directly or indirectly, to Woodrow Wilson's classic study *Congressional Government*. For those especially interested in committees the debt is direct, since a major thesis of Wilson's book concerns committee dominance of congressional decision-making. It was Wilson who first labeled the committees "little legislatures."[8] It was Wilson who described Congress as "divided as it were into 47 seignories, in each of which a standing committee is the court baron and its chairman the lord proprietor."[9] It was Wilson who stated that "Congress in session is Congress on public exhibition, while Congress in its committee rooms is Congress at work."[10] And it was Wilson who summed up by saying, "It is no great departure from the fact to describe ours as a government by the standing committees of Congress."[11] His quotable aphorisms and his forceful generalizations are copybook maxims in political science. They have dominated our monographs and our textbooks since 1885.

It is an historical curiosity worth noting, however, that subsequent students of the national legislature repeated Wilson's views about the importance of committees while at the same time concentrating their scholarly

[8] Woodrow Wilson, *Congressional Government* (New York: Meridian Books Inc., 1956), p. 89.
[9] *Ibid.*, p. 70.
[10] *Ibid.*, p. 69.
[11] *Ibid.*, pp. 55–56.

attentions elsewhere. Logically, it seems, his sweeping generalizations should have unloosed an avalanche of empirical research on committee activity. But they did not. One reason for the paradoxical outcome may lie in the fact that Wilson deeply deplored what he described. His study had, therefore, a normative-reformist component as well as a descriptive one. And Wilson's disciples, too, have deplored. They read Wilson's book as a call for congressional reform and not as a call for empirical research. It is as if the very eloquence of his description plus the abstract logic of his plea for change rendered further empirical research superfluous. In any case, *Congressional Government* has nourished a long train of plans to bring about the reform of Congress through the reform of its committees. Still, the empirical side of Wilson survives. And, in recent years, less reform-minded students of Congress have begun utilizing his insights for more descriptive purposes.

Especially helpful in developing the present study have been the ground-breaking committee analysis of Ralph Huitt[12] and the observations on Senate committees by Donald Matthews.[13] Somewhat more contemporaneously wrought have been the instructive single committee studies by Holbert Carroll, Harold Green and Alan Rosenthal, Charles Jones, Robert Peabody, and James Robinson[14] and the cross-committee studies of Charles Clapp, George Goodwin, and Nicholas Masters.[15] *The Power of the Purse* belongs to the same genre as each of these studies since their main thrust is descriptive rather than reformist. None of these studies, however, serves as the model for this one. For none employs quite as broad a range of data, encompasses quite the same complexity of relationships, and quite so selfconsciously purports to be a committee-centered analysis of a total legislative decision-making process. Though the analysis which follows places heavy stress on the House Committee on Appropriations, most of what is not devoted to that group *is*

---

[12] Ralph K. Huitt, "The Congressional Committee: A Case Study," *American Political Science Review* (June, 1954), pp. 340–365.

[13] Donald R. Matthews, *U.S. Senators and Their World* (Chapel Hill: University of North Carolina Press, 1960), Chapter 7.

[14] Holbert N. Carroll, *The House of Representatives and Foreign Affairs* (Pittsburgh: University of Pittsburgh Press, 1958); Harold P. Green and Alan Rosenthal, *Government of the Atom* (New York: Atherton Press, 1964); Charles O. Jones, "Representation in Congress: The Case of the House Agriculture Committee," *American Political Science Review* (June, 1961), pp. 358–367; Charles O. Jones, "The Role of the Congressional Subcommittee," *Midwest Journal of Political Science* (November, 1962), pp. 327–344; Robert L. Peabody, "The Enlarged Rules Committee," in R. Peabody and N. Polsby, *New Perspectives on the House of Representatives* (Chicago: Rand McNally, 1963), pp. 129–164; James A. Robinson, *The House Rules Committee* (Indianapolis: Bobbs-Merrill, 1963).

[15] Charles L. Clapp, *The Congressman: His Work as He Sees It* (Washington: Brookings Institution, 1963), especially Chapters 5 and 6; George Goodwin, "The Seniority System in Congress," *American Political Science Review* (June, 1959), pp. 412–436; George Goodwin, "Subcommittees: The Miniature Legislatures of Congress," *American Political Science Review* (September, 1962), pp. 596–604; Nicholas A. Masters, "Committee Assignments in the House of Representatives," *American Political Science Review* (June, 1961), pp. 347–357.

devoted to the Senate Committee on Appropriations. Thus a comparative note is introduced, and a concentration on committee activity can be said to characterize description at every stage of appropriations decision-making.

CONCEPTUALIZATION

Empirical descriptions of complex political activity generate facts without end — and the appropriations process in Congress is no exception. For a description to make sense, facts must be culled and related one to another. For a description to have relevance for other descriptions, the relationships among facts must be stated in generalized form. For these conversion tasks, description requires theory. And a committee-centered description requires committee-centered kinds of theory. The book which follows is eclectic in borrowing various kinds of theory which seem particularly helpful in describing varieties of committee activity and in facilitating generalizations about that activity. No single all-embracing body of theory has been adopted and none is on trial. Indeed, students of Congress have already benefited by many elements of the book's theoretical apparatus. Hopefully, the usefulness of these elements will be confirmed, while less well-tested bits of theory may be judged equally appropriate for committee-centered research. Such, at least, is the third goal of *The Power of the Purse.*

Since three-quarters of the book centers on the work of the House Committee on Appropriations, the important theoretical notions are those used to organize facts about the Committee. Most basically, the study conceives of the House Committee (and the Senate Appropriations Committee) as *a political system* — having certain identifiable, interdependent, *internal parts*, existing in an identifiable *external environment*, and tending to *stabilize* both its internal and external relationships over time. The study distinguishes between the Committee's internal and external relationships. Both sets of relationships are examined — separately and as they affect one another — in an effort to discover and to explicate enduring patterns of interaction. As an aid in the identification, examination, and explication of important relationships, the study focuses attention on some basic problems which every political system must solve in order to stabilize its activity or "survive" over time. Externally, there is the problem of *adapting* to the demands of other political entities. Internally, there are the structural problems of *decision-making* and *integration.*[16]

[16] Obviously, this amalgam of ideas has various sources, most especially in: George Homans, *The Human Group* (New York: Harcourt Brace, 1950); Talcott Parsons and Edward Shils, *Toward a General Theory of Action* (Cambridge: Harvard University Press, 1951), pp. 190–234; Robert K. Merton, *Social Theory and Social Structure* (Glencoe: Free Press, 1951), Chapter 1; David Easton, "An Approach to the Analysis of Political Systems," *World Politics* (April, 1947), pp. 383–400; Scott Greer, *Social Organization* (New York: Random House, 1955).

This amalgam of theoretical notions seems especially congenial to a committee-centered description of congressional activity. In the first place, the idea of system is a broad and comprehensive idea. As such it accommodates itself to the fact that we can gather data on the full range of a committee's internal and external relationships. A committee is small enough so that, empirically, one can encompass a greater complexity than is possible with a political system as large as a city or state or nation. What the idea of system sacrifices in precision, therefore, is compensated for in the large number of interrelated variables that can be accommodated. In a situation where these variables can be investigated empirically, a general level of theory seems particularly useful in organizing an empirical description.[17]

Granted that it is possible to "get all the way around" a congressional committee, the idea of system is valuable intellectual baggage in the conduct and presentation of research. If, that is to say, one does committee research with the notion of system constantly in mind, he will be forced to ask what consequences, if any, one kind of observed activity has for other kinds of observed activity. Particularly, he will be forced to relate various forms of activity to the solution or nonsolution of a variety of survival problems. By asking such questions, the researcher may discover relationships that had not occurred to him before. And in this way, the idea of system has great heuristic value. But whether the relationships be suspected or unsuspected, the important result is that the researcher asks questions about relationships, organizes his findings in terms of relationships, and presents, as the heart of his empirical description, those relationships that form enduring and significant patterns.

In addition, the idea of system seems particularly well adapted for the analysis of a set of interrelated activities which do in fact recur fairly frequently and which do in fact persist for considerable periods of time. Most congressional committees display these properties most of the time. It is difficult to be more specific than this. But the point is that the idea of system assumes a reasonable degree of stability, directs a great deal of attention to the problem of maintaining stability, and seems best suited to describing activities that already evidence some stability. Conversely, the idea of system appears to be less appropriate to the ordering of data about a set of activities whose relations to one another change rapidly, frequently, and fundamentally. This does not mean, however, that the notion of system precludes the analysis of change. Where a set of activities is fairly stable, most changes are incremental and small-scale. And this kind of change can be identified, explained, and, perhaps, predicted within the rubric of system description. In any set of on-

[17] Cf. the general discussion of this "interesting paradox" in Heinz Eulau, *The Behavioral Persuasion in Politics* (New York: Random House, 1963), p. 31.

going relationships, the existence of tension can be described and the potentialities for change as a result of existing tensions can be estimated. The description of patterned relationships existing at one point in time can provide a base line against which to measure change in those relationships over time.

Given a commitment to the idea of system, the immediate task becomes one of identifying the important elements of the system. Most concretely, in the case at hand the elements are the individuals and groups of individuals who participate in the appropriations process. If the House Appropriations Committee is viewed as the system, its elements are the 50 Committee members plus the Committee's staff *internally* and several kinds of groups — the House of Representatives, the Senate, executive agencies, and clientele groups — *externally*. We will be interested in describing those relationships between and among these various elements which exhibit some patterning and, hence, make generalization possible.

A statement of description does not settle the question as to the materials to be used in that description. In this book, the basic materials of description are the *normative expectations* of the various participants, the *perceptions and attitudes*, or *images*, of the participants, and the *behavior* of the participants. Both internal and external relationships are described (insofar as the data allow) by means of these categories.

The idea that, in a political study, one wants to describe what people do (i.e., behavior) needs no comment. And if one did nothing more than observe behavior among the appropriations participants and report the patterns as observed, the results would be immensely valuable. Simple descriptions of behavior do not by themselves, however, constitute explanation or prediction. One can know what happened without understanding why, and one can know what happened without being able to make a reasonable guess as to what will happen. It may also be the case — as it is in the study of all congressional committees — that crucial kinds of behavior cannot be observed at all. Here, the need to supplement the study of behavior is imperative. In this book considerable emphasis is placed on two such supplementary materials of description, in hopes of producing better information, better explanation, and better prediction.

In their relations with others, people usually have an idea as to how they and others ought to behave in given types of situations. These ideas are referred to in this book as expectations. And, unless otherwise indicated, the term expectation is always employed in this normative sense. For every committee-important relationship, external or internal, an attempt is made to find out what each set of participants believes should happen or wants to have happen. In describing external relationships, it has been found useful to distinguish *goal expectations* (*what* others think the committee should do) from *maintenance expectations* (*how* others think the committee should do it). For each set of external relationships the committee members' normative expectations about their own behavior are similarly elaborated and contrasted with the expectations of others. Where conflict exists, the techniques for reducing such conflicts and the conditions under which they are employed are analyzed.

In the description of internal relationships, the emphasis on normative expectations is expressed via the idea of *norms.* A norm can be defined as "an idea in the minds of the members of a group, an idea that can be put in the form of a statement specifying what the members or other men should do, ought to do, are expected to do under given circumstances."[18] Clusters of norms define *roles,* which state how a person in a given position is expected to behave. Individuals occupying positions (e.g., chairman, subcommittee chairman) and, therefore, expected to follow certain specified norms (i.e., play roles) constitute the basic elements of the system's internal relationships. The distinction is made between *role* (how an individual in a position is expected to behave) and *role behavior* (how that individual does in fact behave). The degree of correspondence between role and role behavior and the mechanisms for maintaining a correspondence between them are investigated. The presence of such mechanisms is central to the idea of a norm. For "a norm exists when there are (1) agreements or consensuses about the behaviors group members should or should not enact and (2) social processes to produce adherence to these agreements."[19] *Socialization* and *sanctioning* mechanisms are, therefore, described, and so too are the conditions under which these "social processes" come into play. Thus the description of internal activity follows a pattern roughly similar to the description of external activity in examining expectations, behavior, and their interrelationships.

To the degree that a structure of external and internal expectations can be described alongside a structure of behavior, to that degree will knowledge, explanation, and, possibly, prediction be advanced. In the first place, in a reasonable stable system, patterns of behavior tend to coincide with patterns of expectations. People usually do what they are expected to do. The substance of expectations will, therefore, affect behavior. In this way, knowledge of expectations helps to explain observed behavior. The reverse relationship holds too. People come to expect others to do what in fact they usually do. Behavior affects expectations; and knowledge about behavior, therefore, helps to explain expectations.

[18] George Homans, *op. cit.,* p. 123. The ideas of norms, role, and role behavior used in this book owe a great deal, in addition to Homans, to John Wahlke, Heinz Eulau, William Buchanan, Le Roy Ferguson, *The Legislative System* (New York: John Wiley, 1962), to John W. Thibaut and Harold H. Kelley, *The Social Psychology of Groups* (New York: John Wiley, 1959) and to Neal Gross, Ward Mason, and Alexander McEachern, *Explorations in Role Analysis: Studies of the School Superintendency Role* (New York: John Wiley, 1958), pp. 11–69.

[19] John W. Thibaut and Harold H. Kelley, *The Social Psychology of Groups* (New York: John Wiley, 1959), p. 239.

In the second place, and again in a reasonably stable system, patterns of behavior will vary in the degree to which they coincide with patterns of expectations. The closer the correspondence between a set of expectations and observed behavior, the more likely that pattern of behavior·is to endure. And the more stable a pattern of behavior, the greater is the likelihood of making accurate predictions.

Third, should conflicts exist among expectations or should behavior and expectations remain discordant, actions will be taken, in a reasonably stable system, to change some expectations and/or some behavior so as to promote a greater degree of congruence. Such cases will provide instances of small-scale changes which can be explained and, perhaps, predicted.

Fourth, in instances where one cannot observe behavior, it may be possible to infer some behavior from expectations. Obviously, this is a second-best way to acquire knowledge about behavior. But if a consensus on expectations is found to exist and if the correspondence of expectations to behaviors is found to be close in related areas, it may be possible to make fairly accurate inferences about non-observable behavior. It would seem, in sum, that to know something of both expectations and behavior puts one's knowledge of a political system on a surer footing than if only one or the other were examined. Indeed, once the commitment has been made to study a whole system empirically, it becomes virtually impossible to avoid description in both normative and behavioral terms.

The third ingredient of description is the blend of perceptions and attitudes, or images, which participants hold. Here again, the assumption is that behavior can be more fully·explained (if not predicted) when one understands something of the premises of behavior. Perceptions (what a person sees when he observes the world around him) and attitudes (how a person evaluates, favorably or unfavorably, for example, what he sees) are two such premises. These perceptions and attitudes are formally separable. But in this study they cannot be and, for the most part, have not been. The difficulty is that the participants themselves rarely make the distinction, and what a respondent has joined together this researcher cannot put asunder. In recognition of this cognitive-evaluative entanglement, the two elements have been run together deliberately and labeled *images*. This term is the one most often used. Thus an attempt is made in the book to understand how participants think they and others ought to behave (expectations), how participants believe they and others do behave together with approval or disapproval of this behavior (images), and how everyone involved does, in fact, behave (behavior).

In describing the materials which have been used, it might be noted briefly that two kinds of material have not been used. No attempt has been made to use individual personality data. The relevance of personality as a variable is fully recognized and is discussed, at length and by example, at several points. But no attempt has been made at a systematic interpretation of the behavior of individuals in terms of their psychological characteristics. If anything, reference to specific individuals has been systematically underplayed. In one sense, this is a self-denying ordinance, since the Washington researcher inevitably gets drowned in a flood of personality-centered talk — each item of which purports to explain some specific event. There are two ways, at least, to deal with personality data. One is to take meaningful psychological categories, collect the appropriate data across a large number of participants, and relate these data to behavior.[20] The second is to see how far one can go toward an empirical description — not of isolated events but of repeated events — using a minimum of personality data. The first approach is necessary in doing a sophisticated analysis of the personality variable. The second approach may help in later efforts to relate the personality variable to other variables. It is out of necessity rather than virtue, however, that this study follows the second approach. It hopes to show how much generalization is possible short of a heavy reliance on personality data.

In a second sense, too, this study lacks depth. It has not been organized to employ materials dealing with the developmental history of appropriations decision-making generally or of the House Committee particularly. As in the treatment of personality, important historical events are treated as they exemplify important relationships. But that is not the same thing as attempting to explain existing behavior patterns in terms of their development through time. As A. R. Radcliffe-Brown has stated the difference,

> One explanation of a social system will be its history, where we know it — the detailed account of how it came to be what it is and where it is. Another 'explanation' of the same system is obtained by showing . . . that it is a special exemplification of laws of social psychology or social functioning. The two kinds of explanation do not conflict but supplement one another.[21]

This study pursues the second line of explanation.

The book has a time dimension, covering more or less the period from 1947–1965, in an effort to consider a sufficient number of events to support generalization. But the attempt is to generalize about persistence and change in appropriations patterns during that one period alone. The origins of appro-

[20] An excellent study along these lines has been done for the Connecticut House of Representatives. See James David Barber, *The Lawmakers: Recruitment and Adaptation to Legislative Life* (New Haven: Yale University Press, 1965).

[21] As quoted from A. R. Radcliffe-Brown, "On The Concept of Function in Social Science," *American Anthropologist*, New Series, 37 (1935), p. 401 in Seymour Martin Lipset, *Political Man* (New York: Doubleday, 1959), p. 71.

priations politics certainly pre-date the Constitution, and the origins of the two Appropriations Committees lie in events of the 1860's. Doubtless, contemporary expectations, images, and behavior took root in the intervening period. But this study takes them as they can be observed from the late 1940's to the mid-1960's. It asks what they are and how they relate to one another. It does not ask where the varieties of expectations, images, and actions came from. Some may feel, of course, that a study of a political process and a political system lacking psychological and historical depth is not worth the energy consumed in writing it. But, again, it is the hope of the author that the weaknesses of the book will not overshadow its strengths as a contemporary description and as an aid to related research.

DATA

The data for the study come from two main sources. They come from the public record of appropriations activity — e.g., from the *Congressional Record*, committee hearings, committee reports, and House and Senate documents. And they come from interviews with the participants — e.g., with members of the House and Senate Appropriations Committees, the staffs of those members, the staffs of the two committees, other members of the House of Representatives, and executive agency officials who deal with congressmen on appropriations matters.

The basic decision governing the use of data from the public record was the decision to select a representative group of executive agencies and to chart their appropriations case histories in dollars-and-cents terms over an extended period of time. The purpose was to collect some comparable and quantifiable evidence concerning the content of appropriations decisions. A group of 36 executive agencies of the bureau level representing 7 of the 10 Cabinet departments were selected. Their appropriations requests were recorded together with 5 subsequent decisions on those requests (e.g., by House Committee, whole House, Senate Committee, whole Senate, conference committee) for a period of 16 years, 1947–1962. The criteria of selection for the 36 bureaus were first, that their activity be dominantly domestic in scope; second, that their organizational integrity have been maintained throughout the 16-year period,[22] and, third, that their activity have been funded by means of direct appropria-

[22] Bureaus excluded from consideration by this criterion were those which underwent the following kinds of organizational changes during the period: *relocation in a new department*, e.g., Bureau of Employees Compensation moved from Federal Security Agency to Labor Department; *new organizational status*, e.g., Civil Aeronautics Administration removed from Commerce Department and made into the independent Federal Aviation Agency; *bureau consolidation*, e.g., regrouping of agricultural research activities in November, 1953; *bureau division*, e.g., splitting up of Bureau of Foreign and Domestic Commerce; *went out of existence*, e.g., Civil Aeronautics Board; *came into existence*, e.g., Office of Automation and Manpower in Labor Department.

tions for the entire period.[23] A total of about 40 bureaus met these criteria. Of these, 36 were selected for study. The omission of 4 was dictated by considerations of time and was essentially arbitrary. But the characteristics of the 4 seemed to be duplicated by bureaus that were selected and no underrepresentation is believed to have resulted.[24] The 36 bureaus constituted a virtual population rather than a sample.

The bureaus chosen from the 7 Departments were *Agriculture* — Extension Service, Farmer's Home Administration, Forest Service, Rural Electrification Administration, and Soil Conservation Service; *Commerce* — Census Bureau, Coast and Geodetic Survey, National Bureau of Standards, Patent Office, and Weather Bureau; *Health, Education, and Welfare* — Food and Drug Administration, Office of Education, Office of Vocational Rehabilitation, Public Health Service, and Social Security Administration; *Interior* — Bonneville Power Administration, Bureau of Indian Affairs, Bureau of Land Management, Bureau of Mines, Bureau of Reclamation, Fish and Wildlife Service, Geological Survey, and National Park Service; *Justice* — Federal Bureau of Investigation, Federal Prison System, and Immigration and Naturalization Service; *Labor* — Bureau of Labor Standards, Bureau of Labor Statistics, Wage and Hour Division, and Women's Bureau; *Treasury* — Bureau of Customs, Bureau of Narcotics, Bureau of the Mint, Bureau of the Public Debt, Internal Revenue Service, and Secret Service.

The appropriations case histories of the bureaus were collected in the following manner. The budget estimates (or the appropriations request) and the final appropriation (the conference committee decision) were found in the annual Senate Document, *Appropriations, Budget Estimates, Etc.*, and taken from the section therein entitled "Itemized Comparison of Budget estimates and Appropriations arranged by Appropriations Acts."[25] The budget

[23] The Bureau of Engraving and Printing and the Farm Credit Administration, for example, went off direct appropriation and onto funding via a revolving fund and contract authorization, respectively. Two bureaus that remain in the group exchanged some direct appropriation for contract authorization. For the case histories of these bureaus, Extension Service and Farmers Home Administration, only their "salaries and expenses" have been used.

[24] The 4 omitted were: Southwestern Power Administration (Interior), Bureau of Apprenticeship (Labor), Bureau of Employment Security (Labor), and Bureau of Accounts (Treasury). Also omitted was the Coast Guard (Treasury) whose status as a domestically oriented bureau was uncertain. With regard to the 4 omissions, it might be noted that 2 Interior Department bureaus concerned with public power were studied, that the Labor Departments budget is the smallest (save for Justice, which is represented by 3 bureaus) of the departments studied and is represented by 4 bureaus already; and that 2 Treasury Department bureaus being studied have operations very similar to that of the Bureau of Accounts. Despite the arbitrariness of the selection, the 36 bureaus give adequate representation to each Department and every kind of bureau.

[25] For 1962, for example, the document is U.S. Senate, *Appropriations, Budget Estimates, Etc.*, Senate Document No. 162, 87th Congress, 2nd Session (Washington: U.S. Government, 1962). The relevant appropriations data were taken, in this volume, from Section VIII, pp. 717–721. This annual document can be found in any library that is repository for government documents.

estimates in this document were then checked against the estimates as recorded in the House Appropriations Committee report containing information for a given bureau in a given year. Where a discrepancy existed, the budget estimate as listed in the Committee report was the one used. In such cases, the estimate that appeared in the Senate document mentioned above was used only for the discussion of Senate Committee action.[26] The House Committee's decision was always located in the relevant House Committee report. The whole House's decision was taken from the relevant Senate Committee report (which always lists the final House determination), and this report also yielded the Senate Committee's decision. The whole Senate decision was located by reading the account of Senate floor action in the *Congressional Record*.

These 576 appropriations case histories (36 bureaus, 16 years) did much to focus the use of the written public record — since reading tended to center on those documents which aided in understanding these 576 sets of decisions. Thus, the author read (in the *Congressional Record*) the appropriations floor debates for each of the 7 departments involved, in House and Senate, for all of the 16 years. No attempt was made, though, to examine all of the relevant volume of committee hearings and committee reports, but some were read covering every bureau and covering every year. In addition, all floor debates covering State Department, Post Office Department, and Corps of Army Engineers appropriations for the 16-year period have been read. Generous samplings of floor action on Defense Department and foreign aid appropriations have been made. In one case — the analysis of amendments proposed on the House floor — the quantitative analysis is expanded to include 8 departments plus public works. But for the most part, the quantitative evidence of the study supports generalizations only about a range of domestic government activity.

The second major source of data is the body of approximately 175 interviews conducted by the author with individuals involved in appropriations decision-making. Data from these interviews cover all fields in which appropriations decisions are made. The first of the interviews was held in May of 1959 and the last was conducted in June of 1965, all in Washington, D.C. Since the interviews provide so much of the study's qualitative data, a brief chronology and a description of interview style may be helpful in assessing their value.

Interviewing began when conversations were held with 43 of the 50 members of the House Committee on Appropriations and with 5 staff assis-

---

[26] Normally, there is no discrepancy; but in about 60 of the 596 case histories, the budget estimate changed between the time the House Committee received the budget and the time the Senate Committee acted upon it — often as a result of programs newly authorized in the interim.

tants to these members in May and June of 1959. A year later, in May and June of 1960, a parallel effort in the Senate yielded interviews with 15 Senate Appropriations Committee members, 6 staff assistants to Committee Senators, and 4 members of the Committee's professional staff. At the same time, 5 members of the House Committee were interviewed, 2 for the first time and 3 for the second. Executive officials from the great bulk of the 36 executive agencies were contacted in December of 1960. Interviews were held with the chief budget officers of all 7 departments, with 18 bureau chiefs, 6 assistant bureau chiefs, and 10 bureau budget officers. Bureau representatives came from 23 of the 36 bureaus. In January of 1961, interviewing centered on sessions with 8 members of the House Committee's professional staff. But conversations were also held with 3 Senate Committee members (bringing the final total of Senators to 18), 2 Senate Committee staffers, 2 House Committee members (1 for the first time), and 2 Representatives active in choosing House Committee members.

Interviewing continued in April of 1963[27] via talks with 10 House members who had been especially active in the process whereby Appropriations Committee members were chosen. This brought to a total of 12 (7 Democrats, 5 Republicans) the number of such people interviewed — 6 of whom spoke from the leadership perspective of Speaker (1), or majority floor leader (3), or minority floor leader (2), or majority whip (3), or minority whip (3), or some combination of these. At the same time, interviews were also held with 2 House Committee members (1 for the first time) and 2 House Committee staff members (both repeats). Though sporadic personal contact with House Committee personnel had continued since 1959, no concentrated interviewing had been conducted with the group since then. So, in the spring of 1964, a series of 24 interviews were held with House Committee members. Of the 24 interviewees, 11 were people who had come to the Committee since 1959 (bringing the final number of different House Committee members interviewed to 58), and 13 were re-interviews with Committee members with whom conversations had been held in 1959. In May of 1965, one final re-interview with a House Committee member and one with a member of the Committee's staff ended the formal interviewing for the study.[28]

The interviews were semistructured. Certain key questions, all open-ended, were asked of all respondents holding similar positions. But the inter-

[27] In June of 1961, in the course of research for a separate study, interviews were held with 19 members of the House Committee on Education and Labor. Occasionally, the subject matter of the Appropriations Committee was pursued with these men. Similarly, in 1963 and 1964, interviews held by a group of 6 political scientists with a dozen or so Representatives produced information relevant to appropriations politics.

[28] In June of 1965, a series of interviews held with Congressmen — some of whom were active in the selection of Appropriations Committees members — were helpful as confirmation of earlier conclusions.

view was kept very flexible in order to permit particular topics to be explored with those individuals best equipped to discuss them. The interviews averaged from 45 to 60 minutes in length and ranged from a low of 10 minutes to a high of 3 hours. In a few cases, where respondents encouraged it, notes were taken during the interview. Typically, however, notes were not taken but were transcribed immediately after the interview. Unattributed quotations in the text, therefore, are as nearly verbatim as the author's power of immediate recall could make them. These techniques were used in the belief that they encouraged what the author believes to be the quintessential condition of successful interviewing of political elites — *rapport* between interviewer and respondent.

Obviously, the data of the study are of two quite different sorts. The 576 appropriations case histories provide some relatively "hard" dollars-and-cents data on appropriations decisions. Since these data are susceptible of quantification, appropriations decisions (at least those decisions recorded in money terms) can be described quite precisely. Whether one wishes to generalize about the outcome of the appropriations sequence or whether one wishes to generalize about the output of a committee as a system, one must know what kinds of decisions get made. Decisions, that is, are a critical dependent variable in process-oriented and system-oriented research. Too often in legislative research, we describe the process of decision-making in great detail yet cannot relate process to outcome — because we simply cannot describe the decisions that result. It is enormously helpful, in this case, to be able to characterize appropriations decisions and base generalizations about them on quantified evidence.

On the other hand, reading the public record and conducting 175 interviews have yielded quite a different sort of data — verbal, imprecise, impressionistic, and, for the most part, nonquantifiable. These data have provided most of the evidence with which to support generalizations about expectations, perceptions and attitudes, norms, roles and role behavior, plus the mechanisms operating to maintain harmony among these elements of a political system. Once a commitment has been made to these materials of description, qualitative interview data become essential. The requirements of description, therefore, and not an *a priori* devotion to particular kinds of data, have dictated the use of data. An effort has been made to follow David Truman's wise advice to the student of political institutions "to perform his task in quantitative terms if he can and in qualitative terms if he must.[29] In describing the appropriations process in Congress, one "can" and one "must."

[29] Social Science Research Council, Items (December, 1951) as quoted in Robert A. Dahl, "The Behavioral Approach in Political Science: Epitaph for a Monument to a Successful Protest," *American Political Science Review* (December, 1961), pp. 767–768.

ORGANIZATION

One final word about the organization — or the two organizations — of the book. The 12 chapters have been ordered so that they follow the fixed appropriations sequence — from House Committee on Appropriations through to the conference committee. But at the same time, the 12 chapters have been weighted so as to allot most of the coverage to the work of the House Committee. Where the House Committee is at the center of the analysis, the organizing idea of a political system is superimposed on the organizing idea of stages in the appropriations process.

The "two organizations" show up most noticeably in the treatment of Senate appropriations activity in Chapters Ten and Eleven. The book begins with a discussion of the House Committee on Appropriations because this group acts first in the sequence, and the discussion is extended because this group is the most influential one in the entire process. Chapters One through Nine are unified in that they describe the external and the internal relationships of the Committee, ending with a description of Committee success in defending its decisions on the House floor. At this point, senatorial activity can be regarded either as the next step in the appropriations process or as one of the external relationships of the House Committee. It is, of course, both. Hence, Senate activity could be described in great detail quite apart from House activity or Senate activity could be described as it relates to House activity. The choice was made to treat the Senate Committee as a political system and to telescope the same line of analysis as was used for the House Committee in Chapters One through Nine into Chapters Ten and Eleven for the Senate. The idea of system was used, but for Chapters Ten and Eleven, it is the Senate Committee and not the House Committee under investigation. So the book becomes an examination of two systems whose most important interrelationship is discussed in Chapter Twelve in the context of the final stage of decision-making — the House-Senate conference.

In the end, the book has twin foci — the House Committee on Appropriations and the total appropriations process in which the Senate as well as the House plays a part.

THE POWER
OF THE PURSE

*Appropriations Politics
in Congress*

CHAPTER ONE

The House Committee and the House
I: House Expectations and Images

THE COMMITTEE–HOUSE RELATIONSHIP

When the President sends the proposed federal budget to Congress every January, the first legislative body to act on it is always the Committee on Appropriations of the House of Representatives. Appropriation bills "originate" in the House by virtue of tradition rather than (as is the case with revenue bills) by constitutional prerogative. But tradition has legitimized and fixed a sequence for appropriation bills that is equally inflexible.[1] Chronologically, therefore, a description of the appropriations process in Congress should start with a look at the House Committee. And that is where the present study does begin. The House Committee, however, is not only the first legislative body to act, but the most important one as well. And this additional fact means that the Committee can usefully be singled out for extended analysis. The present chapter begins that analysis — of the House Committee as a political system.

Granted that the House Committee be described both first and foremost, the question arises as to the order in which its internal and external relationships should be examined. If organized in strict accordance with chronological sequence, the analysis would have to focus first on the internal Committee activity immediately following receipt of the budget and

[1] The Senate continues to maintain what it regards as an equal claim to originate appropriation bills. See, for example, U.S. Senate, *The Authority of the Senate to Originate Appropriation Bills*, Senate Document No. 17, 88th Congress, 1st Session (Washington: U.S. Government Printing Office, 1963). The most recent (1962) House-Senate clash over their respective prerogatives is detailed in Chapter 12.

proceed from there to a treatment of the Committee's external relationship with executive branch agencies which come to Capitol Hill in support of their budget requests. From there, the flow of activity would be traced back inside the Committee to record its internal decision-making activity and thence to a discussion of external relationships on the House floor. If the description is organized according to the idea of system, however, it makes sense to locate the Committee in its environment before attempting to say what it does. We can, thereby, gain a perspective on the Committee as one political entity among other political entities; and we can gain some sense of the outer constraints on Committee activity before investigating that activity directly. The second line of reasoning undergirds the construction of the first two chapters.

A necessary condition for the survival or stability of any political system is that it do what people want it to do in a way that people want it done. A political system, that is to say, must satisfy expectations in order to survive. But two questions immediately arise: what expectations and whose expectations? An answer to the query "what expectations?" would yield a compendium of expectations held by all individuals and groups interested in or affected by the system. Once such a listing is made, however, the crucial question becomes one of "whose expectations?" Among the multiple sets of expectations pertaining to system activity, which ones have the greatest impact on that activity? Or, among the many individuals and groups making demands on a system, which ones have the resources to make their demands effective? Answers to the question "whose expectations?" must be sought in two directions — from among the members of the system itself and from among interested groups in the environment of the system. Whether one starts by examining the expectations of those inside or those outside the system is an arbitrary choice. In the case of the House Appropriations Committee, we have decided to begin by examining the expectations of people outside the Committee. And among those entities, the one having the most direct, the most pervasive, and the most continuous influence over its activity is the parent House of Representatives.

The initial perspective one needs for an understanding of the Appropriations Committee is a view of it as a subsystem of the House of Representatives.[2] This relationship puts the most crucial restraints on the Committee. And it is here — with a description of committee-parent chamber interaction — that the study of any congressional committee could profitably begin. For the parent chamber creates all committees, legitimizes their

---

[2] When specific reference is being made to the House-Committee relationship, the Committee may be referred to as a subsystem. Ordinarily, however, the Committee is referred to as system, since it is the focus of analysis.

every activity, and supplies them with such necessary resources as time, money, and members. The question as to how much influence the parent chamber exercises may bring a different answer for each committee. But it is an appropriate first question to ask. It was, interestingly, the central empirical question of Woodrow Wilson's 1885 study. And it was one which Wilson himself answered with the blanket generalization that the parent chamber exercised relatively little influence over its committees and that the committees were virtually autonomous legislative units.[3] One consequence of the lack of empirical research on committees in the period following Wilson has been the acceptance of his generalization.[4] It is, therefore, one virtue of beginning a single committee analysis with the committee-chamber relationship that one addresses himself directly to our most hoary and hallowed proposition about committees.

Chapters One and Two are concerned, then, with the question of House influence on Appropriations Committee activity or the relative autonomy of the Committee. The description works its way toward an answer, however, through the following sequence of questions. Do the members of the House have a well-developed and identifiable set of expectations as to how the Appropriations Committee ought to behave or what it ought to do? What are they? What perceptions do House members have of actual Committee behavior? What attitudes do House members have toward Committee activity as they perceive it? Considering House member perceptions and attitudes, is there any evidence that House members are satisfied with Committee performance? Is there any evidence, in other words, that actual Committee behavior meets House member expectations? Conversely, is there any evidence of House member dissatisfaction, any evidence that Committee behavior does not meet House expectations? And, where the two are in conflict, does the House have sanctions available to it to bring about Committee compliance with its expectations? Finally, does the House ever want to exercise and does it in fact exercise any effective sanctions over its Appropriations Committee? Answers to these questions will provide a fairly full description of the Committee-House relationship from the point of view of the House Committee.

[3] See, however, Woodrow Wilson, *Congressional Government* (New York: Meridian Books, 1956), pp. 69, 113, 129–130, where he specifically exempts the Appropriations Committee from some of his generalizations.

[4] Recently and authoritatively, for example, by George Galloway. "These miniature legislatures have acquired such power and prestige that they are largely autonomous of the House itself which created them and whose agents they are supposed to be . . . The role of the House is now largely limited to ratifying decisions made by its committees." George Galloway, *History of the United States House of Representatives* (Washington: U.S. Government Printing Office, 1962), p. 87.

3

HOUSE EXPECTATIONS

It may appear presumptuous to speak of House expectations concerning the Appropriations Committee. And in the absence of a survey of House members, perhaps, it is. But there can be little doubt, from the kind of semi-structured interviewing that has been done, that the Committee is a highly visible, well identified, and much talked about unit in the chamber. One of the House's most prominent spokesmen described the Committee, for example, in language so graphic as to leave small question as to its prominence in the minds of other members:

> They're a dedicated committee, a powerful committee, and a tireless committee. They are the hardest workers in the Congress. They get no glamor, no fanfare, and nobody even knows what they are doing until it gets to the floor. They sit morning and afternoon and sometimes at night — plodding, plodding, plodding, and figuring. I could never do it. Appropriations is the last committee I would ever want to go on. I like to deal with broad policy questions which affect people or large segments of the population. I may do some figuring, but if I do it's incidental to some broad legislative question. But I couldn't sit there day after day and figure up dollars and cents, dollars and cents. With them it's a state of mind, a way of life. They have a missionary spirit on that Committee. I admire them for it; and I respect them. You walk over in the morning to the House just before ten o'clock, and you will see all of them pounding through the tunnel on their way to subcommittee meetings. Down that long tunnel they come, hurrying along and afraid they are going to be late. They shouldn't be going so fast — some of them are too old — but they do it just the same. It's that dedication they have. They're like missionaries.

Whatever may be true of other committees, House members have expectations and images of the House Committee. Indeed, the vivid commentary above expresses and implies some of them.

Two conditions, probably, induce such striking expectations and images. One condition relates to the perceived importance of the work of the Committee to the power of the House of Representatives. The other relates to the frequency of contact between Committee and House.

The power of the purse has long been considered the spearhead of the House's legislative power. The special importance of the House in money matters (revenue matters) is enshrined in the Constitution. Concern for the maintenance of its financial power has led the House to relatively frequent scrutiny of its Appropriations Committee. In the Legislative Reorganization Act of 1946, for example, the Appropriations Committee was the object of more provisions than any other House committee. But in addition to such episodic attention the Appropriations Committee is on display before the

4

parent House more frequently than any other single committee — on 15 to 18 appropriation bills every year, year in and year out. Each of these occasions becomes an opportunity, at least, for the development and testing of expectations about their tasks. It seems reasonable to assume that the more the activity of any committee is perceived as being important to the power of the House, and the more frequent the contact between that committee and the other members of the House, the more fully articulated will be House member expectations regarding the committee's tasks.

Historically, House expectations have been expressed when Appropriations Committee activity was under critical review. Three times in the life of the committee — 1865, 1885, and 1920 — its activities have been scrutinized and significantly altered at the hands of the House. On other occasions, such as those leading to the Legislative Reorganization Act of 1946, the Accrued Expenditures Act of 1958, and during the hearings of the Joint Committee on the Organization of Congress in 1965, special attention has been focused on the Committee. In the specific period under study, House expectations have occasionally been articulated by a clear majority of House members on a roll call vote. For the most part, however, House expectations have to be inferred from the words of those individual members with some claim to represent an important subsystem of the House. Given the oligarchical structure of influence in the House, individuals may represent such subsystems as party, other committees, state delegations, or informal factions. Such leaders, as well as others, will express House expectations when they commend the Committee or, more likely, when they protest that "the Committee is not doing its job." Although the idea of House expectations will be employed, an attempt will be made throughout to specify as precisely as possible what body of opinion is involved in each expectation.

House expectations can be divided into two related categories. In the first place, the Appropriations Committee is expected to assist the House in attaining House goals whenever these goals involve the subject matter of appropriations. Committees are created to perform certain goal-oriented tasks which their parent chamber as a whole lacks the ability, the time, or, perhaps, the will to perform adequately. Second, in seeking to accomplish the goals prescribed for it the Committee is expected to observe certain rules of the game — formal and informal — established by the parent chamber. This set of expectations pertains more to the procedural "how" than to the substantive "what" Committee behavior. Since all House-prescribed rules of the game are designed to stabilize the system-subsystem relationship, they can be categorized as maintenance expectations as distinguished from goal expectations.

5

GOAL EXPECTATIONS

The Appropriations Committee was established by a House resolution in 1865 which gave some Ways and Means Committee tasks to two new committees, Appropriations and Banking and Currency. The rationale for the creation of an Appropriations Committee was the growing inability of the Ways and Means Committee to perform its two traditional tasks of raising revenue and allocating appropriations. The resolution's sponsor opened the debate by saying that "in relation to the division of the Committee on Ways and Means, I desire to show the importance and immensity of the labor imposed upon the Committee with a view to a division of the labor."[5] A study of the existing committee's tasks had led the Select Committee on the Rules of the House to the conclusion that

> No set of men, however enduring their patience, studious their habits, or gigantic their mental grasp, when overburdened with the labor incident to the existing monetary condition of the country growing out of this unparalleled civil strife, can do this labor as well as the people have a right to expect of their Representatives. Therefore, we propose to divide the labor of the Committee on Ways and Means.[6]

If the brevity of debate and the paucity of opposition are indicative, general House agreement existed then, as now, on the need for a Committee on Appropriations to help the House in the attainment of its goals.

The most general goal of the House is to participate in making laws for American society. House members expect the Committee on Appropriations to deliberate, decide, and make recommendations which will then be acted upon authoritatively by the House. The Committee members are the House's specialists in appropriations lawmaking. And their principal task as seen by the House is to make educated recommendations as to the amount of money to be appropriated for the various operations of the government. Their recommendations are expected to be accompanied, should the Committee deem it necessary or wise, by the specification of conditions governing the availability and use of appropriated funds. On closer inspection House lawmaking expectations break down into two more specific expectations — one involving program support and the other involving economy. A third House expectation prescribes Appropriations Committee help in overseeing the activities of the executive branch — in exercising that "continuous watchfulness" over administration called for in the Legislative Reorganization Act of 1946. Finally, a fourth House goal involves the necessity of negotiating with the Senate in conference committee sessions so as to iron out differences in bills passed by the House and the Senate.

[5] *Congressional Globe*, 38th Congress, 2nd Session, p. 1312.
[6] *Ibid.*

6

The vast majority of public laws passed by the House of Representatives should be viewed as stating a goal expectation for the Appropriations Committee. They say, on behalf of the House, "We have decided that the federal government should engage in the following specified activity. You, the Appropriations Committee, are expected to vote sufficient funds to support that activity." The spending of money by the government ordinarily involves a two-step process. First, Congress must authorize a program or activity and authorize the expenditure of money to finance it. Second, Congress must give some official the authority (i.e., obligational authority) to spend money in connection with the program or activity which has been authorized. These separate steps are usually carried out by two distinct pieces of legislation — an authorization bill and an appropriation bill. The Appropriations Committee, in other words, is called upon to grant obligational authority to someone to spend money for a program that has already been voted into existence by an act of Congress. Since, presumably, everyone who votes for a program expects it to be financed adequately, every authorization bill expresses the expectation of a House majority that the Appropriations Committee should provide financial support for the activity specified therein.

An understanding of this very basic goal expectation serves to place Appropriations Committee activity in perspective from the outset. The Committee's money decisions are expected to conform broadly to expenditure patterns established by authorization statutes. And any particular authorization is expected to circumscribe the Committee's decision-making freedom. The Committee is given discretion; it may be allowed to stretch the limits of that discretion quite far; and the exercise of its discretion brings the Committee considerable influence. When, however, the Committee confronts a budget request for an appropriation to support an authorized program, its decisions are expected to have a marginal or incremental effect on the program. The Committee is not expected to appropriate every last nickel requested. But it is not expected to vote so little money that the program, as conceived by the House, cannot survive.

Between these extremes, conflict will arise over what constitutes "adequate" or "sufficient" financing and what constitutes the "survival" of a given program at a particular time. Hence, House expectations as to the Committee's area of discretion are hard to pinpoint. One can only generalize that when a majority has declared support for a program, the Appropriations Committee is expected to appropriate most of the money authorized or requested for it. A vastly larger portion of a request is expected to be beyond the reach of the Appropriations Committee than is expected to lie within its area of discretion. The Committee's independent influence is expected to be marginal or incremental. Such is the dominant demand of every authorization statute.

Expectations of program support get expressed by House majorities. But other expectations calling upon the Committee to vote financial support come from individual House members or small clusters of Members. These Members press very specific, constituency-oriented demands upon the Committee. Occasionally a Member expectation calls for unsympathetic treatment of a government agency whose action he perceives as inimical to the interests of his constituency. Normally, however, individual congressmen seek sympathetic consideration and money for their "pet projects." And these are likely to be items of a sort which do lie within the Committee's area of discretion — a dam, a research laboratory, a field office, a federal building, etc. The intensity of such demands stems from the belief of most Members that their reelection may well depend on the Committee's decision in such matters. "The biggest thing in electoral politics, in Congressional politics," said an experienced House member, "is boodle and the reputation you get back home for being able to get boodle." True or not, many congressmen believe it is. They express their expectations clearly and urge them upon the Appropriations Committee. Taken together, expectations of support for programs and projects emphasize the spending side of House goal expectations.

Finance Programs and Projects Economically

Since the time the Appropriations Committee was created most House members have expressed a second kind of expectation about Committee recommendations. The Appropriations Committee is expected to assist the House in achieving the most economical expenditure of federal money. The expectation that the Committee should finance programs and projects has usually been taken for granted. The expectation that it should finance them as economically as possible has frequently been articulated as the most special goal to be sought by the Committee.

In addition to a redistribution of the work load, the architects of 1865 were seeking a means of holding down as far as possible the appropriation of money in the face of the increasingly strenuous demands being pressed upon them. They believed that the closer the scrutiny of appropriations and the more single-minded the group which performed this operation, the greater would be the likelihood of economies. The resolution's sponsor described the Committee's substantive goal in these words:

> I need not dilate upon the importance of having hereafter one committee to investigate with nicest heed all matters connected with economy. The tendency of the time is to extravagancies in private and public. We require of this new committee their whole labor in the restraint of extravagant and illegal appropriations.[7]

[7] *Ibid.*

8

Even in the most critical period (1885) of the Committee's history, when the House cut its jurisdiction in half (see Chapter Two), a consensus existed with regard to the need for economy. As might be expected those who argued against assigning six of the twelve appropriation bills to substantive legislative committees grounded their opposition in the language of economy expectations. The author of the minority report defended the proposition that

> Whenever we relax that rigid grasp which the Appropriations Committee can alone keep upon the purse strings of government, whenever we wrest from it the key of the national Treasury, we will at once enter upon a vast field of public expenditure that has no bounds, and embark upon a turgid ocean of public extravagance which will soon swallow up our entire public resources.[8]

Though the advocates of change challenged this line of reasoning, they did not challenge the assumption about the need for economy on which it rested:

> With solemn shakings of the head and ominous rolling of the eye we are constantly admonished by the more experienced members of this House that the expenditures of the government will be vastly swollen if this proposed change is effected. This, sir, is nothing in the world but naked assertion. The truth is that the logic of the situation conducts to a different conclusion; that is unless it is claimed for the Committee on Appropriations that they are possessed of higher intelligence and a greater disposition to frugality than the members of other committees.[9]

The attack on the Committee centered on the alleged pervasiveness of Committee influence within the House — its control over House business, its power to legislate on appropriation bills, and its subsequent dwarfing of other committees. There remained agreement on both sides that it was the unquestioned duty of the House of Representatives and of every committee dealing with appropriations to insure the economical expenditure of federal money.

When, in 1920, the House restored full jurisdiction to the Committee, the clearly expressed expectation was that the move would effect greater economy than had been obtained under the post-1885 arrangement. The enactment of the Budget and Accounting Act of 1920 to alter budget-making within the executive branch, precipitated the complementary drive to alter the appropriations process on the legislative side. To take the new single executive budget and scatter it among several appropriating committees would, in the eyes of its sponsors, inevitably inflate appropriations and defeat the very ends of the Act. The Act and the resolution restoring full jurisdiction

---

[8] 17 *Congressional Record*, p. 172.
[9] 17 *Congressional Record*, p. 237.

to the Appropriations Committee were laced together in House debate as the twin imperatives of economy.

In 1920, as in 1865, the Committee's supporters (a majority in both cases) based their expectations on the proposition that "real economy in appropriations and government expenditures cannot be effective unless all appropriations bills originate in a single committee devoted primarily to that task."[10] The man who was the chief House sponsor of both the Budget and Accounting Act and of the resolution restoring the Appropriations Committee jurisdiction spoke to those who, following the ethos of 1885, feared the increase in Committee power:

> This resolution should not suffer because it gives additional power to a committee that must produce strict economy. If you want real economy, if you want a reduction in the high cost of living, a reduction in expenditures, a reduction in taxation, if you want a real budget, you will vote for this resolution.[11]

In each of these classic confrontations of House and Committee, the record indicates that a firm consensus existed among House members that the Appropriations Committee should produce recommendations embodying the most economical expenditure of the taxpayer's money. Again in 1946, the clear purpose of Section 138a of the Legislative Reorganization Act, setting up the legislative budget, was to effect a reduction in expenditures. It is worth noting that 1865, 1920, and 1946, years of especially significant displays of economy sentiment, were all post-war years. Periods of abnormally large expenditures, it seems, are likely to be followed by periods of abnormally strong concern for economy within Congress.

Though their intensity fluctuates over time, economy expectations have probably never been absent from the chamber. And this is because they appear to represent a dominant theme of American public opinion. In voicing their demands for reduced government expenditures House members speak for a breadth of sentiment which no representative body could ignore. It is, moreover, a sentiment deeply rooted in the ethics of a capitalist society. Ideologies get telescoped, for public discourse, into labels. And in the world of labels where they must operate, every congressman shuns the label "spender." Short of the labels of treason, a House member would rather be called anything else than a spender. In 1957, for instance, the *Congressional Quarterly* developed from selected roll calls an index of "economy voting" and proceeded to rate members of Congress according to their economy-mindedness. Legislators rated low on "economy voting" objected strenuously. So strong was their adverse reaction to the index — really, to the label

[10] 59 *Congressional Record*, p. 8117.
[11] *Ibid.*, p. 8116.

"spender" — that the *Congressional Quarterly* switched to another index which divided congressmen in about the same way but which was labeled, less perjoratively, as "federal role score."[12]

A series of American Institute of Public Opinion polls taken periodically from 1949 to 1959 revealed the pervasiveness and persistence of the public demand for economy. See Table 1.1. Though the wording of the question varied slightly, a majority of the respondents, in all but one of the four instances, favored the reduction of expenditures. And once we eliminate those respondents having no opinion at all on the subject, the dominance of the economy sentiment — as opposed to sentiment for maintaining or increasing expenditures — is even more impressive. A set of similar questions asked by the Institute between 1936 and 1941 elicited the same range of responses — with majorities consistently in favor of reduced federal spending.[13] At this most general level, a desire for economy in government may well be among the most durable strands of American public opinion.

TABLE 1.1

PUBLIC OPINION ON REDUCTION OF FEDERAL EXPENDITURES

	Per Cent in Favor of Reduced Federal Expenditures — All Respondents	*Per Cent in Favor of Reduced Federal Expenditures — Respondents with Opinion*
1949[a]	54	70
1953[b]	59	72
1957[c]	47	59
1959[d]	52	—

[a] Question: "Is there anything the Federal Government spends money for now which you think should be reduced or cut out?" AIPO, 3/17/49.
[b] Question: "Do you think it is possible to further reduce government expenses without cutting down on important services to the people?" AIPO, 10/7/53.
[c] Question: "Do you think the budget should be cut or not?" AIPO, 5/15/57.
[d] Question: "Do you think there is anything for which the government should be spending less money than it is at present?" AIPO, 3/3/59.

House members must reckon, however, not only with the existence of economy opinion but with its salient properties. One such property is diffuseness and lack of focus. That is to say, while many are in favor of reduced expenditures, far fewer are willing or able to specify the exact areas in which reduction should take place.[14] When respondents who favor economy in gen-

[12] See *Congressional Quarterly*, "Economy Voting," August 2, 1957, pp. 916 ff., October 25, 1957, pp. 1199 ff. 98 *Congressional Record*, pp. 1759–1760.
[13] Hadley Cantril (ed.), *Public Opinion: 1935–1946* (Princeton: Princeton University Press, 1951), pp. 917–922. See especially Nos. 4, 16, 31, 54.
[14] Compare, for example, Nos. 4 and 16 with Nos. 37 and 38, *Ibid.*

11

eral are asked, in an open-ended inquiry, to pinpoint the places where economies should be made, many fail to do so in detail. Of the 1,184 people favoring reduction in 1949, only about half named "specific" areas for reduction (e.g., foreign aid, military expenditures, veterans' programs). Half of the respondents took refuge in even greater generalities (e.g., too many employees, high salaries, red tape, too many bureaus, or "everything"). In the 1953 poll, 860 people who thought expenses could be reduced "without cutting down on important services" were asked to be specific. Of the responses to this somewhat more directed but still open-ended question, 78 per cent produced either the same amorphous bill of particulars or (in the case of 19 per cent of the respondents) no answer at all.

To some degree, people do not pinpoint economies because they cannot. Their lack of knowledge about government — their diffuse perception of "the government" — explains the diffuseness of their economy opinion. Of equal importance in understanding the properties of economy opinion is this additional fact; people do not specify economies because they do not favor specific economies. As soon as the pollster moves from questions calling for "a reduction in expenditures now" or "a reduction in general government running expenses," to questions which pinpoint the program to be reduced, economy opinions fall away sharply. To ask someone to suggest program areas to which cuts might be applied is to call to mind the extent to which government spending serves his own interests. If he is familiar with specific programs, the chances are that he is a beneficiary of that program and will not want to see it reduced. The only specific program area which was regularly offered up as able to absorb cuts was the foreign aid program — the rewards of which are not very tangible for the average respondent.[15] Not only, therefore, may people be unable to specify economies; they may also be unwilling to do so.

Table 1.2 illustrates the American public's great willingness to economize in general and its reluctance to economize in particular.

Given a choice, Americans in 1950 indicated their overwhelming support for decreasing "the general expenses of government." They also declared in favor of decreasing program expenditures in two areas, farm subsidies and foreign aid — neither of which bestows tangible or direct benefits on any very sizable proportions of the population. But the public declared against decreased expenditures in five other program areas, and in three of these, opinions favoring increases outweighed the combined opinion in support of decreases plus the status quo. The five programs which drew the least economy sentiment do benefit, directly and tangibly, either a majority or a sizable minority of Americans. And this explains their reluctance to prescribe re-

[15] Even this involved a small percentage of the total number of respondents — 17 per cent in 1949, 4 per cent in 1953, 10 per cent in 1957, 17 per cent in 1959.

TABLE 1.2

PUBLIC OPINION ON REDUCTION OF FEDERAL EXPENDITURES
IN SPECIFIED AREAS — 1950[a]

Specific Area	Per Cent Decrease Expenditures	Per Cent Keep Expenditures the Same	Per Cent Increase Expenditures	Per Cent No Opinion
General Government Expenses	66	21	7	7
Farm Subsidies	52	21	16	10
Foreign Aid	46	33	12	10
Federal Housing	24	21	46	9
Veterans' Benefits	18	47	30	5
Social Welfare	16	37	42	5
Public Works	14	27	52	7
Defense	7	24	63	5

[a] Rows may not add up to 100 per cent because of rounding. Question: "Do you think U.S. Government spending should be increased, decreased or remain the same on the following?" AIPO, 3/24/50.

ductions. It is of interest to note that economy opinion varies from program to program. It is also true that for any given program economy or spending opinions fluctuate over time.[16] One should not overdraw, therefore, the specificity of opinions recorded in Table 1.2. Still they lend support to the gross generalization that, the more nonspecific the governmental activity involved, the more prevalent will be economy opinion regarding it. Conversely, the more clearly specified a program area, the more likely it is that economy sentiment will decline.

Aside from its amorphous qualities, economy sentiment exhibits a high degree of latency. It represents an enduring element in American public opinion; and its existence sets some outer boundaries to appropriations decision-making — "opinion dikes" in the terms of V. O. Key.[17] But if public economy sentiment is to have any differential impact from year to year or from program to program, it must be activated and brought to bear on appropriations decision-making by specifically interested individuals and groups, in or out of government. Members of the House pride themselves on being (because of their two-year election cycle) uniquely close to "the people." They view themselves as sensitive, but by no means passive, interpreters of

16 For example, when the same question regarding defense expenditures as was asked in 1953 was repeated in 1957, the distribution of responses was 22 per cent in favor of increased expenditures, 60 per cent in favor of the same level of expenditures, and 9 per cent in favor of decreased expenditures — a marked change from 1953.

17 V. O. Key, Jr., *Public Opinion and American Democracy* (New York: A. A. Knopf, 1961), Chapter 21.

public opinion. As such, they may, on their own initiative or under prodding from the President or economy-minded interest groups, activate latent economy opinions and communicate them to the Appropriations Committee.

Appropriations Committee members themselves are fully sensitive to the existence of latent sentiments in favor of economy in government. Indeed, they may decide for reasons of their own, to activate and canalize such opinion. Nonetheless, the expression of economy expectations by House members can produce an intensity of demand that the Committee would not otherwise feel and could not generate on its own. The House economy drive of 1957 is a case in point. In that year, a national survey revealed considerable public sentiment in favor of economy characterized by typically low intensity. Those respondents (47 per cent of the sample) who favored reductions in the 1957 budget were asked further: "Do you think that there should be a major cut or not?" Only 42 per cent were willing to support a "major cut." Forty-seven per cent opposed a "major cut" and 11 per cent offered no opinion. Clearly, a ready resource existed (as always) with which to fuel an economy drive, but, left unactivated, the opinions expressed hardly added up to a decisive public demand for decreased expenditures. In 1957, however, Secretary of the Treasury Humphrey and President Eisenhower became especially alarmed about the size of the budget and began to voice extraordinarily strong economy expectations. Conservative groups around the country (especially the Chamber of Commerce) picked up the theme. So did economy-minded members of the House. And, in loose coalition with one another, these groups sought to activate some broader public sentiment. House members drew upon such sentiment as was expressed and upon the undoubted existence of untapped sources of economy opinion to press intensified economy expectations upon the House Committee. In 1951 and 1952, years of the Korean War, House members generated and communicated similarly intensified economy demands, and they did so quite independently and without prodding from extra-congressional forces. As the direct transmission line from the larger public to the Appropriations Committee, the House regulates the intensity of public demands for economy.

To say that House expectations may register an intensity of economy sentiment much greater than that generated by the public at large is not to say that House and public economy opinion differ in other respects. Most House economy expectations, whatever their intensity, are expressed in the same amorphous and diffuse fashion as the public sentiment they claim to represent. "The public demands economy in government this year." "All nondefense expenditures must be cut to the bone." "We must keep the budget as close as possible to last year's levels." It is in formulas like these that House economy expectations get communicated to the Committee. Thus the House, too, sets up "opinion dikes" for the Committee — prescribing a general direction and some outer boundaries rather than issuing specific instructions. Gabriel Almond has observed that America's political decisions generally may be affected by "intervention in policy making through the transient impact of public moods."[18] And it is useful to think of House economy expectations in terms of "transient moods," which wax and wane depending on conditions external and internal to the chamber.

One partial measure of House economy moods can be gained by examining over time the nature of changes in Appropriations Committee recommendations made on the House floor. In those years when a large number of changes are made and when a preponderance of these changes are decreases, one can assume that an economy mood exists in the chamber. For purposes of studying floor action (in Chapter Nine), all floor amendments involving the appropriation bills for eight departments (all but Defense and Post Office) plus public works, from 1947 to 1962, were examined. In terms of the kinds of amendments passed on the floor, there were three years in which more than three decreases in Committee recommendations were voted on the floor. The years were 1951, in which 31 decreases were voted; 1952, in which 19 decreases were voted; and 1957, in which 13 decreases were voted. What makes the existence of an economy mood in these three years all the more unmistakable is the fact that the changes made on the House floor ran overwhelmingly in the single direction of further reductions. Thus, only one amendment calling for an increase over the Committee recommendation passed in 1951 and 1952; and none passed in 1957. (For these totals, see Table 9.6, p. 452.) With House expectations so intensely and so one-sidedly expressed, there seems little doubt but what the Appropriations Committee would get the general message. As to specifics, however, the Committee would be left pretty much to its own devices.

However strongly an economy mood may run in the chamber, the Committee is not expected to make such reductions as will place on-going or newly authorized programs in jeopardy. Thus it bears repeating that, whatever independent influence the Committee exercises, it is expected to be marginal in any one year and incremental over time. House expectations do not specify what dollars and cents decisions the Committee should make. But they do set limits to Committee discretion through the equipoise of program and economy expectations. Expectations of program support allow for marginal economies; yet economy expectations assume a substantial expenditure for program support. The Committee is asked to exercise discretion in balancing these expectations, but the arena of discretion is kept circumscribed and modest.

[18] Gabriel Almond, "Comparative Political Systems," *Journal of Politics* (August, 1956), p. 400.

In exercising its discretion, the Committee faces two potentially conflicting expectations. Though they need not conflict irreconcilably with one another, program and economy expectations do pull the Committee toward a different balance of decisions. One set of expectations calls on the Committee to take more money out of the Treasury; another calls on the Committee to leave more money in the Treasury. One asks the Committee to spend; the other asks the Committee to save. Ordinarily the House does not tell the Committee how to resolve the dilemma. Some guidance may come by way of dominant House moods. In 1951, 1952, and 1957, the Committee was expected to tip the balance toward economy. By contrast, in 1953, 1954, and 1955, the cues coming from the House ran in the other direction. In these latter three years, a total of 45 changes were made on the House floor and every one was an increase over Committee recommendations. One might describe the mood of these three years as a permissive mood — relative, at least, to the proposals of the Committee. With economy sentiment remaining latent and with recession psychology present, the House approved of attempts of individual Members or clusters of Members to secure increased appropriations for specific pet projects.

Just as demands for budget reduction tend to be amorphous, demands for budget increases tend to be specific. Throughout the appropriations process, as we shall see, the more specific the budgetary item under discussion the more likely it is that the dominant pressure will be for increases. And this tendency is clearest when individual Members plead for individual constituency-oriented projects. The conflict between program and economy expectations is acknowledged, and Member demands for increases are pressed in the formula of "economy, but. . . ."

In the words of a veteran Texas Member:

> I am for economy in Idaho and perhaps in Maine and a considerable amount down in Oklahoma. Then in the districts of some of my [Texas] colleagues, I am for economy over there unless it would injure and hurt my colleagues; but when you come into my district I am for "economy, but."[19]

Hardly an appropriation debate goes by without some speaker rising to say, "I am in favor of economy but I am not in favor of false economy."[20] Or, "I doubt if I have failed to support it in its efforts at economy at any time since we went into session . . . but I am vitally interested in [an airport] in my district."[21] Members feel obliged to pay lip service to economy with such

---

[19] 103 *Congressional Record*, p. 4561. On the "economy, but" theme, see also Allen Otten, "Economy Anyone?" *Wall Street Journal*, March 28, 1963, pp. 1, 13.

[20] 103 *Congressional Record*, p. 5035.

[21] 95 *Congressional Record*, p. 5373. See also 102 *Congressional Record*, p. 8441.

rhetoric as "false economy," "penny wise and pound foolish," and "saving at the spigot and wasting at the bung." But the Committee is expected to resolve their particular cases by tilting the balance of decision toward the "but" and not the "economy."

The Committee is not always left without clear prescriptions as to how the demands of program support and economy should be balanced. But in general and within the limits fixed by the equipoise of the two, the House presents potentially conflicting expectations and leaves the House Committee to devise its own pattern of responses.

Oversee Executive Activity

A third House goal expectation holds that the Appropriations Committee should engage in oversight of administration. The Committee is expected to keep itself and the rest of the House informed on the way in which the executive agencies use the money granted to them and, indeed, to influence the use of public funds in ways prescribed by law. The Committee has been specially authorized by House rules (Rule 11, Section 2) to

> conduct studies and examinations of the organization and operation of any executive department or other executive agencies . . . as it may deem necessary to assist it in the determination of matters within its jurisdiction.

There are, of course, numerous techniques for congressional committees to watch over administrative activity. But "the power of the purse" has long constituted the major legislative weapon in its struggles to control executive institutions. The weight of informed judgment continues to support the view that revenue and expenditure controls represent the most effective legislative sanction over the federal bureaucracy.

House oversight expectations are undergirded by that sense of institutional rivalry which most members of the body harbor with regard to the executive branch. To be sure, party ties with the Chief Executive or alliances of mutual interest with particular administrative agencies mitigate and blunt legislative-executive antagonism. But it seems reasonable to assert that House members perceive of the oversight task as predominantly a negative or checking one. At best it functions to legitimize executive actions. What seems amply evident is that the House does not expect its Appropriations Committee to "rubber stamp" executive requests for funds. Every member identifies to some degree with his own group "on the Hill" and carries some suspicions of "the people downtown." The existence of this set of attitudes nourishes the expectations that the Committee's oversight activity will have a predominantly negative thrust. One attitude distributed fairly widely among House members holds that federal executives, in their enthusiasm for their policies, tend to request more money than they really need. Such sentiments

17

will be heard during the authorization as well as the appropriations processes. To the degree that House members do perceive administrators in this way they expect the Appropriations Committee to perform its oversight task by eliminating every proposed expenditure which lacks a convincing justification in the estimates. Here, oversight expectations frequently dovetail with economy expectations in encouraging Appropriations Committee reductions in administrative budget requests.

The Committee is expected to utilize both statutory and nonstatutory oversight techniques. The most obvious kind of statutory control flows from the Committee's dollars and cents appropriation decisions. Money levels control program levels. And if, for example, an agency or a part of an agency is deemed not to have used its funds in accordance with House desires, the Committee is expected to use its money leverage to ensure compliance. In addition, and where appropriate, the Committee is expected to place language in the bill specifying conditions under which the money can or must be obligated. Thus the Committee may choose to "earmark" a sum of money for a certain use by stating typically that "not less than $10,000 shall be used for (a specified purpose)." Or the Committee may "limit" the use of funds by stating that "no part of this appropriation shall be expended for (a specified activity)." Or the Committee may fix the length of time over which the money can be obligated — usually for a single fiscal year, but sometimes over several years ("multiple year" appropriations) or indefinitely ("no year" appropriations). House members may not always approve of the uses to which these prerogatives are put, but they grant the Committee the right to use them.

Beyond the letter of the appropriation bills it writes, the Committee is expected to pursue its oversight tasks in nonstatutory ways. The Committee holds hearings each year for the purpose of examining agency budget requests and questioning agency officials. Both "on" and "off" the record, ample opportunity exists for the Committee to scrutinize agency behavior and communicate legislative desires to the agency officials involved. Another oversight technique involves the intentions, admonitions, and directions conveyed to the agency by means of Committee reports. Ostensibly written to convey the reasoning behind the Committee's recommendation to the House, the criticisms and suggestions carried in the reports accompanying each bill are expected to influence the subsequent behavior of the agency. Committee reports are not the law, but it is expected that they be regarded almost as seriously. A third nonstatutory method of oversight involves the informal contact, face-to-face or written, between individual Committee members and the Committee staff on the one hand and the chief executives and budget officers of executive agencies on the other. It is expected that Appropriations

18

Committee influence, like that of all House committees, should be wielded in fairly continuous personal communication with executive agency personnel.

The traditional primacy of the Appropriations Committee in implementing legislative oversight tasks derives not just from the fact that it holds the power of the purse nor from the variety of techniques available to it. It stems also from the frequency of opportunity for control. The fact that appropriations decisions are made annually makes the Committee more "continuously watchful" than any other. Committee hearings for the purpose of taking testimony number upward of 400 each year. Informal oversight activity surrounds each one of these hearings and formal oversight activity takes root there. Appropriations Committee oversight is expected to be intensive, repetitive, and constant. But in specifics, as always, House expectations leave the Committee with a significant degree of operating freedom.

Negotiate with the Senate

A final set of expectations relates to the House's need to negotiate with the Senate in all cases where their appropriation bills reveal disagreement. In 576 bureau case histories studied from 1947 to 1962, the two bodies passed identical provisions in 186 (32 per cent) cases. In 390 (68 per cent) instances, therefore, conference committee negotiations were necessary between the representatives of the two chambers. The Appropriations Committee or, rather, a few of its members act as the spokesmen for the House in these negotiations. They are expected to drive as hard a bargain as possible on behalf of those provisions approved by the House.

House expectations may be registered in different ways and with different degrees of intensity. In some instances the House may, by special roll call vote, "instruct" its conferees, i.e., bind them, to a certain position. Ordinary roll calls may also register House expectations. In these cases, the more lopsided the roll call votes the more firm is the House expectation that its position should be upheld. In other cases, individual Members will simply exhort the Committee to "stand hitched" or to "fight until the snow comes if necessary to maintain the position of the House in effecting reduction in these bills." The House expects, however, that the Committee will have to compromise if a bill is to be produced. They hope that Appropriations Committee conferees will draw upon a sufficient reservoir of institutional patriotism and skill to produce compromises which they can claim as "victories" over "the other body." But House members do not expect to fix the terms of the compromise themselves. Again, within certain guidelines, the specifics of decision-making are left to the Committee.

19

The central proposition of this section is, very simply, that "the House" does express certain expectations concerning the goals to be pursued by its Appropriations Committee. The Committee should support programs and projects, support them as economically as possible, oversee executive activity, and negotiate with the Senate. As House members see it, these expectations describe what the House should do. They prescribe the broad channels of Committee activity. A second proposition of the section is that each set of expectations leaves the Committee with a sizable degree of operating freedom. In performing the tasks defined by House goal expectations, the Committee is expected to determine more specific, day-to-day objectives for itself. House expectations, therefore, assume a degree of dependence and a degree of autonomy for the Committee.

MAINTENANCE EXPECTATIONS

Just how much autonomy and how much dependence should characterize the Committee's relationship to the House? This is the question with which House maintenance expectations are concerned. And, of all expectations, the most basic is this: Whatever House-prescribed goal the Committee seeks to achieve it should always act as a dependent subsystem of the House of Representatives. The Committee's status as a subsystem is set by the fact that it depends for its very existence — let alone its jurisdiction, its members, and its money — upon the House. When House members declare that "the Committee on Appropriations is the servant and not the master of the House," or "the Appropriations Committee is the creature of the House," or it is "a mere agent of the House and within the control of the House," they are expressing what they consider to be the fundamental rule of the game in House-Committee relations. As the Chairman of the Rules Committee once put it to his colleagues,

> You all know and it is not necessary for me to repeat it to you, that the Committee on Appropriations cannot do one thing — they cannot appropriate money and they cannot prevent the appropriation of money unless that is the will of this House. You have an opportunity on every annual appropriation bill that comes up to express your will.[22]

Committee members are not allowed to forget that they owe their legitimacy to the House and that each of their decisions must be legitimized by a subsequent House decision.

To preserve this basic system-subsystem relationship, the House articulates a set of subsidiary maintenance expectations — formal and informal — which Committee members are expected to observe. Insofar as these norms

[22] 105 *Congressional Record*, p. 8673.

are followed, the Committee's autonomy is a limited, contingent autonomy; and the Committee remains in a fundamentally dependent relationship to the House.

Follow Consensus-Building Procedures

All Committee decisions are expected to reflect "the will of the House." Precisely what that "will" requires in substantive terms may be quite unclear — especially, as we have seen, when one moves from the generality of a mood to the specificity of a discrete decision. It is for this reason, perhaps, that the House stresses the procedures of decision-making at least as much as the substance of the decision. The Committee is expected to arrive at its decision by searching out the terms of widest agreement among conflicting demands. And they are expected to present their decision to the House as such — not to throw a whole series of insoluble conflicts into the lap of the House. The House, as a practical matter, expects the Committee to do the bulk of all appropriations decision-making. What the House wants, however, is some assurance that the Committee's decision is likely to command widespread support in and out of the chamber. If the Members can be assured that the Committee recommendations are politically viable, they will more readily make the recommendations legally authoritative. Hence the emphasis on the way in which the Committee decision was arrived at.

House expectations concerning the procedures of consensus-building become most evident when the Committee's recommendations reach the floor. At that stage, House members seek assurance that the Committee has exposed itself to all sides of a question, that every interested individual or group has been able to secure access to the Committee, and that everyone has had a courteous, "fair" hearing. Members may want to know whether actual or possible conflicts between the two parties have been successfully resolved. They may want to know if the relevant substantive legislative committees have been consulted. They expect that the Committee will have spared no effort of time or procedure in seeking out differences of opinion and working for a viable, broadly based settlement of conflicts. These are the practices that produce, in congressional parlance, "a good bill." To the degree that the Committee meets the expectations of consensus-building, their recommendation, whatever its substance, is more likely to be accepted as carrying out "the will of the House" and, hence, maintaining the basic dependence of the Committee.

Appropriate: Don't Legislate

The Appropriations Committee is a product of the division of labor; but so, too, are all the standing committees of the House. The House, in its rules and precedents, has produced an elaborate corpus of maintenance expectations to govern Appropriations Committee–substantive committee relations. The rule of the House (Rule 21, Section 2) which states that "No appropriation shall be reported in any general appropriation bill or be in order as an amendment thereto, for any expenditure not previously authorized by law . . ." is the formal basis upon which a separation of tasks between the Appropriations Committee and the substantive committees is maintained. In Rule 21, however, an exception is made if the legislation reported by the Committee "shall retrench expenditures" — a proviso known as the Holman Rule. With this exception, the Appropriations Committee cannot legislate on an appropriation bill. And, under Section 4 of Rule 21, legislative committees cannot appropriate money. As a practical matter, however, the separation between appropriation and legislation is difficult to maintain — both because of inherent definitional problems and because the will to maintain it may not exist. Legislative committee members are greatly concerned that when the Appropriations Committee attaches conditions to an appropriation bill, it will in effect make changes in substantive legislation. Just what constitutes "legislation on an appropriation bill" and what does not, what actions "retrench expenditures" and what do not, are the subjects of an elaborate and complicated body of rulings — which occupy more space in *Cannon's Procedure in the House of Representatives* than any other section save one.[23]

House rules provide that legislation on a general appropriation bill is subject to a point of order and can be stricken from the bill by one objection from the floor. Frequently, Member expectations are not so seriously violated by particular pieces of legislation as to produce objections. Thus, much legislation does appear in appropriation bills. Indeed, a provision prohibiting legislation on an appropriation bill was included in an early version of the Legislative Reorganization Bill and deleted because, presumably, House members find such legislation useful. Occasionally, the Appropriations Committee will obtain a rule from the Rules Committee waiving all points of order on a given bill. Normally, though not without protest, the House will vote approval of the rule — thus permitting appropriations legislation to affect some substantive area. The Committee is allowed to function with a degree of autonomy in the area of "legislation"; but the dominant House expectation remains — that Committee activity proceed at the sufferance of the House.

A pair of House veterans commented typically: "It is not the business of the Committee on Appropriations, in the minds of most of us in the House, to engage in legislative undertakings about which they are not thoroughly familiar."[24] "Congress writes the checks. You are supposed to

[23] Clarence Cannon, *Cannon's Procedure in the House of Representatives* (Washington: U.S. Government Printing Office, 1963), pp. 24–74.
[24] 97 *Congressional Record*, p. 2695.

carry out the intent and purpose of the legislative committees of the Congress."[25] Substantive committee members expect the Appropriations Committee to support programs as authorized and not tamper with the program itself. As one Member said, "The Appropriations Committee should check into waste and inefficiency and they should decide whether too much money has been authorized to meet the goals of the program." But the problem of funding a given program adequately without affecting the program substantively is not easily solved. The potential for conflict between the House (i.e., its substantive committees) and the Appropriations Committee is obvious. In the interests of harmony the Committee is expected to observe procedural restraints.

Collect and Distribute Information

Another area of special concern to Members centers around problems of information-gathering by the Committee and the communication of this information to the House. It is one chronic source of legislative-executive friction that congressmen feel underinformed by the executive branch. And Member expectations are that the Appropriations Committee should provide a major channel by which information flows from the executive branch to the House of Representatives. These expectations have been formally articulated through the adoption of procedures designed to facilitate the collection of information by the Committee. It was the only House Committee, for instance, which was left free under the terms of the Legislative Reorganization Act of 1946 to hire as large a staff as it wished. Necessarily, therefore, the Committee's annual budget is left expandable by the House. At the beginning of each Congress, the Committee receives blanket authorization "to sit during the sessions and recesses" of the House. And, most importantly, it is allowed to hold all of its hearings in closed, executive session.

Each of these special considerations is designed to encourage a heavy flow and a free flow of information from the executive branch to the Committee. For it is deemed that the achievement of lawmaking and oversight goals require a maximum of information. The Committee is expected to exercise some judgment in the disclosure of its information. But the dominant expectation is that the Committee should disseminate most of the information it has assembled to the other members of the House to form the basis on which their authoritative decisions can be made. "I do not believe," said a House member during the Reorganization Act hearings, "that the information so obtained ought to be the exclusive prerogative of the Appropriations Committee, nor that members of such committees ought to come on the floor and say our investigation has revealed so and so but the rest of you

<hr>

[25] *Congressional Record*, Daily Edition, May 11, 1960, p. 9324.

23

members cannot see it."[26] In recognition of their subject matter importance, the Committee's bills are allowed to bypass the House Rules Committee for a preferentially swift trip to the floor, where they become privileged matters.

A cluster of further expectations involving Committee-to-House communications were underscored by their inclusion in the Legislative Reorganization Act of 1946. It was in the interest of overall clarity that the Act "authorized and directed" the Committee to join with the three other financial committees of House and Senate to present to the House a legislative budget, estimating revenue and expenditures for the next fiscal year and recommending a ceiling on expenditures. Also in the interest of clarity in communication, the Committee was directed (in Section 139b) to develop and place in its printed hearings "a standard appropriations classification schedule which will clearly define in concise and uniform accounts the subtotals of appropriations asked for by agencies in the executive branch of the government." Finally, and most importantly, in the language of Section 139a (now House Rule 21, Section 6) the House registered its desire that the Committee communicate its recommendations well in advance of floor consideration:

> No general appropriation bill shall be considered in the House until printed Committee hearings and a Committee report thereon have been available for the Members of the House for at least three calendar days.

The idea is that increased communication between Committee and House will tie the two units more closely together. The idea is, too, that although the Committee will exercise an important degree of independence, these procedural norms will underscore its ultimate dependence.

Observe Integrative House Norms

The solidarity of the House as an on-going political system is maintained, to an important degree, by the existence of certain integrative norms together with substantial Member conformity to them. These norms — for the most part informal — prescribe behavior that will tend to minimize or control internal House conflict. Such, for example, are norms which call for bargaining and compromise as methods of decision-making, reciprocity as a key to interpersonal relations, subject matter specialization as a key to intercommittee relations, consultation as a key to interparty relations, and seniority as a criterion for distributing influence. Underlying and interlinking all of these is the norm which prescribes a loyal attachment to the House as an institution and which proscribes, in general, all behavior which will diminish

---

[26] Joint Committee on the Organization of Congress, *Hearings on the Organization of Congress,* 79th Congress, 1st Session (Washington: U.S. Government Printing Office, 1945), p. 33.

the power and prestige of the House within the American political system. In the interests of the cohesion, the stability, and the influence of the House, all Members are expected to conform to these integrative norms. Not all, of course, do — at all or to the same degree. But House leaders consider it necessary that members of the more influential, and hence potentially most disruptive, committees exhibit a higher than average degree of conformity. And one such influential committee is the Appropriations Committee.

Expectations regarding Committee observance of internal, informal, integrative House norms get articulated when House leaders discuss the selection of new Committee members. Nicholas Masters, in his study of selection for the Appropriations, Ways and Means, and Rules Committees, stresses the selectors' desire for "responsible legislators" — Members who sympathize with and conform to basic House norms. In the eyes of the House leadership, says Masters,

> A responsible legislator is one whose ability, attitudes and relationships with his colleagues serve to enhance the prestige of the House of Representatives. He is one who has a basic and fundamental respect for the legislative process and who understands and appreciates its formal and informal rules.[27]

The desire for a responsible legislator or for a man who will conform to integrative norms is a linchpin expectation. That is to say, the likelihood that all other House maintenance expectations will be met is increased significantly if such men can be found for the Committee. A responsible legislator will be responsive to the House and sensitive to his Committee's dependence on the House. He will more likely seek consensus than run roughshod over others. He will be less likely to prosecute internecine war with the substantive committees, and he will be less likely to risk conflict by hoarding information.

For the Appropriations Committee, specifically, one important component of "responsibility" or of responsiveness to the House is a willingness to work hard at legislative tasks without the compensations of personal publicity. In the language of one House member the Committee's task is "all drudgery and no romance." An important Democratic committee-maker stated,

> We want to know whether he has the ability and whether he will work and attend the meetings. That committee works very hard and has laborious hearings. There's a lot of detail work. The chairman of those subcommittees want men on their subcommittees who will do the job.

[27] Nicholas Masters, "Committee Assignments in the House of Representatives," *American Political Science Review* (June, 1961), p. 352.

A Republican leader agreed:

> They have to be willing to work. They can't be lazy. They have to attend the meetings. It's a laborious job, so diligence is one thing. And they have to be men of integrity. They have to have — I don't know what you call it — plenty of political stamina.

Conversely, these expectations do not countenance positions on the Committee for those seeking public recognition through personal aggrandizement.

A man who devotes himself whole-heartedly to the work of his committee is likely to become enmeshed in the internal life of the chamber and more attuned to its most general integrative norms. But, House committee-makers believe, some members may be constrained to adopt other legislative styles. Members with hairline election margins, it is felt, may be so attentive and so beholden to narrow constituency concerns as to leave them quite inattentive and quite unresponsive to internal House concerns. An influential Republican committee-maker explained:

> We don't just go by the fact that he's been elected. We go back in his community and we ask around. "Is he able? What's his background? Has he got the stuff to stand up under pressure? Or can he be gotten to by other interests? . . ." We make up a chart on his vote margin in past elections. If we put a man in from a close district, his committee assignment could defeat him in the next election. Maybe he couldn't stand up. We need someone who can do what he thinks best, who has the backing and whose district will say "We're with you no matter what you do up there."

When Committee selectors acknowledge their preference for men with safe districts over men without, they articulate in another form their concern for maximum Committee conformity to the general integrative norms of the House.

Most important, perhaps, among House norms are those which state the expectation that Members work with others in a style based on cooperation, mutual respect, and a willingness to compromise. Committee-makers speak frequently of wanting for the Committee "the kind of man you can deal with," "a guy you can get along with," "a fellow who is well-balanced and won't go off half-cocked on things," "Members who are more popular than others," "someone who's stable . . . and acceptable," "someone who isn't a screwball," or someone who "doesn't go around kicking everyone in the teeth." And they actively guard against the appointment of an uncompromising ideologue.

In particular, cooperative relationships are expected to exist between Committee members and their respective party leaders or party contingents. Given the pervasiveness of party influence on the internal structure of the House, a special responsiveness of Committee Democrats to other Democrats and of Committee Republicans to other Republicans is viewed not as an impediment but a necessary condition of internal solidarity. When party leaders state their expectation that Committee members should work harmoniously with them, they are voicing not just a party norm, but a House norm as well.

Specifications are expressed by party leaders in the form of criteria for Committee membership. One criterion to which both parties subscribe states that Committee responsiveness to party will be maximized by attention to geographical representativeness — keeping in mind the geographical distribution of party strength. A Republican leader pointed out that

> Every section of the country is entitled to a seat on the Committee. You wouldn't want to stack the Committee with all Easterners. That wouldn't be right. Of course, you take the big states, they pay most of the taxes and they should have representation. But still you wouldn't want to stack the Committee.

His Democratic counterpart concurred:

> If there's a state or a section of small states that is not represented on the Committee, we'll give it to them. It's good for the party and it's good for the country to spread it around. You don't want membership concentrated in one area. That's not good.

Since all members of a party, wherever situated, have expectations as to what the Committee should do and how, considerable disruption could result from a failure to achieve broad representation on the Committee. The likelihood of achieving a Committee consensus that represents "the will of the House" is enhanced by the regional representativeness of the Committee. It is further advanced by the sheer size of a 50-man Committee — the largest by far of the committees of the House.

Republican and Democratic bills of specifications differ in one important respect on what it takes to achieve a special responsiveness of the party contingent on the Committee to the party contingent in the House. Republican party leaders emphasize a policy requirement. In their view, no Republican could be sufficiently responsive to House Republicans if he did not first display a special set of attitudes toward government spending. Three of the most influential Republican committee-makers described their expectations as follows:

> We want someone with a thorough background in economics and who has the Republican point of view on these matters . . . there are some big spenders on the Republican side. But they don't get on the Appropriations Committee.

> You want a man who is solid and sound. You want someone who has had experience in spending money and knows what the value is. That's

the big thing. Some people don't know what money is — they are too liberal with money, with other people's money. You don't want people who are too liberal with other people's money.

We don't want anybody who will just spend and spend and spend. We ask ourselves will he be — I don't want to say conservative — but will he be as thrifty with other people's money as he is with his own money? Is he a sound businessman? If this were his money, would he invest in this bank or in this program? Don't you see what I mean? We can't spend more than we take in.

These leadership expectations run with the grain of Republican party doctrine, and they match the policy views of a majority of House Republicans.

Among Democratic leaders, expectations run less to substantive questions of economy than they do to personal legislative style. Some Committee selectors say that "I wouldn't vote to put a wild-eyed spender on that Committee," or "I want someone who isn't too liberal on spending." But, given the disparate elements among House Democrats, it would be impossible to select a responsive Committee if unity on spending policy were made a governing principle. Three Democrats, wielding great influence in the selection process stated their expectations this way:

We don't ask them whether they are spenders or not. That doesn't enter into it. It isn't an ideological matter. We don't care about his stand on policy.

We look at his standing in the House, what he's done and how he's done it. After all that touches on his effectiveness as a member of the House and as a member of his party . . . . We never lay the political philosophy of a man out on the table. It's more an instinctive reaction to a man than a studied one.

If you have a wild spender, he'd have a pretty hard time with the Committee on Ways and Means. But on the other hand if he were very conservative he'd have a difficult time too. I'd say that in four out of five cases the man is chosen for a balance between conservatism in spending money and responsiveness to the party leadership and the party position. He can't be fighting the leadership all the time on foreign aid or public power and the things like that which you have to have.

The only controlling principle is that Committee members be responsive to party expectations — to the end that internal House solidarity be preserved. Party expectations differ from, as well as duplicate, one another.

House members, in sum, express expectations pertaining to the "how" as well as the "what" of Committee decision-making. Most basically, these "how" or maintenance expectations hold that the Committee should recognize and act in keeping with its ultimate dependence on the House. This overarching expectation governs Committee activity in areas of consensus-building, legislating on an appropriation bill, collecting and disseminating information, and obeying integrative House norms. In every case, however, the House proceeds on the assumption that the Committee collectively and its members individually will enjoy a good deal of procedural leeway. House concern is simply that Committee autonomy not become excessive.

House maintenance expectations express a desire, also, for stability in House-Committee relations. Nearly all of the expectations examined center on some potential source of conflict between the two entities — between Committee decisions and the will of the House, between the Committee and the authorizing committees, between the Committee and those seeking information from the Committee, between the Committee and House leaders. In every case, the House-prescribed rules of the game call for the minimization of that conflict. The House wants a relationship with the Appropriations Committee characterized by an ultimate dependence, a considerable degree of operating independence, and overall stability.

HOUSE IMAGES

Granted that House members hold and express a set of expectations as to what the Appropriations Committee should do and how they should do it, the question arises as to whether House members express any perceptions or attitudes about actual Committee behavior. And the answer clearly is that they do. There are few members who fail to observe its behavior or to pass judgment upon it. In the answers to open-ended questions, however, Members' perceptions and attitudes get so closely intertwined that it has been impossible to separate them. When we wish to stress the cognitive aspects of Member statements, we shall use the term perception. When we wish to emphasize the evaluative side of a comment we shall use the term attitude. But most frequently (in keeping with the replies of House members) the two aspects have been blurred and fused in the more ambiguous term, image.

We want to find out what images House members have of the Committee because we want to know, ultimately, whether such images as do exist lead to relationships of satisfaction and support or to relationships of dissatisfaction and conflict as between House and Committee. If House members perceive the Committee as meeting their expectations, they will hold favorable images of the Committee. If they evaluate it favorably, they will be satisfied and will tend to support and defend the Committee. Conversely, if members perceive the Committee as failing to meet their expectations, they will express unfavorable attitudes toward the Committee. And if members evaluate it unfavorably, they will tend to come into conflict and to oppose the Committee. Actual perceptions, attitudes, and their conse-

29

quences will not be as black and white as this. But the degree to which they fall into one or the other of the above clusters will shape patterns of Appropriations Committee behavior and will affect the stability of those patterns. Leaving aside, for the moment, the degree to which each cluster of perceptions and attitudes is held, it is clear that images leading to House satisfaction and images leading to House dissatisfaction are held by the Members.

Favorable Images

Favorable images concerning the Committee's performance in meeting goal expectations have historically emphasized its success in meeting House demands for economy. In the great debate of 1885, defenders of the Appropriations Committee praised "the unselfish devotion of this very Appropriations Committee standing at the door of the public Treasury, between the Treasury and those making raids upon it," "the steadfast gentlemen who have staid the march of triumphant extravagance and confederated greed," and "the granite integrity and sterling honesty of the men controlling the Appropriations Committee."[28] Again in 1920, those who sought to restore the full jurisdiction of the Committee grounded their proposals in the same image:

> The time has come when the Congress has got to stop spending the people's money indiscriminately. That time will never come unless the appropriations power is put in the hands of an appropriating committee. Where every small committee here and there indiscriminately has power of appropriation, extravagance will never stop.[29]

In 1885, the favorable image was held by a minority; in 1920 it was held by a majority. But the image was always present in the chamber.

When asked, 40 years later, how House members view the Appropriations Committee, two House veterans highlighted the same economy theme. Said one, a key Democratic committee chairman,

> The Committee has a very good reputation. I think the Committee is accepted as doing work of high standards. They present their bills well. They are very seldom amended on the floor. Years ago we used to take a week or ten days on an appropriation bill, and you would have many amendments. Now we pass appropriation bills in a few days and they are seldom amended. They are accepted as doing a good job. They usually have cuts — not all in one place but in many different places. So you know they have gone through it with a fine tooth comb.

And the other, the leader of a large Republican delegation, echoed,

> They do a very good job. They're a highly respected group of men. It's a very economical committee on both sides of the aisle. If the Committee

[28] 17 *Congressional Record*, pp. 281–282.
[29] 59 *Congressional Record*, p. 8105.

were left alone, they would cut a lot more than they do. They offer the cuts, but they are sometimes overridden on the floor. That's the truth of the matter.

The Committee does draw praise for meeting expectations of program support — most frequently from individual Members who compliment the Committee for including their pet projects in the bill. On the whole, however, Committee action of this sort is taken for granted; and Committee action in meeting economy expectations draws the more consistently favorable comments.

House members hold a favorable image, too, of some aspects of Committee behavior in meeting maintenance expectations. The Committee, for instance, is almost universally admired for the diligence which it displays in processing its enormous work load. Even substantive dissatisfactions, it is said, cannot dim the esteem which the Committee garners through sheer industry. Said a Republican party leader,

> It's a dog's life. Nobody gives you any credit. You go down into the dugout the first of December and don't come out again until after adjournment. It's a hard Committee. Everybody knows that. It's a labor of love and a devotion to duty that keeps you on that Committee. People have a lot of respect for them. Oh, sometimes they get mad because they can't have what they want but after they cool off they have a high regard for the Committee.

Though the image of the dedicated, diligent committee focuses in the first instance on maintenance expectations, it predisposes House members to approve of the Committee's substantive decisions. Lacking evidence to the contrary, House members may assume that a Committee which does so much work must be doing a good job:

> They do a good job. I don't think there's any doubt about that. They have so much work to do they have to break up into subcommittees. I don't have the time and no congressman who was frank about it would say he did, to read all the appropriations hearings. You have to rely on someone.

Or, to put it another way, favorable images of the Committee in the area of maintenance expectations tend to produce or reinforce favorable images of the Committee in the area of goal expectations.

The Committee commands a good deal of respect in the chamber. But it is important to note that Member respect is flavored with a prudent regard for the Committee's acknowledged power. Favorable images of the group are rooted as much in fear and caution as they are in love and affection. And the respect that the Committee commands partakes of that variety of "healthy respect" which one expresses for a talented and influential adversary. "They're a hard-working bunch; but they aren't going to win any popularity contest," summed up one Ways and Means Committee Democrat. And another veteran of the same committee elaborated on Member reaction as follows:

> It's a mixture of awe, fear, and envy. Awe because of the power of the Committee, fear because of the effect that the Committee can have on the future of a member in his district, and envy because of the attractiveness and enhancement the position gives to any Member who is on it. But I say God bless them all and go to it. Get on the Committee as early as you can and stay on it as long as you can.

The perception of a powerful committee is universal. And most Members cannot and do not take so benign an attitude toward the group as the senior member just quoted.

"Everybody trembles before the Appropriations Committee," writes one Member.[30] And, it should be added, no one is eager to oppose the Committee by word or deed. Should Members speak against a Committee recommendation on the floor they often begin with an open confession of trepidation. "I certainly have a very high regard for the gentlemen of the Appropriations Committee, because we are all under the gun when we start criticizing this powerful Committee."[31] Or, "I have been told that it is always unwise for a younger member of this body to get into any kind of squabble with anybody on the Appropriations Committee."[32] Speeches in opposition to the Committee are more often than not preceded by protestations of respect:

> I think all of us here recognize and I want to say once again for the record that they do a tremendous job and do it well. Specific points raised regarding individual programs are not intended to detract from the overall commendation of these gentlemen. . . .[33]

Members who have received the blessings of the Committee may supplement hymns of praise with hymns of thanksgiving:

> I am so grateful to the distinguished gentlemen. I want to thank you Mr. Chairman for these funds for the buildings . . . for which we have been waiting for four years and which are needed so desperately. May I again, Sir, say thank you and tell you what an excellent job you have done.[34]

The prudent respect of the Members helps account for this exaggerated public deference to the Committee. It also helps account for the vicarious delight which Members experience when someone succeeds in overthrowing the Committee on the floor. Tales climaxed by the conquest of "the powerful Appropriations Committee" quickly become epic David and Goliath,

---

[30] Clem Miller, *Member of the House* (Scribners: New York, 1962), p. 40.
[31] 105 *Congressional Record*, p. 8669.
[32] *Congressional Record*, Daily Edition, August 30, 1961, p. 16472.
[33] *Congressional Record*, Daily Edition, March 20, 1962, p. 4226.
[34] *Congressional Record*, Daily Edition, July 30, 1962, p. 13981.

Jack the Giant Killer legends in the corridors and cloak rooms of Capitol Hill. Members sometimes express favorable images of the Committee (at least publicly) because they feel they might have to pay a price for expressing an unfavorable one.

Unfavorable Images

The House view that the Committee fails to meet goal expectations centers around the lack of adequate Committee support for programs and projects. In the debates of 1885 and 1920, for example, those Members who favored placing or keeping jurisdiction over appropriations in the hands of the relevant substantive committees seemed to feel that more generous program support would result. Most recently, criticism of the Committee has tended to come from liberals who support programs requiring huge outlays of federal funds, and who have viewed the Committee as excessively dedicated to economy. In a time of rapidly expanding governmental expenditures for socio-economic purposes, the Committee has sometimes come under fire for its failure to provide adequate financing. If this recent criticism by House liberals reflects a secular decline in the saliency of economy sentiment in the public at large, the tasks and the influence of the Committee could, of course, be substantially altered.

At the level of individual "pet projects," House member complaints seem to be destined, always, to center on the parsimony rather than the open-handedness of the Committee. As one experienced member summarized, "There's a latent hostility to the Committee. It's an obstructionist Committee with regard to the projects that Members want." When the House is in an economy mood, expression may be heard that the Committee is insufficiently tight-fisted. In the area of goal expectations, however, favorable images are constructed from the Committee's perceived fulfillment of economy goals; and unfavorable images stem mostly from a perceived failure to achieve House prescribed programs and project support goals.

Unfavorable images of Committee activity in meeting maintenance expectations flourish in both general and specific form. Overall, a set of perceptions and attitudes have long been held which views the Committee as excessively powerful or excessively autonomous — thus threatening the prescribed relationship of dependence on the House. In 1885, the Committee's opponents felt that, despite the virtues of the Committee, their relationship to the chamber was badly out of balance. Said one,

> I have ever entertained, and doubtless shall continue to entertain, the profoundest respect not only for the personnel, but for the integrity and industry of said committee, but have been compelled at times to note its encroachments upon the rights and privileges of other committees . . . the

33

Committee on Appropriations . . . like some gigantic oak of the forest, has sent out its roots and spread its branches until it has absorbed all the wealth of the soil around it and no vegetation can live and flourish in its shadow.[35]

And again in 1920, the critics prophesied that with the reinstitution of a single Appropriations Committee,

They will become the sole power in this House, and the other committees will be mere nonentities without power to do anything, and this House will have one committee, which will be the Appropriations Committee.[36]

In the 1960's, two top House leaders expressed the identical criticism. "The Committee likes to grasp for power," said one. "It's that tendency to concentrate. It's bad. They're a tremendously powerful committee, but sometimes they try to go a little too far."

Sure, there is resentment against the Committee. They have special privileges, let's face it, and the other Members get jealous. They meet all the time when Congress is in session. Their bills are privileged and come to the floor without a rule. They get special treatment from the departments. Their colleagues must reckon with them. They have a life and death power over things. You hear people say, "That isn't fair." You hear that a lot.

Criticism of the Committee for its failure to meet maintenance expectations is voiced more often and more openly than criticism involving the fulfillment of goal expectations. Many Members probably state substantive disagreements with the Committee in the language of excessive independence, since in this way they can avoid being labeled as "spenders." More Members, that is to say, can be found to agree to the proposition that the Committee is too powerful than can be found to criticize any single decision. The Committee's power affects all members; and the common perception that the Committee is powerful fuels the image that the Committee is too powerful.

Unfavorable images of Committee behavior get expressed with regard to most of the specific maintenance expectations described earlier. The Committee is sometimes regarded as getting into too much legislation, communicating too little information, or as being insufficiently responsive to House norms. Apropos of the injunction "appropriate, don't legislate," substantive committee members sometimes perceive and resent Appropriations Committee encroachment on their jurisdiction.[37] Almost every substantive committee has felt at one time or another the effects of legislation on an appropriation bill, and public protests against Appropriations Committee

[35] 17 *Congressional Record*, p. 202.
[36] 59 *Congressional Record*, p. 8105.
[37] An excellent case study of one such conflict is: Edith Carper, *The Defense Appropriations Rider* (University: University of Alabama Press, 1960), published by the Inter-University Case Program.

expansionism occur regularly. Committee action altering the salaries of several civil service employees elicited the following protest:

> As Chairman of the Committee on Post Office and Civil Service, I must protect the rights and authority of my own Committee. As the gentleman knows, this is clearly an infringement and usurpation of the rights of the Committee on Post Office and Civil Service. . . . I wish the powerful Appropriations Committee would quit stepping on the toes of the Committee on Post Office and Civil Service.[38]

The issuance of a rule waiving all points of order and hence protecting all Appropriations Committee legislation produced this complaint:

> I am speaking now not only as a member of the House but as Chairman of the Committee on Agriculture and by direction of the Committee in opposition to this rule. There are in this bill at least six provisions that are pure legislation . . . what we are in effect doing is setting up the Committee on Appropriations as a great super-Committee of the House of Representatives which will undermine the authority, activity and importance of the legislative committees. When I say this, I am speaking not only for the Committee on Agriculture, but for every legislative committee of the House.[39]

A member of the Rules Committee itself echoed the same sentiment when he said, on another occasion,

> Now I think well of the Appropriations Committee. The Appropriations Committee are fine boys, and they are all good friends of mine. But they have enough power already. If you give them any more power to legislate on an appropriation bill, you might as well do away with the standing committees altogether and let them legislate the whole ball of wax.

Beyond the view that the Committee is legislating on an appropriation bill, therefore, may lie the complaint that the Committee has even taken over policy leadership in a given area. A House Republican expressed great resentment toward Committee action regarding foreign aid.

> They decide the objectives. The worst example of this is the foreign aid program. Of course, you've got a very weak Foreign Affairs Committee and that contributes a lot to it. But every year, the big debate isn't on the authorization; it's on the appropriation bill. The authorization doesn't mean a thing. The Appropriations Committee doesn't just say we need so much money to implement a judgment which was made elsewhere. They make the judgment themselves. They say, this is a bad program. And they have no damned business doing that. They're God-like.

[38] 102 *Congressional Record*, p. 6995. For other disputes between the Appropriations and Post Office and Civil Service Committees, see 106 *Congressional Record*, pp. 3276–3280, and 107 *Congressional Record*, p. 5028.

[39] 93 *Congressional Record*, pp. 5874–5875. See also the comment of Rep. McCormack, 94 *Congressional Record*, p. 6632.

The image of an imperialistic Appropriations Committee may be related specifically to legislative oversight tasks. A substantive committee or the House as a whole may feel that its ability to exercise ultimate oversight authority is being jeopardized by Committee action. One substantive committee chairman complained:

> Since when did the appropriations Committee arrogate to itself such mighty powers as to say that Congress authorizes an act but we will cut it off, notwithstanding the views, the unanimous views of all the Committee on Agriculture, Republicans and Democrats alike? It seems to me this is a kind of test. Who is going to run the Department of Agriculture? The subcommittee on appropriations or the legislative committees of this Congress and the Members of the Congress themselves?[40]

The exercise of the Committee's nonstatutory techniques of legislative oversight can induce a considerable amount of House member frustration, should he try to assert the chamber's ultimate authority. When, for example, the Committee directs an agency to do something by way of a committee report, the direction carries great weight — and yet the ordinary House member cannot change it. It was this situation which triggered the following anguished comment from an experienced House member:

> Suppose the will of the House is not in accord with the will of the subcommittee and the House would like to change that recommendation? How can one offer an amendment to a Committee report? You see, the House is prevented from working its will . . . the recommendation is in a Committee report and I am helpless to do anything about it. If it is binding, it ought to be in the law, and if it is not in the law then it ought not to be considered binding and that ought to be understood here and now.[41]

The perceptions and attitudes revealed in these examples feed an image of the Committee as operating with so much autonomy as to place it beyond the control of the House.

The expectation that the Committee will collect information on behalf of the House is, as has been noted, a strongly rooted one. While the Committee is guaranteed a high degree of independence in their collection process, they are expected to recognize their dependence in the distribution process. House dissatisfaction regarding the dissemination of information has a recorded history dating back at least to 1885, when a Committee opponent proclaimed, "Let us have no more closed corporations, no more star chamber proceedings."[42] Intervening years have changed neither the charge of a Committee monopoly over information nor the vocabulary in which it is

[40] *Congressional Record,* Daily Edition, May 11, 1960, p. 9324.
[41] 100 *Congressional Record,* pp. 2700–2701.
[42] 17 *Congressional Record,* p. 202.

couched. Indignant attacks are frequently leveled against the closed hearings. In the words of two very senior members,

> It is a star chamber proceeding. If you happen to be a witness, now, the door is open for a little crack and you are permitted to slide in and say your little piece and slide out; but there are no public hearings . . . they close the doors. Nobody hears anything about it except the Committee and then they report out a bill.[43]

> I thought I could come over here and stay and hear witnesses. I came and testified. Although treated with every courtesy . . . I was told "you have to go out now; we are going to hear other witnesses." Can I wait and find out what is being brought up against it? "No, you cannot do that. You will get that information when the bill comes before the House, then and not before." Imagine a member of this body being denied the right to know about a problem he is vitally interested in.[44]

Complaints about the flow of information appear at each stage of the process. When appropriation bills reach the floor, Members often complain that Committee hearings have not been made available to them sufficiently in advance of debate. One veteran Member expressed his exasperation at the opening of debate on a conference report brought in by the Committee:

> I know the gentleman can explain this conference report because the gentleman sat in on the conference. But I doubt if any of the rest of us know what is in it. I have great faith in the gentleman from Texas [Mr. Thomas] but I am getting tired of taking everything on faith . . . why is it not made available to members on the floor of the House as it should be, and as the gentleman knows it should be, and as I know it should be, because we have both been here for a long time?[45]

For those House members attempting to assert leadership on the floor, the image of "a third House" restricting the output of information may be especially exasperating. "They work in secrecy," complained one House leader,

> I can't get any information. You can't find out anything until they get to the floor. And it's hard to lick 'em at that stage. They're a closed corporation. When they stick together, you can't lick 'em on the floor.

The image here is clearly one of excessive autonomy.

Members of the Committee are chosen in accordance with the expectation that they will be especially responsive to the integrative norms of the House and, hence, will work cooperatively with House members. Party leaders, especially, express this expectation. Associated, however, with perceptions of "star chamber" and "closed corporation," is the perception that, once placed on the Committee, its members become excessively Committee-

[43] 101 *Congressional Record*, p. 10945.
[44] 92 *Congressional Record*, p. 1092.
[45] *Congressional Record*, Daily Edition, July 23, 1962, p. 13437.

oriented. Committee norms may conflict with House norms and the Committee member may respond to the former rather than the latter. House leaders express their dissatisfaction in exclamations like these: "You talk about the Senate being exclusive. It's a sideshow when you put it beside a subcommittee on appropriations." "You get on one of those subcommittees and they are a clan. They're more of a club than the Senate." Occasions when Committee members congratulate each other publicly for their work on a bill are viewed by House members as symptomatic of an excessive clannishness or Committee-mindedness. One expressed a widely felt irritation when he exclaimed on the floor,

> I have heard the gentlemen of the Committee compliment each other all afternoon here for doing their duty. It seems to me when a committee comes to the floor and spends most of its time complimenting its members rather than discussing the merits of the bill under consideration it seems desirable for some of us to inquire why this mutual admiration society goes on. You gentlemen are only doing your duty when you do your Committee work on this bill, and I do not know why you should spend so many minutes on the floor complimenting each other for doing your duty.[46]

To the degree that a responsiveness to internal Committee norms produces a corresponding lack of responsiveness to integrative House norms, House members will react unfavorably. A party leader rehearsed an episode which requires little comment:

> When young men go on there, you notice a change of mind. They begin to get that indoctrination. Maybe that's too strong, but you can see it. I remember once when a Member asked me to help him with a project. I called in one of the fellows on the Appropriations Subcommittee . . . I helped put this man on the Committee; and I asked him about the project. He said, "I'll look into it." I felt like saying, "Why don't you tell me yes or no;" but I didn't. There was that drawing away attitude, that veil of secrecy. I know these fellows want certain subcommittee assignments on the Committee. I know they have to behave that way sometimes. I understand; but I put this fellow on the Committee, and he was acting very funny. So I asked him a second time about it; and he gave me the same story, "I'll look into it." Well, I said to him, "Stop this. Tell me yes or no, yes or no. If it's no, tell me. If it's yes, tell me. But tell me, yes or no." I said, "I helped put you on this Committee, but I don't want your help on that account, I'm glad you're on there. But I want a straight answer." . . . Well, he said yes he would, and he did. I had to put it to him hard. He's a nice fellow and I like him. I'm glad he's on the Committee. But I did it to shock him — for his own good. I had to shock him for his own good. Some of them get that power and get in there in secret and it takes a very differentiating mind to know how to act. They begin to see power as a personal attribute instead of a trust. And that's no good.

[46] 108 *Congressional Record*, p. 13610.

House members are expected to "go to school" in their committees. But the expectation is that behavior learned in the Appropriations Committee will conform to and not violate the expectations of the House and its leaders. When Committee-oriented behavior reveals a creeping lack of concern for House norms, the unfavorable image of a "servant" committee beyond its "master's" control will be evoked.

HOUSE SATISFACTION AND DISSATISFACTION

Given the existence of both favorable and unfavorable images of the Appropriations Committee, do House members, on balance, feel that their expectations are or are not being met by the Committee? Short of a sample survey of Member attitudes, the question cannot be answered with certainty. Subject to further ramification in the later chapters, however, the available evidence supports two general conclusions. First and on balance, House members believe that Appropriations Committee behavior meets their expectations. The dominant image of the Committee is, therefore, a favorable one from which flows House satisfactions and House support for the Committee. Secondly, though the Committee may have some confirmed enemies and some steadfast fellow travelers in the House, the vast majority of Members hold both favorable and unfavorable images of the Committee. Though they do not represent dominant sentiment, various and widespread dissatisfactions exist in the chamber. Viewed from the perspective of the House, therefore, House-Committee relations are characterized primarily by agreement and support and secondarily by underlying conflicts.

The most convincing evidence of satisfaction with the Committee's achievement of House-prescribed goal expectations can be found in the record of House support for Committee recommendations. For the period 1947 to 1962, appropriations case histories of 36 executive bureaus were studied. Of the 575 separate Committee recommendations involved, the House accepted 517 — or 90 per cent — of them. Such House changes as were made, furthermore, were fairly well balanced between increases (30) and decreases (28). These figures would seem to indicate that Committee action was never too far away for too long from House goal expectations. In the calculations made for the appropriation bills covering eight departments plus Public Works, floor changes were somewhat more overbalanced, with 93 increases and 70 decreases. Still, these results do not indicate any very lopsided or very persistent (floor changes averaged only about 1 per department per year) House dissatisfaction. Added to the view most commonly expressed in interviews that "the Committee does a good job," the overwhelming House acceptance of Committee decisions seems indicative of a dominant satisfaction and support.

39

With regard to Committee fulfillment of House-prescribed maintenance expectations, summary evidence is difficult to come by. Most convincing, perhaps, is the simple fact that, despite repeated proposals to alter the basic House-Committee relationship, it remains in 1965 virtually as it was mandated in 1920. Forty-five years of "reform" ideas, agitated for both in and out of the House — the legislative budget, the omnibus appropriation bill, the item veto, the Joint Committee on the Budget, the alternate budget year, etc. — have virtually come to naught in the chamber. Nothing remotely resembling the fundamental alterations of 1885 has recurred. Member complaints about the state of the House-Committee relationship are easy to locate — easier, indeed, than statements of satisfaction with the relationship. But this happens because Members articulate their dissatisfactions more freely than they do their satisfactions. The state of House support cannot be assessed, therefore, through frequency counts of criticism and praise. More impressive is the longstanding lack of success which reform-minded Members have had in trying to convince House majorities to alter existing maintenance relationships.

It is not easy, of course, to bring about fundamental changes in the tasks and authority of a congressional committee — much less a powerful one like the Appropriations Committee. An important increment of House support flows to the Committee by virtue of support for the committee system itself. So long as a division of labor is required in order for the House to achieve its goals, for that long will the House require a committee system. And so long as the House requires a committee system, for that long will the Appropriations Committee (or any other committee) enjoy a cushion of support quite independent of anything it may or may not do. The committee system is the key to the House's internal structure, and House members will not put the committee system or any part of it in peril except under extreme provocation. To some degree, therefore, a surface stability in House-Committee relations could be deceptive. A substantial accumulation of dissatisfactions can be held in check by sentiments of support for the committee system — coupled, perhaps, with Member reluctance to risk the personal price of an unsuccessful attack on this particular Committee. Should dissatisfactions build up beneath the surface, very little by way of a catalyst might be needed to rupture existing House-Committee relations. Conclusions about the persistence of House satisfaction and, hence, the stability of existing House-Committee relations depend on an assessment of the areas of conflict.

Given the number and variety of expressions of dissatisfaction, it seems reasonable to conclude that, despite overall support for the Committee, serious areas of House-Committee conflict do exist. From the perspective of the House, the House-Committee relationship should be viewed as one of precarious harmony and perpetual tension. Whether the harmony will be ruptured depends largely on the degree to which House dissatisfactions are persistent and cumulative. One significant factor in dissipating House dissatisfactions, however, are some basic dualities in House expectations. Goal expectations prescribe both program support and economy. These are often expressed by evanescent, noncumulative moods — now pressing for economy, now being more permissive. And, even though Members usually want more money for pet projects than they get, they know that the Committee cannot grant every request. House maintenance expectations prescribe both a degree of Committee dependence and a degree of Committee autonomy. House members want to curb the independent power of the Committee; yet they have deliberately created a powerful Committee, commensurate with the importance of appropriations decisions. The two-sidedness of House goal and maintenance expectations helps to keep House images bifurcated and House dissatisfactions short-run, piecemeal, and noncumulative. The existing distribution of House expectations, perceptions, and attitudes, therefore, helps promote stability in House-Committee relations.

The House Committee and the House
II: *House Sanctions*

THE IMPORTANCE OF SANCTIONS

At the heart of the Committee-House relationship lies the question of the House's capacity to secure Committee compliance with House expectations. It is interesting, of course, to know what expectations and images House members hold. But the knowledge is of little value to an analysis of Committee activity if the House lacks the capacity to enforce its expectations and the Committee is left free to disregard House dissatisfaction. Some House members believe that the House has the capacity. "After all," threatened one dissatisfied House member of the Joint Committee on the Organization of Congress, "the Appropriations Committee is a creature of the House. . . . May I say that unless the Appropriations Committee straightens itself out then the House is going to have to straighten the Appropriations Committee out."[1] Is this a plausible or an empty threat? The question needs to be answered before conclusions can be drawn about Committee autonomy or about external House influence on the appropriations process.

The specific questions which need to be answered for any congressional committee–parent chamber relationship are these: What sanctions are available to the Members? Under what conditions are the sanctions applied? Who applies them? How successful is the application of sanctions in bringing about the fulfillment of expectations? The difficulty in answering these questions results from the fact that, whereas it is easy to secure evidence of

---

[1] Joint Committee on the Organization of Congress, *Hearings on the Organization of Congress*, 79th Congress, 1st Session (Washington: U.S. Government Printing Office, 1945), pp. 205, 208.

House dissatisfaction, it is hard to locate and document specific examples of House-Committee conflict. For this reason we have been thrown back on the use of a mélange of illustrative materials of uneven quality. Roll calls involving serious system-subsystem conflict have been used whenever they could be found. But there are not many; and at their best roll calls describe a conflict at only one moment in time. They may describe very imperfectly the position of many Members. Interviews, too, have their weaknesses in the sense that each informant has a unique perspective. And the task of securing the perspective of everyone concerned via interviews is virtually impossible. The ensuing discussion of House sanctions draws, then, on such materials as are readily available. The cases described should be considered, therefore, as identifying types of House-Committee conflict, types of sanctions available, uses to which these sanctions have been put, and the variety of House groups which have used them.

MANIPULATING COMMITTEE JURISDICTION

1885

The House of Representatives exercised its most basic form of control over the Appropriations Committee when it gave the Committee its legitimacy and fixed its jurisdiction in 1865. And what the House has the authority to create, the House has the authority to abolish. Though the House has combined and eliminated committees from time to time, the total abolition of such an important group as the Appropriations Committee would appear so nearly an attack on the committee system itself as to render it the most remote of practical possibilities. Less drastically, however, the House can reduce the Committee's jurisdiction. Even this action might appear to be a remote possibility were it not for the fact that, between 1877 and 1885, the House did strip the Appropriations Committee of its jurisdiction over eight out of fourteen appropriation bills. The appropriation bills dealing with Rivers and Harbors (1877), Agriculture (1880), Army (1885), Military Academy (1885), Navy (1885), Consular and Diplomatic Affairs (1885), Post Office and Post Roads (1885), and Indian Affairs (1885) were taken from the Appropriations Committee, where they had been since 1865, and placed under the control of the appropriate substantive legislative committees. In so doing, the House removed nearly one-half of the total federal budget, and many of that budget's most controversial items, from the purview of the Appropriations Committee. Short of abolition, the House's action was as effective an emasculation of a committee's influence as could be imagined.

The source of House dissatisfaction in 1885 lay primarily in the image of an excessively independent Appropriations Committee, with an under-

43

current of criticism of an excessive economy-mindedness.[2] The depth of the dissatisfaction is reflected in the overwhelming 227 to 70 margin by which the House voted to sanction the Committee. "The House" in this case consisted of 75 per cent (128 members) of the majority Democratic party and 78 per cent (99 members) of the Republican minority. The Appropriations Committee position was upheld by 42 (25 per cent) Democrats and 28 (22 per cent) Republicans. Since the measure drew bipartisan support and won party majorities of the same relative size, the conflict cannot be understood in partisan terms. On the other hand, most evidence does support an analysis in terms of House-Committee or system-subsystem conflict.

In the first place the sitting members of the Appropriations Committee (those who were on the Committee in the 48th Congress, since committees had not been chosen for the 49th Congress at the time the vote took place) voted 7 to 1 against the change. And the sitting members of the 7 committees that either had taken away or under the terms of the resolution would take over Appropriations Committee jurisdiction voted 47 to 8 in favor of the change. These votes by those who stood most directly to lose and those who stood most directly to gain were significantly more lopsided than one would have expected at random.

The House drive against the Committee was promoted, also, by the other powerful committees of the House. The sitting members of 5 other prestigeful committees (Ways and Means, Rules, Judiciary, Banking and Currency, Commerce) voted 30 to 5 in favor of the change. Considering the votes of the highest ranking Democrat who voted and of the highest ranking Republican who voted on each of all 12 committees (7 who stood to gain plus 5 other prestigeful ones), we find that 21 votes were cast in favor of sanctions and only 2 against. Furthermore, the floor fight was led by the Chairman of the Committee on Ways and Means. The Appropriations Committee drew 12 votes from the home state of the Committee's Chairman (Pennsylvania) and 20 more from the neighboring states of Ohio, New Jersey, and New York — all on a bipartisan basis. Nineteen more votes came from the South and the rest were scattered without apparent pattern. Freshman members of the House apparently supported the powerful bipartisan coalition of their elders. "The House" which effectively exercised control over its Appropriations Committee in 1885 consisted of the sitting members of the most powerful House committees and, especially, their more senior members. And, as the debate makes clear, they acted on the basis of an image of Appropriations Committee imperialism.

[2] The 1885 debate and vote can be found in 17 *Congressional Record*, pp. 138–320 passim. An excellent first-hand account will be found in Joseph G. Cannon, "The National Budget," *Harpers* (October, 1919), reprinted in *Congressional Record*, Daily Edition, July 16, 1962, pp. A5408 ff. Cannon emphasizes the hostility to Committee Chairman Samuel Randall.

In the context of the Budget and Accounting Act of 1920, a majority of House members supported a revitalized Appropriations Committee to be brought about by reversing the decision of 1885.[3] Once again, therefore, the ability of the larger system to control the activity of one of its subsystems was demonstrated. In 1920, the position of "the House" was less distinct than in 1885 — as revealed by the fact that a rule calling for debate on the resolution passed by only 158 to 154. The resolution itself later went through by the more substantial margin of 200 to 117. On the critical vote on the rule, "the House" consisted of 104 members (65 per cent) of the majority party Republicans and 54 members (36 per cent) of the Democratic party. In opposition to the House majority and to the Appropriations Committee were 57 (35 per cent) Republicans and 97 (64 per cent) Democrats. Unlike 1885, party majorities were found in opposition to one another. The measure was introduced by the Republican majority, which supported it in markedly greater measure than did the Democratic minority. To some degree, therefore, the 1920 conflict must be viewed as a partisan one. However, the more than one-third minority vote within each party and the low index of cohesion for both parties which resulted would indicate that the explanatory power of partisanship is limited.

The 1920 conflict must be understood to some degree also as a House-Committee conflict. The Appropriations Committee, which stood to gain most directly, voted unanimously (15 to 0) in support of the rule. And the members of the 7 committees which this time stood to lose most directly voted 67 to 38 against the rule. A majority of both the Republicans and the Democrats on these 7 committees opposed the rule — in each case voting more strongly in opposition than their party groups as a whole. Opposition by such margins as 17 to 2 from Naval Affairs members, 13 to 5 from Military Affairs, 11 to 2 from Post Office and Post Roads, and 11 to 5 from Agriculture speaks for itself in evidence. Opposition to the Appropriations Committee was clearly heaviest in those substantive committees which stood to lose jurisdiction.

Unlike 1885, however, hostility to the Committee was not evident in the 5 other powerful committees examined. With the exception of Ways and Means, they turned in strong majorities in support of Appropriations — and the combined vote of all 5 was a significant 47 to 24 in support of the Committee. Within this overall support figure, though, 16 of the 24 highest ranking and voting Republicans and Democrats on each of the 12 committees voted against the Appropriations Committee — which may indicate a continuation of opposition among senior House members.

[3] The 1920 debate and vote can be found in 59 *Congressional Record*, pp. 8102–8121.

The 1920 opposition to the Committee, while it contained a hard core very similar to that of 1885, was less broadly based. For that reason it was not likely to be as potent a restraining force as the 158 to 154 vote would indicate. "The House" operated in 1920 on the basis of an optimistic and mutually-supporting image of House–Appropriations Committee relations. The 158 to 154 vote on the rule constituted a clear reminder of potential "House" control over the committee units of the system. Yet the subsequent 200 to 117 vote on passage is indicative of a felt need to give contingent grants of considerable power to those committees.

"Backdoor Spending"

A more roundabout method by which the House can alter the scope of Appropriations Committee activity is to provide for the financing of federal programs by methods other than the regular appropriations process. There are a number of such techniques — known to their opponents as the techniques of "backdoor spending." A commonly used technique is that of direct Treasury financing — or a public debt transaction — pioneered in the financing of the Reconstruction Finance Corporation. Since then it has been used to finance such agencies as the Commodity Credit Corporation and the Export-Import Bank and programs involving urban housing and aid to depressed areas. Under this method, the House votes to authorize an agency to borrow its funds, in amounts as specified, directly from the Treasury, and the Treasury is authorized to sell bonds to get the money to lend to the agency. Most of the programs so financed are of a sort (loan programs frequently) that there is some expectation that the Treasury loan will be repaid by the agency. But sometimes the Congress cancels parts of the obligation — 12.9 billion in the case of the RFC. In other cases, Congress sets up a revolving fund so that loans paid back to the agency can be loaned out again — in several cases without further congressional action. From the perspective of this study, the essence of a public debt transaction is that it bypasses the Appropriations Committee. From 1947 to 1960, approximately 81 billion dollars were withdrawn from the Treasury by public debt transactions in lieu of the regular appropriations process.[4]

The House has available to it (when concurred in by the Senate, of course) other techniques which severely narrow the scope of Committee influence. The House can by substantive legislation authorize an agency to contract for the things it needs before the agency has received an appropriation. Then, when the agency does come before the Committee, it will already have created an obligation on the part of the government which the Com-

[4] For summaries of the use of public debt transactions and of the controversy, see: *Congressional Quarterly*, May 19, 1961, pp. 849–851; *Congressional Record*, Daily Edition, February 15, 1961, pp. A911 ff.; February 23, 1961, pp. A1173 ff.; February 23, 1961, pp. A1178 ff.; May 11, 1961, p. A3345.

mittee must honor. Urban renewal housing, for one, is financed in this manner. Similarly, when Congress authorizes a grant-in-aid program and promises to match state contributions, the Appropriations Committee must honor the commitment. Or, Congress may place certain revenues in a trust fund (social security or highways) over which the Committee has little or no control. In these and still other ways, the House can authorize the appropriation of money from the Treasury without allowing the Committee to exercise its discretion. Each step diminishes the jurisdiction of the Appropriations Committee. And though Committee members may sometimes feel constrained to support such action, they are in general — and quite naturally — opposed to any erosion of their authority. Since the question of renewing old financing arrangements occurs periodically and since some House members favor the expansion of direct Treasury borrowing to new areas (such as foreign aid), this major source of House-Committee conflict remains unresolved.

What House members initiate and support the more controversial efforts to bypass their Appropriations Committee? The best available evidence comes from a roll-call vote on an amendment to the Housing Bill of 1959.[5] The amendment (offered by an Appropriations Committee leader, Albert Thomas, D., Texas) provided for the financing of public housing programs through the regular appropriations process and for the elimination, therefore, of a financing provision (public debt transaction) which had been put in the bill by the Banking and Currency Committee. The amendment drew support, 39 to 8, from an unusually cohesive Appropriations Committee. The amendment carried by a close vote of 222 to 201. For the moment, therefore, the Committee evaded a potential House sanction. But, regardless of who won, this showdown roll call furnishes our best evidence as to the composition of the House group which has sought to restrict the jurisdiction of the Committee. It seems likely, moreover, that this group will be similar in character to those found in opposition to the Committee on other programs involving heavy federal spending.

On the 1959 vote, the Committee's opponents were dominantly Democratic and liberal. Proponents were, though less markedly, Republican and conservative. The 201 opposing votes were cast by 194 Democrats and 7 Republicans. In support of the Committee were 80 Democrats and 142 Republicans. If support for the opposition to the strongly held Committee position is related to degree of liberalism, it becomes evident that the more liberal the voting record of a Representative, the more likely he was to oppose the Appropriations Committee. To demonstrate this relationship, a liberalism

[5] The debate on the Thomas amendment will be found in 105 *Congressional Record*, pp. 8667–8674. The vote is on pp. 8844–8845. The subsequent debate and vote on the acceptance of the conference report, which deleted the amendment will be found in *ibid.*, pp. 11615–11624.

rating was given to each non–Appropriations Committee Representative, based on the AFL-CIO ratings for the 86th Congress.[6] These ratings were then correlated with the vote on the Thomas amendment. Democrats voted more strongly in opposition than did Republicans. But among members of both parties, opposition increased as degree of liberalism increased. Eighty-two per cent of the opposition to the Committee came from members who ranked in the top one-third in regard to liberalism. See Table 2.1.

TABLE 2.1

HOUSE MEMBER OPPOSITION TO THE APPROPRIATIONS COMMITTEE: BY PARTY AND DEGREE OF LIBERALISM — THOMAS AMENDMENT 1959

Per Cent Liberal Votes — AFL-CIO	Democratic Votes Opposed to Appropriations Committee Majority	Republican Votes Opposed to Appropriations Committee Majority	Totals
	Per Cent	Per Cent	Per Cent
70 to 100	153 (80.1)	4 (2.1)	157 (82.2)
30 to 69	25 (13.1)	2 (1.0)	27 (14.1)
0 to 29	7 (3.7)	0 (0)	7 (3.7)
Totals	185 (96.9)	6 (3.1)	191 (100)

The reverse relationship held for the supporters of the Appropriations Committee. Republicans of every degree of liberalism were more likely to support the Committee than were Democrats. But among members of both parties support for the Committee increased as the degree of liberalism decreased. See Table 2.2. Sixty-seven per cent of the support for the Committee came from members who ranked in the bottom one-third in regard to liberalism.

The overall, combined vote totals confirm the relationship between degree of liberalism and the degree of opposition to and support of the Committee. See Table 2.3. The more liberal a member in terms of AFL-CIO rankings, the more likely he was to oppose the Appropriations Committee on the Thomas amendment and, it is hypothesized, on similar system-subsystem conflicts involving "backdoor spending."

[6] Liberalism-conservatism scores were those given to members of the 86th Congress by the AFL-CIO Committee on Political Education (COPE) as reported in *Congressional Quarterly*, October 7, 1960, pp. 1660–1661. A very few Members are not included because they received no AFL-CIO rating.

TABLE 2.2

HOUSE MEMBER SUPPORT OF THE APPROPRIATIONS COMMITTEE:
BY PARTY AND DEGREE OF LIBERALISM — THOMAS AMENDMENT 1959

Per Cent Liberal Votes — AFL-CIO	Democratic Votes in Support of Appropriations Committee Majority	Republican Votes in Support of Appropriations Committee Majority	Totals
	Per Cent	Per Cent	Per Cent
70 to 100	7 (3.9)	7 (3.9)	14 (7.8)
30 to 69	17 (9.4)	28 (15.6)	45 (25.0)
0 to 29	35 (19.4)	86 (47.8)	121 (67.2)
Totals	59 (32.7)	121 (67.3)	180 (100)

TABLE 2.3

HOUSE MEMBER SUPPORT OF AND OPPOSITION TO APPROPRIATIONS
COMMITTEE: BY DEGREE OF LIBERALISM — THOMAS AMENDMENT 1959

Per Cent Liberal Votes — AFL-CIO	House Votes in Support of Appropriations Committee Majority	House Votes in Opposition to Appropriations Committee Majority	Totals
	Per Cent	Per Cent	Per Cent
70 to 100	14 (3.8)	157 (42.3)	171 (46.1)
30 to 69	45 (12.1)	27 (7.3)	72 (19.4)
0 to 29	121 (32.6)	7 (1.9)	128 (34.5)
Totals	180 (48.5)	191 (51.5)	371 (100)

There was some verbal evidence during the debate of the resentment which House members have for "the powerful Appropriations Committee." Referring to the fact that the original bill had been written by the Banking and Currency Committee, majority leader John McCormack said,

> I respect the Committee on Appropriations, I realize the power of the Committee on Appropriations, I realize that money is power and I have felt the impact of it. But I also believe that the standing committees of the House of Representatives should not be put in a subordinate position to the Committee on Appropriations.[7]

[7] 105 *Congressional Record*, p. 8674.

But the core of opposition to the Committee came from those liberally oriented supporters of the housing program who did not wish to subject the program to what they perceived to be an economy-minded, budget-cutting Appropriations Committee. In the colorful language of the bill's sponsor, Albert Rains (D., Ala.),

> You know Mr. Chairman, when I heard my distinguished friend, and I love Al Thomas, say, "I asked for a vote," and when he was referring to this as just a little simple amendment, it reminded me of what happened in Alabama one time. I was out on a fishing bank fishing, and saw a little tiny boy, and he had a fish about that long. That fish was just wiggling and wiggling and wiggling and the little boy said, "Hold still, little fish, I ain't going to do nothing to you except gut you."[8]

Committee opponents lost the Thomas amendment skirmish. But they won their battle when the conference committee restored Treasury borrowing and the House voted to sustain it on the floor. On the final vote, the 201 originals were joined by House members for whom, at that point, support for a public housing bill was the overriding consideration. In the end, therefore, sanctions were effectively levied by the House against the Appropriations Committee. And it should be noted that the House can and did (in conference) draw upon the considerable resources of the Senate to make its sanctions effective.

In every session of Congress since 1959, battles over backdoor spending have been fought. And the war promises to continue without complete victory for either side. Supporters of backdoor spending have succeeded, repeatedly, in stopping a resolution which would prohibit all forms of direct Treasury financing. It is a resolution made necessary by a crucial ruling made from the chair in 1949 that public debt transactions are not to be considered as appropriations.[9] Active supporters of the resolution have typically been Republican and conservative. Of the 119 signatories to the 1963 version, 102 were Republicans and the rest conservative Democrats.[10] That resolution, like its two predecessors (H. Res. 161 in 1959 and H. Res. 115 in 1961), was blocked in the Rules Committee — this time by 7 to 7 tie vote, 7 Democrats against 5 Republicans and 2 Democrats. The following 1961 exchange in the Rules Committee illustrates the position of the two sides.

> MR. BROWN: Of course, boiling this thing down to the real content of it, those who oppose legislation of this type are the interests that want an easy way to get money out of the Federal Treasury without having to present their cases in an open hearing before Congress and show the necessity thereof. And those who support the legislation feel that the Appropriations

8 *Ibid.*, p. 8668.
9 See *Congressional Quarterly*, May 19, 1961, p. 851.
10 For the entire list of 1963 sponsors, see *Congressional Record*, Daily Edition, January 24, 1963, pp. 965–977.

Committee of the House and the House itself as well as the Senate should have some opportunity to pass upon the matter.

MR. O'NEILL: I think you put that very mildly.

MR. BROWN: I am a mild man, generally.

MR. O'NEILL: I think the proponents of this legislation would like to scuttle housing and urban renewal and long-range programming.

MR. BROWN: Any program that cannot stand on its own feet before the Congress or the House has to go around by the back door.

MR. O'NEILL: This is scuttling legislation.[11]

Or, in the words of one key Democratic leader, "What can you do when you have these broad programs like housing? You can't take a program like that to the Appropriations Committee where they are planted and ready to cut you down."

Those House members who would preserve and enlarge Appropriations Committee jurisdiction did score a significant victory in 1963 when they succeeded in changing the method of financing the Export-Import Bank from Treasury borrowing to direct appropriations. So strong was House sentiment that the Democratic leadership was forced to abandon its strenuous efforts to maintain Treasury financing and capitulate without a fight on the House floor. The question eventually became such a bone of contention in the conference committee (due, again, to Senate support for Treasury financing) that the entire matter of financing was shelved for one year.[12] The rollback decision in the House reveals, again, the strong cushion of support for the Committee which exists among Members. On the other hand, the existence and use, from time to time, of backdoor spending techniques reminds Committee members that House majorities can wield important sanctions over Committee activity.

SELECTING COMMITTEE MEMBERS

The recruitment and selection of Committee members is a less direct and less visible sanction than the manipulation of jurisdiction. But it probably represents the single most important long-run source of House influence over the Appropriations Committee. One week after its victory over the Committee in 1885, for example, the House filled all six of the vacancies on the Appropriations Committee with men who had opposed the Committee — doubtless hoping to bring the Committee more in line with dominant chamber sentiment. In 1921, the House moved to reduce House-Committee conflict by filling seven of the ten Committee vacancies with men who had opposed the Committee and whose own committees had suffered at its hands.

[11] *Congressional Record,* Daily Edition, February 23, 1961, p. A1179.
[12] *Congressional Record,* Daily Edition, May 1, 1963, pp. 7064–7073.

Although the processes by which political leaders are chosen are among the best-established topics of research in American national politics, students of Congress have barely begun to examine the process of Committee selection.[13] Thus far, moreover, analyses of Committee selection have not been cast in system-subsystem terms. That is to say, little attention has been paid to selection as one among several sanctions available to the House in case of House-Committee conflict. If, however, the House has a set of recognizable expectations about Appropriations Committee behavior and if these expectations become the criteria by which Committee members are recruited and selected, there is surely an increased likelihood that Committee members will subsequently behave in accordance with House expectations. And to the degree that this is so, traditional assertions about Committee autonomy and House impotence may need modification.

At the outset, it should be noted that the very size of the Appropriations Committee is subject to House control, and that the group's size has been altered several times during the period under study. So, too, does the House fix the majority-minority party ratios on the Committee — and that ratio has been altered from time to time. Normally, size and ratio are set by negotiation between party leaders and are formally established by House rule or special resolution. In the words of Speaker McCormack,

> That has always been a matter of discussion from Congress to Congress between the leadership of the two parties. Then when there is a little embarrassing situation in one party or another, we recognize that and we sort of get together and take care of it . . . we have increased any number of committees . . . the Committee on Appropriations under the rules is 43. It is now 50.[14]

In 1949 the House passed a special resolution changing the size of the Committee from 43 to 45; and by a similar 1951 resolution, the group was increased to its present size of 50 members.

From 1949 until 1965, the party ratio was held constant at 3 to 2. See Table 2.4. The 45-man Committee was composed of 27 majority and 18 minority members; until 1965, the 50-man Committee had 30 majority and 20 minority members. The House did not require that the partisan composition of the group reflect changes in the partisan complexion of the chamber as a whole. In 1965, however, Democratic membership in the House soared to its highest peak since the 1930's, and the party's leaders were faced

[13] Two excellent studies are Charles Clapp, *The Congressman: His Job as He Sees It* (Washington: Brookings Institution, 1963), Chapter 5; and Nicholas Masters, "Committee Assignments in the U.S. House of Representatives," *American Political Science Review* (June, 1961), pp. 345–357.
[14] 109 *Congressional Record*, p. 20.

TABLE 2.4

PARTY COMPOSITION AND VACANCIES FILLED
BY EACH PARTY, 80TH TO 89TH CONGRESS

Congress	Committee Membership by Party	Vacancies Filled by Each Party	Vacancies Filled with Freshman Members of Congress	Total Member- ship
80th (1947–1948)	18D — 25R	3D — 9R	1R	43
81st (1949–1950)	27D — 18R	11D — 0R	4D	45
82nd (1951–1952)	30D — 20R	3D — 8R	1D	50
83rd (1953–1954)	20D — 30R	0D — 13R	6R	50
84th (1955–1956)	30D — 20R	10D — 0R	2D	50
85th (1957–1958)	30D — 20R	5D — 3R	0	50
86th (1959–1960)	30D — 20R	2D — 8R	1R	50
87th (1961–1962)	30D — 20R	4D — 3R	0	50
88th (1963–1964)	30D — 20R	5D — 3R	1R	50
89th (1965–1966)	34D — 16R	9D — 5R	1D	50

with an unprecedented task in finding Committee positions for the huge majority. Accordingly, the majority was increased by 4 seats at the expense of the minority. The change does not appear to embody a permanent requirement that the Committee ratio reflect the partisan ratio in the chamber; rather it appears as an emergency measure to ease pressure on the Democratic leaders to make some choice Committee seats available to deserving Members.

Membership selection is a recurring sanction for which some pattern can be described. And since the results of the process yield identifiable persons, some estimate can be made of House success in applying the criteria for selection discussed earlier. It is impossible, however, to determine at this point in the analysis whether success in fulfilling expectations as to personnel has any payoff in actual behavior. For the present, the selection process will be treated as the independent variable and Committee personnel as the dependent variable.

"The House" in Committee-Making

"The House," as it engages in committee recruitment and selection, consists of two kinds of subgroups — party leaders and the state or regional delega-tions of the respective parties. For the Democrats, their official decision-makers are their members of the Committee on Ways and Means. But the Speaker and majority leader (or the minority leader and whip in years of Republican control) normally exercise a strong influence over the selection of Ways and Means Democrats and sit with them when they are in the process of allocating committee assignments. A Democratic leader assessed the various influences:

> I talk about it with the Speaker and with the members of the Committee. I have candidates, of course, and will talk about them . . . many times the Speaker makes the selection and the Committee just goes along. But once in a while the Committee goes against the wishes of the Speaker. And I've had candidates of mine rejected. On the whole I try not to interfere in what the Committee does. They are the constituted authority and once you start meddling with them you get into trouble. They are set up to do the job. So I try to stay out of it as much as I can. The only time I say anything is when I think the thing is serious.

Because the Ways and Means Democrats perform the selection function, care is taken in selecting its membership to include representatives from all the large Democratic state delegations and from other regional clusters of states. Each member then "looks after" the interests of the House members from his state or regional cluster in the bargaining process which attends the allocation of committee assignments.

House Republicans make committee selections by means of an official Committee on Committees. The minority leader (or Speaker when the Republicans are in control) sits as the Chairman of that Committee, and the minority whip (or majority leader) has usually been a member of it. Hence the party leaders exercise an important influence over committee selection. One seat on the Committee on Committees is given to each state delegation having at least one Republican member. But voting in the Committee is weighted so that each member casts as many votes as there are members in his state delegation. Normal practice is for the party leader to appoint a subcommittee dominated by the representatives from the large Republican delegations to make recommendations to the full Committee — a subcommittee on which the party leaders also sit. Since the bulk of the votes are cast by these same representatives, their recommendations are likely to be accepted. Just as some small-state Democrats gain membership on the Ways and Means Committee, so are some small-state Republican delegations represented on the subcommittee of the Committee on Committees.

A former Chairman of the Committee on Committees discussed the realities of the process:

> We had five states — New York, Pennsylvania, Ohio, Illinois, and California. I didn't give a damn whether the other states were there or what they wanted. We would make up a slate and push it through.

A leader of one of the large-state delegations completed the description:

> Then we report back to the full Committee. Now they could make a fuss there and change this and change that, but I can't remember when that has happened. That's because we've done a pretty good job if I do say so. Then that Committee reports back to the [Republican] conference. They could change the result there too and claim that this man or that man had been treated badly. But no changes have been made there for years.

Both processes of committee selection accord special weight to party leaders, to large-state delegations, and to regional clusters of state delegations. For purposes of selection, the influential men in these groups constitute "the House." As a matter of practice, however, one very important addition has to be made to the list of selectors on the Republican side. The Republicans have given (at least up until John Taber's retirement in 1962) great influence to their senior man on the Appropriations Committee itself. Referring to Taber as "our top guy on Appropriations," one floor leader explained, "He and I collaborated on that. We would check together to see who he wanted on the Committee." And a veteran member of the Committee on Committees said of Taber:

> He was more influential than any other committee chairman in that way. He'd check over all the applicants very carefully and he'd come around to our meetings every time with a list of the men he wanted on his Committee. And he got just about every one he wanted. He'd talk very frankly about people. He would say, "I don't want that man on my committee. I just can't work with that guy. He's not my kind of man." That's why we got such good people on that Committee.

By contrast, Clarence Cannon, senior Committee Democrat until 1964, never exerted more than an occasional influence over Democratic selections. Hence, the notable failure of Democrats to mention him in explaining how they got on the Committee. ("The Speaker has the power here, not Mr. Cannon. Mr. Cannon doesn't have anything to say about it.") Hence, too, Cannon's own lament that "Sam packed the Committee against me."[15] Cannon preferred the Republican to the Democratic selection machinery:

> The Speaker can use his influence to dictate the selection of members of the Ways and Means Committee and thereby dictate the selection of all these other committees. Usually he consults with the chairmen of the committees but not always. When that man from Texas was the Speaker — the man who was here for so long, Sam Rayburn — he would go around to some Members and say "We'd like to put you on the Ways and Means Committee. But when you come to appoint members to the other com-

15 *Time Magazine*, February 2, 1959, p. 14.

55

mittees, we'd like to be able to come around and speak with you. If there's any problem we would like you to listen to what we have to say and so on, and so forth." And the Member would say, "Certainly, Mr. Speaker." That wouldn't happen under the Republican system. On our side, men are chosen for committees because they are politically acceptable.

The regular inclusion of Taber and the frequent exclusion of Cannon may have resulted in part from the greater personal affection which his party cohorts had for "old John Taber." But Taber's successor, representative Ben Jensen, exercised some of the same influence in at least one decision made in 1963. And Cannon's successor, George Mahon, had no great influence over Democratic selections in 1965. A deeper explanation may be found in the greater homogeneity of economy-related attitudes among Republican House members. In either case, the differences point to a Committee-House relationship somewhat less conflict-ridden on the Republican than on the Democratic side.

The Search for Responsiveness

The intangibility of House expectations — that Appropriations Committee members be especially responsive to integrative House norms — makes the assessment of prospective members tremendously difficult. Committee-makers, therefore, proceed with painstaking deliberation in order to minimize their mistakes. Since the safest guide is the previous behavior of prospective members, selectors impose an informal apprenticeship of one or two terms in the chamber. "We don't often appoint a freshman to this Committee," said a Republican leader. "The boys figure he's got to prove himself first." And a Democratic selector concurred: "Members serve a few years before the mast — a period of probation. If they are good men, they are taken off the other committees and put on the Appropriations Committee." Committee-makers thus buy time with which to observe the House activities of Committee prospects. "I've always tried to get out on the floor as much as I can to see what part these young fellows are playing," said a key Republican. "And I talk to the older members of their state delegations because they are the ones that keep the closest contact with the younger men." Thus proceeds the collection of intuitive personal assessments so necessary to judgments about "the responsible legislator."

A leader of one of the largest Republican delegations provided insight into the expectations and activities of House leaders like himself in the following description:

> We want people of maturity. Sometimes we give it to a person who has been standing in line for some time. ———— is a good case. . . . I thought he was about ripe — he had about two terms of experience. I thought he was ready. So I called him into my office one day and I said to him, "I know

56

you and I knew your father before you. I know what stock you are made of. I know your background, your experience, and your character. I think you are ready to go on the Appropriations Committee." I knew he was unhappy because he felt he wasn't getting any place. I said to him, "I have only one question about you. Damn it all, if I put you on that Committee, will you work? Will you go in there and work hard? Will you start early in the morning and burn the midnight oil if necessary?"

In cases where suitable recruits cannot be found "standing in line" inside the House, Committee-makers may have to choose among freshman applicants. In this case, they will frequently reach back into the district, as well as into the state delegation, in pursuit of relevant information and judgments. Two Republicans, who were chosen for the Committee in their freshman year, described what one referred to as a "security check" conducted by John Taber in their constituencies:

> It wasn't until afterward that I found out that I had been pretty thoroughly checked out in my home community with the bankers and businessmen and judges — to see if I measured up to the job. Enough of my neighbors lied about me, so I got the job.

> The Chairman (Mr. Taber) I guess did some checking around in my area. After all, I was new and he didn't know me. People told me that they were called to see if I was — well, unstable or apt to go off on tangents. . . . Well, to see whether or not I had any preconceived notions about things and would not be flexible — inflexible about things — whether I would oppose things even though it was obvious.

The prolonged and intensive search measures something of the importance which the House attaches to the activity and personnel of the Committee.

Table 2.5 summarizes the length of prior service in the House of the 119 members who served on the Appropriations Committee from 1947 through 1964.[16] Their House apprenticeship averaged 3.7 years, nearly 2 full

TABLE 2.5

LENGTH OF CONGRESSIONAL SERVICE BEFORE APPOINTMENT TO APPROPRIATIONS COMMITTEE — 119 MEMBERS 1947 TO 1964

Number of Years in House Before Selection to Appropriations Committee	0	1	2	3	4	5	6	7	8	9	10	11	17
Number of Men	18	10	25	8	22	7	10	4	8	2	3	1	1

[16] The total of 119 men used in Tables 2.5 through 2.7 does not include Rep. W. R. Hull (D., Mo.) elected to the Committee in June, 1964. Rep. Clarence Cannon, who died in May, 1964, is credited with serving the entire year 1964.

terms. Only 18 (15.1 per cent) gained membership in their freshman year. As Table 2.4 indicates, 13 of these 18 came to the Committee in years of party turnover — 1947, 1949, 1953, and 1955. In these cases, the party found itself with from 8 to 12 vacancies to fill and appointed some from the accompanying influx of freshmen. Nonetheless, House committee-makers have been more successful in maintaining an apprenticeship for the Appropriations Committee than they have been with all but three of the other House committees.[17] Insofar as a lengthy and painstaking scrutiny helps to ensure the selection of responsible, responsive Committee members, House expectations seem likely to be met.

By enforcing a House apprenticeship, the selectors helped to bring about the selection of Committee members with safe election margins. The putative "one-termer" is automatically eliminated from consideration, and the man whose electoral circumstances will not allow him to adopt the House as an important reference group can be spotted. Considering their victory margins in the election just prior to their appointment to the Appropriations Committee, the members come — by a margin of nearly 3 to 1 — from safe districts. If 55.0 per cent or more of the total vote is used as the measure of a safe seat, then 87 (73.1 per cent) members originally came from safe seats and 32 (26.9 per cent) members originally came from marginal seats. These seats are distributed equally among Republicans and Democrats. The Republicans represented 43 safe and 16 marginal districts; the Democrats represented 44 safe and 16 marginal districts. If, instead of looking at the election prior to their selection (which is, of course, the way Committee-makers look at it) one examines the safeness of the sitting members' districts, the proportion of safe seats will be even more impressive. For the 50 men on the Committee in 1961, for example, 41 of them had election margins of more than 55 per cent in 1960. The preponderance of members with safe seats represents a fulfillment of some House expectations.

Since regional or state influences are built into the normal selection procedures, House expectations regarding the Committee's geographical representativeness are generally well met. Once on the Committee, it is assumed regional representatives will be especially responsive to regional expectations. And the net result, it is hoped, will be to enhance Committee responsiveness to the House and to party contingents in the House. Consensus-building, especially, should be facilitated by the geographical representativeness of Committee members. Table 2.6 presents a regional breakdown of Committee membership from 1947 to 1964 in terms of man years of service.

[17] The three Committees are Rules, Ways and Means, and Foreign Affairs (for which the percentage is about the same as that for Appropriations). See Donald Stokes and Warren Miller, *Representation in the American Congress* (New York: Prentice-Hall, forthcoming).

TABLE 2.6

REGIONAL DISTRIBUTION OF COMMITTEE MEMBERS — MAN YEARS OF SERVICE AND AVERAGE SERVICE PER MAN: 119 MEMBERS 1947 TO 1964

REGION[a]	MAN YEARS OF SERVICE			AVERAGE YEARS OF SERVICE PER MAN		
	Democrats	Republicans	Total	Democrats	Republicans	Total
East	87 (18%)	122 (31%)	209 (24%)	7.9 (11 men)	8.1 (15 men)	8.0 (26 men)
South	199 (41%)	10 (3%)	209 (24%)	10.5 (19 men)	10.0 (1 man)	10.5 (20 men)
Border	54 (11%)	12 (3%)	66 (7%)	7.7 (7 men)	4.0 (3 men)	6.6 (10 men)
Midwest	93 (19%)	184 (48%)	277 (32%)	6.2 (15 men)	6.1 (30 men)	6.2 (45 men)
Far West	57 (11%)	59 (15%)	116 (13%)	7.1 (8 men)	5.9 (10 men)	6.4 (18 men)
Total	490 (100%)	387 (100%)	877 (100%)	8.2 (60 men)	6.5 (59 men)	7.4 (119 men)

[a] East: Conn., Del., Me., Mass., N.H., N.J., N.Y., Pa., R.I., Vt.
South: Ala., Ark., Fla., Ga., La., Miss., N.C., S.C., Tenn., Texas, Va.
Border: Ky., Md., Mo., Okla., W.Va.
Midwest: Ill., Ind., Iowa, Kans., Mich., Minn., Nebr., N.D., Ohio, S.D., Wisc.
Far West: Alaska, Ariz., Calif., Colo., Hawaii, Idaho, Mont., N.M., Ore., Utah, Wash., Wyo.

Every major region has been represented on the Committee with, perhaps, some slight overrepresentation of the Midwest and underrepresentation of the East. The regional distribution of members by party reflects the regional distribution of party strength — of Democratic strength in the Southern-border regions and of Republican strength in the Midwest. In 7 of the 9 Congresses studied, every Southern state had a representative on the Committee. For representational purposes, both parties think in terms of subregions — like those superintended by each Ways and Means Democrat. Nearly every state represented on the Ways and Means Committee has a member on the Appropriations Committee. No large state (New York, California, Pennsylvania, Illinois, Ohio, Texas, and Michigan), regardless of region, has lacked for representation during the seventeen-year period. And, with the exception of Texas, these big delegation, heavy tax-paying states usually enjoy representation on both sides of the aisle — frequently by more than one person. Conversely, no small state is likely to be represented by more than one man on either side of the aisle.

Since influence within the Committee is conditioned by seniority, length of service per man becomes consequential. Table 2.6 reveals one very important regional variation in this regard. Southern Members not only get to the Committee in ample proportions, but they stay on the Committee longer than Members from any other region. The average length of service of 10.5 years stands in sharp contrast to the average for the other four regions of 6.8 years. Given their longevity and their seniority, one would predict that Southerners on the Committee will have held a disproportionate share of such influential jobs as subcommittee chairmen from 1947 to 1964.

Table 2.7 lists the state party delegations which, in the seventeen years studied, enjoyed representation of better than one member per year. As one

TABLE 2.7

STATE PARTY DELEGATIONS AVERAGING BETTER THAN 1 MAN PER YEAR
ON APPROPRIATIONS COMMITTEE, 1947 TO 1964

DEMOCRATS		REPUBLICANS	
State	Man Years Service	State	Man Years Service
Texas	34	N.Y.	44
N.Y.	27	Ohio	30
Calif.	26	Pa.	29
Ill.	26	Mich.	24
		Ill.	21
		Wisc.	19
		N.J.	19

would expect, it is the large states which gain the most representation. The difference, however, between Democratic and Republican rankings reflects the relative importance of state party delegations in the House. As measured by their success in the selection process the Texas Democrats, the New York Republicans, and the Ohio Republicans would appear to be important sanctioning groups within "the House." And conversely, the lack of success of such party delegations as the Pennsylvania Democrats and the California Republicans may point to their relative impotence within the chamber. The strength or weakness of state delegations rests in turn on the presence or absence of influential and unifying figures like Speaker Sam Rayburn (D., Texas), Thomas O'Brien (D., Ill.), John Taber (R., N.Y.), and Clarence Brown (R., Ohio).

Continuity in the representation of regions, subregions, and states is retained by the customary practice of replacing a deceased, defeated, or retired Committee member with another from the same area. The practice is least likely to hold for small states and for states with declining representation in the House. Most explanations by Committee members of how they attained membership included the statement that "by tradition" the member's state or region was "entitled to" or "eligible for" a recently vacated seat. Or, members speak of waiting until "there was a slot for me" due to state or regional vacancy. Should they come from a subregion that is lacking in representation, they may "make a pitch" on these grounds. Thus geographical considerations set limits on the availability of candidates for the Committee. And to a degree, therefore, limits are set on the sanctioning ability of "the House." But the custom can, of course, be broken. When it is, the results are normally traceable either to differentials in the attractiveness of candidates or in the skill of Committee-makers.

A Democratic leader recalled, for example,

> Sometimes a man is so popular with the Committee on Ways and Means that he gets on the Committee in violation of all the ordinary rules. That was the case with Henderson Lanham of Georgia. He got on the Committee even though Prince Preston was already on the Committee from Georgia. But he was just one of the most well-liked men in the House.

The New York Republicans lost one of their three seats on the Committee in 1963 and another in 1965 — partly because the relative size of the delegation declined, but also because the man who had obtained some overrepresentation in the first place (Rep. Taber) was no longer around to exercise his influence.

In 1963, an important break in tradition was engineered by a majority of House Democratic Committee-makers. Seats formerly occupied by Democrats from New York, Washington, Illinois, Arkansas, and North Carolina

61

were vacant. And they were subsequently filled by Democrats from New York, Washington, Illinois, New Jersey, and Connecticut, respectively. Arkansas lost a Committee seat which it had held for 30 years, and North Carolina a seat it had held (except during the Republican interval 1953–1954) for the same length of time. And Southern representation on the Committee was thereby significantly reduced. The change gives clear evidence of the ability of the House — in this case liberal Democrats — to levy sanctions on the Committee via membership control. One Ways and Means Democrat explained,

> The new ones are a progressive group. We had to liberalize the Appropriations Committee this year. You're in trouble over there. So we put some people on who would support the administration and the party position. They just squeaked in, but we got the votes.

Appropriations Committee Chairman Clarence Cannon was not consulted on any of the five choices and, as a matter of fact, approved of only one.

In 1963, there was a somewhat greater than normal emphasis on policy criteria among the Democrats. But other factors proved decisive in some cases. An insight into the circumstances under which the 1963 changes occurred is provided by two Ways and Means Democrats — one a Southerner and one a Northerner — both of whom ascribe the break in tradition to relative skillfulness in playing the politics of selection. With reference to the contest in which the Northern candidate Robert G. Giaimo (Connecticut) defeated the Southern candidate Robert Ashmore (South Carolina) for the traditional North Carolina seat, the Southerner said,

> North Carolina didn't put up a candidate. We talked to some of the fellows and asked them to run, but they were all situated on committees. South Carolina had a candidate. They had had a member and lost him. . . . Ashmore should have been elected. But he just didn't get around to speak to enough people. You have to do that, it's very important. You have to go around and visit with the members of the Committee and let them know you really want it.

The Northerner attributed Ashmore's failure to politick successfully to the inexperience of his regional spokesmen on the Ways and Means Committee:

> The real surprise was Bob Giaimo. He took away a Southern seat. Pat Jennings was the new member from that district and his newness worked against him. The rest of us took advantage of his inexperience. He just couldn't put his man across. He came to me and said, "I was elected by the Southern delegation and I've got to get that job for my region." Well, I didn't say anything. I knew how his man got licked . . . next time, two years from now, he'll know how to put his man across. The first year I came down here I didn't have any success with my candidates. This year I got all my men on the committees. It's quite a workout.

House members who approved of it considered the outcome a revolution in their efforts to promote Committee responsiveness. But it needs to be stressed, as an analytical matter, that successful "House" control of the selection process cannot guarantee Committee behavior that will meet House expectations.

Self-Starters, Inner-Circle Choices, and Coopteds

When the recruitment and selection process is viewed from the candidate's perspective, additional light is shed on the exercise of "House" selection controls. Descriptions by Committee members of how they gained Committee membership revealed three distinguishable patterns, which can be labeled — after categories set up by Lester G. Seligman — as self-starting, inner-circle recruitment, and cooptation.[18]

Self-starters refer to applicants who propel themselves into consideration because of a self-initiated desire to serve on the Committee:

> It's been my objective from the first moment I came here. I declared my preference for it from the start, and I've been watching it as long as I've been here.

For the self-starter, his problem is to make himself known favorably to the key "House" people involved. He begins by getting the support of his state delegation — via the "dean" of that group. A Western Republican deliberately attached himself to a senior man in his delegation:

> I became a protégé of his. I ran errands for him. I read what he wrote. I went to him when I was in trouble. I kept pretty close to it for a long time, I'll say that.

If the "dean" or senior man of the group happens also to be a member (or better still an influential member) of the Ways and Means Democrats or the Republican Committee on Committees, the applicant already has privileged access to those decision-making bodies. In the company of his delegation head or with his approval, the aspirant will then present his case, orally or by letter or both, to other members of the decision-making groups and party leaders. The process is variously described as "a lobbying proposition," "just like running for office," "like getting elected to this body in the first place," "hard work and hand-shaking — you know, the old routine." A Republican and a Democratic self-starter recalled typical efforts:

> In 1957, I let my wishes be known. Mr. Martin was the leader then, and I talked to him, but there were no vacancies. I talked to most of the people from my area of the country. And, of course, Mr. Taber — I talked to him two or three times about it.

[18] Lester G. Seligman, "Recruitment in Politics," *PROD* (March, 1958), pp. 14–17.

I lobbied the members of the Ways and Means Committee for a whole year. The Speaker [Rayburn] had a lot to do with it. If he hadn't supported me, I doubt that I would have made it. He will indicate to the Ways and Means Committee who he thinks ought to go on the Committee. I don't say they will always take his advice, but 95 per cent of the time they do.

Insofar as candidates for Committee membership are self-starters, House Committee-makers exercise their influence by screening out applicants who do not promise to meet their expectations. Since the number of applicants usually far exceeds the number of vacancies, this negative influence is considerable.

Table 2.8 summarizes from 1953 to 1963 the relation of applicants to vacancies by party.[19] Though little is known about the 82 individuals who

TABLE 2.8

APPROPRIATIONS COMMITTEE VACANCIES AND APPLICANTS
FIRST SESSION OF EACH CONGRESS, 1953 TO 1963[a]

CONGRESS	DEMOCRATS[b]		REPUBLICANS[c]	
	Vacancies	*Applicants*	*Vacancies*	*Applicants*
83rd Congress	0	10	13	23
84th Congress	10	16	0	0
85th Congress	3	3	3	15
86th Congress	1	8	8	15
87th Congress	2	4	2	9
88th Congress	5	10	3	19
Total	21	51	29	81

[a] Vacancy totals may not correspond to those in Table 2.4 which include both sessions of Congress.
[b] From the records of the Committee on Ways and Means.
[c] From the records of the Republican Committee on Committees.

[19] Table 2.8 should not be read as a complete listing of vacancies and applicants but only as a listing of those which occurred at the beginning of each Congress. Such a list does include the great majority of cases. Quite often, however, an appointment will be made close on the heels of the death of a Committee member. Or, a Committee member who knows he will not be returning for the next Congress may resign from the Committee early so that his replacement can be selected at the end of one Congress rather than at the beginning of the next. State or regional groups who wish to make certain that they retain a seat on the Committee will find it advantageous to make these kinds of in-term selections. By moving quickly and by avoiding the January traffic jam, they increase their chances of success. The immediate replacement of Clarence Cannon of Missouri by W. R. Hull of Missouri, after Cannon's death in May, 1964, is an example of one in-term selection. The early resignation of H. Carl Andersen of Minnesota who had been defeated in a primary and his immediate replacement by Odin Langen of Minnesota in October of 1962 is an example of another kind of in-term selection.

lost, it is a reasonable guess that nearly all of them were self-starters. For one reason or another they were kept off the Committee (though some of them doubtless persisted and later won) by those who speak for "the House" in exercising its control over selection. Only a single case was turned up in which a self-starter, relying on his seniority within his delegation, won election to the Committee contrary to the wishes of the leadership:

> I was opposed by labor — they didn't want me on the Committee and some others didn't. I don't know why. I talked to the leadership. McCormack tried to discourage me because of my seniority on my other committee. Then I began to get some calls. That's when I decided I really wanted it. I'm a little bastard that way. As soon as I got those calls telling me not to take it, I decided to go after it all the way. That's the kind of person I am.

Inner-circle recruitment describes a pattern where a House member is urged by influential individuals or groups to campaign for Committee membership. The move is initiated, then, by others — usually a Committee-maker or a state delegation. In such cases the House exercises a positive kind of influence. A Ways and Means Committee leader said, "Sometimes we'll talk around and urge certain fellows to run. But we always have more applicants than places." A Southerner recalled that "Friends of mine on the Ways and Means Committee said there was a chance that I could get on Appropriations. When I heard there was a chance, I jumped at it. I'm only the fifth man from my state to get on Appropriations." A Northerner explained how he reached the Committee: "It's simple. The member of Ways and Means from my state and I were old friends. We were alumni of the same law school. He came to me and asked me if I wanted to go on Appropriations." A Republican spoke similarly of his long friendship with the ranking minority member of the Committee and added,

> He came to me and said, "I want you on the Appropriations Committee," so I followed that up with a letter back thanking him for the idea. He told me what other people I should see like Clarence Brown — and I went around. He said that as ranking minority member his wishes would be given consideration, but that he couldn't do it all by himself.

Another inner-circle pattern occurs when a state delegation, seeking to maximize its influence, selects its candidate and runs him for the Committee "for the good of the delegation." "Very frankly, when I came up, I wanted to be on the Ways and Means Committee," said a Southerner. "But we had a man on Ways and Means, so I couldn't get on. My delegation didn't have a man on Appropriations and we wanted to get one on. The delegation met and proposed me for the position." When asked how they got on the Committee, two Northern Democrats responded:

> When I came here, I was on the ———— Committee and was very happy. In my first term Mr. X of my state, who was on the Appropriations Com-

65

mittee, died. The members of my delegation wanted to keep a man on that Committee. The leadership spoke to me and the members of the delegation spoke to me. They felt that since ours was a large state and had had a man on the Committee that we could get it if an acceptable person could be found.

I didn't want it exactly. I was on the ———— Committee and was happy doing creative and exciting work. But I was prevailed upon to take it — prevailed upon isn't exactly the right word. I didn't have to have my arm twisted. Our state didn't have a person on the Committee on either side of the aisle, and I thought it would be good for the state. Our whip came to me and said there was a vacancy on the Committee and that our state could have it and did I want it. I said they should give it to the new man in the delegation. He said they wouldn't have a freshman on the Committee. So I said "Yes."

Members recruited in this manner will start their campaign with the blessing of influential House members. And they will normally win. Insofar as they actively suggest and promote the candidacy of acceptable individuals, House members exercise an independent control over selection.

Cooptation refers to a process by which members are picked for the Committee without having either requested it or campaigned for it. Here the influence of the Committee-makers is total. They unilaterally select a man deemed to meet their bill of specifications and then notify him of his selection. In such instances, "the House" can get the kind of individual it wants. Four Members describe their experience.

The first thing I knew about it was when I was reading the assignments. I talked to Mr. X and he said, "You go over there and raise hell with them." On the way over I met McCormack who said, "I'd keep quiet and go along if I were you. This is a better committee; you can help your constituents a lot more." So I did.

I'm probably one of those rare instances, but I didn't want to get on the Appropriations Committee. When I came here I wanted to get on the legislative committee on agriculture. Mr. Rayburn called me one day and said that he was very sorry that it was not possible to put me on the Agriculture Committee. Then he asked me what committee I wanted. I said I was interested in doing the work of a congressman and that he knew more about it than I did. He said "Fine" or something like that. Two years later I went on the floor one day and someone said, "Congratulations, you're on the Appropriations Committee." That's how I got on the Appropriations Committee.

I didn't . . . in fact, I refused it, and even suggested who I thought ought to have it. They laughed at me and said, "Why don't you quit while you're ahead?" . . . Well, the more you don't want a thing the more they want you. So the leadership asked me to take it again.

66

I didn't ask to go on the Appropriations Committee. I just wanted to get off the ———— Committee. . . . Then they came and told me after the meeting that of all the ones talked about I had been selected for the Committee. It wasn't a case of my asking them for the job but the other way around. They asked me if I would take the job. I said I'd take it; but I hadn't put any drive on at all. The leadership wanted me.

A Republican who described himself as happy on his committee recounted the pressure applied by the Committee-makers. Speaker Martin called first to inquire if he would like to go on Appropriations. When the reply was "No," the Speaker tried to persuade him, but to no avail. Later, a clinching call came from John Taber, which went as follows:

Why don't you want to come on my committee?
Don't put it that way Mr. Taber. I just said I was happy where I was.
Well, I picked you for my committee.

In cases like these, the hand of the House lies heaviest on Committee selection.

Additional light can be shed on the selection process and on House controls by asking the further question, "What Committee members gain membership by what processes of selection?" Table 2.9 presents a summary correlation (for those members whose interview answers made classification possible) between partisan categories and recruitment patterns.

TABLE 2.9

PARTY GROUPINGS AND RECRUITMENT PATTERNS

Party Grouping	Self-Starters	Inner-Circle Choices	Coopteds	Total
Republicans	17	1	2	20
Southern and Border-State Democrats	6	6	0	12
Northern Democrats	9	5	5	19
Total	32	12	7	51

A clear majority of Committee members were self-starters, who made a unilateral decision to seek membership and who were chosen in preference to other less acceptable contestants. The proportion of self-starters among Republicans is, however, significantly greater than that on the Democratic side. The difference reinforces the evidence of Table 2.8 (on applications and vacancies) that the Committee is, initially at least, a more attractive Committee to Republicans than to Democrats. Doubtless, the Committee's power makes it attractive to all groups of congressmen. But the marked extra appeal that it has for Republicans probably stems from the fact that House goal expectations concerning the Committee dovetail more closely with Republican party ideology than with Democratic party ideology. Economy expectations and, to a lesser degree, oversight expectations may come more naturally to Republicans than to Democrats. The surfeit of Republican self-starters accounts for the paucity of Republicans who get recruited in other ways.

Democrats, however, differ among themselves in their initial enthusiasm for the Committee. Southern and border-state Democrats come to the Committee via self-starting or inner-circle routes. Inner-circle choices make up a significantly larger proportion of this group than they do for Republicans or Northern Democrats. This fact may reflect the extraordinary keenness with which, as state delegations, Southern and border-state Democrats have increased their influence inside Congress by deliberately spreading themselves across influential committees. It may also reflect a superior intraregional communications network where legislative perquisites are involved. It is noteworthy that Southern and border-state congressmen leave nothing to chance or to others in these matters and that not a single one was coopted by the Committee-makers.

Northern Democrats are the most evenly distributed across the recruitment categories. Of particular interest is the fact that they comprise five of the seven members who were coopted. Northern Democrats may be less attracted to the Committee because they lack conservative predispositions about saving money or, conversely, because they are positively attracted to committees more actively engaged in writing legislation in controversial policy areas. It is suggestive, perhaps, that by a margin of six to one those Democrats who came to the Committee as representatives of the New York City or Chicago delegations came via the inner-circle or the cooptation routes. Liberal Democrats from large urban centers may not find the Committee on Appropriations very visible or, when visible, very appealing. The Committee's work patterns — long and hard — may not attract, for example, New York City congressmen who like to remain in Washington only 3 days a week, Tuesday to Thursday. It might also be noted that, as a group, the ten Northern Democrats who were inner-circle choices or coopteds seem notably nonideological in their approach to politics — thus enhancing the likelihood of their being responsive to "the House."

Evidence of Success

It is impossible to know for sure the degree to which House Committee-makers can meet House expectations. The notion of the responsible or responsive legislator defies hard and precise measurement. But there is ample evidence that certain related and measurable expectations are met — prior experience, safe election margins, and geographical representativeness. And there is ample evidence of House control over the selection process as a whole. To this can be added the direct testimony of House leaders or candidates involved. Responsiveness to party leadership, for example, bulks large in House expectations; and there are two clear examples that this was controlling in 1963. Republican Committee-makers, faced with a vacancy from the northeast rejected the bid of an experienced man from New Jersey and chose a freshman from New Hampshire instead. A Republican leader explained, "New Jersey was pushing awfully hard to get a man on the Committee. I don't want to get into names, but that delegation has been jumping the track on us too damned much. They were pushing a fellow, but the boys just wouldn't buy it." Another attempt to fulfill House expectations was described by a Democratic leader:

> There was a vacancy in that whole northwest Rocky Mountain region. You had two candidates — Walter Baring of Nevada and Julia Hansen of Washington. They both wanted it. Baring was a man you couldn't have. The administration didn't trust him. The party couldn't trust him. He was an enemy of foreign aid and other things. The job was given to Mrs. Hansen.

Within their capability to estimate responsiveness, party leaders certainly fulfill their expectations in cases such as these. And it is reasonable to assume that these two cases are not unique.

Evidence that the two party contingents apply their special criterion of responsiveness with success comes from the testimony of those who gained membership. When asked why they were chosen, nearly all of the Republicans who went on the Committee in 1959 stressed their devotion to economy. One described his campaign:

> I wrote a letter to Mr. Taber. I said, "Mr. Taber, I know you are acquainted with my conservative views and I'd like to get on the Committee." I know how John works and I knew that would score points with him. . . . We stacked our Committee with conservatives this year.

A second newcomer recalled that he was selected in competition with a more senior man from his region — a man spurned by Taber as "a spender." "If you have any wild ideas on our side, the Republican side, you just don't get on the Committee," he added. A third Committee freshman noted, "Of course I had to convince John Taber that I wasn't a wild-eyed spender or anything like that." Given the importance of economy in Republican ideology, a random selection would produce more economy-minded individuals among Republicans than among Democrats. But Republican selectors operate — successfully it would seem — to increase the odds. Speaking of 1959, a high-ranking veteran of the Appropriations Committee said, "This year we lost

69

eight men. Four quit and four were defeated. We took the list of Republicans, John Taber and I, and we picked eight young energetic fighting conservatives."

In explaining why they were selected, young Democrats give particular weight, as befits the expectations of Democratic leaders, to their legislative style. This involves responsiveness to leadership, cooperativeness, and a devotion to legislative give and take. One Northern Democrat said that he had been chosen for membership over eight competitors because "I had made a lot of friends and was known as a nice guy." He especially mentioned his friendships among the Southern Democrats. A Western Democrat said, "I got the blessing of the Speaker [Rayburn] and the leadership. It's personal friendship. I had done a lot of things for them in the past, and when I went to them and asked them, they gave it to me." Another Northern Democrat said,

> You've got to look at the long pull. I've based my whole legislative career on that. You can't shoot your mouth off and be effective. You have got to learn what you're doing and keep your mouth shut. I know that's why I'm on the Committee. They want sober people on the Committee.

Conversely, a man who was finally chosen for the Committee explained that he had first been denied the seat to which he was entitled because he failed to support Speaker Rayburn on the Rules Committee enlargement in 1961. Doubtless, these members have a pretty accurate explanation of why they were chosen. And they certainly dovetail with the preselection ambitions of Democratic Committee-makers.

The House, acting through its two designated sets of Committee-makers, wields an important sanction when it superintends the selection of the Committee on Appropriations. And it seems reasonable to assume that the makeup of the Committee will help account for Committee behavior. But sanctions over membership are not sanctions over behavior. The ability of the House to select Committee members probably represents a necessary condition of House control over Committee behavior. But it is by no means sufficient.

AMENDING COMMITTEE RECOMMENDATIONS

One obvious and fundamental sanction which a House majority (and normally far less than that) can exercise over the Appropriations Committee involves the acceptance, rejection, or alteration of any Committee recommendation at the time it reaches the floor. An analysis of Committee recommendations and their disposition on the House floor will be undertaken in Chapter Nine — which chapter constitutes an extension of the present one. All that needs to be said at this point is simply that the House can and the House does alter Committee proposals. In the 16 years from

1947 to 1962, 547 separate floor amendments were offered to the appropriation bills of 8 executive departments plus Public Works. Of these, 162
(30 per cent) passed. Of the total that were passed, 46 or about one-quarter
passed over the protests of an Appropriations Committee united in its spoken
opposition. Similarly, when Committee members seek approval of their decisions as House conferees, the House has an opportunity to change this
decision. On at least 6 different occasions (as discussed in Chapter Twelve)
the House altered or caused the conferees to alter their decisions at this final
stage in the congressional legislative process. Without for the moment calculating orders of magnitude, the point can be made that the House does
have and does exercise these important sanctions over its Committee on Appropriations.

CONTROLLING PROCEDURE

Annual Authorization

A dominant set of House maintenance expectations focuses on the flow of
information from Committee to House. Insofar as House members perceive
Committee restrictions on the flow of information, they complain about
their dependence on the Committee. The House has moved recently to
countervail this dependence by increasing the number of items for which
authorization must be obtained annually. Appropriations are not in order
unless authorized by law. Many appropriations, however, are the subject
of permanent authorization and, hence, receive annual consideration only at
the hands of the Appropriations Committee. Other items, according to law,
must receive a fresh authorization each year and, hence, must be considered
first by a substantive legislative committee and then by the Appropriations
Committee. Permanent authorizations are made for such items as departmental salaries and expenses and for long-term, well-established departmental
programs. Annual authorizations are required for such agencies as the Agency
for International Development, the Peace Corps, the Atomic Energy Commission, and the National Aeronautics and Space Administration. Biennial
authorizations are usually passed for the rivers and harbors projects of the
Corps of Army Engineers. Where substantive House committees hear testimony on a given program as a prelude to recommending an authorization
figure, the House develops a body of subject-matter experts in addition to the
Appropriations Committee. House members can avail themselves of two
channels of information, thus helping to free them from their sense of dependence on the single Appropriations Committee.

In recent years, the House has significantly increased the number of
programs for which two annual "look-sees" are required. One very sig-

nificant step in this direction occurred when Congress in 1959 altered existing procedure and provided, henceforth, for the authorization of all expenditures for "aircraft, missiles, and naval vessels." Language calling specifically for annual authorization was deleted in conference. But one student concludes that "the intent of annual authorization, however, was not dislodged."[20] And annual authorizations have been made ever since. When, in 1960, the House Armed Services Committee reported out its first authorization measure, Chairman Carl Vinson stressed the degree to which House dependence on the Appropriations Committee had been diminished:

> Up to this time the Departments merely had to request and obtain appropriations for the procurement of these items under these very broad authorities. I am afraid that the end result of this procedure was that members of the Appropriations Committee were the only ones in the Congress who actually had very much knowledge of the tremendous programs and expenditures which the Congress was called upon to pass on each year. It is my hope that Section 412 has called to a halt this situation. If it did nothing else, it brought 37 more members of the House into the heretofore exclusive areas of knowledge of these very large programs.[21]

Open system-subsystem conflict did not break out, but a distinct lack of enthusiasm was expressed by the members of the Appropriations Committee in private.

In the same year, when provision was made for the annual authorization of funds for the National Aeronautics and Space Administration, Committee-House conflict did reveal itself. A member of the Science and Astronautics Committee defended the legislation in terms that clearly relegated the Appropriations Committee to a lesser task:

> By that provision we require that they (the Space Agency) come specifically before the authorizing committee so that those who have been following these scientific advances can add the benefit of their knowledge as well as that of the Appropriations Committee who will look after the housekeeping.[22]

Several veteran Appropriations Committee members spoke against the annual authorization section — not in the language of influence but in the language of efficiency:

> I doubt if it is necessary to have a complete and total authorization each year plus a review by the House and Senate Committees on Appropriations.[23]

[20] Raymond Dawson, "Congressional Innovation and Intervention in Defense Policy: Legislative Authorization of Weapons Systems," *American Political Science Review* (March, 1962), p. 53. More generally, see the testimony of Arthur Maass in Joint Committee on the Organization of Congress, *Hearings on the Organization of Congress*, 89th Congress, 1st Session (Washington: U.S. Government Printing Office), pp. 942 ff.

[21] *Congressional Record*, Daily Edition, May 24, 1961, p. 8218.

[22] 105 *Congressional Record*, pp. 8290–8291.

[23] *Ibid.*, p. 8279.

On the vote to institute the annual authorization procedure, the Appropriations Committee members voted 33 to 15 against the proposal. The members of the Science and Astronautics Committee voted unanimously in favor.

The result, as in the case of military procurement, was a sharing of influence in what had previously been the Appropriations Committee's private preserve. The House seems increasingly enthusiastic about the annual authorization technique as a device to keep themselves from becoming hostaged to the Appropriations Committee. In 1962, they voted to require prior authorization for all new military research and development programs. A year later, they extended annual authorization provisions to Coast Guard construction and procurement programs.

Existing authorizing committees conceive of themselves unmistakably as experts on whom House members should rely. They go out of their way to stress the care with which they have considered the authorization figure. Thus, in presenting the NASA authorization in 1962, the Chairman of the Science and Astronautics Committee cited the 11 weeks of hearings, the 2298 pages of testimony, and the 85 witnesses as evidence of his group's thoroughness. He spoke of his Committee's members as

> Sitting day after day, week after week, for long hours, with near perfect subcommittee attendance, going over each of the programs and items with a dedication to searching out the facts so that the Science and Astronautics Committee — as your representatives — could bring to you this most thoroughly studied legislative measure.[24]

More than this, authorizing committees conceive of themselves as assisting in the tasks of the Appropriations Committee. In the same NASA debate, the Committee's dominant Republican exclaimed,

> The Committee on Science and Astronautics is watching the money. We are not abdicating our responsibility by saying to another committee, the House Committee on Appropriations, that "We are establishing the programs and you take care of the money." Each one of these items has been gone over carefully and argued.[25]

Still another member concluded, "Committee recommendations by no means put a rubber stamp on the NASA requests. We made a number of cuts and in some places we cut deep."[26] Annual authorization procedures constitute a sanction on the Appropriations Committee. To the present time, no serious conflict has occurred. But should an accelerated trend develop, it is possible that privately expressed doubts would be more openly and aggressively entertained.

[24] *Congressional Record,* Daily Edition, May 23, 1962, p. 8382.
[25] *Ibid.,* p. 8394.
[26] *Ibid.,* p. 8421.

House members have a set of expectations as to procedures to be followed by the Committee in the performance of its tasks. To the degree that these procedures are amenable to House control, they provide further evidence of the range of sanctions available to the parent chamber. The Committee enjoys all of its special procedural prerogatives — from the privileged character of its bills to its executive session hearings — at the sufferance of the House. And though the House is unlikely to attack these, lest the entire committee system be threatened, the authority to do so exists. A small procedural control which is occasionally used to police House expectations forbidding legislation on an appropriation bill is the parliamentary point of order. House rules prohibit legislation on a general appropriation bill, but the Committee does — overtly and covertly — insert such provisions in its measures. It may secure House assistance for its action through a Rules Committee decision to prohibit points of order from being registered on the floor. Ordinarily, objections to such a ruling will come from the affected legislative committee, and a sharp conflict may occur between that committee and the Appropriations Committee before the Rules Committee. If the substantive committee loses, it may take the case to the floor. There, despite bitter protest, it will, on the record, lose. Barring such action by the Rules Committee, however, House members can, by raising a point of order, have stricken from the bill any item ruled to be legislative in nature. One Member explained,

> I make more points of order on appropriation bills than anyone else. And I do it to keep them in line. They'll bring in items that haven't been authorized by the legislative committee. I don't make points of order on all legislation on an appropriation bill, because some may be necessary due to changing conditions. But you've got to hold them down. If they're going to do all the appropriating without authorization, we might as well give up the legislative process. And they don't make any mistakes. They know what they're doing. I just want to keep the legislative process working according to the rules of the House.

Ordinary Members may occasionally find this a useful way of setting boundaries to Appropriations Committee activity. Whether used or not, the existence of the point of order technique acts as one more reminder to the Committee that its activities cannot run counter to House expectations.

Prescribing Budgetary Procedure

In 1958, an open House-Committee conflict did occur in the area of Committee procedures. In pursuance of a Hoover Commission recommendation, the House revised the method by which budget estimates would be presented to the Appropriations Committee and transmitted to the House by the Committee. The aim, as far as the House was concerned, seemed to be to state estimates on an annual accrued basis so that Members could know exactly how much money was being expended in any given year, including money appropriated in previous years but not spent until the current year. As one supporter summed up, "The bill would return more control to the House itself . . . there would be fewer decisions by subcommittees and more review by the individual members of the House."[27] When the change was proposed in 1957, 40 members of the Appropriations Committee signed a letter opposing the change and circulated it to the House membership. The two House members from the Government Operations Committee who sat at the speakers' table to lead the fight for the bill recalled that they could not recruit others to sit beside them. No one wished, they felt, to incur the obvious displeasure of the Appropriations Committee.

The Appropriations Committee majority left no doubt that it viewed the change as an attack by members of the larger system upon the members of the subsystem. During the debate, the Committee's leaders exclaimed,

> If the members of the Committee on Appropriations have come out against this proposal, and they have, do you mean to say that the House of Representatives is going to kick them in the teeth? . . . Has the Committee on Appropriations . . . done anything to warrant a vote of no confidence by the members of the House of Representatives?[28]

> I cannot conceive that you will force this bill down the throats of the Committee on Appropriations. . . . If you vote for such a measure as this you will be forcing upon practically the entire Committee on Appropriations who must work on this matter day in and day out, month in and month out, something which they do not want and which they think is wrong. We would not do that to the Committee on Foreign Affairs or the Committee on Ways and Means or any other of the great committees of the House.[29]

On a Committee-sponsored motion to recommit the bill, its members were recorded 36 to 12 in favor.

The Committee was, however, overwhelmed — on the recommittal motion by 119 to 275 and on final passage by 86 to 311. On the recommittal vote, which found the Committee at maximum strength, both party contingents in the House voted against the Committee majority. The Democrats voted 80 to 100 and the Republicans voted 7 to 161 against the Committee. Committee Democrats supported the motion 22 to 5 but Committee Republicans

[27] 104 *Congressional Record*, p. 3616. The debate runs from pp. 3466–3478, 3607, 3621.
[28] *Ibid.*, p. 3467.
[29] *Ibid.*, p. 3613.

split 10 to 7 in favor. Most noteworthy is the nearly unanimous opposition of non-Committee House Republicans. GOP members were cross-pressured by loyalty to the administration and to their Committee. They chose to vote against the Committee, a vote made especially easy by the sharp division among the Republicans on the Committee itself.

Support for the Committee came mostly from House Democrats — a vote made more compelling by the degree of solidarity among Committee Democrats. The vote did not involve Appropriations Committee–substantive committee relations. Indeed, there was general agreement in debate that it was the Appropriations Committee and only the Appropriations Committee whose procedures would be affected by the change, and this recognition had an effect on the makeup of Committee supporters. The Committee seems to have drawn a noteworthy amount of support from the leaders of other House committees, who may have perceived the issue in terms of system-subsystem relations generally. If a set of procedures uniquely affecting one committee can be altered in the face of the strenuous objections of that committee, it could be done to other committees as well. The Chairmen of the Committees on Ways and Means, Rules, Armed Services, Judiciary, Education and Labor, Banking and Currency, and Merchant Marine and Fisheries supported their fellow Chairman in his fight to recommit the bill. Speaker Rayburn, too, as a protector of the committee system, was opposed to the bill. A key Democratic sponsor said later, "Rayburn was against the bill, but he didn't speak against it. He got mad at McCormack [majority leader] for speaking for the bill. But McCormack likes to tweak the nose of the Appropriations Committee."

CONCLUSION

In cases of House–Appropriations Committee conflict "the House" (or other subsystems of the House) possesses a battery of sanctions, large and small, direct and indirect, formal and informal, to bring Committee performance into closer conformity with House expectations. Indeed, no other group in the environment of the Committee possesses sanctions of comparable quality or quantity. The House uses its sanctions, and enough evidence has been collected already to suggest that, by using them, the House can influence Committee behavior. The House could, indeed, do more than it has. It could impose financial sanctions by withholding operating funds from the Committee. Or, it could choose to enact a few of the many reform proposals which have been suggested during the past 45 years. The House has not chosen to use these sanctions presumably for the same reason that it has exercised its other sanctions so sparingly. It is mindful of the importance of the Committee's work, satisfied with the largest portion of

Committee behavior, and aware of the damage which the excessive application of sanctions might inflict on the committee system as a whole.

The successful use of one sanction at one point in time, moreover, may exert a kind of multiplier effect. If the Committee is assumed to be listening, use of a sanction may constitute a standing reminder of House authority and of ultimate Committee dependence. Once a sanction has been levied successfully, the threat of its use can become doubly effective as a preventive. To the degree that sanctions succeed, though only occasionally, House members may gain a sense of efficacy in their relationship with the Committee. And that sense of efficacy may, in turn, blunt the edge of their dissatisfaction with specific Committee actions. If, that is, Members feel confident that they can bring the Committee to heel when they have to, they may feel less uneasy about the degree of day-to-day Committee autonomy. They may, therefore, not feel it necessary to levy sanctions simply to prove a point, and the stability of relations may be enhanced. All of which is to say that the effectiveness of sanctions cannot be measured simply by the frequency with which they are applied.

It seems clear, from the examples studied, that the precise composition of "the House" will vary with the type of conflict and the type of sanctions being applied. "The House" which selects Committee members is not the same as "the House" which implements backdoor spending. And neither is exactly the same as "the House" which has extended annual authorization. The effectiveness of sanctions varies, in turn, with the composition of "the House." Whether, for example, "the House" contains majority party leaders would seem to make a considerable difference. House members, it also must be remembered, can call upon others for assistance in levying sanctions on the Committee. But for the help of the Senate, dissatisfied House members could never have sustained proposals for direct Treasury financing. And it was the support of the Eisenhower administration which ensured the passage of the Accrued Annual Expenditures Bill. "The House" is not, therefore, wholly dependent on its own resources in controlling the activity of the Appropriations Committee. To recognize this fact is to remind ourselves that the system-subsystem relationship we have chosen to analyze is, after all, part of a more comprehensive interacting political system.

The discussion of House sanctions completes the answers to a set of questions suggested at the beginning of Chapter One as basic to an understanding of House-Committee relationships. The House, it now appears, does have an identifiable set of expectations, perceptions, and attitudes concerning its Appropriations Committee. On balance, Committee behavior has met House expectations and has elicited images in the chamber which have led to House satisfaction and support. Still, a pattern of unmet expectations persists which has led to some unfavorable images of Committee performance among House members and, hence, to dissatisfaction and House-Committee conflict. Where such disagreement exists, the House has available to it sanctions which it can and does use in an effort to keep or bring Committee behavior into a tolerably close conformity with House expectations.

At the minimum, Chapters One and Two indicate a Committee-House relationship more complicated than the one suggested in traditional generalizations about House desuetude. Clearly, a description of the appropriations process cannot begin with assumptions about a powerful, independent Appropriations Committee set within a weak, dependent House of Representatives. The House does not require strict or continuous accountability. It seeks only to maintain ultimate Committee dependence and a long-run conformity of Committee behavior to House desires. The House prescribes therefore, some outer boundaries to Committee activity. But its capacity to enforce its prescriptions sets constraints on Committee activity. Without question, House-drawn boundaries allow the Committee considerable day-to-day autonomy. The largest measure of that autonomy, however, is granted by the House deliberately and willingly. Hence, such Committee independence as exists cannot be interpreted as a sign of a predisposition or a capacity on the part of the Committee to disregard the parent chamber. The sheer amount of House involvement in Committee affairs, as revealed in Chapters One and Two, indicates by itself a substantial interaction between the two entities. From the House perspective, at least, Committee and House, subsystem and system, are linked in a closely interdependent relationship.

CHAPTER THREE

The House Committee
I: Committee Expectations and Adaptations

ADAPTATION AND COMMITTEE MEMBER EXPECTATIONS

As viewed from the perspective of the parent chamber, Appropriations Committee behavior partly satisfies House expectations and partly fails to satisfy them. We have identified these satisfactions and dissatisfactions. But we cannot explain the process by which they have come about nor can we estimate their likely persistence until we examine Committee-House relations from the Committee's own point of view. What, for example, are the Committee members' goal and maintenance expectations and how closely do they correspond to those of the House? What self-image do Committee members possess and how closely does it correspond to the image which House members have of them? What personal satisfactions or dissatisfactions do Committee members gain from their activity and how does the distribution of their satisfactions and dissatisfactions compare with that demonstrated by House members? How do Committee members respond to the threat and use of House sanctions? Answers to these kinds of questions are indispensable to an explanation of Committee behavior. They are indispensable also, to any assessment of the likelihood of stability or change in such behavior patterns as do exist at the first stage of the appropriations process.

From the perspective of the Appropriations Committee, its relationship with the parent chamber can be stated, most abstractly, as one which centers on the problem of adaptation to the environment. Given the kinds of sanctions which the House can and has exercised over the Appropriations Committee, the Committee cannot survive unless its behavior satisfies House expectations as to what that behavior should be. The development of expectations and the response or adaptation to those expectations should not be conceptualized, however, as a one-way process. We are not describing a relationship in which the House independently develops a set of expectations to which the Committee must then respond or suffer drastic consequences. We are describing a relationship in which House expectations may be significantly shaped either by Committee expectations or by an adjustment to Committee responses. The Committee and the key element of its environment are interdependent and the "feedback" is as basic to the relationship as the "feed in." The essential idea is that, from the Committee's point of view, its behavior patterns must somehow or other be kept in substantial correspondence with House patterns of expectations.

We have not investigated the historical development of either kind of pattern and cannot, therefore, untangle their interrelations through time. We have described House expectations and Committee behavior as we find them and concerned ourselves with the degree of correspondence between them. The problem of maintaining some correspondence is the problem of adaptation faced by the Appropriations Committee. And its behavior cannot be understood apart from its concern for the solution of this problem.

Committee adaptation to House member expectations is complicated by one very important condition. Committee members have one set of expectations about their behavior which they develop independently of anything House members may desire. These expectations are the personal desires which Committee members wish to have satisfied through Committee activity. Quite apart from ideas coming from the environment as to what the Committee should do, a set of ideas comes from the Committee's members as to what the Committee should do — *for them as individuals.*

Membership on a committee can fulfill important desires for an individual congressman. It can, for example, satisfy his desire for power, for prestige, for re-election, for recognition, for information, for achievement, for self-fulfillment, for a sense of social solidarity, or for the furtherance of specific career ambitions. In the 435-man House, where fewer avenues for the fulfillment of such personal desires are open than in the Senate, committee membership may constitute the most fundamental source of gratification for the individual legislator. Appropriations Committee members express most, if not all, of the wants listed above. Indeed, they have sought Committee membership in the hopes of satisfying them. Once on the Committee, and this is the point, they will behave in ways calculated to fulfill their personal expectations.

If the behavior required to fulfill individual Committee member expectations is the same as that required to meet House member expectations, the Committee's problem of adaptation will be easily solved. If, however, the two sets of expectations call for different forms of behavior, the Committee's problem of adaptation to House expectations becomes complicated. This chapter begins with a description of personal Committee member expectations during which it becomes evident that such conflict does in fact exist.

Where conflict exists, Committee behavior taken to meet House expectations will be tempered by a calculation as to the cost in terms of individual satisfactions. A Committee satisfying no personal desires will not be deemed worth preserving. On the other hand, insofar as Committee members are satisfying their personal expectations via membership on the Committee, action taken in further pursuit of these expectations will be tempered by a calculation as to the cost of not adapting to House expectations. For, in such a case, the cost may be the survival of the Committee and, hence, the loss of personal satisfaction the member presently derives from it. From the perspective of the Committee member, therefore, the problem of adaptation is not a straightforward matter of adapting to House expectations. It becomes a matter of balancing House expectations against his personal desires. Committee behavior must be explained in terms of the search for such a balance.

In addition to their *personal expectations* ("What do I want Committee membership and Committee behavior to do for me?") Committee members express a set of expectations that parallel the concerns of the House. Committee members have some well-developed *goal expectations* and *maintenance expectations*, which can be described and compared with those of the House. It is through these latter two sets of expectations that Committee members express their overall conception of what Committee behavior should be. These goal and maintenance expectations are influenced both by the array of House expectations described in Chapter One *and* by the personal expectations of Committee members just discussed. Indeed, the individually oriented expectations of Committee members make their contribution to Committee behavior as they are incorporated into and expressed through the more Committee-oriented goal and maintenance expectations. For it is, after all, the correspondence or noncorrespondence of House and Committee expectations at this level that provides the important explanations of behavior and informs our estimates about the stability of Committee-House relations. The latter part of this chapter is devoted, therefore, to a description of Committee goal and maintenance expectations and a comparison of them to the same kinds of expectations as are expressed by the members of the House.

81

INDIVIDUAL MEMBER EXPECTATIONS
AND SATISFACTIONS

Power and Prestige

Members reveal their individual, personal expectations when they discuss their reasons for seeking membership on the Appropriations Committee. In answering the question: "Why did you want to come on the Committee in the first place?" they spoke also of present satisfactions and of the favorable features of life on the Committee. In every case, their expectations and satisfactions centered on the power and the prestige of the Committee. And in every case they recognized that the source of Committee influence rests in its control over the financial resources of the federal government. "Money is power" and "Where the money is that's where the power is" serve as the base line against which to understand Committee member expectations and satisfactions alike. Members have been attracted to the Appropriations Committee from nearly every other committee in the House. See Table 3.1. And they have not voluntarily left the Appropriations Committee to join any other House committees except Ways and Means and Rules. What Donald Matthews discovered for the Senate holds equally true for the House.[1] Some committees are considered more desirable than others by the Members. And on the basis of subjective Member choice in committee assignments, an objective prestige ranking of House committees emerges. An analysis by Warren Miller and Donald Stokes of the pulling and holding power of House committees ranks the Appropriations Committee a very close third (behind Ways and Means and Rules) in its ability to attract members from other House committees and hold them.[2] Mere membership on the Committee, therefore, can satisfy an individual's need for prestige and recognition in the chamber.

The Appropriations Committee is prestigious because it is influential. And, for most members, the two are synonymous. Many remembered their decision to change committee assignments as a decision to try to increase their influence. An inner-circle choice, requested by his state delegation to run for a regional vacancy, recalled,

> I said, "No, thanks." I was on the —————— Committee, and doing very well in seniority — second to the chairman. They said that I should go on Appropriations — that the anchorman on Appropriations was more important than being chairman of most other committees.

[1] Donald Matthews, *U.S. Senators and Their World* (Chapel Hill: University of North Carolina Press, 1960), pp. 148–152.

[2] Warren Miller and Donald Stokes, *Representation in Congress* (New York: Prentice-Hall, forthcoming).

82

TABLE 3.1

COMMITTEE MEMBERSHIPS HELD AT TIME OF ASSIGNMENT
TO APPROPRIATIONS COMMITTEE — 119 MEN

Committee	No. of Men Leaving for Appropriations
Interior and Insular Affairs	26
Veterans Affairs	18
Public Works	16
House Administration	14
Post Office and Civil Service	13
Education and Labor	10
Banking and Currency	9
Judiciary	9
Merchant Marine and Fisheries	8
Government Operations	6
Agriculture	5
Armed Services	4
District of Columbia	4
Foreign Affairs	2
Rules	1[a]
Total[b]	145

[a] One man was "bumped off" Rules due to party changeover and came to Appropriations, therefore, involuntarily.

[b] The total exceeds 119 because many of the new members gave up more than one committee assignment.

A self-starter reflected, in similar vein, on his previous committee assignment:

I'd be fifth in seniority, with twenty years in age between me and the next man above me. So I probably could have been chairman of that committee some day. I'll never get to be Chairman of Appropriations. But you have to ask yourself whether you want to wait around to be a chairman some day or whether you want to get in on things and wield a little influence around here before that time.

And a third said,

I served seven years on the Public Works Committee and I had a lot of water projects. That's very important in my district. I had them all authorized and was getting some money for them. But I thought the power would be important. Like Kennedy said about the Presidency — "That's where the power is."

All but one of the Committee members interviewed ranked their Committee on a par with, or higher than, the Ways and Means Committee in terms of power and prestige. A number included Rules in what they called "the big three" or "the blue ribbon committees." The opinion of a veteran member probably hits close to majority sentiment:

> The Appropriations Committee is the most powerful committee in the House. It's the most powerful committee in the Congress. This is where all the money starts rolling. . . . the chairman of the Appropriations Committee is the third most powerful man in government — the President, the Speaker, and the Chairman of Appropriations. Only the Speaker has more power in the Congress.

Members proudly reminisce about the rugged competition they survived to win what they agree is "a prize plum," "a much sought after assignment," "a coveted position," "an honor and a promotion." From their success, they derive the feeling that they are a fairly select group. And they say proudly "They know who they want" or "They wanted me; make no mistake about that" or "By the time you get on the Appropriations Committee, you're not supposed to be an amateur. You're supposed to be a son of a bitch in your own right. That's the idea of waiting around for a while." In support of their self-estimate, they cite the House rule designating Appropriations (along with Ways and Means and Rules) as one of three exclusive, or single membership, committees. And they mention, too, the special procedural prerogatives conferred on the Committee by the House.

Power and influence are relative notions. And the question arises: Over whom do Committee members hope to exercise their power? Collectively, the answer would be: Over everybody who participates in the political process nationally. Individually, however, each member voices some specific combination of desires.

At the broadest level, there are some who seek Committee membership in the hope of having some measurable impact on the national economy. They are alarmed at the high cost of government and at the ever-increasing rate of spending, and they want to exercise some influence over "the spenders" generally. (None voiced the reverse desire to fund some national program.) As one might expect from the selection process, such individuals are almost exclusively Republicans. What is interesting, however, is the fact that only a minority of Republicans gave any special emphasis to this broad economy goal; and none of those gave it as their sole reason for seeking Committee membership. Nearly all the Republicans on the Committee are conservatives, and all are interested in saving money. But most of them take the realistic view that their effect on the economy will be marginal and, hence, seek additional satisfactions from their Committee-based power. Those few who came to the Committee with the thought of making major contributions to the economy are likely to remain partially unfulfilled. Said one,

> I ran for Congress because I wanted to see if I couldn't do something to hold down unnecessary spending. We have to live within our means. We have to have a balanced budget. . . . And I thought that membership on the Committee would help me redeem some of my campaign promises. . . . Now I'm frustrated. I thought I'd be able to do a lot more than I can.

Even this member has derived other satisfactions from using his Committee-based influence — satisfactions of the sort which have amply fulfilled the expectations of 90 per cent of his Committee colleagues.

Far less apocalyptic than a desire to alter the economy, yet of far greater personal immediacy, is the unanimously held member belief that Committee membership will enhance one's ability to get projects for his constituents — thereby satisfying their need for service and his need for re-election.

Several members changed to the Committee because, as one put it, "I can do more for the people back home." "Most people feel," said another, "that a place on the Appropriations Committee gives them more personal influence, for themselves I mean. They feel they can get more for their districts, and that's true." And a man who had a good chance of becoming chairman exclaimed "Don't you think I couldn't get anything I wanted for my state as chairman of Appropriations. Why, certainly." Still another member explained why Appropriations was more appealing to him than the other exclusive committees.

> Some Members want to get on the Ways and Means Committee or Rules. Neither of those interest me in the least. And I don't understand why anyone would want to go on those two committees. They aren't any help to you in your district. They may give you a high prestige threshold, dealing with national issues. But they don't help you to be of any particular help to your constituency.

From their prior experience in the chamber, congressmen seeking membership on the Committee recognize the importance of subcommittees in Committee decision-making. And they seek general Committee membership in the hopes of gaining privileged access to (if not membership on) the subcommittees most vital to their constituency interests. Two members explained:

> Naturally, you want to do as much to help the people in your district as you can. . . . When you are interested in something, any Appropriations subcommittee will listen to you a lot more if you're a member of the Committee than if you aren't.

> [Once on the Committee, your influence] depends on the friends you can make on other subcommittees. There's the fellow who asked me about a

85

hospital he's got coming up. Then when I want something done, I will go and see him. They'll pay more attention to me when I'm a member of the Committee. You trade back and forth across subcommittees that way. . . . It's a matter of scratching each other's backs, I suppose. But that's the only way you get any specific project accomplished around here.

In speaking of their ability to serve their constituents, Committee members voice their expectations and their obvious satisfactions.

A Republican member from Ohio, in a typical year's-end report to his constituents, listed among his accomplishments an airport "that came about as a result of my work on the Appropriations Committee" and a highway which "I was able to initiate largely because of Appropriations Committee activities."[3] A final excerpt from a speech by a veteran Committee member from Mississippi speaks for itself:

My membership on the Committee which controls the purse strings means that I am in the middle of the show and have a real opportunity for service. Certainly, my membership on this Committee has contributed in my own state to the Boll Weevil Laboratory, the Poultry Laboratory, the Soils Laboratory, the many flood control and watershed projects, soil conservation, REA, Extension and 4-H Club programs, the Greenville and Pascagoula Harbor projects, the Agricultural Conservation Program, and many others which I have been able to promote. . . . This year I am proud to say we provided increased funds for watershed protection and flood prevention, for domestic public works — including $70,725,100 in funds for the lower Mississippi, increased funds for the Big Sunflower, provided for additional surveys, increased funds for other Mississippi projects and kept work on harbor development going forward.[4]

Accomplishments such as this comprise the guts of most Members' appeal for re-election. And it may be significant, from Table 3.1, that more Members come to the Committee from the Interior and Insular Affairs Committee than any other. Interior, and the same may hold for Public Works, is a constituency-oriented committee to which Members are attracted when they have "pet projects" to be authorized. Service on these committees and success in getting projects authorized may make these Members especially appreciative of and desirous of a place on the money-granting committee — still for constituency service reasons.

Any financial resources a congressman channels into his district must come via contact with an executive agency. And membership on the Appropriations Committee was sought by most members for the power over agency conduct it would bring. In some cases influence with the agencies is tied exclusively to the desire to get things for one's constituents. A senior member summed up his reasons for seeking membership: "It's the committee that

[3] *Congressional Record*, Daily Edition, October 3, 1962, p. 20782.
[4] *Congressional Record*, Daily Edition, September 18, 1961, p. A7391.

gives you the most power with the government agencies; and you're in touch with them all the time for your constituents." Another complained that where his pet projects depended on direct Treasury financing he had been unsuccessful. "It's like talking to a blank wall. But if they had to come to the Committee, I'd get it — just like that — no questions." And a newcomer observed,

> You can get the ear of the agencies downtown a lot easier on Appropriations than you can on other committees. I've noticed when my staff calls downtown now, the agencies respond a lot quicker and with more concern then they did when I was the lowest ranking minority member on Agriculture.

In other cases, influence over the executive branch is related to more generally formulated expectations and satisfactions. One member generalized,

> The way things work around this town, the administrators will listen to you more on the Appropriations Committee than on a legislative committee. I'd prefer to work on the drafting of legislation — to work on the substance of bills. But the facts of life are that you can be more effective on the Appropriations Committee. We passed a program on my former committee, but they didn't administer it anywhere near the way we intended. And they didn't care. They had their bill. The only people they cared about was the Appropriations Committee. That's a fact of life. So it's not as enjoyable but it's more effective.

And another was even less specific in his summary statement. "The Committee," he said, "is a good grab bag place. Bureaucrats kowtow to you a lot more when they sit across the table asking you for money than they do in a legislative committee." There is no doubt but that any increase in influence, specific or general, over the bureaucracy is a source of immense satisfaction to most congressmen.

Finally, membership on the Appropriations Committee is prized as a source of leverage in the constant round of negotiation accompanying decision-making in the House. House leaders who pick the Committee seek members who are oriented toward careers in the House. From the members' perspective, an assignment to the Committee "gives you power in the House" or "makes you influential in the House." A member who had just come to the Committee after a long wait summed it up:

> The process here is one where consent must be obtained before anything gets done. If you are one of those from whom consent must be obtained, then you are a more important person in the House. When you're on the Appropriations Committee, you are that kind of person. That's all. It's a question of power.

Committee members know that power in the House rests at bottom on their perceived capacity to affect the electoral fortunes of fellow Members

87

by granting or withholding funds for pet projects. "Any Member's pet project can be killed or made to flower by the Appropriations Committee," declared one Committee member. Nearly every Representative is believed to have some pet project — a project which he believes may affect his chances or his margin of re-election. "They are very polite to us. They've all got projects in over here and they know what we can do to them." The Committee wields its sanction both negatively and positively. A man who had been denied made a public plea for which there surely are one hundred reasonable facsimiles in private:

> My people are up in arms. They want at least a study made of these problems. They do not mind me voting for worthy projects all over the United States: but I can tell you, I am not much to look at, but unless I get some money to be spent down in southern Illinois to study these problems you may not be seeing me next year.

On the other hand, a member of the Subcommittee on Public Works (which received 350 separate pleas for pet projects in 1964)[5] pointed out that the Committee does keep such considerations in mind. "We keep an eye out for a fellow who needs something in his campaign. If he can bring back a little something and we can help him in his campaign, we naturally go along." Committee membership, concluded a veteran of the group, "gives you a lot of prestige in the House. After all, if you control the purse strings, that's where the power is." The theme is repeated for every context in which the Committee member finds himself.

Taken together, the several contexts in which the Committee member exercises his influence (added to the fact that an Appropriations Committee member is likely to be a "responsible" legislator) give him a potential for pyramiding his legislative power beyond the specifics of the appropriations process. In the nineteenth century, it was not uncommon for Appropriations Committee Chairmen (e.g., Samuel Randall and Joseph Cannon) to become the party leaders of the House. And, though the sequence has not been followed recently, the ranking minority member of the Committee, Gerald Ford, was selected as his party's floor leader in 1965. Committee leaders have, typically, filled lesser positions of leadership in the party hierarchy — thus extending their influence beyond the scope of appropriations. In the 88th Congress, for instance, it is worth noting that Rep. Albert Thomas was the Chairman of the Democratic Caucus, Rep. Michael Kirwan was Chairman of the Democratic Congressional Campaign Committee, Rep. Harry Sheppard was Chairman of the Democratic Patronage Committee, and Rep. Gerald Ford was Chairman of the Republican Conference. When Ford

[5] *Congressional Record*, Daily Edition, June 16, 1964, p. 13467.

became minority leader in the 89th Congress (and gave up his Committee membership), Rep. Melvin Laird became Chairman of the Republican Conference and Rep. John Rhodes became Chairman of the Republican Policy Committee. When Rep. Sheppard retired from Congress, he was replaced as Chairman of the Democratic Patronage Committee by Rep. Joe Evins. All of these men have been Appropriations Committee leaders as well. Without assessing the power of each of these positions, the point is that Appropriations Committee members would seem to have a better chance than most Representatives of achieving that rare commodity in Congress — influence beyond the subject matter of one's committees.

As one example of the pyramiding of influence from an Appropriations Committee base to a broader scope in the chamber, the case of Rep. Michael Kirwan (D., Ohio) is especially noteworthy. From 1949 to 1953 and from 1955 to 1964, Kirwan was the Chairman of the Appropriations Subcommittee on the Interior Department. In that position, he has sat astride the granting of money for the pet projects of all the Western congressmen and most all the rural Easterners as well. The activities of all Interior bureaus are geographically based, which means that installations can be distributed on a congressional district basis. Bureau of Reclamation irrigation projects, Fish and Wildlife hatcheries, Bureau of Mines research laboratories, national parks, Bureau of Indian Affairs offices, hospitals, and schools, public power installations, and (under Subcommittee jurisdiction since 1955) national forests are of the utmost importance to individual Members. Kirwan also sat for most of these years as a member of the Public Works Subcommittee, which dealt almost exclusively with pet projects; and in 1964 he became chairman of that Subcommittee. Kirwan's influence over the fortunes of other Members is considerable, and he has been known to exercise it both positively and negatively.

In 1948, Kirwan became Chairman of the Democratic Congressional Campaign Committee which gave him some control of funds to be used for the re-election campaign of House Democrats. He has resisted attempts to cover his committee's funds into the National Committee's funds; and they continue to be collected and disbursed independently — that is, by Kirwan's committee. Thus Kirwan has come to have more influence than any single House member over two of the most important sources of money available to help congressmen — and to help the Democratic party leadership with efforts at persuasion. Small wonder it is that Kirwan gets eulogized from the floor — at the drop of a hat — eloquently and perfervidly. Small wonder it is that, when Kirwan is attacked by someone outside the House like Drew Pearson, a sizable portion of the membership — on both sides of the aisle — rises in his defense. Small wonder it is that half of Congress turns out for his annual St. Patrick's Day party. In a recent book by a House member, he is

89

characterized as one of the reigning oligarchs of the House. He is virtually unknown outside of the Chamber, yet his influence there is enormous. And it is his position on the Appropriations Committee that has made most of it possible.[6]

The Scope of Committee Activity

A source of Committee attractiveness, related to but separable from power and prestige, is the government-wide scope of Committee activity and the fund of information available to members as a result of it. Relatively few governmental activities escape the purview of the Committee. "Every program needs money," they say, "and if it doesn't, it isn't worth worrying about." Members derive great satisfaction from their feeling that "Everything comes to a focus in the Appropriations Committee. You learn about everything, not just one area." They contrast their breadth of operation favorably with their previous assignments:

> If you want to learn about the whole government and how it operates, the Appropriations Committee is the best place to learn it. You don't on other committees. On Merchant Marine and Fisheries you learn about merchant marine and fisheries and that's it.

The ordinary congressman may feel that he has too little knowledge of and too little control over his environment. Appropriations Committee membership compensates for this feeling of helplessness by increasing his contact with and his information about the world of the executive branch. Members come to possess the sense that they, to a degree that is rare in the House, "are in the middle of things" and "know what is going on." The feeling of being engaged brings satisfaction. And the objective possession of a broad range of information underpins the member's especially wide scope of influence.

The Style of Hard Work

Closely related to the scope of their activity in the minds of members is the intensiveness of their activity. The Committee's review and oversight activities are initiated annually, but in fact they are never-ending. For the House leaders who select the Committee the willingness to work hard is a major criterion. For those who seek the job, too, hard work may appear as the road to legislative self-fulfillment. One of the reasons most often cited for leaving other committees was the feeling that they "weren't doing anything most of the time." Members expressed themselves as being "unhappy," "disgusted," "frustrated," and "dissatisfied" by service on committees where "if we met once every three weeks we were lucky." "You have to live with yourself,"

6 See, for example, 106 *Congressional Record*, pp. 6687–6694; 107 *Congressional Record*, pp. 96–98.

reflected a Committee veteran who said that he derived no "inner sense of satisfaction" from his earlier committee service. "They'd introduce me back home as 'that great congressman.' But I wasn't doing anything." Not so on Appropriations most of whose members work very hard and derive immense satisfaction from so doing.

The satisfaction they find from working hard probably far exceeds their original expectations. And the reason for this is that the deepest satisfactions derived from hard work flow to the Committee as a collectivity and not just to the members as individuals. More than anything else, it is hard work that provides Appropriations Committee members with a satisfying sense of group identification and sentiments of group solidarity. Every lasting social group develops distinctive characteristics which form the basis for sentiments of pride, of exclusiveness, and of loyalty. Members of the Appropriations Committee distinguish the "we" from the "they" on the basis of their recognizable and distinctive political style — the style of hard work. Their badge of identification is that of "the hardest working committee in Congress." As one of them said on the floor, "Mr. Chairman, we on the Appropriations Committee are very proud. We are proud because we work hard and we work long hours."[7] In a political culture which honors industriousness as a prime virtue and in a legislative body where "He does his homework" is highest praise, the Committee member wears his badge conspicuously. And he believes, furthermore, that the pursuance of his political style enables him to preserve and to capitalize the power and the prestige of his Committee.

When senior Committee members are asked to prescribe the ideal qualifications for new members, they give highest priority to a willingness to work. "If you want to play, there's no room for you on the Committee. The Committee meets all the time." Or, "Don't come on unless you want to work. It's a man-killing Committee. You work harder than on any other committee." One of the Committee's most senior men caught the pervasive spirit of the style when he exclaimed with regard to new members,

> They have to be hard-working. This Committee is no place for a man who doesn't work. It's a way of life. It isn't just a job, it's a way of life.

When Committee newcomers are asked about life on their new Committee, they speak of the "culture shock" involved. And many specific elements of that shock center on the necessity for changed work habits. One commented that he could not get out and participate in floor actions as much as he had previously. A second said that he had been forced to rearrange his

[7] *Congressional Record*, Daily Edition, April 18, 1962. When Committee members die, the eulogies spoken from the well of the House always characterize the individual for his willingness to work hard. See for example the eulogies in the *Congressional Record*, Daily Edition for January 16, 1960, pp. 705 ff.; March 9, 1960, p. 4661; January 23, 1961, pp. 1125 ff.; February 9, 1961, pp. 1909 ff.; February 16, 1961, pp. 2120 ff.

office schedule and the working hours of his staff to accommodate his own extended work day. A third new member spoke more specifically:

> It's an especially hard Committee for a New York City member. It's a Monday through Friday job. Hearings are held every day and you have to be here a lot more than you do on a legislative committee. So I'm down here more than I ever was before. It's quite a change for me.

A fourth expressed the contrast as follows:

> It's a thankless task. You work at it all the time. You miss your constituents when they come to see you, and you weaken your political fences back home. It's a consuming mistress. On a legislative committee, you don't have to be there all the time. You have fourteen witnesses and you go to hear the one you care about. But you can't do that on Appropriations. You miss one day and you miss a whole agency.

A fifth new member was impressed by how much of the informal "horsing around" among Committee members was devoted to mock self-commiseration about life in "the salt mine of Congress." He recalled meeting ex-Committee member Hamer Budge in the House barbershop and teasing him by saying, "I'll bet you don't work as hard on Rules as you did on Appropriations."

The Committee members' self-perception colors, as we shall see, their perception of others with whom they come in contact. They tend, for example, to respond sympathetically to those administrators who conform to their own self-image — the hard-working executive whose testimony gives evidence of steady and thorough application to duty. Conversely, they respond unsympathetically to the Senate Appropriations Committee, because they do not feel that Senators meet high standards of diligence. Even the members' view of their constituents is affected. When asked whether his constituents understood his job, a member replied,

> No, not in the slightest. They call me up and wonder why they can't talk to me. They say, "I can't reach my congressman." Well, when I'm over there presiding over my subcommittee, I don't stop for anything. People don't understand the work of the Appropriations Committee.

It's heavy work schedule imposes upon the Committee a style singularly lacking in political glamor. The Committee's method of operation is that of "dig dig dig, day after day, behind closed doors." It discourages individualized performances of the sort that attend the flamboyant legislative investigations or the major legislative battles that win coverage in the mass media. As three members put it: "There's no public relations value in it. You don't report any bill in your name. They all come out under the Committee." "It's no fun to sit in there. You get no publicity, and for all you know the people back home think you're sitting on your prat." "I sit be-

hind closed doors four hours every day and nobody knows I'm in Congress."
These comments help to highlight the other side of the coin. The style of
hard work is positively conducive to the development of internal Committee
solidarity. With individual publicity-seeking proscribed, with the same work
conditions enforced on all, and with the members constant interaction with
one another, internal esprit grows. Hard work is a private virtue and it
encourages sentiments of mutual regard and sympathy. "Members of the Committee get along very well together. There's an esprit de corps, a comrade-
ship." "The Committee is a tightly knit group. We don't leave each other
very often [in voting]. We do favors for each other and for each other's
friends."

The mere existence of some identifiable and valued style or way of life
is a cohesive force for a group. But the particular style of hard work is one
which increases morale twice over. A leader on the minority side summarized,

> I think it's more closely knit than any other committee. Yet it's the biggest
> committee, and you'd think it would be the reverse. I know on my sub-
> committee you sit together day after day, you get better acquainted, you
> have mutual sympathy for each other when the other fellows go off to play
> golf. There's a lot of esprit de corps in the Committee.

Conversely, out-group attacks on the Committee get explained in terms of
the Committee's style. "I think there's some jealousy involved. Some of these
committees who don't do very much — they see you working all the time
and getting into big problems." The sense of Committee unity, of in-group
solidarity fostered by the style of hard work brings immense satisfaction to
individual Committee members. They will behave, therefore, in ways calculated to preserve it.

Only one Committee member failed to take pride in the Committee's
political style. "When the boys are out having a good time," he complained,
"you have to work." He regretted having come on the Committee and
added, "I wouldn't advise anyone to go on Appropriations." The significant
thing about this lone dissent is that this is the same man (and the only
one) who placed both Ways and Means and Rules higher in the prestige
hierarchy of the House. This deviant case suggests what Committee members
themselves believe, that there is a close correlation between their prestige
and their reputation for hard work. They are perfectly aware that, without
the formal delegation of authority from the House, they could not survive.
But they believe that they earn and receive the respect of the House by their
example of hard work. When they take their bills to the House floor they
back their plea for support with assertions about their industriousness. And
they do this because they believe it counts heavily in their favor with the
Members. Committee members believe, in other words, that House expecta-

tions and their own expectations are equally well served by the style of hard work.

It is clear that legislators seek and find the fulfillment of important personal expectations through service on the Appropriations Committee. Persuasive confirmation can be provided by the simple fact that, whereas Members are attracted to it from nearly every other House committee, very few leave it for service on other committees. Of the 119 members in the 1947 to 1964 period only 2 men left the Committee, and neither of them initiated the move. One, Thomas O'Brien (D., Ill.), was personally requested by the Speaker to move to Ways and Means. The second, Hamer Budge (R., Idaho), was chosen by a caucus of Western Republicans to be their representative on the Rules Committee.[8] Of the 23 members who were forced off the Committee for lack of seniority during a change in party control or who were defeated for re-election and later returned, 22 sought to regain Committee membership at the earliest opportunity.[9]

Where Committee membership brings such great personal rewards to its members, they will develop a strong psychological attachment to it. "There's a tendency on this Committee for people to think of themselves as members of the Appropriations Committee first and members of the House second." And members will identify their personal satisfaction with Committee survival. From the Committee members' perspective, therefore, there clearly exists a strong incentive to adapt to House expectations. Yet, in the very process of adapting, Committee members may find their personal desires less requited than they wish. The point is that the optimum fulfillment of House and of Committee member expectations calls for different patterns of behavior. Herein lies the most important source of Committee-House conflict and of the House dissatisfactions recorded in Chapter One.

Committee members will want to act so as to preserve their power and prestige; but House members will seek to reduce what they regard as the Committee's excessive power. Committee members will wish to maintain their insiders' position relative to the flow of information; but House members will want to pry more information out of what they feel is a "closed corporation" and "a star chamber." The Committee's members will nourish their political style and the group esprit which it fosters; the House members may be irritated and wish to diminish the separateness of "the exclusive club," "the clan," and "the third House." Tensions are inherent in the Committee-House relationship. Short of a total convergence of system and subsystem, these tensions cannot be eliminated. But they can be controlled so

---

[8] Letter from Thomas O'Brien to author, June 30, 1959; letter from Hamer Budge to author, July 6, 1959.

[9] The exception was Otto Kreuger (R., N.D.) who was "bumped" from Appropriations in the party changeover of 1955, but failed to return to Appropriations when a vacancy opened up in 1957. The circumstances of his choice are not known.

that the relationship remains reasonably stable. The House, for its part, can control the relationship by applying sanctions and by exercising self-restraint in that application. The Committee can help control the relationship by adopting, to a large extent, House goal and maintenance expectations and by acting in such a way as to satisfy, at some point less than optimal for either House or Committee, the expectations of both.

COMMITTEE GOAL EXPECTATIONS
AND ADAPTATION

The Appropriations Committee's view of its goals is patterned in faithful response to House expectations calling for program support, economy, oversight, and negotiation. These responses come naturally and without verbal embroidery as the rock-bottom price for Committee survival. But Committee members (quite correctly) view these expectations as the very broadest of directives, establishing the outer limits of substantive Committee activity while leaving to the Committee the job of charting its own day-to-day behavior. Furthermore, Committee members perceive (also correctly) that surveillance by the parent chamber is sporadic and that its sanctions are enforced sparingly. And they interpret this loose hold on the reins as a deliberate grant of considerable, albeit contingent, autonomy. And so, within a general framework of acceptance, the Committee articulates for its own use a more elaborate and a more precise set of goals. These, in turn, are buttressed by a set of perceptions and attitudes which comprise the Committee's self-image and its image of others. On this more complex basis, the Committee acts in response to the House. And, while acting, it seeks always to accommodate the performance of its House-prescribed tasks to the satisfaction of its own members' expectations.

One of the most significant features in connection with the set of goals elaborated by the Committee is the remarkably solid consensus on which these goals rest. They are articulated most often by the senior members of the Committee, but they are shared equally by veterans and newcomers alike. They are shared also by Democrat and Republican. The two party contingents do not develop different sets of goals. In any specific situation, the members may differ as to which action best serves a goal — or as to which goal ought to be applied. Hence agreement on goals ought not to be equated with unanimity in action. But at the level of articulation, Committee members exhibit substantial agreement. The solidarity of the Committee's consensus makes it more likely than otherwise that the House will adopt the Committee's own elaboration of its goals. That is, a committee that could not agree on what it should be doing would present the House with alternatives to choose from. But a committee that is unified becomes singularly

95

persuasive. To the degree this is so, the very fact of the Appropriations Committee's consensus on goals generates important feedback, which will bring and keep a reasonable correspondence between Committee and House expectations.

Protect the Power of the Purse

The Committee's articulation of its goals rests, first of all, on a belief that, within the separation of powers, the power of the purse is the essential bulwark of congressional power. "Of all the legislative prerogatives," writes its chairman,

> The power to appropriate is the most vital. Not a wheel of government can turn without motivation of an appropriation. Basic authorizing statutes for the most part are broad in scope and grant to the executive rather wide latitude. The one continuing and recurring procedure for congressional control over governmental activities within such statutes is the annual appropriation review and the legislative provision of funds.[10]

House expectations, as reflected in the goals they set for the Committee, rest on a similar assumption. But the members of the Committee to which has been delegated House tasks in this area have a heightened sense of the connection between legislative power generally and the power to appropriate specifically. Committee members put it bluntly to their fellow House members — "If we don't have the power to appropriate, then what have we got?" So, the Committee adopts as its overarching goal, on behalf of the whole House, the preservation of the legislative power of the purse.

The Committee gives expression to this most abstract goal when it spearheads or tries to rally House opposition to some fundamental alteration in the appropriations process. For example, the Committee rests its opposition (as a general proposition, though not always in specific instances) to direct Treasury borrowing on the argument that the legislature is surrendering its most essential power. A leading Republican Committee spokesman writes,

> Backdoor financing raises questions vital to the orderly processes of representative government. The Congress, as the directly elected representatives of the people, has but one certain and continuing way to effectively control the government. That is the power of the purse. No other certain way exists.[11]

Chairman Clarence Cannon saw it as a loss of House influence:

> The Senate has never been reluctant to initiate backdoor appropriations — and they are trying it on this bill. . . . It is incredible that Members would

[10] Clarence Cannon, "Against the Item Veto," *Harvard Law Record*, April 21, 1960, as reprinted in *Congressional Record*, Daily Edition, May 6, 1960, p. A3916.
[11] *Congressional Record*, Daily Edition, August 10, 1961, p. A6279.

96

in any way encourage and support erosion of this all-important position of the House as the body closest to the people and to their pocketbooks.[12]

When Members conduct their floor battles against backdoor spending they implore the House to consider the overall consequences. In pleading for the Thomas amendment, its author argued,

> As the Committee bill now stands, you, and you, and you, every member of this Congress, has given away the rights of your people. You have absolutely given away the rights of your people to control the purse strings. . . . I do not want to put anybody on the spot, but I mean the bill has given away the rights of the members of Congress to control the purse strings to the tune of four billion dollars. Now, who's going to spend this money? Not a single person who has ever been voted upon by the people will spend this money. Do not say that the President is going to spend it, because the President has too much to think about. It is going to be someone appointed in the various bureaus. I suggest to you that now is a good time to recoup the authority that the people back home who elected you think that we have.[13]

Similarly the members of the Appropriations Committee are in the vanguard of opposition to the often-proposed item veto on the grounds that it would tip the entire check and balance system irrevocably in favor of the President and away from Congress.[14]

Committee concern for legislative power draws much of its intensiveness from the assumption that the House of Representatives is the prime mover in the legislative appropriations process. Every Committee member knows, and most of them volunteer, that House primacy is legitimized by no less an authority than the Constitution. The constitutional clause (Article 1, Section 7) that "All bills for raising revenue shall originate in the House of Representatives" does not legally include appropriations. But under "immemorial custom" it has been interpreted to include appropriations as well as revenue measures. While acknowledging their periodic dispute with the Senate on this question (see Chapter Twelve) the official Committee position is that,

> Unfailingly, throughout over a century and a half of the existence of the government, the House has asserted and successfully maintained its exclusive rights in this matter.[15]

[12] *Congressional Record*, Daily Edition, July 1, 1963, p. 11361.
[13] 105 *Congressional Record*, p. 8688.
[14] See Clarence Cannon, "Against the Item Veto," *Harvard Law Record*, April 21, 1960, as reprinted in *Congressional Record*, Daily Edition, May 6, 1960, pp. A3916–3917; see also 99 *Congressional Record*, p. 4928.
[15] *History of the Committee on Appropriations*, House Document 299, 77th Congress, 1st Session (Washington: U.S. Government Printing Office, 1941), p. 4.

It is the House of Representatives, then, to which the Constitution and tradition grant exclusive prerogatives. But it is a very short step for the Committee on Appropriations, as the "efficient" part of the House in this area, to assume that the Constitution has endowed it with a special grant of authority. They feel, at any rate, that the exercise of their power rests on the rock of the Constitution — a firmer foundation than that of any House committee save Ways and Means. The conviction that the Constitution speaks almost directly to them is a source of considerable satisfaction and pride.

Though the Committee is, in formal organizational terms, one decision-making unit in a complex appropriations process — extending back into the executive agencies, through the Budget Bureau and the President, through both houses of Congress, and back again to the President — Committee members do not envisage their status as a coordinate one. To its members, the Appropriations Committee is *the* repository of the House's special constitutional prerogatives over appropriations. And, therefore, it is the most important decision-making unit in the appropriations process. In the words of a veteran member,

> Great responsibility rests upon the shoulders of the Director of the Budget and on the Secretary of the Treasury, but an even greater responsibility rests upon the shoulders of congressmen, and more especially on the shoulders of the members of this Committee, the Appropriations Committee of the House of Representatives where all appropriations are supposed to originate.[16]

In Committee parlance, the primacy of their task is often summed up by the statement that they, after all, "get the first crack at the budget." They expect every other participant in the process to help them, but their perception of others is based on the centrality of the position they assign to themselves. In its conflicts with the House, the Committee draws strength from its argument that to weaken the Committee is to weaken the House itself.

Guard the Federal Treasury

Money in the federal Treasury cannot be made available for governmental use except by act of Congress (Article I, Section Nine). Most of the authority is granted by Congress through annual appropriation bills processed through the Appropriations Committee. Committee members accept the House-prescribed goal of program support. They assume that appropriation bills should provide sufficient funds to finance government programs as authorized by congressional majorities. They know (and they sometimes complain) that

---

[16] Committee on Appropriations, *Hearings on the Budget for 1958*, 85th Congress, 1st Session (Washington: U.S. Government Printing Office, 1957), p. 17.

prior authorizations sharply circumscribe their own area of discretion. There is no question, therefore, that Committee goal expectations include the positive aspects of the House's two-sided law-making expectations.[17]

The House goal expectation which the Committee most centrally and enthusiastically adopts as its own, however, is that which calls for the economical financing of programs. When Committee members articulate their own goal expectations, the language is almost wholly negative — screening requests for money, checking to make certain that the taxpayer gets his money's worth ("a dollar's value for every dollar spent"), and protecting the nation against ill-advised expenditures. In the Committee's own view its main goal is to guard the federal Treasury. Only thus, they believe, can it preserve the power of the purse for the House of Representatives. And to the extent that House members perceive the Committee as being more economy-minded than open-handed, they perceive correctly. The Committee intends to behave that way.

"You may think my business is to make appropriations," declared Joseph Cannon, one of the Committee's most illustrious chairmen, "but it is not. It is to prevent their being made."[18] Cannon's predecessors and successors — known variously as "the watchdog of the Treasury," "the great stone man," and "Cerberus of the Treasury" — have expounded the same Committee goals. All have shared the view that the federal Treasury is besieged and beleaguered by people trying to extract its contents. And all have cultivated the Committee's self-image as the heroic underdog in the endless battle against the "wolves," "pirates," and "thieves" who eye the Treasury waiting for a relaxation in Committee vigilance. In the official history of the Committee another former Chairman described the job of each member as "constantly and courageously to protect the federal Treasury against the thousands of appeals and imperative demands for unnecessary, unwise, and excessive expenditures."[19]

Chairman Clarence Cannon voiced Committee orthodoxy in this fashion:

> The greatest duty devolving upon the Congress, and one of the most difficult, is that of protecting the money of the taxpayers in the federal Treasury. There are today some people who want to get in the federal Treasury, want federal money, so many lobbyists, and unfortunately so many members of the Congress who, in a determination to have federal funds for personal or local purposes, will use every possible effort, will resort

[17] See, for example, *Congressional Record*, Daily Edition, March 7, 1961, p. 3153.
[18] As quoted in William R. Gwinn, *Uncle Joe Cannon: Archfoe of Insurgency* (New York: Bookman Associates, 1957), p. 63, from "Speaker Cannon: A Character Sketch," *Review of Reviews* (December, 1903), p. 674.
[19] *History of the Committee on Appropriations, op. cit.*, p. 11.

to every device, to get money out of the Treasury put there by the taxpayers and put there under realizations of the responsibility of the Congress to protect the resources of the nation.[20]

And Chairman George Mahon, in commemorating the Committee's 100th anniversary, made the same point:

> It is probably one of the safest of premises that the interests, wherever they lie or whatever they be, will rarely if ever neglect advocacy of the truly essential needs; that these needs will more or less automatically present themselves, abundantly accompanied by justification. It not unreasonably follows that the appropriation function — however organized — is to look at all demands objectively with the attitude that not everything is essential or indispensable. For with public money hardly ever in sufficient abundance to cover all that is desirable, a first and foremost function is the allocation of resources among competing demands — setting priorities of purpose and amount. Thus has it been a natural consequence for the system to veto or diminish the budget requests as often as reasons deemed sufficient to do so could be found.[21]

The Committee's own dominant goal expectations are primarily negative; and the Committee's dominant self-image is "guardian of the federal Treasury."

The self-image of guardian gets reinforced and further defined by the perceptions and attitudes which Committee members express concerning other participants in the appropriations process. In brief their image of these "others" is simply that they either cannot or will not adequately protect the Treasury. Thus the Committee is strengthened in the conviction that it must give special emphasis to this one goal. Committee members have achieved a consensus in stressing the negative tasks of guardianship not because they oppose the programs for which they must appropriate (though, of course, some members do act on this basis for any given program) but because they believe that *someone* in the political system must perform these tasks. The Committee accentuates the negative partly because, in their view, nearly everyone else in the larger system accentuates the positive. Several members have hung a Calvin Coolidge aphorism on their office wall: "Nothing is easier than the expenditure of public money. It does not appear to belong to anybody. The temptation is overwhelming to bestow it on somebody." The job of the Committee, on behalf of the entire government, is to resist temptation.

The Committee members' image of the Senate, for example, leads them to conclude that they cannot expect much assistance from that quarter. It is a threadbare Committee jibe that the Senate is called the "upper body" because it always "ups" appropriations. House members see Senators as lacking in fiscal responsibility. A veteran Committee spokesman exclaimed,

[20] Committee on Appropriations, *Hearings on the Budget for 1961*, 86th Congress, 2nd Session (Washington: U.S. Government Printing Office, 1960), p. 82.
[21] *Congressional Record*, Daily Edition, March 2, 1965, p. 3866.

The Senators are interested in chicken feed politics. They go back to their states and go around to every little town to see where they can use some money. And they say, "The House won't take care of you, but the Senate will. We want to give you some money." They didn't use to do that. They were above it. We bring them over a good bill, but every time they raise it.

Furthermore Committee members view the Senate as a club in which each member willingly grants the appropriations requests of his fellow members, thereby piling up ever-larger totals:

It's just like a fraternity. You've got all this courtesy business — and it's not party line at all. The Democrats and the Republicans do favors for each other. If one of them wants a special project, they'll throw it in the bill for him. It doesn't make any difference whether he's a Democrat or a Republican — they'll give it to him. They load up the bill with all these special things. . . . I've never known the Senate to cut an appropriation bill. They always "up" appropriation bills. Over there it's just a fancy game of give and take. They give each other what they want and everybody takes.

And withal, it is felt, Senators do not do the necessary work. Committee members agree (with evident satisfaction) that "Senators don't work as hard as we do" and that "all the work is done in the House." The House Committee, its members believe, is the only reliable and responsible legislative guardian of the Treasury.

The Committee's consensus on goals is reinforced, too, by its perceptions of the Budget Bureau. The Committee's view is that the Bureau does not, cannot, and should not function as an adequate guardian of the Treasury. A sizable minority of the Committee members interviewed expressed outright antagonism toward the Bureau. Their attitudes ranged from derision ("Who has the best information in regard to the bill? The subcommittee who heard the witnesses or the pencil and paper boys down at the Bureau of the Budget?") to disgust ("I don't have any damn use for the Bureau of the Budget. I'd vote today to abolish the Bureau of the Budget."). The critics expound the theme that the Bureau is "arrogating unto itself" the constitutionally grounded task of the Committee. And the Budget Director has, on occasion, encountered considerable hostility in his appearances before the Committee.[22] A slightly larger number of members are more sympathetic to the Bureau. Their attitudes range from realistic acceptance ("It's a balance wheel; and if the President didn't have this, he'd have to create another one. It's either this or something else like it.") to praise ("They do a good job. We couldn't get along without it.").

Whatever the attitude — and this is the crucial point — all members agree that the estimate prepared by the Budget Bureau is the place to begin

[22] For an example of a clash between the Budget Director and a Committee leader, see Committee on Appropriations, *Hearings on the Budget for 1960*, 86th Congress, 1st Session (Washington: U.S. Government Printing Office, 1959), pp. 53 ff.

101

and not a figure that should be accepted as authoritative. The Bureau can only propose; the Committee must dispose. The whole Committee takes the attitude expressed by its chairman that, "It has always been our contention that the Committee has the last word on fixing the amount of money that should be spent by the departments." This is in accord, moreover, with the expectations of the President:

> The President's budget is an overall ceiling. He does not expect us to go above it, nor does he expect us to adhere to it where conditions do not warrant it. But he expects us to cut where cuts are possible.[23]

In this spirit, Committee members take action and defend it. Consider this floor exchange:

> CONGRESSMAN: Is it not true that the department has been through one wringer over at the Budget Bureau?
> SUBCOMMITTEE CHAIRMAN: They might have gone through a soft rubber wringer rather than a hard rubber; and that is what we need to do, to squeeze out a little more.[24]

The Committee may be divided on whether to view the Budget Bureau as an ally, or rival, or a pretender in the realm of guardianship — but there is no doubt in their minds that the Committee on Appropriations must be, should be, and is, king.

Reduce Budget Estimates

Since "guarding the Treasury" lacks specificity, the Committee defines for itself a related but more explicit goal. This instrumental goal, to be sought in pursuit of the more general goals, is to reduce budget estimates. All other things being equal, Committee members feel the Treasury can be most effectively guarded by cutting budget requests. Budget reduction, being reasonably specific, becomes the Committee's most central guide to action. Members feel it is the core of their appropriations task. Committee members believe that the long-run goal of guardianship and the short-run goal of budget-cutting meet basic House expectations regarding economy as they have persisted since the creation of the Committee in 1865. "When you're on the Committee," said one member, "people expect you to cut — the other Members and the general public." Furthermore, the members believe that if they strike a highly critical and aggressive posture toward all requests for expenditures they will also fulfill House expectations regarding oversight of executive agencies. Budget-cutting is the essential sanction which the Committee wields in its effort to control executive activity.

[23] 94 *Congressional Record*, p. 1880; also *Congressional Record*, Daily Edition, June 18, 1963, p. 10405.
[24] 103 *Congressional Record*, p. 2330.

The Committee pursues its budget-cutting goal in direct confrontation with executive agencies. And, again, the Committee's self-prescribed goal expectation is shaped and reinforced by the image its members have of some "other" group — in this case the agencies themselves. The Committee's image of executive agencies is that each wants to expand and that a good deal of such expansion is unnecessary. (Each member has his exceptions, of course, but it is the generalized perception that is important here.) It is accepted as a fact of life that all bureaucrats want to enlarge their domains. "The appetite of bureaucracy is insatiable," said the chairman. "If their appropriations were doubled or tripled they would still ask for more."[25] Some members look upon this expansion as a "cancerous" growth, and others see it as a sign of commendable executive vitality. But all agree that this "natural tendency" is due to the parochialism of the bureau. "I know," said a young member of the Defense Subcommittee, "that there never was an admiral who had enough of a fleet, there never was a general who had enough soldiers, and there never was a newspaper editor who had enough reporters." Each agency feels that its program is the center of the universe, and if the Committee were to endorse each claim with an appropriation, the government would soon collapse. In taking the overall financially responsible view, the Committee naturally will have to reduce budget requests. Said one powerful subcommittee chairman,

> They don't ask for more money than they need to do what they want to do. They just want to do more than what we think is necessary and we think they can do it with less than they do.

Even when one considers the "necessary" programs, it is "a number one assumption" of the Committee that executive agencies "usually ask for more than they need."

Given this assumption, Committee members operate with suspicion as their rule of thumb. A Committee newcomer explained, "We've got to see that these agencies don't get a blank check. If they want the money, they've got to walk the hard road to get it." And a second member put it more strongly, "You've got to be critical. You've got to take the attitude that 'you people are coming up here and asking for too much . . . trying to feather your own nests and your friends' nests, too.'" Committee members assume furthermore, that each agency head will stand fast and insist that his budget estimates cannot be reduced. The agencies, therefore, cannot be expected to be of any assistance to the Committee:

> The departments come down here bound to the budget estimates, item by item, as representatives of the executive department. Now if they cannot

25 *Congressional Record*, Daily Edition, September 1, 1960, p. 17587.

show us where we could save some money, all right, then we will have to show them.[26]

And, armed with the assumption that the agency is after all seeking more money than it needs, Committee members proceed to "show" agencies where cuts can be made.

Here, for example, is one subcommittee chairman in action on an agency request for a new building:

> My question is, how much can you take off when you rework the plans a second time and how much can you take off when you rework the plans a third time. The first time you take all the lace out. The second time you take all the gingerbread out, you take all the wasted space out, and you narrow the corridors. The office building is not quite as spacious and the laboratories are not quite as big. You will put a little terrazzo in there rather than some more expensive material. How much can you cut this and still have a usable functional building? Can you not cut it 25 or 30%? . . . Have you ever seen any quick plans which, if they were reworked and reworked could not be reduced, where you could come up with a reduced price and a better job? This Committee has considered funds for a lot of buildings around here, and we are not virgins in the forest in this construction business.[27]

Committee members are not persuaded by bureaucratic assertions that the entire estimate can be or has been spent. For members credit all executives with the ability to spend everything they get whether they need it or not.

A related Committee perception which supports it in its budget-reducing task is in the nature of a self-fulfilling prophesy. Committee members believe that agencies adjust their budgets upward in anticipation of Committee cuts. "There's a certain amount of padding in every budget." or "Padding has an unsavory connotation. Let's say they put a little cushion in there." "They've been through it before — they expect to be cut and that's why they put in everything they need." A subcommittee chairman explained, "They get cut year after year and so they say, 'They're going to cut us, so let's put in everything we think is necessary.' I'd do that if I were in their place." The Committee can, indeed must, reduce agency budgets, because agencies expect them to and are behaving accordingly. A good deal of strategy in the appropriations process is, as we shall see, based on anticipated reactions such as this one.

The product of these perceptions and attitudes toward executive agencies is the belief that every budget can be cut. In the words of two Committee veterans and one newcomer: "There has never been a budget sub-

---

[26] *Hearings on the Budget for 1958, op. cit.*, p. 44.

[27] Committee on Appropriations, *Hearings on Commerce Department Budget for 1958*, 85th Congress, 1st Session (Washington: U.S. Government Printing Office, 1957), p. 215.

mitted to the Congress that couldn't be cut." "There isn't a budget that can't be cut 10 per cent immediately." "There are soft spots and fat in every budget that I have ever come in contact with."[28] At the very least, it is believed, every agency can absorb "a token cut." The belief in the token cut derives from the Committee's assumption that no matter how diligently they search, they can never find all the unnecessary expenditures in a budget. This does not mean that the Committee always cuts. It does not. But it does mean that this belief is one of the key predispositions affecting Committee action. And this belief becomes an important part of the Committee's ethos. "It's a tradition in the Appropriations Committee to cut," observed a senior member. And another agreed, "You're grounded in it . . . it's ingrained in you from the time you get on the Committee."

It is a mark of the intensity and the self-consciousness with which the consensus on budget-cutting is held that it is couched in a distinctive occupational vocabulary. The workaday jargon of the Committee is replete with negative verbs, undesirable objects of attention, and effective instruments of action. Agency budgets are said to be filled with "fat," "padding," "grease," "pork," "oleaginous substance," "water," "oil," "cushions," "avoirdupois," "waste tissue," and "soft spots." The action verbs most commonly used are "cut," "carve," "slice," "prune," "whittle," "squeeze," "wring," "trim," "lop off," "chop," "slash," "pare," "shave," "fry," and "whack." According to their regional backgrounds, members speak of "doing a little woodshedding," "picking the sour apples out of the barrel." "doing some selective logging," or "thinning out the herd." The tools of the trade are appropriately referred to as "knife," "blade," "meat axe," "scalpel," "meat cleaver," "hatchet," "shears," "wringer," and "fine-tooth comb." Members are hailed by their fellows as being "pretty sharp with the knife." Agencies may "have the meat axe thrown at them." Executives are urged to put their agencies "on a fat boy's diet." Budgets are praised when they are "cut to the bone." And members agree that "you can always get a little more fat out of a piece of pork if you fry it a little longer and a little harder."

The characteristic dilemma for the Committee is not whether or not to cut, but how to cut wisely. Here, members make it clear that judiciousness ought not to be confused with timidity. The Committee's rule of thumb is that when in doubt it is better to be on the hard side than to be too lenient. "Our experience indicates," says a veteran spokesman,

> that we should cut to the point that there will be no necessity for any executive trimming of the budget, that we should fix the low figure rather than fix the high figure which gives the department wide latitude in deciding how much they can spend.[29]

[28] *Hearings on the Budget for 1961, op. cit.*, p. 114.
[29] *Hearings on the Budget for 1958, op. cit.*, p. 21.

In plain language, this means not to be afraid of cutting too much. One senior member used a rustic metaphor in advising his colleagues to operate according to the lesson he had learned pruning his grandmother's grape arbor:

> She said, "Cut them until you think they are going to die and you will have some grapes." And that has been the way I have operated . . . I have only this to say to you. Do not be afraid of killing them. Cut hell out of them and you will have some grapes.[30]

From here it is but a short step to the assumption that the more you cut the better job you are doing. And, more often than not, members subscribe to this view. "There's the tendency after you've been here a while to think that any cut is good," declared one member. And the chairman expounded the same view publicly:

> It has long been an unwritten rule of the Committee on Appropriations that the budget estimate is to be taken as the maximum and the efficiency of the subcommittee has been judged — and the chairman of each subcommittee has prided himself on — the amount he was able to cut below the budget estimate.[31]

Committee members temper the seeming harshness of this view with self-restraint — often born of constituency interest. And countervailing external pressures operate in support of all executive agencies. Within the appropriations process, moreover, the Committee finds at least two safety valves. Members believe that, if an agency is severely crippled, it can always come back again and make its case for a supplemental appropriation. Hence, a denial is not necessarily irrevocable. Second, the Senate will probably raise the amount above the House figure anyway. Agencies that are grievously wronged may seek an effective remedy at the hands of the Senate. Said one member, "Sometimes we make mistakes for lack of information; but we have several backstops if we make any serious ones."

These goal expectations elaborated by the Committee — protecting the power of the purse, guarding the Treasury, reducing budget estimates — help the individual member to fulfill his personal expectations. Each one of them, together with their supporting images, constitutes a reminder of the Committee's importance and a rationale for the exercise of influence. The very fact that a consensus on goals exists promotes the unity and the esprit of the group. And the specificity (or "operationality") of a goal such as budget-cutting increases both the sense of identification with the group and

[30] *Ibid.*, p. 84.
[31] 102 *Congressional Record*, p. 11128. Also *ibid.*, p. 8699.

the individual sense of satisfaction with a task measurably well done. "They talk a lot about it," said an experienced member. "They take — not exactly pride — but a lot of satisfaction in cutting the budget." But for the veteran Committee member, pride is the correct description. The Committee's ranking minority member exclaimed,

> I am proud to say that no bill has ever come to the floor of the House from a subcommittee of which I have been a member that was not below the budget and as you know, Mr. Speaker, I have been a member of the Appropriations Committee for the past twenty years.[32]

By emphasizing the negative aspects of House expectations, the Committee develops a distinctiveness which is also a source of satisfaction — and pride:

> We're a different breed of cat — we members of the Appropriations Committee. We're different from the members of all the other committees. It just grows on you. . . . You listen to the conversation among the members of the Committee, when we are visiting among ourselves, and we'll be talking about a program and everyone will want to know, "How much did it cost?" That's automatic with us, we're money conscious and we talk about everything in terms of dollars and cents.

Influence and a sense of distinctiveness bring individual satisfactions. And it is hard to see how either would result if the Committee should suddenly decide to emphasize program support as their special goal or their unique contribution to the legislative process.

Committee members feel, too, that their goals of guardianship dovetail nicely with their style of hard work — the style from which they derive so much evident satisfaction. They believe that hard work will inevitably produce "the facts." If you "get the facts," you will usually uncover waste in the bureaucracy. And the revelation of waste will be followed by cutting the budget. Therefore, according to Committee syllogism, hard work will result in cutting the budget. Occasionally, digging out the facts will produce sympathy for an agency's plight and a budget increase. But Committee members are convinced that if they work hard, they will end up cutting the budget. Conversely, if you want to cut a budget, you must work hard. Goal expectations, Committee style, and individual satisfactions are tightly interrelated.

Do the goals which the Committee has set for itself help them to adapt to House expectations? The answer, as was made clear in the previous chapter, is "yes" and "no." And the details of the answer will be filled in throughout the book. There is no question, however, but that the Committee's goals dovetail with those House demands involving economy. Committee members

---

[32] *Congressional Record*, Daily Edition, January 17, 1963, p. 516.

believe that they are acting in full accord with House expectations when they cut budgets. A Committee newcomer observed that "a lot of the older members feel they have to go before Congress and say they cut the hell out of the budget." And they do. The floor definition of "a good bill" is one that has been reduced as much as possible. And a bill that can be "improved" is one that can be cut even further. Committee members solicit House support in precisely these terms.

In support of his bill, one subcommittee chairman argued typically:

> All in all it looks like a big bill and the percentage cut does not look very large, but I think we have cut more out of this bill this year than any subcommittee has ever cut since I have been a member of it . . . in practically every agency, we show a cut below 1951. That is why I say I think this Committee has done a splendid job.[33]

On the other hand, a subcommittee chairman whose group has cut very little may feel constrained to apologize. "We have been over this bill very carefully and, frankly, I feel like making some apologies. I believe we are recommending the smallest cut this committee has ever made."[34] Committee members believe, too, in pursuing their goals of guardianship, they are helping to fulfill House oversight expectations. And they further believe that by working hard and getting the facts they are acting in a manner best calculated to meet House demands for economy and oversight. They appeal for, and win, House support on all these grounds.

Serve Member Constituency Interests

The three Committee goals so far discussed are not especially responsive to those House expectations which stress support for programs and projects. The controversy over backdoor spending reflects the failure of the Committee to meet some of these expectations. Committee members are perfectly aware that "House members think we are too conservative — at least, the liberals do." For most programs, the Committee does (as we shall see) provide most of the money authorized. But it declines to prescribe for itself the goal of rubber-stamping all authorizations: Within its area of discretion it pursues economy and suffers some liberal-based House antagonism as a result.

House members' expectations calling for Committee support for pet projects, however, are sufficiently widespread and insistent to require some kind of special recognition from the Committee. Out of collegial sympathy for their elected brethren and out of a sense of necessity, the Committee defines for itself a fourth goal — serving the constituency interests of House

[33] 97 *Congressional Record*, p. 4009.
[34] 104 *Congressional Record*, p. 3403.

members. But they give to this goal a subordinate place in their hierarchy of goals — a short-run exception to a long-run pattern of behavior. Chairman Cannon elaborated the goal this way:

> It is the intent of every member of this Committee to provide as economical a budget as possible. Every member of this Committee and every member of Congress has pledged to his constituents back home to observe the strictest economy here — of course, except in places where local interests are involved.[35]

Committee members adopt the servicing of constituency interests as a legitimate goal because, in one sense, they must. To yield in this matter is to yield to the facts of political life in a representative body. Furthermore Committee members are impelled by their status as congressmen to recognize that increases may be necessary and cuts impossible. Each Committee member, that is, may wish to get in and remove the contents of the Treasury. It is, after all, in precisely these terms that they seek membership on the Committee and express satisfaction with it. A senior House leader talked about the Committee's chairman in this vein:

> Cannon wants to cut, cut, cut — unless Missouri is involved. He fights hard for Missouri, and I admire him for it. But he'll go out there on the floor and cry and cry "Support the Committee. We've got to cut" — but not on Missouri.

Committee members find themselves holding to the same potentially conflicting views as other House members. Thus the same Committee member can make two such contrasting statements as these — the first as the apostle of economy and the second as the servant of his district:

> APOSTLE OF ECONOMY: Just as surely as the sun will set tonight, unless we stop this constant criminal waste by the billions in almost every department of our federal government, we will all drown together in a sea of rot, mud, and muck.[36]

> SERVANT OF HIS DISTRICT: I am proud of the fact that I have supported every dime which has been recommended by the Agriculture Subcommittee on Appropriations for the Rural Electrification Program and for the entire agricultural program every year since I have been a member of this body, for surely farming is the greatest free enterprise in our blessed land.[37]

The budget-cutting and district-oriented goals are believed to be compatible so long as moderation is observed and the latter does not predominate in the

[35] *Hearings on the Budget for 1958, op. cit.*, p. 27.
[36] 98 *Congressional Record*, p. 2864.
[37] 104 *Congressional Record*, p. 5976.

109

long run. When the constituency service task is paramount, the member is expected to exercise self-restraint and not to let this interest influence most of his activity. Committee newcomers will be told that it may be all right to "go local" for one year but that "after you've had your run, you've got to be national."

What the Committee accepts for itself, it accepts for other Members as well. Overlapping membership produces a different set of perceptions and attitudes than the institutional rivalry implicit in the check and balance system. Committee members are suspicious and sharply critical of executive requests. But they understand a request (often the same request) if it is made by a fellow congressman in terms of representing the folks back home, servicing the district, and getting re-elected. Given the geographical representativeness of the Committee's members, every member of Congress can gain access to one of them. And Committee members frequently forego projects of their own to support those of a fellow congressman. One of the Committee's leaders discussed internal Committee processes in these terms:

> Every member of the Congress has a friend on the Appropriations Committee. And they say, "Jim wants this project; let's help him out. Jim needs to be elected; let's help him out."

When Committee members feel that they must deny a legislator's request for money, they do not level accusations of waste nor do they employ the axioms about cutting which guide them in dealing directly with the executive branch. (Any legislator's project, of course, will require action by the executive branch.) In private they will say, "I just can't do that" or "you know how things are" or "maybe next year." "If we have to cut out some pet project," says a Committee member, "they are pretty understanding":

> They'll go out on the floor and make a fuss; but I'm surprised at how good they are about it. And we try to be accommodating with them. If some man comes before the Committee and makes a good presentation and we have to deny it, we may write him a letter and say that he made a good presentation but that we were unable to grant the request this year. This makes him feel better and clears him with the home folks. That's just good business. I do that every chance I get.

On the floor, Committee members will begin by expressing understanding and end by arguing against the particular request in the name of the larger goals of the Committee and of the whole House. In the words of the Committee's chairman,

> We do not inveigh against any man in this House, or any man to be in this House in the future, for coming before the Committee on Appropriations and requesting an appropriation for his district. That is what he is here for. He is merely performing his duty to his constituents who sent him here.

110

But I do say the rest of us ought to consider every application made by everybody from every district and say, "Now, my boy, you are on the right track, but let us be a little reasonable. We are going to have to cut you down a little bit to serve the whole country and put what little taxes are paid in where it will best benefit the most people."[38]

Allowances are made for the constituency-oriented, budget-increasing syndrome of the elected representative; but the Committee assigns top priority to the goals of guardianship throughout.

Committee members recognize that the dilemma involved in balancing demands for money against the goal of protecting the Treasury presents one of their most serious problems in adaptation. Dissatisfaction of individual Members or clusters of Members on this score are concrete; they are communicated in face-to-face contacts; and they are highly visible to Committee members. With a sense of pride and the slightest tinge of martyrdom, Committee members freely acknowledge their unpopularity. "This is a committee where you do not win friends and influence people. You lose friends and disrupt people. But it is a job that members of Congress have to do."[39] "If you stay around here long enough, you will have every single Member mad at you," said one subcommittee chairman. "You can't win on this Committee."

Committee members believe that unrequited requests for pet project money is one of the most important sources of House-Committee conflict. "Oh, they don't like the Appropriations Committee," chuckled one member.

> You step on too many toes. Any Appropriations Committee does this. If a Member has a pet project, he thinks that the most important thing in the world. It has a great deal to do with his future. If he doesn't get it, he may carry a grudge for a long time.

And a subcommittee chairman agreed,

> They remember the one they didn't get. You get a lot of requests to help Members. You help them out and they come to you the next year with an impossible project. And if you don't get it they never forget it. It's like the old story, "What have you done for me lately?"

Committee members are fully resigned to complaints. Indeed, complaints are a positive indicator that the Committee is doing its duty; and the volume of complaints represents important feedback:

> Members of the Appropriations Committee always have a rather peculiar feeling when we hear applause and words of congratulation from other Members because we are not used to that. We are not too certain, when everybody congratulates us, that the bill is not overly generous.[40]

[38] 102 *Congressional Record*, p. 8700.
[39] 102 *Congressional Record*, p. 8705.
[40] 102 *Congressional Record*, p. 3941.

In many instances, member dissatisfactions are isolated and fairly random. But Committee members recognize that, should they allow House dissatisfactions to become cumulative, a serious threat to the survival of the Committee might be posed.

COMMITTEE MAINTENANCE EXPECTATIONS AND ADAPTATION

Dependence, But . . .

House expectations regarding the maintenance of system-subsystem relations may be summed up in this way: Whatever goal the Committee pursues, it should follow the will of the House which, after all, creates and legitimizes it. In support of this basic rule of the game, the House elaborates many more specific procedural expectations — all designed to keep the House-Committee relationship in balance. Committee members readily acknowledge the ultimate authority of the House and their position subordinate to it. But again, they recognize that they have been granted considerable leeway in writing their own canons of procedure. Committee members, therefore, develop specific maintenance expectations of their own — expectations with quite a different thrust than those of the House. And these differences complicate the problems of adaptation. Maintenance expectations deal, as we have seen, with relationships of influence between the House and the Committee. House maintenance expectations emphasize the influence of House over Committee and, hence, the dependence of the Committee. The personal expectations of Committee members, however, stress the influence and, hence, the autonomy of the Committee within the House. The problem of adapting to House maintenance expectations presents a more direct conflict for the Committee than does the problem of adapting to House goal expectations.

The Committee's response to House maintenance expectations can only be described as one of inevitable ambivalence. On the one hand the Committee seeks to maintain harmonious relations with the parent chamber. On the other hand, it seeks to fulfill its self-prescribed goals and the individual desires of its members — for power, prestige, information, and group solidarity. At the most fundamental level, the Committee fully accepts House expectations as to House-Committee relations. In the words of the Committee's chairman,

> All that the Committee on Appropriations does in bringing in these budget estimates in a bill, is to give you an opportunity to consider, debate, modify, and vote. We do not ask you to approve them. We merely ask you to consider them and then vote them up or vote them down . . . the fact that the

Committee on Appropriations puts an item in a bill does not mean that the House has to agree to it. We leave that to you. All we do is to give you an opportunity to exercise your prerogative, representing the people of your congressional districts.[41]

And the Committee prides itself on its ability to sense and to follow the mood or temper of the chamber. "A mere novice in Congress without experience might not know generally what Congress is going to do, but experienced members of the Appropriations Committee generally can sense what the Congress will do with respect to the budget estimates." The House's record of acceptance is proof of considerable success in Committee attempts to subordinate its behavior to the will of the House.

Yet, as we know, House members level a great variety of criticism, the most common of which is that the Appropriations Committee exercises excessive power within the chamber. The Committee does not seek such conflict directly. But it does take what it considers to be legitimate and necessary action in pursuit of Committee member expectations. And it is not so anxious for House-Committee harmony that it willingly foregoes its own goal or maintenance expectations. Committee members believe, for example, that closed executive sessions are necessary to protect Committee deliberations from pressure generated through publicity which would, in their view, increase appropriations and prevent them from protecting the Treasury. Similarly, they believe that the flow of information to House members must be carefully guarded to prevent the leakage of information that would precipitate a raid on the Treasury. They acknowledge House resentment:

> They think we're a powerful committee. And they're a little jealous. They think we are high-handed — maybe high-handed isn't the word for it — but they think we are too much of a closed corporation, because of our executive sessions.

But the Committee continues this practice, nonetheless.

Appropriations Committee–Substantive Committee Conflict

At the heart of the Committee's problems in adapting to House maintenance expectations is its relationship with other House committees. House criticism of Committee encroachment upon the legitimate jurisdiction of its substantive legislative committees is as old as the historic dispute of 1885. The tension in this relationship arises from the Committee's belief that its goals can only be achieved by placing all appropriations controls in the hands of a single committee and the House's fear that centralization of appropriations controls may result in an excessive concentration of power. It has been renewed whenever the Committee has come under the special scrutiny of the

[41] 101 *Congressional Record*, pp. 11058–11059.

House (1920, 1946). And it has been articulated regularly and persistently — most often by substantive committee chairmen protesting, on behalf of the entire House, the imperialism of the Appropriations Committee. The criticism, when raised, is especially sharp and bitter because in a conflict between committees the most vital interests of the participants are at stake. A number of House criticisms can be related to or subsumed under this one complaint. The House provision for direct Treasury financing has been spearheaded by substantive legislative committees (Banking and Currency on housing; Foreign Affairs on development loans) seeking to keep programs nurtured by them from being cut back by the Appropriations Committee. Similarly, House complaints about the Committee's communications monopoly stem in large part from substantive committees which feel at some disadvantage in their own areas of competence. Many of the specific procedural rules elaborated by the House aim at the maintenance of proper Appropriations Committee–substantive committee relations and, through them, at the maintenance of proper overall House-Committee relations.

In the Committee's eyes, the activities which excite substantive committee criticism are activities which must be undertaken in pursuance of the Committee's goals. It recognizes fully that authorizing committees must act before money can be appropriated, but in order to guard the Treasury it feels that it must take a fresh and independent look — guided but not fettered by the authorization figures sent to it via substantive legislation. Committee members describe their group as "the saucer into which the hot cup of legislative tea is poured to cool." Their expectations regarding the authorizing committees are stated as follows:

> The legislative committee goes through the hearings, evaluates the evidence before it, and tries to determine the amount of money which is the ceiling that the committee could possibly justify as far as the activity is concerned. Then it is up to the Appropriations Committee to determine how much of the money can be spent in that particular year, and that is the amount which is made available. . . . Each committee works for a different objective. The objective of the legislative committee is and ought to be to establish a ceiling for a program. The objective of the Appropriations Committee is and ought to be to establish the proper sum of money which can or should be spent by law in any given year.[42]

In 1962, when the Armed Services Committee wrote into an authorization measure that Congress "directs" the expenditure of certain monies (for the B-70 bomber program), the Appropriations Committee succeeded in substituting the word "authorizes" in order to protect its prerogatives in taking an independent look.[43]

[42] *Congressional Record*, Daily Edition, September 5, 1961, p. 17022.
[43] *Congressional Record*, Daily Edition, March 21, 1962, pp. 4305–4335.

114

The Committee's perception of the authorization as a ceiling allows it to implement freely its goal of budget-cutting. And the clear implication is that the authorization figure should be reduced. Exclaimed one member, "May I say to my distinguished friend if this House appropriates all the money that has been authorized by Congress, then God help us — that is all."[44] Normally, therefore, the Committee appropriates less than is authorized, which action brings it into conflict with the authorizing committee. In areas such as public works and foreign aid, the differences between the two sets of committees may be especially marked. And this is highly irritating to House members who have sought to make the authorizations as economical as possible. As a Public Works Committee member put it, "We do not wave a doubtful project through hoping it will get stuck in the money committee for lack of merit."[45] From the Appropriations Committee's point of view, its actions are legitimate and necessary and cannot be surrendered to others.

Hand in hand with their idea of the fresh, independent look goes an attitude of self-sufficiency which also nourishes conflict. That is to say, Appropriations Committee men consider themselves perfectly competent to handle the same range of problems as substantive committee members. Indeed, they have served on most of them before coming to Appropriations. And they may simply feel no need or have no time for communication with the members of such committees. Consider this illuminating exchange between a House member and a veteran subcommittee chairman:

HOUSE MEMBER: I am concerned about one phase that I think we are drifting farther and farther apart from all the time, and that is the affinity and the contact and the consultation as between the subcommittee on appropriations and the real experts who live with the problem every day of the year, the members of the Committee on Foreign Affairs. Do you call them in? Do you consult them as to some of these proposals to cut or to increase? I think there is an inexhaustible source of unimpeachable information that you can get directly from your own source right here in the country.
SUBCOMMITTEE CHAIRMAN: No member of the Committee on Appropriations will agree to that or admit that it is so. The members of the Committee on Appropriations feel that they have a pretty good knowledge of all the matters that are contained in their appropriation bills.
HOUSE MEMBER: I am mindful of the load you carry, but I think you might advance your own position and make it stronger if you did consult the real experts, who are right here in the family, the members of the Committee on Foreign Affairs.
SUBCOMMITTEE CHAIRMAN: As a member of the Committee on Appropriations, I cannot make such a concession.[46]

44 91 Congressional Record, p. 11206.
45 Congressional Record, Daily Edition, August 20, 1962, pp. A6299–6300.
46 96 Congressional Record, p. 5468.

An attitude like this, quite honestly taken in pursuance of Committee expectations, is not likely to endear its members to the remainder of the House.

Committee members know that the rules of the House forbid them to legislate on an appropriation bill. Yet they assert the necessity of doing so in order to protect the money they appropriate and prevent wasteful expenditures:

> We are criticized for legislating on the appropriation bill. I think we should have some facility for protesting the work of the legislative committees when their authorization bill will embarrass us financially.[47]

The Chairman of the Committee addressed the House and asserted that his group could not do their work without some legislation. "I do not have to call the attention of the House to the fact that owing to the vast coverage, to the intricacy of the problems involved, every appropriation bill must necessarily carry some legislation."[48] House members often agree and may not wish to maintain their rule against legislation inviolate. But they protest what they regard as its excessive use or its use against particular interests in particular cases.

Sharp Appropriations Committee–substantive committee fights may occur should the Committee seek House passage of a rule waiving all points of order and hence protecting legislation in an appropriation bill. The leaders of the substantive committee affected normally are not happy about this invasion of their territory. But Appropriations Committee members are not likely, either, to be bashful about asserting the necessity for their action. Few public exchanges, however, will be as blunt as this one:

> CHAIRMAN OF SUBSTANTIVE COMMITTEE: Personally, I resent very much waiving all points of order against certain provisions which should be considered by the appropriate legislative committee. It is an infringement on the legislative committee of this House by a subcommittee on appropriations. As Chairman of the Committee on Public Lands, I resent it very much . . . this rule will make possible the very thing that was done over the unanimous vote and wish and will of the Committee on Public Lands.
>
> . . . .
>
> SUBCOMMITTEE CHAIRMAN: Abuses no end have been carried on in the Interior Department which should have been corrected a long time ago by legislation. I want to say that the reason we found ourselves compelled to put some language in this bill, to which the Chairman of the Public Lands Committee objected, is because of the fact that he as Chairman of that Committee has refused to act and do something about bringing out the legislation that would correct those abuses.[49]

[47] Committee on Appropriations, *Hearings on Agricultural Appropriations for 1950*, 81st Congress, 1st Session (Washington: U.S. Government Printing Office, 1949), p. 925.
[48] 101 *Congressional Record*, p. 11058.
[49] 94 *Congressional Record*, pp. 6595–6596.

On such occasions, the Committee's fate is in the hands of the parent chamber. Almost always, however, it is successful — thus revealing that in specific situations House members, too, entertain ambivalent expectations.

In writing an appropriation bill the Committee can employ several techniques — not judged to constitute legislation — which enable it to influence programs. The Committee can reduce a program by placing "limitations" on the use of money. Or, the Committee can foster a program by "earmarking" funds for it. The Committee uses similar techniques to exercise control over agency personnel. The most famous of these was the so-called Jensen rider used in the early 1950's, which specified that none of the money appropriated to an agency could be used to fill more than three out of every four vacancies that occurred. By the systematic use of such techniques as these, Committee action obviously affects programs.[50] And its members recognize their ability to enforce their independent judgment by "vetoing or enlarging a program." One member summarized,

> We can't put law into an appropriation bill. If we do, it's subject to a point of order. But we can put a limitation on the amount to be spent on certain things. That's legal; and in that way, we can control the flow of money into a program . . . we control appropriations; but we control programs, too.

Through the less formal device of language included in the Committee report, it also wields considerable influence over substantive programs. For example, in the case of programs for the aged, the Committee wrote in its report that it was "disappointed" in the "poor showing" of the Department of Health, Education and Welfare in this field and expressed its "considerable concern." And it ended the report with this admonition, "It is certainly to be hoped that in another year something substantial in the way of a program will be developed." And the subcommittee chairman made the group's influence amply clear when he stated on the floor,

> When we mention in the report, that we expect the Department to come up with a real program next year, I believe we will get it . . . I am pretty sure that they will come up with a program, as they have in connection with other recommendations of this Committee on other programs.[51]

Another subcommittee chairman spoke similarly about the potency of a report:

> I will guarantee you that you can depend upon this report, because . . . we will see that they live up to this. . . . When I have an agency which

[50] For the effects of "limitations" on a program see William L. Morrow, "Congress and ICA: A Study in Legislative Control of Administrative Discretion," unpublished manuscript (State University of Iowa, 1961). For an analysis of the effects of the Jensen amendment, see 98 *Congressional Record*, pp. 4484–4487.

[51] 102 *Congressional Record*, p. 3951.

tells me they are going to do something and they do not do it, they wish they had done it. That has been true all during the 10 years that I have been chairman of that subcommittee, and you can put that down.[52]

Committee members recognize the report as another of their programmatic weapons to be included in their guardianship of the Treasury:

Now you take these reports. They aren't law. They're just an expression. We sometimes indicate dissatisfaction with the program. It's in the nature of a directive to the agency.

The House acknowledges the report as a requisite technique of legislative oversight; but the use of it may, as we have seen, bring irritation and frustration.

Committee influence over programs brings pride and satisfaction to its own members. It is, indeed, one of the important components of the Committee's power, prestige, and information. "A legislative committee proposes and the Appropriations Committee disposes. There's more power in Appropriations," one member asserted in explaining why he had come to the Committee in the first place. "The Appropriations Subcommittee on Agriculture," exclaimed one of its members, "has more power over agriculture than the legislative Committee on Agriculture. We look at every program every year . . . why, we've started many important legislative programs right here in this [subcommittee hearing] room." The chairman of the same group agreed and recalled a specific example. "Our subcommittee, without budget approval, provided $5 million to set up 56 pilot plants over this nation. That was the beginning of the great watershed program we have today."[53] In cases of this nature, the expectations of House and Committee may come into direct conflict.

Committee members are perfectly aware of legislative committee criticism. Second only to their denial of pet projects, they ascribe their unpopularity to what they see as a "built-in conflict" between themselves and other House committees. A subcommittee chairman said,

It's an unpopular Committee in the House. Maybe you are popular as an individual, but not as a committee. We get into legislation on an appropriation bill — quite often we do — and the members of the legislative committees resent it.

A ranking subcommittee member discussed the same conflict and the Committee's need to protect itself:

[52] *Congressional Record*, Daily Edition, February 29, 1960, pp. 3425–3426.
[53] *Congressional Record*, Daily Edition, November 19, 1963, p. 21183. See David C. Knapp, "Congressional Control of Agricultural Conservation Policy," *Political Science Quarterly* (June, 1956), pp. 257–281. Also, Robert J. Morgan, "Pressure Politics and Resources Administration," *Journal of Politics* (February, 1956), pp. 39–60.

I think there is a feeling that the Appropriations Committee cuts too many sensitive programs. That's one reason why you need to keep the Appropriations Committee large. If you have fifty men and have them well-situated, you can always do pretty well on the floor.

In 1965, Chairman Mahon emphasized to the Democratic leadership the need to fill the nine vacancies on his side of the aisle with men of "top quality," to help the Committee withstand "the increasing attacks of the legislative committees."

Adaptation and Nonadaptation

In their conflicts with the legislative committees of the House, Appropriations Committee members prepare for the worst, but they also adapt to legislative committee resentment by trying to reduce it wherever and however they can. Inside the Committee, "The Chairman keeps driving it into us that we shouldn't encroach on the jurisdictions and prerogatives of the legislative committees." On his own initiative, in 1961, Chairman Cannon made up a list of all legislative provisions of appropriation bills and sent the relevant ones to each substantive committee chairman. Frequently, appropriations subcommittees will try to keep their opposite number substantive committee informed of matters of mutual interest.

The Chairman of the Committee on Interior and Insular Affairs complimented the Chairman of the Appropriations Subcommittee on Interior in one case as follows:

I particularly wish to commend the chairman and the committee for his and the committee's willingness to work with the authorizing committee. This has been a relationship that has developed within the last few years. It makes it much easier for the authorizing committee to know the problems of the appropriating committee.[54]

The relationship between these two committees on Interior Department matters has yielded a critical increment of support for the Appropriations Committee — even for its legislative activities. In 1964, for example, the chairman of the legislative committee gave blanket approval to the Interior Department Appropriation Bill and the accompanying report:

Once again Mr. Chairman, I want to commend the [Appropriations Subcommittee Chairman] and his committee for the responsibilities that they have always taken care of so well. I have made a close study of the report and I find it is another one of those reports which to me is not open to any serious question. What has been placed before us is in line with our thought about what should be done . . . I also wish to suggest that the

[54] 108 *Congressional Record*, p. 5449.

limitations and legislative provisions that are to be found in this bill and referred to in the report should be accepted by this body without any question whatsoever.[55]

In view of the fact that a sizable proportion of Member pet projects must be processed through these two Interior-oriented committees, the establishment of a reasonably harmonious relationship represents an important success in Committee adaptation to House expectations. It may be that the exceptionally large number of ex-Interior Committee members on the Appropriations Committee (see Table 3.1) helps explain this instance of comity.

Other examples of successful adaptation may find the Committee acting aggressively on behalf of the substantive committee. The Chairman of the Armed Services Committee, for example, took the floor to praise Committee action in earmarking funds for the B-70:

> I congratulate the Appropriations Committee . . . the Appropriations Committee has been the trail blazer in the field of the B-70. Indeed, I can say in a very real sense the Armed Services Committee is following the leadership furnished by our great Appropriations Committee.[56]

Or, individual members of the two kinds of committees will cooperate closely in areas of mutual concern. Two senior Iowa Republicans — one on the Committee on Public Works and one on the Appropriations Subcommittee on Public Works—revealed a successful instance of adaptation:

> MEMBER OF APPROPRIATIONS SUBCOMMITTEE: Fred and I have had to work closely together since he came to Congress, so I have become aware of this ability his constituents respect so much. He is on the Public Works Committee; I am on Appropriations as a member of the flood control projects, etc. which clear through his committee . . . [and] come up to the Appropriations Committee for the necessary funds. . . .[57]

> . . . .

> MEMBER OF PUBLIC WORKS COMMITTEE: He comes from the Missouri River side of our state, while my district lies along the Mississippi River. But when it comes to a sympathetic ear for funds to create necessary public works, my constituency could have no greater friend. I'm extremely pleased to have him in his position of prominence on the powerful Committee on Appropriations.[58]

[55] *Congressional Record*, Daily Edition, March 17, 1964, p. 5307. For a similar expression of mutual support by the appropriations subcommittee and the legislative committee dealing with the District of Columbia, see *Congressional Record*, Daily Edition, March 3, 1964, pp. 4087–4088.
[56] *Congressional Record*, Daily Edition, March 21, 1962, p. 4311.
[57] *Congressional Record*, Daily Edition, October 2, 1962, pp. 20609–20610.
[58] *Congressional Record*, Daily Edition, August 20, 1962, p. A6299.

For several years, the Chairman of the Appropriations Subcommittee which appropriates for NASA and the Chairman of the Science and Astronautics Subcommittee on Manned Space Flight were Texans. The Appropriations Committee member had the Manned Space Flight Center erected in his district; he, in turn, fought hard to give the Science and Astronautics Committee the authority to make annual authorizations for the NASA budget. Through a great variety of quid pro quos — of program, of pet project, and of information — the Committee pursues harmonious relations with the legislative committees of the House.

On the House floor, the pursuit of harmony continues with public disclaimers of expansionist aims. In the words of Chairman Cannon:

> The Committee has too much jurisdiction to suit the Committee on Appropriations. We have far more business than we want. We certainly have no desire to encroach upon the prerogatives or the jurisdiction of any other committee. God forbid.[59]

Committee members take time during floor debate to demonstrate to the House their awareness of the problem and their great self-restraint:

> Mr. Chairman, the Committee on Appropriations over the years has been castigated because of the allegations that it has invaded the jurisdiction of the legislative committees. Of late, we have sought to restrain ourselves and absolve ourselves of any legitimate criticism in that regard.[60]

Another approach is to assuage House fears via a public confession of guilt. George Mahon, later Chairman of the Committee, once followed this tack:

> As a member of the Committee on Appropriations I have sometimes been embarrassed by the efforts of some members on rare occasions to more or less abolish other Committees of the Congress and arrogate to themselves the right to pass legislation.[61]

The reassuring implication is that any such transgressions are a thing of the past.

Another Committee response to legislative committee criticism is to deliberately de-emphasize the programmatic effects of appropriations decisions. Members seek, first of all, to calm House fears by placing Committee activity in perspective. They emphasize, therefore, the degree to which they are in fact bound by prior House determinations. For example,

> Many people have an exaggerated idea of the power of the Committee on Appropriations and what they do. Our troubles are made in this Committee of the Whole House and we have no choice but to activate and appropriate for the many activities that this House authorizes.[62]

[59] 101 *Congressional Record*, p. 11058.
[60] *Congressional Record*, Daily Edition, May 5, 1960, p. 8951.
[61] 93 *Congressional Record*, p. 4098.
[62] 95 *Congressional Record*, p. 4093.

Thus the Committee stresses the narrow limits within which they exercise discretion. Secondly, Committee members underplay their policy impact by projecting the image of a "business" committee rather than a "policy" committee. By highlighting their concern for waste, inefficiency, and unnecessary expenditures, Committee members hope to play down programmatic concerns and avoid conflict, on the verbal level at least, with substantive committees. Such assertions may seem like a subtle form of self-deception — a lesson in how to influence programs without really seeming to. But they must be understood primarily as a serious effort to adapt to House expectations.

The House has, of course, a variety of sanctions available to it which it can use, or threaten to use, to bring about Committee responsiveness. And the existence of these helps account for Committee efforts at harmony. Chairman Mahon noted in 1965, for example, that excessive legislation on appropriation bills via the Holman Rule (permitting legislation that retrenches expenditures) was one reason for the application of House sanctions in 1885. He went on to acknowledge the wisdom of contemporary Committee restraint in the area:

> We have seen the grief that came from operations under the Holman Rule in the Committee's early days. Yet significantly, the House itself has seen fit to clothe the Committee with the abrasive, contentious, negatively oriented retrenchment rule, *vigorous assertion of which would certainly again bring down the displeasure of many members*.[63] [Italics added]

In gauging the use of their autonomy, Committee members also gauge the likelihood and the consequences of House sanctions.

On the other hand, it must be noted that the Committee possesses its own sources of power and may adapt by blunting the effectiveness of House sanctions. When, for example, the House wrote its expectation into the Legislative Reorganization Act of 1946 that Committee reports should be available three calendar days prior to floor action, the Committee paid scant attention to it. In the very next year, 1947, the Committee violated the rule in eleven instances. Since then, it has honored the provision in the breach as well as in the observance. Also approved by the House in the same Act was a Legislative Budget to be drawn up each year by the members of the four revenue and appropriations committees (two in the House and two in the Senate). This provision was scuttled, after a one-year trial, by the noncompliance of the House Committee on Appropriations. A House member who helped write the provision explained, "old Clarence Cannon and old John Taber decided that the Senate had no business getting in on appropriations this way; and they threw it in the wastebasket."

[63] *Congressional Record*, Daily Edition, March 2, 1965, p. 3866.

When the House passed the Annual Accrued Expenditures Bill in 1958, prescribing new budgetary forms for the Appropriations Committee to follow, the Committee informed the department to submit their budget as usual. A departmental budget officer recalls,

> I went up there and sat down with the [Committee] clerk. I asked him, "How do you want this? I want to give it to you just the way you want it." Cost basis, accrued expenditure basis — pooh. He said, "I don't care how you gave it to the Budget Bureau. We want it just the way you did it last year."

In 1959, President Eisenhower submitted accrued expenditure limitations for six different appropriations items. In 1960, he submitted twelve items with accrued expenditure limitations attached. The very first subcommittee to be faced with the proposition ignored it with these words, "In the opinion of the Committee, the facts are conclusive that this proposition is an absurdity and would not save any money and the Committee has acted accordingly."[64] In all of the other instances, too, the Appropriations Committee eliminated the accrued expenditure from its bills. In 1962, the trial period prescribed in the Act ran out. "Cannon doesn't like accrued expenditures," a Committee member said in 1964. "John Taber didn't either. The subcommittee chairmen don't like it. Either they won't learn any other way of reading the budget or they just won't use it."

In each of these cases House sanctions were rendered ineffective because they conflicted with the expectations of the Appropriations Committee itself and because the House did not feel sufficiently aggrieved to conduct open warfare against the Committee. The House remains critical, but the ability of the Committee to maintain some autonomy has been successfully asserted.

So long as each unit possesses a capacity for enforcing its own expectations on the other, smashing victories are not likely to be recorded by either. Far more likely is a sequence of semivictories. Such, for example, has been the history of the dispute over frontdoor and backdoor spending. The Committee successfully prevented backdoor financing in the Foreign Aid Bill of 1961 and the Export-Import Bank renewal in 1963. But it eventually lost the same battle in conflicts over the Housing Act in 1959 and over the Area Redevelopment Act in 1961.[65] In each of these latter two pieces of legislation

[64] Committee on Appropriations, *House Report No. 227*, 86th Congress, 1st Session (Washington: U.S. Government Printing Office, 1959), p. 12. See also, *Congressional Record*, Daily Edition, May 17, 1961, pp. 7709–7711.

[65] On the Foreign Aid Bill see 107 *Congressional Record*, pp. 15737 ff., 15812 ff., 16022 ff., 16188 ff., 17851 ff. On Export-Import and Housing, see Chapter 2, footnotes 5 and 12; for Area Redevelopment see 107 *Congressional Record*, pp. 6717 ff. For another minor Committee setback, see *Congressional Record*, Daily Edition, March 23, 1964, pp. 5697–5711.

the Committee position was sustained in the House version of the bill; it was then lost in conference with the Senate, and its loss was sustained by a vote in the House on the conference report. This sequence reveals yet another crucial factor which prevents clear-cut victories. Conflicts between the Appropriations Committee and the House are rarely cast in a pure form. They are conflicts continually cross-cut by other conflicts. When the issue of backdoor spending is made paramount, the Committee can normally win the support of the chamber. But when a substantive issue (in these instances, the enactment of public housing and depressed areas bills) is superimposed upon it, a new conflict is present and the Committee may lose.

Even for Committee members themselves the issue posed by backdoor spending may become not one of Committee power but one of their own program goals. One Committee member who voted against the Thomas amendment reflected,

> You say to yourself, "Somebody's got to look after all this money." Then you realize what will happen to the program if it comes to our Committee. They oppose it. So you vote to keep it away from the Committee.

On the same 1959 housing bill, 9 Committee members voted for the Thomas amendment but then voted for the final bill with backdoor financing in it. The issue had changed. Indeed, it is fair to say that no member of the Committee considers the question of backdoor spending of such paramount importance that he will support it regardless of what other substantive issues are superimposed upon it. Most of them heartily support programs such as veterans' loans and surplus grain disposal and such agencies as the Commodity Credit Corporation and Home Owners Loan Corporation which are financed by backdoor spending. Only 17 Committee members signed the 1961 and 1963 petitions for a change in the House rules so as to prohibit backdoor spending.[66] Maintenance issues are, therefore, never wholly maintenance issues. A single type of House-Committee conflict may take different forms in concrete circumstances. And, according to the form, the makeup of supporters on both sides may change. So long as such conditions exist, permanent victories will be hard to come by.

CONCLUSION

Appropriations Committee expectations regarding what it should do and how it should do it differ somewhat from House member expectations. Among the goal expectations set by the House, the Committee gives primary emphasis to implementing those related to economy. Among the House-prescribed

[66] *Congressional Record*, Daily Edition, February 9, 1961, pp. 1916–1917; January 24, 1963, p. 977.

maintenance expectations, the Committee stresses its own autonomy and influence. These Committee expectations are, of course, interrelated. Committee members believe that only by adopting the negative goals of Treasury guardianship can they maintain any considerable degree of influence in the House. And it is precisely this influence that individual members expect to derive from their assignment to the Committee. The price of satisfying Committee member expectations, however, is House-Committee conflict. House members consider the Committee excessively economical — in the case of liberal programs and, most aggravatingly, in the case of individual Member pet projects. They view the Committee as excessively autonomous and influential — most especially in its relations with substantive legislative committees. The Committee acts in pursuit of its own expectations; but at the same time, in the interests of survival, it adapts to the expectations of the House.

Over all, the Committee seems to have adapted sufficiently to House expectations — sufficiently, that is, to avert drastic House-induced changes in its behavior. Some adaptation has resulted from the Committee's own feedback activity designed to change House expectations and images. Some has resulted, too, from the nature of the House's feed-in activity in terms of its expectations and sanctions. Committee success rests, first, on the considerable overlap in expectations which, despite signal differences, does exist. The Committee does develop its goal and maintenance expectations within the general framework set by the House. Moreover, it loses no opportunity to press the legitimacy of its own goal and maintenance desires before the House. Thus, the Committee can exercise some control over House expectations. And specific conflicts can be minimized by references to overall agreement. Second, Committee adaptation is increased by the serious efforts which the Committee makes to blunt resentment. With regard to pet projects, the Committee has adopted the servicing of Member constituent interests as a goal — albeit a subordinate one. In the area of legislative committee relations, the Committee has taken remedial action and has spoken the language of reassurance. The Committee is wholly aware of House criticism, and many of its actions must be understood as efforts to reduce this criticism. Third, Committee adaptation is made easier by the existence of considerable ambivalence in the House. In any of its specific actions, the Committee can always rely on substantial House support, however threatening the long-run implications of that action for House-Committee relations may be. And, finally, it must be remembered that some adaptation is forced upon the Committee, through no action of its own, by the intermittent application of House sanctions. Committee adaptation is a piecemeal form of adaptation. Its success derives partly from the fact that House resentment, criticisms, and sanctioning actions are also piecemeal.

125

Committee adaptation is only partially successful, however, and any summary statement of the relationship must emphasize the persistence of tension. Committee members express it when they say, "There's a question about the future of this Committee." Or, "There may be a revolt against the Appropriations Committee some day, but not yet." Or, "I'm afraid there's going to be a knockdown drag out fight sometime. I don't know when." Or, "On a secret ballot they'd beat our brains out every time; but on a roll call vote, they don't dare." The unanswered question here is not "Why is there tension?" but "Why has it not been resolved decisively?"

The answer in general is that the tension has not become so great that either side is willing to risk the benefits of the present arrangement in exchange for a less ambiguous one. Should Committee members seek to expand their influence without restraint, they risk losing the important personal and career satisfactions that flow from Committee membership. Should House members, in the spirit of 1885, reassert their dominance over the Committee, they risk the demise of a Committee which implements some of their most crucial values. They also risk widespread tension and disruption inside the chamber and they risk, most basically, jeopardy to the committee system as a whole. Tensions exist, but they have not moved either side to decisive action.

In the final analysis, House-Committee interaction is maintained because conflicts between them are episodic and piecemeal rather than persistent and cumulative. House criticisms are piecemeal; they find different foci at different times; they are put forward by different groups of people. A long-established, interrelated pattern of expectations, perceptions, attitudes, and actions can be disrupted, it would seem, only by an accumulation and a concentration of dissatisfactions to a degree of magnitude which has not occurred. So long as the present consensus on expectations survives, and so long as conflicts remain basically noncumulative, the existing patterns of influence and of tensions between the House and the Appropriations Committee will remain. And the state of the relationship will have important consequences for the behavior of House members and Committee members alike.

CHAPTER

FOUR

The House Committee
II: *Structure for Decision-Making*

DIVISION OF LABOR, ROLES, AND ROLE BEHAVIOR

The Committee's goal-oriented and maintenance-oriented tasks are set for it by a blend of House and Committee member expectations. Committee success in satisfying this blend of expectations depends primarily on its appropriations decisions — how it makes those decisions and what kinds of decisions it makes. At this point the solution of the Committee's external problem of adaptation requires the solution of an essentially internal problem or, rather, two problems. In the first place, the Committee must develop an institutionalized decision-making structure. In the second place, the Committee must maintain or stabilize the decision-making structure it has created. In solving these problems, the Committee is left to its own devices. Chapter Four describes the decision-making structure as it has existed in recent years. Chapter Five describes the ways in which and the extent to which that structure has been maintained — or, in the term to be used, integrated — during the same period.

The central question in creating a decision-making structure is: "Who, within the organization, shall do what?" Since the alternative of having all fifty members perform all Committee tasks is not practicable, an allocation of positions and tasks among the various members has developed. This allocation provides for an internal division of labor. Individual positions have been established, whose occupants are expected to perform certain specified tasks. Also, individual positions have been combined to form subgroups — that is, collectivities smaller than the Committee itself — whose members are expected to cooperate in the performance of certain specified tasks. This

127

differentiation of individual positions and of subgroups, together with the differentiated expectations associated with them, produces the basic elements of the Committee's internal structure.

To use a shorthand description, the basic elements of the Committee's internal structure are its differentiated roles. A role is simply "the ways of behaving which are expected of any individual who occupies a certain position."[1] Here, as elsewhere in the book, the idea of "expectations" and, hence, of role is a normative idea. A differentiation of roles, that is to say, describes "who should do what" and not necessarily "who does do what." Committee members develop certain agreed-upon expectations as to how people occupying certain positions (taken singly or in combination) should behave. These expectations, in turn, get expressed as Committee norms. A norm can be defined as "an idea in the minds of the members of the group, an idea that can be put in the form of a statement specifying what the members or other men should do, ought to do, are expected to do under given circumstances."[2] Each of the Committee's differentiated roles gets defined, therefore, by a set of norms or a set of statements prescribing expected or appropriate behavior. Thus "Roles consist of clusters of norms providing for a division of labor or specialization of function among members of a group."[3] An understanding of the Committee's internal structure depends upon an understanding of Committee roles which, in turn, depends upon an understanding of the Committee's norms.[4] And by discussing individual behavior in this manner, it should be added, the need for an analysis of individual personalities may be minimized.

In the final analysis, however, what we want to understand is not the Committee's structure of normative expectations but the Committee's actual behavior. To talk in terms of role is to describe how an individual in a certain position should act. But if one wants to describe how individuals in those positions do act, we must talk in terms of role behavior. In some instances, role and role behavior may correspond. In other cases they may not. One could, of course, find out how the Committee behaves simply by observing its behavior and dispensing altogether with the examination of the structure of expectations. But one could not explain the behavior he has observed nor

[1] Theodore M. Newcomb, *Social Psychology* (New York: Dryden, 1950), p. 280.
[2] George C. Homans, *The Human Group* (New York: Harcourt Brace, 1950), p. 123.
[3] John W. Thibaut and Harold H. Kelley, *The Social Psychology of Groups* (New York: John Wiley, 1959), p. 148.
[4] A statement of expected behavior was taken to be a Committee norm when it was expressed by a substantial number of respondents (a dozen or so) who represented both parties and varying degrees of experience. In nearly every case, moreover, no refutation of the norms was encountered; and ample confirmation of their existence can be found in the public record. Their articulation came most frequently from the more senior members of the group.

base any predictions upon it. If, however, one knows whether or not observed behavior meets or does not meet expectations, explanation and prediction are advanced. If the observed behavior meets expectations, then the behavior represents a normal, stable, explainable, predictable pattern of behavior. If a lack of congruence shows up between behavior and expectations, then the behavior is recognized as deviant. It can then be accorded special attention, in order to determine what expectations were not met and why, how the Committee prevents deviant behavior from recurring, or how, if it does recur, the Committee adjusts its expectations to accommodate change.

It is thus important to maintain the analytical distinction between role and role behavior. But in studying and describing an on-going political system, it is extremely difficult to do so. The difficulty is especially great in studying the Appropriations Committee, since much of its decision-making behavior cannot be observed. It can only be known through interviews with participants. Yet these participants are the same persons who set the norms defining various Committee roles. Sometimes it is clear that they are talking about expectations, and at other times it is clear they are talking only about behavior. Frequently, however, they infer expectations from behavior and extrapolate behavior from expectations. And it is difficult to maintain the separation in the kind of open-ended interviews conducted. To put the problem another way, Committee members act both as respondents and informants at the same time, and the interviewer must use them as he finds them in this respect.

The Committee's internal problem of who shall do what is partly the question of goal-attainment. And that question can be stated: "Who shall make the Committee's authoritative decisions and how?" The Committee fulfills most of the goals set for it by making decisions. Its internal role differentiation pertains mostly to decision-making. Roles such as Committee Chairman, subcommittee chairman, ranking minority Committee member, ranking minority subcommittee member, subcommittee member, subcommittee clerk, and Committee newcomer[5] are defined primarily in terms of norms relevant to decision-making.

Throughout the chapter, the effort is made to describe the role associated with each position and then to give some evidence that role behavior does correspond to it. Whether because there are none or because the author found none, no Committee roles are reported for which there is no evidence of congruent role behavior. And no role was discovered for which there was not substantial evidence of congruence. For each of the roles discussed, then,

[5] Throughout the study, "newcomers" are defined as men who have served no more than 2 terms on the Committee. "Experienced members" are those with 3 to 5 terms of service. "Veterans" or "senior members" are those who have 6 or more terms of Committee service.

129

evidence is given first for the existence of the role and second for the existence of corresponding role behavior. The problem of deviant behavior will be discussed in the next chapter. Pending that investigation, however, it is assumed that what is being discussed in this chapter is the normal, dominant pattern of decision-making by the Committee on Appropriations. It is further assumed that the pattern has sufficient stability to serve as a basis for gross predictions about the behavior of individuals and of the group.

SUBCOMMITTEES: DIVISION OF LABOR

The Committee's goal-oriented tasks center around the annual examination of budget estimates submitted to them by the President. These estimates summarize in terms of dollars and cents nothing less than the full scope and complexity of the activity of the national government. Committee members point with pride to the magnitude of their task — to the fact that so great a proportion of federal activity must pass in budgetary review before them. In 1964, for example, the Committee acted on a set of original budget estimates (exclusive of supplementals) totaling 95 billion dollars. These estimates were subdivided into hundreds of separate line items. The Committee's work centered on these line items; and its basic decisions were recorded in hundreds of separate dollars and cents recommendations. But each of these decisions was the resultant of innumerable component decisions. And still other decisions of 1964 were recorded authoritatively through limiting language in the bills or, informally, through the language of Committee reports and through the private communications between Committee members and federal executives. Obviously, a division of this decision-making labor is required.

In keeping with the response of the House itself to the problem of decision-making, the Committee has sought its solution through the establishment of standing subcommittees. Each subcommittee deals with a segment of the budget, and each segment, in turn, becomes a separate appropriation bill. Thus, in 1964, the Committee divided its work among 12 subcommittees. Each subcommittee was given jurisdiction over a group of budget estimates, and each group of estimates formed the basis of an appropriation bill. In large part, the subcommittee structure parallels the structure of the executive branch, with one department or one cluster of related agencies coming under the jurisdiction of a single standing subcommittee. For reasons discussed later, however, a few significant deviations do occur.

Considerations of personnel, of strategy, and of circumstance may affect the number and composition of the subcommittees. During the period from 1947 to 1963, there have been as few as 9 subcommittees and as many as 15. The membership of each subcommittee has ranged anywhere from a low of

5 to a high of 17. The pattern existing in 1964 was more or less typical of the period since 1947. The subcommittees, their jurisdiction, the amount of the budget estimate included therein, their size, and their partisan composition — as of 1964 — are listed in Table 4.1.[6] With the change in party ratios in 1965, most of the subcommittees were enlarged slightly and the partisan composition of each was made more Democratic. But the subcommittees and their jurisdictions were not changed.

TABLE 4.1

APPROPRIATIONS SUBCOMMITTEES — 1964

Department of Agriculture and Related Agencies

Department of Agriculture (except Forest Service)
Farm Credit Administration

5.5 Billion
5 men (3D, 2R)

Department of Defense

47.4 Billion
12 men (7D, 5R)

District of Columbia

.1 Billion
5 men (3D, 2 R)

Foreign Operations

Foreign Assistance
Export-Import Bank
Inter-American Programs
International Development Association
Peace Corps
Refugee Programs
Ryukyu Islands (Department of the Army)

3.4 Billion
11 men (7D, 4R)

Independent Offices

Civil Aeronautics Board
Civil Defense Activities
Civil Service Commission
Federal Aviation Agency
Federal Communications Commission

---

[6] An additional, special subcommittee, the membership of which remains a secret, allocates funds for the Central Intelligence Agency. These funds are hidden among conventional line items (as was done for the Manhattan Project) and do not appear separately in the budget. See David Wise and Thomas Ross, *The Invisible Government* (New York: Random House, 1964), p. 266.

Independent Offices (Continued)

Federal Home Loan Bank Board
Federal Power Commission
Federal Trade Commission
General Accounting Office
General Services Administration
Housing and Home Finance Agency
Interstate Commerce Commission
National Aeronautics and Space Administration
National Aeronautics and Space Council
National Capital Housing Authority
National Science Foundation
Office of Emergency Planning
Office of Science and Technology
Renegotiation Board
Securities and Exchange Commission
Selective Service System
Veterans' Administration

 14.2 Billion
  7 men (4D, 3R)

Department of Interior and Related Agencies

Department of Interior (except Bonneville Power Administration, Bureau of Reclamation, Southeastern Power Administration, and Southwestern Power Administration)
Commission of Fine Arts
Federal Coal Mine Safety Board of Review
Forest Service
Historical and Memorial Commissions
Indian Claims Commission
Indian Health Activities
National Capital Planning Commission
National Capital Transportation Agency
Outdoor Recreation Resources Review Commission
Smithsonian Institution
Transitional Grants to Alaska
Virgin Islands Corporation

 1.0 Billion
 5 men (3D, 2R)

Departments of Labor and Health, Education, and Welfare and Related Agencies

Department of Labor
Department of Health, Education, and Welfare (except Indian Health Activities)
National Labor Relations Board
National Mediation Board
Railroad Retirement Board
Federal Mediation and Conciliation Service
Interstate Commission on the Potomac River Basin
United States Soldiers' Home

 7.8 Billion
 5 men (3D, 2R)

Legislative

    .2 Billion
    5 men (3D, 2R)

Military Construction

    1.8 Billion
    5 men (3D, 2R)

Public Works

    Atomic Energy Commission
    Bonneville Power Administration
    Bureau of Reclamation
    Civil Functions, Department of the Army
    The Panama Canal
    St. Lawrence Seaway Corporation
    Southeastern Power Administration
    Southwestern Power Administration
    Tennessee Valley Authority
    Water Study Commissions

        4.4 Billion
        10 men (6D, 4R)

Departments of State, Justice, and Commerce, the Judiciary, and Related Agencies

    Department of State
    Department of Justice
    Department of Commerce
    The Judiciary
    American Battle Monuments Commission
    Arms Control and Disarmament Agency
    Commission on Civil Rights
    Federal Maritime Commission
    Foreign Claims Settlement Commission
    Small Business Administration
    Subversive Activities Control Board
    Tariff Commission
    United States Information Agency

        2.0 Billion
        7 men (4D, 3R)

Departments of Treasury and Post Office and Executive Office

    Treasury Department
    Post Office Department
    Advisory Commission on Inter-Governmental Relations
    Executive Office of the President
    President's Advisory Committee on Labor-Management Policy
    Tax Court of the United States

        6.2 Billion
        5 men (3D, 2R)

If there is any generalization about Appropriations Committee activity that is fully supported by past research, it is the proposition that the tasks of the Appropriations Committee are accomplished by its subcommittees. The full fifty-man committee does not transact much of its business as a unit. Normally, it meets only to organize itself at the beginning of each Congress and to give a majority vote of approval to the recommendations of its subcommittees. It has met on rare occasions to consider an urgent internal committee matter, to take testimony from the Secretary of the Treasury or the Director of the Budget on a new budget and the state of the economy, or to hear the views of some other public official, such as Admiral Hyman Rickover on education. The day-to-day appropriations tasks, however, are performed in the subcommittees. And, so long as the subcommittees can command support in the full Committee and in the House, their decisions are the most important ones in the entire appropriations process.

When the President sends his budget to Congress — and sometimes even before he does — the members of each subcommittee receive from the agencies under their jurisdiction detailed "budget justifications." This basic subject matter document, explaining, comparing, summarizing, supporting, and justifying — in words and in tables — each agency's "estimates of appropriations," goes only to members of the relevant subcommittee. When these "justification books" have been received, they are summarized and annotated in a "subcommittee print" which then becomes the subcommittee's working document. After this preparation, each subcommittee proceeds to hold its own hearings — all in closed executive session. Agency leaders and, in some cases, interested parties such as congressmen or clientele groups explain and justify their estimates orally and answer the questions of the subcommittee members.

After the hearings have been concluded, the members of the subcommittee meet in executive session to "mark up" the bill — to decide, for each budgetary item, what their dollars and cents recommendation will be. They may also decide upon other actions of a statutory or nonstatutory nature. Then, the subcommittee writes a subcommittee appropriation bill together with an explanatory subcommittee report to accompany the bill. And it takes both of these documents to the full Appropriations Committee for approval. With changes, if such were made in the full Committee, or without changes, the subcommittee bill and report then become the Committee's bill and the Committee's report and both are sent to the House floor. The subcommittee members organize and lead the debate in the House until its appropriation bill, amended or not, has been passed. And, finally, should a conference with the Senate be necessary, subcommittee members customarily become House conferees on their respective bills. Such, in brief, is the appropriating sequence in the House.

134

Each subcommittee works in virtual isolation from every other one. "We tend to be," says Chairman Mahon, "more an aggregation of autonomous subcommittees than a cohesive Appropriations Committee." Members participate in the labors of those, and only those, subcommittees of which they are official members. One subcommittee chairman exclaimed,

> Why, you'd be branded an imposter if you went into one of those other subcommittee meetings. The only time I go is by appointment, by arrangement with the chairman at a special time. I'm as much a stranger in another subcommittee as I would be in the legislative committee on Post Office and Civil Service. Each one does its work apart from all the others.

A veteran staff member agreed:

> If another Committee member wants to come into a hearing real bad, he may be invited. I've seen that done. But even that would be super-special. They don't ask. If they have questions, they write them out, give them to the subcommittee chairman and he asks them.

Members of one subcommittee will not lend their "justification books" to Committee members not on the subcommittee. And nothing save the incapacitation of an official subcommittee member will bring a nonsubcommittee member into the group's crucial markup session.

The Committee at work is the Committee compartmentalized. It is not quite accurate to say, as one new member did, that "There is no Appropriations Committee — just twelve secret principalities, each jealously guarding its own domain." But, for the ordinary Committee member, compartmentalization does mean that 90 to 95 per cent of his Committee time and energy will be expended in the work of his subcommittees. His Committee experience will be, in effect, his subcommittee experience. The other Committee members he works with, travels with, reacts to, bargains with, and learns from are most likely to be other subcommittee members. Men who have served together on the Committee for ten years, but whose subcommittee paths have never crossed, will say that they "know" each other "only just to say hello." Had they served on the same subcommittee or had lateral communications normally existed between their subcommittees, they could not have remained virtual strangers.

In conversation, Committee members do not usually use the word "subcommittee." They talk about their subcommittees as "my committee" or "the committee"; and only the context reveals whether they are talking about the full Committee or their subcommittee. Nearly always, they are referring to their subcommittee — a habit of speech which underscores the importance of subcommittees in meeting the individual needs of the individual member. Not only, that is to say, does the division of labor help the

Committee to meet House-prescribed goals, but it makes possible a division of influence, of prestige, and of information which helps Committee members to fulfill their expectations. It produces, also, primary group attachments which may fulfill their desires for social solidarity. Whether the individual Committee member could satisfy his own expectations as readily and as thoroughly if there were no subcommittees is an open question. But the fact is that many of his expectations are met by the existence of relatively independent subcommittees; and, therefore, he has a stake in preserving a maximum of subcommittee autonomy. Through subcommittee independence comes subcommittee influence, and through subcommittee influence comes subcommittee member influence. The Appropriations Committee's decentralized structure of decision-making represents a response to the goal expectations of the House and of the individual Committee members.

COMMITTEE CHAIRMAN AND RANKING MINORITY MEMBER: ROLE AND ROLE BEHAVIOR

The special saliency of subcommittees directs attention immediately to the processes by which these subcommittees are created, their members selected, their jurisdiction defined, and their staffs chosen. For each of these allocative decisions the key figure is the Chairman of the Committee. And of secondary importance in such matters is the ranking minority member of the Committee. An examination of the Committee's role structure must begin with these two.

The position of Chairman and ranking minority member are created and filled not by the Committee but by the House. As such, they represent the continuing influence of the House on the Committee. In the first place, it is the party composition of the House which determines the party affiliation of the occupant. Secondly, it is the House norm of seniority which determines which member of each party shall occupy the position. The Chairman of the Appropriations Committee is that member of the House's majority party with the longest continuous service on the Committee. The ranking minority member is the man from the House minority party with the longest continuous service on the Appropriations Committee. Finally, the Chairman of the Committee is formally elected not by the Committee members but by the whole membership of the House. Those men who become Chairman and ranking minority member do so in compliance with House norms. Subsequent to their selection, they are granted a status in the parent chamber which carries with it prestige, prerogatives, and influence.

Committee members do not select their Chairmen, but they do share with the House as a whole in the definition of his role. House norms define certain aspects of every chairman's role. For example, the Appropriations

Committee Chairman is expected to call meetings of the Committee, fix its agenda, and preside over its meetings. He is expected to create subcommittees as he thinks necessary and to appoint the majority party members to each subcommittee. And it is within his prerogative to participate in the work of any or all subcommittees. He is expected to suggest (subject to formal appointment by the Speaker) the House conferees on appropriation bills. And it is within his prerogative to participate in the work of all appropriations conference committees. He is expected to exercise surveillance over the flow of Committee work, from hearings to markup, to full Committee. This may involve setting dollar targets for the subcommittees or setting a general "line" for the Committee in terms of its posture toward the budget. Or it may involve the timing of subcommittee activity. He decides when an appropriation bill will go to the House floor, and he negotiates with the Senate on the timing of conference committee meetings. He is expected to hire the Committee's staff members and supervise their work. And he is expected to be the major spokesman for the Committee to the House or to other groups in the environment. All of these expectations are fixed by the traditions of the House. Though a Committee majority can alter them, any wholesale changes would run against the most hallowed norms of the parent chamber.

These expectations define a role with a great potential for influence over Committee decisions and over the legislative life of its members. The degree to which the Chairman capitalizes on this potential will be affected, however, by the degree to which he plays his role in accordance with other, Committee-established norms. "If he can handle people and plays his cards right," said one subcommittee chairman, "he can have a lot of power. But if he can't carry the Committee with him, he'll lose it." He may choose subcommittee members, but he is expected to observe seniority in the advancement of members on the subcommittee and in his choice of subcommittee chairman. He is not expected to be arbitrary or vindictive or attempt to aggrandize his personal position at the expense of others. His surveillance over and participation in subcommittee work is expected to be minimal. He is expected to support subcommittee autonomy and display confidence in their decisions. He is expected, in all his actions, to be the exemplar of the Committee's style — a model for the imitation of others. He is expected, therefore, to work as hard as, if not harder than, any member of the Committee. He is expected to be as well informed as, if not better informed than, any member of the Committee about the subject matter and the technicalities of the appropriations process. He is expected to work harmoniously with others and compromise in case of differences. He is expected to consult with others in making key decisions — especially with the ranking minority member. Thus he is expected to tone down partisanship wherever possible.

137

These Committee expectations are not very precise, and they allow for plenty of slippage in the Chairman's role. What they do fix, in the minds of Committee members, are some outer boundaries of the role. The members agree that he should exercise his formal prerogatives, but they expect that he will observe certain Committee norms in so doing. Should his role behavior exceed the boundaries set by these norms, the implication is that the members would attempt to enforce conformity to the role as they have elaborated it. In sum, then, the role of the Chairman is defined by both House and Committee expectations; the Chairman's influence on Committee activity will depend upon the degree to which he meets both sets of expectations.

The role of ranking minority member of the Committee is set by the same amalgam of formal prerogatives and Committee norms. The ranking minority member is expected to designate the minority members of the various subcommittees. It is expected that he will work closely with the Chairman on problems, such as the scheduling and the timing of Committee work. It is expected that he will exercise surveillance over the work of subcommittees through contact with the minority members. It is expected that he will speak for the Committee's minority members when such a voice is required — to the Committee's majority, to the whole House, or to the members of his party in the House. But in the final accounting, his impact on the Committee's work is contingent upon his allegiance to the same set of norms which shape the role of his majority counterpart.

Subcommittee Selection

The central expectations of the Chairman's role and of the ranking minority member's role are those which carry a potential influence over subcommittee activity. Among these expectations, probably the most fundamental are those relating to subcommittee selection. Since, as we have seen, Republican House leaders add the special expectation that their senior man on Appropriations help select Republican members of the Committee, his ability to manipulate subcommittee assignments may be a somewhat less vital aspect of his role. But for the senior Democrat, whose role includes very modest expectations of influence over original selection, subcommittee selection is the main source of his intracommittee influence.

The expectation is clear that subcommittee selection is the prerogative of these two Committee leaders. And, in terms of role behavior, it appears that, whenever the Chairman or the ranking minority member has a particular reason for making an assignment and has determined on a course of action, it is done. Several Democratic subcommittee chairmen stated flatly that they had no influence whatsoever on the selection of men for their subcommittees. "I had as much to do with it as you did," said one. "He did it without consulting me at all. He put some new ones on last year, and the first I knew

138

about it was when I was introduced to them in the subcommittee hearing." A second subcommittee chairman grinned broadly to convey an implication of helplessness as he explained Chairman Cannon's procedure. "He'll come to me and say 'I've got a good man for that vacancy on your committee. What do you think?'" A third said that he had never even made any suggestions to Mr. Cannon one way or another because, "It wouldn't do any good . . . Mr. Cannon rules with an iron hand in this respect." In those cases where a Chairman has made up his mind, this judgment seems to be eminently correct.

But the Chairman will listen to the argument of subcommittee chairmen and occasionally yield. One subcommittee chairman recalled that he had been successful in keeping someone off his subcommittee. "I didn't want one fellow who wanted to get on. He was from west of the Mississippi and there are too many people from west of the Mississippi." Another claimed that "Sometimes I have been very influential in getting men on my subcommittee. I may go and tell the Chairman what I want. That's because of my personal relationship with Mr. Cannon. I've been here long enough and worked with him." But he added that he had been totally unsuccessful in an attempt to keep someone off the subcommittee. "I went to Mr. Cannon and told him I didn't like it." But the man was appointed anyway.

Mr. Taber exhibited the same pattern of behavior. Some of the ranking minority subcommittee members said that their wishes had been considered, but others claimed little or no influence. Said one, "When X was put on my subcommittee, Mr. Taber knew he was opposed to my views. He didn't consult me at all. It was a lack of courtesy on Mr. Taber's part." Another complained similarly, "I honestly feel that if I continue on, I'll have real trouble getting along with him [a new man on his subcommittee]. It's nothing he's done; it's just that his conception of what he's doing is so different from mine." Several of the Committee's senior Republicans, all ranking minority subcommittee men, tried without success on one occasion to influence assignments to the Defense Subcommittee. A less senior ranking subcommittee member recalled, "Carl Andersen and Ben Jensen and those fellows, they wanted to take it over. They made a fight of it last year, but old John kept things in line on that."

From the viewpoint of members seeking subcommittee membership, their leaders' control is equally evident. In many, but not all, cases individuals are asked to state subcommittee preferences. Some report that their requests were granted; others report that they were not. A plurality of members recall that they were "just put on" their subcommittees by the senior man on their side. On what basis, then, do the Chairman and ranking minority member allocate subcommittee positions? Doubtless some choices spring from personal motives — such could hardly be ruled out of any selection process. But

139

they are probably random and cancel each other out. The dominant patterns of subcommittee selection follow a system-oriented rationale. That is to say, the two patterns of subcommittee selection which are clearly identifiable represent attempts to structure the Committee internally so as to further the achievement of Committee goals.

One pattern follows the norm most frequently applied in the House to overall Committee selection — that men having a special interest in a given subject should serve on the Committee dealing with it. "Interest" may refer to constituency interest or to an individual's expertise or both. To the extent that subcommittee selection takes these factors into account, it follows the same pattern which places farm state Representatives on the Agriculture Committee, seacoast Representatives on the Merchant Marine and Fisheries Committee, urban Representatives on the Education and Labor Committee, reclamation state Representatives on the Interior and Insular Affairs Committee, bankers on the Banking and Currency Committee, or lawyers on the Judiciary Committee. Furthermore, one of the Committee's goals as set by the House is to serve the constituency interest of House members. And one of the Committee members' own goals is to serve their individual constituency interests. By placing men on those subcommittees in which they have a particular interest, the attainment of House and Committee member goal expectations may be facilitated.

For fifteen of the nineteen years from 1947 to 1965 a Democrat from a heavy cotton-producing area has been chairman of the Subcommittee on Agriculture. During two of the other four years the chairman was a Republican farmer from what he called "one of the few strictly agricultural congressional districts in America."[7] From 1947 to 1962, these men headed their respective party contingents on the subcommittee. A man representing a tobacco-growing area has sat on that same group from 1955 to 1965.[8] And a Representative from a fruit-producing area held subcommittee membership from 1947 to 1964. One of the few Committee members to have held an official position in the ranks of organized labor has been Chairman of the Subcommittee dealing with Department of Labor for fifteen of the past nineteen years. The only man on the Committee from the Tennessee Valley area has sat on the subcommittee handling the TVA budget from 1955 to 1965.[9] For fourteen of the past nineteen years, the subcommittee dealing with the Bonneville Power Administration has had a State of Washington representative on it. From 1955 to 1964, the Subcommittee on Military Construc-

[7] On the constituency benefits accruing from his service, see the remarks of Rep. Whitten in *Congressional Record*, Daily Edition, May 19, 1964, p. 10971.

[8] On the constituency benefits accruing from his service, see the article from the Nashville *Tennessean* as reprinted in *Congressional Record*, Daily Edition, March 12, 1963, pp. A1331–1332.

[9] 101 *Congressional Record*, p. 3874.

tion was led by a former consulting engineer, and in 1965, subcommittee leadership passed into the hands of a General in the Army Reserve. A man who was previously a state tax commissioner headed the Treasury Subcommittee for fourteen years until 1964. In all but four years since 1947, the subcommittee passing judgment on the Justice Department has had a former district attorney as its chairman.

An interest-dominated pattern of selection is common enough among the committees of the House. More than likely, interest will produce sympathy; and sympathy on the part of an appropriating committee will more than likely produce clientele-oriented appropriations decisions. Of course, this is one of the Appropriations Committee's goals. But clientele-oriented decisions (where clientele is taken to include both constituency or other reference group based on background) are likely to produce larger rather than smaller budgets. And the group's own dominant goal is to guard the Treasury through budget reductions. The interest-sympathy-leniency syndrome is perfectly acceptable for substantive committees. But it was to escape from this pattern that the revolution of 1885 was reversed in 1920. The pattern of mutual interest alliances between substantive committees doubling as appropriating committees, executive agencies, and constituency interest, it was felt, had produced steadily increasing appropriations and reduced the likelihood of critical scrutiny.

Following this line of reasoning and in pursuit of the Committee's budget-cutting goal, the Chairman and ranking minority member have employed a second, countervailing, pattern of subcommittee selection. That is, they have deliberately appointed individuals to subcommittee membership where no clientele interest exists. Members who feel no stake in the appropriations of an agency, it is felt, will not come to the job favorably disposed toward its budget and will be more likely to cut. Indeed, members with opposing clientele interest may be appointed to subcommittees in order to ensure budget reduction. Chairman Cannon, pointing to a portrait of a predecessor and namesake on his office wall, commented,

> When Uncle Joe was Chairman, he had a plan. If a man had a shipyard in his district or a naval base, he put him on the Interior Subcommittee, or if he had Interior projects in his district, he put him on Naval Affairs. . . . Sometimes we have to follow that practice. No member of the Committee should be obligated by his supporters to a certain appropriation. He should be able to take a judicial view of appropriations, a neutral view.

John Taber agreed:

> I'd rather put a man on a subcommittee where he doesn't have any special interests. If a man has a Navy yard in his district, I would not put him on [the] Military Construction [Subcommittee]. I'd rather not put a farmer on the Agriculture Subcommittee. He couldn't see things so clearly.

141

And Chairman Mahon has expressed his approval:

> Putting men on subcommittees where they have a vested interest in the subject matter should be avoided wherever possible. However, it is hardly possible to find anyone whose constituency interest is completely disassociated from all activities for which appropriations are made. The factor of objectivity is one of the considerations in making selections.

The end product of the "judicial view," "the neutral view," seeing things "clearly," or being "objective" is expected to be a cut rather than an increase in budget estimates.

Committee members recognize the same pattern. A Democratic subcommittee chairman said,

> You could ask Mr. Cannon to go on a subcommittee, but if you did he'd probably put you on some other committee, because he'd be afraid you were a partisan and would want to spend money.

And younger Democrats often stated the rule that, under Cannon, "The one sure way not to get an assignment is to ask him for it." "They tell me he tries to keep people away from a subcommittee where they have an axe to grind," said one newcomer. "Maybe that's why I'm on the subcommittee I'm on. I certainly don't have any axe to grind with the people we see." A second newcomer recalled going over to talk with a subcommittee chairman before a Committee meeting to solicit membership on his subcommittee: " 'Get away,' the subcommittee chairman told me. 'Don't let Cannon see you talking to me. You'll never get it that way.' " Similarly, a young Republican from the Far West, who sought and was denied membership on the Public Works Subcommittee, complained,

> There's a tendency, and I don't mean to be critical of John Taber, but he doesn't like to appoint you to a committee dealing with reclamation if you have reclamation in your district. I think that's wrong.

During the past nineteen years (from 1947 to 1965), the Subcommittee on the Interior Department has not had a chairman from west of the Mississippi River. For fourteen of those years, its leader was a Congressman from Youngstown, Ohio. Of the 108 man years of service on that subcommittee from 1947 to 1964, 81 man years have been served by men from east of the Mississippi, and only 27 man years by men from the area most served by that department.[10] Since 1955, the Bureau of Reclamation budget has been under the jurisdiction of the Subcommittee on Public Works. Of the 126 man years served on that subcommittee through 1964, 11 man years have been served by representatives of the 17 reclamation states and 115 man years have been

[10] In appointing two Republicans to the subcommittee in 1963, however, ranking minority member Rep. Ben Jensen changed the pattern for his side of the aisle. See Jensen's comments in *Congressional Record*, Daily Edition, April 2, 1963, p. 5137.

served by people in whose districts the Bureau does no work. These distributions are diametrically different from the membership pattern on the authorizing committee — the Committee on Interior and Insular Affairs — most all of whose members (20 out of 33 in 1964) come from the 17 reclamation states west of the Mississippi River.

On the basis of a 1960 district-by-district analysis of military installations, 3 of the 5 members of the Military Construction Subcommittee and 7 of the 14 members of the Defense Department Subcommittee were without a single military installation in their districts. The average number of military installations per member of the latter subcommittee was 1½; whereas the average number per member of the authorizing committee — the Armed Services Committee — was 3.[11] The Chairman of the Foreign Operations Subcommittee from 1955 to 1965 is one of the most devoted opponents of foreign aid in the House. And the two Republicans who have sat on the Subcommittee for Labor and Health, Education and Welfare Departments have, characteristically, opposed most of the legislation authorizing the program for which they make appropriations decisions.[12] In 1958, a New York City representative from East Harlem was put on the Agriculture Subcommittee; and when he was defeated for re-election in 1962, his Subcommittee slot was given to a man from a district in nearby Queens. Normally, once a person secures subcommittee membership, he rises in accordance with seniority norms in subcommittee status. One subcommittee member recalled, however, that Mr. Cannon removed him from a subcommittee assignment shortly after he had received it.

> The reason he took me off was because I was in favor of the program [under the subcommittee's jurisdiction]. I asked him to put me back on the subcommittee last year and the Speaker even intervened for me. But Cannon said he had to put someone else on the committee. That's crazy.

Subcommittee selectors have deliberately followed this balance wheel pattern of appointment (and in a rare case, removal) in an attempt to buttress the primacy of budget-cutting while at the same time meeting the House-prescribed goal of program support and the Committee's self-prescribed goal of constituency service.

Subcommittee Manipulation

Two additional sets of expectations expand the opportunity for the Chairman and ranking minority member to influence subcommittee membership. The first is their acknowledged prerogative of deciding which subcommittees

[11] *Congressional Quarterly*, March 24, 1961, pp. 463–478.
[12] See 103 *Congressional Record*, p. 4412 and 108 *Congressional Record*, p. 4750 for the remarks of Reps. Laird and Michel.

they will join. Officially, they sit as chairman or ranking minority member of one subcommittee and, perhaps, a regular member of another. House norms also grant to the Chairman the right to sit ex officio as a voting member of each and every subcommittee — which he does. Furthermore, the Chairman, for so long as Cannon and Taber alternated in this position, extended the same right to the ranking minority member. In 1963, when Ben Jensen became ranking minority member, Cannon declined to grant him the ex officio status. But George Mahon and Frank Bow resumed the Cannon-Taber tradition in 1965. Thus the Chairman and ranking minority member extend their personal influence. Committee norms hold, however, that their role as ex officio subcommittee members be played with great restraint. And, since the two men place themselves on active duty as regular working members of at least one subcommittee, they function in large part within the subcommittee framework.

A second set of norms surrounding the Chairman's role further expands his potential for influence. The Chairman, working, perhaps, with the ranking minority member, is expected to create and abolish subcommittees, to fix their jurisdiction, and to determine the number of members for each subcommittee. By manipulating these factors, the Chairman influences subcommittee membership and, hence, subcommittee decisions. It gives him more opportunity to create suitable subcommittee positions for himself and for others. When the Chairman uses these additional sources of his influence it has been, again, to maintain a balance between the goals of program and project support and budget reduction.

One area in which constituency-induced pressure to appropriate money has always been strong is that involving public works projects. Membership on the subcommittee is highly valued for the influence it brings in the chamber — which probably accounts (see Table 4.1) for the out-sized number of members relative to the size of the budget being handled. From 1947 to 1962 Mr. Cannon and Mr. Taber (except for one two-year period) took membership for themselves on the subcommittee dealing with the Corps of Army Engineers. In 1955, with the acquiescence of Mr. Taber, Chairman Cannon created a new Public Works Subcommittee and gathered under its jurisdiction the budgets for the Army Corps of Engineers, the Bureau of Reclamation, and the Atomic Energy Commission plus all of the agencies dealing with public power. (See Table 4.1.) He then assumed the chairmanship of the Subcommittee. Representative Taber, too, designated himself as a minority member of the Subcommittee and remained on it until he retired in 1962. In 1963, the new ranking minority member of the Committee, Mr. Jensen, became the ranking minority member of this Subcommittee. A student of public works legislation has noted, predictably, that "the Corps (of

144

Engineers) does not enjoy the same uncritical support from the Appropriations subcommittees that it does from the Public Works Committees."[13]

Committee leaders have positioned themselves in this manner partly to devote personal attention to holding down pork-barrel spending. For a while, Mr. Cannon experimented with an internal subcommittee organization to help achieve the desired goals. He divided the Public Works group into panels: one panel for the public power agencies and three geographical panels — one to pass on all projects in the East, one for Midwestern projects, and one for the Far West. As members of each panel, he and Mr. Taber then designated men who had no immediate interest. The chairman of the Far Western panel, for instance, was a man from Tennessee and it had as its members Representatives from Rhode Island, Illinois, Iowa, and New Jersey. The chairman of the Eastern panel was from Minnesota, and the chairman of the public power panel was from Detroit.[14] And to further prevent "interested decisions," as we have already noted, Westerners were kept off this subcommittee to begin with. Mr. Cannon's main effort was to reduce constituency-induced leniency in an area fraught with pressures to increase budgets. But, as a secondary theme, it must be noted that public power represented one of Mr. Cannon's own great legislative passions and the area in which he was most willing to spend money. His desire to sit in judgment of the public power agencies and the Atomic Energy Commission (in the days of Dixon-Yates) represents the sympathetic, clientele-oriented side of his committee activity.

Another subcommittee which has long received extra solicitude from the committee's leadership is the one which appropriates for the foreign aid program. Both Mr. Cannon and Mr. Taber viewed the program as a place where potentially great savings to the taxpayer could be made and where large budget reductions were possible. When he became Committee Chairman in 1953, Mr. Taber chose to become the chairman of this Subcommittee on Foreign Operations. And he remained on the Subcommittee as its ranking minority member until his retirement. Mr. Cannon placed himself on the Subcommittee, too, in 1953. And he always maintained a Southern, anti-aid majority on the Democratic side. Table 4.1, for example, shows this Subcommittee with the most lopsided Democratic majority of all. Cannon removed himself four years later, however, once he had become convinced that with Otto Passman (D., La.) as Subcommittee chairman, a maximum budget-cutting pattern would prevail on the Subcommittee. At the

[13] Earle Wallace, "The Politics of River Basin Appropriations: A Case Study of the Roanoke River Basin," unpublished manuscript (University of North Carolina, 1959), p. 168.

[14] 101 *Congressional Record*, p. 8324.

145

time Passman was selected in 1955, the man slated to become Subcommittee chairman via seniority was representative Vaughn Gary, who had been chairman of the Subcommittee in 1951–1952 and its ranking minority member from 1953–1954. But Cannon wanted Passman and so he announced a new Committee norm — that no member could be chairman of two subcommittees. This ruling eliminated Gary, who had long been senior Democrat on another subcommittee. It also eliminated the next senior Subcommittee Democrat, Representative John Rooney. And it surprised Passman. "I didn't ask for the job. I didn't know I had the job until I read about it in the papers."[15] Mr. Passman is a man who has voted against every foreign aid authorization since the Greek-Turkish loan and who acknowledges that "in principle I am very much against foreign aid." In view of the very considerable publicity attending the budget-cutting activities of Mr. Passman, it needs to be emphasized that his selection as Subcommittee member and his elevation to the chairmanship follows one perfectly normal committee pattern. In 1965, Chairman Mahon definitely "liberalized" the membership of the Passman subcommittee (replacing 2 pro-aid Democrats with 2 anti-aid Democrats) in an attempt to balance program support against what he regarded as excessive budget-cutting.

Mr. Taber's choice of becoming the ranking minority member of the Labor, Health, Education and Welfare Subcommittee from 1956 to 1960 reflected his desire to help hold down budgets in areas like Public Health Service, where an extraordinary rash of spending had broken out. Taber's 1951 choice to take membership on the Defense Subcommittee coincided with the outbreak of the Korean War and an upsurge of defense spending. Table 4.2 shows the way in which Representatives Cannon and Taber distributed themselves in terms of their working subcommittee memberships.

The Chairman can and has manipulated subcommittee structure and, hence, subcommittee assignments in other ways in an effort to promote budget-cutting activity. In 1956, for example, he abolished a long-standing system of three panels — one each for the Air Force, Army, and Navy — on the Defense Subcommittee. Believing that a long acquaintanceship had produced evidence of the interest-sympathy-leniency pattern, he moved to sever the association between each subcommittee panel and its particular armed service. A veteran member of the subcommittee explained,

> Interservice rivalry in the Pentagon was being transferred to the panels over here. The Navy panel wouldn't let the Army or the Air Force get anything they couldn't get. The Chairman got upset.

[15] *Washington Evening Star*, April 3, 1963.

In 1963, Cannon abolished the Subcommittee on the Commerce Department and Related Government Matters and returned jurisdiction over Commerce Department appropriations to the subcommittee handling the State and Justice Department budgets. A member of the latter subcommittee said,

> I heard he wasn't satisfied with the composition of the Commerce Committee. He didn't think the Commerce Department was being watched closely enough. They were getting too buddy-buddy. So he wiped it out.

Another example of jurisdictional maneuvering for budget-cutting ends occurred on the Civil Defense shelter program. In 1961, the President transferred part of the Civil Defense shelter program to the Defense Department. One intended effect of the transfer was to take the program away from the jurisdiction of the Independent Offices Subcommittee which had been hostile to it and place it under the jurisdiction of the more sympathetic Defense Department Subcommittee. Mr. Cannon countered by specifically ordering the Civil Defense appropriations back to the less sympathetic Independent Offices Subcommittee.

In 1958, the Chairman established a special Subcommittee on Deficiencies to deal with all deficiency (requests for money to enable an agency to finish out the current year's activities) and supplemental (requests added after the budget has been submitted to cover the next fiscal year) budget requests. The recent history of the committee was this. In the 80th Congress there was a separate Subcommittee on Deficiencies populated by the Committee's most senior members. In the next two Congresses its jurisdiction was expanded to include control over Army Civil Functions (Corps of Engineers). But in the 83rd Congress the processing of agency deficiency and supplemental requests had been turned over to the subcommittees which handled their regular appropriations. In the 86th Congress, because he perceived the close relationship as producing budget leniency, Mr. Cannon returned to the older arrangement. He and Mr. Taber staffed the new subcommittee from among the toughest budget-cutters on the Committee. In January of 1964, however, when Mr. Cannon believed that the Subcommittee (headed by Texas Representative Albert Thomas) was prepared to be especially lenient with President Johnson's $2.2 billion supplemental request (see Chapter Five), he abolished the Deficiencies group. The abolition of the armed services panels, the death of the Commerce Subcommittee, the Civil Defense jurisdictional maneuver, and the re-institution and demise of the Subcommittee on Deficiencies point up, again, the fact that the Committee's own goal expectations have a marked effect on the Committee's internal structure. The attempt to ensure Treasury guardianship — while admitting the necessities of program and project support — is reflected in the manipulation of subcommittee membership and subcommittee structure.

147

TABLE 4.2

SUBCOMMITTEE MEMBERSHIPS HELD BY COMMITTEE CHAIRMEN
AND RANKING MINORITY MEMBERS

YEARS	MEMBERS				
	Clarence Cannon (Chmn. 1949 to 1952; 1955 to 1964 Rank. min. 1947–1948; 1953–1954)	John Taber (Chmn. 1947–1948; 1953–1954 Rank. min. 1949–1952; 1955–1962)	Ben Jensen (Rank. min. 1963–1964)	George Mahon (Chmn. 1964–)	Frank Bow (Rank. min. 1965–)
1947–1948	1. Agriculture (Rank. min.) 2. Deficiencies	1. Deficiencies (Chmn.) (ex officio all others)			
1949–1950	1. Deficiences and Army Civil Functions (Chmn.) (ex officio all others)	1. Deficiencies and Army Civil Functions (Rank. min.)			
1951–1952	1. Deficiencies and Army Civil Functions (Chmn.) (ex officio all others)	1. Armed Services (Rank min.) (ex officio all others)*			
1953–1954	1. Civil Functions and Military Construction (Rank. min.) 2. Agriculture 3. Foreign Aid (ex officio all others)*	1. Foreign Aid (Chmn.) 2. Civil Functions and Military Construction (ex officio all others)			
1955–1956	1. Public Works (Chmn.) 2. Foreign Aid (ex officio all others)	1. Foreign Aid (Rank. min.) 2. Labor-HEW (Rank. min.) 3. Public Works (ex officio all others)*			
1957–1958	1. Public Works (Chmn.) (ex officio all others)	1. Foreign Aid (Rank. min.) 2. Labor-HEW (Rank. min.) 3. Public Works (ex officio all others)*			
1959–1960	1. Public Works (Chmn.) (ex officio all others)	1. Foreign Aid (Rank. min.) 2. Public Works (ex officio all others)*			

TABLE 4.2

SUBCOMMITTEE MEMBERSHIPS HELD BY COMMITTEE CHAIRMEN AND RANKING MINORITY MEMBERS (*Continued*)

1961–1962	1. Public Works (Chmn.) (ex officio all others)	1. Foreign Aid (Rank. min.) 2. Public Works (ex officio all others)*			
1963–1964	1. Public Works (Chmn.) (ex officio all others)		1. Public Works (Rank. min.)		
1964–1965				1. Defense (Chmn.) (ex officio all others)	1. State, Justice, Commerce (Rank. min.) (ex officio all others)*

* By invitation of the Chairman

In the light of the two main patterns of subcommittee membership and organization, some persistent sources of Appropriations Committee–legislative committee conflict can be better understood. Some — though not all — Appropriations subcommittees are deliberately peopled with members who are either disinterested in or opposed to the programs which they vote to "support." The substantive legislative committees are more likely to be populated by members having a special interest (constituency or ideological or professional) in promoting programs in their policy area. In such cases, the economy-oriented behavior of the Appropriations subcommittee is likely to conflict with the program support-oriented behavior of the legislative committee. In those cases where the Appropriations subcommittees are most heavily weighted with members who themselves have interests to promote, the subcommittee may find itself competing with the legislative committee for policy leadership. In either case, the Appropriations Committee can and may reap the antagonism of the legislative committees of "the House."

Staff Selection

The role of Chairman includes, as it does on every House committee, norms which accord him important controls over the staff of the committee. The Appropriations Committee employs two separate and distinct kinds of staff — one a permanent professional staff and the other a temporary survey and investigations staff. Both are under the ultimate control of the Chairman. He hires them, allocates their tasks, and supervises their work. Their combined expenditures, for 1963, totalled almost $1 million. His prerogatives in

149

shaping these aspects of Committee structure carry considerable potential for influence. And he plays his role, again, in such a way as to promote the goals of the Committee.

The regular Appropriations Committee staff consists of 20–25 full-time professional employees — officially designated as "staff assistants" but known in the Committee as "clerks." Their salaries, fixed by the Chairman, ranged from $10,000 to $19,000 per year in 1963.[16] As described by the Chairman, the criteria for their original selection includes, "former service in some budgetary capacity in a federal department . . . [and] they must be technical, scholarly, objectively minded men and, of course, men of immaculate integrity."[17] Party affiliation is not a criterion of appointment. "I have not known at the time of appointment — and I do not know today — to what political party . . . a single one of [them] belongs,"[18] said Mr. Cannon. This means that the staff does not change with changes in party control of the committee. "The staff of the Committee on Appropriations," in Cannon's words, "is permanent. It is made up of career men who serve for life . . . we have our own system of civil service."[19]

Of the 15 men on the staff in 1961, 9 had been in budgetary work in the executive branch. They had been recruited from the Departments of Agriculture (2), Navy, Post Office, and Defense, from the Atomic Energy Commission, the Central Intelligence Agency, the Federal Housing Administration, and the Civil Aeronautics Administration. The remaining 6 men had varied backgrounds — as FBI agent, civil engineer, labor department employee, assistant to a member of Congress, public school teacher, and graduate student in public administration. The rationale for the budgetary experience pattern is provided by Cannon. "In order to know how to tear down a budget the clerk must have had experience in building up a budget." The staff, it seems clear, is expected to assist in the task of budget reduction. In the hiring process, great care is taken to eliminate anyone who might have a personal interest to promote. This is in part the reason why, in Mr. Cannon's words, "No one who applies for a position is ever appointed . . . any man who makes application to us for one of these jobs thereby automatically eliminates himself from consideration."[20]

The professional staff works for the Chairman of the Committee. In formal organizational terms, their work is supervised by a person designated by the Chairman — variously entitled Chief Clerk or Staff Director or Clerk

---

[16] *Congressional Record*, Daily Edition, July 17, 1963, pp. 12102–12103; January 24, 1964, pp. 1122–1123.

[17] *Congressional Record*, Daily Edition, April 17, 1962, pp. 6319–6320.

[18] *Ibid.* See also Committee on Rules, *Hearings on H.R. 7888 and S. 913*, 82nd Congress, 2nd Session (Washington: U.S. Government Printing Office, 1952), p. 38.

[19] *Ibid.*

[20] *Congressional Record*, Daily Edition, April 17, 1962, pp. 6319–6320.

and Staff Director, which title was for a while given to two co-equal men. This top staff man (or men) works on behalf of the Chairman in a room in the Capitol, H-218, sandwiched between the main Appropriations Committee office and the Chairman's office. The other staff members, however, are assigned to the various subcommittees and carry on their day-to-day work in association with these subgroups. Staff allocation is suggested by the Chief Clerk and approved by the Chairman, usually in consultation with the sub-committee chairman involved. Thus the ordinary committee clerk has a formal allegiance to the Chairman and a working allegiance to his Subcom-mittee chairman. Should his two superiors have different expectations, the problem of role conflict arises. One clerk recalls,

> When I first went to work for my subcommittee chairman, he said, "Who are you responsible to?" I said, "I work for you and for Mr. Cannon. I'll work for you 100 per cent of the time until your views conflict with those of Mr. Cannon. When they do, I work for Mr. Cannon. If that time comes, I'll let you know.

Since, however, the Chairman is expected to observe the norm of minimal interference in subcommittee affairs, staff members do not find the problem a serious one. Two of them commented:

> Sometimes I find myself in a bind because I know Mr. Cannon wants some-thing and my subcommittee chairman feels differently. I'm caught in a cross-fire but usually it isn't too bad and I can resolve it pretty easily.

"Your boss is the subcommittee chairman. And, of course, the Chairman of the committee; but that isn't much of a conflict there." Committee clerks play their role as a part of the subcommittee structure.

In making staff member assignments, the Committee leaders follow a pattern very similar to that of subcommittee selection. Expertise is assured by choosing as clerks men who know how "to tear down a budget." But they are not allowed to operate on the same budget they worked on in their executive branch job. A staff member explained that

> When I came here the Chief Clerk told me, "It's a policy that no staff man will work on the agency he came from." And that's a good policy; he'd have an axe to grind one way or another. Either he would have some friends in the agency he'd like to help or someone he was mad at when he left and that wouldn't be healthy.

The aim is to guard against both excessive hostility and leniency — but the main effort is to hedge against the possibility of the special interest-sympathy-leniency syndrome from developing on the part of the staff.

> We don't assign a person to a subcommittee which handles the department where he used to work. He might be too friendly and too soft. On the other

151

hand, he might be more familiar with the work of the agency and know where the soft spots are. There are two schools of thought on that and the arguments have gone on for a long time. One chairman thought a man had reached his peak of usefulness after three or four years — that he'd begun to be soft. I know some places in my old agency that need clearing up, but on the other hand I was very sympathetic with their whole program.

Staff selection operates as another internal structural device for shoring up the budget-cutting activity and guarding against its excessive erosion by clientele-oriented program support activity.

In view of the fact that Congress grants the Committee an open-ended budget for professional staff, the size of the group is determined by the Chairman. He has deliberately kept it small, but has supplemented it by allocating to each subcommittee chairman and to each ranking minority member a sum of money with which to hire a "clerk-stenographer" of his own choice. This enables the members of the Committee with the heaviest duties to augment their regular office staff. This person will work in the congressman's office on subcommittee-related matters or in normal office routine. In 1963, the Committee carried 26 such "clerk-stenographers" on its payroll and paid amounts of money to them ranging from $500 to $8,600.[21] Though their salaries are paid by the Committee, they are not in any sense a part of the Committee's staff. They are not allowed to work in the Committee's offices nor attend any of the Committee meetings. One of these extra-staff individuals is titled "Clerk to the Minority," but he is housed in the Cannon Building where he does research — and where he stays. The salaries of these people are a kind of special subvention allocated by the Chairman to those Committee members who are expected to carry the heaviest work load.

In addition to its relatively small permanent staff, the Committee has maintained, since 1943, a larger yet more temporary investigations staff. Whereas a permanent Committee clerk works with a subcommittee in all its operations, an investigative staff man deals with particular problems in particular agencies. Prior to 1943, the Committee had been "without a staff on which we could call upon for examination and study of pre-appropriations matters."[22] House Resolution 20, later incorporated into the Legislative Reorganization Act, empowered the Committee to conduct such investigations. At the official request of the Chairman and ranking minority Committee member plus the chairman and ranking minority member of a subcommittee, temporary investigators are hired to obtain information for the Committee. Committee leaders stress the "wholly nonpartisan" character of this procedure. In the words of Chairman Mahon, "No investigative study is made without the approval of two members of each party. As a

[21] See footnote 16 *supra*.
[22] 89 *Congressional Record*, p. 887.

152

matter of fact there is a minimum of partisanship in the Appropriations Committee."[23] The intent, as expressed at the time the staff was inaugurated, was to recruit "entirely from Civil Service positions in the various departments."[24] When an investigator (or team of investigators) has forwarded his report to the Chairman, he will return to his regular job in the executive branch.

The Director of the Surveys and Investigations Staff is an FBI agent, loaned to the Committee for a three-year hitch. The first two years he serves as an Assistant Director and then as Director. These two men come, says one FBI official, "from among our top flight investigators . . . men with at least 15 years of experience in every type of investigation." They earn approximately $15,000 a year, and have an office staff of 5 or 6 people. It is they who assign specific investigators to specific projects. From 1962 to 1964, for example, the investigative staff worked over 100 man years and produced 67 separate reports.[25] As for the temporary investigators themselves, more of them come from the FBI than anywhere else. In 1963, the Committee listed 57 investigators, 28 of whom were FBI agents.[26] The rest were permanent employees of nearly every major executive agency. Sometimes, though not usually, the investigator comes from the same agency that is being investigated.

More than the permanent staff members, whose bread and butter attachment is to the subcommittee and its chairman, the investigative staff is controlled by the full Committee Chairman. Different Chairmen have implemented slightly different conceptions of the investigative staff. But they have pursued the intent of the 1943 resolution — which they all supported — as stated by Mr. Cannon. "The purpose of the resolution is to promote economy. Its object is the retrenchment of expenditures and the reduction of disbursements of funds from the United States Treasury."[27] Mr. Cannon consistently favored the original idea of a temporary staff. Mr. Taber, however, looked with favor on a more permanent arrangement. In the Republican-controlled 80th Congress, Taber set up a permanent investigation and research staff, drawing part-time assistance from men outside the government. A veteran committee Republican described it:

> We had . . . a staff of some 10 permanent investigators with FBI and General Accounting background. We had in addition some 25 part-time members on the staff, including outstanding leaders in the accounting pro-

[23] Joint Committee on the Organization of the Congress, *Hearings on the Organization of Congress*, 89th Congress, 1st Session (Washington: U.S. Government Printing Office, 1965), p. 1732.

[24] 89 *Congressional Record*, p. 887.

[25] *Hearings on the Organization of Congress, op. cit.*, pp. 1631–1637, 1651.

[26] See footnote 16 *supra*.

[27] 89 *Congressional Record*, p. 886.

fession and in the research profession throughout the length and breadth of this country . . . numbered among these men were 10 of the country's outstanding accountants picked as a special committee by the American Institute of Accountants.[28]

The Republicans defended their system on the grounds that it produced greater budget reductions than ever before.[29] When the Democrats assumed control, Mr. Cannon reverted to the previous system. When he resumed the chairmanship in the 83rd Congress, Mr. Taber retained the existing system but supplemented it with a staff of his own choosing recruited mostly from outside the government. He hired 75 business and management experts to do a six-week special investigation called "Operation Economy." He reverted after that to the existing pattern — which has remained intact ever since.

House members, who have granted the Committee an expandable budget for their staff purposes, sometimes urge the Committee to increase its permanent staff. Chairman Cannon defended his idea of a temporary, flexible staff. He defended it, first, on the grounds that it can do the job just as expertly, efficiently, and impartially as a permanent staff. "The Committee on Appropriations has the best experts that can be secured, the best trained and the most efficient that could be supplied." And he relied on the reputation of the FBI to carry his assertion that, "It is in every respect impartial and non-partisan, the fairest and most experienced and best trained system of investigation to be found anywhere in the world today." Second, Cannon believed that the current type of staff is more easily kept under the control of the Committee. "They are available in unlimited number. That is the advantage of our system. It is elastic. It can be expanded or contracted."[30] A permanent staff, on the other hand, might become a "Frankenstein which could not be controlled or dislodged."[31] He further believed that a temporary staff is less likely to develop the potentially dangerous interest-sympathy-leniency syndrome:

> What happens when you put men permanently on the staff? They get careless, they get lazy, they develop friendships with the departments . . . they develop a camaraderie with the members of the Committee and get their salaries raised. Everybody downtown knows them. When they enter the door, the word is passed around, "Here comes that man from the Committee."[32]

[28] 96 *Congressional Record*, p. 4699.
[29] 96 *Congressional Record*, pp. 4701 ff.
[30] 97 *Congressional Record*, pp. 2803, 2805–2807.
[31] 89 *Congressional Record*, p. 887.
[32] 97 *Congressional Record*, p. 2804.

154

The investigations staff — like the permanent staff — has been structured by the Committee so as to facilitate the goal of budget-cutting and Committee guardianship of the Treasury.

In resisting a substantial expansion in permanent staff personnel, the Committee's chairmen have argued, too, that they presently have all the staff help they can effectively use. The Committee regularly receives all reports issued by the General Accounting Office, and uses the GAO to make special studies. This agency keeps accounts and conducts audits of all executive branch expenditures and reports them (at the rate of about 250 a year) to the Congress. The Committee may find these helpful in pinpointing waste and inefficiency. The GAO, indeed, prepares one summary report especially for the Appropriations Committee. Chairman Mahon explained,

> We have had them in addition prepare for us material, each year, which is embraced in this *Report to the Committee on Appropriations, House of Representatives, Selected Significant Audit Findings.* It is a report of "significant findings" whatever it might be. One volume is in the area of defense and one volume is in the area of non-defense . . . They help us. They help direct the attention of the Committee to areas of their regular audit reports that might be especially important to us.[33]

The Committee's chairmen have felt that its permanent staff plus these ad hoc staff extensions are capable of meeting the Committee's information needs. George Mahon has looked a bit more favorably on the expansion of the permanent staff. But his basic stance is strikingly similar to that of his predecessor. In 1965, he said,

> I think we are somewhat understaffed and have been for years . . . I think we will increase our staff as we go along, and should, but I would like to say unequivocally that a real large staff is not the answer to our problems.[34]

Insofar as the Committee can control its destiny in such matters, the existing staff arrangements seem likely to endure.

Committee and Subcommittee Participation

When the full Committee holds its organization meeting and adopts its rules at the beginning of each Congress, the Chairman has an opportunity to confront the whole group. He may say something about the allocative decisions to be made by himself and the ranking minority member — the list of subcommittees, the membership of each subcommittee, the jurisdiction of each subcommittee, the assignment of the permanent staff to

---

[33] *Hearings on the Reorganization of Congress, op. cit.,* pp. 1638, 1734. See also p. 1754.

[34] *Ibid.,* p. 1630.

subcommittees, and any other new staff arrangement. He also has the chance, before the Committee breaks down into its working subgroups, to remind the members of their broadest goals and, if he wishes, to set overall targets for them to shoot at. He may, for example, urge each subcommittee to keep its recommendations for next year below the current year's appropriation. And he will always charge the subcommittee chairmen to produce appropriations figures that are lower than the budget estimate. What he customarily tells them is something like this:

> The budget traditionally required the Committee on Appropriations to conserve the taxpayers money and protect the capital and national Treasury. We always take the position that we should not exceed the budget. We judge the efficiency of chairmen of subcommittees by the extent to which they are able to cut the budget. We take for granted that under the circumstances unless there is some special emergency each subcommittee will report a bill under the budget estimate. The budget estimate is supposed to be the ceiling.[35]

The ranking minority member may also use the full committee as a forum in which to transmit some overall sense of purpose to the members.[36] The Republican Committee members may meet by themselves once or twice and never more than three times a year to discuss their posture and strategy or both. But the Democrats have not held a caucus for at least a dozen years. However, "Two or three times a year the Chairman [Cannon] will call in the subcommittee chairmen and talk to us," said one Committee elder. "But that depends on his wishes. It's not regularized. He may talk to us about the budget generally or about how we have to hold down or about something special that has come up."[37]

What the leaders never say when they confront the Committee is as important as anything they do say. Budgets must be reduced, the Treasury must be saved — yes. But the subcommittees are left free to decide for themselves where the cuts shall be made, how much shall be cut, and by what combination of choices the Treasury is to be saved. The prime concern of the Committee's leaders is that subcommittee totals be lower than total estimates for the agencies under their jurisdiction. It is easiest, of course, to achieve such overall reductions by cutting each segment of the budget. But some segments can be increased if others are reduced. And the extent of reduction or

---

[35] *Congressional Record*, Daily Edition, September 26, 1961, p. 20071. See also 96 *Congressional Record*, p. 4616.

[36] Full Committee meetings held at the beginning of a session with the Secretary of the Treasury and the Director of the Budget are also useful for this purpose. Such meetings were held in the late 1950's and early 1960's, stopped for a few years and resumed in 1966. See *Congressional Record*, Daily Edition, January 24, 1966, p. 871.

[37] When he was Chairman, John Taber did the same thing. See Committee on Appropriations, *Hearings on Labor Department Appropriation for 1948*, 80th Congress, 1st Session (Washington: U.S. Government Printing Office, 1947), p. 237.

increase can vary. Within the goals set by Committee leaders, therefore, a wide range of alternative courses of action remain. And as far as the leaders are concerned, a subcommittee is normally free to choose among them.

The two leaders do not wholly withdraw from subcommittee decision-making. Since about 1951 (with the exception of the 88th Congress), both have been ex officio members of all subcommittees. Committee norms prescribe, however, that the leaders' intervention be minimal and governed by great restraint. They are expected to exercise a close and continuing influence only over those subcommittees on which they choose to sit as regular members. The leaders do participate ex officio in the executive sessions where the subcommittee marks up the bill and as conferees on each bill. They are, therefore, physically present on the two occasions when the subcommittee makes its most important decisions. In those instances where they choose to intervene actively, they can probably have an important impact on subcommittee decision-making. In a more general sense, their very presence at so many different points in the process magnifies their potential for influence. In a Committee where jurisdictions are splintered, where information is de-centralized, and where decision-making units operate autonomously, only the Chairman and ranking minority member comprehend the whole. They and only they can possess a breadth of vision, sources of information, and a degree of participation that encompasses the full scope of the Appropriations Committee's work.

In markup sessions, their role behavior appears to demonstrate both restraint and influence. "Sometimes they inject themselves into the discussion, and sometimes they just listen to the members," said a member. John Taber described their mode of operation as one which followed committee norms against arbitrariness:

> We don't force them to do anything. If we see that they are doing something that is wrong, we tell them frankly and most of the time they agree. We don't bludgeon them or anything. There are lots of ways to tell a fellow he's wrong other than by using a bludgeon.

And a Committee member described Mr. Cannon's role behavior similarly,

> He's very faithful and attends every subcommittee markup. He doesn't come in there to dictate. He doesn't make recommendations or suggest figures or anything like that. He may say, "Our experience with this item has been thus and so," or something like that.

Most of the time, the Committee's leaders play the role of brooding omnipresence — brooding, usually, on behalf of greater budget reduction than the subcommittee members may be inclined to make. "They never miss a markup," said one subcommittee chairman, "and if you get extravagant,

157

you've got two pretty sharp boys riding on your neck." A second subcommittee chairman emphasized that when the two men do act in his subcommittees, they maximize their influence by acting in concert:

> Of course, Mr. Cannon and Mr. Taber are always in favor of the low figure — always looking for a cut. In all the markup sessions I've attended, I've never seen any friction between Mr. Cannon and Mr. Taber. They may disagree in full Committee but not in subcommittee.

Given the three to two or four to three makeup of most subcommittees prior to 1965 (eleven out of fourteen in Mr. Taber's last year, 1962), the joint intervention of Chairman and ranking minority member constituted a potential swing vote.

Any very palpable intervention, practiced or promised, stirs jealous resentment of subcommittee members. In 1947, Chairman Taber exercised influence over his Interior Subcommittee simply by threatening to intervene and to vote should they fail to follow his budget-reducing injunctions. Subcommittee members registered their disapproval by nicknaming Taber the "Big Bad Wolf." On such occasions, members are protesting what they see as a lack of respect for their expertise and, hence, their relegation to "second class citizenship."[38] Their resentment may be centered on markup activity:

> During the markup of the bills, we discovered we had another member of the committee, the gentleman from Missouri [Mr. Cannon]. He had not sat for one single minute in the hearings on this bill. This bill, as it comes to the floor of the House is, in effect, the Cannon bill, not only in amount but in language.[39]

When Chairman Cannon did intervene to promote budget-cutting, a favorite tactic was to propose an outrageous reduction and then bargain to a compromise. In the process, however, he predictably incurred the displeasure — even wrath — of his subcommittee chairman. And the key person in effecting an eventual compromise was very likely to be the ranking minority member of the subcommittee. Two instances, related at some length by key participants, fall into this pattern. A Democratic subcommittee chairman recalled one of them:

> Mr. Cannon always supported his subcommittees, but once in a while he got some funny ideas of his own. I went to Mr. Cannon before our markup once and said, "Mr. Chairman, don't you think we ought to get the members on

[38] 96 *Congressional Record*, p. 4939.
[39] 95 *Congressional Record*, p. 3418. Where Mr. Cannon's own interests such as public power were involved, his intervention during markup would militate against reductions. One such markup came to light, in which Mr. Cannon protected several Interior Department bureaus. But he was forced, late in the day, to catch a train for Missouri. His departure cost the Southwestern Power Administration 47 million dollars. 96 *Congressional Record*, p. 5543.

our side together before the markup and decide what we are going to propose?" He said, "Oh, no, we'll take care of it in the committee, don't worry." Then when we got in the markup, he said, "I make a motion that we cut the estimate two billion dollars." That would have wrecked the program. So I talked around and stalled and waited until we got some bells for a quorum call or something, and then adjourned the meeting. I got ahold of the ranking minority member and said to him, "You know we can't have a cut like that. It will wreck the program." He and I always worked well together. We straightened it out.

A Republican ranking minority member of a different subcommittee described another incident in which he argued for a $400 million reduction in a certain item and was supported by Chairman Cannon. The subcommittee chairman, however, was opposed to any cut and, during the first markup session, he "banged the gavel and adjourned the meeting."

The next morning when I went over to the Committee room, there was the old man sitting in the hall waiting for me. I said, "What are we going to do, Mr. Chairman?" He said, "We'll do the best we can." We went into the meeting together. "Mr. Cannon made my motion for me — a $400 million cut. The vote was 4 Democrats on one side and 3 Republicans plus Cannon on the other side. We were deadlocked. Then the subcommittee chairman offered a cut of $50 million. And again, the vote was 3 Republicans plus Cannon versus the subcommittee chairman and the other 3 Democrats. The Democrats were voting with their chairman but against the big Chairman. Then Cannon started to make another motion and the subcommittee chairman said, "I don't recognize you." And Cannon said, "I've got a right to make a motion and I make a motion." And the subcommittee chairman said, "I don't recognize you." And they started to go at it shaking their fists at each other. I know the subcommittee chairman pretty well and so I turned to him and spoke in a low voice with all the home spun tones I could get. The old man is deaf and can't hear you all the time — though you never can tell whether he hears you or not. I said, "Let's not let our emotions get the better of us. You've got to be reasonable. If you don't cut this budget someone else is going to do it for you." So I proposed a $200 million cut and it was voted in. The full Committee accepted it, the House did, and so did the Senate.

In each of these two cases, the influence of the Committee Chairman, the resentment of the subcommittee chairman, the mediation of the ranking minority member, and the desire of all concerned for compromise are constants.

Similar protests may be made when the Chairman exercises his prerogatives during a conference committee:

RANKING SUBCOMMITTEE MEMBER: The gentleman from Missouri sat there and voted and decided this issue . . . by making himself a super-member of the Subcommittee on the Department of the Interior Appropriations. . . .

159

Mr. Speaker, for the first time in the history of this Congress, the Chairman of a full Committee has seen fit to make himself a super-member of the conference committee.

FULL COMMITTEE CHAIRMAN: Of course it is not necessary for me to call attention to the rule which has been in effect in the Committee on Appropriations ever since its establishment in 1865 under which the Chairman of the committee has been ex officio a member of all subcommittees.[40]

Although such intervention is permitted, it does violate the expectations of subcommittee autonomy. The Chairman can capitalize on his potential only if he intervenes occasionally and sparingly. The dominant expectation is that Committee decision-making shall be subcommittee decision-making.

The limitations imposed on the role of the Chairman confirm the basic expectations as to subcommittee autonomy. But, since the Chairman holds such a potential for influencing subcommittee behavior, his role sets limitations on subcommittee independence. Obviously, the key to the internal structure of the Committee rests in the kind of relationships — of roles and role behaviors — worked out between the Committee Chairman on the one hand and subcommittee leaders on the other. And, since the decision-making roles of the two do seem to intersect, it seems likely that the relationships involved will have to be worked out through some process of mutual testing and mutual accommodation. This process and its results will be discussed in the next chapter — after the ordinary day-to-day role and role behaviors of the other Committee members have been described.

SUBCOMMITTEE MEMBER: ROLE AND ROLE BEHAVIOR

The norms which define the role of Committee member are virtually coterminous with those which define the role of subcommittee member. Both are roles shared by every member of the Committee. And since the key work units are the subcommittees, the most general Committee role discussed will be the role of subcommittee member. This refers to the cluster of norms which all members of all subcommittees are expected to follow. Insofar as these norms are observed, they will describe the configuration of Committee decision-making — first of all within each subcommittee and secondly, among the various subcommittees.

For all members the overarching norm is that of *hard work*. As recognized by both the House and the Committee, the norm of hard work gives to

[40] 95 *Congressional Record*, p. 14041. Committee members similarly protested his (and Mr. Taber's) dominance of the House conferees on the omnibus appropriation bill of 1950. 96 *Congressional Record*, p. 4939, 4949.

the Committee its distinctive political style. No matter what phase of Committee work is involved, members are expected to conform to the highest standards of diligence. Enough has already been said on this point. All that needs to be added is that an individual member's influence in the subcommittees, like the Committee's influence in the House, depends on his working hard and acquiring the reputation for working hard. Hard work brings information, and the two together constitute a necessary condition of internal Committee influence.

An important norm of the House of Representatives is that of *specialization*. The fact of subcommittee autonomy gives the norm an intensified application on the Committee. Each member is expected to play the role of specialist in the activity of one subcommittee. He will sit on from one to four subcommittees, but he is expected to specialize in the work of only one. If he is a subcommittee chairman or ranking minority subcommittee member, he will specialize in the work of that group. If one of his subcommittees represents a constituency interest or a personal interest, he may choose to specialize in that. Or, if all of his subcommittees are areas about which he knows little, he may choose on some other basis — his seniority, the attitude of his subcommittee chairman, etc. Within one subcommittee he may specialize by concentrating on the work of one agency or one program. This kind of specialization twice over occurs in such subcommittees as Agriculture, Interior, and Defense.

"We all have a tendency in our subcommittee to specialize along some line or other," said a member of the agriculture group in 1962.[41] A man whose father was the first county agent in Minnesota specialized in the work of the Extension Service and the Farmers Home Administration. A man from Washington specialized in the Forest Service. The two senior men specialized in soil conservation. And the New York City member worked on the school lunch and meat inspection programs. On the Interior Subcommittee, in 1962, a man from a constituency with badly eroded soil specialized in soil and moisture conservation programs. A Pennsylvania congressman whose father was a coal mine inspector and who was himself an M.D., specialized in the work of the Bureau of Mines and Indian health programs. In earlier years, a man from Oklahoma specialized in the Bureau of Indian Affairs, and a man from Idaho specialized in the activities of the Bureau of Land Management. On the Defense Subcommittee men became known from their prior service on subcommittee panels, as experts in the Army, Navy, Air Force, or the Marines. And, said a minority member of the State-Justice-Commerce Departments Subcommittee, "Some of those agencies I don't bother with at all. On some I do a lot of digging. I get assignments to take care of — and the same with the others."

[41] 98 *Congressional Record*, p. 4585.

Committee members believe that specialization is especially appropriate to the task of guarding the Treasury. Only by specializing can they unearth the volume of information necessary for the intelligent, critical screening of budget requests. Only by developing their own expertise can Committee members successfully counter the battery of experts sent down by each executive agency to defend its budget. Since expertise is based on facts and since the facts can only be acquired through industriousness, he who is a specialist will, perforce, adopt the Committee's style of hard work. Thus the goal of budget-cutting, the norm of hard work, and the norm of specialization are interlinked and mutually supporting.

A Committee member who cherishes a dream of ranging widely throughout the area covered by the Appropriations Committee and who expects to wield influence in that broad arena, will find himself operating in the least congenial system imaginable. If, on the other hand, he curbs the scope of his activity, works hard, and becomes an acknowledged expert within a restricted area, he will win respect, deference, and, hence, influence in Committee decision-making. Within his own subcommittee, specialization can become the source of considerable influence for an individual member. Thus it may be said of a subcommittee specialist,

> We on the subcommittee feel that we have in the gentleman from Washington a specialist in research and a specialist in problems relating to the great forest industry in America. We look to him when details relative to those general problems come up.[42]

> During the six years he had been on the subcommittee we have turned over the job of looking after the health of Indians to him and he has really done a job. We never question his position when it comes to the health of the Indians, because we know he has looked into it thoroughly. The committee has also turned over the job of looking after the Bureau of Mines to the gentleman from Pennsylvania. He spends a lot of time on that.[43]

If it is to guide Committee decision-making, the norm of specialization must be supplemented by the norm of *reciprocity*. According to this norm subcommittee members are expected to act on the basis of mutual respect for one another's work. They are expected to acknowledge each other's specialized information and expertise and defer to it. Said one member, "After you have been here for a while, you become sort of a semispecialist with respect to legislation which interests you. And you say of the rest, 'I trust you to see that nothing wrong is done.' "[44] Within and between subcom-

[42] *Ibid.*
[43] 98 *Congressional Record*, p. 2941. See also *ibid.*, p. 3070.
[44] Joint Committee on the Organization of Congress, *Hearings on the Organization of Congress,* 79th Congress, 1st Session (Washington: U.S. Government Printing Office, 1945), p. 340.

mittees, trust is expected to be reciprocal. It is expected that reciprocity should be observed within subcommittees and among subcommittees. Insofar as it is observed within subcommittees, it shores up the influence of individual members. Insofar as it is observed among subcommittees, it becomes a basis for preserving subcommittee autonomy.

Members of each subcommittee are expected to observe reciprocity with respect to the recommendation of every other subcommittee. When a subcommittee brings its appropriation recommendations to the full Committee — that is to say, to the other subcommittees — for approval and legitimation, the full Committee could choose to reargue the recommendations *de novo*. But it is not expected to do so. In accordance with the norm of reciprocity, it is expected to defer to the subcommittee which has specialized in the area, has worked hard, and has "the facts." "It's a matter of you respect my work and I'll respect yours." "You don't go barging into another man's field unless something is patently wrong." "It's frowned upon if you offer an amendment in the full Committee if you are on the subcommittee. It's considered presumptuous to pose as an expert if you aren't on the subcommittee." Thus articulated, the norm of reciprocity shores up the autonomy and the influence of each subcommittee. "Trust," "confidence," "respect," and "faith" are the lubricants of full Committee activity.

It is impossible to know for certain the degree to which reciprocity is observed — that is, how often the full Committee accepts the recommendations of its subcommittees. No public records exist and private records, if such there be, are not systematically kept. Fortunately, however, the off-hand estimates of Committee members do not vary much. Subcommittee recommendations, they agree are "very rarely changed," "almost always approved," "changed one time in fifty," "very seldom changed," "usually go through," "go smiling through," etc. A man with over ten years of service as a subcommittee chairman said, "I don't believe I've ever had a change made in full Committee in my bills." The optimum conditions for changing a subcommittee recommendation would seem to be present when the fight is led by a dissident member of that subcommittee — by a member, that is, who can draw on the norm of specialization and its concomitants of information and hard work. But insofar as it is observed, the norm of reciprocity is a foundation stone of subcommittee autonomy and influence.

Since no subcommittee is likely to command deference of the full Committee unless its recommendations have widespread support among its own members, a third norm — that of *subcommittee unity* — is expected to be observed by all subcommittee members. Unity refers to a willingness to support (or not to oppose) the recommendations of one's own subcommittee. Reciprocity and unity are closely dependent upon one another. Reciprocity would be difficult to maintain if subcommittees were badly divided, and subcommittee unity would have little appeal unless intersubcommittee reciprocity was likely to be observed. The norm of reciprocity functions to minimize intersubcommittee conflict; the norm of unity functions to minimize intrasubcommittee conflict. Committee members believe that both must be observed if subcommittee influence in decision-making is to be maintained.

In a positive way, members believe subcommittee unity should be achieved by applying the basic House norm of *compromise* to subcommittee action. In making their decisions, subcommittee members are expected to be flexible and to give and take in order to produce recommendations which all subcommittee members can support. Again, it is not possible to know for certain how frequently this norm is observed. But the high rate of acceptance of subcommittee recommendations by the full Committee is prima facie evidence to that effect. Subcommittee members also describe their markup sessions — which are the key points of subcommittee decision-making — as governed by efforts to achieve unity through compromise. A subcommittee chairman asserted,

> Sometimes there are different ideas. We kick it around and we give a little, take a little. I've worked on the subcommittee with some pretty sharp people and we always like to have what we call a "round book." They do it at the race tracks and we do it here.

A ranking subcommittee member described his subcommittee markup sessions:

> If there's agreement, we go right along. If there's a controversy, we put the item aside and go on. Then after a day or two, we may have a list of ten controversial items. We give and take and pound them down until we get agreement.

A Committee newcomer observed, with regard to still another set of markup sessions,

> If there's any way to bring out a unanimous report, they'll do it. They'll sit there long hours. They'll backscratch and give and take and compromise.

In a negative way, Committee members believe that subcommittee unity can only be achieved by minimizing the most divisive force in legislative politics — partisanship. Every subcommittee is expected, therefore, to observe the norm of *minimal partisanship*. That is, under most conditions, Committee members are expected to minimize their party-oriented behavior. Nothing would be more dysfunctional for the observance of reciprocity, subcommittee unity, or compromise than bitter and extended partisan controversy. On the evidence, the norm seems to be widely observed. Nearly every respondent emphasized, with approval, that "very little" or "not much" or "amazingly little" partisanship prevailed on the Committee. Many new-comers find that this feature of Committee life provides the sharpest contrast with their previous committee:

> Usually we come to an agreement and compromise things out. Most sub-committee reports are unanimous reports. I never saw a unanimous report on anything in my last committee. I guess you could say there's a lot less partisanship on Appropriations.

"Well," concurred a subcommittee chairman, "partisanship naturally enters in, but the surprising thing is how little there actually is." And a ranking minority subcommittee member said, "You might think that we Republicans would defend the budget of the [Eisenhower] administration; but we don't." We have already observed that the roles of Chairman and ranking minority member place far less emphasis on partisan leadership than they do on con-sultation across party lines. No committee operating within a party-organized system like the House is immune from the temperature of party conflict. But Committee members believe that their boiling point should be kept high. Minimal partisanship is believed to be a necessary condition of subcommittee unity and, hence, tightly intertwined with all of the other norms thus far elaborated.

Once subcommittee unity has been achieved, Committee members believe that they should stand behind their internal bargain. "There is a strong feeling that the subcommittee should stick together." "Sometimes," said one ranking minority member, "we compromise in committee on the understanding that we will stick together come hell or high water." The payoffs, they believe, are these: Only by presenting the full Committee with a united front can they win acceptance of their recommendations; only by winning acceptance can they preserve their influence on decision-making. Whatever behavior increases subcommittee influence will, in turn, preserve for each member that degree of influence which led him to seek Committee membership in the first place. Since his personal satisfactions depend upon the degree of subcommittee unity, subcommittee members will be constrained to play the role expected of them.

The norms of hard work, specialization, reciprocity, subcommittee unity, compromise, and minimal partisanship help define the role of every Committee member. They constitute an interdependent set of norms which, insofar as they are observed, help explain the sources of individual influence and the dominance of subcommittee influence in Appropriations Committee decision-making. They prescribe an overall decision-making configuration. They do not prescribe particular decision-making roles. And they do not, therefore, reveal much about who makes decisions within the subcommittees themselves. Every subcommittee member does not exercise equal influence on

165

decision-making. Therefore, the Committee's role structure must be further elaborated.

COMMITTEE NEWCOMER: ROLE

The differentiation of roles between senior and junior Committee members provides one basic definition of who is expected and who is not expected to influence subcommittee decisions. Here, as in the case of specialization, the Committee's system of norms is strengthened because it follows that of the parent chamber. Seniority rules are among the most hallowed of congressional norms. So, too, on the Appropriations Committee. Of a junior member, it will be said, "Oh, he doesn't count — what I mean is, he hasn't been on the Committee long enough." He is not expected to play an active part in decision-making. A Committee newcomer — a man of one or two terms of Committee service — is expected to play the role of apprentice.

In answer to a question, "What advice would you give to a new member if he came to you and asked how he should behave on the Committee?" three subcommittee chairmen agreed:

> Follow the Chairman until you get your bearings. For the first two years, follow the Chairman. He knows. He's been around a long time. Then take more of a part yourself.

> Work hard; get to know what you're doing as quickly as you can. Be a good member of the Committee. Get along with the other members, and the rest comes easy. Don't be what we call a rabble rouser.

> Work hard, keep quiet, and attend the Committee sessions. We don't want to listen to some new person coming in here. But after a while when you know what you're doing, we'll listen to you.

These norms define the role of apprentice. The newcomer is expected to work hard, to amass information, to learn the business of his subcommittee, to listen to the senior men, and to follow them. He is expected to devote himself whole-heartedly to the routine proceedings of the subcommittee. And, except in the case of pressing constituency needs, he is not expected to wield or to attempt to wield influence.

For their part, the Committee's veterans extol the virtues of the seniority rule which links influence to Committee experience:

> On this Committee, it takes a long time to learn. They ridicule the seniority rule. God have pity if we didn't have it. It's like anything else, this business, your business, or anything, there's no substitute for experience. I'd hate to get in a plane and have the pilot tell me that this was his first solo flight.

166

Newcomers do not know the ways of the Committee, and they do not have enough information to merit the attention of others. Apropos of subcommittee hearings, a powerful subcommittee chairman asserted,

> Newcomers look every bit as wise as the older members. But they don't know what the score is and they don't have enough information to ask intelligent questions.

And another exclaimed, with respect to markup proceedings,

> When we get a compromise, nobody's going to break that up. If someone tries, we sit on him fast. We don't want young people who throw bricks or try to slow things down.

As far as floor action is concerned, the newcomer is expected to get out on the floor (if he has time) to observe. But he is not expected to speak out (except in the case, again, of constituency needs) until he stands on a foundation of hard work and information which only subcommittee experience can provide. A subcommittee chairman put it this way,

> When I came down here . . . I was full of pep. So I asked Mr. Rayburn how long a congressman had to be here before he went on the floor and made a speech. He said to me that you should attend Committee meetings and learn about your subject. Then, when you bring a bill out onto the floor, you will know more about it than anyone else except the members of the subcommittee. Then people will listen to you.

As the Rayburn advice indicates, the apprentice role is common to all new members of the House. But it is wrong to assume that each committee will give it the same emphasis. Some House committees pay it scant heed. The Appropriations Committee makes it a cornerstone of its decision-making structure.

SUBCOMMITTEE CHAIRMAN AND RANKING MINORITY MEMBER: ROLE AND ROLE BEHAVIOR

If the newcomer is the person least expected to influence decisions in the subcommittee, it is the chairman who is most expected to do so. "Members expect them to lead the committee. You've got to have leadership." Subcommittee members may, accordingly, praise a bill on the House floor as the handiwork of a subcommittee chairman:

> The bill has been pared to the barest minimum consistent with the necessary operations of the military services. It is another outstanding achievement in a great congressman's career. This bill is Harry Sheppard's bill. It

167

is Harry Sheppard's language and Harry Sheppard's thinking. It is a good bill. Harry Sheppard does not bring any other kind to the floor.[45]

Since Members normally succeed to subcommittee chairmanships via seniority, the men who occupy these positions will be the most senior and the most experienced men on the Committee.

Tradition grants to the subcommittee chairman impressive formal decision-making prerogatives. He is expected to allocate tasks to subcommittee members, set the timetable for subcommittee hearings, preside over the hearings, preside over subcommittee markup sessions, initiate action in those sessions, write (or oversee the writing of) the subcommittee report, present the subcommittee's recommendations to the full Committee, manage the floor debate on his subcommittee's bill, lead the House conferees in conference on the bill, and speak for the subcommittee to the agencies of the executive branch. Given the fact that all Committee members are expected to obey a cluster of norms that preserve and protect subcommittee autonomy, these formal prerogatives provide subcommittee chairmen with unlimited opportunities for the exercise of internal Committee influence. An experienced Committee member exclaimed,

> They are the lords with their fiefs and their duchys — each with power over his own area of appropriations. There's a power elite on this Committee. And these subcommittee chairmen are as powerful as other legislative chairmen.

One cannot, however, infer such vaunted power from knowledge about their formal prerogatives — formidable as they may be. These prerogatives constitute a potential for influence, on which the subcommittee chairman must capitalize before he, in fact, can do what he is legitimately allowed to do. Other norms define for him how he should go about exercising his prerogative. And it is by observing these "norms of style" that the subcommittee chairman capitalizes on his potential for influence. In the main, these norms of style are those which apply to all subcommittee members, and which the subcommittee chairman is expected to observe to an exemplary degree. And the same holds true for the man who has the second greatest potential for influence on the committee — namely, the ranking minority member of the subcommittee.

All subcommittee members are expected to obey its norms, but the man who is the legislative leader of the group is expected to set an example and steer the rest in the right direction. The subcommittee chairman and its ranking minority member are expected, for example, to specialize in the work of their subcommittee. They are expected to work harder and to be in

[45] *Congressional Record*, Daily Edition, May 26, 1964, p. 11566.

possession of more information than any other subcommittee member. They are expected to work closely together, compromise with one another, and to minimize partisanship in an effort to achieve subcommittee unity. The ranking minority member is, after all, a kind of shadow chairman, and good relations between the chairman and himself are expected to lubricate every area of subcommittee activity. By their observance of subcommittee norms, they will enhance their own influence within the subcommittee and the influence of their subcommittee in the full Committee. Other norms especially relevant to the role of subcommittee chairman state that he should be fair and not arbitrary in his dealings with subcommittee members. This refers to the desirability of smooth interpersonal relationships — which the chairman can nourish by observing standards of fairness — at the hearings, during the markup, etc. A subcommittee chairman declared that he was summing up the whole question of internal structure when he said, "It's all a group of people on the subcommittee and on the Committee, and the way they get along together."

Committee members are in unanimous agreement that the subcommittee chairman is the most influential decision-maker within this group. And from the way in which they describe his dominance it seems clear that it derives from his observance of his formal prerogatives and his "norms of style." A ranking subcommittee member summed up,

> Subcommittee chairmen have the respect of their members. They are honest, courteous, and tactful. You can't beat a popular chairman . . . but they should be fair and give everyone a chance to ask questions.

The dominance of two subcommittee chairmen at the time of subcommittee hearings is described in these two comments:

> He knows the bill backwards and forwards. He works hard, awfully hard, and the members know it. He's worked with these people for years and he knows them like a book. He does more work on the bill than all the other members combined. I know I don't do as much as I would if I knew I had to have the information. But in the hearings, he develops his case so completely. He has his questions ready and takes maybe two days questioning the witness. When he's through, there isn't much left to ask about — it's all in the record. I'd say it's his performance.

> He knows more about it than anybody else. He works harder than any other subcommittee chairman. He takes a witness and digs and digs and digs and digs, page by page and line by line.

These remarks are not complaints. They are compliments. They reveal subcommittee admiration for the degree to which the basic norms of hard work and specialized information have been met. Through his questioning of

169

witnesses, the subcommittee chairman reveals to his colleagues his knowledge and his understanding of the agencies for which they are appropriating. Subcommittee members expect that he will carry the load in the hearings, attend all sessions, ask the leading questions, and dig out the important answers. When subcommittee members say of their chairman that "He has done his homework" or "When [he] finishes with a witness most of us can usually say the job is done and refrain from further questioning," they are acknowledging that he has met their expectations and is deserving of their support.

A subcommittee chairman who had just completed hearings on his very first appropriation bill, received the praise of an experienced subcommittee member:

> It was clear at all of the hearings during a period of seven weeks in which we sat that the [subcommittee chairman] had done his homework well and concientiously. Mr. Chairman, I believe I may safely say that it was more than evident to the members of the subcommittee that such a grasp of the subject area covered during our hearings could only be grasped by untiring and thorough study which was demonstrated daily by our chairman. . . . He asked penetrating and searching questions of these agency heads and bureau chiefs in fields with which he had had no previous contact. And I assure you they were penetrating questions. They opened the door to the committee immediately upon the start of our hearings.[46]

These remarks constitute highest praise. They represent the kind of verdict for which every subcommittee chairman labors. For it is the underpinning of his influence within the group. A veteran subcommittee chairman discussed the basis of his success in budget-cutting:

> I couldn't do what I have been doing if I didn't have the confidence of the subcommittee and the House. They know that I study this program. I live with it. It is my life. I work twelve to fifteen hours a day, seven days a week. I haven't taken a Sunday off in nine years.[47]

When the hearings have ended, and in advance of subcommittee markup, the subcommittee chairman is expected to look over the transcripts carefully, consult with the subcommittee clerk, seek additional clarification from agency people if that seems necessary, and then to prepare an agenda for the markup session. It is expected that this agenda will normally include suggested appropriations figures and whatever language may seem to him appropriate. On some subcommittees, printed mimeographed sheets entitled "Suggested Items for Consideration in Markup" may be circulated to the subcommittee members. On the sheet will be listed a series of suggested recommendations (usually reductions) together with a brief rationale for

---

[46] *Congressional Record*, Daily Edition, June 13, 1961, p. 9439.
[47] *Washington Evening Star*, op. cit.

the suggestion as found in the hearings or elsewhere. Subcommittee members, in other words, grant to the subcommittee chairman the initiative in subcommittee decision-making. And this they do because they acknowledge that he has spent more time, has more information, and has more experience with the agencies involved than anyone else — he, that is, and the ranking minority member.

Markup proceedings are hidden from public view. And so at the most critical point of subcommittee activity we have to rely, again, on those who participate and to use them as respondents and informants. Their reports differ somewhat depending on their perspective. Subcommittee newcomers and more experienced members perceive subcommittee decision-making in quite different ways. But the sum total of their observations confirms the influence of the chairman together with his observance of important subcommittee norms.

In discussing markup proceedings, the view of the subcommittee newcomer etches in sharpest relief the role played by the chairman. Newcomers paint a picture of utter dominance by the chairman. Two of them said typically,

> The chairman runs the show. He decides what he wants and he gets it through. In the markup, they skip along so fast that you have to really be on your toes to follow. If I say, "Did we delete such and such," or "Are there funds in here for such and such," the chairman may say, "Yes" and move right on.

> The chairman has a tremendous advantage. He and the clerk work for two weeks setting the figures. The other members of the committee, especially the minority, are kind of lost. They come in and say, cut $3 million here, $1 million here, and unless you follow pretty closely and do your homework you don't have much of a chance.

Remarks like these indicate pretty clearly that newcomers do in fact play the role of apprentice. They are not expected to and do not participate actively in markup sessions.

Exceptions will be made if they feel strongly about an item of special concern to their constituency. One Republican newcomer noted that the Democratic chairman of his subcommittee wrote into the committee report that construction should begin immediately on the newcomer's pet project. "That was my introduction to the Committee," he said. "A Democrat helped me out and got that put in the report for me." In broader areas newcomers are still apt to be impressed with their own lack of information, just as they are with the advantage which accrues to the chairman because he possesses it. "I've got one or two amendments I want to get through. But most of the time, I follow the more experienced members of the Committee,"

171

said one model freshman. "I'm a novice and I don't understand the workings of all these agencies. I admit my ignorance and my limitations. This chairman knows a lot more than I do."

More experienced subcommittee members paint the chairman's role behavior in subtler tones. The chairman, they agree, dominates proceedings. He "carries the ball," "is the prime mover," "puts the propositions," and "virtually fixes the appropriation." But they voice the expectation that he should observe standards of fairness. They judge him according to his disposition to allow everyone to participate and his willingness to seek subcommittee unity by compromise rather than by arbitrary imposition. "I've learned that he knows ten times more about it than I do. But I think he knows I know my material. And he gives me all the time I want. I ask all the questions I want to and he never cuts me off." "We expect the chairman and the clerk to have recommendations. He presents them and then if someone feels differently, we argue it out." These descriptions of the chairman's role behavior come from more experienced subcommittee members:

> He works very understandingly and cooperatively with the subcommittee. He is very diplomatic — a right fine gentleman. Usually his ideas get into the bill.

> He has a pretty good idea of what he wants, but he's friendly to compromise . . . the first couple of days are usually a knockdown, drag out affair until a pattern begins to form of things we can agree on.

> He and the clerk go over it, and when you come in for markup, it's all laid out cold, and the members almost always agree. He goes very fast in markup, and sometimes you find that something you were interested in has gone by. And maybe he knows you were interested in it. But he's courteous and fair if you call it to his attention.

The perceptions of experienced subcommittee members run as much to the chairman's style as they do to his influence.

The special concern of these members for the fairness of the subcommittee chairman and for his receptivity to compromise stems from their expectation that they should participate in the markup session. They acknowledge the leadership of the chairman, but they also expect him to preserve a bargaining structure which provides them with opportunity to exercise influence. If, for example, they specialize in certain areas of subcommittee work, they are expected to have a good deal to say on those topics, even prior to markup session. "It's an informal thing. If you sit next to the chairman in hearings or you are visiting with him, you will tell him what your feelings are about something."

172

Last year, two of us — one Democratic member and myself — thought that one item shouldn't go in the bill. We mentioned it to the chairman after one of the hearings. When we got to markup, that item had already been taken out. There was no controversy at all.

Experienced members are allowed, furthermore, to bring a few strong preferences to the markup sessions and bargain for them there. Frequently, the chairman will trade them their preferences in return for their pledge to support the subcommittee's recommendations. One ranking subcommittee member described his group's procedure for achieving unity:

We have a unanimous agreement on everything. If a fellow enters an objection and we can't talk him out of it — and sometimes we can get him to go along — that's it. We put it in there.

Experienced subcommittee members understand this desire for unity and rely upon it in bargaining for their preferences.

The role of the experienced member prescribes more active participation than that of the newcomer. Ultimately, though, he is expected to support the chairman during markup. Normally, his attention will be dispersed among his two or three different subcommittee assignments. He will not have the time to participate continuously in the work of all his subcommittees. He may, therefore, appear at little else except the markup session, to which he comes to bargain and to support the chairman. A newcomer explained that, on his subcommittee,

The hearings lasted three months and the markup was over in less than two hours. That was the first time, at markup, that the whole committee showed up. Usually, just one or two men were there and the others might come in once in a while when they were interested. Then they all showed up to support the chairman on markup.

The subcommittee chairman alone will have concentrated his entire effort on the appropriation bill under discussion and will have the most information. At markup time, indeed, he has been known to be in possession of the only transcript of the hearings that is available.

For the subcommittee chairman, the most crucial increment of support he seeks is that of the ranking minority member. Thus it is particularly necessary that he observe the norm of minimal partisanship during markup proceedings. Said one subcommittee chairman of his markup role, "My job is to keep down partisanship." If the chairman is to preserve his subcommittee's unity he must establish good working relationships with the ranking minority member. If the subcommittee is to reach its decisions by bargaining, the most consequential bargains are those struck between the chairman and the rank-

173

ing minority member. Two ranking minority members described the style of their subcommittee chairmen as models of comity:

> Frequently, the chairman has a figure which he states. Sometimes he will have no figure and he'll turn to me and say, "What do you think?" Maybe I'll have a figure. It's very flexible. Each member has a chance to say what he thinks, and we'll move it around. Sometimes it takes a long time . . . he's a rabid partisan on the floor, but he is a very fair man in the subcommittee.

> He and I are political opposites. But in committee, he's very fair. He bends over backwards to protect our rights, to see that we have all the time we need. He's not arbitrary. If we make a suggestion that is reasonable, he'll help us. He goes way overboard to make us feel an integral part of the committee. And that's proper. We don't want to have minority reports. If we have a sticky problem we sit down and talk it out. If any of us wanted to be stubborn, we could wreck the appropriations process.

The following exchange on the floor testifies to the consummation of an effective compromise by the two key subcommittee leaders:

> SUBCOMMITTEE CHAIRMAN: Because of my sincere friendship for the gentleman from Oklahoma, and knowing his great desire for economy in this particular bill, I went further than I ordinarily would have gone, because of his influence on me in the marking up of the bill.
> RANKING MINORITY SUBCOMMITTEE MEMBER: I think there is no doubt about that, and I want to thank the gentleman publicly for acceding to my requests in many instances.[48]

And finally, the sentiments expressed by still another ranking minority member reflect an optimum fulfillment of norms:

> [I want to] express my admiration and warm personal regard for the chairman of the subcommittee under whom I have served for the past four years. An abler, harder working, better informed chairman I would find it hard to imagine. On top of that he is fair, he is easy to get along with and it is a pleasure to sit on the same side of the table with him.[49]

Only occasionally do the majority (at least the Democratic) members of the subcommittee caucus prior to markup. But the minority (at least the Republicans) very often do meet before the markup. Frequently, therefore, the ranking minority member speaks for the other subcommittee members on his side of the aisle when he bargains with the chairman.

The subcommittee newcomer, the experienced member, and the ranking minority member each sees an aspect of the subcommittee chairman's role and his role behavior at markup time. The role is defined first by expectations that he take the lead and move the subcommittee toward the goals set for

[48] 97 *Congressional Record*, p. 4014. See also *ibid.*, p. 4102.
[49] 103 *Congressional Record*, p. 8886.

it by the full Committee and by the House. He is expected to lead. But in leading, he is expected to observe such norms as fairness, willingness to compromise, and minimal partisanship. The role allows for variations in behavior according to the content of the appropriation bill and the personal idiosyncrasies of individual subcommittee chairmen. A chairman may be placed under greater pressure to bargain, for example, in the public works bill than he is in the Justice Department bill. Or, one chairman may be temperamentally "more autocratic" and less inclined to bargain than another. The role permits slippage, but it also prescribes one distinct pattern of behavior for all subcommittee chairmen. Descriptions of actual markup proceedings cited in the last several pages suggest that the expected pattern of behavior is observed.

Both role slippage and role observance are confirmed in the following descriptions by three subcommittee chairmen of their own markup behavior:

In subcommittee we take the bill up item by item. I throw out a figure and someone may name another. I may say, "That sounds a little high to me," or "a little low to me; but I'll split the difference with you." That's the way I operate. Some chairmen take it personally if you oppose their figure. I don't.

The day before we are going to mark up the bill, I sit down with my clerk and we go over the committee print. I ask him to look back over the testimony and what was said and we talk it over. Then I write down a figure that I will suggest the next day. If I don't do this, there would be chaos. Some fellow would say, "Let's cut the hell out of this crowd," maybe because of a pet peeve of his. And someone else might have a project or have a good friend of his in an agency. So when markup comes, I suggest the figure and explain why I think that should be the one. Ninety-five per cent of the time, that figure prevails. Oh, there may be a lot of discussion, but in the end that usually is accepted. After discussion, I'll say, "Are there any objections to the figure $2 million? If not, let's pass to the next item." Sometimes there is controversy, and if there is, we talk it out. We never take a vote in subcommittee. There is no partisanship on the subcommittee, and you don't get any rigid party-line votes. We talk it out and compromise. The subcommittee chairman is the key person here.

Usually, I have a figure, and I'll say to one of the people on my side, "What do you think?" If he shakes his head, that's it. There are no greenhorns here. We've worked together for a long time and we've developed ways for getting a compromise. If there's disagreement, I'll usually take the judgment of —— and —— [two experienced subcommittee members, one a Democrat, one a Republican]. I'll say, "You two get together and whatever you come up with, that's it."

The subcommittee chairman leads and bargains; he promotes the subcommittee's goals; and he maintains subcommittee unity.

175

One factor which impels the chairman to seek subcommittee unity and which affects his decisions at markup time is his concern for success in the full Committee. No subcommittee chairman wants a fight in the full Committee. Even less so does he want to lose, thereby damaging his prestige inside the Committee. Explained one member,

> They take their presentation before the full Committee very seriously and they work very hard at it. That's one reason why they want to work things out in subcommittee. That's the place to iron out our differences. One of the considerations will be, "Can we sustain this item in the full Committee?" And if we can't, we'll throw it out. They don't want to flub in there. If they can't justify something to the full Committee — or if some members are against something — a chairman will be in for a rough morning or a rough afternoon. And they don't want that.

Action at one stage of committee deliberations is affected by the anticipation of reactions at each subsequent stage.

When the subcommittee finishes marking up the bill, the subcommittee chairman with the help of the clerk (sometimes the relationship is reversed) writes a subcommittee report to accompany their recommendations to the full Committee. The report lists the money recommendations, explanations for money reductions (or increases), and expresses in a variety of literary forms the opinions, recommendations, attitudes, warnings, and directives of the subcommittee to the agency for which the money is being appropriated. Here is another point at which the chairman's superior information (or access to information) and the continuousness of his participation give him an advantage over other subcommittee members. And it is expected that he take the lead by writing the report. He is expected, however, to maintain comity through consultation with the ranking minority member of the subcommittee. Consultation with others is not deemed essential. Again, newcomers are struck by the raw influence of the chairman:

> A subcommittee report is, as a matter of fact, the chairman's report. That's the thing that impressed me. On a legislative committee you get much more of a chance to contribute to the report than you do here.

This means, of course, that subcommittee members ordinarily go to the full Committee meeting on their own bill without having seen the accompanying report. Another newcomer explained, "The first time you see it is at the full Committee — or maybe a little before. You hardly have any time to find out what's in it."

More experienced members view the report procedure with less alarm. A man of eight years of service remarked that, "I don't think I've ever seen a subcommittee report before going to the full Committee." He recalled a conversation with a committee newcomer on the subject:

176

——— came up to me one day and said, "What goes with these reports? Don't you ever see them?" I said, "Come to think of it, I don't think I ever have." I guess that's just SOP around here . . . members sometimes say, "What if it happens that someday your subcommittee reports out a bill that you don't see and aren't in favor of at all?" But it never happens that way. Maybe a sentence here or there, but never the general report.

Ranking minority members are usually even less concerned. Said one, "I wasn't taken by surprise by the report. In fact, I suggested revisions." If, of course, they have been ignored, they will protest it as a violation of the norm of minimal partisanship:

> I had nothing to do with writing the report, because I was not consulted when the report was written and neither was [the other minority subcommittee member]. The report was completed and printed without either of us having a chance to look at it until it was made public which is quite out of the ordinary.[50]

When he is accorded deference, the ranking minority member is expected to contribute to subcommittee unity by throwing his weight behind the subcommittee report. The following sequence on the House floor triggered by the criticism of ordinary subcommittee members that they had not seen their subcommittee's report, could be predicted:

> SUBCOMMITTEE CHAIRMAN: I had the counsel and advice from the various members of the committee, and made the report available to them. . . . Insofar as the preparation of it is concerned, I helped to put it together and submitted it to the members of my committee in line with what we ordinarily do here.
>
> $\cdot$ $\cdot$ $\cdot$ $\cdot$ $\cdot$
>
> FIRST MINORITY MEMBER OF SUBCOMMITTEE: We were invited to the committee. We got to the committee. The gentleman was explaining the bill when I got in, about three minutes late. Of course it was more interesting to hear him explain the bill than to begin to read the committee report, and that is the first time I had seen it. Consequently, I took it to my office with me and an hour after the committee adjourned I started to read the report. I was a little surprised . . . because I had hardly expected the criticism in the report that I found.
>
> $\cdot$ $\cdot$ $\cdot$ $\cdot$ $\cdot$
>
> SECOND MINORITY MEMBER OF THE SUBCOMMITTEE: That majority report was made available to us only when we sat down in full Committee.
>
> $\cdot$ $\cdot$ $\cdot$ $\cdot$ $\cdot$
>
> RANKING MINORITY MEMBER: The [chairman] did tell me that a copy of the report was available in our clerk's room to look over and scrutinize. That is

[50] 96 *Congressional Record*, p. 6012.

the usual procedure in our subcommittee. . . . It has been my experience during the 11 years in which I have helped handle the annual . . . appropriation bill that the report is the responsibility and is prepared largely by the chairman of the subcommittee. Certainly, the other members, including the minority members, had the privilege of looking over the rough drafts, but in the main the report is the work of our chairman.[51]

This defense of the chairman by the ranking minority member represents a tangible payoff for the observance of minimal partisanship between the two.

When the full Appropriations Committee convenes to pass upon subcommittee recommendations, the proceedings are, again, controlled by the subcommittee chairmen. The Chairman of the full Committee presides:

He always calls first on the chairman of the subcommittee who explains what the subcommittee has done. Then he calls on the ranking minority member. If there are any questions, they try to answer them.

In this forum, too, the subcommittee chairman possesses overwhelming advantages — especially if he is supported by the ranking minority member, his other subcommittee members, and the full Committee Chairman. As one rank newcomer viewed the proceedings:

The subcommittee chairman and the ranking minority members speak and explain the provisions. But they work hand in glove and there is no conflict between them. Then the Chairman says, "Without objection, the report is approved." There are no votes. I haven't seen a vote yet. You would have to stand up and say, "I object." And if you did, all hell would break loose. So we just look at each other and no one objects. That's another example of the power the Chairman exercises.

Committee norms prescribe that members of the other subcommittees defer to the recommendations as stated by the subcommittee chairman. He and his group are the only ones who have done the work, have specialized in the subject, and have the information. To raise proposals that have not been previously considered by the subcommittee violates Committee norms. A subcommittee chairman spoke disapprovingly of one such proposal which was offered and rejected:

We sat for five months and heard hundreds of witnesses and not once was that project mentioned until someone in full Committee jumped up and made a motion. That's no way to do it. The purpose of a subcommittee is to hear testimony, get the facts, to let everybody have a chance to tell his story and come to a deliberate and considered judgment.

When the Committee meets, only the subcommittee chairman and ranking minority member of the subcommittee and their opposite numbers on the

[51] 101 *Congressional Record*, pp. 3832, 3844, 3874.

full Committee may have seen the subcommittee report. The ordinary subcommittee member is at some disadvantage, but the ordinary full Committee member finds it even more difficult to follow the proceedings. He will not have participated at all up to that time, and he will not have seen the subcommittee report until he enters the full Committee meeting:

> No member except those on the subcommittee knows what's in the defense bill. The other members come in and they find in front of them five volumes of hearings a foot high, and a thirty-page report — neither of which they have ever seen before. George Mahon gets up and explains the bill. And Gerry Ford supports him. And no one in that room can ask an intelligent question. Then everyone votes aye. They go out of the Committee united.

> Take the defense subcommittee report — it is thirty-five pages long. The chairman of the subcommittee starts to explain it and he may say, "Read page eight for an explanation." Well, you look at that briefly but you don't have any time to think about it or to check it with the hearings.

And time is something that is not available. Full Committee meetings do not meander to a conclusion. Full debate is allowed, but even under the most favorable conditions only those who know precisely what they want are likely to get it. Votes may be held, but only when subcommittee recommendations are under serious challenge:

> From the time the gavel sounds the opening of a session until the gavel bangs it shut, parliamentary rules are in effect. We don't waste time on details. Everyone knows what he wants on the big items. You have to be quick on your feet to swing things your way.[52]

When the Committee in 1950 packaged all of its bills in one omnibus appropriation bill, the combined subcommittee reports were made available to all Committee members on Saturday. The full Committee met at 10:00 A.M. on Monday morning, and it approved and sent to the House floor a $41 billion appropriation bill in the time of three hours and seven minutes.[53] Ironically, the primacy of subcommittees was never more convincingly illustrated than on the very bill which was designed to reduce the decentralization of Committee decision-making.

For Committee newcomers, no aspect of the group's internal decision-making structure is more striking and more puzzling than full Committee action. Many of them, it will be recalled, sought Committee membership in the belief that their activities would be government-wide in scope. The working autonomy of subcommittees does no violence to their expectations, but their

---

[52] Quoted in Dwaine Marvick, "Congressional Appropriations Politics," unpublished manuscript (Columbia University, 1952), p. 234.

[53] 96 *Congressional Record*, p. 4936.

lack of impact on decisions outside their subcommittee bailiwick, in full Committee, is startling and somewhat disappointing. The efforts of two new-comers to reconcile themselves to the realities of the situation are especially informative:

> The subcommittee report is only made available just before the full Committee meeting and only then to the subcommittee members. You can get one, but you have to take the initiative. If I want one, I have to go to one of the members of the subcommittee and ask him for a copy. And there's a reason for that. If everybody got ahold of it, pressure would build up just like that before the Committee met and we'd have a harder job. It would start controversy and we'd have a lot more partisanship than we do. That's a real good reason and I agree with it. But I would like to see a little more consideration by the full Committee. There isn't any problem with the rules. But it's gotten to be a tradition. The subcommittee reports and every-one says it's going to pass anyway so why get excited about it. I don't say every item should be considered all over again — oh heavens no — we'd never get anything done. But we shouldn't go through it quite as quickly as we do now.

> I didn't know the function of things. You walk in there and they say, "Here's a report, here's the bill and that's it . . ." But you are really not shut off — you can read the hearings and most everything is there. Of course you don't have the time or may not take the time. And it would be easier if you could get the report a day earlier. You could pick up things you might be against. If you can't do things the easy way, you do them the hard way. And you can always get up on the floor and say what you think. You have time there to get prepared. It would be better the other way, but it's not going to change. They've been doing it for tens of years and no one has proven he's been hurt by it. The subcommittees are the ones who work on the bill. I see it on our subcommittee. We are the ones who sit there all the time and we know more about it than anyone else. So it's right that they should have most of the say.

If a member wishes to influence the decision of a subcommittee of which he is not a member, he must do it informally and prior to the full Committee meeting. Otherwise, he must content himself with the considerable influence that he can exercise within the limited scope of his own subcommittee.

When the full Committee meets, they realize that the defense of their bill on the House floor is just around the corner. And, faced with this prospect, their awareness of unfavorable images held by House members is quickened. Believing that their disunity will encourage and facilitate attack on the floor, they strive in full Committee meeting to produce a maximum of unity. "We fight it out in Committee; and if someone loses he's not supposed to cry baby about it on the floor," explained one experienced member,

> We iron out our differences in Committee. We argue it out and usually have a meeting of the minds, a composite view of the Committee . . . if we went on the floor in wide disagreement, they would say, "If you can't agree

180

after listening to the testimony and discussing it, how can we understand it? We'll just vote on the basis of who we like the best."

It is, of course, not as easy to maintain unity among a full Committee of fifty members as it is among a subcommittee of five or seven or nine. But full Committee members are expected to support (or not to oppose) Committee recommendations on the floor. In full Committee, subcommittee chairmen warn the membership that if they go to the floor in disarray they will be "jumped," "rolled," or "run over" on the floor. And they repeat a cardinal maxim of the Committee, that "You can't turn an appropriation bill loose on the floor." A veteran subcommittee chairman described it as part of his role in full Committee to warn the members:

> I tell them we should have a united front. If there are any objections or changes, we ought to hear it now and not wash our dirty linen out on the floor. If we don't have a bill that we can all agree on and support, we ought not to report it out. To do that is like throwing a piece of meat to a bunch of hungry animals.

Committee members believe that their influence at every stage of appropriations decision-making is dependent upon their internal unity. Whenever the subcommittee chairman is called upon to lead, he is also called upon to preserve internal unity.

The role of the subcommittee chairman and ranking minority member on the House floor will be discussed in Chapter Nine. But in terms of internal subcommittee decision-making, it must be noted that the two subcommittee leaders are expected to act as official spokesmen for the subcommittee to elements of their environment other than the House. With respect to executive agencies, the subcommittee chairman is permitted to make decisions on behalf of the subcommittee during those periods when Congress is not in session. Should agency officials find it necessary to have some of their authority to spend revised, or to shift money from one program to another, or to have an authoritative interpretation of the language of the report, the decision will be given by the subcommittee chairman and the ranking minority member. Thus these two men speak (as committee newcomers do not) of being in touch with the executive agencies the year round on behalf of their subcommittees. "Almost every night when I get home, there is a communication from the ———— Department informing me of something they want to do," said one subcommittee chairman. And another explained,

> I'm in contact with them all the time. They want to show us something or they're having trouble with the budget. We've appropriated money for some purpose and they want to shift it . . . it's an unwritten rule that when Congress is not in session the subcommittee will stand behind anything the chairman does — with the consent of the ranking minority member.

181

In this way, also, the subcommittee chairman and ranking minority member remain in the midst of the information flow regarding appropriations matters.

Given the great potential for influence carried in the role of subcommittee chairman, it is amply evident why the position is considered one of the prizes of congressional service. It is evident, too, why Committee members want it so badly, why they adopt behavior patterns deemed helpful in achieving it, and why the control over these positions constitutes an essential source of the full Committee Chairman's power. It is evident, too, why sitting subcommittee chairmen are likely to fight against proposals (e.g., omnibus appropriation bills or joint budgetary committees) which threaten to dilute their influence by centralizing the decision-making process.

SUBCOMMITTEE CLERK: ROLE AND ROLE BEHAVIOR

In the structure for subcommittee decision-making, a prominent role is prescribed for the member or members of the Committee's permanent staff. There may be more than one clerk assigned to work with a subcommittee (six are assigned to the Defense Subcommittee full-time or part-time), but each clerk has one subcommittee to which he is primarily attached. Everything he does must be supported and legitimized by his subcommittee, but subject to that proviso his informal prerogatives are impressive. They prescribe for him close contact with every stage in decision-making and continuous immersion in the stream of information consequent to decision-making.

For his subcommittee, each clerk is expected to schedule and oversee the routine of the hearings, suggest areas of inquiry for the hearing, make up specific questions for use in the hearings, prepare the transcript for publication, help prepare for the markup session, oversee the routine of the markup, participate during markup, help write the subcommittee report, and the subcommittee bill, participate in full Committee, sit with and advise subcommittee members during floor debates, help schedule and prepare for conference committee meetings, prepare materials for use by House conferees, participate in conference proceedings, receive and digest reports from the investigation staff, keep in constant communication, in season and out, with agency officials, and accompany committee members when they travel to visit agency installations. His role requires that he process all the committee's working documents and that he be present physically at every stage of decision-making. "There may be some part of the process that I miss or don't know about," said one staff man, "but I doubt it."

In playing each part of his role, it is expected that the clerk's basic working attachment be with the subcommittee chairman. As one clerk put it, "You're his boy. It's his show and your job is to help him get his work

182

done." To a lesser degree the clerk is expected to assist the ranking minority member; and the expectations with regard to other subcommittee members are relatively minimal. One long-time clerk explained,

> I think the members of the subcommittee recognize that the clerk is primarily attached to the chairman, who has the major responsibility in the subcommittee and certainly does more of the work than anyone else. If any other members of the committee ask me for help, or want some figures worked up, I do it. Mostly the chairman wants this; and next to him is the ranking minority member. He may even want me to work up an argument for him against what the majority wants. If he does, I'll do that. Sometimes I work up both sides of the argument.

The clerk's potential for influence lies in the information he comes to possess, but he can capitalize on it only insofar as he has established a relationship of confidence and trust with his subcommittee chairman. This he can gain by sharing Committee goals, obeying Committee norms, and by proving his individual worth over a period of time.

The Committee's staff perceives the Committee's goals in terms identical to those of the members. "Our job," said one veteran clerk, "is to say 'no' as often as we can find a reason for doing so." "If we're not negative," agreed another, "then I don't know why in the world we exist. Otherwise we are traitorous to the reasons we were reconstituted in 1920. If you want a rubber stamp, any one of these committees around here can do it just as well." Still another man viewed the Committee's job in terms of public demands made upon it:

> We're a country of multitudinous minorities. Each group is a king unto itself with a program it wants to get through. They've all got a bed to feather . . . all these projects are good ones but you would bankrupt the country in a year if you appropriated for all of them. What we need is a great leveler. That's the Committee's job.

A fourth clerk discussed the Committee's job in terms of its relation to the House. "The Committee has to stand against the pressure of all those other House committees. They are all special pleaders for their programs — that's all they are. Our Committee puts on the brakes." Staff members do worry about becoming "too negative," and they talk about it among themselves. But, on the whole, they share the budget-cutting goals of the men with whom they work. And it is expected that they will act accordingly.

Staff members, like Committee members, have certain norms of style, obedience to which increases the likelihood of their influence. One is hard work, which is as much of a norm for the staff as it is for the member. During peak periods of Committee business, clerks speak of missing lunch for two weeks in a row, not getting home for dinner for two weeks at a time, working

183

weekends, and working "under an ungodly amount of pressure." By sharing the work load, it would appear that their relationship would be enhanced. Subcommittee chairmen praise them as "the employee who does most of the work" and as men "unselfish with [their] time." Another important expectation is that the clerks should work in anonymity and with a minimum of fanfare. The Committee Chairman has said that "You do not hear much of these devoted men because it is a breach of Committee procedure to praise them . . . in the report of the subcommittee to the whole committee or in the report of the whole Committee to the House."[54] The norm was expressed by one clerk this way, "My job is to help the members do theirs. They make the decisions. We're the anonymous assistants. They can have all the glory." They are among the few staff members on Capitol Hill who do not list themselves in the unofficial *Congressional Staff Directory*.[55] Their office hideaways and subcommittee workrooms are not easily located in the labyrinthine Capitol and they do not readily assent to interviews. They try to remain as faceless in the world of congressional staffs as their Committee members are in the world of political celebrities. And this behavior makes possible a closer relationship with the subcommittee chairmen whom they serve.

Third, and most important, they are expected to observe the norm of nonpartisanship. As stated by the Chairman, "These men are available to any member of the Committee irrespective of whether he is a minority member or a majority member."[56] The injunction against staff partisanship is stronger than that which obtains for Committee members — for whom, after all, the legislative party is an important reference group. The staff is not chosen and it is not retained on the basis of party affiliation. In the words of the Committee Chairman, "We have our own system of civil service" and "We do retain them for life as long as they will stay with us."[57] By not subjecting its staff to changes with each change in party control, the Committee ensures for itself that this expert knowledge will be preserved and increased. The clerks, for their part, are expected to behave in a scrupulously nonpartisan manner. One of them described his role behavior this way:

> Ninety-five per cent of what we do in the subcommittee is bipartisan. There are seven men sitting around the table and they are all interested in the programs and in finding out how these agencies are spending the money we gave them. I work equally well with both sides; and if the Republicans came

[54] *Congressional Record*, Daily Edition, April 17, 1962, p. 6320.
[55] Of the 20 regular staff members, the biography of only *one* (Chief Clerk Kenneth Sprankle) appears in the 1964 *Congressional Directory*, and it lists an abnormally small number of facts about him. See Charles B. Brownson (ed.), *Congressional Staff Directory 1964* (Washington, D.C., 1964).
[56] *Congressional Record*, Daily Edition, April 17, 1962, p. 6320.
[57] *Ibid.*, pp. 6319–6320.

in, we'd swing right in. During markup I'll run down to the end of the table and say to one of them, "This is what you were interested in. This is the one you wanted to make a fuss about." We keep it all out in the open.

Evidence from the point of view of the subcommittee member that the role does get played can be found in this comment by a ranking minority member about his subcommittee clerk:

> Every week I talk with —————— [subcommittee clerk] about how things are going. When he makes out his questions for the hearings, one copy goes to me and one copy goes to the chairman. He tells me all he knows and doesn't hide things from me. I learn more from him in one short meeting than I do sitting in for days of the hearings.

Still it must be noted that some minority members feel that on some occasions with some clerks their role behavior is not (and, perhaps, cannot be) completely bipartisan. One nonranking minority member explained:

> The chairman has the clerk — and a damn good one — sitting at his elbow all the time. If I go to him and ask him for background material, he will help me all he can — up to a point. And that point comes when I'm trying to work up a challenge to the chairman's position. And that's right. He can't be expected to supply the ammunition that will scuttle the chairman in the full Committee or on the House floor. Given the ethics of the clerk's position, I'm sure he tells the chairman just what direction I'm moving in. So when I'm working up an amendment to challenge the chairman, he knows all about it. But I have no place else to turn.

Still, the dominant behavior of the clerks is held to be bipartisan. When subcommittee members introduce their bills on the House floor, the clerks are usually included in the ceremony of mutual congratulation. And the praise comes equally from both sides of the aisle.

In the final analysis, subcommittee clerks are important elements of the Committee's decision-making structure because the subcommittee chairmen find their assistance useful and necessary. Subcommittee chairmen vary in the degree and kind of assistance they want. But all of them need some help at key stages. One stage is that of the hearings which will be discussed in some detail in Chapter Seven. The other important stage involves subcommittee markup and the writing of the report.

In all cases, the clerk works with the chairman in preparing figures or recommendations to the subcommittee at markup. "Or, sometimes we won't have a figure but we'll decide what the line of attack will be." In some instances the clerk prepares the figure all by himself. Said one, "I write the markup. I do it and then show it to the chairman. We meet to go over it and he agrees on a markup before we take it to the subcommittee. Sometimes it's changed from mine and sometimes not." During markup, the clerk may be

185

called upon to explain the markup recommendations to the subcommittee members. "Sometimes the staff man is expected to sell the markup to the committee. The chairman sits back and the staff does all the talking." On subjects of internal controversy, he may work up arguments for both sides.

Invariably the clerk will be called upon to supply information. And he in turn may use his contact in the agency to make delicate inquiries on the spot. Said one clerk, "In markup I may call up the budget man [in the department] and say, 'We're going to whop you on this. Now, tell me the real truth. Is it going to hurt you?'" An experienced Committee member illustrated this particular aspect of the clerk's role in recounting a subcommittee decision in markup:

> The agency was asking $88 million for next year. The chairman said, "I think they ought to be cut to $50 million." I said, "Wait, Mr. Chairman, $88 million is about as low as it can go." We haggled about it and other members expressed their opinion. Then the chairman said, "Well, what do you think it should be? We ought to give them a token cut at least. How about $75 million?" I turned to the clerk and he said, "The agency expects to be cut on some items but not on this one. They say $88 million is as low as they can go; and that they will have to appeal any cut to the Senate." So the chairman said, "O.K., let's leave it at $75 million; and it will give us something to bargain with the Senate about. Maybe we can hold some other places where we think it has to be cut."

The clerks (see Chapters Six and Seven) are the most continuously operating conveyor belt for the transmission of budgetary intelligence from the executive branch to the Appropriations Committee.

If for no other reason, the clerk has to attend markup because it is he who is expected to write the subcommittee report recording the appropriations figures and explain what the subcommittee had in mind. "You could never catch the tone and spirit of what is said at markup if you weren't there." The process may move along so quickly and in such confusion that there is some doubt as to what the decision actually was. One clerk said that he always takes another staff man with him to double-check his accuracy. And a second said,

> Sometimes in markup they won't say exactly why they are doing something. Maybe it's perfectly clear why from the hearings and they don't feel it is necessary to say any more. So they just cut it and I usually know what the explanation is. If I don't, I'll check with the chairman before the report goes out to make sure that the language is correct. And I may check with the ranking minority member, too.

The clerks are expected to write the report and then show it to the chairman. The chairman may read all of it, some of it, or — once in a while — none of it.

The idiosyncratic nature of the process is revealed in this comment by a clerk whose subcommittee chairman takes an extraordinary amount of care with his subcommittee report:

> My boss doesn't use staff. He wants to be on it himself. Take the committee report. He's very particular about what goes in there. He fusses over that report for two weeks. He reads every word. It makes it tough for me. He and I sit here all day and then he leaves and then I have to stay here and work. Some chairmen never read a word of the report. Their name is on it but they never even see it before it goes out. Or, if they do they don't so much as change a comma. But not my boss. That's one of the things you learn to live with.

In the final analysis only by "learning to live with" his subcommittee chairman can the clerk capitalize his potential for influence:

> Confidence is our product. You work with a chairman and he has confidence in you. . . . I remember one time when another fellow was assigned to my bill with me. The chairman just didn't have confidence in him. When I came to the part of the program he had prepared, the chairman said, "You didn't write this did you?" I said, "No." He said, "Well, let's pass over this and take it up some other time. You work it over and we'll take it up some other time." . . . He didn't have confidence in that man even though he was a very competent person. The man knew it and he transferred out.

Another clerk testified to his compatibility with the subcommittee chairman in these words, "He's a very hard man to work with. . . . I think they leave me here because I'm the only one who has learned to get along with him."

The fact that relationships of confidence and influence do develop can be inferred from the length of time which clerks stay with one subcommittee. Despite the committee's fear of the interest-sympathy-leniency syndrome, and despite the fact that clerks are assigned to subcommittees where they have no "axe to grind," subcommittee clerks tend to remain permanently on the subcommittee to which they are assigned and this is because the chairmen insist upon it. Said one clerk, "I was scheduled to be moved to another subcommittee once and my subcommittee chairman wouldn't hear of it. He said that he had to have me. It wasn't that I was any ball of fire, but I knew all the ins and outs of the bill and he didn't want to lose me." A subcommittee chairman reported a different incident involving his clerk, "Mr. Cannon was going to shift my man to the ——— subcommittee. I went to Mr. Cannon and said that I didn't mind if he were number two man, but that I didn't want him to short-change my subcommittee. I'd be sunk if he left. It would change my whole job."

When a clerk shares the goals of the Committee, obeys the norms of style set for him, demonstrates his usefulness, and gains the confidence of his subcommittee chairman, he becomes influential in subcommittee decision-making. One ranking subcommittee member commented, "They stay on one subcommittee and become a repository of all the information about a subcommittee's work. Then they become 'Mr. Indispensable' and the first thing you know, they run the whole show." One staff man concluded of his subcommittee chairman, "He wouldn't move an inch without me. I have his confidence and he trusts my judgment. Oh, someone may catch him on the floor and say 'I need something or other.' Otherwise, I'm in on it. I'm his alter ego, you might say." But they realize that their influence is derivative. Two of them summed up:

> A clerk can have a lot to do with a bill in the questions he prepares and suggestions he makes at markup. He can do almost anything he wants — within limits, of course. The clerk can have a lot of influence on an agency budget, but if he steps too far out of line with the chairman's approach on things, he won't be around long.

> We've got a lot of influence. Sometimes I think we have more influence than we should have. Last year, the markup I recommended to the subcommittee chairman was the same one that went to the floor. Is that influence? I don't know. I tried to do what I knew they would want done.

Where a close relationship between staff and subcommittee chairmen does exist, the title of "clerk" may well qualify as Capitol Hill's most massive misnomer.

CONCLUSION

The House Committee on Appropriations exhibits a well-differentiated decision-making structure. Seven key roles — Committee Chairman, ranking minority Committee member, subcommittee member, Committee newcomer, subcommittee chairman, ranking minority subcommittee member, and subcommittee clerk — have been described in terms of separately identifiable (though closely related) clusters of norms. These norms do prescribe a well-patterned decision-making structure, and considerable evidence of behavioral conformity to the various roles has been adduced. Pending additional confirmation of role–role behavior congruence and pending an assessment of the stability of the Committee's internal role relationships, we can assume that the normal, stable, and reasonably predictable internal decision-making processes of the House Committee on Appropriations has been described. By way of a concluding commentary on those processes, two points might be kept in mind.

First, we cannot know what constitutes a particular role nor can we estimate the influence of any role in the Committee's decision-making structure until we have discovered the informal as well as the formal norms which define it. The Committee Chairman and the subcommittee chairmen possess impressive and readily identifiable formal prerogatives. But these formal expectations carry only a potential for influence —a potential which they must capitalize through their observance of less formal and less conspicuous norms.

Obedience to informal, Committee-grown norms goes furthest toward winning for the Committee's leaders the "respect," "trust," and "confidence" of their fellows. And these attributes represent the most enduring (if not the most spectacular) sources of influence inside the Committee. One suspects the same generalizations can be made for other committees. The content of the norms will, of course, differ. But the point is that one cannot produce ascriptions or descriptions of a committee chairman's (or any putative committee leader's) influence simply by making reference to some generalized catalog of his formal prerogatives. On the basis of this one study, at least, a close and careful look at a committee's informal norms is essential to a description of its decision-making structure.

A second summary observation involves the degree to which the Committee's solution to its internal problem of decision-making is shaped by a concurrent concern for the solution of its external problem of adaptation. The Committee's decision-making arrangements seem well designed to achieve the kind of balanced response to House member and Committee member desires that was deemed to be the key to successful adaptation. In the realm of goal expectations, for example, the manipulation of subcommittees and subcommittee memberships can be explained, in large part, as attempts to balance the satisfaction of program support expectations (emphasized by "the House") against the satisfaction of economy expectations (stressed by the Committee members). In the realm of maintenance expectations, the pervasiveness of such norms as reciprocity, compromise, and minimal partisanship help to meet House expectations that consensus-building procedures be followed; but at the same time observance of these procedures will help produce the high degree of unity that Committee members believe will enhance their influence — collectively and individually — within the House. The structure of semi-autonomous subcommittees is well adapted to process, with decisiveness and with some variable degree of expertise, the enormous work load which the House piles on the Committee. This decentralized subcommittee structure also facilitates a fairly widespread distribution of influence and prestige among the Committee's members — thus helping to satisfy basic personal desires.

Since it comes as no revelation that a committee's decision-making structure is set up to do what the House tells the committee to do (i.e., make decisions in a given subject matter area), the more interesting of the two findings is that a committee's decision-making structure is set up to do what its own members want it to do — *for them,* individually and collectively. At least this is true for the Appropriations Committee. Though one can fabricate discrete descriptions of the Committee's (and, presumably any committee's) attempts to solve its external and internal problems of survival, the pattern of behavior developed for the solution to one problem will be affected by the necessity to solve the other problems as well. It will be of little help to the Committee to solve one only to find that it has undone the solution to another. A patterned solution to the internal problem of decision-making that also helps in meeting the external problem of adaptation can be assumed to have a certain degree of stability. This seems to be the case with the Appropriations Committee, and, therefore, we can speak with a bit more confidence about the stability of the structure we have described. A final assessment of the Committee's internal stability, however, awaits the analysis of the next chapter.

CHAPTER
FIVE

The House Committee
III: Structure for Integration

THE PROBLEM OF INTEGRATION

The House Appropriations Committee solves its internal problem of decision-making by dividing the work among a number of subgroups and a number of individual positions with their associated roles. The creation of a differentiated structure, however, produces a second internal problem for the group. "How shall these diverse elements be made to mesh or function in support of one another?" This is the problem of integration. Committee integration can be defined as the degree to which there is a working together or a meshing or mutual support among its subgroups and roles. Conversely, integration can be defined as the degree to which the Committee is able to minimize conflict among its subgroups and roles, either by heading off conflict or resolving it when it does arise. The problem of integration is the basic one of how any political system holds itself together. No political system is perfectly integrated — that is, totally free from internal conflict. But no political system can survive without some minimal degree of integration. The Appropriations Committee must be capable of making decisions without flying apart in the process.

The problem of integration has both normative (i.e., do prescribed roles mesh?) and behavioral (i.e., do actual role behaviors mesh?) dimensions. Chapter Four has, in effect, treated the normative aspect of the question by describing an arrangement of roles which fit smoothly together. The norms which most prominently define the Committee's decision-making roles — norms like reciprocity, unity, compromise, minimal partisanship, fairness, minimal interference in the work of others — surely bespeak the

191

Committee's extraordinarily strong commitment to integration on the normative side. The questions which still need to be answered are behavioral ones. How closely does Committee member role behavior correspond to prescribed roles? How can the correspondence or noncorrespondence be explained? What are the consequences of each for Committee activity? What kinds of internal conflict among individuals or groups do arise? How are internal conflicts, potential and actual, dealt with? What are the consequences of internal conflict for the stability of the Committee's decision-making structure?

Some of these behavioral questions have been partially answered in Chapter Four. Descriptions of actual decision-making indicate that Committee members usually do behave as they are supposed to behave — that there is, in other words, a fairly close correspondence of role behavior to role. On the assumption that some such correspondence exists, the decision-making structure outlined (both normatively and behaviorally) in Chapter Four was further asserted to have produced a relatively stable, normal, predictable decision-making process. If these assumptions and assertions are valid, then the Appropriations Committee can be said to be highly integrated. But their validity needs to be examined and tested by confronting the question of integration directly.

To assumptions about the congruence of role and role behavior, one can add evidence of regularized internal mechanisms which function (or fail to function) to produce and maintain such correspondence. To assertions about stability, one can add evidence of the Committee's capacity to cope with internal conflicts that threaten stability. Or one can produce evidence illustrating how internal conflicts can generate change. To assertions about normal decision-making, one can add evidence about deviations from the norm and thereby gain perspective on what is normal. Chapter Five examines the actual management and consequences of internal Committee conflict. It attempts to develop a more definitive empirical underpinning for generalizations about the behavior of Committee members and about the stability and the normality of Committee decision-making.

Above and beyond any relevance it may have for generalizations about decision-making, a description of integration focuses on an important structural property of the Committee. Since the House Committee dominates appropriations decision-making, its ability to manage its own internal conflicts will affect the stability of the entire appropriations process. Furthermore, the Committee's continued influence on congressional appropriations politics may hinge on its capacity to solve the problem of integration. For it seems unlikely that a Committee consumed by uncontrollable or unpredictable internal conflicts could long retain much respect, confidence, deference, and influence within its parent chamber. Nor could a conflict-ridden Committee meet the personal desires of its own members for power, prestige, or social solidarity. A decline in influence could come about either through the application of sanctions by the House or through the apathy, withdrawal, or discouragement of Committee members. The description in Chapter Five will indicate that the Committee has exhibited and maintained a high degree of integration. This internal structural fact surely helps to account for the stability of the appropriations process in Congress and for the House Committee's preeminent influence in that process.

FACILITATING CONDITIONS OF INTEGRATION

Before considering the processes of integration directly, there are some facilitating (one hesitates to call them either necessary or sufficient) Committee-related conditions of integration which have already been mentioned or alluded to and which should be elaborated upon. Most basic, perhaps, is the exceedingly *high value which Committee members themselves place upon internal integration.* Their concern is registered throughout the decision-making structure via the norms of reciprocity, unity, minimal partisanship, and compromise. Each one of these norms expresses the expectation that conflict should be minimized. They help define the role of the Committee's Chairman, of the Committee's ranking minority member, of each subcommittee member, and of the subcommittee chairman and ranking minority member. Within the Committee, there exists a consensus on roles, and that consensus stresses the desirability of integrative behavior. Those who have influence over the decision-making are expected to exercise it in such a way as to avert irreconcilable internal conflict. The Committee's norms of style are expected to have integrative consequences.

Beyond the value placed on internal integration, a facilitating condition is the existence of the *consensus on goals* which exists within the Committee. Members are in substantial agreement on the goals of protecting the power of the purse, guarding the Treasury, reducing budgets, and serving constituency interests. They are also in substantial agreement on the personal goals of influence which they seek. Of course, these goals themselves may sometimes conflict — budget-cutting versus constituency service or House-determined goals versus personally determined goals. But even here general agreement exists. These conflicts should, in the long run, be resolved in behalf of Treasury guardianship. Political systems with a low degree of consensus may minimize the disruptive consequences of conflict by having so vast a number of overlapping conflicts that no single conflict can rend the system. The Appropriations Committee, on the other hand, evidences a high degree of consensus to begin with, which increases the likelihood that sharp conflict can be averted by reference to a commonly accepted set of standards.

193

A third facilitating condition is the fact that so many Committee *decisions are dollars and cents decisions.* The Committee, of course, makes decisions on the same controversial issues as do the committees handling substantive legislation. Committee members know this, and they know that, after all, their ability to affect policy is the root of their influence in American national politics. If their actions had no programmatic consequences, they would hardly merit their reputation as "the powerful Appropriations Committee." Yet the decisions Committee members make are money decisions. And a money decision — however vitally it may affect national policy — is, or certainly can be perceived as, less directly a policy decision. Members refer to this Committee as a "business" or "technical" committee as distinguished from a "policy" committee. In the words of its Chairman, the Committee "deals with national finance and economics and not with politics. It is a business committee."[1] If this is so, decisions can be reached by bargaining and compromise easier than if the point at issue were acknowledged to be one of social philosophy. And differences of opinion with fellow Committee members are not converted into ideological conflicts. Money decisions are continuum decisions rather than dichotomous, yes or no decisions. One does not fight, bleed, and die if he perceives his disagreement with someone as a disagreement over a figure of $100 million against $125 million for the funding of a program already authorized. Besides, every program gets some money and a member can always say honestly that he did support any given program.

Committee members have their cake and eat it too. Their dollars and cents decisions affect programs. Yet they believe (and they act as if) in the words of one, "A disagreement on money isn't like a legislative program — it's a matter of money rather than a difference in philosophy." Or, as another put it, "Policy has been thrashed out ad lib, in extenso, and ad nauseam in the legislative committees. Our only problem is whether to appropriate $20 million or $15 million or nothing." "We consider things in dollars and cents," said a third member, "that's what we talk about."

> We don't get into policy the way the other committees do. We'd like to — and we can in the report and all that — but not in the bill. So there isn't much room for partisan controversy. We are always talking about dollars and cents.

To the degree that members accept their own definition of the situation they can remain relatively free agents, thus promoting intra-Committee maneuvering and blunting philosophical or partisan conflict.

Members do not have to commit themselves to their constituents, either, in terms of precise money amounts. And their constituents do not

[1] *Congressional Record,* Daily Edition, September 12, 1963, p. 16050.

194

punish and reward them for dollars and cents votes. Nor do members pledge themselves in any such concrete fashion to those who select them for the Committee. Members of committees that deal with recognizably controversial issues are often pressured into taking concrete stands on substantive issues by their constituents during election campaigns or by House committee-makers during negotiations preceding committee appointment. Consequently they come to their committee work with fixed and hardened attitudes. This leads to unavoidable, head-on, intracommittee conflict and renders integration attempts relatively useless. Such, for example, is the situation on such House committees as Education and Labor, where differences in social philosophy can hardly be ignored or sublimated. Appropriations Committee members, on the other hand, can convince each other that their money decisions keep them well behind the main battle lines over public policy.

Committee members sell this self-perception to others when they advertise themselves in terms of style rather than policy. When they play up their hard work, their long hours, and their preoccupation with tedious detail, they encourage others to see them, also, as a committee preoccupied with housekeeping routine rather than policy innovation. Insofar as they avoid publicity and maintain low public visibility, they help foster the same image. And they protect themselves from the intrusion of ideological conflict from the environment. The fact that most appropriations decisions are money decisions fosters internal bargaining. It also helps to perpetuate the image of a committee removed from the eye of social controversy. Both conditions facilitate internal integration.

The *legislative orientation of House members selected for the Committee* is another facilitating condition of Committee integration. Responsible or responsive legislators are those who have demonstrated an ability to work cooperatively and flexibly with others and a willingness to engage in legislative give and take. They are selected because they are especially attuned to and receptive toward the norms of the House; and such men will be temperamentally inclined to adopt the dominant norms of any legislative group to which they belong. Appropriations men, by their own admission, seek influence inside the House. Most of them aspire to careers in the House, and most of the others aspire to careers in Congress generally. Table 5.1 gives some indication of the dominant legislative orientation of the members by summarizing the reasons why the 82 men who left the Committee permanently, 1947 to 1965, did so.

Seventy-six per cent of the members (62 of 82) left public life with their Appropriations Committee boots on. They came to the Committee as early as they could and stayed as late as their health, their desire for public service, or their electoral fortunes permitted. The 50 members of the Committee in 1961, for example, had served an average of 13.1 years in the House

TABLE 5.1

REASONS FOR PERMANENTLY LEAVING APPROPRIATIONS
COMMITTEE — 1947 TO 1965

Reasons	Number of Men
Retired from Public Life	22
Defeated in General Election	20
Death	13
Ran for U.S. Senate	8[a]
Ran for or Appointed to Other Public Office	8[b]
Defeated — Primary Election	7
Transferred to other House Committee	2
"Bumped" Off Committee for Lack of Seniority	1[c]
Elected Party Floor Leader	1
Total	82

[a] Two others ran for the Senate, were defeated — one in the primary and one in the general election — and subsequently returned to the House and the Committee.

[b] Ran for: state governor (2), city mayor; appointed to: state treasurer, federal judge, local judge (2), Federal Communications Commission.

[c] Was defeated at next general election, thus preventing reapplication for Committee.

of Representatives. Men who seek legislative careers of such duration could be expected to promote cooperative rather than disruptive modes of behavior. They would be most amenable, therefore, to legislative and Committee norms providing for integration.

The legislative orientation of Committee members has, for one of its consequences, another facilitating condition of integration — *a great stability of Committee membership.* In the period from the 80th to the 87th Congress, for instance, 35 per cent of the Committee's membership remained constant. That is to say, of the 43 members on the Committee in March, 1947, 15 of them were still on the Committee in 1961. The 50 members of the Committee as of 1961 averaged 9.3 years of prior service on the Committee. In no single year from 1947 to 1965 has the Committee had to absorb an influx of new members totalling more than one-quarter of its membership. And this figure was approximated only 5 times in that 18-year period (see Table 2.4).[2] At all times, in other words, at least three-quarters of the members have had previous Committee experience. And its top leadership has been even more stable. When the 87th Congress adjourned in 1962, for instance, John Taber had been the Committee's most senior Republican

[2] Fourteen vacancies were filled in 1965, but two of the men assigned had previously served long terms on the Committee, left Congress, and been re-elected.

since 1933, and Clarence Cannon had been the Committee's most senior Democrat since 1942. Top leadership changes did occur subsequently; and they will be discussed later. This noteworthy stability of personnel has extended into the permanent staff as well. As of June, 1961, for example, its 15 professionals had served an average of 10.7 years with the Committee. In more than 100 years of its existence, the Committee has had but 7 different Chief Clerks — including the two highest ranking clerks as of 1965. Rapid, large-scale turnovers in personnel, carrying a potential for the internal disruption of the Committee, have not occurred. And, it might also be noted, personnel stability and integration have probably been aided by the fact that party control of the House has not changed very often in the period under study.

Membership stability provides the kind of continuity which allows the Committee's integrative norms to develop and take root. Since these norms are, for the most part, informal and traditional — handed down from one Committee generation to the next — membership stability is essential to their survival. It is striking how often Committee and staff members reply to questions about internal procedure by saying, "I don't know why it is, but it's been done for a generation." Or, "Well, I don't know why, it's just not a practice on our Committee." Or, "It's just a tradition, I guess." The following floor exchange with regard to closed hearings typifies Committee responses:

> HOUSE MEMBER: All right, can he stay here and listen to other witnesses?
> APPROPRIATIONS COMMITTEE MEMBER: No, sir, he cannot.
> HOUSE MEMBER: Well, that is what I am complaining about. That is undemocratic according to my opinion.
> APPROPRIATIONS COMMITTEE MEMBER: That rule has been in force since the days of George Washington.[3]

The Committee's senior men (especially Clarence Cannon) become the Committee's memory — nourishing the traditions, the lore, and the history of the group. Staff continuities are important in this regard too. For, should Committee members themselves be pressured by external demands to forego Committee customs for a while, staff men are less likely to be affected and will guard the Committee norms until the deviation is over. Personnel stability encourages a prescriptive reliance on established practices. These practices tend to stabilize and integrate rather than to disrupt the Committee internally.

Stability of membership means that the Committee's influential positions do not change hands frequently and it means that the group's younger

---

[3] 92 *Congressional Record*, p. 1092; see also 87 *Congressional Record*, p. 7916.

men rise to higher seniority rankings with glacier-like speed. An experienced Democrat said resignedly,

> I'm not moving very fast on the Committee. I'm not going to move much faster either, because there are Southerners above me. Lots of people who came in [to the House] with me are chairmen, ranking minority members, or high on their committee . . . you just have to wait your turn. It's like the Vice President — you know the Dawes story, "Every day you get up, look at the weather, and inquire about the state of the President's health."

An experienced Republican echoed similar sentiments about his subcommittee seniority:

> I have to speak as the very junior member of the so-called Gary-Canfield Committee. I have been on that body for a long time, but people who run for election and who are members of that committee never get defeated and people who are on that committee, thank God, never die. None of them ever resign, so that I am now on that committee just where I started seven years ago.[4]

The very gradualness with which seniority rankings change gives each member a long exposure to the Committee's integrative norms prior to the time he attains an influential position. And, so long as Committee members accept slow change — or are resigned to it — the probability of internal conflict is lessened and integration increased.

When a committee has developed a set of integrative norms, length of exposure to them increases the likelihood that they will be understood, accepted, and followed. So, too, does *repeated and concentrated exposure to Committee norms*. In this regard three factors peculiar to the appropriations process are relevant to internal integration. Repeated exposure follows from the fact that appropriation bills must be processed annually. Committee members perform the same operations with respect to the same subject matters every year, year in and year out. Familiar problems are faced and ample opportunity is provided for testing and confirming the usefulness of Committee norms in dealing with them. Moreover, the absolute necessity that appropriation bills do pass gives urgency to the adoption of norms designed to terminate rather than prolong conflict. Concentrated exposure to Committee norms is abetted by the stipulation that no Committee member may serve on another standing committee.[5] This House rule is a deterrent against the kind of fragmentation of activity which might expose a

---

[4] Committee on Appropriations, *Hearings on the Budget for 1958*, 85th Congress, 1st Session (Washington: U.S. Government Printing Office, 1957), p. 84.

[5] The only exception to this rule in recent years has been the dual service of Republican Glenard Lipscomb on the Appropriations and House Administration Committees. Several members sit on Select and Joint Committees; e.g., Joe Evins has been Chairman of the Select Committee on Small Business since 1963 and Albert Thomas sat on the Joint Committee on Atomic Energy from 1959 to 1966.

Member to contradictory sets of committee norms. Double exposure, in turn, might be a source of difficulty in gaining acceptance of the Appropriations Committee's integrative norms and, hence, holding that group together. Concentrated exposure to norms is produced, also, by the secrecy of Committee hearings. The fact that so little Committee action takes place in public helps insulate the group from externally generated norms which might conflict with internal ones.

A final facilitating condition of integration is *the continuing attractiveness which the Committee has for its members.* For, all things being equal, the more attracted a member is to the Committee, the more likely it is that he will obey its integrative norms. Members seek appointment to the Committee initially to satisfy their personal expectations for influence, for prestige, for information, for a sense of involvement. And to the degree that they find satisfaction, they will find membership attractive and rewarding to them. But continued Committee membership brings additional satisfaction in terms of a sense of group identification and group solidarity. As discussed earlier, the Committee's style of hard work is an especially important factor in this regard. What needs to be re-emphasized about that style is that it entails almost continuous interaction among members of the Committee — particularly in their subcommittee units. The members work long hours in close association with one another while at the same time being cut off by the injunctions of secrecy from outside intrusions. They work, fight, and negotiate behind closed doors. This intense internal interaction seems to increase their personal liking for one another and, hence, the attractiveness of Committee membership over and above or apart from any original reasons that they may have had for seeking Committee membership. The psychic rewards of friendship add to the continuing attractiveness for its members and, hence, to their willingness to abide by its integrative norms.

Some hint of the positive "affect" involved can be gleaned from public comments of members extolling "the spirit of friendship, mutual esteem and admiration, and even fraternal affection, that prevails in our [sub]committee."[6] When Committee members take the floor for the last time before leaving the Committee they are frequently moved to expressions of affection for their long-time subcommittee colleagues:

> Mr. Chairman, I will say that the one thing I take with me when I leave this Congress is my memory of the prodigious work of this subcommittee and a memory of its members which I shall cherish to my dying day.[7]

> Mr. Chairman, I take the floor at this time with a profound feeling of sadness. This will be the last time I address myself to the Independent Offices Appropriation Bill as a member of the Independent Offices Subcommittee of

[6] 100 *Congressional Record*, p. 2021.
[7] *Congressional Record*, Daily Edition, March 24, 1964, p. 5918.

the House Committee on Appropriations. One cannot easily take his leave from close friends with whom he has worked for the last fourteen years without having some sentiment stir. The bonds established in Committee over the years are very firm. . . . I have enjoyed the work of the subcommittee very much. I've enjoyed the work of the entire Appropriations Committee and the opportunities which it gave to build the close friendships which I have with its members.[8]

When the normal discount rate is applied for the syrupy amenities common to the House floor, these sentiments reveal a genuine warmth of association in subcommittee. Networks of friendship develop on nearly every subcommittee which run across party lines. Both the growth of integrative norms and an obedience to them are thereby encouraged.

SOME EVIDENCE OF INTEGRATION

Since party conflict represents the most pervasive form of conflict in the House of Representatives, a major problem in achieving Committee integration is the minimization of partisanship. The norms which define the Committee's various decision-making roles emphasize that Committee decisions should not be majority party decisions. They should be majority and minority party decisions, worked out cooperatively at every stage and whenever possible. Committee members believe that interparty agreement is a prerequisite for their influence in the chamber. Normally each subcommittee would rather produce a bill which satisfied the minority than a bill which maximizes the advantages for a majority. They want to be able to go to the House floor and say — as they normally do —

> This is one [sub]committee where you will find no partisan politics. We carry on the hearings and we mark up the bill and we compromise our differences. We bring a bill to the floor of the House each year with the unanimous approval of the [sub]committee members.[9]

> The subcommittee's approach has never been partisan and the subcommittee was unanimous in its findings. The recommendations were unaltered by the full Committee and the bill was reported to the House by a unanimous vote.[10]

If these public statements accurately describe private reality, they reflect a high degree of integration.

Subcommittee integration holds the key to Committee integration. And, for the subcommittee, the condition of integration is that the key roles

[8] *Congressional Record*, Daily Edition, July 30, 1962, p. 13985.
[9] 107 *Congressional Record*, p. 6123.
[10] 93 *Congressional Record*, p. 1873.

of chairman and ranking minority member mesh rather than conflict. The attempt to achieve such role reciprocity is reflected in the expectation that the two cooperate and consult in Committee decision-making. When they do, partisanship will automatically decline. Thus one ranking minority member described his relationship with his chairman:

> I have worked closely with him and can say that we have never had a minute's disagreement during the time we served together. As ranking minority member, I received every consideration which could possibly be expected from [the] chairman. In fact it can be safely said that under [his] chairmanship there were no parties in the subcommittee — we were all working for the same goal and working shoulder to shoulder.[11]

To the degree that partisan role behavior is minimized, an important exchange of rewards occurs. The chairman gains support for his leadership and the ranking minority member gains intracommittee influence. The Committee as a whole ensures against drastic change in its internal structure by giving to its key minority member a stake in its operation. Chairmen and ranking minority members will, in the course of time, exchange official positions. To the degree that the roles associated with the positions mesh, a switch in occupants will not heighten conflict in the subcommittee.

Two subcommittee chairmen described situations in which they had exchanged positions while maintaining internal harmony through cooperation:

> When I have served as chairman of this committee [he] has given me the utmost cooperation and support. I have tried to reciprocate and together we have carried on the work of the committee without any friction, without any partisan politics.[12]

> One thing that has impressed me about [him] is that at all times during these ten years he has shown a great disposition to cooperate with the leadership of the committee, and by virtue of that fact [he] received cooperation when he served as chairman.[13]

A Republican chairman testified to the considerable sharing of information and skill which takes place when he said of the Democrat he had just succeeded,

> He has been very generous with his knowledge and experience in assisting and counseling me during my first year as chairman . . . it has been a pleasure to work with him and I hope to continue to draw on his knowledge and guidance in the future, as I have in the past.[14]

[11] *Congressional Record*, Daily Edition, January 16, 1962, p. 232.
[12] *Congressional Record*, Daily Edition, February 23, 1960, p. 3006.
[13] 103 *Congressional Record*, p. 8880.
[14] 99 *Congressional Record*, p. 5327.

And a Democratic chairman referred to his ranking minority member as "my old professor who trained me how to handle the bill."[15]

Still another pair of senior Committee men who traded official positions for fifteen years painted a picture of substantial role reciprocity resulting in integration. Said Tweedledum, "I have served under [his] chairmanship and it has been said that it did not make much difference which of us happened to be presiding officer of the subcommittee."[16] Said Tweedledee, "He and I have worked together . . . many members say we have worked so closely that seldom if ever do our views differ."[17] These comments, related to five different subcommittees, depict considerable success in the minimization of partisanship.

To some incalculable degree, harmony between chairman and ranking minority member is a function of the stability of membership which allows a pair of particular individuals to work out the kind of personal accommodation just described. The close working relationship of Clarence Cannon and John Taber, whose service on the Committee (at the close of the 87th Congress) totaled seventy years, and who exchanged the position of Committee Chairman and ranking minority member for twenty years, highlighted and strengthened the reciprocity of roles existing in the group. Despite their radically different personalities and voting records, the two men concurred that "We have a lot in common," "We stand shoulder to shoulder," "We usually agree," and "We are both on the conservative side" when it comes to the business of the Committee. "Many times," said Cannon, "the two of us could sit right here at this table and go over the whole schedule — authorizations and all. If we saw something that ought to come out, we'd take it out; if we saw something that ought to go in, we'd put it in."

It was Cannon and Taber who inaugurated and sustained the powerfully integrative arrangement whereby the ranking minority member as well as the Chairman served as ex officio member of every subcommittee. Committee members who watched them in action reiterated that, "They work very closely together," "They fight for the same things," or "They've been here so long they understand each other." "Mr. Cannon confides in Mr. Taber and he confides in absolutely nobody else," said a veteran subcommittee chairman. A senior staff member described the mutual understanding which had been built up over the years and which checked the force of partisanship:

> They understood each other. They knew they were members of opposite parties and that party loyalties would pull. But they knew where they each

[15] *Congressional Record*, Daily Edition, September 20, 1962, p. 19041.
[16] *Congressional Record*, Daily Edition, May 10, 1960, p. 9166.
[17] *Congressional Record*, Daily Edition, June 6, 1961, p. 8922.

stood. They differed widely on such things as public power. But they would vote against each other on that and then join the next day and take up the fight together. They knew where to find each other on the issues. They knew each other's idiosyncrasies. But they forgot past battles and didn't dwell on old issues. In this way they were both big men. They had been together for a long time. They went through many eras together. They were old men and they grew old together.

In a system where the teaching of Committee norms and role behavior is accomplished primarily by example, the impact of the Cannon-Taber comity multiplied itself as a model for others. Their counterparts on the subcommittees — long-time chairman/ranking minority twosomes such as Representatives Gary (D., Va.) and Canfield (R., N.J.) (1949 to 1961); Whitten (D., Miss.) and Andersen (R., Minn.) (1949 to 1963); Kirwan (D., Ohio) and Jensen (R., Iowa) (1949 to 1963); Fogarty (D., R.I.) and Laird (R., Wisc.) (1959 to present); Mahon (D., Texas) and Ford (R., Mich.) (1959 to 1965); Thomas (D., Texas) and Ostertag (R., N.Y.) (1959 to 1965); Rooney (D., N.Y.) and Bow (R., Ohio) (1959 to present), have had an example to follow as well as time to work out such idiosyncratic techniques of accommodation as might be necessary.

No matter how well meshed the roles and the role behaviors of party leaders, internal conflict cannot be eliminated from the Committee. But, even where it persists, Committee members attempt to minimize its disruptive impact by containment. Toward this end, the most functional Committee practice is its tradition enjoining the use of minority reports. A minority report, written in opposition to the majority report of a committee, is the outward visible symbol of inward invisible committee disunity. It publicizes, prosecutes, and sharpens internal committee conflict. By custom, Appropriations Committee members do not often file minority reports.

A few have been written, but on only 12 of the 197 original appropriation bills in the period 1947 to 1962. That is to say, 94 per cent of all original appropriation bills during a 16-year period were reported out to the House floor without public dissent from any Committee member. Six reports that were written registered disagreement by more than 1 person. Five of these cases involved interparty differences. Five cases were one-man expressions of sentiment. With the possible exception of the Armed Services Committee the record as summarized in Table 5.2 is unmatched in the House of Representatives.

When there are no minority reports, Committee members can proclaim to the House, "For the twelve years since I have been chairman of this subcommittee, we have had unanimous reports," or "For the past many, many years this bill has come to the floor by unanimous agreement of the

TABLE 5.2

MINORITY REPORTS ON ORIGINAL APPROPRIATION BILLS
1947 TO 1962

Year	Total No. of Original Appropriation Bills	No. of Minority Reports	Subcommittee Involved	No. of Signers and Their Party
1947	12	1	Agriculture	2 (majority)
1948	13	1	Government Corporations	3 (minority)
1949	11	1	Foreign Aid	2 (minority)
1950	11	0	—	—
1951	11	2	Treasury–Post Office	1 (minority)
			Legislative	1 (minority)
1952	11	0	—	—
1953	11	0	—	—
1954	11	0	—	—
1955	13	1	Agriculture	2 (minority)
1956	13	2	Treasury–Post Office	1 (minority)
			Public Works	4 (minority)
1957	13	2	Treasury–Post Office	1 (minority)
			Defense	1 (minority)
1958	14	0	—	—
1959	14	2	Agriculture	1 (minority)
			Foreign Operations	4 (minority)
1960	14	0	—	—
1961	13	0	—	—
1962	12	0	—	—
Total	197	12		

subcommittee."[18] Committee members believe that public displays of cohesion will enhance their influence on the floor.

The custom against minority reports does not mean that internal disagreement is suppressed. The Committee has its own functional equivalent of the minority report. It is the custom of "reserving." When a subcommittee member cannot agree with the majority decision, he simply informs his colleagues informally by expressing his "reservations" on the item involved. Thus he puts his colleagues on notice that he may, at some later point in the proceedings, disagree openly. It is his way of telling them that he may seek a change or support a change in that particular item in the full Com-

[18] 108 *Congressional Record*, p. 4728; 105 *Congressional Record*, p. 4966.

mittee or on the floor. But he does not publicize his dissent. Also, by restricting his disagreement to specific items, he does not universalize internal differences. The Committee then makes and publicly announces a "unanimous" recommendation.

A member explained how the technique operates in subcommittee:

> If there's something I feel too strongly about, and just can't go along, I'll say, "Mr. Chairman, we can have a unanimous report, but I reserve the right to bring this up in full Committee. I feel duty bound to make a play for it and see if I can't sell it to the other members." But if I don't say anything, or don't reserve this right, and then I bring it up in full Committee, they'll say, "Who are you trying to embarrass? You're a member of the team, aren't you? That's not the way to get along."

The individual member retains some freedom of maneuver without firm commitment. Since "If there's anything members don't like it's someone who keeps quiet in Committee and then pops up on the floor with an amendment," the technique of reservation protects him with his associates. He may, as many do, signal his disagreement by "reserving" but take no further action. Thus the Committee has a technique for ventilating internal disagreements which keeps their disruptive consequences to a minimum.

A threat even of "reserving" may trigger an intracommittee effort at compromise. One ranking minority subcommittee member recalled an instance in which the subcommittee chairman yielded his preferences rather than go to the floor with a reservation hanging over his bill:

> We had a gentleman's agreement in markup to make a $50 million cut — let them take it anywhere they want it. It was an across the board kind of cut. Well, I got thinking about it afterward and got pretty unhappy. So I went to see the subcommittee chairman. I said, "That's not a big enough cut. I've got to reserve on that." He said, "Well we've got to go in together on that; let's go down to my office and talk it over." So he got the Chairman of the Committee and a few others and we sat down and they said, "How much of a cut will you take?" I said, "$150 million." Well, we talked it back and forth. I argued that they wouldn't be hit by it, that $50 million was no better than nothing and that if we couldn't cut here we couldn't cut anywhere. I said they had more than they knew what to do with anyway and so on and so on. Finally the subcommittee chairman said, "Will you take $100 million?" I finally said, "All right. I'll take $100 million."

When the Committee succeeds in eliminating or in containing internal conflict, it displays its "unanimous" recommendations on the floor amidst a veritable orgy of self-congratulation. The subcommittee chairman expresses his thanks to each member of the group — especially, of course, to the ranking minority member. He praises each member in turn, stressing his hard work, length of service, sterling individual qualities, or unique contributions.

205

"I am very proud of the team which makes up the subcommittee on appropriations handling the Treasury and Post Office Department funds. In passing, I want to say a word about each member of that team."[19] And each member responds in kind, explaining what privilege it is to work with such an able chairman and such a fine group of colleagues. "I want to preface the remarks I am about to make by expressing my sentiments toward my fine colleagues on the subcommittee."[20] "It would not be a complete presentation by a subcommittee," said one member on the floor, "unless all of us were to take the floor and tell you how much we love each other."[21] Subcommittee love feasts exceed the normal expression of legislative amenities. They express the Committee's sense of togetherness and an exclusiveness which House members, as we have seen, resent as evidence of "a clan," "a club," and "a closed corporation."

Chairman Cannon asked members to refrain from the practice — and one subcommittee, at least, has a rule (not enforced) against it — but it continues. Evidently Committee members feel that they can preserve and increase their internal integration by reminding each other in public how highly integrated they are. At the same time, they can remind each other of the reasons for this integration. And each member can indulge his pride in membership on the Committee. The practice is functional, too, as a means by which each member helps his colleagues to a bit of publicity. Many Committee members get no other public recognition. For them the emergence of their subcommittee's bill into the light of day represents their main opportunity to let the folks back home know they are on the job. The distribution of kudos is for the public record. It might not be quite so lavish if it were not a major publicity outlet for many Committee members.

Subcommittee self-congratulation normally ends (again, despite the chairman's self-proclaimed "rule" against it) with a paean of praise for the subcommittee clerk — "the man without whose help . . ." The Committee's permanent staff functions to promote Committee integration as well as decision-making. Primarily, it does so by maintaining a scrupulous nonpartisanship. But, starting from this base, the staff builds its own internal esprit and sense of identification which is a mirror image of that on the Committee. The job is attractive to them and they derive great personal satisfaction from it. Only two men have left the staff since 1951. "When I came here," said one, "the Chief Clerk told me 'once you've been on this job, it'll spoil you for any other one.' He's right. You have the feeling that you're at the center of decision-making and that you can do some good. You get a lot of satisfaction from the job." Members refer to the

[19] 99 *Congressional Record*, p. 4922.
[20] *Congressional Record*, Daily Edition, May 10, 1960, p. 9162.
[21] 96 *Congressional Record*, p. 5627.

staff as "a lodge." Their close working harmony is lubricated by informal ties. Two members described a highly integrated staff operation in this way:

There are no cliques on the staff. We help each other out and discuss any problems we have with each other. It's a diversified group — lawyers, accountants, public administrators, engineers. There isn't any problem we can't work out. Things get coordinated much better down here than they do on the Committee. . . . We keep our luncheon appointments to a minimum and we eat together and talk over our problems with one another.

We have a lot of contact back and forth on the staff. It's small and very informal and we work closely together. We have coffee in the morning and talk things over and try to coordinate our approach across bills . . . we are small and can work together easily. When we have a party, 21 places will do for all of us — typists and all.

A third staff member highlighted internal integration by stressing the degree to which staff roles are both complementary and interchangeable. Referring to his own lack of a budgetary background, he said,

My great deficiency is budgeting. I've picked up a lot, but on some real technical problems I need advice. ———, ———, and ——— [subcommittee clerks] are experts. So I'll go to them and they'll help me out. We'll put our feet on the table or go to lunch and I've got it made. We're a very closely knit group and we can do that sort of thing. If I'm sick and unable to handle a hearing, another man can step right in. I've handled other hearings when I didn't know a damn thing about the bill; but you know the procedure and you know the members, and you can go right along. One time I had to get out a report in 36 hours. It was impossible. Three or four others came over and we pitched in and we sat until 3 A.M. We got it out.

Negatively, the highly integrated Committee staff eliminates a possible source of internal disruption. But it seems likely, as well, that by their efforts they increase the degree of harmony among the Committee members for whom they work.

INTERNAL CONTROL MECHANISMS

The Committee's internal structure has been described in terms of the clusters of normative expectations which define who should do what with regard to decision-making and integration. For each of the behavior patterns so prescribed, evidence of corresponding actual behavior has been presented. That evidence is persuasive. But, necessarily, it is' incomplete. Too much of the Committee's internal activity remains beyond the pale of systematic observation. Empirical generalizations about Committee norms, about Committee behavior, and about the relation of norms to behavior, therefore, are in the nature of inferences made from a substantial though still fragmentary body of data. The reliability of these generalizations could be substantially increased, however, if it were known that the Committee had systematic and effective internal mechanisms for bringing about the observance of Committee norms. To the degree that such mechanisms operate, it becomes highly probable that norms or roles (as expressed by Committee "respondents") and actual behavior or role behavior (as observed through the public record and Committee "informants") do correspond to one another. If that is true, the Committee's internal structure can be seen as a stable set of expectations which underlie and relate to stable patterns of behavior. The validity, therefore, of inferences made from norms about behavior or about behavior from norms is markedly increased.

The idea of control mechanisms completes the definition of an operative social norm. It will be recalled that

> A norm exists when there are 1. Agreement or consensuses about the behaviors group members should or should not enact and 2. Social processes produce adherence to these agreements.[22]

When the norms of the group are, as in this case, highly integrative and only minimally disruptive, control mechanisms operate to promote and preserve internal integration. Two such mechanisms are of special importance to the Committee on Appropriations. The first is the socialization processes through which Committee newcomers are taught the norms of the group. The second is the sanctioning mechanisms applicable to all members of the Committee which operate to reward the observance of appropriate norms and punish deviations from them.

If, of course, there were no deviations and no inclinations to deviate from Committee norms, control mechanisms would be unnecessary. Conversely, in order to observe control mechanisms in action, there must be some observable deviation from norms. Indeed, it seems essential to the effectiveness of internal control mechanisms that some deviation should occur. The mechanisms must be used occasionally to remain effective. Their use reminds members of the existence of such mechanisms and keeps them in good working order. They function to promote a pattern of behavior which remains in general accord over time with expectations, to bring deviations within the bounds of expectations — but not to ensure perfect accord between behavior and expectations. The discussions that follow will center upon the capacity of the Committee's control mechanisms for minimizing deviation and for correcting it.

[22] John W. Thibaut and Harold H. Kelly, *The Social Psychology of Groups* (New York: John Wiley, 1959), p. 239.

New members do not come to the Committee equipped with the full complement of expectations, perceptions, and attitudes held by the incumbent members of the group. They must be taught and they must learn — and the process of teaching and learning Committee perceptions and Committee norms is called the process of socialization. Not all newcomers will have to be taught the same things. For the liberal Democrat the goal of budget-cutting may have to be learned; for the economy-minded Republican, the Committee's integrative norms may be little understood. The point is that Committee selection produces no fully socialized members. Committee-makers, indeed, stress responsiveness to the chamber and *not* responsiveness to Appropriations Committee norms as their main criterion. But the selection process does produce a group of Committee newcomers who are legislatively oriented and, hence, have a built-in responsiveness to the socialization processes of any legislative group of which they are members. Furthermore, since most Committee newcomers are strongly attracted to the Committee, they are more susceptible than otherwise to in-Committee training. In terms of aptitude for learning and of motivation for learning, therefore, the selection process produces excellent raw material.

The function of the apprentice role assigned to the newcomer is that it provides time during which socialization can proceed. It helps ensure continuities in Committee behavior by denying influence to those members who remain untutored in its ways. For the member who performs his apprentice role creditably and learns his lessons well, the passage of time holds the promise of Committee influence. But for his first term or two, he is viewed by his elders as a man with relatively little to contribute to the proceedings. His socialization begins by acquainting him with the role of apprentice and impressing upon him — as one newcomer put it — that whatever his previous House accomplishments, "You are a freshman all over again."

The prime technique of socialization on the Committee is that of learning by doing. Senior Committee members teach by the "do as I do" not the "do as I say" method. When asked to put apprenticeship norms into words, they advise "Keep quiet," "Follow the chairman," and "Learn the business of the Committee." Experienced members who had, within memory, sloughed off their apprenticeship role typically answered the question "How did you learn the ropes?": "You pick it up by ear" or "It's like anything else in the House — you learn it by yourself." Two others agreed that they were not taught by the lecture method:

> Nobody tells you. You just go to subcommittee meetings and gradually assimilate the routine. The new members are made to feel welcome, but

209

> you know that you have a lot of rope learning to do before you carry much weight.

> Nobody tells you anything around here. You find out for yourself by living with it. It's like any other experience — you live with it, that's all. There's a lot to be said for experience.

Two experienced members asserted that they did not have to learn any ropes. But the rest felt that they had something to learn, that apprenticeship was beneficial to them — and, most importantly, they were now prepared to enforce it on the current crop of newcomers.

Newcomers themselves are not as universally well disposed toward the role they are called upon to play. Most of them do what is expected of them; a few rebel. But all of them watch, listen, and imitate the older members. They speak freely about their learning experience, and, however painful a process it may be, they begin early to accept for themselves most salient aspects of the Committee's political culture.

For example, most of them become quickly aware of their own relative ignorance. Said one, "Sometimes I go home sick at night. When they start talking about these missiles and things, they just leave me. But I'm getting an education, and I study four or five hours a day." Said another, "If I became ranking minority member now, I'd be scared to death. I don't know my stuff yet." As the newcomers experience their first set of subcommittee hearings, they typically find themselves in a losing scramble to keep up with the detailed lines of questioning being advanced by senior members. One complained that in his first year his subcommittee "went along so fast I never did have time to get a grasp of things." Thus they come to learn early the need for information. One freshman declared, "I attended all the hearings and studied and collected information that I can use next year. I'm just marking time now." They discover, too, the value of hard work which one newcomer related in a perverse sort of way:

> There are some old war horses on the Committee, some pretty dull-witted guys. They plug and plug and plug. And they get more than the smart fellow, because they're there all the time working at it.

If it is their first set of hearings that impresses upon them the need for specialized information, it is their first markup session that makes them conscious of the impulse toward unity. Several reported feeling "the great pressure to conform." Another observed that "Many times the older men stuck together on votes. They had things under control. Some of them have been on the subcommittee for 15 or 20 years." "These fellows want to report a bill they can all agree on," another recounted. "They don't want any minority reports. About all you can do is say, 'I reserve on that point, Mr. Chairman.'"

Since the Committee's norms are so largely informal and traditional, they cannot be internalized overnight. Rather they are absorbed after frequent and extended exposure. One very sensitive first-year man expressed his feeling that

> The Appropriations Committee is a club. As one of the younger members of the club, there are a lot of things you don't understand. You don't understand them but you sure can feel their presence — like cosmic rays.

Another commented simply, "It's strange and mysterious." Slowly, however, the newcomer imbibes the important elements of the Committee's political culture. And as he does he comes to feeling increasingly like a member rather than an observer of "the club." A second-year man discussed his newly acquired sense of group identification:

> It's like anything else in Congress. You have to sit in the back seat and then edge up little by little. I've made a lot of friends on the Committee and I feel like a member of the Committee now. In the beginning you have a lot of trouble keeping up with the complications and intricacies of appropriations.

A man who feels like a member of the Committee will begin to act like one. His first public opportunity to demonstrate his allegiance comes when his subcommittee first brings its bills to the House floor. A newcomer who, before his service on the Committee, resented their rite of self-congratulation, may have acquired a new appreciation of its integrative function:

> As a new member of this Committee who has been sitting here for the last four years, I have noticed that every time one of these committees came in here with a bill they started handing out orchids to the Chairman and other members of the Committee; and it made me a little shaky. It rather got under my skin. But I have had an education. I really want to add my word to this hard-working Committee and our Chairman, to the members on the minority side . . . if you worked mornings and afternoons and nights trying to keep up with them, then you will see that you have a job.[23]

Evidence that their socialization is progressing satisfactorily can be gleaned from comments such as these by Committee members making their maiden speeches as Committee men:

> Mr. Chairman, during the past three months I have had my initiation as a member of the Committee on Appropriations, and as a member of the subcommittee that handled the bill under consideration at this time. It has been a pleasant revelation to me to see the vigor and the ability and the high

[23] 93 *Congressional Record*, p. 1883.

211

purpose that the . . . members of the Committee displayed in examining the witnesses and really pursuing questions to the point where we had just about all the information that it was possible to bring out from them. I feel that the older members of the Committee, who have had a great deal of experience have done just an excellent job, and I appreciate the opportunity of having been a member of this Committee and working with them.[24]

Mr. Chairman, in view of the fact that I only joined this subcommittee this present year, I have not sought to take part in general debate on the bill here today. I rise only for the purpose of publicly expressing the high esteem and appreciation I have developed for my colleagues on that subcommittee and for the fine conscientious job that I know they have done in bringing this bill here today. I also want to take this occasion to say that I have followed this bill and the leadership of my colleagues on the Committee as closely as I know how and that I am here supporting the bill as it was reported by the Committee.[25]

These men have accepted the role of apprentice and have begun to internalize norms of hard work, specialization, and unity. They have begun to develop positive affect toward their fellow members and have expressed it publicly. The consequences of these attitudes and actions are highly integrative for the Committee.

Socialization is in part a training in perception. Before members of a group can be expected to observe its norms, they must see and interpret the world around them with reasonably similar results. This kind of learning proceeds, too, during the apprenticeship period. The newcomers' perceptions are brought sufficiently into line with those of the older members to serve as a basis for integration. Radically different perceptions of political reality could promote different sets of expectations and attitudes with seriously disruptive consequences for the group. Most important, perhaps, is the training of Committee newcomers to perceive their environment in terms that lead them to accept the Committee's definition of its goals. Their elders, for example, already perceive that all executive agencies ask for more money than they need. And this perception buttresses their goal of budget-cutting. A subcommittee chairman explained,

When you have sat on the Committee, you see that these bureaus are always asking for more money — always up, never down. They want to build up their organization. You reach the point — I have — where it sickens you, where you rebel against it. Year after year, they want more money. They say, "Only $50 thousand this year"; but you know the pattern. Next year they'll be back for $100 thousand, then $200 thousand. The younger members haven't been on the Committee long enough, haven't had the experience to know this.

The Committee's young must be trained to see things in this same way.

[24] 98 *Congressional Record*, p. 3412.
[25] 103 *Congressional Record*, p. 2268.

212

The Committee's self-starting, economy-minded Republicans and its conservative Southern Democrats are predisposed to accept such goals as Treasury guardianship and its supporting perceptions. But one-half of the Committee's Democratic members are Northerners and Westerners (primarily from urban constituencies) who come to the Committee favorably inclined toward domestic social welfare programs and the high level of federal spending necessary to support them. Their voting records are as "liberal" on behalf of such programs as non-Committee Democrats from like constituencies. For some of them, the Committee had no initial attraction; and they had to be coopted by their party's committee-makers. It is crucial to Committee integration that these men learn to temper their potentially disruptive welfare state ideology with a conservative concern for saving money. They must change their perceptions and attitudes sufficiently so that they view the Committee's goals in nearly the same terms as their Southern Democratic and Republican colleagues.

The Committee's liberal Democrats were not selected because of their economy-mindedness, but because of their political flexibility. And, though this is hardly their intention, Democratic Committee-makers send to the Committee precisely those individuals who are most easily socialized through Committee experience. In the early months of one "liberal's" service on the Committee, he received a call from the White House asking for his support (given in the past) on the administration's plan to continue financing the Export-Import Bank by direct Treasury borrowing. When the fledgling Committee member hesitated, saying "Well, I don't know," the White House liaison man shot back, "Do you have some deep philosophical objection or something?" The Committee member replied, "You're damn right I have." And, a few weeks later he explained, "I had some doubts about it before. But since I've been on the Committee, they have been re-enforced. What else have we got in Congress but the power over spending." Clearly, he had already adopted the Committee's broadest goal — protecting the power of the purse — and his socialization was well under way.

Within one or two terms, Democratic liberals are differentiating between themselves and the "wild-eyed spenders" or the "free spenders" in the House. "Some of these guys would spend you through the roof," exclaimed one experienced liberal. And another newcomer explained, "I'm a liberal. But I can see myself getting more conservative." Repeated exposure to Committee work and to fellow members has altered their perceptions and their attitudes on money matters. Half a dozen new or experienced Northern Democrats agreed with two of their members who said,

> Yes, it's true. I can see it myself. I suppose I came here a flaming liberal; but as the years go by I get more conservative. You just hate like hell to spend all this money. It's an awful lot of money. I used to look more at the pro-

213

gram, but now I look at it in terms of money . . . you come to the point where you just say "by God, this is enough jobs."

Yes, I think you do [get more conservative on the Committee]. You get to sympathize more with the taxpayer. You get insight into where the money comes from and where it goes. You want to save as much as you can. You get to feel it. It's like a wage earner. He knows where the money comes from and how hard it is to get it, and he's careful in spending it. There's an inherent desire to economize in the members of the Committee.

These men remain more inclined toward spending than their Committee colleagues; but their perceptions and attitudes have been brought close enough to the others to support a consensus on goals. They are responsive, now, to appeals for budget-cutting that would not have registered earlier and which remain meaningless to liberals outside the Committee. In those cases, therefore, where Committee selection does not and cannot produce individuals predisposed toward guarding the Treasury, an equivalent result is achieved by socialization.

For the more conservatively inclined newcomer, Committee socialization has the effect of reenforcement. Committee elders state as a rule applicable to all members that, "The longer you are on the Committee the more conservative you become." And a senior staff member highlighted the extent of the learning process within the Committee in describing his own experience:

The more I stay around this branch the more conservative I get, the more mossback I get. Necessarily, we have to be negative, necessarily we have to be unpopular, and necessarily we have to develop a philosophy. You observe the growth of bureaucracy and you can't help developing a conservative philosophy. I've noticed that the congressmen can't escape this.

Another important perception which newcomers must learn involves the degree to which the internal influence of Committee leaders depends upon their adherence to Committee norms. As we have seen, the Chairman and the subcommittee chairmen (and their opposite numbers) have impressive formal authority. But they win the respect and deference of other members just as much because of their obedience to group norms of style. Newcomers do not immediately perceive this. The Democratic freshmen of 1963, for example, tended to exaggerate Clarence Cannon's influence and the importance of its formal sources.

Cannon exercises a constant surveillance. Nothing escapes him. He abolishes subcommittees and decapitates subcommittee chairmen. All the Committee's actions have the stamp of the Chairman on them.

214

The Republican newcomers of 1959 seemed to convert their own sense of powerlessness (felt the more strongly, perhaps, because of their minority status) into the perception that their subcommittee chairmen possess "inconceivable," "absolute," and "inordinate" influence. "If you're a subcommittee chairman, it's your committee." "The chairman runs the show. He decides what he wants and he gets it through." "He's the boss. He gets about what he wants." "Nine times out of ten what he says goes." "Some chairmen act like God Almighty." When the newcomer lists the resources of the subcommittee chairmen he tends to find them either in his formal prerogatives or in some deus ex machina such as the staff member.

Experienced members see through a different set of lenses. They perceive internal influence much more in terms of a contingent and revocable grant by which the deference of the members is tendered for so long as the leader meets their expectations. They do not see arbitrary or awesome power. Regarding Cannon: "Of course the Committee wouldn't follow him if it didn't want to. He has a great deal of respect. He's an able man, a hardworking man." Regarding subcommittee chairmen: "Occasionally one comes along that is too cocky: then one of the members of the Committee cuts him down to size and trims his whiskers a little." Newcomers must come to share these perceptions about internal Committee influence before they can understand and fit easily into Committee activity.

The Socialization of Fred Santangelo

Newcomers get trained, for the most part, by the subcommittee members with whom they work. And special perceptions may have to be taught to particular subcommittee newcomers. The man, for instance, who has been appointed to a subcommittee partly because of his lack of interest in the subject matter under its jurisdiction and in the hopes that he will further reduce budgets presents a special problem. If his perceptions are not brought within tolerable limits, he may disrupt a well-established pattern of subcommittee behavior. An interesting case of this sort (i.e., subcommittee socialization in the direction of interest and generosity) was the education of Representative Fred Santangelo.

Congressman Santangelo, a New York City Democrat representing an east Harlem constituency, came to the Committee in 1958. He was immediately assigned to the Subcommittee on Agriculture. The appointment seems to have been designed to countervail a marked interest-sympathy-leniency syndrome operating within the subcommittee. (The relative liberality of the Agriculture Subcommittee is shown in Chapter Eight.) The rhetoric of the appointment was that of "balancing things up" and "representing the consumer interest." A very influential subcommittee member protested the

215

appointment to Cannon. "I told him I didn't like it." Committee wags talked about the cross section now represented on the subcommittee — "You've got corn, cotton, tobacco, wheat, and the marijuana farmer from New York." And Santangelo himself was bitterly disappointed. In an early full Committee meeting he spoke openly, pointedly, and sarcastically against Mr. Cannon's decision:

> I stated at that time to the Chairman that I appreciated the significance of this appointment and I knew that the farmers in my area, with their tremendous plantations and farm land in the rear of a tenement house, amounting to 18 feet by 12 feet, and with their truck gardens on the fire escapes and the window sills, would also appreciate the significance and importance of this assignment.[26]

The subcommittee wanted a newcomer with a similar interest in and perceptions about agriculture as they; the man they got admitted believing that REA was a foreign-made automobile. The liberal Democratic newcomer wanted an assignment from which he could help his urban constituency; the Subcommittee on Agriculture seemed to him the most remotely related one of all.

During his first year, Santangelo kept quiet and listened. In so doing, he discovered that his subcommittee did, indeed, have jurisdiction over some things of direct interest to his constituents — particularly the school lunch program. He also found an area of special personal interest — given the fact that his father had been a butcher — the meat inspection program. With these as a foundation, he gradually learned to perceive the overall interests of farm and city as intertwined rather than separate from one another. And he came to value his subcommittee associations. When the subcommittee brought its bill to the floor, the chairman singled out Santangelo for praise, saying "He has rendered excellent service [and] has shown great interest in the operation of the Department."[27] Translated, it meant that a proper apprenticeship was being observed. Santangelo was given five minutes to speak, during which time he praised the chairman for his "brilliant cross-examination of many witnesses which elicited . . . a wealth of information," praised his other colleagues, and spoke in support of the school lunch program. In his words of appreciation to his subcommittee colleagues, he revealed the extent of his socialization:

> I want to take this opportunity of thanking the . . . members of the subcommittee . . . for giving me the benefit of their views, and for the courtesy, comfort, and encouragement which they have given to me as a neophyte member of the subcommittee, a person coming from the city dealing with

[26] *Congressional Record*, Daily Edition, February 15, 1961, p. A916.
[27] 104 *Congressional Record*, p. 5961.

matters which seem not to be germane to city life. Because of their cooperation and because of their help I have found work on this subcommittee to be very inspiring and it made me realize very clearly that the welfare of the farmer is intimately connected with the welfare and the dignity of the laborer in the city. . . .[28]

With his perceptions altered and the attractiveness of his role increased, Santangelo was well on the way to being fully integrated into the work of the subcommittee.

During his second year on the subcommittee, he was asked to specialize in the school lunch program. When the chairman was invited to address a convention of school lunch administrators, he passed the opportunity to Santangelo. Soon, the New York City congressman was the acknowledged authority on the subject. Later, he added meat and poultry inspection to his list of specialities. And he, in turn, acknowledged and deferred to the expertise of the other members in forestry, agricultural research, soil conservation, production payments, or in dealing with specific crops. By the end of the second year, the man who had originally protested Santangelo's appointment was delighted with the outcome. "My fears were needless," he said. "He's a hell of a fine fellow and a good friend of mine. I didn't know him so well before, but he's cooperated and gone along and everything's worked out fine." In 1960, Santangelo's horizons were broadened by his being included on a trip with two subcommittee members — to western United States and Asia. When the Agriculture Appropriation Bill of that year came to the floor, Santangelo praised the chairman for helping "to educate a city member of the committee." And he thanked especially his two companions on the trip "who have taken a city boy in tow in the rural electrification program, in the rice paddies of Asia, and in the pens among the hogs and the pigs and the cattle in Nebraska and Illinois." And, once again, he reaffirmed his new perception:

I am no farmer. I have no farmers in my district nor do I have any farm in my district except rock gardens and small backyard plots. I do not even represent those crabgrass weekend farmers of suburbia, but I do know and am firmly convinced that in America there is an economic unity between the man who toils on the farm and the worker who labors in industry.[29]

The subcommittee chairman, representing a rural Mississippi district, reciprocated:

. . . The gentleman from New York, and I mean downtown New York . . . is a splendid lawyer and a tireless worker who is interested in the subject. He works untiringly not only in the Committee but out in the field. He has

[28] *Ibid.*, p. 5985.
[29] *Congressional Record*, Daily Edition, May 10, 1960, p. 9171.

more energy than most members . . . he has brought essential balance to this subcommittee which is a tribute to the arrangement which put him on this subcommittee. The gentleman from New York has done a great service on this Committee, a great service; and I am glad to say so.[30]

For two more years, a well-established role reciprocity inside the Committee and a harmony in perceptions were displayed in an ever more lavish exchange of gratitude and felicitation. A thoroughly socialized Santangelo became a distinct asset to the subcommittee. By 1961, the man who once thought REA was a car had extended his area of competence to include rural electrification. And he was invited to speak to the National Rural Electric Cooperative Association convention on the unity of farm and city. Saying that he had become "particularly interested in REA," he admitted that "it has not always been thus."

> Before I came to Congress I had not been aware of REA. . . . As a member of the Appropriations Subcommittee on Agriculture, I have sat through hearings, listened, read, and inquired. I have been compelled to think about our soil, the trees, our streams, our electric power. . . . I've come to realize that they affect my way of life, my constituency, and my nation.[31]

More importantly, he worked to win urban allies for the farm appropriations in a time of declining political strength for agriculture. On the floor he spoke as an urban representative to urban Members: "I would like to direct my attention to those of my colleagues who come from the cities and urban areas."[32] And he was assigned to handle the criticisms from such Members. Consider this floor exchange:

> CONGRESSMAN: I have almost no farmers in my congressional district. There are literally no farmers in my district. I represent a great urban district which pays $355 million in federal taxes. After reading this report, may I ask if the Committee is urging someone like me to vote for this appropriation? . . . Should I vote "Aye" when my name is called on this bill? The report would seem to indicate we have been pouring money down a rat hole here.
>
> . . . . .
>
> SANTANGELO: I believe I have the same type of district as the gentleman. . . . I believe you have some school children who are sharing in the school lunch program; is that not correct?
> CONGRESSMAN: That is correct.

[30] *Ibid.*, pp. 9171–9172. See also a similar exchange in *Congressional Record*, Daily Edition, June 6, 1961, pp. 8925–8927.
[31] *Congressional Record*, Daily Edition, February 15, 1961, p. A916.
[32] *Congressional Record*, Daily Edition, July 24, 1962, p. 13604.

SANTANGELO: And your people are also sharing in the special milk program; is that not correct?

CONGRESSMAN: That is correct.

SANTANGELO: People in the gentleman's district are sharing in food donations for needy people. Therefore, to a large extent the people from the city districts are sharing in this abundance that the farmers are producing.[33]

Santangelo's behavior obviously met with the approval of Chairman Cannon. In 1959, Santangelo was given a second (relatively unimportant — but still a second) subcommittee assignment on the District of Columbia Subcommittee. And late in 1962, he was given a "midnight" appointment to the important Labor-HEW Subcommittee. This latter appointment seemed to be designed to help him during his re-election campaign. But Santangelo had been redistricted out of any realistic chance for re-election, and he was defeated. Chairman Cannon gave his place on the Agriculture Committee to the Committee's newcomer from New York City — Representative Joseph Addabo from Queens. With the successful education of Fred Santangelo as precedent, the Subcommittee was unruffled. The Subcommittee chairman rose, when his bill reached the floor in 1963, and said,

> The only new member on our Subcommittee this year is the gentleman from New York, Congressman Addabo. I say candidly that some years ago when the first member from the city of New York, Fred Santangelo, was put on the committee, who was my personal friend and a fine person, the question arose in the minds of some as to why a man from the city of New York would be interested or why he would be chosen to serve on a committee dealing strictly with farm appropriation bills. But . . . I do not think there is anything more fitting than to have a representative . . . from the consuming areas of our nation on the Agriculture Appropriations Subcommittee . . . we are proud to have our new colleague, the gentleman from New York [Mr. Addabo] on the Committee because the gentleman does understand the consumer aspects of these matters.[34]

And the socialization process began anew.

Socialization: Rewards, Frustrations, Punishments

The case just discussed is a special one only because it began under the most inauspicious circumstances and proceeded to the most successful of conclusions. It reveals, more generally, that changed perceptions may be necessary if acceptable behavior is to follow. And it reveals also the use of rewards as an encouragement to learning. The Committee newcomer who plays the role of apprentice and imbibes the appropriate perceptions and norms will find his

[33] *Congressional Record*, Daily Edition, May 11, 1960, p. 9319.
[34] *Congressional Record*, Daily Edition, June 6, 1963, p. 9788.

personal expectations gradually fulfilled. At the least, there are the rewards of camaraderie; and beyond this are the essential rewards of influence.

One newcomer described his second-year apprenticeship behavior as follows: "I'm not provocative. I'm in there for information. They're the experts in the field. I go along." And he added that he had already begun to reap some subcommittee influence — albeit in a very narrow area — through specialization:

> The first year, you let things go by. You can't participate. But you learn by watching the others operate. The next year, you know what you're interested in and when to step in. For instance, I've become an expert on the ———— program. The chairman said to me, "This is something you ought to get interested in." I did; and now I'm the expert on the subcommittee. Whatever I say on that, the other members listen to me and do what I want.

The first taste of influence is normally sweet enough to compensate for the frustrations of apprenticeship and increase receptivity to further role training.

A more experienced Committee member who had just attained to a higher level of Committee accomplishment said he had suffered through several political campaigns back home fending off charges that he was a do-nothing congressman. But present rewards seemed worth his efforts to be a model Committee member:

> When you perform well on the floor when you bring out a bill, and Members know that you know the bill, you develop prestige with other members of Congress. They come over and ask you what you think, because you've studied it. You begin to get a reputation beyond your subcommittee. And you get inner satisfaction, too. You don't feel that you're just down here doing nothing.

In his later years on the Committee, at any rate, John Taber came to rely heavily on a group of middle seniority Republicans of proven capacity for work in preference to the more senior Committee Republicans. One such man said in 1961,

> Mr. Taber runs the Committee with the men from Gerry Ford [sixth in seniority] on down. He works very well with us, consults with us about things — even about subcommittee assignments for the other members. And that's because he knows we'll work. If you work hard, there isn't anything he won't do for you. He's a hard worker himself and puts a high value on it. He's afraid the older men won't do the work. That's why he works closely with the younger members.

These "younger men" whose Committee service ranged from three to five terms had begun to reap the most satisfying of rewards. It is essential to

220

Committee integration that apprenticeship be temporary and that it carry the certainty of such rewards. By learning and observing Committee norms, members can be assured of fulfilling the expectations that first directed them to the Committee.

Though they may not approve of the Committee's norms, most newcomers are wise enough in the ways of the House to realize that time is on their side if only they will wait. Said one Republican and one Democrat,

> There are a lot of things around here that I'd change. But I've been around here long enough to know that you don't rush in here and say "Do this and do that."

> It's frustrating as hell. You feel shut out — and you are . . . but I'm just looking around and feeling my way. I want to know where I'm going before I flywheel off in public.

For such newcomers, socialization proceeds by present example coupled with the promise of future rewards. A few newcomers, however, register their disapproval of Committee norms by openly deviating from the apprentice role. For them, rewards must be replaced by punishments.

Socialization is, of course, a training in behavior as well as in perception. Punishments operate directly to teach expected behavior when overt behavior threatens some disruption of the Committee. Depending on the extent of nonconformity, the deprivations involved can range from the gentle subtlety of a raised eyebrow to the formal severity of removal from a subcommittee assignment. An experienced Republican recalled his first quite inadvertent encounter with the tradition against minority reports. He announced he was going to file a minority report:

> The Chairman [Cannon] was pretty upset about it. It's just a tradition, I guess, not to have minority reports. I didn't know it was a tradition. When I said I was going to write a minority report, some eyebrows were raised. The Chairman said it just wasn't the thing to do. Nothing more was said about it. But it wasn't a very popular thing to do.

He persisted in writing it. (He would have been less likely to have done so were he a Democrat.) But this simple reproof was not lost upon him. Like any attempt at socialization, deprivations may not prove wholly successful. This is especially true where deeply held convictions or ingrained temperamental differences are involved. But the newcomer will certainly be made aware of the difference between proper and improper behavior. And whether or not he mends his ways, he is certain to be discomfited by the unpleasantness of the experience.

One frustrated freshman objected strongly to playing the role of apprentice:

> The appropriations system is lousy, inadequate, and old-fashioned . . . you don't know what's going on. Nobody tells you. They try to keep you one step behind them . . . the traditions of the Appropriations Committee result in a lot of talented people going to waste. And that's no way to run a railroad.

Of the Committee's formal leaders he exclaimed, "Their power is inconceivable to me. They work together, decide things, build up friendships, and don't tell anybody what they're doing." His lack of sympathy for Committee norms, especially as they applied to him, led him to violate several of them on the occasion of his first disagreement with the Committee. He spoke out in full Committee against the recommendation of a subcommittee of which he was not a member. This effort, he recalled, was "not appreciated." "I got gaveled down when I tried to speak. I had to rescind a motion in order to get to speak." He made a statement recording his opposition to the subcommittee's position. When the full Committee remained unmoved, and the bill reached the floor, he publicly reiterated his criticism against the (by now) position of the full Committee.

His fellow members did not look with favor on his performance:

> They want to wash their linen in the Committee and they want no opposition afterward. They let me say my piece in Committee . . . but I just couldn't keep quiet. I said some things on the floor, and I found out that's about all they would take . . . if you don't get along with your Committee and have their support, you don't get anything accomplished here.

By speaking up, speaking in relation to another subcommittee's work, and by opposing a Committee recommendation on the floor, he had violated the norms of apprenticeship, plus reciprocity, plus that of Committee unity. He was a rebel three times over. Afterward, he reflected upon the lessons of his experience.

> I'm trying to be a loyal, cooperative member of the Committee. . . . You hate to be a stinker; but I'm still picking at little things because I can't work on the big things. There's nothing for the new men to do. So they have to find places to needle in order to take some part in it.

He added, however, that with regard to other Committee practices which he vigorously opposed before he joined the Committee, he had remained loyal to Committee views. "They've got me in a funny spot now," he said. "I take a lot of ribbing about it. I'm silenced and can't speak out against the Committee." Several years later, he seemed relatively content with his lot.

"There hasn't been any rebellion," he said. "There's a hell of a lot of difference between being a new member and being here a while. You have a chance to work your way in if you do your homework. The only limitations are time and staff. And we don't have enough of either. You'll find," he added, with evident satisfaction, "that all of us are more active now."

Socialization via punishment began for another newcomer when he violated apprenticeship norms (some of which he described as "nauseating") during subcommittee hearings in his first year. His reactions during this first year were strong:

> Some of these old men don't know how to get right down to a question. They say your first year here you should keep quiet and listen; but I'm asking a lot of questions. . . . I try to pick up what I can, and just hope I hit on something. . . . I'm having a field day. I'm asking as many questions as the subcommittee chairman.

At first, deviation brought a mild rebuke. "The subcommittee chairman has made some insinuations that the Committee has gotten along fine long before I got here. And I guess they'll get along after I'm gone." Insinuations, however, were not enough. The newcomer decided to file a minority report opposing his subcommittee's recommendations. He found, however, that this, too, violated a Committee norm. At this point, he decided to conform. "I tried to write one," he said, "but I got talked out of it. They said it was very unusual." The subcommittee chairman then levied a far less subtle sanction than the previous "insinuations." In selecting members from the subcommittee to accompany him on an extended trip during the recess, he pointedly passed over the offending newcomer.

The fact of his punishment was not lost on the young man in question. But he continued, during his second year, to violate apprenticeship norms. By this time, personal relations between himself and his subcommittee chairman had begun to deteriorate. Accordingly, sanctions meted out against him became open and not at all subtle. During the second year, he said,

> In the hearings, I have to wait sometimes nine or ten hours for a chance; and he hopes I'll get tired and stay home. I've had to wait till some pretty unreasonable hours. Once I've gotten the floor, though, I've been able to make a good case. Sometimes I've been the only person there . . . he's all powerful. He's got all the power. He wouldn't think of taking me on a trip with him when he goes to hold hearings. Last year, we went to ———. He wouldn't give me a nudge there. And in the hearings, when I'm questioning a witness, he'll keep butting in so that my case won't appear to be too rosy.

223

During this same year, the newcomer tried again to file a minority report. This time, the Chairman of the full Committee intervened and sat on him hard:

> I tried to file additional views, too, but got caught with my pants down. I got knocked down by the Chairman on a technicality. That's the way you get to be a good congressman — by getting your knuckles rapped. Next time, I'll know . . . you can't argue with Cannon. He wrote the books.

Attempts to preserve normal legislative courtesy between this newcomer and his subcommittee chairman degenerated into sarcastic exchanges on the floor. One attempt to subliminate their differences beneath the customary amenities — based on the Committee's norm of hard work, produced only this laughter-provoking colloquy between them:

> NEWCOMER: Mr. Chairman, I have great respect for my chairman. I have worked very diligently with him through the sixteen weeks of our hearings, and he has done an excellent job. I believe there is not a harder working man in the Congress.
>
> SUBCOMMITTEE CHAIRMAN: Mr. Chairman, will the gentleman yield?
>
> NEWCOMER: I yield.
>
> SUBCOMMITTEE CHAIRMAN: I appreciate that comment. I am glad to see that the gentleman has changed his mind. Yesterday he accused me of running a sideshow here.
>
> NEWCOMER: Well, a lot of people who run sideshows work hard just the same.

His rebelliousness received precious little approval from his elders, not because he disagreed with the subcommittee chairman — disagreement is accepted as the stuff of political life — but because he was not pursuing his disagreement in accepted ways. A ranking minority subcommittee member discussed the episode:

> He was having trouble with his subcommittee chairman. He was sounding off in the hearings; and it got to be a personal thing. You're not supposed to agree with your subcommittee chairman on everything or polish for him or anything like that. I don't; and if you did, you wouldn't be doing your job. But there are ways to do it. He didn't get much support from the other [members of his party on the subcommittee] . . . he was hurting their cause. They tried to slow him down and tone him down a little. After all, your decisions are made in markup and not out there in the hearings. There are ways to do things.

The socialization of this particular newcomer has been only partly successful. It has been uniquely unpleasant and unremitting. "It's been a frustrating five years," he said recently. "I've been an outsider looking in the whole time." He has gained satisfaction outside the subcommittee, but very little inside. "The only plus is that I've been able to work with the administration on some things. But that has only fanned the flames inside the Committee." Conformity seemed nowhere in sight.

In 1963, the five new Democratic members complained a good deal among themselves about their assignment to subcommittees in whose work they had (with one exception) no special interest. And, when the second appropriation bill came to the full Committee, they were further irritated by their inability to find out what was going on in other subcommittees. Said one,

> We're going to take up the Interior Bill on Thursday in full Committee. So I asked my secretary to get me a copy of the Committee print. And I couldn't get one. Now how am I supposed to go in there and vote intelligently on that bill? Maybe there are reasons why you can't release the figures prior to the meeting, but I haven't heard them. . . . I hear some of the young men are going to kick up a fuss at the Committee meeting Thursday. They are talking about it anyway.

At the meeting, a second newcomer raised the question, "I'm new around here," he said, "but I wondered if we could get subcommittee reports about 48 hours in advance so we could study them." A veteran subcommittee chairman, assuming the role of teacher, stepped in and replied, "You must be new here. If we put those reports out early, they would get out and subject you to pressure [for increased spending] from the lobbyists." And he went on to advise the newcomer to read the hearings. That was all that became of the "fuss." No other member, old or new, supported the request that the traditional flow of information be changed.

One of the newcomers, however, felt especially trapped within the confines of his single subcommittee. Having come to the Committee in the hope of increasing the scope of his knowledge and influence, the fact of subcommittee decision-making and full Committee ratification left his expectations unfulfilled. "The full Committee meeting is a big joke," he exclaimed,

> You can't get the report of the subcommittee until you get there. So you file in and the clerk hands you a copy of the report. The Chairman starts right in and says, "This item is $1 million more than last year but $1 million less than they asked for. All those in favor say aye — nays? — the item is passed." In the meantime, you are riffling through this big report trying to find intelligent questions to ask. Then the meeting is adjourned. You are just another body in there.

Frustrated, the newcomer tried to become active at the full Committee stage of decision-making — thus violating most of the Committee's integrative norms. First, he tried to get hold of another subcommittee's report the day before the full Committee was to meet:

> I called the clerk a day before the Committee meeting and I asked him, "Do you have the report?" He said he did. I said, "I'm coming over and

225

I'd like to see a copy of the report." The clerk said — the clerk, mind you, and I'm the Member — the clerk said, "You can't see it, Chairman's orders."

Having thus been rebuffed in his attempt to become something "more than a body" in full Committee meeting, he decided to file a protest minority report to one of the Committee's reports anyway:

> I tried to file minority views on the foreign aid appropriation. I said that I had not been able to see the report before the full Committee meeting. I said that the money may be enough or it may not be enough — but that I didn't have the information and couldn't get it. I said I just was not a party to the Committee report. I handed it to the clerk. When the report was put out, my views were not there. The Chairman had ordered it not printed. I didn't make an issue of it.

The newcomer was left without any doubt as to what the key Committee norms were and as to the fact that he had violated them. Furthermore, he was conscious of being punished for his violation. "They don't come right out and say it directly, but you know you are an outcast." For him, his subcommittee had become not a source of influence but a prison. The harder he fought to break out, the more securely was he imprisoned. The internal structure of the Committee is deliberately inhospitable to individual efforts at surmounting barriers.

The newcomer's sense of deprivation was very acute. And he realized that the course he had chosen was neither the only course available nor the wisest:

> The only way to change is to get 10 or 12 young Turks to join you. But I'm the only one who has said anything. There are four other new ones — Northern liberals, supposedly. They are hoping that next year, when a vacancy comes up, they will be rewarded for being good little boys. And they are probably smarter than I am. I have spoken up and what has it gotten me — nothing. I'm in the doghouse. And I'll probably stay there. I'll never get another subcommittee.

As fate would have it, the shifting of personnel in 1965 opened up the possibility that this young man might become a subcommittee chairman. Under those conditions, he did receive another subcommittee assignment!

Evidence obtained from interviewing Committee newcomers from 1959 to 1964 indicates that the problem of socialization increases in proportion to the number of newcomers. The two occasions on which the greatest amount of open dissatisfaction, threatened rebellion, and actual rebellion occurred coincided with the two greatest personnel turnovers. The first two cases discussed occurred when the Republicans absorbed eight new members in 1959. And, when the Democrats took on five new Northern members in 1963, restlessness rose to its highest level on that side of the aisle. The spirit of rebellion is more likely to flourish when a sizable number of newcomers can communicate with each other about their grievances and can entertain some hope of redress based on their numbers. What they learn, of course, is that sheer numbers do not count for much on the Committee — the less so when they are newcomers. If, however, the tendency to rebellion increases as personnel turnover increases, the very stability of Committee membership appears, once again, as a vital condition of integration.

Appropriations Committee integration is no social accident. It is, in part, the result of effective socialization processes by which newcomers are taught and learn appropriate perceptions and behavior. All newcomers learn and the vast majority conform — even though they may not, at first, understand or approve of what they observe. The restlessness of 1963 did not turn into a concentrated rebellion for the simple reason that four of the five newcomers were willing to observe an apprenticeship and await its rewards. Two of them spoke in 1964 in tones of which their elders would approve:

> There's more resignation this year. We are resigned to waiting around for a while. In a year or two the young people will begin to speak their piece. Even the middle guys — the number two and three men on the subcommittees — don't speak up much either. If you want a change, it's hard to know how to go about getting it. You can scream, but what good will it do you? There's no point in screaming if you can't be effective.

> There are five of us and maybe we could pick up five more and say, "We've got a bloc of ten votes and we'll go along with you if you will do this." We could demagogue that way and cause a lot of trouble, but we didn't. There's a job to be done and you do it. After you've been here a while you realize the obligation you have to the Committee and to your people back home and to your fellow Representatives. They are busy with their Committees and they lean on you. They come and ask you what you think — "Are they spending too much or too little?" So you have to do your job. You do your job and wait to see how the cookie crumbles.

Given the legislative orientation of these people, time will bring understanding — and, later, approval.

Among experienced Committee members wholesale criticism of Committee norms and of socialization has disappeared. A Republican beginning his fourth term and a Democrat beginning his fifth term illustrated the change in outlook:

> When I came here, I used to say certain things and the older members would look at me with a jaundiced eye or jump me. But as time went on, I didn't say these things any more. It's a matter of knowing the score, the history of things, and the facts of life.

> You've got to have fresh blood. The young men make some very fine contributions sometimes. But they get a little drastic, I might say that. I had

227

stars in my eyes, too, when I came here; but I got them out. Experience is a great thing. You get more influence — that's natural — the more experience you have.

A senior staff member, when asked about the actions of the bumptious newcomers discussed earlier, philosophized, "They'll grow out of it. They always do." By the time experienced members become subcommittee chairmen or ranking minority members, their devotion to Committee perceptions and norms will be even stronger — as, indeed, it must be, for to them falls the task of teaching the Committee's newcomers.

The fact that satisfaction with the Committee's internal structure increases with length of Committee service has important consequences for internal integration. The new member, who from untutored perceptions, from ignorance of norms, or from rebellion against the apprentice role violates Committee expectations, presents some threat to internal integration. But the threat is minimized by the fact that the deviant newcomer does not possess sufficient resources to affect adversely the established Committee behavior. Even if he does not respond immediately to the application of sanctions, he can be held in check and subjected to an extended and (given the frequency of interaction among members) intensive period of socialization. To state it in another way, internal integration is strengthened by the fact that those Committee members who have sufficient resources to disrupt the internal structure are precisely those most satisfied with it. It follows that the most serious threats to Committee integration come when, for one reason or another, the more senior members of the Committee fail to act according to expectations. In such cases, the Committee's integration is preserved by the use of sanctions levied by one leader (or group of leaders) against another leader (or group of leaders).

The Chairman: His Use of Sanctions

The Committee Chairman possesses the greatest capacity for rewarding conformity or punishing deviation on the part of other Committee members. Most tangibly, he controls the size, number, jurisdiction, and membership of subcommittees. Newcomers, whose future hangs in the balance on their subcommittee assignment, feel the weight of these sanctions most heavily. But many an experienced member covets a more favorable subcommittee berth or, indeed, a subcommittee chairmanship. In less tangible ways, too, the good will or good offices of the Committee Chairman are valuable assets for any member to whom they are extended. And these less tangible sanctions assume a greater importance to the more secure Committee member. By giving or withholding his confidences, for example, the Chairman may sanction the behavior of the most senior men of the group. Some of the same capacity is possessed, for his side of the aisle, by the Committee's ranking minority member. And should they so desire, the two Committee leaders could move jointly to ensure conformity to Committee norms.

Chairman Clarence Cannon was known by his Committee members as a man who "deals by rewards and punishments" or "deals on a promise-reward basis." "When Cannon wants someone to go along," said one senior member, "he says, 'Maybe there's a chairmanship of a committee coming up for you.'" Through the years, he divided, subdivided, combined, and recombined subcommittees, expanded or contracted their jurisdiction, increased or decreased their membership — creating or calling in these currencies as the circumstances required. During the period 1947 to 1963, for instance, the number of subcommittees changed by Congresses as follows: 9, 9, 11, 11, 13, 14, 15, 14, and 14. And even when the total did not change, the number of available positions per subcommittee did. In 1947, 45 members were distributed equally among 9 subcommittees — 5 men to a subcommittee and each man with but 1 assignment. Cannon gradually altered this symmetry so that, by 1961, 50 members were distributed among 14 subcommittees which varied in size from 5 to 15 members each. Seven men had 1 subcommittee assignment, 27 men had 2, and 16 had 3. By this system of controlled inflation, 64 additional appointments were put at the disposal of the Chairman during the years 1949 to 1961. Most all were dispensed by Cannon. One member explained how he worked to get one:

> You fight with Cannon. But I've gone along with him, too, a couple of times when he needed the votes. I went along. And I was the only member of my [state] delegation who did. You've got to if you want a better assignment. I called him up and said, "I'm too valuable to be wasted on this Committee. I want another subcommittee." He said, "You're doing a good job . . . I hear good things about you."

The member was rewarded the following year with an extra assignment.

When the Chairman (or ranking minority member) levies a sanction of this sort, it is often impossible to know precisely what behavior it was designed to reward or punish. Caution is needed in drawing conclusions about such a thing as the manipulation of subcommittee assignments and its intended effect on integration. Yet there are some suggestive examples. In 1959, every Republican member save one had at least two subcommittee assignments. The exception was Representative Gordon Canfield (N.J.), a fourteen-year veteran of the Committee and ranking minority member of the Treasury–Post Office Subcommittee. But that was his only assignment. In his seven terms of service on the Committee Canfield was never given more than one assignment by John Taber. The eight freshmen members of 1959 were all better treated in this respect than he. The other noteworthy fact about Representative Canfield was that throughout his service on the Committee his voting record was incomparably the most liberal, on behalf of social welfare measures, of all the group's Republicans.[35] Twice, moreover, he wrote minority reports protesting excessive subcommittee cuts. His one subcommittee assignment seems not to have been an accident. It is hard to escape the conclusion that Taber viewed Canfield as a potentially disintegrative force — a member whose perceptions left him insufficiently devoted to economy — and acted to restrict the range of his influence.

On the Democratic side, two similar cases are observable. In early 1962, three men remained on the Committee out of the group which had been selected in 1949. Representative Robert Sikes (Fla.) had assignments on three of the most important subcommittees and Representative Otto Passman (La.) was chairman of an important subcommittee plus having another assignment. But Representative Sidney Yates (Ill.), the third member of the class of 1949, had but one subcommittee assignment. A year earlier Yates had fallen heir via long service and seniority to the chairmanship of the Subcommittee on the Commerce Department. But Chairman Cannon had denied it to him by abolishing the subcommittee and transferring jurisdiction over the Commerce Department to another subcommittee. By the standards of roll-call voting, Yates was one of the Committee's most liberal members. It is not possible to know whether Cannon considered him a threat to integration on these grounds, though it is possible. Sikes and Passman and Representative George Andrews (Ala.), the chairman of the subcommittee to which Commerce was given, were certainly more devoted to economy than Yates. Another fact is that Yates (for all his affection for his one subcommittee cited on pages 199–200) never displayed the requisite legislative orientation expected of members. His rumored desire for a federal judgeship was common corridor conversation on the Hill. In the fall of 1962 he left, at the behest of the Chicago Democrats, to contest a Senate seat he had little chance to win. Two years later, however, the Chicago Democrats prevailed upon him to return to the House. He sought and gained reassignment to the Committee. But he did not suffer a better fate under Chairman Mahon. Placed next to last in seniority among nine Committee newcomers, he failed to win back his old subcommittee assignment and was placed, instead, as the lowest ranking Democrat on a far less important subcommittee. The subcommittee, furthermore, was one of the two most lopsidedly Democratic in its membership — thus reducing even more Yates' potential for influence.

In early 1962 there remained on the Committee, also, five men who had come to the group in 1955. Three of these men served on three separate subcommittees and one served on two subcommittees. The fifth member of

[35] See AFL-CIO Committee on Political Education, *How Your Senators and Representatives Voted, 1947–1956* (Washington: AFL-CIO, 1957). See also the voting patterns in Chapter 9, page 485.

the class, Representative John Shelley (Calif.) served on only one. Furthermore, Shelley had never served on more than one subcommittee in his seven years of service. One cannot know for sure why he was treated in this way. But he, too, had one of the most liberal voting records on the Committee, had been a trade union leader, and was an advocate of most all large federal spending programs. Furthermore he, too, displayed less of a legislative orientation than his colleagues. He had long harbored the desire to be mayor of San Francisco. And, in 1963, he was elected to that post. It is possible that the sanctions levied against Yates and Shelley contributed to their decision to leave the Committee. Or, it is possible that Cannon levied sanctions against them because he felt they were insufficiently oriented toward the Committee, and hence, "unteachable." It seems likely in any event that Committee integration was increased by the leanness of their assignments if not their departure.

The Chairman (or ranking minority member) may levy sanctions to promote conformity to a key Committee norm or he may act simply out of the most personal of motives. It is often impossible to know whether rewards and punishments are intended to promote integration or just some personal end. No doubt there are some instances of pure personal pique. But to some degree even these are relevant. Integration is best served by cordial personal relationships, and personal conflict is surely a disintegrative force. In many cases, the personal and the Committee-oriented motive probably get mixed. A subcommittee chairman reported just such an instance. He had violated the Committee's integrative norms by offering an amendment in full Committee to the recommendation of a subcommittee of which he was not a member. In justification of the move, the amendment pertained to a matter involving his constituency. He lost the fight, and proceeded to violate another norm by offering his amendment on the floor in opposition to the Committee. What is more, the chairman of the affected subcommittee was Clarence Cannon himself. And, what is still more, the subcommittee chairman won. The deprivations which the Chairman levied were of the most intangible sort, but they were so effective that the subcommittee chairman, one year after his victory, had come to rue the entire incident:

> We won. Mr. Cannon has hardly spoken to me since. I wish I'd gotten rolled. When you think of that man, being here 50 years, the Parliamentarian of the House, the Chairman of the Committee getting rolled by a country boy like me — that's rough. I wish I'd have been rolled.

Idiosyncratic and occasional deviations from Committee norms, no matter who the violator may be, present little more than a temporary threat to Committee integration. And it can be so treated by the Chairman — even as a kind of personal affront to be dealt with by ostracizing the offender.

231

More serious nonconformity will call forth appropriately stronger sanctions. An important case in point has been the persistent nonconformity of the Subcommittee on the Departments of Labor–Health, Education and Welfare. Of all the units of the Committee, this one has been consistently the least enthusiastic about the goal of budget reduction, the least susceptible to perceptions supporting that goal, and the most receptive to clientele interests supporting budget increases. More specifically, the subcommittee has adopted the interest-sympathy-leniency syndrome with regard to the Department of Health, Education and Welfare; and within that Department (as the figures of Chapter Eight make clear) their budget-increasing behavior has centered on the Office of Education, the Public Health Service, and the Food and Drug Administration. Whereas the size of the original budget estimates for the entire government doubled (from $47 billion to $96 billion) between 1953 and 1963, the size of the original estimates for the Department of Health, Education and Welfare tripled (from $1.9 billion to $5.7 billion) in the same period. And, as the data in Chapter Eight will show, the Committee frequently appropriated for the individual bureaus more money than requested in their estimates. If such a pattern of behavior were to become infectious and permeate the operation of all subcommittees, it would constitute nothing less than a revolution in the system we have been describing.

Two main forces seem to have produced this behavior — first, a greatly increased and more effective demand for HEW programs coming from the environment of the Committee and secondly, a uniquely sympathetic subcommittee chairman. Committee leaders could do nothing to affect the first condition. But they brought a number of sanctions to bear in trying to affect the second. Since 1949 (with the exception of the Republican-dominated years 1953–1954) the subcommittee chairman has been Representative John Fogarty (R.I.), whose interest in the subject matter stems both from his pre-congressional career in organized labor and his medical history of heart trouble. He did not request service on the subcommittee, but was "just put on" by Chairman Cannon in 1947. After a one-term apprenticeship on the minority side, he suddenly found himself the most senior Democrat of the group and, in 1949, succeeded to the chairmanship. It was a meteoric rise, unsurpassed in speed by any in the period under study, and it meant that an abnormally short period was available for subcommittee socialization. Furthermore, the subcommittee had functioned in an abnormally partisan fashion during his brief apprenticeship, and he himself had been stepped on very hard by his subcommittee chairman.[36] Both conditions probably de-

[36] See, for example, Committee on Appropriations, *Hearings on Labor Department Appropriations for 1948*, 80th Congress, 1st Session (Washington: U.S. Government Printing Office, 1947), p. 65.

creased the chances for successful socialization. Such early factors may or may not have been contributory. But of the results and of the consternation of Committee leaders there can be little doubt.

In 1956 Chairman Cannon spoke disapprovingly of Fogarty when his subcommittee's bill came to the House floor:

> In recent years we have had now and then chairmen of subcommittees who took the view that the budget estimate was the floor and that they should increase the appropriation as high as the situation permitted over the budget estimate.

And Fogarty acknowledged the rebuke plus the facts behind it:

> The gentlemen from Missouri and I have never agreed on any of these items so far as research and public health are concerned in the ten years that I have had the privilege of serving on this subcommittee — for six years as its chairman.[37]

"I've differed with Mr. Cannon so many times that I can't count, and Mr. Taber too" said Fogarty. "They think the Appropriations Committee ought to cut every budget; but I think that we ought to raise it where it's a good program and cut it where it's necessary." Given the strong environmental support for many HEW programs, which is reflected in the near adulation which Fogarty receives on the House floor, he has been able to carry the Democratic subcommittee members with him without difficulty.[38]

As early as 1950, the Chairman began to countervail the subcommittee by asserting his authority during markup. In that year, the subcommittee's ranking minority member complained that

> The Chairman of the Appropriations Committee was not there at a single hearing when this matter was discussed, yet he came before the subcommittee when the bill was marked up and insisted on cutting this program [hospital construction] right square in two.[39]

In 1955 John Taber designated himself as ranking minority member of the subcommittee to see if he couldn't help hold down what he called "the sob-sister bill." Mr. Cannon cooperated by deliberately holding the subcommittee membership to five men. Thus the two Republicans together with Cannon could force a tie vote three to three in subcommittee markup sessions; and they could extract a price from Fogarty before allowing the bill to move forward. It occurred to the two leaders, however, that under this arrangement Taber was simply canceling his own vote, since he was entitled to vote at markup as an invited ex officio member. As soon as he was

[37] 102 *Congressional Record*, p. 11128.
[38] See Chapter Nine, pp. 478.
[39] 96 *Congressional Record*, p. 4710.

confident that his replacement would carry on, Taber removed himself from the subcommittee. With Taber and Cannon both voting ex officio, they outvoted Fogarty and his two Democratic supporters four to three from 1959 to 1962.

Taber acted to ensure the four to three outcome by appointing to the subcommittee people who were especially suspicious of most of the welfare programs under its jurisdiction. The present ranking minority member, Representative Melvin Laird (Wisc.), picked and trained by Taber to be his successor, said during his first debate on the bill,

> I think it is well for us to look over some of the new programs which the President and the (Budget) Bureau included in this particular bill. Every one of these new programs was authorized by the 84th Congress. I might add that I voted with the minority on the establishment of those programs.[40]

The second Republican member of the subcommittee exhibited the same budget-cutting predispositions when he spoke on the bill in 1962.

> I find myself Mr. Chairman, in rather a perplexing situation on this subcommittee, for there are a number of enactments of the Congress which I have not supported at the authorizing stage but feel compelled to appropriate funds to implement the will of the Congress.[41]

Despite the fact that the Labor–HEW bill was the fastest growing appropriation bill and despite the fact that its hearings were more voluminous than any bill save Defense, the size of the subcommittee was (until 1965) held constant at the strategic number of five.

The effect of these countervailing sanctions was to make the markup sessions the longest and hardest fought of all the subcommittees. But in these sessions all members of the group observed the Committee's integrative norms. Fogarty's nonpartisanship and his good personal relations with the ranking minority member were models of their kind. Fogarty pushed normally for a high figure, the ranking minority member for a low figure, and the result was nearly always a compromise supported by all concerned. Sometimes the two met privately before the markup, agreed to a compromise, and presented it to the rest — Fogarty speaking for the Democrats and the ranking minority member speaking for the Republicans plus Mr. Cannon. Fogarty prided himself on the fact that his subcommittee always produced unanimous reports.[42] But reservations were, of course, made. And in 1957 (see Chapter Nine) these reservations resulted in a full-scale floor attempt to cut back the

---

[40] 103 *Congressional Record*, p. 4412.
[41] 108 *Congressional Record*, p. 4750.
[42] *Congressional Record*, Daily Edition, March 27, 1962, p. 4728. For representative sentiments concerning Fogarty's fairness, from the subcommittee's minority, see 97 *Congressional Record*, pp. 4013–4014; 98 *Congressional Record*, pp. 2843 and 2847.

bill. None of the subcommittee participants welcomed such a floor fight, however — Fogarty because it reflected on his prestige as a subcommittee chairman and the more conservative members because they realized that, given the popularity of the programs involved, they were likely to lose. Fogarty occasionally carried his fight to the full Committee and won a victory over his opponents there. He, therefore, could use the threat of a full Committee fight or a floor fight to raise the level of the compromise. The budget-cutters for their part searched for the lowest figure which Fogarty would pledge himself to support at all future stages in the process. By concerting their available sanctions and by forcing Fogarty into a hard bargaining situation, the Committee's two leaders were able (from 1953 to 1962 at least) to contain subcommittee behavior within limits that were satisfactory if not of optimum desirability for the integration of the system.

The Subcommittee Chairmen: Their Use of Sanctions

It might be wondered why Chairman Cannon did not utilize his formal authority to the fullest by removing the subcommittee chairman. Part of the answer may be that the battery of sanctions as applied were deemed sufficient to his purpose. But the more basic answer is simply that he could not have done so without risking either a complete failure or the most serious kind of internal disruption. As we have already noted, the Chairman can capitalize on his formal authority only by meeting the less formal expectations that define his role. Perhaps the most important of all such expectations for the preservation of the Committee's decision-making structure is that which prescribes minimal interference by the Chairman in subcommittee activities. The aim here is to maintain subcommittee autonomy. The removal of a subcommittee chairman against his will constitutes, on its face, one of the grossest possible violations of that norm. Such a move would constitute a standing threat to every other subcommittee chairman and hence to the entire internal structure. As one veteran subcommittee chairman said,

> The rules of the Committee permit the Chairman to constitute and reconstitute the subcommittees as he sees fit. But if he went around helter skelter removing subcommittee chairmen, he would find himself outvoted by his own Committee. The subcommittee chairman and the subcommittee members would find a community of interests in seeing that the same thing did not happen to all of them. If he tried to do that, he'd be set down pretty fast. He can't be a dictator. But he can almost be a dictator if he has the loyalty of his subcommittee chairmen.

It is the subcommittee chairmen who have the greatest stake in subcommittee autonomy; it is they who help fix the Chairman's role by prescribing the norm of minimal interference in subcommittee activity; and it is they who must be reckoned with by the Chairman should he deviate from such a norm.

235

The Chairman knows that he needs a well-integrated Committee if he is to be of maximum effectiveness as a leader — inside and outside the group. Up to a point, he can promote integration by exercising his sanctioning authority. Beyond that point he risks open conflict with his Committee members — or, most importantly, his subcommittee chairmen. If the conflict is one to be decided by a vote, the Chairman knows he may lose; if the decision is to come by a test of will, he knows that the subcommittee chairmen can in more subtle ways refuse to give him their cooperation and support. The Committee's veterans see the situation the same way. They view the Chairman's authority as a grant from the Committee and revocable by them whenever he violates their expectations. The role they prescribe has, as we have seen, a great deal of slippage, but it has its bounds. Should the Chairman venture beyond these bounds, the subcommittee chairmen are prepared to take such action as will ensure compliance with the role they have prescribed.

When senior men give expression to this posture toward the Chairman, they say, "What the Committee has given the Committee can take away." Or, "He can be stubborn and do things wrong once in a while, but not too often." Or, "He runs the Committee. He has a lot of power. But it's all done on the basis of personal friendship. If he tries to get too big, the members can whack him down by majority vote." Even when they bow to a sanction they may say, "I didn't feel like opposing him. But I've taken him on before and he knows that I will." The subcommittee chairmen do have sanctions available to them. The Committee Chairman not only knows it but will act accordingly — which doubtless explains why he never undertook to remove Representative Fogarty.

The most important generalization to be made is this, that Committee integration depends on the extent to which all roles mesh and the extent to which all members observe the norms that prescribe their role. That includes the Committee's Chairman. If he is to be kept functioning within the Committee's internal structure, then those who prescribe his role must have sanctions available to use against him just as he has sanctions available to use against them. On the Appropriations Committee, integration is achieved by interaction — particularly between the Chairman and the subcommittee chairmen. The reciprocity of their roles is ensured by their reciprocal capacity to levy sanctions.

Testing the Limits of Leadership Roles:
Chairman and Subcommittee Chairmen

In a case such as that posed by the removal of Representative Fogarty, the Chairman would have no difficulty calculating the magnitude of Committee reaction. As one member said, "If he tried it, he'd run into a hornet's nest." And a veteran clerk elaborated,

236

Mr. Cannon always wins in full Committee. But he won't go into a full Committee fight unless he's got the votes to win. For years John Fogarty has gone against Cannon in increasing the HEW budget; but Cannon doesn't do anything about it because he knows he hasn't got the votes.

But in many instances, the metes and bounds of the Chairman's role and the role of other Committee members can only be ascertained by a mutual testing to find the practical limits. Examples of such testing are hard to come by, for they involve the most sensitive area of internal activity. No one talks freely about his success or failure in the art of arm-twisting and in-fighting. A few rather random examples — illustrative of the process of interaction — have come to light. In most cases what is involved is the reaction of the Committee (or elements thereof) to initiatives by the Chairman which come close to or exceed the permissible limits of his role.

The original assignment of Committee members to their subcommittees lies wholly within the unchallenged area of the Chairman's role. He is not bound by any norm of seniority. Nor is he bound to observe that norm in the original appointment of men to subcommittee chairmanships. He can deny a subcommittee chairmanship to a man who is entitled to it by seniority so long as he can avoid an outright denial. Representative Yates was denied by abolishing the subcommittee; Representative Gary was denied (see page 146) by the new rule that no man could have two subcommittee chairmanships. Cannon could have denied the subcommittee chairmanship to Fogarty in 1949 on some such grounds as these; but once he decided to maintain the subcommittee and the ground rules, he could not have denied it to him. John Taber, when he was Chairman, once tested the limits of the role by seeking to have a man voluntarily renounce a subcommittee chairmanship he was about to inherit. The prospective victim recalled,

> Francis Case came to see me and wanted to be chairman of the subcommittee. Maybe he and John Taber had gotten together. He came in here and asked me if I wanted it. He was a senior man on the Committee, but I was senior man on the subcommittee. I said I was going to stand by my rights and said I hoped there wouldn't be any trouble about it. He said, "No, of course not," that he just wanted to see if I was serious about it. I always thought maybe John Taber would have liked it if Frank had been chairman of the subcommittee.

Once a person becomes a member of a subcommittee, it is expected that the Chairman will leave him there. In only two or three cases since 1947 has the Chairman (or ranking minority member) removed a member from a subcommittee against his will. One of these removals was initiated by a subcommittee chairman. Said the victim, "He wanted me off the Committee; so Cannon did it. You could raise hell about it I suppose if you can stir up a revolt. But they won't back you against the Chairman." Whether this man's

237

assessment was correct or not, he did not contest his removal. It appears that against the ordinary member the removal power can be exercised, with greatest care; against a subcommittee chairman, not at all.

In 1955 Chairman Cannon tested for and found some limits to his authority to manipulate subcommittee jurisdiction. When, at the beginning of the session, he circulated the usual list of subcommittee memberships and jurisdictions, one of the subcommittee chairmen who had lost considerable jurisdiction protested. One of his losses was that of the Atomic Energy Commission which had been allocated to the new Public Works Subcommittee whose chairman was Cannon himself. The affected subcommittee chairman decided to make a fight of it on the grounds that the Chairman's interference with his subcommittee jurisdiction was excessive. He lined up support among the other subcommittee chairmen. Two of them recalled the episode:

> Mr. Cannon, for reasons of his own, tried to bust up one of the subcommittees. We didn't like that. He was breaking up the whole Committee. A couple of weeks later a few of the senior members got together and worked out a compromise. By that time he had seen a few things, so we went to him and talked to him and worked it out.

> There were a lot of changes [in the subcommittee jurisdictions] but it looked like it was targeted at Thomas . . . Thomas had AEC and some others which made his subcommittee next to Defense the most powerful one. A group of us got together and worked out a compromise. We took it to the Chairman and he accepted it, because he knew he was going to lose.

The Chairman's action represented a threat to all the subcommittee chairmen, and they in turn threatened to outvote him if necessary to keep him functioning within permissible limits.

When the Chairman established the Subcommittee on Deficiencies in 1959, he thereby reduced the jurisdiction of every one of the other subcommittees. Whereas each of them formerly handled, within its area, all estimates submitted after the original budget estimates, subsequently all supplemental or deficiency requests were funneled into the single subcommittee. In these terms it was a clear violation of the norm of minimal interference in subcommittee activity. And, by setting up one subcommittee to intervene in the affairs of other subcommittees, it endangered violation of the norm of reciprocity among subcommittees. The change triggered off considerable criticism, and it created a source of tension within the Committee. Yet the change stood intact until 1964 — when Cannon decided that it no longer served its purpose and abolished it. A discussion of its survival and its demise helps to delineate more clearly the contours of the Chairman-subcommittee relationship.

Several factors differentiate this seemingly more drastic subcommittee change from the proposed shakeup of 1955. In the first place, the Committee had previously had a deficiencies subcommittee. Thus the move could be described as a return to an old tradition, by a tradition-conscious Committee.[43] In the second place, it was taken not to increase the personal influence of the Chairman, but in pursuit of a goal, budget reduction, to which all members subscribed. A related point is that the committee was seen as a device to cut down the number of deficiency and supplemental requests, a practice which many Committee members deplore. In the third place, by choosing one of the most powerful of the subcommittee chairmen (Representative Thomas) and giving him the authority to pick the Democrats on the Committee, the Chairman made himself a key ally. Similarly, since Mr. Taber sat on the committee ex officio and chose his membership, another important ally was won over. Finally, since the committee's seven members also sat as members of the regular subcommittees, those subcommittees could feel that their interests were being protected.

While few Committee members (or members of the subcommittee for that matter) expressed enthusiasm for the device, the most vocal criticism came from the two major subcommittees having no member on the Deficiencies Subcommittee — the Subcommittees on Agriculture and on Treasury–Post Office. The leaders of these two subcommittees criticized the move. First, they criticized the way it was done without consulting them:

> He's a difficult man to work with because he's a lone wolf. He never tells you what he's going to do. He doesn't consult with his Committee, just pops out and announces things like this deficiency subcommittee. The old system was working just fine and all of a sudden he goes back to the old deficiency system. We were as surprised as people on the outside.

But more substantively they criticized the fact that the business of their subcommittee was being processed by people who did not know what they were doing.

A leader of the Agriculture Subcommittee complained,

> No one committee can say grace over the whole of government with these supplementals. Some of the agencies lie in wait when they go through my subcommittee and then bring it up in the supplemental committee where they didn't have the background. There isn't a finer group of people than that bunch on the committee, but no one can have all the background. It's an unsound procedure.

And a leader of the Treasury–Post Office Subcommittee felt similarly bypassed:

> When you had supplemental bills, the agencies used to come before a grass roots committee that knew the bill. But a couple of years ago, Cannon set up the deficiency subcommittee and gave it to Al Thomas, a real axe man.

[43] See remarks of Rep. Edward Boland, *Congressional Record*, Daily Edition, April 9, 1963, p. 5702.

The idea was to give them a cursory hearing and knock them down — and they do. They range over the whole of government and they don't know the bills they're dealing with. So when they come to the floor, we have to change them. Or, we have to go to the Chairman and say, "You're all wet here. You don't know what you're doing." Of course, you take John Rooney — he sits on that committee. So when they come to the Immigration Service they say, "John, you know all about that"; and he says, "Don't cut them." But it hurts our agencies, Post Office and Treasury. Maybe it was an honest to goodness effort to hold things down. But it looks like it reflects mistrust of our regular committees.

Confirmation of this latter fear could be had by talking to the Deficiencies Subcommittee members themselves. One of them said that,

I never had such a frustrating experience. When they brought in items from [my subcommittee] bill I knew what they were talking about; but on agriculture and defense, I was lost. We made meat-axe cuts on pay raises ten per cent across the board. I wouldn't let them do it on items from [my subcommittee] bill but in other cases where there was nobody there to defend them, they got a meat-axe cut.

Some agencies on the other hand received more favorable treatment from the Deficiencies Subcommittee. But in those cases, too, the affected subcommittee protested — on the same general ground — that the committee which had the information and was the expert in the area had not been deferred to. The Agriculture Subcommittee leaders protested an increase in agricultural research. Said the ranking minority member,

We are being bypassed entirely. This is the first I have heard about this. . . . I think this ought to be stricken out of the bill just to maintain at least the authority of the various subcommittees involved. I resent a thing like this. . . . I just want to say how necessary it is to approach a situation of this kind through the subcommittee which really knows what this problem is all about. . . . I am attempting . . . to defend the integrity of my subcommittee.[44]

The tension expressed here results from a violation of the norm of reciprocity between subcommittees. If more subcommittees had been adversely involved, the threat to integration would doubtless have been greater and the likelihood of the Subcommittee's survival might have been lessened.

Actually, the survival power of the Subcommittee was increased by the converse type of action. Members of the Subcommittee expressed their devotion to the norm of reciprocity and sought, in informal ways, to comply with it and reduce tension. When, for example, the Agriculture Subcommittee launched the protest just recorded, members of the Deficiencies Subcommittee

[44] *Congressional Record*, Daily Edition, April 4, 1962, pp. 5460–5467; April 5, 1962, pp. A2645–2646.

moved immediately to assuage the bad feeling. Representative Thomas expressed his devotion to the norm of reciprocity when he replied,

> We should have consulted the gentleman and I humbly apologize and I assure him that in the future we will do that. . . . I humbly apologize and I ask the gentleman's forgiveness at this time. . . . We certainly do not want to usurp any jurisdiction that the gentleman may have. . . . We would have been glad to turn it over to you.[45]

A good deal of conflict was headed off by action taken at the staff level. Normally, the clerk of the Deficiencies Subcommittee consulted with the clerk of the affected subcommittee. In fact, the clerks of the regular subcommittees did much of the preliminary work for the Deficiencies Subcommittee. In later years, moreover, the chairman of the relevant regular subcommittee was allowed to sit in on the appropriate portions of the hearings and the markup — though not as a voting member. Among Committee members the sensitivity to the slightest loss in jurisdiction is, however, great, and their sense of injury remained; but the remedial actions of the Subcommittee surely helped make the arrangement tolerable.

In 1964, President Johnson was able to keep his fiscal year 1965 budget low by including a considerable number of budget requests in supplementals for fiscal year 1964 — to be presented to the Committee early in 1964. Chairman Cannon, perceiving that Texan Albert Thomas was likely to be lenient with Texan Lyndon Johnson's supplemental requests, abruptly abolished the subcommittee. A member of the Deficiencies Subcommittee agreed with Cannon's assessment of the situation. "We would probably have given them most of what they wanted," he said. "Under the circumstances Cannon was right. He's a very wise man and it was a wise move on his part." Two circumstances doubtless made the change both appealing and easy for Cannon. In the first place, he knew that an overwhelming majority of the Committee was opposed to the existing arrangement. Doubtless he had been under criticism for some time and, perhaps, as several suggested, "The criticism was just catching up." He knew, in other words, that in any showdown, he could count on support from his subcommittee chairmen, most of whom would gain in jurisdiction. The only person who was really hurt by the change was Thomas, the Subcommittee chairman. And, since he and Cannon had engaged in one or two heated controversies during the preceding year (and since, in addition, Thomas retained his chairmanship of an important regular subcommittee anyway), Cannon felt no compunctions about losing Thomas as an internal ally.[46] The Committee had served its original purpose, and, in

---

[45] *Ibid.*

[46] See John Pomfret, "U.S. Funds Tied Up by House Leader," *New York Times,* February 19, 1963, p. 1.

the absence of any great cost to himself, Chairman Cannon did away with it — successfully.

The capacity of subcommittee chairmen to take action against the Chairman stems in part from the fact that they can usually rely upon the support of their subcommittee members — at least those of their own party. In the case of the Labor–Health, Education and Welfare Subcommittee, the Democrats always tendered their loyalty to Fogarty in his contests with Cannon. Given the central decision-making activity of the subcommittee and given its normal cohesiveness, this is hardly surprising. Thus the opposition of subcommittee chairmen becomes in effect the opposition of most other members as well. An experienced member recalls just such a resolution of allegiance when Mr. Cannon and his subcommittee chairman engaged in a severe head-to-head clash in full Committee:

> We had a roll call on it. I didn't know whether to vote with my subcom-mittee chairman or with my Chairman. I voted with my subcommittee chairman. I don't know whether I was right. My relations with the Chair-man haven't been the same since. Oh he's polite and smiles at me but when I ask for things I don't get them. But I do get things from my subcom-mittee chairman.

As newcomers come to understand the decentralization of decision-making in the Committee, it seems likely that they will learn to perceive that both the Chairman and the subcommittee chairman are capable of wielding sanctions — on each other and on them as newcomers. One fresh-man related an early Committee experience which had led him to this con-clusion. He attended a full Committee meeting at which one subcommittee chairman's proposal for a Committee resolution was defeated by action of his fellow subcommittee chairmen:

> Those subcommittee chairmen just cut him up. Cannon didn't say a word. He just sat there. They told him he wasn't going about in the right way and that he ought to take it back to subcommittee. Thomas, Whitten, Mahon, Rooney, Sikes, they all got into it. . . . What smoothies those men were. They are real artists. I just sat there. What a show. Why it's better than the theater. I'd pay a hundred dollars a week if I could see a performance like that.

His reaction was one of respect bordering on awe. Out of the experience he came to a new perception of the internal Committee structure. And the net result was to increase his compliance with apprenticeship norms:

> Cannon doesn't bother me. I don't care what he thinks of me or whether he gets mad at me or not. But it's those other subcommittee chairmen. Some of them are very influential guys, and if they get mad at you they can finish you. That's what sobers me. I don't want to fly off like a loud mouth and get in trouble with them.

242

This experience may be unique. But the accuracy of the perception suggests it is not. Sooner or later, newcomers will recognize that, within the full Committee structure, subcommittee chairmen can punish and reward — the Chairman, each other, and the newcomer. This perception, in turn, will strengthen loyalty to subcommittee chairmen in cases of conflict with the Chairman. And this loyalty will enlarge the capacity of the subcommittee chairman to levy sanctions within the system.

In cases where the Chairman clashes with one of his subcommittee chairmen, the subcommittee members will often determine who will apply sanctions against whom.[47] And though they will usually support their subcommittee leader, they may decide under special conditions forcibly to restrict his role. One such case was recalled by several members of a subcommittee in which their chairman clashed openly and seriously with the full Committee Chairman. A majority of the subcommittee (including members from both sides of the aisle) voted on a key measure to support the full Committee Chairman and in so doing incurred the displeasure of their defeated subcommittee leader. To a substantial degree, the subcommittee's members were levying sanctions on their chairman for what they regarded as his excessive violation of key informal norms in playing his role. In their eyes, he had behaved unfairly and arbitrarily. He had been personally abusive. And he had, in his dealings with executive agencies under his jurisdiction, dimmed the reputation of the Appropriations Committee.

In sharpest contrast to the language normally used to describe the role behavior of subcommittee chairmen, several of the members explained,

> He would call the agency people by the worst kinds of names. He thought they were all crooks and liars and that they had to be squelched. He browbeat the witnesses before his committee. I sat there and listened to him for years till I became disgusted. I wouldn't take it any more and I wouldn't go over any more except when some of the important agency officials were there. He wouldn't let the witnesses answer the questions. He did all the talking.

> He would get mad at me because I opposed him. He wanted to be the whole show on his committee and have everyone rubber-stamp his ideas. If you opposed him on anything, you were against him and all that. He was the most biased man I knew. He couldn't see anything objectively.

> He ran roughshod over people and bullied the other witnesses and Committee members for so long that he had lost the sympathy and respect of many members of the subcommittee. He had run that committee with an iron hand. And he had abused so many members of the subcommittee — with verbal abuse, with tongue lashing that cut deep — that [when the vote came] he didn't have the support he might have had.

[47] Another illustration of this point, relative to conference committee roles, can be found in Chapter 12, pp. 646–647.

243

The behavior described here is the very antithesis of the behavior prescribed by those informal expectations defining the role of subcommittee chairmen — expectations of fairness, reasonableness, compromise, and self-restraint. No individual could have hoped to retain the respect, trust, and confidence of his subcommittee members in the face of such behavior. The deviation from norms was extreme. And the alliance of Committee Chairman and subcommittee members against the subcommittee chairman was extraordinary. But the incident illustrates the existence of internal control mechanisms for punishing any Committee member whose role behavior remains grossly and persistently out of line with his role.

No Committee member high or low is immune from the Committee's sanctioning mechanisms. The Committee Chairman has his role fixed and enforced for him largely by the subcommittee chairmen. The subcommittee chairmen usually have their roles fixed and enforced for them by the Chairman. The decision-making structure, in which they share influence, is supported by the integrative structure in which they each have the capacity to fix the other's role and to sanction deviations from it. The number of times when such sanctions are employed, however, is rare. When they are, they come as responses to a probing or testing action whereby one seeks to ascertain the practicable limits of his role. In such circumstances, the allegiance of subcommittee members is likely to be the determining factor. On the whole, the Chairman and the subcommittee chairman observe a treaty under which each gives to the other a sphere of operating freedom cast in the form of a role. A Committee newcomer surmised,

> If the subcommittee chairmen wanted to push Cannon around, they could. But they don't. So I assume they don't want to. They must get together with Cannon and agree on things.

Doubtless, they do. But the terms of the treaty need not be all that explicit. The limits of their respective roles are pretty well known to each by tradition and by experience. Each pledges, implicitly or explicitly, to support the other so long as he acts within the limits of his role. And together, therefore, they promote the integration of the Committee as a whole.

INTERNAL DISINTEGRATION

The internal integration of the Committee is maintained by the existence of certain facilitating conditions, by habitual obedience to integrative norms, by mutually satisfactory bargains among its members, and by the operation of effective control mechanisms. So long as such integration persists, the Committee's decision-making structure will remain stable and predictable. Temporary or minor deviations may occur causing some disruption within

244

the Committee, thwarting short-run prediction. But these deviations have not brought about long-run alterations in Committee structure; indeed they have served to keep the Committee's control mechanisms visible and in working order — thus helping to maintain integration. It is clear that one can have deviation from expectations and still speak of a highly integrated Committee. That is to say, the state of being integrated is not a fixed form of behavior. It is a condition that admits of conflict so long as it does not go beyond certain limits. But it is the problem of limits (or the boundaries of a system) that has long been the thorniest one for students of political systems. The drawing of precise limits beyond which, for example, an integrated committee becomes so disintegrated that it can no longer be described as the same committee is an arbitrary matter. And it will not be attempted here. What can be done is to consider the most serious disruptions which have in fact occurred in the Committee's structure and to assess qualitatively their consequences, both short-run and long-run, for Committee integration. If this investigation does not fix a precise boundary for us, it will at least identify empirically the limits to which Committee disintegration has proceeded. And, by considering the consequences, we shall learn still more about the tendencies for change and for stability in Committee behavior.

External Sources of Disruption: Maximum Partisanship

Minimal partisanship is a necessary condition of Committee integration and extreme partisanship represents one of the most serious disruptive conditions. It is not surprising therefore that Committee integration was stretched to its outermost limit by the sharp rise in partisanship which occurred in the 80th Congress. It did not originate in the Committee. It originated when the Republicans regained control of the House of Representatives for the first time in fourteen years. They were pledged to reverse the trend of the New Deal years and bring about drastic reductions in federal spending. They interpreted the 1946 elections as a mandate to do just that. After fourteen years of minority frustration, they were hardly in any mood to temporize and to compromise. Instead they wanted to press their advantage by taking unequivocal actions. The Democrats, led by their President, counterattacked just as vigorously in defense of their record and their programs. And the years of the 80th Congress leading up to and culminating in the election of 1948 became probably the most partisan of all the post-war periods. Appropriations Committee Republicans and Appropriations Committee Democrats were engulfed in that controversy — partly because they wanted to be and partly, perhaps, because they could not have reversed the tide of partisanship if they had tried. Given the primary Republican emphasis on economy and budget reduction and cutbacks in the bureaucracy, the Appropriations Committee majority became its party's cutting edge.

The subcommittees working in those areas where party differences were most marked (labor, social welfare, public power, agricultural price supports) evidenced the greatest internal disruption. Conversely, the fact that partisanship was restrained within some subcommittees helped to keep the Committee minimally integrated throughout its time of maximum disruption. The subcommittee handling the Labor Department and Federal Security Agency (precursor of the Department of Health, Education and Welfare) budgets reported their bill in March of 1947, and a story unfolded which revealed the wholesale violation of Committee norms. Republican subcommittee members expressed considerable hostility toward the Labor Department saying,

> We have come to the time when we must wean the bureaucrats. The public is demanding that. That is what they said on November 9th . . . we have been spoon feeding, we have been nursing the bureaucrats too long . . . let us wean the bureaucrats. They are old enough to wean. Most of them have been in the government for fourteen years.[48]

Subcommittee Democrats charged the Republicans with wrecking the Department and stated, "I could never understand how any man who works for a living let alone any member of a labor organization in this country could ever be a Republican or vote the Republican ticket in these United States of ours today."[49]

Instead of the usual soothing words about subcommittee unanimity, there was the terse statement by the ranking minority member that, "The minority did not agree with the majority in any instance concerning the appropriations for the Department of Labor."[50] None of the outward visible signs of Committee integration appeared — no self-congratulation, no praise across party lines for working hard or for being fair, no expressions of affection for the group. In their place were accusations of poor attendance, lack of interest, lack of constructive effort, obstructionism, and dictatorship. Subcommittee members refused to yield to one another, told each other heatedly to sit down, and made such personal attacks that their words had to be stricken from the written record.

For example:

> RANKING MINORITY MEMBER OF SUBCOMMITTEE: Mr. Chairman, being a member of this great subcommittee, I suppose I should defend my chairman, the gifted gentleman from Wisconsin . . . the gentleman from Wisconsin is really a charming fellow, when you get to know him. I spent nine weeks with him as a member of this subcommittee, and it was just one grand tea-party. If you did not agree with him whether you were a member of the minority or the majority, it did not get you anywhere. He wrote the bill.

[48] 93 *Congressional Record*, p. 2546.
[49] *Ibid.*, p. 2474.
[50] *Ibid.*, p. 2473.

You saw him on the march here a while ago, strutting as he usually does from one side of the floor to the other, and you have listened, I am sure, to all those fancy expressions of his . . . when anyone who disagrees with him is talking, that Member is using dilatory tactics — tactics designed to interfere with what? With the gentleman's full sway as a dictator and as a czar of this appropriation bill? He might well stop, look, and listen.[51]

MAJORITY MEMBER OF SUBCOMMITTEE: Mr. Chairman, I regret exceedingly to hear the kind of speech that has just been delivered on this floor, when a member of the Subcommittee on Appropriations for Labor and the Federal Security tries to make the members of the House believe that the chairman of this particular committee is a swaggering czar, strutting, etc., and so on; and that the chairman of the subcommittee has written this bill without consultation with his colleagues . . . very little interest was given in the hearings by either of the two members of the minority on that committee. Scarcely ever did they offer anything constructive . . . the majority members of the committee must virtually carry the entire load by themselves. Certainly we had to write the bill, the four of us in the majority. There was no cooperation from the others whatsoever.[52]

The picture is one of a subcommittee totally split on party lines and functioning, therefore, with a degree of integration sufficient only to hold them together as a formal unit.

The Interior Department Subcommittee was equally riven by partisanship — though personal relationships had not deteriorated as far as they had on the Labor–FSA group. The subcommittee chairman expressed the Republican view of subcommittee action,

We are not going to let the Department of the Interior doublecross our anti-inflation program and we have brought in a bill that, in my opinion, is still too high . . . only four members of this subcommittee of seven are trying to hold this position against this great department's inflationary movement. We have only four members of the subcommittee trying to hold down inflation.[53]

And a minority subcommittee member illustrated the unbridgeable partisan gap when he stated,

I objected to every markup except one . . . while there were not more than two or three items in the bill in which we concurred with the majority, nevertheless relations between all the members of the subcommittee were most cordial and friendly. I have no personal fault to find with the intentions of the chairman of this subcommittee or the other members of the majority side. I believe they are sincere in what they are doing to the Department of the Interior — wrecking it.[54]

[51] *Ibid.*, p. 2557.
[52] *Ibid.*, p. 2558.
[53] *Ibid.*, p. 3958.
[54] *Ibid.*, p. 3969.

247

Democrats complained about the "well-oiled steam-roller" of the Republicans that moved the bill without change through the subcommittee, the full Committee, and the floor. Republican subcommittee unity was threatened, however, by a newcomer, Representative Lowell Stockman (Ore.), a Westerner whose sympathy for the Interior Department programs led him to disagree "violently" with his party colleagues. It is some indication of Republican thoroughness and zeal that Chairman Taber threatened to vote with the subcommittee (ex officio), cause a tie vote, and, hence, stop any appropriations from being made unless Stockman voted with the other Republicans on all matters. Subcommittee Democrats nicknamed Taber "the Big Bad Wolf" and remonstrated against his heavy-handed pressure:

> Every time any of the members on the majority side got a liberal idea or a progressive thought in their minds and were going to execute it, they were threatened, "If you do, I will take in the big bad wolf — who was the Chairman of the full Committee on Appropriations — and he votes."[55]

Stockman was silenced in Committee, but he protested vigorously on the floor:

> I want to tell you just exactly why it is not a report of the majority. It was announced in our committee hearings on a certain day that in case of variance of opinion among members of the committee as to the general policy that would be outlined to us, that if the majority of the committee could not see fit to go along, another very important member of the Congress was ready, willing, and waiting to come down and assist us in our work, that he would be only too happy to assist us in our work, and that he as a member of the full Committee would be allowed to cast a vote in our deliberations.[56]

The normal subtleties of subcommittee bargaining had been replaced by complete majority party domination, a policy of no concession to the minority, and the crudest pressures to maintain majority party unity.

On the State Department and the Agriculture Department appropriations, subcommittee disagreement fell rigidly along party lines and again it was abetted by Chairman Taber's remote control. Before the subcommittee on the State Department began its hearings, Taber announced publicly the reductions they were to make. And by pushing the subcommittee to meet this target, he divided Democrats and Republicans who, according to their testimony, could otherwise have come to a compromise. After the Agriculture Subcommittee had marked up its bill, Taber and Speaker Martin ordered it back into session to cut out another $40 million. And, once again, decisions were made on party lines, in violation of all expectations and in deviation

[55] *Ibid.*, p. 3963.
[56] *Ibid.*, p. 3977.

from normal practice. A Democratic member, with 6 years of experience, reported on the floor,

> Last Friday when the full Committee on Appropriations met to give final consideration to the measure we [Democrats] demanded and secured twelve roll-call votes in Committee in an effort to stop the steam-roller of the majority, but to no avail. They had the votes. Let it be said for the record, that when the roll call was taken on reporting the bill, every Democrat on the Committee, with possibly one exception, voted against the bill. During my brief service in the House of Representatives, I had never seen that before.[57]

At one point during the subcommittee's deliberations, two of the members were reported to have engaged in a pushing match in the Committee's rooms just off the floor of the House.

In 1948, the evidence of decision by partisan majorities remained in the public record. But the Democrats had resigned themselves to restricted opportunities for negotiation and did little by way of open protest. The only serious altercation occurred when the Labor–FSA conference report was being debated. The ranking minority member brought to the surface, again, the charge that the Republicans were engaged in "a concerted effort . . . to break down organized labor and to decimate and annihilate the Department of Labor." The subcommittee chairman called this speech "a snarling harangue," accused him of "injecting a note of sour measly dirty politics" into the debate, and said the minority was making "a lot of dirty nasty political cracks."[58] Otherwise, the semblance of normality prevailed.

When the Democrats took control of the Congress in 1949, however, they took some retaliatory steps which rekindled open partisan warfare within the group. This was the year that Chairman Cannon abolished the Republicans' permanent investigating staff and reverted to the temporary FBI-led staff arrangement. He did it, however, without consulting the minority, announced it in the first full Committee meeting, and pushed it through in peremptory fashion. Two senior Republicans described the meeting. Said one,

> [It was done] by the unanimous vote of the Democratic members at that meeting over the unanimous opposition of the Republican members and without permitting a word of debate or a single question by any Republican member present.[59]

The other recalled,

> We stood up and tried our level best, the gentleman from New York and I to offer amendments, but got no recognition from the gentleman [Mr. Cannon]. He would not even look our way.[60]

[57] *Ibid.*, p. 5954.
[58] 94 *Congressional Record*, pp. 7604–7607.
[59] 96 *Congressional Record*, p. 4700.
[60] 95 *Congressional Record*, p. 4618.

One of the staff members would not leave, so Cannon first removed the furniture from his office, then removed him from the payroll, and finally changed the lock on his office door. So great was the unpleasantness surrounding the staff change that a year later the Republican minority was still complaining about their "pretty rough treatment." "It is a little difficult," said one senior Republican, "for the minority on this side of the table to forget, even after approximately fifteen months, just what happened when the minority side of the table did try to offer amendments."[61] But by the time they returned to power in 1953, the Republicans had accepted the temporary investigator arrangement.

It is possible to view this action at the beginning of the 81st Congress as a retaliatory sanction against the Republican deviation from Committee norms in the 80th Congress, the aim of which was to bring the system back into its previously well-integrated state. The capacity of the Democrats to levy sanctions during the previous two years had been minimal. And they may have felt that Republican action had left an imbalance which needed to be reduced by some kind of equal and opposite reaction — at least to the point of satisfying themselves that a serious deviation had not gone unsanctioned. A Democratic subcommittee chairman described one series of events in his subcommittee in the 1947 to 1949 sequence:

> If a subcommittee chairman is vindictive or out to get an agency, he can do it. A fellow on the other side of the table is pretty helpless. In the 80th Congress, our chairman was out to get the ———— agency, without rhyme or reason or justification — just so he could say he cut the ———— agency. They cut them 25 per cent the first year and 20 per cent the next. When I became subcommittee chairman in the 81st Congress, I went the other way. I told the subcommittee I was going to see to it that ———— agency got every cent they asked for; and we got the bill through without anybody dotting a single "i."

The reaction, of course, was as much a deviation from normal behavior as the original action. But the net result of the two deviations was to return the situation to a point more satisfactory in the eyes of the Democrats than previously. It is not a case of two wrongs making a right but of an action and a reaction bringing the system back into a more stable kind of equilibrium. The subcommittee chairman just quoted was quite satisfied once his counterattack was completed. He did not press partisan advantage further, but resumed his obedience to the norm of minimal partisanship. Gross partisanship extending over a period of time would doubtless change the entire system we have been studying. But that has not occurred. Partisan conflict has, of course, waxed and waned, but the intensity of the 1947 to 1949 conflict has not reappeared.

[61] 96 *Congressional Record*, p. 4934.

Two other isolated and short-lived episodes illustrated the important tendency for any sharp increase in partisanship to be met by a retaliatory increase in partisanship. In both cases the outcome of the deviation and the counter-deviation was to halt heightened partisanship and bring about a return to its normally low level. In 1951 Chairman Cannon was probing the outer limits of his authority to manipulate the majority-minority ratio on the subcommittees. He drastically altered the long-standing ratio of three majority and two minority members on each subcommittee. He did it without so much as consulting the ranking minority member. It was suspected that he did it, in part, out of personal pique at the failure of Taber and the other Republicans to support him in his desire for an omnibus appropriation bill. Taber protested on the floor that Cannon's action was an unacceptable violation of Committee traditions and practices:

> The Appropriations Committee met yesterday and organized. . . . I want to call the attention of the House to one of the most shocking examples of packing committees that I have ever witnessed in my 28 years in Congress. Although the historic ratio between majority and minority members has been three-two, the Democrats yesterday packed two subcommittees of the Appropriations Committee five-two and three others at the four-two ratio.[62]

Four ranking minority members then rose to echo Taber's protest against the move, which had so violated the norms of minimal partisanship. After this counterattack from the floor, the Chairman added Republicans to each of the unbalanced subcommittees save one — which remained at four to two. Such lopsided ratios were not proposed by either party, until the full Committee ratio was altered in 1965.

In 1956, after President Eisenhower had vetoed the soil bank bill of that year, the angry and frustrated Appropriations Committee Democrats — led by their Agriculture Subcommittee members — wrote and reported out a bill appropriating $1.2 billion for a soil bank. The move was wholly partisan and anti-Eisenhower in intent and effect. The bill was written without notice or hearings, and the minority members on the Committee were not shown copies of it till one-half hour before the Committee met. The Republicans retaliated by violating the Committee norm against minority reports. Thirteen minority members (nine more signatures than were affixed to any minority report from 1947 to 1963) wrote the dominant opinion and five others wrote additional views. Quite apart from any policy differences, the Republicans complained that "We questioned the procedure and express regret that the minority members were not consulted in any way concerning the issuance of the Committee report and formation of the bill itself." They underscored the importance of minimal partisanship for the Appropriations Committee by charging the Democrats with "a departure from the better

[62] 97 *Congressional Record*, p. 1172.

251

traditions of the Appropriations Committee" through an "unusual disregard of and lack of consideration for other members of the Committee."[63] The action and counteraction were abnormal in the extreme. The issue died with the majority and minority reports, and no conflict of this nature has shaken the Committee since.

These two cases had no long-run effect on Committee integration. This is so partly because they were isolated in time and in scope. But it is also because the equal and opposite reaction seems to have had (one cannot "know" this) a sobering effect on the party which had disturbed the normal pattern in the first place. Without the counterattack, it is possible that further initiatives in the direction of partisanship would have been attempted, bringing Committee partisanship to a new and higher level. Should higher partisanship become normal on the Committee instead of a deviation, integration would be threatened and the Committee's internal structure would undergo drastic change. Given the desire of all parties inside the Committee to maintain the existing structure and to maintain a high degree of integration, the threat of increasing partisanship is a sanction which either party contingent has over the other. This may be of special importance as a weapon whereby the minority party can moderate the actions of the majority and wring bargaining concessions from it.

The serious internal conflict of 1947 to 1949 originated in the environment and was the Committee's response to an external demand that it display greater partisanship. Should a similarly strong demand arise again, the Committee's majority party would surely respond. In this light, the Appropriations Committee's normal level of integration is made possible by the absence of a centralized, tightly disciplined congressional party which makes demands upon legislative committees. Left free by the congressional parties to establish an internal system of their own, the Appropriations Committee has set up a Committee-oriented as well as a party-oriented set of expectations, norms, or rules. Most of the time, Committee-oriented norms are followed and party-oriented norms are minimized. But in circumstances of great externally induced partisanship, party norms become dominant and Committee-oriented norms are pushed aside. In the case of the 80th and 81st Congresses, at any rate, they were only pushed aside. They appear to be too well recognized, too well established, too coherent, and too functional a body of norms to be scrapped or forgotten. When the external demands for partisanship recede, Committee-oriented norms with their thrust toward internal integration are reasserted. In the examples just discussed, the Committee demonstrated two important characteristics of a political system — a responsiveness to its environment and a resilient capacity to snap back to its stable patterns of action after being subjected to the most serious (thus far) disruption.

[63] Committee on Appropriations, *House Report No. 2016*, 84th Congress, 2nd Session (Washington: U.S. Government Printing Office, 1956), pp. 6–9.

Disintegrative influences can come from inside as well as from outside the Committee. Some minor deviations and the control mechanisms used to keep them in check have already been discussed. The most serious internally induced disruption occurred when the 20-year working relationship between Clarence Cannon and John Taber was dissolved by Taber's retirement in 1962 and Cannon's death in 1964. The duration of their dual hegemony was so great, their devotion to Committee norms so similar, and their impact upon Committee integration so obvious, that one of the most natural questions to pose concerns the disintegrative effects of recent leadership changes. More than any other, this query has dogged every step of the research — "What changes will occur when Cannon and Taber leave?" It must be emphasized that this question cannot be answered yet. More time must elapse before a definitive answer can be essayed. Still, a preliminary guess, on the available evidence, can be attempted. And that guess would be that each of the successive changes in leadership has had structural and behavioral consequences but that the internal and external relationships of the Committee are too firmly established to be seriously disrupted by personnel changes even of this magnitude.

JOHN TABER — BEN JENSEN

John Taber's retirement and Ben Jensen's succession to the position of ranking minority member brought a few disintegrative changes in its wake. But they were, on the whole, gradual, marginal, and temporary in their effects. To begin with, Taber's loss was in no sense sudden. He had been persuaded, against his inclination, to run in 1960 and had, during the 87th Congress, delegated most of his day-to-day Committee work to the middle seniority Republicans. In 1964, several Committee members expressed the idea that Taber's acumen had been in slow decline in the two years before his retirement. Hence, they explained, the gradualness of the decline made transition "smooth and operational." "One reason there has been so little change" said one, "is because John Taber in his last years was slipping away. He wasn't as sharp as he used to be." On the other hand, one source of influence which Taber retained to the end — and even beyond — was the respect and affection of his fellow Committee members, high or low on both sides of the aisle. Well after his retirement, Committee Republicans continued to pattern their actions in his image. As one of them put it, in 1964,

> Our thinking is the same as it always was. Mr. Jensen worked with Mr. Taber. I was schooled under John Taber. We carry on the same tradition. Often times we'll say, "John would have said this," or, "John would have said that." You hear that a great deal. There's a carry-over of respect.

253

Taber's successor, Ben Jensen, had been a Committee member since 1943. He was no less acquainted with or devoted to Committee norms than Taber and, indeed, articulated them far more readily than did his predecessor. While Taber was still in Congress, Jensen gave public notice of the thought he had been giving (as Members typically do under the seniority system) to his new job together with his decision to play the role as Taber had played it. Speaking of their "close association of 20 years," he addressed Taber saying, "John, next session, should I step into your place on the Committee, I pledge to do my very best here to carry on in a manner pleasing to you."[64] On the whole, he did behave that way during his two-year tenure. But Jensen experienced difficulty in fully redeeming his pledge. He did not possess the same capital of respect that enabled Taber to maximize the potential of the ranking minority member role. His difficulties were especially evident in his relations with Chairman Cannon, but they extended to his relations with Democrats and Republicans throughout the Committee.

Clarence Cannon and Ben Jensen never enjoyed the ties of mutual regard that maintained (despite one reported fist fight) the close working relationship between Cannon and Taber. Indeed, Jensen and Cannon had a fairly lengthy history of angry personal disputation on the House floor. In 1950, for example, they exchanged such heated charges with one another that a quorum call was resorted to as a way of restoring decorum to the chamber. Again in 1959, they staged such a loud, acrimonious, fist-shaking debate that Speaker Rayburn had to gavel them into silence.[65] An experienced Democrat described their relationship inside the Committee:

> Taber was a much sharper guy. Jensen always wants to cut — but his arguments aren't too good. I think Cannon sort of laughs at Jensen. They have some violent arguments and they almost come to blows. But Cannon just rides over him.

From Cannon's own reaction to the retirement of John Taber, we can sense, too, a bond the depth of which could not be duplicated with a man for whom Cannon lacked an equal amount of respect. Said Cannon in 1964,

> My old and dear friend John Taber, one of the ablest men who ever sat in Congress, promised me he would return this session. I think he intended to; but his health failed him and he decided he'd had enough. So he retired — most unfortunately.

The outward visible symbol of the Cannon-Taber relationship was the arrangement whereby each, when he was Committee Chairman, would allow

[64] *Congressional Record*, Daily Edition, September 20, 1962, p. 19039.
[65] *Congressional Record*, Daily Edition, September 20, 1962, p. 19039. See also *ibid.*, October 6, 1962, p. 21501; 96 *Congressional Record*, pp. 4936–4937; *Congressional Record*, Daily Edition, June 23, 1959, p. 10542; *Washington Post*, June 24, 1962.

the other to be an ex officio member of all subcommittees. And it was precisely this arrangement that broke down when Jensen succeeded to the role of ranking minority member. In contemplating Committee organization in 1963, Jensen fully expected the ex officio tradition to be continued. Though he gave every Republican two subcommittee assignments, he gave up his own seat on the Interior Subcommittee (which he had held for 20 years) and retained only a single assignment on the Public Works Subcommittee. Mr. Cannon, however, did not cooperate. In the first place, he caused Jensen a good deal of embarrassment by arbitrarily trimming one Republican member from each of four subcommittees. Jensen, who had begun to cement his influence as Republican leader by allocating subcommittee seats was forced to renege on some of his promises. To Committee Republicans, of course, the episode indicated a less influential minority voice in Committee affairs. A more important sign of change came when Cannon declined to designate Jensen as an ex officio member of any subcommittee and, hence, of any conference committee. Early in the session, the Chairman called two or three of the more senior Republicans to his office to explain. One recalled,

> He said he was thinking of changing some of the Committee procedures — in the markup, for instance. He said that he had always recognized John Taber and that he had voted ex officio in the markup. But he said that he didn't have to recognize him, that he [Cannon] was the only ex officio member. He said he couldn't recognize Ben Jensen the way he recognized John Taber. "Taber did it for me and I did it for Taber, but I'm not going to do it any more." He didn't ask us our opinion. He just called us in and told us what he was thinking.

The denouement was described by an experienced Democrat.

> Jensen took himself off the Interior Committee because he assumed he'd be a member of all of them. When he started wandering into some of the committees, the Chairman said, "He's not a member." He was going to make an issue of it, but he would have lost in the full Committee. The Democrats would have lined up solidly against him. He was going to appeal to the full Committee, but he decided against it.

Cannon, it appears, was led to alter an existing integrative arrangement because the underpinning of personal respect no longer existed. His success in breaking a precedent depended, however, on the predispositions of other members not to challenge his decision. An influential Republican stressed this aspect of Cannon's move in the context of the leadership change:

> I always considered John Taber a tower of strength on the Committee. And he was. He commanded a great deal of respect. For that reason, Cannon had to be careful in what he did. If he tried to do anything shady or arbitrary, John Taber would get mad and put up an awful stink about it. And

255

if Taber did that, Cannon knew he might lose, because Taber would get support from some of the Democrats. Ben Jensen doesn't have that standing in the Committee . . . [the ex officio change] is an example of that arbitrariness I mentioned before. Whatever their differences, Cannon and Taber had good rapport. Cannon and Jensen didn't have that relationship. I guess Cannon thought this was a good time to break the precedent. Cannon could do that to Jensen. No Democrats would take up the cudgels for Ben Jensen. But if Cannon had ever tried to do that to John Taber, he never would have gotten away with it. The Democrats would have supported Taber.

Cannon's move set up an initial test of Jensen's ability to capitalize the full potential of his role. He could not. The outcome meant, therefore, that the influence of the ranking minority member role — its scope and its weight — was held to a minimum during Jensen's tenure.

Not only did Jensen fail to command support from Cannon and his fellow Democrats, but he conspicuously failed, also, to win the backing of the Committee's Republicans. Taber himself had frequently tunneled around Jensen to work directly with his younger middle seniority colleagues. And the Republicans did not feel any very immediate sense of loss when the ex officio arrangement was altered. "I'd much rather take my other subcommittee to conference with me," said one ranking subcommittee Republican. "He's [Jensen] awfully windy." "The change won't make any difference at all in our subcommittee," agreed another ranking minority member:

> I know what I want and how to get it. Maybe some ranking minority members aren't as good at rough and tumble as I am and can't get the best deal possible. But not on my subcommittee. Mr. Jensen can't come in and say anything about our bill. We take it line by line and item by item, and he doesn't know anything about it.

When Cannon made known his move, no Committee Republican "took up the cudgels" on Jensen's behalf. It seems likely that most of them shared the assessment of a Democrat who had sat in subcommittee for many years with Jensen:

> Actually Cannon saved the subcommittees a lot of trouble. Jensen doesn't know one thing from another in most of these areas. On some committees, he does — but not on a lot of them. He would have come in and just wanted to cut — cut personnel and all that — the meat-axe approach. And he would have given long speeches — interminably. So Cannon actually helped that way.

It is an open question whether subcommittee members ever want the Chairman and ranking minority member to join in their deliberations. Taber was, however, a net asset because of his influence with the Committee Chairman

256

and because of the respect which his knowledge had earned him among other Committee members. Given subcommittee aversion, on principle, to external influence, and given the fact that Jensen had neither of Taber's assets to the same degree, there was little reason for Republican subcommittee members to contest Cannon's initiative.

In the normal conduct of Committee affairs, subcommittees function with a minimum of interference by the Chairman and ranking minority member of the full Committee. At the subcommittee level, therefore, the change in relationships had only a marginal effect — limited, perhaps, to those few decisions where an extra vote would make a difference. Subcommittees tend to develop fairly stable working relationships which in no way depend upon or are affected by the two topmost officials of the Committee. The autonomy of subcommittees insulates them from the effects of personnel changes at the higher levels. Subcommittees, with their proprietary interests and their operating autonomy, constitute a stabilizing and integrating force in the face of change.

The Committee does, of course, carry on a few activities outside of subcommittees. And in these areas — such as the allocation of subcommittee positions reported earlier — the deterioration of the Chairman–ranking minority member relationship had one noticeable consequence. After the rebuff by Cannon and early in the session, Jensen established — for the first and only time in the period being studied — a special subcommittee of Republican members to fix a set of budget-cutting goals for the minority. The subcommittee was known as the Bow Task Force after its Chairman Frank Bow; and it was comprised of Jensen, Bow, and four other ranking minority subcommittee members. Its job was to conduct "a detailed line by line survey of the budget and make firm recommendations as to where savings could be made."[66] The group hired its own expert staff, headed by former Budget Director Maurice Stans and former Deputy Budget Director Robert Merriam, which proceeded to formulate their own targets for budget reduction. They acted, therefore, outside of and in opposition to regular Committee processes. Not only did they set themselves up in competition with Chairman Cannon and his subcommittee chairmen but, in further violation of Committee norms, they met in the offices of minority floor leader Charles Halleck in order to receive a maximum of publicity for their efforts.

It is not possible to say categorically that the Bow Task Force was a retaliatory gesture by Jensen. Republican members agreed that Jensen "authored" the plan, and it did follow in sequence the deterioration of relations between Cannon and himself. Furthermore, it is hard to imagine such a project taking root during the hegemony of John Taber. In any event,

[66] *Congressional Record*, Daily Edition, March 4, 1963, p. 3236.

the Task Force was a potentially disruptive mechanism because, to the degree that it solidified the Republicans in the Committee in opposition to the Democrats, the key norm of minimal partisanship would be threatened. Its earliest consequences seemed to be just that — as Republicans from Eisenhower to Halleck used the Bow Task Force recommendations as the point of the lance in jousting with the Kennedy administration. A staff member described the immediate repercussions on one subcommittee:

> The Republican attack has hardened party lines. The Democrats have drawn together in defense of the budget. Two weeks ago, we could have cut the defense budget by $2 billion. Today, I don't think we were doing it — all because of party politics. Partisanship is killing us.

As it turned out, however, partisanship inflicted no more than a few superficial scratches; surely it did not kill.

At one level, the activity of the Bow Task Force followed the path of most heralded economy drives. It began with a burst of publicity, slowly lost visibility, and then petered out. In March of 1963, the Task Force issued four press releases and a fact sheet. In April, six more press releases followed. But from May through December, the Task Force issued but two public statements — one in May and one in December. In 1964, Jensen revived the group, and in February of that year five press releases reflected another flurry of activity. Thereafter — virtual silence. Whatever sting the idea had packed when it began had long since been drawn.

On another level, the Bow Task Force failed to heat up partisanship because individual subcommittees proved immune from its impact. They preferred business as usual. For example, in the case of the Interior Subcommittee whose bill was the first to reach the floor and which therefore bore the full brunt of Task Force efforts (and on which the Republican representation consisted of two unsocialized Committee freshmen), the minimization of partisanship was evidenced by a unanimous report and a public display of great good feeling across party lines.[67] What seems to have happened, again, is simply that the decentralization of decision-making kept the subcommittees from feeling any direct or compelling impact from recommendations prepared outside their normal processes. Changes at the full Committee level — whether changes in personal relationships or in partisanship — had relatively little effect on the well-established integrative patterns of behavior in the subcommittees. In conclusion, then, the Republican leadership turnover of 1963–1964 demonstrates the Committee's capacity to endure minor disintegrative changes — permanent or temporary — without altering in any basic way the highly integrated character of the system.

[67] *Congressional Record*, Daily Edition, April 2, 1963, pp. 5135–5138.

A year and a half after John Taber's retirement, the Committee's internal structure was tested anew. Clarence Cannon died and was succeeded by George Mahon. A 25-year veteran of the Committee, Mahon's work as Chairman of the Defense Subcommittee had earned him universal respect inside and outside the Committee.[68] He was a close ally of Mr. Cannon's and in sympathy with the full range of the Committee's integrative norms. "I'm trying to carry on in the best traditions of the Committee," said Mahon in the spring of 1965. "We are carrying on in much the same way as we did under Mr. Cannon." On March 2nd, the new Chairman signalized the Committee's 100th anniversary with a floor speech emphasizing his devotion to Committee practices and warning against ill-considered or drastic change.[69] It is obviously premature to assess the consequences of the succession. Surely changes will result. Some have been touched upon earlier and some others will be mentioned later. But most of them, so far as one can tell after one year of Mahon's chairmanship, are marginal. What is more, such changes appear, on balance, to have been markedly integrative rather than disintegrative in their consequences.

Two early innovations by Mahon are noteworthy. First, he acted as soon as it became feasible to restore the close working relationship between himself and the ranking minority member. He did not reverse Cannon's decision during the remainder of the 88th Congress. But when Representative Jensen was defeated for re-election and was succeeded by Representative Frank Bow, Chairman Mahon designated Bow an ex officio member of all subcommittees. "I am taking Mr. Frank Bow with me to all subcommittee markups and conference committee meetings," reasoned Mahon, in classic Committee terms, "because it is very helpful in giving more unity and cohesiveness to the Committee." His action was facilitated by the fact that Bow was a respected member of the Committee, had been a close working ally of John Taber's, and (despite the "Bow" Task Force) had observed the integrative norms of the group as a long-time ranking subcommittee member of the State, Justice, Commerce Subcommittee.

Thus, after a two-year deterioration, the Chairman–ranking minority member role relationship became a more harmonious one. And an important symbol of minimal partisanship was restored. Only time will tell whether Mahon and Bow will carry out their formally reciprocal roles with an informal collaboration on the model of Cannon and Taber. Both have the

[68] See, for example, William S. White, "All Nice Guys Don't Finish Last," *Washington Star*, May 15, 1964; "Frugal Funds Chief," *New York Times*, May 13, 1964; "Mahon to be House Appropriations Committee Chairman," *Congressional Quarterly* (May 15, 1964), pp. 969–971.

[69] *Congressional Record*, Daily Edition, March 2, 1965, pp. 3863–3867

experience of having done so with their opposite subcommittee numbers — Gerald Ford in the case of Mahon and John Rooney in the case of Bow. And it is noteworthy that Bow did not head the Task Force in 1965. For now, however, the point is that the disintegrative changes of the Cannon-Jensen period were quickly reversed. After being subjected to a bit of internal conflict, the Committee would seem to have snapped back in the direction of a more integrated system.

Chairman Mahon also acted in his early days to give the Committee's newcomers a greater sense of participation and efficacy than they had enjoyed in the later years of Cannon's chairmanship. By no means did he seek to abolish the norm of apprenticeship. But he sought to speed up and spread around the satisfactions associated with that apprenticeship. Mr. Cannon had, for example, drifted out of personal contact with the newer members of the group — or so, at least, they felt. "He smiles at me," said one Democratic newcomer, "but I doubt if he recognizes me. He probably recognizes my name though." "I don't think he even knows who I am," said another. "I can't remember that he has ever spoken to me. I may meet him and speak to him and he mumbles something back. But he doesn't recognize me." Cannon probably kept a very watchful eye on the Committee's newcomers. But it was accomplished from afar, and most of the young Democrats believed, with one of their number, "He doesn't even know who I am."

Mahon moved to alleviate this feeling of remoteness. He visited with them and talked with them individually. He asked some of them to sit temporarily as ad hoc nonvoting members at the hearings of his Defense Subcommittee. When the Defense and Military Construction Subcommittees took testimony on the 1965 emergency appropriation for Viet Nam, he invited all Committee members to attend and participate. He improved the subcommittee assignments of most of them. And he designated them as conferees on their subcommittees' bills. Mahon was proud of the change. "The younger members are happier than they have been in years," he said. "They know the Chairman knows them and wants them to grow in influence and understanding. I think I have a fine relationship with the younger members."

The dissatisfactions of the Democrats who came to the Committee in 1963 have already been mentioned. And though most of them became "resigned" to their lack of participation, their restlessness did constitute a potentially disintegrative internal force. Had Cannon faced these five sophomores plus the nine Democratic newcomers in 1964, there is no telling whether he would have distributed rewards in such a way as to maintain or reduce the existing level of dissatisfaction. In any case, Mahon certainly did discern the potential for internal conflict represented by the outsized group of newcomers, and he did take steps to head it off. Thus, in dealing with the younger Democrats the new Chairman acted so as to preserve Committee integration.

To some extent, the changes engineered by Mahon reflect his temperamental distaste for conflict. He prefers to make decisions by talking to everyone concerned, by being "amenable and conciliatory" and developing the broadest consensus possible. Yet this personal variable would seem to be a minor explanation for the two integrative changes just described. Clarence Cannon was a temperamental opposite, inclined to be independent, cantankerous, and careless in provoking conflict. Yet he ran the very model of a tightly integrated Committee. The personal styles of the Chairman will produce some variation in the techniques used to promote integration. For instance, it seems likely that the socialization of the young will involve fewer overt negative sanctions under Mahon than under Cannon. But these are not basic in the structure for integration. The Committee's concern for integration is a logical derivative of its attempts to satisfy the amalgam of expectations confronting it — the more general ones set by the House and the more specific ones set by its own members. Committee members believe, especially, that they cannot meet their own goal or maintenance expectations unless they are highly integrated. And these beliefs do not depend on the individual personality of the Chairman (or ranking minority member) — certainly not one who has been socialized by decades of service on the Committee. Even if a Chairman or ranking minority member with potentially disintegrative predispositions happened along, the autonomy of the subcommittees and the expectations of their members would blunt — at least for some time — any disruption that might occur. The evidence of the Cannon-Mahon and the Taber-Jensen-Bow leadership changes, at least, supports such a view.

Lacking a lengthy time perspective, any conclusions must be tentative. But, tentatively, we can accept the assessment of a veteran staff member in the summer of 1965:

> There's been no revolution here. The Committee has a job to do and it's carrying on just about the same. I've sat under three different Chairmen, Mr. Taber, Mr. Cannon, and Mr. Mahon, and there hasn't been much difference. It's a stable institution and doesn't zig and zag with every change of Chairman.

Committee members like to repeat one of Mr. Cannon's pet descriptions — "The Committee goes on forever, like Tennyson's brook." Despite the presence of disintegrative forces actual and potential, externally and internally induced, the Committee's internal structure has remained stable

261

and integrated. Some disintegrative changes have been absorbed and blunted without permanent effect; some have been turned aside before they developed; some have been endured temporarily and later reversed. The Appropriations Committee's high degree of integration persists because (but only for so long as) Committee members believe it helps them to meet their expectations — and House members do not believe it prohibits them from meeting theirs.

CONCLUSION

The House Committee on Appropriations is a highly integrated political system. A variety of special conditions make this degree of integration possible. Effective internal control mechanisms operate to promote and preserve it. And, once established, the Committee's integrative arrangements exhibit considerable resilience in the face of potentially disintegrative forces.

The fact of Committee integration gives added credibility to all of the summary generalizations of Chapter Four. Our assumption that Committee members do play their prescribed roles is measurably strengthened by evidence that socializing and sanctioning mechanisms operate to bring about this result. For the linkage between role and role behavior is not automatic in a political system; it must be secured by effectively operating internal control mechanisms. Knowledge that these linking mechanisms do exist in the case of the Appropriations Committee reduces the risk in making inferences (as we sometimes have) about nonobservable behavior on the basis of norms.

Evidence tending to confirm the congruence of role and role behavior strengthens, also, our assertions about the stability of the Committee's decision-making structure. A persistent unwillingness to abide by Committee norms or an inability to manage the internal conflict involved would surely produce an unstable decision-making structure. And the unpredictability associated with such a structure would surely vitiate our assertions about a normal or well-patterned decision-making process. Conversely, the ability of the Committee to minimize internal conflict eases the problem of making generalizations about Committee decision-making which cover a period as long as 1947 to 1965. The high degree of Committee integration suggests at least an absence of internally generated upheavals in Committee behavior. And, to the degree that the Committee can stabilize its internal structure, a powerfully stabilizing factor is introduced into the entire appropriations process. Assuming, for the moment that the House Committee does dominate appropriations decision-making in Congress, its high degree of internal integration may help explain why the appropriations process itself has remained so stable — even unchanging — during the period under investigation.

On the whole, the consequences of high integration for a political system are stabilizing kinds of consequences — for its internal structure and its external relationships. But it may promote a stability of relationships in varying degrees. To the extent that this is so, it may be possible to suggest the more likely areas of change. In the case of the Appropriations Committee, it seems clear that integration helps the individual Committee member to fulfill his satisfactions. He believes that a well-integrated internal structure results in Committee unity before the House. And he believes that Committee unity before the House is a necessary condition of Committee influence (hence, his personal influence) in the chamber. Committee integration surely meets his desire for social solidarity. But Committee integration may have mixed consequences in terms of adaptation to House member expectations. House members are likely to view Committee unity as a mark of effectiveness in processing the work load and as some assurance that their representatives on the Committee know what they are doing. But the Committee's internal integrative arrangements, Committee member obedience to Committee-oriented norms, and outward displays of unity also feed House images of excessive autonomy and influence. And these images fuel House dissatisfaction. Committee integration meets the expectations of its own members more completely than the expectations of House members. Viewed from this single perspective, it would seem that, if substantial alterations are to be made in the Appropriations Committee's decision-making structure or its place in the total appropriations process, those changes are likely to emanate from outside rather than inside the Committee.

The House Committee
and Executive Agencies
*I: Agency Expectations,
Images, and Behavior*

THE COMMITTEE-AGENCY RELATIONSHIP

Appropriations Committee behavior is explainable in part by the existing pattern of Committee-House relations and in part by the existing structure of internal Committee relationships — both of which have been described. Committee behavior is also explainable in terms of its interaction with the agencies of the executive branch of the government.[1] It is the specific requests for money made by these agencies that trigger the Committee's decision-making activity. And it is the agencies' need for money that accounts, in the final analysis, for the existence of an Appropriations Committee. The Committee's 400-odd annual hearings are primarily devoted to communicating with agency representatives about their needs; and the same conversations go on continuously in less formal ways. Furthermore, it is primarily by working through or on behalf of executive agencies that the myriad of clientele or interest groups enter the appropriations process. A description of Committee-agency relationships will bring us a step closer to the specifics and the substance of Committee decisions than we have been thus far.

The executive agency, like the parent House of Representatives, is a

---

[1] The term "agency" is used throughout to refer to any and all executive branch organizations whose representatives come before the Committee.

political unit which is part of the environment of the House Committee. Chapters Six and Seven describe this external relationship in the same language of reciprocal expectations, images, and behavior used in discussing Committee-House interaction. There are important differences in the two pairs of relationships. But it should be noted, at the outset, that House and executive agencies may unite their demands and press them upon the Committee in alliance with one another. Some House member can be found in support of every agency demand, and most House member demands will be supported by some executive agency. Committee responses to agency expectations will, therefore, affect Committee adaptation to House member expectations.

The basic difference between the Committee-House interaction and the Committee-agency interaction is the fact that the former takes place within the legislative branch of the government whereas the latter relationship spans two separate branches. The Committee is a subsystem of the House. It is not a subsystem of the executive agencies. Two consequences of this difference are vital. Since the House creates the Committee, legitimizes its activity, and provides its essential resources, the House possesses very direct and very potent sanctions over Committee behavior. Executive agencies, either individually or collectively, do not constitute any such immediate or substantial threat to the Committee. The agencies do have direct control, however, over the pet projects or the constituent services desired by individual Committee members. The ability of the agencies to mobilize the support of clientele groups and House members gives them an indirect method of influencing Committee behavior. And, most importantly, their ability to manipulate complex bodies of information relative to their own area of expertise can be used to influence the activity of the Committee. Still, this is a less threatening array of sanctions than that possessed by the House.

A second difference is the very obvious one of personnel. The Committee-House relationship involves the Committee member with his colleagues. The Committee-agency relationship involves the Committee member with department heads, departmental budget officers, bureau chiefs, bureau budget officers, and others in the ranks of bureaucratic officialdom. The expectations, perceptions, and attitudes of these executive officials will not be the same as those of House members. And they require a different response from the Appropriations Committee. Members of the Committee may occasionally be more responsive to the expectations of the agency than to those of the House. We would not want to generalize in this regard. The point is that differences in personnel, like differences in sanctions, promote a Committee-agency relationship that differs from the Committee-House relationship and, hence, poses different problems for the Appropriations Com-

265

mittee.[2] Chapter Six considers the relationship from the perspective of the executive agency — specifically from the point of view of the executive officials (see Introduction) of 23 of the 36 agencies whose appropriations fortunes have been studied.

AGENCY EXPECTATIONS

Goal Expectations

Agency expectations (or demands) as to how the Committee should behave are of two sorts — those pertaining primarily to substantive goals and those pertaining primarily to the maintenance of a stable relationship between the two groups. They fall into the same categories used earlier in the analysis of House-Committee relations.

Agency goal expectations are revealed most directly in the budget estimates they present to the Committee for decision. The agencies' substantive demand is for money. For them, a budget estimate reflects numberless decisions about programs, about priorities, about personnel, and about other matters of internal agency concern. A budget estimate is, as Aaron Wildavsky has recently re-emphasized, a political document — a resolution of many conflicting judgments and sources of influence.[3] All of the decision-making machinery of the executive branch will have been involved in the preparation, the presentation, the argument, the counterargument, and the appeals up and down the hierarchy which precede the ultimate determination of an agency's goals. These goals then appear in the dollars and cents language of budget estimates. Agency expectations about money are expectations about goals, and money demands on the Committee should be viewed as substantive, programmatic demands.

Judging by the 36 executive bureaus whose appropriations case histories have been analyzed, most agencies present the Appropriations Committee with annual requests for increases in funds. Of the 576 cases examined, there were 465 (80.7 per cent) requests for increases, 20 (3.5 per cent) requests for the same money as the previous year, and 91 (15.8 per cent) requests for decreases in dollar amounts. It is impossible to translate these figures directly into changes in program level. But the magnitude of the increases (and the

<hr>

[2] The full range of executive agency–congressional committee relations are explored via an instructive case study in J. Leiper Freeman, *The Political Process: Executive Bureau-Legislative Committee Relations* (New York: Doubleday, Revised Edition, 1965.)

[3] See Aaron Wildavsky, *The Politics of the Budgetary Process* (Boston: Little, Brown and Co., 1964), a book to which this chapter — especially its discussion of incrementalism — owes many debts. More generally, the debt is to the work of Charles Lindblom. See David Braybrooke and Charles Lindblom, *Strategy of Decision* (Glencoe: Free Press, 1963).

decreases) requested does reveal something about agency expectations. At any point in time, an executive agency will have a widely recognized, well-supported, and well-established core program. And what it requests each year from the Appropriations Committee are additions to or subtractions from that core program. In the language of agency budget people, the core program is known as an agency's budget "base." Agency expectations are that the Committee will accept its base and focus decision-making on the increment being requested. It does not, that is to say, expect that the Committee should (even if it could — which is quite another question) re-evaluate the agency's entire program and hence its entire body of budget estimates. The Committee, the agency feels, should accept the core program and concentrate only on the increments or on recently established aspects of the program.

The sixteen-year summary of estimates by the 36 bureaus reveals the incremental nature of yearly requests. The totals in Table 6.1 represent the annual request as a percentage of the previous year's appropriation — to convey some sense of the magnitude of the yearly increment requested.

TABLE 6.1

ESTIMATES AS A PERCENTAGE OF PREVIOUS YEAR'S APPROPRIATION: MAGNITUDE OF REQUESTED INCREASES AND DECREASES, 36 BUREAUS, 1947 TO 1962

Increases	Number of Decisions	Percentage of Decisions
Over 100.0	14	2.4
90.1–100.0	2	0.3
80.1–90.0	8	1.4
70.1–80.0	6	1.1
60.1–70.0	9	1.6
50.1–60.0	20	3.5
40.1–50.0	11	1.9
30.1–40.0	32	5.6
20.1–30.0	61	10.6
10.1–20.0	122	21.2
0.1–10.0	180	31.3
Same	20	3.5
Decreases		
−0.1– −10.0	55	9.5
−10.1– −20.0	20	3.5
−20.1– −30.0	9	1.6
Less than 30.1	7	1.2
Total	576	100.2*

* Due to rounding.

267

Although the appropriation of the previous year is not the same as an agency's base (normally it would be larger than the base), it is for most agencies a close approximation. As the figures reveal, agencies do not normally expect to be reduced below the last year's dollar amounts; and the tendency is to feel that an appropriation once granted is well on its way to becoming a part of the unchallengeable base. As the figures also reveal, over half of all agency demands were for appropriations increases of from 1 to 20 per cent of the previous year's figure. Thus it is the expectation of most agencies that their base should be expanded slowly and incrementally. A few agencies (the Census Bureau and the Office of Education, for example) have had wildly fluctuating and even cyclical expectations. Some others have requested an exponential expansion during the period under study — sometimes in the pattern of a request for a huge increase followed by the voluntary acceptance of a partial cutback. Agencies of these types account for the presence of rather large incremental requests — increases of over 50 per cent and decreases of over .20 per cent. Usually, the same agencies will account for the extreme cases both on the increase and on the decrease side.

The dominant concerns of agency officials are programmatic. Their incremental expectations are expectations about agency programs. It is this preoccupation with *program* that furnishes the key to understanding agency perspectives on the Appropriations Committee. To begin with, it helps to explain the agency officials' expectation that their budget estimates should not be reduced. The Committee, they feel, should grant them their full requests because each request represents a carefully thought out and necessary program. Every salary item and every procurement item involves the success of a program — or, as they often put it, a service to the public.

Officials representing 22 bureaus together with 5 departmental budget officers, all of whom had been previously interviewed, wrote follow-up answers to this question: "Would you under all circumstances consider a 5 per cent reduction by the Congress in your budget estimates a serious matter and harmful to the operation of your bureau (or department)?" Twenty-one of the respondents answered an unequivocal "Yes." Their answers were typified by three bureau chiefs who wrote: "[We] have a history of efficient and 'close margin' type of operation with the result that a reduction of 5 per cent . . . would hit right at the heart of our service operations." "Estimates submitted to the Congress represent the minimum required to obtain important objectives, and I would view a reduction of 5 per cent as having serious adverse effects." "Our requests to the Congress have been minimal and any reduction, however slight, would have serious results on the programs." All 21 emphasized that programs or services would have to be cut back or eliminated if the budget estimates were reduced by as much as 5 per cent.

The 6 other respondents gave equivocal "yes and no" answers. One departmental budget officer wrote, "Of course it would interfere with program progress, but certainly not to the extent that the world would come to an end." And a bureau chief opined, "I would not consider a 5 per cent cut by Congress harmful if most other bureaus received that or more . . . everything in life is relative. Sometimes a 5 per cent cut would be like a gift, sometimes like an insult." Three replied that the degree of harm would depend on the circumstances; and one bureau head declared flatly that the cut would not be harmful "provided it would assure me freedom to remove from the staff those people whose inefficiency, in my mind, makes them unnecessary." With the exception, perhaps, of this last respondent, none conveyed the expectation that Congress should reduce his budget.

Agency officials express the same expectations in slightly different terms by vigorously denying that their budget estimates are inflated. They are unanimous in asserting that, "I never pad a budget," "There is no fat in our budget," "I don't believe in padded budgets," "We don't fudge on our estimates," "We never put padding in our budget," or "There is nothing in my budget that I don't regard as essential." Since their budget estimates are not padded, it follows that they should be approved in their entirety. This does not mean, of course, that budget-cutting is impossible. What it does mean, again, is that important program values will have to be sacrificed. As a departmental officer put it, "Of course, there isn't a budget that can't be cut. But you'll just have to cut out some services for some programs." A bureau chief agreed, "Of course, our budget can be cut — anywhere — but you'll cut out valuable programs if you do."

Agency officials start from the premise that it is impossible to cut budgets without cutting programs, whereas the idea of the padded budget, they feel, encourages the illusion that such a feat is possible. One department budget officer discussed the question of his department's expectations in precisely these terms:

Just what is a padded budget? If you go in and ask for $1 million and they cut it by $100 thousand, the operation doesn't fold up. But you can't do as much as you would have done with $1 million. Then you come in the next year and they say, "You got along all right with $900 thousand didn't you?" That's where the padded budget idea comes from. Sure, any budget can be cut, but you just have to cut back your activities, that's all. Now if you gave X dollars for some new positions and went around and found people doing nothing, that would be a padded budget. If you mean that a cut can be made without it being fatal, then 90 per cent of the budgets are padded. The agency heads would try to have my job if they heard me say this, but we could cut this department's budget by 10 or 15 per cent. But you couldn't do all the things you are doing now. Right now, the

269

people are getting their money's worth. The question is: "Do you need to do this?" I had an agency director in here this morning and he told me he couldn't operate on the money in the budget. Of course he can operate. But he can't do all that he wants to do. The big question is not padded budgets. It's the policy question — is this operation needed?

Which is to say that, since budget requests express programmatic demands, any and all budget reductions should also reflect programmatic decisions. With this proposition, all agency officials agree.

A corollary agency expectation is that the Appropriations Committee should deal with budget requests in wholly programmatic terms. Officials may not always enjoy the legislative oversight activities of the Committee, but they accept such activity as legitimate — provided Committee attention centers on their programs. They disagree with the Committee's view that budgets are often padded and with the belief that reductions can be made in certain items without damaging agency programs. And they criticize the Committee whenever it moves away from questions of policy to those less obviously oriented in that direction. Agency expectations were expressed by a departmental budget officer:

Some of these [sub]committees want a picture of your appropriations by object classification. And they'll start going into all these separate items. They should get away from that. If you want to cut our program in half, O.K., cut it in half — if you don't believe in it. Or, if you want to say "Can't you take it a little slower in this program and take it in smaller bites?" — O.K. But don't approve the program and then take away the tools. I will say that we try to present the budget in a way that is conducive to that kind of thinking. We try to get them to think of so many people doing such and such work for such and such a program activity — not just so many stenographers, engineers, automobiles, etc.

The same dominant expectation was underscored in the complaints of a bureau chief:

We've been very disturbed by the fact that the [subcommittee's] questions began to turn on the housekeeping chores of the agency and not on our program. The [sub]committee became interested in how we were doing it and not in what we were doing . . . in how we keep our books — the internal audit and things like that . . . the [sub]committee has been treating administration as an end in itself . . . it's very frustrating to go up there and not have a chance to talk about your program.

Agency officials want the Appropriations Committee to talk with them in the language of program. Their assumption is that communication in these terms will increase the likelihood of their budget estimates being approved.

It is relevant to the understanding of Committee oversight activities that, whereas the agencies urge an ever greater program orientation upon them, the House (i.e., its substantive committees) urges an ever smaller program orientation. The legislative committees expect the Appropriations Committee to support agency programs with sufficient funds, but *not* to engage in extensive program review and analysis. The Committee's main task, as they see it, is to inquire into waste and inefficiency and to implement the goal of economy where poor management is discovered. Yet the emphasis on waste leads to the very kind of inquiry into nonprogrammatic detail to which executive agencies object. The Committee is caught between conflicting demands and cannot move too far in either direction without violating the expectations of one or the other external group. If, from the agencies' point of view, the Committee seems insufficiently attentive to program, an explanation may lie in the presence of House expectations and the potency of House sanctions.

Agencies express two major goal expectations: that their entire budget request should be granted, and that all budgetary questions should be treated as program questions. The two goals are interrelated since the budget estimates of an agency represent the agency's judgment about the program it wishes to undertake. In most cases, budget estimates are a reasonably accurate expression of program aspirations. But it needs to be recognized that budget estimates are almost never a perfect representation of agency program desires and that in some cases budget estimates will be a grossly inaccurate representation of agency program expectations. The possibility exists, therefore, that an agency may want substantially more money (or less money) in order to implement its program than expressed in its budget estimates.

The process by which a budget estimate is arrived at is enormously complex, involving primarily the agency, the department, the Budget Bureau, and the President. This process, internal to the executive branch, is not the subject of this book — which takes the final budget estimates as it finds them. But it should be noted that agency budget estimates are a product of conflict within the executive branch over programs, over resources, and over priorities. Typically, any single agency will not be allowed to ask Congress for as much money as it optimally desires. It quite often will have its program and its money demands trimmed by actions within the department and by the Budget Bureau. Normally, the agency fights for its desires within the executive branch, accepts the decision made there (ultimately by the President) as the best it can get, and goes before Congress to defend that dollars and cents figure and no other. When its budget estimates badly distort its program objectives, and when it feels deeply grieved over the decisions made within the executive branch, it is accurate to say that its goal expectations are that Congress should give it *more* money than it has formally asked for. The problem of communicating such expectations is difficult. But

271

it can be done, as we shall see. And, in any event, the point is that intensely felt expectations of this sort may exist and may not be reflected in the budget estimate. In such cases, the Committee will best meet agency goal expectations by granting more money than the agency has formally requested.

It is also a possibility that agency leaders will welcome and even seek reductions in their budget estimates. That is to say, for people who desire changes inside their agency, budget reductions may be a way to induce such changes. Budget reductions may set off reactions inside the agency which bring about long-run gains in program accomplishment. Should agency officials actively seek budget reductions, they will have to communicate with the Committee covertly. This may take the form of statements such as: "If you are going to cut us, here's the place to do it," or, "We can absorb a cut here but not here." But such communications are hidden from view.

After the fact, however, agency officials sometimes express positive satisfaction with the consequences of budget reductions. Two officials whose agencies were among those hardest hit by the Republican economy drive of the 80th Congress reflected on the results:

> In the 80th Congress, it was awfully rough. But it wasn't all bad. Things weren't lost, not by a long shot. You get some old-time bureaucrats who've been in a long time and they do things the same way and never change. Well, the [sub]committee brought in some of the people from the field to testify and just clobbered them. They saw it first-hand. Oh it's easy to be out in the field and say, "We want this." But they went up and had the blaze put to their feet. After the hearing, they came in and said to us, "Don't you ever let that happen again." Well, I had a plan sitting right here in the drawer that I hadn't been able to sell. And some other young fellow had ideas. So we put them through. The results were good — and all because some people got clobbered.

> Maybe it wasn't such a bad thing after all. A kick in the britches is what you need sometimes to take a look at your own program and see if it's running as smoothly as it ought to be. As it turned out, we had overlapping out in the field. These congressmen aren't dumbbells. Their constituents were writing in and saying that three different men would converge on their doorstep when one man could do the job. As a result of that, we did change; and now we are doing [the two jobs] with fewer men than we had [doing one] before. . . . When I was in the legislature, I ran into this. I found there was nothing like messing with the money to bring the boys to the milk in a hurry. The method may have been a little drastic, perhaps, but sometimes it takes a good kick in the britches to bring an agency around.

In his ground-breaking essay on appropriations control, Arthur Macmahon suggested that the most important consequence of Appropriations Committee oversight is to "galvanize the disciplines of administration" inside the agencies.[4] The two cases just cited indicate that the people inside the agencies may want such galvanizing action. In such cases, their goal expectations may be promoted by budget reductions.

Maintenance Expectations

Agency maintenance expectations, too, focus upon money and program. But they relate less to the substance of Committee actions than to the rules of the game observed by the Committee in responding to agency demands. Agency officials, like members of the House, express certain expectations pertaining to the type of relationship they deem desirable between the Committee and themselves. Since the executive branch does not possess the authority (as does the House) to prescribe formal procedures for the Committee, its maintenance expectations are reflected wholly in terms of informally communicated desires, wishes, and hopes. Agency maintenance expectations both differ from and are similar to those of the House. Most House expectations, it will be recalled, focus on the problem of balancing a basic Committee dependence on the parent chamber against a necessary degree of autonomy. But these concerns for dependence and autonomy are less relevant to the relations between elements of two different branches of government. The agencies' dominant concern seems to be for a high degree of *predictability or certainty* in their Committee relations. In other cases, however, House maintenance expectations are echoed by agency officials. Especially they share the desire for an overall *stability* of relationships between themselves and the Committee. Agency leaders (like House leaders) have a set of expectations bespeaking their wish for the minimization of Committee-agency conflict.

The expectation on the part of executive branch officials that the Committee should act predictably stems, again, from the administrator's concern for program. Rational program development requires planning, and planning is fruitless without some reasonable degree of certainty about the availability of funds. Agencies will be hurt by outright budget reductions. But agencies are also hurt when they cannot be sure what the Committee will do from one year to the next, when they do not know why the Committee acts as it does, or when they are unable to assess their own potential for influence on the Committee. The first situation has at least the virtue of being clear-cut. The second keeps the agency harassed and off balance. It precludes long-range program planning, rational personnel policy, and efficient purchasing. Certainty is a prime desideratum for the department or bureau head. Conversely, the manipulation of uncertainty is a key weapon in the hands of the Committee.

[4] Arthur W. Macmahon, "Congressional Oversight of Administration: The Power of the Purse," *Political Science Quarterly* (June, 1943), p. 414.

The expression of the desire for certainty takes several forms. One expression of it is the agency expectation that its budget base should not be disturbed. If, at least, some base amount can be preserved intact, then a degree of predictability and planning will be possible. Agency and Committee communicate with one another in two ways: via the annual appropriations hearings and via informal year-round contacts. And, when agency people express their desire for certainty in relations with the Committee, many of their expectations relate to action at these two points. They want to be certain what the hearings will be about; they want to be informed as to precisely what particular problems are bothering particular Committee members; they want to know the preferences and idiosyncrasies of each Committee member and of the clerk; they want to know exactly which of their programs have the most support; if the Committee is going to cut them, they want some chance to help determine priorities; they want to know exactly what is meant by the language of a Committee report; they want to know the intensity of feeling among Committee members on all matters pertaining to their agency; and they want to be told what needs to be done to win Committee support wherever it is lacking. The Appropriations Committee, they feel, should cooperate to give them this and all other relevant information to the end that misunderstanding will be reduced, that relationships will be predictable, and that agency planning can go forward.

As predictability increases, doubtless stability will increase and agency-Committee conflict will be minimized. Agency officials do express, however, the additional expectation that the Committee should follow *fair procedures* in dealing with them. And, to the degree that these are observed, their observance will minimize conflict. For example, agency officials expect that the Committee give them a full hearing, that the Committee listen with some open-mindedness to their budget justifications, that the Committee deal with them openly and honestly, that the Committee evidence some interest in the agency's problems, that the Committee operate with a minimum of arbitrariness, and that the Committee display substantial trust in the agency's word. The hope is, of course, that the observance of rules such as these will promote Committee support for the agency's substantive goals. But if it does not and if the Committee decides to reduce agency estimates, at least the agency will have received the kind of legislative due process which will hold antagonism to a minimum.

AGENCY IMAGES

An examination of agency perceptions and attitudes involves the relationship between what agency officials want the Appropriations Committee to do and what they perceive the Committee is actually doing. In light of what they perceive as the relation between expectations and behavior, they express certain attitudes toward the Committee. Their perceptions and attitudes (as in the case of the House) blend into images, favorable or unfavorable, of the Appropriations Committee. And agency officials take action on the basis of these images. In analyzing these images and their components, the nature of agency expectations will itself be further clarified.

Insofar as agency expectations are accurately reflected in their budget estimates, it is difficult to decide whether and to what degree agency expectations have or have not been met. We have assumed that in the vast majority of cases budget estimates are a good representation of agency demands. To cut budgets, therefore, is to leave expectations unfulfilled; the larger the cut, the greater the gap between agency expectations and Committee behavior. A description and analysis of 576 Appropriations Committee decisions on agency budget estimates will be presented in Chapter Eight. For now, it is sufficient to point out that the dominant pattern is one of budget reductions and that agency officials perceive it as such. A departmental budget officer and a bureau head commented,

> The attitude of the members of the Committee, their training before they get on the Committee is a highly negative thing. That's the nature of the animal — negative. It's a highly negative piece of machinery.

> In the House it's a policy. They want to show cuts. And every budget they want to cut below the President's budget. It's a tradition there.

Agency officials perceive that their substantive goals as expressed by their budget estimates usually are not met. The degree to which they are not met, however, varies widely. In the cases examined in Chapter Eight, budget reductions range from a low of 0.1 per cent to a high of 100 per cent. Obviously, agency officials will perceive some cuts as being more severe than others, and their attitude toward Committee action will vary with the perceived severity of the cut. The Committee's failure to meet budget estimates, though recognized as the dominant pattern, will not call for the same image or spur the same action on the part of all bureaus.

As a matter of fact the Committee sometimes approves an increase over an agency's budget estimate. In such cases, the agency perception is quite different. The head of an agency which had been receiving more increases than decreases in recent years said,

> Budget Bureau questions to us are always, "Why do you need this?" and "Can't you hold this down?" The House Committee's attitude is, "Why don't you ask for more?" or "Don't you think you could use more?"

This agency perceives the Appropriations Committee as being more friendly than the executive branch hierarchy. In such cases, the Committee technique is to justify budget increases by establishing that the budget estimates are a poor representation of agency expectations. Another bureau head described the pattern:

> Sometimes [the subcommittee chairman] will say, "Do you think this budget is enough for an adequate program?" And I will say, "Well, we can provide an encouraging program." Then he will say, "How much did you ask the department for?" And I will tell him. Then he'll ask, "How much did you ask the Budget Bureau for?" And I'll tell him. Then he'll ask, "And they know more about it than you do, do they?"

The probe, of course, reveals that the agency's original budget estimates and program judgments have been cut back during the internal process of budget-making. And, very frequently, the resulting Committee decision will be an increase rather than a reduction. In such instances, agencies will feel that their goal expectations have been met.

The remainder of this section will be devoted to agency perceptions and attitudes as they pertain to the less measurable of their expectations — to their desire for program communication, to their desire for certainty, and to their desire to minimize conflict through fair procedures. Generalization is hazardous, not the least because of the intangibility of the expectations themselves. But some images of the Committee are uniformly held, and in other cases several varieties of images can be described without precise estimates of their distribution. Emphasis will be placed on those cases in which expectations are not met and in which unfavorable images result. The important aspects of agency behavior can be most usefully viewed as responses to these unfavorable images made in the hope of reducing the gap between agency expectations and Committee behavior.

The Committee and Its Members

All agencies share the basic perception that Appropriations Committee action can be highly disadvantageous to them, and most begin with the view that the most threatening (or influential) legislative unit is the House Committee on Appropriations. When asked about their legislative relations, agency officials invariably begin to talk about the House Committee. They refer to it as *the* Committee or as "our Committee." They talk about the Senate Committee, too, but only comparatively, against the baseline comments they have previously made about the House group. Their preoccupation with the House Committee stems from their perception that the House Committee dominates the process, that its hearings come first, that its hearings are more searching, and that it is more likely to reduce their budget estimates than is the Senate Committee.

When executives speak of *the* Committee, moreover, they really mean the subcommittee that has jurisdiction over them. And when they speak of the subcommittee, they mean first and foremost the chairman. This perception was illustrated at the highest executive level by the invitation to State Department Subcommittee Chairman John Rooney to stay with President Kennedy at Palm Beach shortly after the 1960 election to talk about the foreign service budget.[5] It was behind President Kennedy's special invitation to the subcommittee chairman handling the space budget, Albert Thomas, to accompany him on his "nonpolitical" defense inspection trip of December, 1962 — not to mention the President's presence at a testimonial for Representative Thomas and his lavish praise there, shortly before his death.[6] Foreign Operations Subcommittee Chairman Otto Passman has been invited to the White House on numerous occasions as each of the last three Presidents has sought to ease his problems with the foreign aid appropriation.[7] "On these subcommittees," say agency officials, "90 per cent of it is the chairman." Or, "He's a majority of the subcommittee." And a departmental officer said that, from his point of view, "The most important thing in the whole appropriations process is good working relations between the head of the agency and the members of the appropriations subcommittees, especially the chairman. That's the number one thing."

The subcommittee's ranking minority member and the clerk are also perceived as being influential, and occasionally another member or two of the subcommittee is mentioned. The budget officers of two departments cited circumstances under which they felt the ranking minority member rather than the chairman dominated a given subcommittee. All perceive the existence of minimal partisanship and the necessity that their own behavior be bipartisan. "We get help from both sides. When he was in the minority, Jensen [R.] urged more money on us, and Kirwan [D.] added to our appropriations when he was in the minority. So — we've had splendid cooperation from both parties." Or, "You've got to keep friends on both sides of the aisle. You'll never know which party is going to be in power. When the Southern Democrats dominated, I had an awful time with them, so I had to get help from the Republicans."

The subcommittee clerk, too, is seen as a man whose actions have important consequences for the agency. "An unsympathetic or sympathetic clerk could make a considerable difference." "The staff man can be a very important influence in there." One bureau chief recalled, "Clerks can give

[5] See William L. Rivers, "The Foreign Policy of John J. Rooney," *The Reporter*, June 22, 1961.
[6] See excerpts from President Kennedy's press conference of September 13, 1962, as reprinted in *Congressional Record*, Daily Edition, September 14, 1962, p. 18429.
[7] See Rowland Evans, "Louisiana's Passman: The Scourge of Foreign Aid," *Harpers* (January, 1960), pp. 78–83.

you a lot of trouble. We had one some time ago. He had his nose out of joint over us . . . nothing we could do would make him change his opinion." And another lamented present difficulties:

> Our subcommittee chairman is a busy man and an older man. We get the feeling that he is taking the advice of the clerk a lot more than he used to. During the hearings the clerk is constantly priming the chairman with questions. He's not unobtrusive. The chairman is the kind that makes quick decisions and then you can't change him. That's what bothers us about this situation — the clerk is feeding him his conclusions and the chairman is not paying as much attention to us as he used to.

When agency officials concerned with their budgets look toward the Congress, they see a picture of a subcommittee of the House of Representatives dominated by the figure of its chairman, flanked on one side by the ranking subcommittee member and on the other side by the clerk — with an image of the Senate Appropriations Committee somewhere in the background. The predispositions of the legislators in that picture toward the agency and its program are a matter of the greatest concern to its officials.

Agency perceptions of the Committee's decision-making structure provide an element of the certainty the agencies desire, and the degree of predictability is advanced immeasurably when the same individuals occupy key Committee positions for long periods of time. Continuities in subcommittee personnel may work to the detriment of an agency if the legislators involved are permanently unsympathetic to it. But, save for the most egregious instances, agency officials look favorably upon personnel stability. They believe that changes in personnel impede the stabilization of agency-Committee relations. Should their subcommittees be shifted, for example, they will find the change unfriendly — as many agencies did when the Subcommittee on Deficiencies was suddenly created in 1959. One agency official, none of whose regular subcommittee members sat on the Deficiencies Subcommittee, discussed his first appearance before the group:

> We had to go up there for a supplemental before the Deficiencies Subcommittee. I didn't know what to expect. We clipped out parts of the hearings that these boys had conducted and found some questions of a sort that never came up in our hearings. We don't have any beat-up artists like that on our committee.

Most agency officials are willing to suffer the problems they have known rather than risk the unknown. Moreover, they also believe that legislative interest and sympathy are more likely to increase with personnel continuity than without it. And they worry whenever they must confront a new subcommittee, a new chairman, a new ranking minority member, or a new clerk.

When interviews were being conducted with Commerce Department

278

officials in December of 1960, a change in the chairmanship of their subcommittee was imminent. Representative Prince Preston, subcommittee chairman for the past six years, had suffered a primary election defeat. Perceptions voiced during the interregnum bespoke agency uncertainty and consternation. Department officials could not be sure who was to be the next chairman. Seniority rules indicated Representative Sidney Yates as the logical successor, but agency officials knew that other factors might well govern the decision. One department leader painted a picture of confusion:

> People in the Department keep asking me if it will mean a change. I don't know who will get it — it could flip a lot of ways. They don't even know how it's going up on the Hill yet. Three of the congressmen involved have come in to talk to me about it already.

Bureau chiefs for their part speculated that, "I think Yates will be a good man to work with," or "If [Representative Daniel] Flood becomes chairman of the committee, it might be a real help, who knows." As if to prove how well-founded Commerce Department uncertainty was, Clarence Cannon finally designated Representative George Andrews (see Chapter Five) as the new subcommittee chairman. And one year later he switched jurisdiction over the Commerce Department to a different subcommittee entirely — this time under the chairmanship of Representative John Rooney.

In the context of the interregnum, two bureau heads discussed the consequences of the impending change:

> I was awfully sorry that Prince Preston, chairman of our committee, won't be back. Continuity is very important on both sides. You see the same faces every year and you get so you know what they are thinking about and they know what you are talking about.

> That's the rub. You get so that over the years you establish a rapport with a congressman — especially a chairman of your committee — and then he gets defeated. I'm very anxious to know who the next chairman will be. It might make a big difference, especially since we are planning new construction and are coming up for an appropriation. After some period of time, Prince Preston had accepted it, and he wanted to see it through.

In instances such as this where personnel continuities had produced interest and sympathy on the part of the key subcommittee leader, changes are perceived as having important effects — not only on the maintenance expectations of predictability but on the goal expectation of approved budget estimates.

Another consequence of personnel stability is increased respect on the part of executive branch officials for the knowledge and capabilities of legislative participants. To a marked degree, too, they tender respect independent

279

of the treatment they are receiving at the hands of the subcommittee. A commonly expressed agency sentiment is that veteran subcommittee members "know as much about our program and problems as we do. They've been around a long time." "Some of these men have been on that Committee for 20 years," exclaimed a department budget officer, "you think they don't know those programs? Why they know those programs better than most of the men downtown operating them." A newly appointed agency head recalled that, "When I went to my first appropriations hearing, there were four men there. And I knew damned well that at least three of them knew a hell of a lot more about my bureau than I did." The attitude extends to the subcommittee clerk as well. "The permanent staff men on the Committee," said one bureau chief, "know a lot more about our program than do any of the staff people upstairs . . . in the Secretary's office." It might be suspected that comments of this sort are the better part of valor for agency officials having an on-going relationship with the Committee. But the frequency, the apparent sincerity, and the vigor with which they were expressed support the impression that they are genuine. More importantly, agency officials base much of their appropriations conduct on the assumption that the men with whom they deal are substantively knowledgeable as well as politically influential. Executive branch officials who have had little or no contact with legislators or who have no sense of dependence on them may, of course, have quite a different perception.

The Hearings

Since all agencies face the Committee at the time of appropriations hearings, many of their commonly held images of the Committee involve the hearing room contact. If for no other reason, hearings are essential to legitimize all agency requests for money. Agency officials perceive their appropriations hearings as being an opportunity to communicate information about their program to others whose support they wish to gain or retain. They share the basic perception that "it's one of the most important events of the year and a great challenge to put across the program of the bureau." They perceive the hearings as being a means of communicating with three distinct groups of listeners: the appropriations subcommittee, other congressmen, and the interested public.

"We look upon them as an opportunity to tell the story of our agency to the Congress." "One of the few places an administrator has a chance to show his wares to the public is through an appropriations hearing." In the first instance, of course, the message is conveyed to the subcommittee. For some agencies, the formal hearing is "the only contact we have with Congress to tell our story," and so they see its prime function as informing Committee members. But even here the general agency view is that most members already have a basic predisposition toward the agency which cannot be drastically altered by a profusion of information. Experienced members are considered to be thoroughly familiar with the program already, and it is felt that only the newer members of the subcommittee really take in the information conveyed. The hearing does become more important in terms of informing the subcommittee when a new program is involved. Here, moreover, is where the agency perceives that it is communicating with other members of Congress. If a new program is to be supported with funds, the subcommittee members may have to explain it and defend it in the full Committee and on the House floor. And if they are to explain it and to defend it successfully, they must have a thorough knowledge of it. This thorough knowledge can be gained through questions and answers during a hearing. The agency communicates to the rest of the House through its hearing room contact with the subcommittee on appropriations. Indeed, since interested members of the Senate (particularly the Senate Appropriations Committee) may read the House's Committee hearings, agency officials can communicate to all interested legislators in this fashion.

Agency officials do not operate with any grand illusions about the hearing as a means of communicating program information to congressmen. Many of them, in fact, perceive the interested public outside the Congress as being their most important listeners. "It's one of the few opportunities we have to get our program on record for the public to read. Maybe it won't be read; but we think it will be." Every program has its interested supporters and a clientele outside the government. And agency officials view the hearings as a way of keeping them informed, of stimulating their interest, and of maintaining their support. They view the hearings record as serving this vital function:

> I'll admit its only a small but special segment of the public that reads it and that's important. We prepare our opening statement with that in mind. It's not to be read by the Committee, but by the interested people outside.

> I'm amazed at how many people outside of government read these hearings. Our program impinges on many groups and they want to know what we are doing.

For these clientele groups the hearings may be a prime source of information.

If interested outsiders do not read the hearings directly, the people of the mass media may — and information will spread in a two-step fashion:

> Every newspaper man is interested in what happened in his bailiwick. They read them; and you'd be surprised at the telephone calls and mail I get as a result — from all over the country. These hearings are a very important part of the democratic process. They affect public opinion.

An appropriations hearing is only the first stage in a communications process that extends beyond the hearing room. The Committee members are listening, perhaps. But just as important from the agency's point of view are those in Congress and outside Congress who are listening, too.

If agency officials view hearings as a communications opportunity, it follows that a "good" hearing is one in which their expectations about communicating in program terms have been met. Favorable images of their hearings emphasize the degree to which program gets emphasized:

> You notice in our hearings they never ask us about the money. They just want to know what we are doing. With some of these fellows they want to know, "Why do you need this money?" and "What are you going to use this for?" They never ask us . . . they want to know what we are doing. . . . I don't know anything about these technical details and they don't ask me.

> Some hearings are good hearings. We come out of there and feel as though we have accomplished something. There has been no needling or politics — just an exchange of information.

When they perceive congressmen as talking program, the attitude of these bureau chiefs toward the hearing is a favorable one. And, as the last bureau chief indicated in his reference to "needling," a good hearing is one in which agency expectations about fair procedures have been met. Said a third bureau chief,

> If you rank hearings as excellent, good, medium, and poor, I'd say that we come out pretty consistently near the top. We have a favorable climate and a favorable reception. Now I can see where it could be an ordeal, and I know some agencies where they just eat you alive; but we've been lucky in that respect . . . when I'm in the hearings . . . [the subcommittee chairman] will say, "You just take your time. You say anything you want and don't you hurry one bit . . . don't you worry about a thing. We're listening to you and you have important things to say."

By contrast, when agency officials perceive that they did not get the chance to talk about their program or had not been accorded a fair hearing, their attitudes are unfavorable. Images of bad hearings are expressed as follows:

> The trouble with appropriations hearings is that you are expected to know so much about everything. For instance, how many people you have on the payroll. That's one of the first things they ask. And if you don't know how many men you have on the payroll, you aren't worth a thing. They must think I count them every morning. . . . I'd rather talk program any day.

> You don't mind them if you've had a chance to present your program, There's a lot of nervous energy expended on it. And you feel it's been wasted if they ask you questions of detail.

I often have a feeling of frustration at the end rather than futility at the beginning — that's the way I'd put it. And that's because ninety per cent of the time is spent in talking about something other than what you went over there to talk about. In recent years . . . we have had to take a lot of hell from the subcommittee chairman. He wants to get in the record his feelings about [other matters]. While that's going on I just keep quiet. I figure that after it's gone on a while, the record will be made and then we'll get around to talking about what we went over to talk about. But sometimes when we go out, we feel disappointed that we haven't been able to get all our message into the record.

Agency officials do not necessarily want the opportunity to discuss their program in its entirety. They may be perfectly content to have the hearing focus on their incremental requests for increases. But whatever the scope of the discussion, they want to communicate in programmatic, policy terms and not discuss, as they say, "technical details" or "politics" or other extraneous matters. Doubtless, all agencies have experienced both "good" and "bad" hearings. Doubtless, too, all agencies harbor both favorable and unfavorable attitudes toward their hearings.

Uncertainty

No matter what their overall image of hearings, nearly all agency officials share a feeling of great *uncertainty* about the proceedings. Before hearings begin, their view is that they do not and cannot know for sure what will happen. During and after the hearings, they are often nonplussed about what has transpired. The hearing is their one certain encounter with the Committee on Appropriations, and they view it as a meeting fraught with uncertainties:

There is not a bureau head here whose blood pressure doesn't go up before the appropriations hearings — even the oldest ones. It's an ordeal. You don't know what questions they might ask or what case they might bring up.

"It would be a wonderful world if we knew what was coming." "We never know where the line of scrimmage is going to be."

One of the most common complaints centers on the unpredictability of subcommittee questioning. "We get some questions every time that we didn't anticipate. They come right out of the woodwork."

We'll know that Congressman X traveled abroad and that he went to such and such and saw such and such. But we don't know what he saw or what impressed him. So we don't know what's coming. And then, first crack out of the box, he'll say, "I went to such and such where you asked for eleven men. I saw them and you don't need eleven men there." Or, "I saw your program. I disagree with it entirely." We have no control over that.

283

Sometimes a congressman will reach in his pocket and pull out a letter from a constituent or another congressman, and we won't know what's coming next. Sometimes these questions don't even pertain to our estimates. And it's like the man who carried his bass viol across town and never got a chance to play.

Subcommittee questioning always can and sometimes does border on the random and haphazard. But it can be more calculating, too, and with the same upsetting results:

The subcommittee chairman was a prosecuting attorney and a pretty good one, and he conducts the hearings that way. You get sucked in. He leads you along with some questions that seem perfectly innocent; and then all of a sudden he closes the trap and you're stuck. You don't realize what is coming until it is too late.

Even if the Committee is discussing the agency's program, there is the possibility that the questioner will "trip you up and throw you off in your line of reasoning with something you don't expect." Most agency officials have experienced the unpredictability of both the scattershot and the booby trap questions. And none of them looks forward to a repeat performance of either sort.

A form of uncertainty to which agency officials react far more strongly — even violently — is the line of questioning which may be launched by a report from the Committee's investigation staff. When hearings revolve around these reports, agency officials feel a hopeless uncertainty. Three bureau chiefs described their experiences:

The Committee sent an investigating team here and they camped on our steps for three months. As near as I can tell, their instructions were not to find any good points or, if they did, not to mention them. Those were rough days. Since then, our hearings have been much easier.

They come down here and they are like the Gestapo. We don't know what they are doing. Then we go to the hearing and they present the evidence. We don't know what evidence they have against us or what information they have. It's a Russian-like inquisition.

They bring in this information from the General Accounting Office, sparked by a witch hunt on the part of the clerk. It's like a criminal investigation. You are confronted by evidence you can't see from investigators you don't know based on an approach quite different from your own.

In their descriptions of hearings such as these, agency officials reveal some expectations about their hearing procedure. They expect a kind of legislative due process which will help to minimize conflict with the Committee. And thus they perceive investigation-based hearings as violating such expectations and creating antagonism.

284

Uncertainty sometimes exists in the minds of agency officials as they sit in the hearings about what is really happening. Things simply may not be what they seem to be. A bureau chief recalled the underlying uncertainty of his relations with a former subcommittee chairman:

> You never could tell where you stood with him . . . to read my hearings with him you would never in the world have dreamed that anything was wrong. He had a prosecuting attorney's type of mind and liked to spring things at the end. He wanted a pleasant hearing and didn't want to let you know what was on his mind. Then he hit us with the most drastic cut in our history.

And another bureau head commented,

> You never can tell about these people. One day [a subcommittee member] was asking me a lot of questions that didn't make too much sense to me. Afterward he took me aside and said, "You didn't convince them. I was trying to help you with my questions."

They learn not to judge by surface appearance alone whether the subcommittee is sympathetic or antipathetic to their program.

One agency official expatiated on what he had learned:

> When you have a long hearing that's a love feast, when everybody's patting each other on the back, and everything goes along just fine and nothing is wrong — watch out. That's just the time you're not going to get any money. It's when all hell breaks loose that you get your increase.

This perception assumes that when congressmen are favorably disposed toward an agency they will want to test that agency as thoroughly as possible in the hearings to make certain it merits their support. Still, it may be hard to accept this as an operating assumption in the hearings. One agency head explained,

> It took me a long time to learn that questions that sounded unfriendly were usually to help you make your point. Of course, there may be one who is just trying to trip you up or rattle you. You have to be careful of him.

Uncertainty persists. The agency official cannot know for sure, even when he is in the hearing room, whether the men on the other side of the hearing are prosecutors or allies — or both.

Confidence and Sampling Patterns

Given their perception that appropriations hearings do not always focus on program, and given their uncertainties about these hearings, agency officials have a need for some compensatory, reassuring, harmonizing element in their relationship with the Committee. That indispensable element, they believe, is *confidence*. If the Committee members have confidence in the ability and the integrity of an agency, the agency can survive "bad" hearings, and it need worry less about the uncertainty of it all. Where confidence exists, the agency will receive the benefit of the doubt. It is less apt to be suspected of padding budgets or of withholding information from the Committee. Where confidence exists, the Committee will be less quick to criticize and more willing to listen to the agency's point of view. From start to finish, the potential for agency-Committee conflict will be minimized.

Confidence, agency officials believe, is tendered on the basis of their performance over time. Bit by bit, agencies acquire a reputation — and the officials value nothing so highly as the "good reputation" which earns Appropriations Committee confidence. "I have developed a reputation with the Committee for bringing in an honest budget. That's important to us and I want to keep it that way." "We have the reputation for being an honest economical bureau and they don't bother us any." Conversely, one bureau head lamented, "We aren't getting our program across to the Committee . . . they just don't have that trust in us that we'd like." Confidence, then, is perceived as the all-important cement of good agency-Committee relations. And an appropriations hearing room is unanimously perceived as a place where the Committee's confidence can be won or lost.

Agency perceptions about the hearings are colored by its view of legislative capabilities. The prevailing attitude of agency officials (especially the more experienced ones) toward the abilities of the Committee members (especially the more experienced members) is one of respect. But, at the same time, people in the executive branch express ideas about the limitations of legislators. One such limitation, they believe, is the press of time brought on by a legislator's many duties. And one consequence of limited time is that there is a level of technicality in detail beneath which congressmen cannot go. "No congressman has the time to know every little item in our budget." Staff, of course, can help. But they, too, have limitations — especially, it is believed, in terms of manpower. "As the programs have increased," said one departmental budget officer, "the Committee staff has remained approximately the same. The result is that they have to keep skimming thinner and thinner. They know less and less about more and more."

In the eyes of executive officials, experienced Committee members will have accumulated a mass of information and wisdom about an agency. But they cannot have perfect information and they cannot ask detailed questions about everything. For this reason, agency officials believe, congressmen often gather information and make decisions by *sampling*.[8] Congressmen

[8] See Nelson Polsby, *Congress and the Presidency* (New York: Prentice-Hall, 1964), pp. 5–6, 97.

use specific questions they can intelligently ask to sample a universe of information about which, for lack of information, they cannot ask intelligent questions. They then view the answer they receive as answers about the universe. A specific answer to a specific question thus provides the information on which to base broad conclusions about agency behavior. And on these conclusions will be based equally broad judgments about program and money. If the Committee member is satisfied with the answers to the questions he asks, he will have confidence in the agency and its program, and agency-Committee relations will prosper. If, on the other hand, the congressman is unhappy about the results of his sampling process, the agency will be in for more difficulty than the scope of the original question could, by itself, have provoked. So runs a commonly held perception of Committee behavior.

The following instance as related by a department budget officer makes the essential point:

> I remember one time we went up before the supplemental committee. Boy, they had some rough ones on there, and it was in the 80th Congress. We gave our justifications, and one of them said, "Ah, you don't know whether your figures are right or not." I had a big book about so thick with all the figures in it. So I whispered to [the agency head] and gave it to him, and he pushed it across the table to the congressman. He thumbed through it, looked at it, pushed it back, and said "O.K." And that's all there was to it. We got the money. But if we'd fumbled around, they'd have had us. They didn't know whether the figures were right or wrong. They couldn't know, though they'd never admit it — but what they wanted to know was whether we thought they were right and whether we had gone into them as carefully as we could. They want to know whether you know your job. That's what some new witnesses don't understand — why the questions are asked as they are. Those congressmen aren't trying to do your job for you. But they want to know whether you can do the job . . . sometimes they'll give you a rough time. Things get awfully rough. But it's a test. They want to test you. . . . They want to test you, and have you satisfy them that everything is as good as it can be.

In this episode, a single question about one set of figures was perceived to be an instance of Committee sampling to test for agency competence. Once the test was passed satisfactorily, Committee confidence was increased. And, with that, the likelihood was increased that agency budgetary expectations would be met.

Given their view that Committee member interrogation is a sampling process, agency officials catalog the variety of sampling patterns and prepare for their encounters with Committee members accordingly. These preparations will be discussed shortly. For now, it will be sufficient to note two other sampling patterns in addition to the general competence test just described. One pattern, for example, which agency people perceive is that a Committee member sometimes judges the success of a program by its success in his particular constituency. The questions he asks, therefore, are constituency-oriented questions. For this is one area of activity he knows, and the problem of inspiring overall confidence becomes one of giving satisfactory answers to district-related questions. Agency officials express the view that experienced Committee members are more apt to ask broad questions than Committee newcomers, who have little information. But they, too, may repair to the familiar ground of the constituency to test the agency. One bureau head described the pattern of questioning in his hearings:

> [The subcommittee chairman] knows what's going on, but he's particularly interested in his state. [The ranking minority member] looks at the whole picture, but he starts with his district. "What's happening in my town?" Some of them see the whole picture, some of them don't give a damn for anything except what goes on in their own district. You'll get some old congressman sitting there not paying a damn bit of attention, and when his turn comes to question, he'll say, "And how are things going in my town?"

While there is, among people concerned with programs, some exasperation at constituency-oriented questions, they recognize it as the congressman's test of the agency.

The sampling pattern to which agency officials probably attach the greatest significance is the Committee's attempt to assess an agency by weighing its impressions of the agency head. These impressions are conveyed primarily in the hearing room. When they talk about the functions of appropriations hearings, agency heads speak more about the function of "sizing you up personally" than about any other save that of communicating information. "Your personality has as much to do with it [appropriations success] as anything." They do not mean that personality is a substitute for a program with well-established support. "Your bureau has to have a solid reputation and a good program. But after that, personality counts a great deal — it's the frosting on the cake." Where agency officials believe that personality counts is not in affecting the agency's base, but in helping it secure incremental increases or preventing excessive incremental decreases. In most years the controversial territory in a budget estimate is relatively narrow. And it is in fighting for success in this area that an administrator's personal image may count for a great deal. One official with a solidly established program put the hearings in perspective:

> I look upon the hearings as an opportunity to get a message in the record. The appropriation, whether it's an increase or a decrease, is much more affected by what the people back home say than it is by anything we bureaucrats say in the hearings. I don't kid myself there. We don't change any

minds in the hearings. The congressman has his finger on the pulse of his constituents. He knows the political climate back home and that's what determines his attitude. The most the administrator can do is to go in there and clinch a few nails. He can't drive any nails; he can just clinch some.

In the process of "clinching nails," the personality of the agency head is believed to be crucial.

One agency head said,

> It took me a long time to learn that they don't want to be educated in those hearings. They want to size you up as a person. They want to know whether you're on top of your job as an administrator . . . You're the Ph.D. candidate. It's you they want to hear, and your program and your bureau fades into the background. You're in front of them at the table and it's you they're interested in.

And a departmental budget officer offered as his rule of thumb, "You can draw up justifications for your estimates — using the king's English and all. But the bureau head's presentation is 75 per cent of what you get." What he meant, of course, was not 75 per cent in terms of the total budget, but 75 per cent in terms of that year's controversial appropriations figures. What agency heads want to convey is the impression that they know their job — from which impression flows the reputation as "a man who knows what he's talking about," "a capable administrator," and from which reputation flows Committee confidence. Agencies whose expectations are met by the Committee will attribute it to a substantial degree to confidence thus derived and reposed by the Committee in the head of the agency.

In a bureau which regularly sustained only the smallest of budget reductions, the departmental budget officer reflected about its former chief:

> He was one of the best witnesses in the department. He had been around a long time and knew all the legal ramifications of his program — and they are plenty. You couldn't stump him. He'd tick the answers right off. They had implicit confidence in him. Well, he retired this year and we'll have a new chief going up there. That will make a big difference.

Conversely, in the case of a bureau whose budget estimates suffered relatively severe cutbacks, another departmental budget officer laid it primarily to the presentation of the bureau chief:

> ———— was the chief then . . . . He was a little pompous though he knew what he was doing. But he wore glasses on a black ribbon. And when he was in the hearing making a point, he would pull those glasses out of his pocket and hold them up in front of his eyes with that black ribbon hanging down. He put them up and he put them down. One day I was in [the subcommittee chairman's] office and he said to me, "What's the matter with ————? I can't stand that damnable black ribbon." So I had to tell ———— not

289

to wear his glasses in the hearing. It was a little thing like that. But it's the personal element. [The subcommittee chairman] didn't like ———; and I just had to do the best I could.

The case of the black ribbon may be unique, but it serves to illustrate the importance which agency officials attach to the personal appeal of their agency heads in promoting Committee confidence. The case illustrates further the vagaries of the process by which one human being comes to trust or distrust another human being. Once attained, confidence will reduce agency uncertainties. But just how one goes about capturing the precious commodity, in the first place, is itself another great uncertainty of Committee-agency relations.

Given their own perception of the importance of personality, it is not surprising that the overall attitude of agency heads toward the hearings should vary depending on their own background and temperament. At one extreme, an agency head enthusiastically welcomed the idea of a personal test with the Committee:

I just love it. I look forward to it as a field day for me. You see, I was in the legislature, and I was on the Appropriations Committee there. I know what goes on in their minds and what they are looking for — and they should do that. I used to sit in Jamie Whitten's position as the grantor instead of the grantee. They have a right to find out whether I can run this agency or not. If I can't answer their questions, then I ought to go home. I didn't come down here hunting a job, and if I didn't think I was doing a good job, I wouldn't stay. A good administrator who knows his agency hasn't a thing to fear. It's a real field day for me.

At the opposite extreme was a career agency head who exclaimed, "I hate appropriations hearings. They're the most loathsome part of the job." Another agency head reported having a predecessor who "dreaded them so much that when the hearings came up he'd manage to be away and send his assistant." Most sentiments, however, are more ambivalent than these extremes of relish and of dread. They see the hearings as a challenge and an opportunity, but full of uncertainties. The following comments of three bureau heads represent the modal response:

Some aspects of it are enjoyable and some are not. It's not recreation. It's not play. There's a lot of tension and a lot of anxiety that goes with it because you know you have a great responsibility and a great opportunity and you want to do your best.

I wouldn't call it an unpalatable chore. It's not — well, I don't dislike it. There are some things I like worse and some things I like better. It's not distasteful . . . it's our most trying time, but it's a tremendous challenge. And I don't mind working like hell at it.

290

Well, it's something you like to get over with. I enjoy it, of course, while I'm there. But I'm glad when it's over. I'm glad when any budgetary problem is over.

Most agency heads have their own private store of anecdotes detailing the massacre of some other agency head by a House subcommittee on appropriations: "His face was ashen when he came out, and he kept saying 'Those SOBs, those SOBs.' " Or, "His hands were clammy and his arms were shaking and I said, 'What's the matter with you?' " Or, "We were standing outside waiting our turn. He was pacing up and down and seemed to be trying to memorize something. I said to him, 'You remind me of a whore in church — nervous.' That fellow takes a licking every year." Or, "I've seen some men before the Committee just shaking in their boots; and I've watched the Committee tear them to bits." Two elements seem to be involved in these stories. The first is the knowledge that "It could happen to me." And the second element is an overwhelming sense of relief to find that it usually does not. The agency official remains with this additional ambivalence about the hearings. He justifies his own fears by reminding himself of how shattering the hearings can be. But he reassures himself with the comforting thought that it usually does not happen to him.

AGENCY BEHAVIOR: REDUCING UNCERTAINTY

Agency perceptions of the Appropriations Committee are dominated by a sense of uncertainty. A major thrust, therefore, of all agency action is toward the reduction of uncertainty. The aim, of course, is the attainment of basic maintenance expectations — that is, a sufficiently stable relationship with the Committee to permit program planning and operation to proceed satisfactorily. Agency officials believe that to the degree that their maintenance expectations are met their goal expectations are also more likely to be fulfilled. Each step they take, therefore, toward the reduction of uncertainty is believed by them to be a step toward the assurance of favorable budgetary decisions.

Obeying Reports

Once the Committee's ability to hurt it is recognized, the most obvious way for the agency to ensure a favorable kind of relationship with the Committee is simply to do each year precisely what the Committee tells it to do:

> We get a report card every year. And we administer during the year with as great a sensitivity as is possible to the wishes of the people who give us that report card. If we didn't, we'd get our heads knocked off.

The agency spends the money appropriated to it for the express purposes for which it was appropriated. If funds are appropriated under one line item

291

in the budget, they should not be reallocated (without express Committee permission) to another category by the agency. Construction money for example, should not be used to pay salaries. In some cases, the language of the appropriation bill will make the limits of agency action clear. But in other cases the formal limits will not be clear. In such cases the Committee may give instructions to the agency in nonstatutory form — the most important of which is the Committee report. Agency obedience to the law is hardly worthy of comment. But an agency's religious adherence to the direction, admonitions, suggestions, and intentions written in the Committee report is noteworthy as a measure of its desire for harmonious relations with the Committee.

Committee reports are filled with running comments about the appropriations being recommended for an agency. They contain reasons for past Committee action plus suggestions and admonitions for the future. They are not, as House members frequently point out, the law — they are a kind of legislative obiter dicta. But the response of agency officials to them elevates them to a status barely distinguishable from statute. "We treat it as the law," said one agency head. And other agency officials echoed the idea that there is a distinction without much difference. "They aren't the law of the Congress, they're the will of the Committee. But we follow their instructions." "We take that as the intention of the Committee and we pay attention to every word of it. It has the force of law." "Someone said they have the force of law. They don't. But they are just as good as it. I sit down here and go over the report and pay special attention to every bit of language in it." "If there's anything in the report about us, I make sure that every top administrator reads it. It's must reading. I've never seen an instance where an administrator looked at it and said, 'Oh forget that.' Just the opposite. They might just as well have put it in the Act." When the agencies send up their justifications for their budget estimates each year, some of them include a report of precisely what action they took regarding each relevant item in last year's Committee report. And if, during the year, they find they cannot comply with the wishes expressed by the Committee, they will go to the Committee informally and tell them why it is impossible for them to do it.

Few indices of Appropriations Committee influence are more convincing than agency behavior in response to Committee reports. Agency officials obey the reports in a negative sense because they may be punished if they do not. But, in a more positive sense, they feel that obedience to the Committee's informally expressed desires will help to build the all-important ingredient of Committee confidence. One departmental budget officer expressed both points of view:

We consider them one step below the law. If you want to destroy that confidence I've been talking about, the absolutely best way to do it is to ignore the instructions of the Committee. If you get the Committee mad at you they can cut you down the next time you go up there for money. And they will.

If agencies fail to do what the Committee asks them to do (formally or informally), other attempts at reducing uncertainty are not likely to be very helpful to them.

Preparing for Hearings

One practice engaged in by many agencies for the purpose of reducing the uncertainty connected with their hearings is a pre-hearing rehearsal of some sort. Since agency officials are uncertain as to what questions will be asked and hence uncertain of their ability to perform well, a practice hearing beforehand may increase the preparedness and reduce their anxieties. The practice is widely used. Some officials indicate that their hearings before the Budget Bureau (about which they typically exhibit far less anxiety) serves as a "warm-up" for the more unpredictable legislative hearings. "It's a very valuable brush-up for the congressional hearings. We get a chance to shake out the items that are weak and to anticipate the kind of questions we'll get." In the majority of cases among the bureaus interviewed, some kind of "mock hearing," "skull session," "dress rehearsal," "briefings," "practice session," or "dry run" was held. The preparatory sessions might be held under the tutelage of the departmental budget officer, two of whom described their practice:

> We have dress rehearsals here. I play [the subcommittee chairman] and we practice. I try to know what's going through their minds. . . . I conceive of myself as a football coach. I train them down here; but up on the Hill I just go and sit on the side lines.

> The bureau heads come in to talk it over, or we'll go to lunch. Then I'll say that I'm going to hold a departmental hearing strictly within the family and throw all the questions I can think of at them to see what they do with them. I throw the questions I know the Committee will ask.

Where the departmental budget officer supervises preparations, he plays a role as "uncertainty absorber" for his bureau chiefs. That is to say, he helps them through their uncertainties by acting as if he knew what they did not know — in this case what sample questions would be asked. In other departments less hierarchically organized, preparations are left to the individual agencies.

Whether or not the bureaus are left to their own devices, they place great stress on preparation and go through its rituals faithfully. Their rituals may be full dress rehearsals held in the agency. One agency head advised his fellow witnesses,

> For heaven's sake, rehearse. We sit around here and the division chiefs fire all the questions they can think of and I answer them. I make my whole presentation . . . you need to get a grasp of what they're going to say so you don't fumble around when the time comes. It's like boning up for a Ph.D. exam. I always know what they're going to ask and I don't think a single question has been asked that I didn't think about in advance in recent years. Ninety-five per cent of it is wasted. But that one nugget that you rehearse may make all the difference in the world.

Sometimes, people in the agency will do the spade work and then brief the chief. An assistant bureau chief discussed the manner in which people at his level helped prepare his agency head:

> We sit around the table and have a bull session on previous testimony and on the things we have prepared for [the bureau chief]. We try to put ourselves in the place of the congressman and say, "Now if I were the subcommittee chairman, what question would I ask on this?" From our own experience we can come pretty close. These bull sessions are extremely helpful. But I always kid and say, "They'll ask some questions nobody in the world would have thought of." And they usually do.

Where no joint sessions of any kind are held, the bureau head takes the initiative and directs the search for answers. But preparations go forward with the same aim in mind. Two assistant chiefs discussed the modus operandi of their superiors:

> He prepares down to the last detail. Two weeks before he goes running around here like the proverbial one-armed paper hanger with hives. He's a stickler for details. And you'd better have it.

> He'll call us in and say, "Now here's a question I know I'm going to be asked. And here's what I'll say — one, two, three. Now is there anything I've left out that should be added? Does that seem O.K.?"

Though they worry about the hearing room questions they cannot predict, agencies do possess some fairly reliable indicators of what is likely to transpire. First of all, they have the record of past hearings. Over the years, the interest of the influential senior members of the subcommittees will have become well known, and certain questions can be predicted on that basis alone. The fact that subcommittee members tend to specialize helps the agency guess which congressman will ask about what program. And the fact that each congressman represents a constituency the nature of which can be known also aids in predicting his interests. In the second place, agencies may receive advance tips from the Committee's staff members on questions being prepared by various congressmen. Committee members themselves may call at any time for information or for service of some kind — thereby indicating a line of special interest which may spawn questions in the hearings. In the third place, all agencies receive feedback by mail from individuals and organizations. When their own mail expresses dissatisfaction, great or small, with some agency activity, the likelihood is great that the subcommittee members will be getting similar complaints. So agency officials will be on the lookout for inquiries in these problem areas. Agencies, therefore, are not without information resources in preparing for hearings.

It is a common complaint among agency people that preparation for appropriations hearings absorbs far too much of an agency's time and effort. And, so the complaint runs, it is time subtracted from programmatic efforts. The facts are indisputable. During the weeks before the hearings, most agencies bend their organizational energies to the task of reducing the uncertainty of the hearings. Viewed from one perspective, program time is lost. Viewed from another perspective, programs may be saved.

Advance preparations are no substitute for a backlog of experience in the appropriations hearing room. Their self-confidence and their attitude toward the hearings change after agency heads have been on the job for a while. "I used to be pretty scared, but I'm not anymore," said one bureau head. And two others agreed:

> You get butterflies now and then; but I enjoy it. If you had asked me that question in my first couple of years, perhaps I'd have given you a different answer. I've been here seven years now, and you build up friendly relations with the members of the Committee. We have free and easy chats on and off the record.

> I remember the first appropriations hearing I attended. I prepared and prepared. The whole thing was entirely foreign to me. I was a little jumpy. But now I don't worry about it. I don't dread it. It's just something that you have to do, like a lot of other things.

It is not possible to draw a cause and effect relationship between length of service and budgetary success — or to determine whether career personnel are more successful than noncareer personnel. But, given the perceived importance of the agency head's presentation, anything that reduces uncertainty — as tenure in office seems to do — should improve bureau-Committee relations.

An assistant bureau chief recalled an appropriations hearing which placed a premium on his experience as a witness and which would have been baffling to the uninitiated. The situation was that the department advocated a program which was opposed by the subcommittee and only weakly supported by the bureau itself. The bureau chief went before the subcommittee to "defend" the request:

> Well, we got into the hearing and [the subcommittee chairman] had a list of questions on a sheet of paper. I don't know who had compiled them, but he started to read them off. And they were all critical. Every one amounted to, "What in the devil are you fellows up here in the first place for?" I didn't indicate our true position. But I just kept giving them the information. I stayed perfectly calm. Finally, [the ranking minority member] leaned forward and said, "Now boys, let's stop this thing. We've gone far enough. We know you aren't going to get it and so do you." Then he leaned back and laughed and said to me, "You did your best." I said, "I tried," and left. They felt they had to go through with it, but they had already decided they weren't going to grant it . . . I knew that [the subcommittee chairman] knew very well what the whole situation was and why we were up there testifying. So did I. If I had been a new man, I wouldn't have understood what those questions were all about, and I might have gotten pretty excited.

Experience helps in anticipating the questions of the hearings. And it helps, too, in understanding what is going on in the hearings themselves.

Agencies employ one other form of advanced preparation designed to produce the kind of hearing they desire. They organize their budget in such a manner that Committee questions, when based on their justifications, will tend to follow along programmatic lines. Manipulation of budgetary form was shown to be a device by which the House may seek greater control over its Appropriations Committee. So, too, is the manipulation of budgetary form a device by which agencies seek to influence Committee action. By drawing up their budgets in program terms rather than in terms of object classification (travel, equipment, construction, personnel, "salaries and expenses") that run across programs, agencies try to seize something of the initiative from Committee members. They try to impose a programmatic frame of reference on the hearings. Committee members may not, of course, accept the agency framework. But it is more difficult for them to make fruitful inquiries if they do not. A bureau budget officer described his success in inducing programmatic hearings:

> Our budget is set up according to program, so whenever the congressmen are talking they are talking about program. So we avoid problems like, "How many typewriters are you buying?" We don't get into administrative expenses and salaries, which can give you a lot of trouble. We try to steer clear of that as much as we can and have the congressmen talk only in terms of program. It's a performance budget, and I think we stay out of trouble that way.

Insofar as Committee members do view an agency's budget in programmatic terms, agency officials believe that their goal expectations will be furthered. Congressmen, they believe, are less willing to reduce programs than items

296

classified by object. If he can, they believe, a Committee member will solve his dilemma by reducing "salaries and expenses" while claiming that he has not reduced any program. If they can, the agencies will so structure their budget as to make it difficult for him to have his cake and eat it too.

Finally, agencies sometimes recruit outside witnesses to testify on their behalf in hopes of impressing the Committee with the breadth and intensity of support for the agency program. Agencies are fully aware of the vital support which they draw from sympathetic congressmen and interest groups. And a programmatic budget may attract clientele groups more easily than one where programs are less easily identified. But agency executives do not put great stock in the value of formal testimony by such groups in appropriations hearings. Informal contact is deemed far more useful. So, too, are communications on substantive legislation. Still, they do not overlook the potentialities of testimony by a "grass roots" delegation from a Committee member's home territory or the expert commentary of a respected scientific organization:

> Last year we had a group of scientists lined up, though all of them couldn't make it. I didn't actually recruit them. I told them that they should go up and give their views. I didn't tell them what to say. But I wouldn't encourage anyone I thought was opposed to us — I'll say that.

By encouraging groups of this sort to testify, the agency may help foster a sense of identification between itself and those clientele groups it will need when trouble arises in the form of a budget cut. Then the agency may mobilize outside witnesses to protest before the Senate Appropriations Committee. As we shall see, pressure from groups outside the agency does more to influence Senate decisions than House decisions. This does not mean that clientele support is irrelevant to House Committee decisions — far from it. The point is simply that agency officials feel that more effective means of communication than appropriations hearings exist and are being used.

Building Confidence in the Hearings

In the hearing room itself, the search for a sympathetic, stable relationship continues. Positively, the agency's aim is to strengthen the bond of confidence between itself and the Committee. Negatively, its aim is to keep from so irritating these legislators as to damage such confidence as already exists. Agency officials, as we have seen, respect the Appropriations Committee members for their knowledge as well as for their influence. On the basis of this respect, they formulate their guide lines for success in the hearing room. First among these guide lines stands the prescription to be honest with the Committee. Honesty, according to agency officials, is not only the best policy ethically, but practically as well. In preparing for the hearings, agency officials tell each other that they should not pad their budget because, "We could never slip a padded budget by the Committee if we tried." "We don't pad our budget," reported one departmental budget officer. "I tell the boys, 'You may pad it one year or two or even three and get away with it. But sooner or later they'll find out. And when they do, watch out.' " Like padding a budget, all other attempts to put something over on the Committee are deemed to be based on a false belief. The assumption is strong that "You can't fool these legislators. They know when you're ducking or when you're trying to get out from under." Or, "These congressmen know all about it, and you can't hide anything even if you want to." Or, "They'll find the weak spot in your armor if you have one." Among the agency officials who deal with the Committee, respect for their ability "to spot a phony pretty quick" underlies their response to the uncertainty of the hearing.

One common hearing room perception, therefore, finds expression in these terms. "Be frank"; "Be sincere and lay your cards on the table"; "Be open and honest and fully disclosing"; "Answer every question to the best of your ability and tell the truth." The only proviso attached is that witnesses must know when to stop. Honesty does not require that the witness make revelations or open up avenues of inquiry which Committee questioning does not require. Agency officials believe that "a good salesman knows when to close up his briefcase and go home." If the Committee member asks him, "Is there anything else you want to say?", witnesses are told to say "No." To resuscitate the questioning is to invite rather than reduce uncertainty. A department budget officer spelled out the entire line of argument as it involves the critical end product — confidence:

> The most important thing in a Committee hearing is creating an atmosphere of confidence — so that you have confidence in the Committee and they have confidence in you. I tell my people to be perfectly honest and to have a full, free, and frank discussion with the Committee, even if it hurts you a little bit. That will mean more than anything else in getting your money. Nobody likes to admit things and cast reflections on his own shop, but don't try to fool the congressmen. You can't. They have a fifth sense when someone is not talking freely and frankly. If you have a perfectly open discussion, they'll have more confidence in you, and your appropriations troubles will be minimized.

Frankness in the hearing room and the confidence which results may help also to minimize future attempts by the Committee to trap agency witnesses with surprise questions or with a baffling line of argument. Where suspicions have been allayed, uncertainties will be kept to a minimum.

If, as agency officials believe, Committee members use their reactions to the agency head as a test of the agency as a whole, the success formula of the agency will center around him. Here again, the payoff is the promotion of Committee confidence. Beyond the admonition to be honest with the Committee, great importance is attached to the ability of the bureau chief to handle the bulk of the questioning by himself. If the Committee is testing him, then he must show his mastery of the job by fielding their questions without recourse to the aid of his underlings. One assistant bureau chief who used "to carry the main load" in the hearings on behalf of his superior, recalled "One day a member of the Committee came to me and said, 'The chief of a bureau ought to do his own testifying.'" Immediately thereafter the chief and the assistant reversed their role behavior. To the degree that the agency has conveyed self-confidence, the Committee will return the sentiment in kind. A departmental budget officer stated this common line of agency reasoning:

> After you've been up here a while, you should try to handle as many of the questions as you can by yourself. If you keep turning questions over to your subordinates year after year, they won't have confidence in you. They'll start evaluating your subordinates and wondering whether they know what they're talking about. They'll come around and say [to me], "What's the matter with X? Can't he run his shop?" . . . if you answer the questions, they will build up tremendous confidence in you. Why, I have some men here in [my department] who could go up and tell the Committee that black was white and white was black and they would believe him. If one of them asked the Committee for fifty new men, they'd give them to him with almost no questions asked. But if he turned questions over to his subordinates, they would start in evaluating again. They would say, "Well, I wonder if what he says squares with what I heard from so and so on that." Or, "I may want to question that." But if they have real confidence in you, they'll believe anything you say.

For all witnesses, agency head and assistants alike, there are some commonly accepted "dos and don'ts" reflecting the agency-eye view of the Committee. For instance, if an agency intends that the Committee should pick up any information from the formal part of its presentation, the admonition is, "Make it factual, objective, and concise. Make it brief. Don't get all involved in detail so that they have to listen closely or go back and read it to understand it. I say use *Saturday Evening Post* language and not *Atlantic Monthly* language." If an agency's opening presentation is pitched on a frequency to which the congressman can readily attune himself, it may give the agency the initiative in the hearings. One way of describing the source of agency officials' uncertainty is to say that they do not ordinarily hold the initiative, and their basically defensive posture breeds a great deal of their anxiety. If, however, they can interest the Committee with their opening

299

presentation, they may fix the frame of reference for the ensuing question-and-answer session. One agency head discussed his agency's opening presentation:

> A good lead-off statement should be about ten minutes. It should single out a few items of performance that we are interested in — hit the high spots. It should show what we are doing, and get the congressmen interested. If we do this, maybe they will think of some questions to ask on these subjects — on the things, in other words, that we want to talk about.

The maneuver is not easy to execute, but the agency has nothing to lose and something to gain by trying it.

In the catalog of hearing room prescriptions there are two major "don'ts" designed to keep agency officials from irritating the Committee. The first is that as witnesses they should be careful not to appear to be superior or disrespectful in any way. Agency officials feel that a sense of institutional rivalry pervades the hearing room and that Committee members will be quick to take umbrage at behavior that indicates a slight to the legislative branch — or, naturally, to them as individual legislators. One department, in its book of hearing recipes, reminds all its witnesses that "the Committee members are assigned one side of the table and departmental witnesses are assigned to one side. Witnesses should not trespass on the Committee's side of the table." Witnesses, it adds, should never ask to use the Committee's telephones. Most to be avoided, however, are the verbal intimations of disrespect. Two bureau chiefs advised. "Don't ever talk down to the congressmen and say, 'Listen to me. I'm it.' They won't take that." "If you act superior or talk down your nose to them, you won't get the kind of treatment you would otherwise get." Two departmental budget officers spoke of the necessity of getting this kind of message across to the inexperienced agency witness. "You get a new man testifying before the Committee and he thinks they don't know what his program is all about. Why, they know more than he does and we have to tell him not to act like the expert — because he's not, they are."

> I tell them that the chairman is running the hearing and they ought to let him ask the questions. That's hard for some of these newcomers to learn — especially the lawyers. They are used to prosecuting, and the first thing you know they are asking questions of the Committee. They start making a case instead of letting the chairman develop the case he wants. That's one thing the Committee doesn't like.

Socialization proceeds within the agencies just as it does within the Committee itself. The inexperienced bureaucrat may have to learn those attitudes of respect and those deferential forms of behavior to which the majority of veteran agency officials already subscribe.

The second negative prescription stresses that witnesses should not engage in arguments with members of the Committee. "I like to go at things directly," one experienced agency head observed. I'm the kind of guy who likes to argue. But you shouldn't argue with congressmen. I learned that a long time ago." Another agreed, "They can badger you but you have to take it. You can't argue back or get emotional about it or you'll be finished. It's a matter of survival." Witnesses who cannot learn this lesson become a drag on agency efforts to maintain good relations. A third agency head pointed out,

> I've been going to appropriations hearings for twenty-five years, and we have learned that there are some members of the staff, no matter how brilliant they are or how good their performance may be, when they get in the witness chair they get belligerent. They don't make good witnesses and the congressmen don't like them. So we just don't take them anymore. We have to leave them at home.

Just as House members take special pleasure in defeating "the powerful Appropriations Committee" on the floor, so do agency witnesses take great delight (heightened by a sense of relief) when they can turn an invitation to take issue with a Committee member to their own advantage. Several officials related — word by gleeful word — their nimble escape from the well-baited traps of Committee questioners. If the questioner ends the dialogue with a compliment, "That's a good answer," or, "I like your answer," the witness's moment of triumph is at hand. He will have turned uncertainty into certainty. And, against the background of uncertainty, it is small wonder that he never seems to forget it.

One line of Committee questioning requires special notice for the problem it presents to the agency official. Interestingly enough, the line of questioning is a predictable one and can be found in almost any set of Appropriations Committee hearings. The problem, then, is not uncertainty; the problem is that agency heads cannot agree on how they should answer this particular question. And the reason they cannot agree is that the line of questioning places them squarely in the middle of a conflict between the Appropriations Committee and the executive branch hierarchy — both of whose support the agency needs to survive. The line of questioning involved encompasses the Committee's attempts to find out precisely what budgetary requests the agency made within the executive branch and which ones were denied it during the process of executive decision-making. In a formal organizational sense, agency officials are presenting, justifying, and defending the President's budget. From this standpoint they do not feel that they should reveal the inner deliberations of the executive branch. To do so would involve disloyalty to the President. On the other hand, their budgetary and program expectations may have been so violated by executive decision-making

301

that they may feel it is imperative to appeal to the Committee for an increase in funds. They can make such an appeal by revealing to the Committee the extent of the Budget Bureau's reduction and, under prodding by the Committee, admit that they could have used the deleted funds to good advantage. Such roundabout appeals to the legislature against the President bring down severe executive displeasure on the offender. Agency officials have no commonly accepted prescription unless it is "Support the President's budget, but . . ." The "buts," however, take a multiplicity of forms.

One agency official stated the executive hierarchy's viewpoint when he said,

> You're bound to support the President's budget. There's a very fine line of protocol you have to tread. You're not a free agent when you're up there. Back of these estimates are twelve months of work inside the executive branch and you have to defend them . . . sometimes it can be pretty embarrassing.

A bureau head who observed this rule in his most recent hearings recalled,

> Last year [the subcommittee chairman] and I had a colloquy, and he asked me, "Couldn't you use more investigators? Couldn't you use more money?" He knew what I'd asked Budget for and he wanted to get it in the record. Well, I have to defend the budget; so I did. I would have loved to have said "Yes," but I didn't.

Another agency official recalls a slightly different response to the Committee's probing action:

> I remember once they asked me whether I couldn't build so many more buildings if they appropriated so much more money. I answered that "Yes, I could." Any administrator who said otherwise would be a darn fool. What I wanted to say was not only "I sure can," but, "And we need those buildings terribly." But I didn't say that.

A third kind of response shows how far an agency head may go in satisfying the Committee's inquiry without giving up his sense of executive commitment. Said an agency chief,

> If they ask me directly what my professional judgment is as to whether we can use any more money, I will tell them honestly. They may ask me what I was planning to do with the money cut out by the Budget Bureau. If they ask me a direct question, I will answer them. I will give them my professional judgment, though I will say that as to a fiscal judgment I cannot say. After all, I'm a member of the executive family.

The shades of difference among agency responses are subtle. So, too, are the understandings which grow up between administrator and Committee:

Sometimes they give us a little more than we ask for. You're not supposed to say you need more, but sometimes they'll ask, "Don't you think you could use more than you are asking for?" If you hesitate a little in your answer, you may get some more. All you have to do is hesitate — they know what it means.

There is one cardinal rule in the game which administrators play in this situation. It is that the witness must never initiate or volunteer information as to those of its expectations which went unmet within the executive branch. They may, however, answer a direct question. Even here, loyalty forbids excessive enthusiasm. "They have to worm it out of you." "You're supposed to wait a decent length of time before you let your arm be twisted." "You are supposed to let them bruise you a little before you give in." The agency head works his way through his dilemma via a kind of ritual mating dance. One department budget official expressed impatience with the ritual. "Why go through this rigamarole about 'taking all things into consideration' or 'the budget problem is'? That's ridiculous, absolutely ridiculous. We just tell them and get it over with." Given the fact that legislature and executive share formal budgetary authority, every agency will respond in accordance with some balance of loyalties or some calculations about support. No balance, however, is likely to resolve its dilemma with any degree of permanence.

Maintaining Informal Contacts

The questions and answers of an appropriations hearing provide the most visible, the most regularized, and the most commonly shared process by which agency officials seek the fulfillment of their expectations. But it is by no means the only — nor necessarily the most vital — form of interaction between agency and Committee. For most bureaus, formal hearings do not last more than a few days. For some it is less than a single day. Even under the best of hearing room conditions, the Committee will not explore the full ramifications of an agency's program, nor will all of an agency's uncertainties be allayed. "We have a tremendous communications problem, and you can't solve it with one hearing a year," one agency head exploded. What is more, few agencies try. For most of them, the hearing room confrontation is but the top of the iceberg. What happens there and what happens in the pivotal subcommittee markup session is the culmination of an agency's informal, piecemeal efforts to curry Committee confidence and build increments of support. The history of such efforts may encompass years. Much can be won or lost in the hearing room. But much has already been won or lost by the time agency and subcommittee face each other across the table.

If it serves no other function, informal communication lubricates the hearing room process. Preparations immediately preceding the hearing go forward between agency and Committee as well as within the agency itself.

These preparations run the gamut from arrangements of time to the transmission of inside information on the subjects to be pursued. When agencies hold their practice sessions, they often will be rehearsing on the basis of knowledge already passed to them through informal channels. Advance information regarding the hearings acts as a powerful tranquilizer for anxious agency witnesses. A bureau head who reported that, "I enjoy the hearings," divulged the basis for such enthusiasm with this subsequent description of prehearing communication:

> Our relations are so good with the Committee that [the subcommittee chairman] will call me up and tell me that [a minority member] is going to ask me such and such a question, or [the ranking minority member] is going to ask such and such so I'll be prepared in advance. If he himself has a question and doesn't call me, it's because he knows I know the answer. But if he thinks it's a hard one, he'll call me.

The relationship is probably unusual, but it demonstrates the potentialities of informal contact for the reduction of uncertainty.

For the most part, agency-Committee communication in preparation for the hearing proceeds at the staff level. The subcommittee clerk on the one hand and the departmental budget officer or bureau budget officer on the other hand constitute the day-to-day linkage between the legislative and executive branches in appropriations matters. Committee members and bureau chiefs are enmeshed in a web of other relationships. Neither has the time or the technical mastery to deal with the complications of budgetary detail. And so, to their respective subalterns they delegate the day-to-day appropriations negotiations. Those negotiations and the personal relationships established underpin the Committee-agency relationship. Uncertainties existing at the staff level reflect themselves in the uncertainties of the hearing room. Confidences established at the staff level reflect themselves in exchanges of confidence between Committee members and bureau chiefs. The reliance of the Appropriations Committee on its staff has already been described. And the reliance of agency heads on their budgetary staff is no less great. It hardly needs to be added that the payoff for good staff-to-staff relations can be found in the dollars and cents line items of the agency appropriation.

Agency budget officials express the common executive concern for "a smooth running hearing." By this they mean a hearing which emphasizes program, which observes certain standards of fairness, and which minimizes uncertainty. Exchanges of information on the staff level contribute heavily to these ends. A departmental budget officer discussed his communications with Committee staff:

> I'm on close personal relationships with the members of the Committee's staff. During the working season [prior to the hearings] we're in constant contact, daily and on weekends, here or at home . . . we want to be sure

they talk about important things and don't go running off into unimportant areas. Or, if there are going to be certain questions coming up, we want to know what they are. The Committee staff will tell us. And that's good. It's much better to be prepared than to say, "I don't know. I'll look it up."

A bureau budget officer described the value of the two-way relationship for his agency:

> We have very friendly relations with the clerk . . . [he] will call us up and tell us that Congressman X is worried about this or that program so we can be ready for it in the hearing. They help us to have a more fruitful hearing in that way. Or, they may ask us for additional data on something . . . that will help them out in understanding our program. Then they may be able to explain it to the congressmen better than we can. The congressmen don't read our justifications very thoroughly — and I sympathize with them — but the clerks do. If we can help them in answering their questions, they may sell our program for us. They will sit in the hearings handing questions to the congressmen, and if we have given them information their questions will be more understandable.

Budget officers give high priority to the maintenance of good relations with House Committee clerks. "I'm going up to a meeting with some of the Committee staff tomorrow," exclaimed one. "I don't know what they're going to talk about and I don't know why they want me there. But I'm surer than hell going to be there. As long as I can walk, I'll go."

A change in subcommittee clerks disrupts established patterns of communication and causes a loss of understanding and of confidence. An agency budget officer who had suffered through such a breakdown and was beginning all over again to establish good staff relations painted a particularly vivid picture of the linkage. He began by complaining that his agency's most recent hearing had gone badly. He blamed the difficulty on the fact that, since he and the clerk had not communicated beforehand, no one in the agency was apprised of what the Committee was driving at. Agency witnesses, therefore, could not answer the questions to the Committee's satisfaction. He went on to stress the necessity for repairing the damage which had been done to staff communications:

> It isn't easy. I was just getting to know the other clerk. Now he's gone and a new one is here. According to protocol, I can't just pick up the phone, call the clerk, and say, "How about coming down here for a chat." I'm trying to work out a program to get him out to look at our facilities. He and I went up to ———— last week to inspect the station there. On the way back I said I hoped we could work together to accomplish just two things. First I hope I can help him understand everything about our operation. We're going out again in two weeks. The second thing I said was that I hoped he would come to have enough confidence in me so that he could pick up the phone and call me and trust me to tell him the truth. I don't say we have to be

close personal friends. Maybe that would bring personalities into it. The important thing is confidence. If I had had that relationship with him, we never would have had that misunderstanding [in the recent hearing]. I think things will be better, and I hope this fellow stays around a long time.

In their relations with the Committee, agencies labor constantly to achieve substantive ("understanding everything about our operation") and maintenance ("confidence") expectations.

Agency officials consider that the mere fact of person-to-person contact between themselves and the legislative participants will help to minimize personal antagonism. For them the most vexing uncertainties are those which come as the result of the personal hostility of a Committee member or clerk. What makes the personality variable so frightening is its essential immunity to rational argument. But agency officials do what they can to bring it under control. When faced with particularly recalcitrant individuals, they seek out personal meetings to ascertain whether the opposition is personal or philosophical. Where it is philosophical, agency officials can try discussion, and where discussion fails, at least an element of predictability exists. Where the opposition is personal, they seek to defuse it by demonstrating their own personal friendliness in face-to-face conversation. "He continued to oppose us, but at least it wasn't a personal thing anymore," may be an important step forward for the agency. Where "The thing is not personal," or, "He's got nothing personal against us," the agency officials believe that the hearing is likely to be a fair one and that a key element of arbitrariness will have been removed.

In the promotion of informal contact between agency and Committee, the importance of the departmental budget officer needs to be underscored. To the degree that the internal decision-making processes of a department are hierarchical (and all of them are to some degree) the departmental budget officer stands as the chief internal coordinator (on behalf of the department head) of the departmental budget. His program concerns and his range of responsibility are broader than that of any single bureau budget officer. He speaks for a whole department to committees whose jurisdictions, by and large, run parallel to departmental lines. He, therefore, is the person in every department who is in most frequent informal contact with the Committee. He may be supplemented in his Committee relationships by departmental officials whose portfolio is more broadly that of informal congressional contact men — men like Otis Beasley in Interior, General Robert Moore in Defense, and Sam Andretta in Justice. But the departmental budget officer is the man who combines formal authority and informal negotiating activity in the appropriations area. His activities are year-round.

To hear departmental budget officers tell what they do is to recognize the kind of informal communications which lubricate agency-Committee

306

relations in the period after as well as before the hearings: "I say to [the sub-committee chairman] you are cutting us too much. Go ahead if you have to, but leave the door open for a supplemental." "If you feel you've got to clip us and you've got to cut the budget, cut us here and not here."

> So I got them together, the subcommittee chairman, the Secretary [of the department], and me for an informal lunch to straighten things out. [The subcommittee chairman] walked in and the first thing he said [to the Secretary] was, "You've got to fire that man." Boy, that was some start, and it was a pretty cold lunch.

"I was up on the Hill all night for a week trying to save our money." "Twenty-five per cent of what we get [over the base] is what I get by horse-trading on the side." "I found out how to get around [the subcommittee chairman] . . . even if he was taking the witness off somewhere I'd let him go. Then I'd go around later and see him in his office and straighten him out . . . I'd go around man to man after the hearings." In conversations of this sort many differences between agency and Committee can be resolved to their mutual satisfaction.

In the course of his negotiating activities, the departmental budget officer builds as close a relationship sidewise to the Committee as he already has hierarchically inside the executive branch. One spoke of his relations with his subcommittee's clerk:

> My relations with [him] are excellent. I know him professionally. And I know him socially. We work well together. Lots of times when he goes on trips I go with him.

The subcommittee clerk involved spoke even more warmly of their relationship:

> I know him [the departmental budget officer just mentioned] more than any of the others. He's the coordinator up there and I'm the coordinator down here. We talk on the phone a good deal. Four or five times a year we get together for dinner and have a few martinis and talk things over. He's a smart man — one of the best budget men in the business.

Over a period of time, the departmental officer develops confidential relationships with both legislative and executive personnel. So long as he retains their mutual confidence, he has the ability to manipulate the perceptions which they have of one another. To the Department he conveys what goals are possible of attainment and which are not, and how best to proceed in reaching them. To the Committee, he conveys the vital interests of the agencies, departmental priorities, and an overall impression which will re-dound to the benefit or the detriment of the agencies. Since he knows more about both parties than either one knows about the other, they both rely

307

heavily upon him. But, since he is limited in what he can reveal about the one to the other, he must act as a kind of one-man uncertainty absorber for both parties — but especially for the executive.

His problems are those of bridging the executive-legislative budgetary gap. Three departmental budget officers discussed the problems of working both sides of the street. The first stressed the difference between his perspective and that of executives who act exclusively within the executive branch:

> We have to tread a pretty thin line and we're always caught in a cross fire between the Budget Bureau and Congress. I just wish those people over there [in the Budget Bureau] had to carry those requests out — just once. They'd learn what the problems were. They make decisions down here, but they haven't any idea what we go through. That's one of the funny things about this process. The budget is made up over there, but we have to carry the ball. The Budget Bureau has just sent over a budget for us that I know Congress won't like. So right now I'm trying to get some adjustments made so that I can have a budget I can take up there with some confidence. They have no understanding of the climate up there, of the pressures, of the personalities.

The second man indicated how his behavior oscillated as he tried to serve two masters:

> Sometimes you wonder just who you are working for. I haven't been in too many embarrassing situations. With my relations with the Congress as they are, I may tell them that, frankly, I don't think I ought to tell them — that I have to maintain my loyalty to the department. Sometimes I go against the department. One year [a bureau] was given extra money, and it was written in the bill that they should expand [a particular program]. Well, they took the money and used it to raise salaries. I didn't defend them. [The bureau chief] called me up and said, "You're going against the department." I said, "You go up there and do a selling job on the Congress and convince them that you should raise salaries. I'll support you. But you have diverted money, and that's contrary to the law." If they do things like that, I'll give 'em hell. You're in the middle.

The third department officer suggested that his effectiveness depends on maintaining confidence with both legislature and executive:

> Sometimes I'll go over to the Committee and talk about something with them. The first time I went, they told me it was confidential. And I said, "When I came through that door, I started working for the Committee. Whatever goes on in here just didn't happen as far as I'm concerned when I leave here." And I tell them that every time. Sometimes, I'm over here and the Secretary or someone will try to worm it out of me what's going on. But they know I won't tell them. I'll say, "I don't have anything I can tell you." And that's the truth. I don't say, "I don't have anything." I just say, "I don't have anything I can tell you." . . . They all know that they won't get anything out of me — on either side. If I break down on one side, I'm all through because the other side will never trust me.

No departmental budget officer monopolizes informal communications with the Committee. But, depending upon the internal organization of a department and upon his own role orientation within that structure, some departmental budget officers come reasonably close. One of them, operating within a hierarchically organized department, said of his agency heads,

> Their contacts with the Committee are limited to the hearings. All communication with the Hill is done at the higher level, through this office and others. That's by design. If every one of them went up on the Hill looking for money, we wouldn't know where the hell we were. They don't have other contacts.

His description of reality was only partially accurate, despite his effort to make it so. Three of his agency heads presented different degrees of compliance with his prescription. The most compliant reported,

> I leave them strictly alone. I don't do any lobbying up there or go around to talk to them on the side. Oh, one time we did. It was a mistake, and I'd never do it again. A bunch of us went up there to talk about our appropriations. . . . We went there and sat around and chatted, and it didn't amount to a hill of beans. That's the only time I've done any lobbying outside the formal hearings since I've been here. Your equities are higher if you follow the routine channels. That's my opinion. These men are busy. They are lobbied to death on all questions.

A second bureau chief in the same department felt restive under departmental restraints:

> That's one of the problems of being in a bureau within a department. I've pressed on a number of occasions and without success for more informal contacts with the Appropriations Committee. But these contacts all have to be authorized by the Administrative Assistant Secretary. There's that restriction and we have abided by it. I think I've been to [the subcommittee chairman's] office about three times to talk — three times in the last six years. . . . It was a great help. It's always easier to sit down informally with a man than to attend hearings. It may be easy for a congressman who is used to it, but making a public record is a great strain for me.

A third agency head described a pattern of greater activity.

> When I first came here, I didn't have any [informal contacts], but we have more now. I've gone out and tried to develop contacts with congressmen, because that's the way the game is played. But I don't like it. You shouldn't have to lobby for your program. But politics being what it is, I've done a little more of that . . . Some people higher up in the department object to our having any informal contacts with congressmen, but we'll just have to get around that, I guess.

It seems reasonably clear that in this case the departmental budget officer carries on most of the communication outside the hearing room himself.

309

A more permissive policy was enunciated by a different departmental budget officer:

> We try to find every legitimate opportunity for the bureau heads to meet the congressmen and make themselves known. But when they go up, they always let me know, because I might be up there horse-trading myself. If you're going to run a department, you have to have a field general somewhere.

His agency heads reported having varying degrees of informal contacts, ranging from one who said, "I don't talk to these people informally the way some bureau heads do," to another who said that he met Committee members "on social occasions and we'll chat a little or they will call me and ask me questions about the program or ask me to lunch to discuss something with them," to a third man who said that, "Saturday used to be my day for roving around on the Hill trying to see who was in. Usually they weren't busy and I could go in and talk with them in a relaxed manner."

The most permissive role of all was played by a budget officer who described his departmental structure as minimally hierarchical. "This is a department of semiautonomous agencies. . . . We let each bureau go up and do their own selling job. We say, 'If you can't sell the Congress on your own program, don't come back and blame us.' " And one of his agency heads painted a picture of informal communication unsurpassed in intimacy when he discussed long-term relations with his subcommittee:

> I had good friends on the Committee. Why, time was when I used to write the report. They'd say, "We've got to cut you, we've got to cut you" — five per cent or ten per cent or whatever it was. "Now you tell us where you want to absorb the cut, and write up the report explaining it." Those relations ended. . . . But up to five years ago, I never had any trouble. I used to enjoy it. I considered those men among my friends.

This relationship, like a few others reported, is unusual. But it is not likely that it would have sprung up if the department had been more hierarchically organized and if the departmental budget officer had tried to control contacts with the Committee.

Another variable which affects the flow of informal communication is the degree to which an agency's program is relevant to the special interests of Committee members. Where it is, and where the agency can be of some tangible service to the congressman, the program-oriented agency head has an easy entree. The agency head who spoke of his Saturday visits to Capitol Hill said, for example, that "I would take something along — a recent publication or something that might be of particular interest to them, a different one perhaps for each man. I would stress service and tell them that if I could ever be of service to them for them to call me." An agency head without tangible services to offer a congressman or his constituents would find access more difficult and be more likely to leave the task to the man who was more a legislative technician. Agriculture Department officials especially stressed services to the Committee members as a natural way to maintain informal communications. One official of the Department discussed his most successful agency head (recently retired) to whom had been left the job of uncertainty reduction for his agency:

> He made it his business to become friendly with the Committee. He was a big, hearty, rough and tumble guy, and he built up wonderful relationships up there on the Hill. He saw to it that they got what they wanted when they wanted it.

More than in any other department, the heads of the agricultural agencies take it upon themselves to mend their own Committee fences. Their services are tangible ones, the community of interest with rural congressmen is great, and the tradition of political maneuvering among agricultural groups is time-tested.

"When we get a new congressman on our Committee," said one Agriculture official, "I make it my business to know all there is to know about him." When Chairman Cannon deliberately confronted them with a great unknown — an urban congressman, Representative Santangelo — departmental officials redoubled their efforts at uncertainty reduction. It is interesting to note that, while Congressman Santangelo was undergoing socialization within the Agriculture Subcommittee, Agriculture Department officials worked informally to achieve goals of program understanding and predictability. The budget officer of one agency reported,

> We've spent a lot of time with Congressman Santangelo, educating him as to what [our program] is all about. With his background he didn't know anything about us and he said so. But he's a smart man. He's an independent man, and he asks very intelligent questions. There was an opportunity for [the bureau chief] to meet with him informally in New York, to explain to him about the institutional and political structure of the agency. Now he's familiar with a number of things. His questions in hearings are very objective. He says, "Where I come from, I never heard of you. What do you do?" I hope he stays on the Committee.

The head of another agricultural bureau commented,

> Well, he wants to learn all he can about it. I had occasion to go to Puerto Rico once, and Congressman Santangelo was on the same trip. Two different evenings we sat together down there and talked about [our program]. He wanted to learn all that he could about it. Naturally, two evenings is not enough time to absorb everything, but he is a reasonable man. You read the hearings. His requests have not been obnoxious or unreasonable.

311

Certainly the net product of Committee and agency education was to produce more program understanding, more sympathy, and hence more predictability on the part of Mr. Santangelo.

Agency officials do not see the pattern in subcommittee selection which places congressmen unsympathetic or uninterested in their program on their subcommittee, but they do perceive the general tendency to reduce budgets. And they seek to countervail this tendency by personal contact with unsympathetic Committee members outside as well as inside Washington. Indeed agency officials are unanimous in believing that, if done right, contacts made "in the field" are the most beneficial contacts of all. So they encourage their subcommittee members to visit their agency to see for themselves what it does. The junket has its hazards, of course, when a Committee member or staff man sees what he is not expected to see or interprets what he sees as he is not expected to interpret it — and when he then pops up in the hearings with an unexpected query. But the long-run payoff of a first-hand look is deemed well worth the risk. It is deemed beneficial precisely because it produces the interest-sympathy-leniency syndrome — the very syndrome which Appropriations Committee leaders seek to prevent.

The natural response to the budget-cutting subcommittee personnel is to get them out to see the agency in action. One bureau budget officer expressed it,

> Most of the congressmen on our committee live in districts where they aren't interested in our program, because they don't know anything about it. That's a real problem for us — to get congressmen interested in what we are doing. . . . Congressmen love to travel, and if we can get them to visit our installations, we feel they will become more sympathetic. Take [the subcommittee chairman] and send him to ———— and he's sold.

Insofar as the uncertainty in Committee relations stems from a lack of knowledge or interest, a visit "out on the ground" is considered a certain antidote.

A departmental budget officer discussed the importance and consequences of visits by his subcommittee.

> Every time I can, and in every way I can, I encourage our committee to get out and see what they are appropriating for. I'll make up a schedule and ask the chairman if he and members of the committee won't come along. . . . I don't think there's a subcommittee in Congress that has seen more of its installations than ours has. I'd say they have seen pretty well up into the thousands of separate parts of our operation . . . one time they asked whether we couldn't mechanize one of our operations a little more commonly and we said, "Certainly, if we had more money." So they said, "You prepare a program here and send it up." We did. So they have taken the initiative sometimes, and have even needled us to move faster than we

would have. And that's good. How could they know about our need for electronic equipment sitting back there. They have to see it . . . it cuts down on our questions at a hearing. When we talk to the chairman about a building, he knows just what we are talking about. We don't have to draw him a map or write him a book. He was there. He can visualize exactly what it looked like when he was there. That cuts down on the hearings and on the justifications.

And, it might be added, it cuts down on the uncertainties which the agency must confront. Agency officials frequently lament their inability to arrange suitable visits to their installations. What they most frequently see as the cause is the relative lack of glamour of their own program. Committee members, they believe, must have their interest aroused by some startling innovation in equipment and technique or some visible improvement in program results. And not all agencies can provide such when it is needed.

CONCLUSION

In their relations with the House Committee on Appropriations, executive agencies want funds for their programs and they want communication to focus on those programs. In terms of maintenance desires, they seek a predictable and stable relationship. They view the House Committee as the most influential group in the congressional appropriations process; and they, like House members, have a well-developed set of images of the group. Unlike the images of House members, however, the most central agency images do not run to the power and performance of the Committee. Because agency officials live within a different branch of government and because agency officials are acutely aware (at least in their moments of face-to-face contact) of the Committee's sanctions over them, their most lively perceptions center on the pervasive uncertainty of the relationship. Their ultimate concern, of course, is for program success. But they believe that a necessary first step is to bring a degree of certainty and, hence, stability into their dealings with the Committee. When executives confront legislators the imponderables of human relations and the difficulties of communication loom larger than when legislators confront fellow legislators.

Agency officials devote a great deal of their behavior to attempts at reducing uncertainty. On every occasion of contact with the Committee, agency people seek to build sympathy and confidence. Sympathetic support is, of course basic to program success. And many agencies will have sympathetic Committee allies. But Committee confidence in an agency's competence, its word, its chief executive is believed to be the essential uncertainty-reducing element. Confidence, they believe, is necessary to hold sympathy — given the negative orientation of most Committee members. How

313

to increase certainty by winning and keeping the confidence of the House Appropriations Committee becomes the central agency preoccupation. Their formulas involve obedience to Committee reports, careful preparation for Committee hearings, confidence-producing behavior in the hearing room, and the maintenance of informal contacts throughout the year. Behavior focused on the Committee hearing is predicated to an important degree on the agency perception that Committee members use sampling procedures to test the agency and to make judgments as to whether their confidence is warranted. Behavior focused on informal contacts is predicated largely on the belief that continuous communication is necessary to win and hold both sympathy and confidence. Agency behavior in and out of the hearing room has been described. The appropriateness of this behavior, however, cannot be judged until we have considered the Committee-agency relationship from the Committee point of view.

CHAPTER SEVEN

The House Committee
and Executive Agencies
II: *Committee Expectations,
Images, and Behavior*

COMMITTEE EXPECTATIONS AND IMAGES

Executive agencies want favorable decisions from the House Appropriations Committee. They try to achieve their goal by adopting certain forms of behavior which, in the light of their image of the Committee, they deem appropriate. The effectiveness of their behavior must be judged by the decisions the Committee makes. And these decisions, for 36 agencies, will be described in some detail in the next chapter. But it helps in understanding why agencies behave as they do and why the Committee decides as it does if we examine the posture of the Committee prior to final decision-making. Committee expectations and images have already been elaborated in Chapter Three. Committee behavior in face-to-face contact with the agencies — especially in the hearings — has not been described, and it forms the main body of the present chapter.

In terms of their expectations, Committee members wish to support the various programs for which they appropriate. Every program, it has been repeatedly stressed, has its body of supporters off and on the Committee. And Committee members individually and collectively desire to maintain most of the agencies as going concerns. They consider, however, that their own particular function should be a negative rather than a positive one. Most generally, it is to protect the congressional power of the purse and especially the House's share of that power. The Committee feels that it must exercise the power of the purse by subjecting agency activity to constant scrutiny and by ferreting out unnecessary expenditures wherever they exist. Subject only to the proviso that constituency interests should be served, the Committee seeks to reduce budget estimates. Its decision-making structure is organized to promote this end. Its integrative mechanisms are designed to ensure and protect budget-cutting decisions from internal and external forces which might work in the opposite direction. Committee expectations, it is clear, diverge considerably from those of the agency. Agency expectations or demands call for long-run increases in appropriations and, in the short run, complete approval of each budget estimate. Furthermore, they call for a stress on program accomplishments. Committee expectations do concern program, but they center more actively and visibly on the discovery of unnecessary expenditures. As it balances demands for program support against demands for economy, the Appropriations Committee throws its institutional weight most strongly on behalf of the demands for economy.

The Committee buttresses its expectations with a commonly accepted image of the typical executive agency. The image holds that every agency considers only its own program, that agency parochialism feeds the desire to expand, that expansion requires money, and, therefore, that the typical executive agency requests yearly increases in its appropriations. Furthermore, Committee members' experience informs them that every agency will defend its budget requests as the minimum needed to do the job. But, given their own view of their job, Committee members develop other perceptions which diverge from those of the agency. They believe that agencies can "get along" with less money than they request and still carry on their "program" at an "adequate" level. They believe, contrary to agency belief, that agency budgets are padded — that they request more money than they actually "need." As one subcommittee chairman put it, "They say they need seven new positions, but you know that if they tightened up and filled them with people already on the payroll they could get by." The "survival" of an agency typically means a different thing to an Appropriations Committee member than it does to an agency official.

In its direct confrontation with agency officials, the Committee performs two of its House-prescribed tasks — law-making and oversight. And it performs them simultaneously. Committee members feel that a detailed and meticulous annual oversight of agency activity is essential, and they believe further that such an inquiry will yield examples of unnecessary expenditure. But, even if no waste is found, they believe it is imperative that some legislative group with a concern for saving money keep the threat of inquiry hanging over the executive branch. One member summed up:

How can you tell the projects which have merit from those that don't? You have to pick them apart. And so you do — you ask them questions about the most meritorious and authentic-sounding proposals to see if they can justify them to you. When you find one that they can't justify you weed it out that way. They say that we're suspicious. We're not suspicious; we just want to be sure they need all the money they ask for. Some of them come over here with padded budgets. We've got to find these out, but we've got to be careful not to cut the man who has his program well figured out. But you give the man with the good program just as hard a going over as the man with a program that may not be quite so well in hand. You have to let all of them know that you are watching them even though you leave the program alone. . . . Sometimes I say to myself afterwards, we didn't go far enough into that item. I know we could have cut more out if we had. You can't know everything. But you keep asking questions just to let them know someone is watching them. You've got to give them that idea — the manager of any shop would do that or the whole thing will go to pot.

A staff member voiced similar sentiments, "You've got to shake 'em up once in a while. No one else will."[1]

Despite such disclaimers as the one just given, the elemental Committee attitude toward the agencies is suspicion. At bottom, perhaps, rests the natural suspicion which a legislative body (especially one that considers its activity to be the bulwark of legislative power) has for an executive body. "These agencies spend all their time — I'm convinced of it — trying to think up ways to hoodwink us. You have to ride them hard all the time." "We have to catch them here and catch them there and find out when they are lying and when they are double-talking us. They all do it. Some of them make a capital production out of it." The attitude becomes more firmly embedded with every example of waste that is discovered. "We take the attitude that something's wrong here and we're going to catch you. . . . The agencies don't come up here and put their cards on the table and say, 'We made a mistake on this one.' They come up here and paint a rosy picture and then we stumble on to something and find it's a mess."

Committee suspicion, it must be emphasized, is not the same thing as Committee hostility. Knowing the Committee's expectations, it might be presupposed that these fifty men would harbor an especially harsh set of perceptions of agency officials. It might be presupposed that here on the Appropriations Committee one would find the hard core of congressional animus toward the federal bureaucracy. Such is not the case. Some Committee members do level wholesale ideological indictments against the sins of the executive branch. And these attacks may be triggered by some special frustration born of their Committee experience. But as a group the Com-

[1] See the comments of Representative Marshall, 105 *Congressional Record*, p. 8673.

317

mittee expresses no greater hostility towards the "bureaucrats" than do House members generally. Occasionally, in a special set of circumstances, Committee members will explode in a denunciation of some particular situation.[2] But neither privately nor publicly do Committee members provide a disproportionate share of antibureaucratic invective. Indeed, on occasions when House members are in a rampaging economy mood, the Committee is likely to furnish a protective shield for the agency against "excessive," "crippling," and "blind" budget reductions. The Appropriations Committee man, however, does begin with deeply held suspicions. He must be "shown" each year by each agency official that his budget is not bloated beyond what is necessary for agency "survival." Whether, in the end, he cuts budget requests or not, he believes it is his job to let the agencies know that someone is watching them.

The Committee perceives its oversight and budget-reducing tasks as essentially incremental operations. When the Committee makes its annual inquiry into agency appropriations, it does not normally range throughout the length and breadth of agency activities. Just as the agency considers much of its appropriation to be beyond controversy, so, too, does the Committee act on this assumption by restricting its purview to those budgetary increments granted in the previous year and requested for the coming year. "We only have the time to study increases and new functions," said one member. "We don't go into existing functions." A veteran subcommittee chairman agreed:

> When I first took over the committee, I went extensively into all the operations of the agencies. But now I consider only the new departures. It's the changes we look at now. The hearings and junkets are necessary in the consideration of changes.

The Committee does not, as a rule, probe deeply into well-established programs with well-established bases of support. What it normally does is to check carefully what the agency did with the increase it was given last year and inquire into the purposes for which the current increase is to be used. A program established last year or proposed for the coming year will receive careful scrutiny; and it is here that the program preferences of a key Committee member can work themselves most directly and decisively into legislative policy-making.

The Committee tendency to perceive agency estimates primarily in terms of current increments is revealed and at the same time promoted by the layout of the documents with which it works during the review of budget estimates. Both the justification books submitted by the agency and the

---

[2] For example, the comments of Representatives Clevenger and Flood, 95 *Congressional Record*, pp. 4094–4095.

subcommittee print drawn up by the Committee present in tabular form last year's appropriation, this year's request, and then, in the final column, the incremental figure for the present year — that is, the amount of increase or decrease represented by this year's estimate compared with last year's appropriation. The subcommittee print also lists in another place estimates and appropriations for several preceding years. These working documents are set up, of course, to show the Committee members what they want to see. Member attention is fixed on the increment and turned away from the established base. The Committee, therefore, tends to consider the budget estimates primarily in terms of the top of the iceberg and concentrates its attention there.

From the agency officials' viewpoint, this is a consummation devoutly to be wished. For they consider their usual problem as "getting more" rather than holding what they already have. What they fear most is a reduction which cuts into what they consider their established base. Constituency complaints, the personal interests of a Committee member or of a staff member may redirect Committee attention to an old program. When this happens, the agency may have to fight for its very life. A newcomer, in criticizing the standard Committee approach, painted a vivid picture of what life would be like for the agencies under a different approach:

> If I ever get to be chairman of this subcommittee, there will be the tightest requirements of proof and justification you ever saw. I'll make them justify the programs they've already got and not just the increases. Let's say some small agency comes in and wants $13 million instead of $12 million and 43 new positions. I'll say to them, "Now this is just preliminary. But I see you want 43 new positions. You aren't going to get the 43 positions. The Committee is unanimous on that and that is settled. Now, the Committee wants you to justify the personnel you already have. We're thinking of cutting you back ten per cent all across the board. Is there any reason why we shouldn't? And if you have any difficulty in determining just what functions you'd like to cut out, you can just leave that to the Committee." Then you'd really see something.

Indeed. But this is the daydream of a newcomer. It does not reflect the perceptions or the practices of the men who make the Committee's decisions.

In its dealings with executive agencies, the Appropriations Committee's problem of adaptation is not so immediate or so acute as the one posed by its relationship with the House. But it is no less serious. Committee survival depends on its ability to satisfy, by means of its decisions, those agency expectations which reflect the important needs of the society. The problem is not one of pleasing each agency in terms of its short-run demands. Though every agency wants all it asks for every year, Committee survival does not depend on meeting this expectation. And there is little the agencies can

319

muster by way of sanctions in ordinary cases of budget reduction. But should a Committee decision or series of decisions be widely assessed as reflecting bad judgment and having very undesirable social consequences, the House, the Senate, clientele groups, and interested citizens could combine to levy the most drastic of sanctions against the Committee. The Committee's adaptational problem vis-à-vis the agencies is that *it must make knowledgeable and wise decisions.* Committee failure will jeopardize its own survival and redound to the great discredit of the House of Representatives and the Congress as well.

Committee members are fully aware of the problem. And their awareness is reflected in their stress on the need for information and experience. From information, they believe, comes knowledge, and from experience comes wisdom. And these are the ingredients of good judgment and intelligent decision-making. Committee members place considerable stock in the value of conscientious, repetitive, incremental examination of agency budgets for producing the experience requisite to good judgment. Their more active concern focuses on the need for relevant information. And the problem of adaptation becomes, in their eyes, largely the problem of information. The Committee-agency relationship, in this respect, is the exact reverse of the Committee-House relationship. In confronting the House, the Committee possesses all the information advantages. But when the Committee faces the executive agency, the agency possesses the same advantages; and it is the Committee which is on the outside "trying to find out what is going on."

Committee expectations, images, and behavior all need to be understood in terms of its information disadvantages. An important maintenance expectation, for instance, holds that the agencies should be frank and open and should not attempt to cover up or hold back relevant information. But an equally central perception holds that agency officials do precisely that. And it is this perception that fuels the attitude of suspicion. Budgets are padded; soft spots do exist; one can never be sure whether the agencies are revealing pertinent information on these matters; the Committee's task, therefore, is to get the pertinent information by its own devices. Committee behavior centers around the search for and the manipulation of information on which to base its decisions. In that search, Committee members are constantly aware of their disadvantage in terms of the complexity and volume of executive-held information. It is in an attempt to offset this permanent disadvantage that the Committee adopts the sampling process which agency officials perceive as a major aid to Committee decision-making. Uncertainties exist, therefore, on *both* sides of the Committee-agency relationship. Agency officials feel they cannot be sure what the Committee will do; Committee members feel they cannot be sure they have the information they need. Both seek increased certainty. In this light, it is easy to see why Committee members would be as anxious to place their confidence in an agency as the agency would be to secure it.

The remainder of the chapter describes Committee behavior in its agency relationships. It focuses on the arena of the hearings and on the adaptational problem of informed decision-making.

COMMITTEE BEHAVIOR

Collecting Information

The Committee's own idea of what it is doing in dealing with the agencies centers on the collection of information — formally and informally. Nowhere, of course, is this quest more forcefully revealed than in the mountainous volume of Committee hearings. But Committee members and their "clerks" begin by stressing their extensive year-round preparations for decision-making. In the words of a subcommittee chairman,

> The members of this Committee worked the year round. We do not hold hearings and then forget about it. The Committee has visited the installations of the Treasury and the Post Office Departments in various parts of the world. We have visited post offices in various parts of the United States. We have visited Coast Guard installations which are scattered far out into the Pacific and into the Atlantic.[3]

Committee people, like agency people, emphasize the value of traveling to see agency activity at firsthand. And it is done by Committee members, by Committee clerks, and by members of the investigation and surveys staff. Another subcommittee chairman explained, "I believe firmly in the visual concept. I can get more knowledge from a few minutes actual experience than from listening to the testimony of experts for ten days in a committee room."[4] A member of a third subcommittee detailed the travels of its members between two sessions of Congress:

> In addition to the hearings, Mr. Jensen, Mr. Schwabe, and myself spent seven weeks last fall visiting various Interior Department projects in the West. Mr. Stockman visited Hawaii and Mr. Kirwan toured [31 states in] the West.[5]

As recent sessions of Congress stretch further into the fall and winter, the opportunities for extensive travel have been reduced. But the weeks following the early November elections have long been one favorite time for

[3] 102 *Congressional Record*, p. 2232.

[4] Harrison Humphries, "California Congressman Insists on First Hand Knowledge of Jets," Associated Press Release, reprinted in *Congressional Record*, Daily Edition, January 29, 1960, p. A765.

[5] 94 *Congressional Record*, p. 6603.

junketing. Congressmen defend these trips as absolutely necessary to well-informed decision-making.

Agency officials perceive junkets as a technique for inducing the operation of the interest-sympathy-leniency syndrome. And though one cannot be sure of the net effect, it seems likely that firsthand inspection does pay off for the agency. A senior subcommittee member described one kind of bonus for the agency:

> Maybe we'll be on a plane going somewhere, and I'll be visiting with the Assistant Secretary and he'll say, "I've got a problem that bothers me." We'll talk about it and maybe come up with a plan. That's how you become an advocate of an agency's position.

Committee members remain open-minded and speak of their visits in the relatively neutral terms of "finding out what is going on." But they certainly do not view these trips as techniques for reducing their budget-cutting proclivities. A suspicious newcomer explained,

> I have a sneaking hunch that some of the people who appear before the Committee are trying to indoctrinate me. But I don't want to make my decision on a personal basis. I want to be objective and decide on the basis of what they need. They want to take me out here and there and show me things to prove to me otherwise. And I may take them up on it sometime. But I'm not anxious to do it.

On visits to agency installations, Committee members sometimes scheme to get out from under the "official" agency planned tour.[6] And when they return they advertise as successes those trips which resulted in the discovery of waste.[7]

Among Committee staff members, who accompany the members on their journeys and who take many solo trips, the perception is very markedly that of a search for "soft spots." They approach their junkets as opportunities to find out what is wrong with agency operation and so justify budget-cutting. Two veteran clerks described their method of operations:

> I'd say I've visited over half the field offices of the department. When you talk to people in the field you find out things that don't ever appear in the justifications — problems they have and things that aren't going so well. You may see some things that look pretty bad and need tending to. Then at the hearings — or before the hearings — you can ask them about it. Occasionally we'll find out things the agencies themselves didn't know about.

> [Travel] is indispensable and I should do more than I do. All you get up here are damned briefings sent over here by the department. . . . I pride myself on being able to look around a place and tell whether it's being run

[6] See *Congressional Quarterly*, September 8, 1961, p. 11555.
[7] For example, see *Congressional Record*, Daily Edition, June 18, 1963, p. 10398.

efficiently or not. If it's really bad and there's a lot of confusion you can tell — and you know they are wasting money. . . . The department can tell you a lot of things, but you have no idea of what's being done unless you see it.

Committee suspicion of the agencies is amply evident here. Since the agencies will not willingly reveal (and may willfully conceal) their soft spots, the Committee will have to find them itself. Agency and Committee have slightly different perceptions as to what an inspection trip is all about. Both, however, are equally confident of their ability to achieve results favorable to them.

The first formal transmission of information prior to the hearings comes via the justification books which are compiled by each agency and which accompany (or occasionally precede) the President's budget message to the Committee. These massive books, jam-packed with detail, present, explain, and justify the budget requests being made by the agency. Together with relevant reports from the investigative staff or the General Accounting Office, they are the basic informational documents which the Committee uses. Just who reads them varies from one subcommittee to another. One subcommittee clerk explained,

> I read the justifications from cover to cover and I'm the only person who does. The congressman [subcommittee chairman] doesn't have time to read them — they make a pile that high. But it's a real part of my responsibility . . . I figure I have to do two day's work on the justifications for every one day of hearings — writing up questions and so forth.

A second clerk described a different pattern:

> One of my responsibilities that I'd better not miss up on is to get the justifications to him [subcommittee chairman] early. He takes them home with him and reads them right through. He knows what the agencies have been doing and he can catch anything by himself. He's a self-starter in these things.

No matter who reads the justification books, the attitude of suspicion prevails. The search is for information that will reveal unnecessary expenditures. A clerk explained,

> At the beginning when you are preparing for the hearings, your attitude is critical. You are trying to find the soft spots and the loopholes. So you are looking for negative information. . . . The departments tell us what they are planning to do and I go through it with a fine tooth comb to make sure there are no sleepers they are trying to slip through. At this stage, it's "buyer beware."

Typically, at this same pre-hearings stage, Committee members and clerks seek out additional information through informal contacts — the members with top agency executives and the clerks with their staff counterparts. And, quite unsolicited, they receive random bits of information from other congressmen, constituents, and informants within the agencies themselves.

The final ingredient needed to make sense out of the information which is collected is the appropriations experience of the individual member. The Committee's influential decision-makers do not approach the hearings or the subsequent decision with one-year's collection of relevant data. Some of them come with an accumulation of information that has been amassed over decades, used as the basis for prior decisions and found to be relevant or irrelevant. Senior members and veteran clerks place great stock in their experience as a guide to decision-making. Out of their continuous, repeated, concentrated, and specialized exposure to agency budgets, they believe they have developed the ability to process information and to make prudent judgments. In the words of one veteran member,

> I might say that some of us on this subcommittee have been in Congress for sixteen years. . . . We feel that we have some knowledge of the problems of agriculture and through the years we have assimilated much information of that kind. We do not consider the budget in any sense sacred. . . . We are here for the purpose of using our own good sound judgment.[8]

On the basis of their experience, the Committee veterans express confidence in their ability to make wise judgments. Committee newcomers generally express no such confidence. But it is the senior members after all who do most of the decision-making. Their stress on experience as the keystone quality in decision-making serves as a bulwark of the Committee's internal structure. The self-perception of the older members squares, it might be added, with the perception that leads most agency officials to tender them their respect.

Making a Public Record

Committee members — at least the influential ones — come to the hearing room with much information and layers of experience at their disposal. There, they listen to the prepared statements of witnesses, interrogate them, and create (though some portions are "off the record") a public record. The overwhelming impression of that record is its sheer bulk. In the First Session of the 88th Congress (1963), the twelve regular subcommittees produced 38,584 pages of published public hearings. Contained therein was a mountain of detail in prepared statements, question and answer exchanges, reprinted agency documents, additional studies worked up at the request of the Committee during the hearings, and the testimony of interested congressmen and

[8] 100 *Congressional Record*, p. 5008.

clientele groups. The impression is inescapable that an enormous mass of information is excogitated in this annual ten-foot shelf of hearings. Doubtless selected elements of it do serve the basic informational needs of the Committee's decision-makers. But just what elements or how is immediately obscured by the pure bulk. Before probing further into the usefulness of the hearing for the Committee members, it should be noted that the very size of the hearings is of considerable use to them. It helps assuage the uneasiness they may feel about the uncertainties of their art; it helps maintain the confidence of House members that the Committee is on the job; and it buttresses the Committee's internal esprit by providing tangible evidence of its hard work. And, of course, the mere fact that hearings were held and a public record was made gives an important element of legitimacy to all subsequent decisions of the group.

The perceptions which Committee members have of themselves in the hearing room provide a basic understanding of what the hearing is all about. Member perceptions, of course, vary. Newcomers see it as educational, for they learn things about agency operation which they never knew before:

> I had no idea that the Commerce Department was as big as it was — no idea in the world. I had been around here for four years, but I never dreamed that Department was that extensive. The only way you can learn is to have them come before you — bureau by bureau — and listen to them describe their job. The hearings are very important for me.

For the more knowledgeable, experienced, and influential Committee member, agency exposition is more likely to be "boring," "routine," and "mentally wearying." He will, however, seek to turn the hearing to his own purposes — most of which have been predetermined. With the assistance of the clerk (whose contribution varies from "90 per cent of the questions" to "a few suggestions") the subcommittee chairman prepares a host of specific questions and fixes the general tone of the hearing. The initiative in the hearing belongs to the Committee member if he can bend the witness to his line of questioning and keep him there. It is for precisely this reason that agency officials feel so much uncertainty in connection with the hearings. Committee people feel that it is to their advantage to maintain the initiative. "We don't always know what tack they [the agency] will take when they come up here," said one clerk. "So I prepare a statement for the chairman in which he says, 'I think the following should be dealt with — one, two, three.' That gives him the initiative and makes it look like he's running the show." Members agree on the importance of keeping the initiative. But they differ on the use to which they put it, depending on circumstances and personality.

The most common self-image to which members subscribe with respect to the hearing is that they are making a public record that will provide

325

justification for budget reduction. In this view, the hearing is an *adversary proceeding* and the Committee member's perception of his role is that of "prosecutor." Committee veterans frequently refer to themselves as prosecutors, and Committee newcomers often praise an elder as "a brilliant interrogator" or "an expert trial lawyer." A prosecutor operates with the suspicion that soft spots exist, that the agency will not willingly reveal them, and that his job is to expose them publicly by means of his questioning. "The Appropriations Committee is the only committee," explained one member,

> where you never hear two sides of the question. The witnesses always defend their appropriation. So you have to be the prosecutor and not the judge. . . . You have to look at [the witness] with a jaundiced eye. He is trying to protect his domain. It's just you and him.

A subcommittee chairman described his hearing room procedure:

> I take the budget when it comes down here and see what I think it ought to be — within limits. Then I make out my case. When I ask questions I just don't go around for curiosity. I have a purpose, like a lawyer or prosecutor making out his case.

An experienced member stated,

> It's our function [in the hearings] to ask questions and to find out where the frills and wastefulness are . . . sometimes the information comes easy, and sometimes you have to sit across the table like a prosecutor and twist the answers out of them.

A subcommittee clerk spoke similarly about his chairman's procedure:

> He's a prosecuting attorney and he knows how to put his point on the record. He doesn't need much staff help . . . once he decides what he wants, he gets it out of the witness.

Experienced Committee members — many of whom have in fact had much prior courtroom experience — express confidence in their ability to support their indictment of waste and win a verdict of budget reduction.

"It's a game between you and the agencies," said one subcommittee chairman. "You are trying to trap them and show inefficiency and they hold practice sessions." This view of the hearings is widely held among Committee members. And some of them can be very hard-nosed and aggressive about it:

> I want to know why, why, why do you need this? When you're in there, it's a trial court. You're trying a case in there and they've got all the witnesses. I don't have any. You have to be tough, you can't believe anything they say. You keep hammering away. That's the lawyer in me. . . . I don't give a damn about them. I don't let personalities enter into it. Outside you may be friends, but when you're in the courtroom you are enemies — not

326

enemies exactly but opponents. They are just employees to me — people on the payroll. I don't care if they invite me to cocktail parties — as they do — and I go to about one in five. I'm tough.

Where Committee members choose not to reveal their line of questioning beforehand, they can, with the aid of investigative reports and staff studies, press a tactical advantage over the witness. The adversary-cum-prosecutor type of hearing is the one which fills the agency official with the greatest uncertainty and anxiety.

There is the "Let's be frank," broadside query. "Have you got this fattened up a little bit along here, Doctor?"[9] There is the "When did you stop beating your wife?" gambit. "Would [you] care to advise the Committee where you believe you could best sustain a curtailment of your activity, assuming that it became necessary to curtail your appropriations ten to twenty-five per cent without any increase in it whatsoever?"[10] And there is the familiar courtroom technique classically illustrated by this dialogue quoted by Wildavsky:

SUBCOMMITTEE CHAIRMAN: I find a gentleman here, an FSO–6. He got an A in Chinese and you assigned him to London.
AGENCY OFFICIAL: Yes, sir. That officer will have opportunities in London — not as many as he would have in Hong Kong, for example —
SUBCOMMITTEE CHAIRMAN: What will he do? Spend his time in Chinatown?
AGENCY OFFICIAL: No, sir. There will be opportunities in dealing with officers in the British Foreign Office who are concerned with Far Eastern affairs. . . .
SUBCOMMITTEE CHAIRMAN: So instead of speaking English to one another, they will sit in the London office and talk Chinese?
AGENCY OFFICIAL: Yes, sir.
SUBCOMMITTEE CHAIRMAN: Is that not fantastic?
AGENCY OFFICIAL: No, sir. They are anxious to keep up their practice. . . .
SUBCOMMITTEE CHAIRMAN: They go out to Chinese restaurants and have chop suey together?
AGENCY OFFICIAL: Yes, sir.
SUBCOMMITTEE CHAIRMAN: And that is all at the expense of the American taxpayer?[11]

Out of encounters like these, agency officials fashion their anecdotal parade of the horribles. They fear this kind of sleigh ride as much as anything save the irrationality of sheer personal hostility. But, as noted earlier, it does

[9] Committee on Appropriations, *Hearings on Federal Security Administration Appropriations for 1948*, 80th Congress, 1st Session (Washington: U.S. Government Printing Office, 1947), p. 457.
[10] Committee on Appropriations, *Hearings on Labor Department Appropriations for 1948*, 80th Congress, 1st Session (Washington: U.S. Government Printing Office, 1947), p. 543.
[11] Aaron Wildavsky, *The Politics of the Budgetary Process* (Boston: Little, Brown and Co., 1964), pp. 96–97.

not happen very often. For the Committee member, the importance of the extreme case lies in the threat that it represents. Members do not see themselves as being particularly rough on agency witnesses. But a senior member of the Subcommittee on Defense smiled when he said,

> These great military heroes who have commanded armies and fleets in battle, some of them are poor witnesses. They don't know their homework and they're scared. They shouldn't be. We're not a bunch of bastards or sharpshooters. Oh, once in a while we may ask some questions that are hard to answer. But basically we're sympathetic. Still, they get butterflies and they get ulcers. They hate to do it. They'd rather be in the front lines than come before this Committee.[12]

Members do derive some satisfaction from the obvious anxiety of agency witnesses. They value the chance it gives them to manipulate agency uncertainty and keep the agency on its mettle.

A variant on the Committee's self-image as prosecutor is the view that it is making a public record which will provide justification for the granting of some or all of the increase in funds requested by the agency. In this view, the hearing is a *pseudo-adversary proceeding*, in which the defense lawyer tests out his own client to determine how strong a case they can make in court. The Committee member who is already predisposed to grant the agency its requests may subject an agency official to a stiff interrogation to reassure himself that the agency case is a defensible one. If the Committee grants all or part of the increase, it may have to defend its action on the House floor. And Committee members dread the prospect of being caught unprepared in floor debate. So, in the hearing, they may subject the agency to the severest questioning — the object of which is to have the agency official make a detailed case which the congressman can use later. A ranking minority subcommittee member explained to an agency witness:

> The important thing, as far as I am concerned, is to get some information, some testimony here, as to why we have to increase a budget. I can assure you that you may think it is a little difficult, but we take this bill to the floor of the House of Representatives; we then become the advocate of the bill that we report. We have to substantiate on the floor of the House any bill which we submit — what it will be we do not know but we have to have testimony here, good reasons why.[13]

It is this type of hearing to which agency officials refer when they opine that the roughest hearing may be the most beneficial and that one cannot tell

---

[12] For a similar view, from the executive perspective, see remarks of Bryce N. Harlow to the Reserve Officers Association of the United States, February 5, 1960, as reprinted in *Congressional Record*, Daily Edition, February 8, 1960, p. 1972.

[13] Committee on Appropriations, *Hearings on State and Justice (U.S. Information Agency) Appropriations for 1958*, 85th Congress, 1st Session (Washington: U.S. Government Printing Office, 1957), p. 118.

from the surface questioning whether the underlying predispositions of the Committee members are hostile or friendly.[14]

Whether the hearing is viewed by the member as a genuine or a pseudo-adversary proceeding, what he does in the hearing is related to the decision he is predisposed to make anyway. Insofar as he is predisposed to reduce the agency estimates, he will seek to produce supporting evidence in the hearing. Insofar as he is predisposed to grant the requested increase, he will conduct the hearing so as to build up the case for that decision.

The least common self-image which Committee members display (but, still, one to which most of them do subscribe at one time or another) holds that they are making a public record which will promote justification for an increase in funds above and beyond what the agency requests. In such cases the hearing is viewed as an *ex parte proceeding*, in which the Committee member acts on behalf of the agencies against the budget-making hierarchy in the executive branch. Committee members begin by getting on the record just how much the original agency request was reduced by the Budget Bureau. The implication is that the original agency request represented its objective needs and that the agency has been forced to submit an insufficient estimate to the Committee. If they can, the Committee members will attempt to get on the record some admission by the agency official that the implication is correct. One subcommittee chairman explained,

> One of my stock questions is, "How much did you ask the Budget Bureau for?" . . . I have to dig it out of them in the hearings. Sometimes I have to ask a question four or five different ways to get the answer I think they ought to give. They are on the spot. They aren't supposed to say — and they are watched carefully. They read the hearings over in the Budget Bureau.

Committee members will tell the worried witnesses that, "When we ask you a question we expect a frank answer, regardless of limitations which are imposed upon you by your superiors."[15]

When the predispositions of the Committee coincide with important expectations of the agency, the incentive to yield is very great:

> RANKING MINORITY MEMBER: Could you use $300 thousand for this particular purpose for which you requested of the Budget Bureau $150 thousand

---

[14] As one agency executive said, "If you have a hard-headed hearing, where the congressmen ask pointed questions and bore in and bore in — that's when you'll get your increase. If you're going to get an increase, these congressmen are going to have to defend it in the Congress. And that's not easy to do. So they want to get everything in the record that they need to support you. They'll ask hard, pointed questions to make sure they can justify the increase."

[15] Committee on Appropriations, *Hearings on Department of Health, Education, and Welfare Appropriations for 1958*, 85th Congress, 1st Session (Washington: U.S. Government Printing Office, 1957), p. 741.

and which the Bureau of the Budget has submitted to us the amount of $120 thousand? Could not you use $300 thousand just as well?

AGENCY OFFICIAL: Well, I dislike to say we could not use it, although I am embarrassed by trying to defend a sum beyond what is in the approved budget.

RANKING MINORITY MEMBER: Why could you not use it?

AGENCY WITNESS: If I must answer it, I would say, "Yes."

RANKING MINORITY MEMBER: You could use it?

AGENCY OFFICIAL: I could use it.

. . . . .

SUBCOMMITTEE CHAIRMAN: We are thoroughly familiar . . . with the reticence you gentlemen have in coming up here and attempting to make statements that go beyond the action of the Budget Bureau; but after all, Congress initiated this program and set it in motion and the Congress is interested in this program's success and its extension. They are responsible to the people; the Bureau of the Budget is not. Now, we want to be sure, when we are implementing a program with money that Congress is definitely interested in and definitely demands some action in, that you get off that old horse of reticence here and tell this Congress exactly what [your agency] believes it can do in this field . . . we do not want you to violate any rule of ethics, regulations, orders, or anything else; nevertheless, [the ranking minority member's] interrogation was right down the alley of what this Committee is interested in.[16]

In the ex parte type of hearing, the typical gambits are the reverse of the genuine adversary hearing. For example, the naive broadside is of this variety: "Are you satisfied with your progress? I am not."[17] Instead of asking where they can absorb a cut, agency officials are encouraged to "blue-sky." "How would you spend another million dollars if it were granted to you for training?"[18] And the patient, dogged kind of interrogation is one in which the Committee member tries to extract from the agency official the confession that he needs more money than his estimate calls for:

SUBCOMMITTEE CHAIRMAN: Are you satisfied then with the progress you are making in building up [this bureau]?

DEPARTMENT SECRETARY: Yes. I feel we made good progress this last year, and I think that with this budget we have got here . . . I think it will make satisfactory progress.

SUBCOMMITTEE CHAIRMAN: It may be satisfactory but are you satisfied?

DEPARTMENT SECRETARY: I am going according to what [the bureau head] tells me, and I think you will find from his testimony that it is satisfactory.

[16] Committee on Appropriations, Hearings on Federal Security Administration Appropriations for 1948, op. cit., pp. 354–355.

[17] Committee on Appropriations, Hearings on Department of Health, Education, and Welfare Appropriations for 1958, op. cit., p. 35.

[18] Ibid., p. 369.

SUBCOMMITTEE CHAIRMAN: He can't say anything else. He is going to come up here and, of course, he isn't going to disagree with you, if he wants to stay on the job.

. . . . .

DEPARTMENT SECRETARY: I think he is going to show you we are making good progress. We are asking for about twenty per cent increase, which in view of the present budgetary situation —
SUBCOMMITTEE CHAIRMAN: I am just trying to find out if you think that is enough.
DEPARTMENT SECRETARY: I would say, in view of the general overall budget situation we are faced with —
SUBCOMMITTEE CHAIRMAN: I am not talking about the overall budget situation. I am talking about this —
DEPARTMENT SECRETARY: We have to take that into account.
SUBCOMMITTEE CHAIRMAN: I know.
DEPARTMENT SECRETARY: We can't disregard it; but compared with the progress that has been made for many, many years, I think we have made very good progress in the last two years.
SUBCOMMITTEE CHAIRMAN: Oh, there is no question about that, but I don't think it is enough. Do you think it is enough?
DEPARTMENT SECRETARY: I of course have to stick to the budget figures which we are presenting.[19]

Another characteristic of the ex parte hearing is for the Committee to call in nongovernmental experts to testify that the agencies in question need more money than their estimate called for. Since these witnesses operate under no bureaucratic restraint, they will freely accede to the Committee's leading questions and create a record favorable to Committee predispositions. This device has been a special favorite of the Subcommittee on the Health, Education, and Welfare Department, whose sympathy for ever-expanding programs has been discussed. Subcommittee Chairman John Fogarty regularly buttresses his predispositions with the testimony of eminent physicians. In 1963, for example, 43 physicians testified to the need for more money for the Public Health Service. Hearings before this subcommittee have long been of a predominantly ex parte character.

The function of appropriations hearings for the Committee member can be understood only by knowing his self-perceptions and his predispositions. Since these vary according to circumstance and personality, it seems likely that most hearings will fulfill each of the functions we have discussed in different combinations. Significantly, however, none of them emphasizes the agency expectation that the hearing should be devoted to programmatic discussion.

[19] *Ibid.*, p. 48.

Sampling for Information

In every kind of hearing, the Committee member encounters the same basic need for information. No matter what predetermined position he seeks to justify in the public record, he needs information with which to do it. Furthermore, although it is clear that the Committee does not behave as an impartial judge or jury in making its decisions, its members can be influenced by what goes on in the hearings. At the very least, members can have their predispositions re-enforced or weakened by the information their questions elicit. And the margin may be critical to their ultimate decision. Members acknowledge that much of their questioning is designed to test the validity of their own predispositions. And they are fully prepared to make marginal modifications as a result of what they hear. Moreover, they sometimes stumble quite inadvertently on information of which they had no prior knowledge. The hearing is, therefore, more than just a proceeding by which a public record is made to support member predispositions. As agency officials are fully aware, the script of the hearings is filled with uncertainties, and what does finally happen has important consequences for the fulfillment of their expectations.

Committee members, then, perceive the hearing as a place where they can find information to assist them in making knowledgeable decisions. They begin this search, however, with two assumptions. The first is that they cannot know or find out all there is to know about an agency's operation. And the second is that the agency witnesses who come before them are in possession of much greater technical information than they, the congressmen, possess. Working from these premises, the Committee member takes the initiative in the hearings and samples the universe of information. By conducting the hearing on his own grounds the congressman minimizes his relative disadvantage in information levels. But he still faces the problem of reducing the enormous, unmanageable technical complexity of agency programs to comprehensible and manageable size. He does this, as experienced agency executives recognize, by a process of sampling. Using bits of information which he possesses and comprehends, he interrogates the agency witness. From the answers he receives to his questions and from his impressions of the witness who answers them, he then extrapolates broader judgments about agency programs and performance. The Committee member does not try to know all there is to know about agency activity. He tries, however, to know some things and treats that which he knows as a representative sample of that which he does not know.

At the point of decision-making, he will use the various items in his sample as a basis for drawing inferences about agency activity. During the hearing, however, he will use each sample item as a kind of trace element which may lead him progressively deeper into agency activity. The sampling process, in this sense, becomes an inductive process whereby the Committee member moves, by successive testing of the witness, from relatively specific bits of information toward increasingly general judgments. "The way I look at the appropriations process," said one member, "you have to get into these nit-picking things if you want to branch out into the bigger areas. They give you leads." A second member spelled out the process in greater detail:

> You just learn these things after you've been here. There are some standard questions. How many new people do you want? What do you want them for? How many stenographers do you want, or desks or wastebaskets? That fellow better be able to snap those things right off or he's in trouble. If he knows them you may be satisfied with the program and move on. But if he hesitates the least little bit, you keep going. If he can't pass that first test you know he doesn't know what he's talking about. He hasn't figured it closely enough. And you keep pushing him and make him justify it. If he can't, you tell him to come back tomorrow.

By sampling for information the Committee member seeks to reduce his area of uncertainty. (On the other hand, agency officials' efforts to reduce their sense of uncertainty revolve around attempts to predict what sample items their subcommittee is likely to use.) Given the necessity of sampling, from the Committee member's point of view, it becomes clear why the hearings become fragmented and frequently disappoint agency officials. The use of trace elements may be quite incompatible with the emphasis on program so desired by the agencies.

(A) EXAMINING BUDGET INCREMENTS

One sample item (which, incidentally, does not displease agency officials) used by the Committee is the incremental increase (or decrease) in each budget. Committee questioning frequently begins by asking detailed justifications for each item for which the agency is requesting an increase over the previous year. These increases will have been singled out and underscored in the justification books sent earlier by the agency to the Committee. Committee members like to hear it for themselves, however, so that they can probe further should their interest be captured. Often their probes take the form of comparing the requested increment with the increment granted in the previous year. Members like to move back and forth from the present request to the previous year's appropriation. This gives them some clue to the rate and the content of program expansion — both proposed and actual. "The past is prologue. Look to the past. That's what I do. I always check this year's testimony against last year's testimony," said one subcommittee chairman in discussing his rules of thumb. Committee members help answer their own favorite question, "What do you want this new money for?" by asking a second question, "What did you do with the money we gave you last year?"

Satisfactory answers given to these questions may suffice as the agency's defense of its entire program. If, however, the agency's defense of its incremental increases proves unsatisfactory to the Committee, it will probe further, and the submerged segment of the agency's budgetary iceberg may come under scrutiny. The Committee may even draw broad conclusions from the absence of incremental requests, as in the following case:

> SUBCOMMITTEE CHAIRMAN: Last year you came into this Committee with the same amount you had prior, not a penny less not a penny more, showing a status quo, that you are not doing a thing down there. That is in the hearings. I gave you a warning. You were right to the penny and were the last year and the year prior. . . . I was a little peeved that for two straight years you came in for the same amount to the penny. One would think you did nothing but open up the office in the morning and go back to the same old stand again.[20]

On the whole, Committee concentration on increments is highly satisfactory to the agency since it leaves the "base" largely unexamined.

One common incremental trace element which influences Committee decisions is evidence that money appropriated in the previous year was used for purposes not authorized by the Committee. Appropriations hearings are replete with dialogues of this variety:

> SUBCOMMITTEE CHAIRMAN: Let us get down to specific answers. You have gone all around the mulberry bush. Did you or did you not transfer from "Printing and Reproduction" $40 thousand for the payment of salaries?
> AGENCY OFFICIAL: Not knowingly, sir.
>
> . . . . .
>
> SUBCOMMITTEE CHAIRMAN: You came in and you gave us a set of hard figures and said, "This is what we want and this is what we are going to do with it." Now I understand, instead of following what you told us you were going to do, you have made other adjustments and juggled funds to suit your own purposes rather than doing what you told us you were going to do. Is that true?
> AGENCY OFFICIAL: I would say it was not with that intent at all.
> SUBCOMMITTEE CHAIRMAN: Let us leave out the intent. No one ever intends wrong; but did you do that?
> AGENCY OFFICIAL: The figures have been changed from the purpose for which we originally estimated, to some extent; yes, sir, they have.[21]

[20] Committee on Appropriations, *Hearings on Department of Interior Appropriations for 1958*, 85th Congress, 1st Session (Washington: U.S. Government Printing Office, 1957), pp. 263–264.

[21] Committee on Appropriations, *Hearings on Department of Commerce Appropriations for 1958*, 85th Congress, 1st Session (Washington: U.S. Government Printing Office, 1957), pp. 90–91. See also, *ibid.*, pp. 506–510.

Similarly, members may turn up evidence that an agency has not followed the directives of last year's Committee report:

SUBCOMMITTEE CHAIRMAN: Is this one instance where you completely ignored the recommendations in the House reports?
AGENCY OFFICIAL: No, sir, it is not.
SUBCOMMITTEE CHAIRMAN: You do not call that ignoring it?
AGENCY OFFICIAL: No, sir, I do not.
SUBCOMMITTEE CHAIRMAN: It says, "The Committee has specifically denied the $5 million for the incentive investment fund . . . ," and you went ahead and started the program did you not?
AGENCY OFFICIAL: Yes, sir.
SUBCOMMITTEE CHAIRMAN: That is all I want to know. I do not need anything more.[22]

If the agency finds itself distressed by Committee directives, it is expected to consult with the subcommittee chairman and the ranking minority member informally and seek permission to reprogram. If it has not, its failure adds to Committee displeasure. Where disobedience is uncovered, the Committee's most elemental suspicions of executive agencies may be aroused. "I would like to know what the Agency's attitude is. Do you give a darn about this Committee or not? . . . I have reached the end of the rope as far as being patient."[23] Committee confidence will be shaken, and other agency programs may be put in serious jeopardy.

When veteran Committee members actually go about trying to locate soft spots in a budget request, they sample in areas which experience has proved useful in judging agency performance. In some agencies, the key is the "work load": how many patents have been processed, how many violators of a certain law have been found, how many prisoners are in the prisons, etc. Everything that an agency wants may be measured by the Committee in some time-tested proportion to a hard, quantifiable figure representing "work load." In such cases "there's no mumbo jumbo about the process," declared one member optimistically. "Some of it comes as close to mathematics as you can get. You can take a slide rule, providing you know the standard specifications of the agency, and figure out almost exactly what they need."

In other cases the key informational short cut involves personnel. Budgets are considered in terms of the number of new personnel being asked for, and the attention of the hearing may be concentrated on this. "Why do you need this many new positions?" "How many new positions did you add last year?" "What will they do?" "How many new supergrades [top level

[22] Committee on Appropriations, *Hearings on Mutual Security Appropriations for 1961*, 86th Congress, 2nd Session (Washington: U.S. Government Printing Office, 1960), p. 2177.

[23] Committee on Appropriations, *Hearings on State and Justice (U.S. Information Agency) Appropriations for 1958, op. cit.*, p. 186.

personnel] are you asking for?" "What proportion of your personnel are in Washington and what proportion are out in the field?" Answers to these questions may be translated into much broader programmatic conclusions by those who ask them. Similarly, answers given to questions about the number and the cost of new automobiles, the number and cost of desks and waste-baskets, the size of travel allowances, the size of per diem payments, or the size of the public relations budget may give the Committee member the informational handle he needs to take hold of a more complex problem. Committee objections to program-oriented budgetary forms have rested in part on its preference for a budget in which personnel items, travel items, equipment items, etc., are separated out conveniently for its scrutiny.[24] It has considered these object classification budgets easier to comprehend (and easier to cut) than performance budgets.

(B) FOLLOWING THE LAW OF THE FAMILIAR

C. Northcote Parkinson enshrined the logic of the sampling process in his "Law of Triviality": "The time spent on any item of the agenda will be in inverse proportion to the sum [of money] involved."[25] And the operation of the law can be easily verified in any appropriations hearing. The law might better be recast as the "Law of the Familiar." Committee members discuss seemingly trivial items because the items are familiar and, hence, comprehensible. And members discuss them for the purpose of drawing much broader conclusions. They may, if they find waste in some familiar areas, test their findings in increasingly broader areas. Or they may draw conclusions directly about overall agency inefficiency. But, given their informational problem, the need to start with comprehensible and familiar items is overwhelming. An experienced member of the Subcommittee on Defense said, "How can you understand what a billion dollars is or five billion dollars? I can't imagine that much money. So I just think of a five dollar bill and then I add zero, zero, zero, zero, zero, zero, zero, zero, zero." The utility of familiar sample items in making judgments about agency budgets explains why Committee members place so much emphasis on agency performance in their own states or districts. It explains why they devote so much attention in the hearings to a letter from a constituent or to something they saw personally on a trip to the agency's field offices:

> The Fish and Wildlife Service has during the past year shown a stubborn and uncompromising attitude in its relations with Minnesota sportsmen. Attempts made by Minnesotans to secure consideration of their complaints . . .

[24] Committee on Appropriations, *Hearings on Justice Department Appropriations for 1951*, 81st Congress, 2nd Session (Washington: U.S. Government Printing Office, 1950), p. 347.

[25] C. Northcote Parkinson, *Parkinson's Law* (Boston: Little, Brown and Co., 1957), p. 24 and all of Chapter 3.

have been ignored or brushed aside. It is time to analyze a service such as this. Let us serve notice upon this bureau that it cannot secure all the funds it wants from the Congress without giving an account of its stewardship to the people we represent.[26]

If something is wrong in the district, or with the treatment of a constituent, or in the place where the congressman traveled, he will pursue it as evidence that something is wrong in the agency — until witnesses can demonstrate otherwise.

(C) EVALUATING THE ADMINISTRATOR

Perhaps the most commonly used sample item is the Committee member's reaction to the agency head and to his presentation. No function of the hearings is more important from the legislator's point of view than the opportunity they give him to size up the administrator. Of course, the sizing-up process goes on the year round, year in and year out, between veteran Committee members and veteran administrators; but the hearings (as agency heads acknowledge) represent the most important testing time. Elective politicians may yield to others in matters of technical competence but they defer to no one in their ability to "size up" a fellow human being. They believe that they can tell a lot about a man by the "impression" he makes — by the firmness of his handshake, the look in his eye, the authority in his voice, the clothes that he wears, the idiom in which he speaks. And they believe, of course, that they can size up a man by the answers he gives to their questions. The small Committee hearing rooms, where interrogator and witness face each other only a few feet away across the hearing table give the legislators their best opportunity. They are in familiar home territory. The initiative is theirs. So, too, is the chance to manipulate uncertainty. Should it suit their purposes, they can take the hearing "off the record." For all the reasons that agency officials express concern over the confrontation, Committee members find it a congenial testing place. And there they test the agency's chief executive as a means of testing the agency. "You learn ways to evaluate an administrator," said one subcommittee chairman, "whether he's doing a good job or just trying to build up — by the way he answers questions. . . . And," he continued, "you can evaluate an agency or tell whether it is doing a good job by the way its case is presented."

The Committee members' self-image emphasizes the dedicated, hard-working master of detail. They react most favorably to the administrator who reflects by his words and by less tangible cues a mirror image of themselves. They react most unfavorably to agency officials in whom they can find few of their own criteria for self-evaluation. A member of the subcommittee which

---

[26] 97 *Congressional Record*, p. 4735.

for years made deep reductions in the budget for the United States Information Agency commented on one contributing factor in that series of decisions: "A lot of these people are artists. Congress is used to dealing with executives and businessmen. These people are motion-picture producers, writers, and a lot of them are — well, they are creeps."

All other things being equal, Committee members establish their most sympathetic rapport with an administrator who has mastered the details of his agency's operation and who gives evidence that he is the executive force within the agency:

> Some of these people have a vast knowledge of their subject. When you see that, you say that you've got to be careful with his budget, because he's doing a good job. When a man comes along and makes a presentation like this he's sure to find some friends within the Committee.

A subcommittee chairman gave thumbnail sketches of the agency heads under his jurisdiction: "He is a good scientist and a good administrator." "He's an old fogey, but he made some changes." "He's no good. He's just a Chamber of Commerce, sky's the limit guy. So we give him a rough time." "He won't delegate. He wants to touch every piece of paper." "He's old, but he delegates to a group of good young men." Doubtless, these impressions have been conveyed in the hearing room; doubtless, too, they carry considerable weight.

One clue to the administrator's competence is the number of subordinates he brings with him to the hearing room and the proportion of the questions he answers by himself. An administrator who delegates too large a proportion of Committee questions to his phalanx of experts is suspected of not "knowing his job" or not being "on top of his job":

> Some men come up here and don't know what their people are doing. They haven't done their lessons. They read a little statement and then can't answer any questions. They have to ask other people to answer their questions for them. That doesn't make a good impression with the Committee members.

The mere act of bringing a coterie of subalterns into the hearing room makes a bad impression on the Committee. To begin with, the battery of experts reminds the Committee of its own informational disadvantages. And second, it exposes an administrator to the Committee's suspicion that he is avoiding a "fair" confrontation with the Committee. Members respect any administrator who eschews, as it were, his bureaucratic advantages and engages in a face-to-face, man-to-man encounter with them. Again, the Committee members' self-image guides their evaluation of the administrator.

Committee members view themselves as frugal guardians of the tax-

338

payers' money, and they react favorably to any administrator who projects this aspect of their self-image. In the Committee's view, economical administration is good administration. They search for evidence of the administrator's concern for saving money. They may, for instance, inquire into his background for evidence of managerial abilities. Or they may ask him bluntly whether "you personally have ever tried to meet a payroll budget on your own as a businessman?"[27] A favorite sampling element is the line item involving the administrator's own office. Since this item is a familiar and manageable one, consisting not of complex programs but of "salaries and expenses," Committee members find it an especially convenient clue. A well-worn Committee theme is that "economy begins at home" — in the administrator's own office budget, that is.[28] Burgeoning requests in that area may be taken as evidence of a spendthrift administrator.

The Committee's judgment of an administrator may be registered in its treatment of the budget request for his office. A subcommittee chairman, for example, explained favorable action on the funds for the office of Agriculture Secretary Clinton Anderson:

> I tried to err on the side of generosity. The Secretary was once a very distinguished member of this body; in fact for 10 years. The Secretary once served as a member of the Committee on Appropriations, and we count him not only as a good public servant, but as a friend.[29]

By contrast, administrators blessed with no such happy credentials may receive less friendly consideration. A chairman of another subcommittee recalled,

> Whenever we got down to the office of the Secretary or the [Federal Security] Administrator, as it was called then, when Oscar Ewing was the Administrator, there was not much I could do about it because the Republicans and the Democrats on the subcommittee for 4 years did not have much use for Oscar Ewing and they just indiscriminately cut every year. It was an across-the-board cut. If it was a 15 per cent cut, some might say 20 per cent, and then, "Oh, let's make it a 25 per cent cut." That was the way it went for 4 or 5 years. His office was cut on an average of 20 to 25 per cent because of a clash of personalities, and because they did not like the way Oscar Ewing ran the office.[30]

[27] Committee on Appropriations, *Hearings on Federal Security Appropriations for 1948, op. cit.*, p. 187.

[28] Committee on Appropriations, *Hearings on Department of Commerce Appropriations for 1958, op. cit.*, p. 526; Committee on Appropriations, *Hearings on the 1958 Budget*, 85th Congress, 1st Session (Washington: U.S. Government Printing Office, 1957), pp. 66, 101, 156; 93 *Congressional Record*, p. 5880.

[29] 93 *Congressional Record*, p. 5960. See also remarks of Representative Plumley, 94 *Congressional Record*, p. 3101.

[30] 99 *Congressional Record*, p. 5332. See also remarks of Representative Williams, 97 *Congressional Record*, p. 4086.

When an agency spends less than it received and returns its surplus to the Treasury at the end of the year, this action is taken as evidence of economical administration:

> If one man is a good administrator and turns back money he didn't use, that makes a good impression. We have two of those cases from last year. If you don't reward him for turning back money and cut him hard the next year instead, he'll never do it again. And we want to encourage that. Sometimes, we'll let a budget request slide right through without touching it just for that reason. We'll keep an eye on him, of course, but we want to give recognition to good administration like that.

Committee members behave in this fashion, it needs to be added, only if they have some confidence in the administrator to begin with. If they do not, they are likely to seize upon the surplus as evidence that they did not cut deeply enough the year before. As a case in point, one subcommittee chairman discussed the case of an agency of which he was already deeply suspicious:

> Last year we cut them pretty close. But just today while I was in subcommittee hearings, a note was passed to me saying that [the agency head] had $23,500 left over and wanted my O.K. to air-condition the first two floors of the administration building. We thought we cut them pretty close, but we didn't get it all.

The Committee's double standard was spelled out by the staff assistant to a veteran Committee member:

> If the subcommittee has trust in an administrator, they may make an understanding across the table that doesn't appear in the record at all. They may say, "We'll give you so much with the understanding that if you don't need it you'll return it to the Treasury." They'll give him all the money he wants. If they don't have confidence in him, they'll give him a cut and say, "If you need more, come back and ask for a supplemental and we'll see."

Confidence begets confidence for the administrator.

In approaching the technically complex, rapidly fluctuating world of the bureaucracy, person-to-person relations seem to furnish a reliable point of reference for the congressman. Personal virtues are stable and recognizable whereas agency virtues may not be. As agency officials recognize, prime among the virtues which count are an essential honesty and frankness. One of the Committee's influential leaders expressed the Committee's emphasis on the face-to-face virtues in this revealing analogy:

> Would your wife buy groceries from a man she didn't like even if she could save a little money? No. You might ask her why she didn't trade at [the supermarket] instead of down at the corner and she'd say, "I don't like those people. I got some bad groceries once." Well, it's just the same with us. Some administrators come over here and lie to us. We cut them just to show them they can't do that.

340

By simplifying his task to a personal assessment, the Committee member seeks to reduce his area of uncertainty. Where the assessment is favorable, he will trust the administrator and act on that more certain basis. The agencies, for their part, would prefer that Committee confidence be invested in a program. But, while the Committee does place a good deal of trust in programs, it will be more comfortable about its budgetary decision if it can add to that trust a personal confidence in the individual administrator.

Seeking Political Intelligence

Of minor importance, in the eyes of Committee members, is the political intelligence which comes from the testimony of interested congressmen and clientele groups. Members, of course, concern themselves mightily with differentials in the nature and intensity of support (or opposition) for the programs for which they appropriate. House member demands, however, are communicated through more effective channels than an appropriations hearing. And the same is true for the demands of clientele groups. For one thing, informal communication outside the hearing is infinitely more effective. So, too, in terms of formal communication is testimony made at the time of program authorization. The political intelligence concerning support and opposition which members take in from outside witnesses at public hearings amounts to very little over and above that which they take in privately.

On the whole, the Committee acts in ways that discourage both outside interest and outside witnesses. Information about the scheduling of hearings is not readily available. Outside witnesses are not normally solicited. All hearings are, of course, in executive session, and no witness can listen to the testimony of another witness. Until the printed hearings are made public at some time before floor debate, no outside group can know what the Committee's predispositions are or what it is that must be fought for or against. To the degree that outside witnesses appear, Committee members feel they will be put under that much more pressure to increase appropriations. The more they can keep outside witnesses at arm's length, the easier will be their pursuit of budget-cutting goals. The appropriations testimony of such witnesses is usually held to a reading of prepared statements. Committee members generally do not (except when making a case in an ex parte hearing) engage outside witnesses in questions and answers. Despite these discouragements, House members and clientele groups are allowed to testify, and they do so in varying numbers. Their testimony lends legitimacy to subsequent decisions. And, from their testimony, Committee members may find bits of information which enlighten, evidence to support their predispositions, or, perhaps, an increment of political intelligence.

Table 7.1 lists the number of agency and nonagency witnesses who put in an official appearance (were acknowledged in the body of the hearings) be-

TABLE 7.1

RATIO OF OUTSIDE WITNESSES TO AGENCY WITNESSES IN
APPROPRIATIONS HEARINGS: HOUSE COMMITTEE, 1963

Appropriation Bill	No. of Pages of Testimony	No. of Agency Witnesses Appearing	No. of Outside Witnesses Appearing	Ratio of Outside Witnesses to Agency Witnesses
Public Works	5,903	122	554 (172)[a]	4.54
Agriculture	3,905	137	257 (59)	1.88
District of Columbia	1,271	112	87 (4)	.78
Labor-HEW	4,246	255	116 (10)	.45
Interior	1,811	162	65 (26)	.40
Defense	4,627	233	39 (8)	.17
Foreign Operations	3,849	155	15 (0)	.10
State, Justice, Commerce	4,990	260	22 (3)	.09
Independent Offices	4,051	410	28 (8)	.07
Post Office–Treasury	1,325	128	5 (2)	.04
Legislative	367	36[b]	1 (1)	.03
Military Construction	2,239	165	2 (2)	.01
Totals	38,584	2,175	1,191 (295)	.55

[a] Figures in parentheses indicate number of House members who appeared.
[b] Witnesses here are legislative branch employees.

fore the 12 Appropriations Committee subcommittees in 1963. Not all of them actually testified, though a sizable proportion did, but their presence can be taken as a rough measure of their interest.[31] Table 7.1 is constructed in such a way as to call attention to the ratio of agency to nonagency witnesses. And it highlights the difficulty of generalizing about the importance of House member and clientele group activity in the hearings.

The most important revelation of Table 7.1 is the fact that agency witnesses outnumber nonagency witnesses by almost 2 to 1. This overall average ratio conceals the fact that for 9 of the 12 subcommittees the proportion is even more heavily in favor of agency witnesses and that a median ratio for the 12 subcommittees would be about 9 agency witnesses to 1 outside witness. Though comparative figures are not available, the supposition is that this ratio is the exact reverse of what it would be for hearings before the substantive legislative committees. The point is that clientele groups are more active in the authorizing than in the appropriating process. This seems

[31] It is possible to calculate what proportion of the witnesses who appeared actually gave testimony. But that task was considered too time-consuming. The assumption of Table 7.1 is that the ratio of those who appeared to those who testified is fairly constant across categories of witnesses and subcommittees.

true in terms of their formal activity and probably holds for their informal activity as well. The stakes are greatest when the program is being voted up or down. When the money is being allocated, the agency is left to carry a larger share of the load. Appropriations Committee members prefer to view the hearing this way — as a matter between themselves and the agency officials. Said one veteran member, "Budget and appropriations are operations in support of the government. It's between the legislators and the administrators, and the public isn't involved — well, they're involved indirectly but not directly."

In addition to the overall pattern, Table 7.1 reveals enormous differences in the proportion of outside witnesses appearing in appropriations hearings. As one might expect, the agencies on whose behalf outside witnesses are most active are those whose services are directly constituency-oriented (i.e., Public Works, Agriculture, and Interior) or those whose clientele groups have been actively encouraged by the subcommittee in the first place (i.e., Labor-HEW). Furthermore, these agencies draw the strongest expressions of House member support. Public Works figures indicate the great concern of Members for their pet projects. The District of Columbia ratio is accounted for by the fact that the Committee is, in effect, the local, municipal finance board for these outside groups. Conversely, agencies whose programs are not notably constituency-oriented tend to attract smaller representations of clientele groups and congressmen. Committee members are correct in their belief that people who come to testify come in support of spending and not budget reduction.

The Committee, it seems, will take in more political intelligence through some hearings than through others. In part, this difference is a function of clientele and constituency-oriented versus nonclientele and nonconstituency-oriented subject matter. The difference also appears to be one of subcommittee practice or subcommittee-agency agreement. The Military Construction Appropriation Bill is almost as much constituency-oriented (said one Member, "It's all pork") as the Public Works Bill. Yet the ratios of nonagency witnesses for these hearings are diametrically opposite. A similar though less strong statement could be made about the Defense Department and Independent Offices bills — each of which contains constituency-oriented pet projects. Yet, in these cases, the agency carries the ball formally, and nonagency people act informally. The pattern probably reflects some lack of clientele group organization, an estimate by congressmen of the relative unimportance of formal appearances, the proved ability of the agency to succeed, and the dampening efforts of the subcommittee involved. Table 7.1 reveals something of the Committee's intake of political intelligence — but by no means all.

ADAPTATION: SELF-CONFIDENCE
AND SELF-DOUBTS

A Committee veteran summarized the Committee's own view of its problem in dealing with the agencies when he said in a meeting of the full Committee,

> There is not a man in this room who would deny that appropriated funds are spent every day which need not have been spent. There is hardly a witness who appears before us but what would admit that this is true. The problem is to anticipate waste and slippage in advance and to intelligently reduce appropriations to correct those things before they happen.[32]

The difficulty in reducing budget estimates is to do so "intelligently." This is the Committee's problem of adaptation.

As members view it, the problem of intelligence is primarily one of combining information and experience in making judgments. They believe that they possess a mass of information — "more bullets than we can ever shoot" — and a wealth of experience in dealing with the agencies for which they appropriate. No member would claim that the problem of intelligent action is easily solved. But most would agree with the overall verdict of the subcommittee chairman who concluded, "The members of the Committee on Appropriations by and large know where the soft places are in the budget requests and in the appropriations measures. They usually, and I may say wisely and intelligently, cut the places that need cutting."[33] Other Committee leaders echoed a similar theme:

> We do as good a job as a group of human beings can do . . . after you sit on the Committee for fifteen years, you know these men and their programs. You become experts on them. The thing just flows along. It gets into a pattern. Believe it or not, we do a pretty good job.

> After you've been here and you've been through the budget before, you know the agencies and you know where to look [for soft spots].

> After you've been on the Committee for a number of years, you get a fifth sense about these things.

> Oh, you just feel it after a while and you've got lots of precedents to go by. We say, "Well, we did this in such and such a case, so why the hell shouldn't we do it now?"

> If it's a program that's been going for a while you can come pretty close. If it's a new program, then you just have the best educated guess you can.

The dominant feeling is one of self-confidence.

[32] Committee on Appropriations, *Hearings on the 1958 Budget, op. cit.*, p. 80.
[33] 104 *Congressional Record*, p. 1998.

Committee members readily acknowledge, however, that necessarily their information is imperfect and their experience is fallible. Therefore, when they make decisions, "there is still a big element of guesswork involved . . . none of us knows enough about it to always be certain we are right in our conclusions."[34] However much information they collect, they can never be sure they have the relevant information with which to make the most knowledgeable decision. "It's not a scientific process. It can't be." "How can you tell whether an agency needs $5.7 million or $5.6 million? Who knows?" They do not sell their decisions to the House as *the* right decisions:

> I do not want to say to the House that this is an exact business we run. Five of us on the Appropriations Committee for agriculture sat for more than two and a half months. We heard witnesses. We went into all these sundry and various programs from A to Z. But you cannot say point-blank that they should have this or that amount, you just have to use your best judgment.[35]

> The bill before you . . . was arrived at as a result of a blending of our collective knowledge of what we have learned from past experience, liberally spiced with some guesswork, some old-fashioned horse sense, and some hunch.[36]

Though their major theme is one of confidence in their own experience, guesswork, horse sense, and hunch, Committee members obviously carry a component of uncertainty to their decision-making activity.

A Committee member's self-confidence is re-enforced by the perception that, relatively, he knows a great deal more about the agencies for which he appropriates than other members of the House — indeed, more than the entire Congress. If other House members must rely upon his intelligence — then he feels that he does a pretty good job and he certainly merits their support. A Committee member's self-confidence is weakened, on the other hand, by the perception that, relatively, he knows a great deal less about the agencies for which he appropriates than do agency officials themselves. Agency officials are perceived as men who spend all of their time immersed in the programs about which they come to testify. By comparison, not even the most senior Committee member with the safest of congressional districts and with the smoothest running office believes that he can give even approximately equal time to the scrutiny of agency behavior. "Just think of all the water in that defense bill. We ought to go into every line item, but we just don't have the time." This is a commonly heard lament. It is accompanied by the complaint

---

[34] Committee on Appropriations, *Hearings on the 1958 Budget, op. cit.,* pp. 78–80.
[35] 96 *Congressional Record,* p. 6816.
[36] *Congressional Record,* Daily Edition, June 7, 1961, p. 8981. See also the exchange between Representatives Frelinghuysen and Rooney, 101 *Congressional Record,* p. 4472.

that "the representatives from the executive branch . . . come up here and have their stories so well in hand that you cannot out-argue them."[37] The Committee members' belief that they are handicapped by the informational superiority of the agencies is a source of self-doubt.

The Committee's perception that it lacks information — absolutely and relatively — has some direct consequences for Committee behavior. The most obvious is the Committee reliance on the straight percentage, across-the-board method of budget reduction, a method which would be less appealing, perhaps, if the Committee had sufficiently discrete knowledge of each and every budgetary item. Basing its decision on certain trace elements, for example, the Committee may settle on one general rather than several specific reductions. Two senior members of the defense subcommittee explained:

> This government is so big I cannot keep up with all its facets. I do not know whether anybody can. However what I am thinking is, you have to do some arbitrary and what appears to be meat-axe operations in the executive branch if you are going to cut expenses in my opinion . . . if we are being frank about it, we have made many arbitrary decisions in these military budgets.[38]

> More often than not it's an arbitrary cut — we look at what they ask for and we say they've got too much money. We look at what they got last year and we say what the hell do they want with so much money. Then we give them halfway between what they ask for and what they got last year.

Committee members do not equate "arbitrary" action with unintelligent action. They may feel that their reasons for cutting are good and sufficient, but in the absence of a certain range of technical information they should move cautiously in applying it. And, it might be added, agency officials may view a meat-axe cut as a relatively intelligent one — in the sense that it leaves them free to use their own judgment in applying the cut in any way they see fit. From time to time, the Committee has added blanket provisions to appropriation bills. The most popular of these was the so-called Jensen amendment of the early 1950's which provided that (with certain exceptions) only three out of every four vacant positions could be filled until such time as the personnel of the department was reduced by ten per cent of its current number of employees.[39]

Committee self-doubt concerning the adequacy of their information may also nourish attitudes of inferiority and defeatism. "You get drunk trying to follow the figures from bureau to bureau."

---

[37] Committee on Appropriations, *Hearings on the 1958 Budget, op. cit., p.*36.
[38] *Ibid.*, p. 36.
[39] For the text of a typical Jensen amendment, see 98 *Congressional Record*, p. 6720.

346

These men from the departments that line up across the table from us —
there are generally from six to a dozen — are schooled in the art of justifying their requests. They have spent years at it. And we are so busy. We just
do not have time to go down and inform ourselves. We ask them as many
questions as possible in order to have an idea of how they plan to carry on.
But in the end, we appropriate blindly.[40]

They come in here with their portfolios — with every expert they can get
hold of. Just look at all the people they bring in. And then outside the
hearing room they've got five people sitting with suitcases full of materials.
We are babes in the woods. We have no experts and not enough investigators.

Members do not express this sense of impotence very often — least of all the
experienced ones. The two comments just given are from Committee newcomers. Both, typically, are spoken in the context of an argument for a larger
Committee staff — a demand more frequently heard among the Committee's
inexperienced young than among its experienced senior members. The Committee's sense of information inferiority, however, is sufficiently widespread so
that agency officials are well advised when they warn their witnesses not to
talk down to the Committee.

Any agency action which can be interpreted as registering superiority may
produce hostility and an overly aggressive response on the part of the Committee. Members of the State Department Subcommittee satirize in private
the coterie of prep school, ivy league witnesses who file into the hearing room
all wearing custom-tailored dark suits and all carrying attaché cases. And it is
certain that the State Department does itself no good by conveying this impression of superiority. Something of the same element may help to produce
the following aggressive reaction to the rather cosmopolitan group of witnesses
who testify on the foreign aid bill:

When you're faced with arrogance, and some of them are arrogant, when
they don't know half the time what they're talking about, when they try to
conceal mistakes . . . damn it, you have to be tough.[41]

A subcommittee chairman reported what happened to an agency whose officials tried to out-argue him. "We gave them a good big cut — twenty-three
per cent. I didn't even look at the budget. I was so disgusted, I threw it in the
drawer and told my clerk I didn't want to see it again." Self-doubt is the minor
theme when members assess their competence. If, however, their latent sense

[40] Joint Committee on the Organization of Congress, *Hearings on the Organization
of Congress*, 79th Congress, 1st Session (Washington: U.S. Government Printing Office,
1945), p. 202. See also the remarks of Representative Clevenger, 96 *Congressional Record*,
p. 4950.
[41] *Newsweek*, September 10, 1962, p. 43.

of inferiority is activated by agency officials, the Committee reaction may prove costly. The possibility adds still another imperative to the agency's effort to cultivate the confidence of Appropriations Committee members.

CONCLUSION

The House Appropriations Committee–executive agency relationship is characterized on the one hand by conflict and uncertainty; it is characterized on the other by a substantial agreement on what should be done and is being done to minimize conflict and uncertainty and, hence, to keep the relationship reasonably stable.

The sources of conflict lie in the difference between the program-oriented goals of the agencies and the combination of economy-oversight goals of the Committee. The agencies want the Committee to think in broad and positive terms about supporting programs. The Committee's own view of its goals leads it to think in dominantly particular and negative terms about reducing unnecessary expenditures. The existence of conflict helps to promote uncertainty. And the sources of that uncertainty lie in the difference in the political worlds inhabited by the nonelected executive and the elected Representative. The agency official cannot be sure what motivations and interests will move the Committee member; the Committee member cannot be sure whether he possesses the relevant information with which to make intelligent decisions. Since neither group is likely to relinquish its goals, and since the worlds each lives in are not likely to merge, conflict and uncertainty cannot be eliminated from the relationship.

Both groups, however, want to stabilize the relationship — want, that is, to keep conflict and uncertainty to a tolerable and predictable level — because it is in their interest to do so. For the agency, a stable relationship is an aid to program planning and implementation. For the Committee, a stable relationship is an aid to adaptation and survival — to its continued ability, that is, to meet House member and Committee member desires. Both groups expend a substantial proportion of their resources in attempts to minimize conflict and reduce uncertainty — the agencies somewhat more, perhaps, than the Committee since the sanctions running from the Committee to the agency are more immediately and directly threatening than those running the other way. Agency executives prepare meticulously for the hearings, conduct themselves in the hearings, and arrange for informal communication in ways they deem appropriate to Committee member motives and interests. Committee personnel collect information — in the hearings and out — and use alternative kinds of information to sample agency activity in ways they deem appropriate to intelligent decision-making. Each acts while keeping one eye on the problem of maintaining stable relationships.

Such success as they have had depends heavily on the fact that mutual concern plus repeated exposure to one another has given each a fairly accurate perception of the other. Each knows reasonably well how the other will, in fact, behave — even if they would wish it otherwise — and has the ability to adjust to realities. In some cases, the adjustment results in a mutually beneficial pattern of behavior. Most important, the incremental approach of the Committee helps the agency meet its program goals while simultaneously serving the Committee as a key sample item. In other cases, the adjustment results in a mutually accepted decision as to the kind of behavior necessary to maintain stability. Above all, both groups recognize the basic need to win and retain the confidence of the other. And they act, wherever possible, to promote it. Both groups believe that mutual confidence will keep conflict and uncertainty within tolerable and predictable limits.

The Committee-agency relationship has achieved sufficient stability so that a general pattern of expectations, images, and behavior can be described. But relationships between specific agencies and specific appropriations subcommittees may vary a great deal from one year to the next. An attempt has been made in Chapters Six and Seven to generalize while giving some idea of the range of possible relationships. It has been done without reference, however, to the content — either general or specific — of the Committee's appropriations decisions. For the agency, these decisions are the acid test of its relationship with the Committee. For the Committee, they are the most tangible evidence of its attempt to meet the variety of expectations pressed upon it from the agency — and elsewhere. The Committee's decisions are the subject of Chapter Eight.

The House Committee's Decisions
I: Patterns and Determinants

THE ANALYSIS OF COMMITTEE DECISIONS

The important results of Appropriations Committee–executive agency inter-action are the Committee's decisions concerning the agency's request for money. Through its decisions, the Committee also adapts to the expectations of the parent chamber. And, through its decisions, the Committee makes its unique contribution to the sum total of congressional output. We have de-scribed the kinds of decisions which House members, Committee members, and agency officials want the Committee to make. We have described the structure by which the decisions are made. And we have described a variety of internal and external relationships which affect the making of Committee de-cisions. The question now arises: What kinds of decisions does the Commit-tee make? Is it possible to generalize about the substance of Committee decisions — to add to our generalizations about how they are made some generalizations about what they are? The answer is that the dollars and cents nature of appropriations decisions does make it possible to generalize, very tentatively, about Appropriations Committee decisions. The explication and explanation of some patterns is the subject of this chapter.

At the outset, certain limitations should be made clear, and they should be remembered by the reader throughout. In the first place, only one kind of Committee decision will be examined — namely, that decision which is ex-pressed in a dollars and cents appropriation. A quick comparison between the sparse, dominantly quantitative language of an appropriation bill and the expanded, more qualitative commentary of a Committee report makes it perfectly clear that many explicit decisions of the Committee are not revealed in the dollars and cents figures. And, given the scope of informal communication between Committee and agency, it is also clear that many other Committee decisions will be hidden from public view entirely. Statutory dollars and cents decisions are supplemented and qualified by a broad range of nonstatutory decisions.

In the second place, dollars and cents figures can be compared only at the obvious cost of losing relevant information about contextual differences. The same dollars and cents figure may be subject to quite different interpretations given contextual differences. For instance, all dollars and cents appropriations figures are assumed to represent the Committee's real preferences in dealing with the agencies. As a matter of fact, we know that some Committee decisions are partly tactical decisions, made in anticipation of Senate or conference committee action. (For instance, the House sometimes grants a smaller appropriation than it "really" wants because it believes the Senate Committee will raise the appropriation and the conference committee will make a decision somewhere between that of the two committees.)

In the absence of accurate information as to what part of each appropriation figure is a tactical bargaining segment, it must be assumed that this segment is either the same or nonexistent across agencies. This is but one of the more obvious losses of information entailed in the comparison of dollars and cents figures.

A third limitation stems from the restricted sample of decisions being examined. All generalizations must be considered tentative for this reason, if for no other — that the desire of the author was to test for some patterns among a limited kind and number of executive agencies. The agencies about which generalizations will be made (see Introduction) come from only seven of the ten major departments of the government. The list includes no agencies which exist outside the departments. All the agencies are concerned primarily with domestic, nonmilitary programs. And the scope of the appropriations decisions concerning them covers only one sixteen-year time span. Generalizations offered here must be considered as hypotheses which remain to be tested for other departments, other program areas, and other times.

A fourth limitation stems from the fact that all the decisions being analyzed are decisions made regarding the original appropriations requests. Action taken on deficiency or supplemental budget requests is not included. Where supplementals represent the inauguration of new programs not in existence at the time of the request, their impact in the budget will be registered in the appropriations figures of the succeeding year. But where an agency returns to the Committee later in the year and is given money originally denied to it, some information will be lost by considering only the original request and the original decision.

Though the generalizations which follow cannot be considered definitive, they will furnish a more solid basis for current understanding and future investigation of appropriations output than has heretofore been available. Whatever their limitations, dollars and cents appropriations decisions are the single most important component of decision-making in this area, as any agency official will quickly acknowledge. In terms of contextual differences, some of the most obvious of these differences will be taken into account in the analysis. And, though the bureaus studied do not constitute a representative sample of all federal agencies, they do constitute nearly all the available agencies in the domestic department. Finally, on the testimony of Committee and bureau participants alike, the inclusion of deficiency and supplemental figures in the analysis would yield relatively minor differences in the gross patterns which will be presented. Despite limitations, therefore, a sixteen-year picture of domestic appropriations politics is rather closely approximated in the output analysis which follows.

OVERALL DECISION PATTERNS

Two summary measures are mentioned most frequently by Committee members themselves in describing their dollars and cents decisions. The first is the relation between the dollars and cents agency estimates and the dollars and cents Committee recommendation. That is to say, Committee members describe their decisions as reducing, increasing, or leaving intact the budget requests of the agencies. When they speak of cutting budgets, they usually refer to decisions recommending less money for the next fiscal year than the agency asked for in its estimates. Less frequently, they speak of "giving them what they asked for" or "giving them more than they asked for." The second common measure of Committee output is the relation between the amount of money already appropriated to an agency for the current year and the amount of money recommended in the Committee's decision for the following year. Members, in other words, compare what they are recommending for next year with what the agency received at the conclusion of the appropriations process last year. During economy moods, they can sometimes demonstrate their frugality by noting that they have prevented bureaucratic growth by holding an agency to the same figure it received for the current year. Or, if they are under fire for reducing an estimate too much, they can demonstrate their support for a program by noting that they are recommending more for next year than the agency received this year. The first measure involves relationships between appropriations and estimates in a single year; the second measure involves relationships among appropriations from one year to the next. They reveal different kinds of Committee decisions, and they have quite different consequences for executive agencies. Both measures, therefore, will be used in discussing Committee decisions.

The overall pattern of Committee decisions relative to agency estimates is described in Table 8.1.

TABLE 8.1

APPROPRIATIONS AS RELATED TO ESTIMATES: DECISIONS OF
HOUSE APPROPRIATIONS COMMITTEE, 36 BUREAUS, 1947 TO 1962

Committee Decisions	Number of Decisions	Percentage of Decisions
1. Increases over budget estimates	46	8.0
2. Same as budget estimates	106	18.4
3. Decreases below budget estimates	423	73.6
Total	575[a]	100

[a] In 1957, the Committee lumped the appropriations for the Soil Conservation Service in a larger total, and the agency figures are unavailable. This accounts for all those instances where the total number of cases is 575 rather than 576.

The Committee does, in fact, make the kind of decisions which its members strongly believe it should make, the kind of decisions which House members less strongly believe it should make, and the kind of decisions which the Committee's own internal structure is largely designed to facilitate. In three quarters of the cases, it does reduce budget estimates — thereby "protecting the power of the purse," "guarding the federal Treasury," and "reducing unnecessary expenditures." In about two out of every ten cases, the Committee deviates from its dominant pattern by allowing the budget estimates to stand as the appropriation. In less than one out of every ten instances does the Committee meet those expectations of program support or constituency service which require increases in budget estimates. The Committee's own hierarchy of goal expectations is reflected in the pattern of its decisions on agency budget requests.

A breakdown of Committee decisions on the estimates reveals that a large majority of these decisions fix on a dollars and cents figure within 5 per cent of the agency estimate. The overall pattern is one of moderation rather than of drastic action in either direction. See Table 8.2.

The dominant pattern is not a wholesale slashing of agency budgets. Most Committee reductions (and increases) in budget estimates are marginal ones, ranging between an increase of 5 per cent and a decrease of 5 per cent in budget estimates. This does not mean that they are inconsequential. Agency officials were nearly unanimous in their assertion that a 5 per cent reduction in estimates would be harmful to them. And over one third (35 per cent) of

353

TABLE 8.2

APPROPRIATIONS AS A PERCENTAGE OF ESTIMATES: MAGNITUDE
OF INCREASES AND DECREASES, 36 BUREAUS, 1947 TO 1962

Per Cent of Estimates Received	Number of Decisions	Per Cent of Decisions
Over 120	1	0.2
115.0–119.9	4	0.7
110.0–114.9	2	0.3
105.0–109.9	10	1.7
100.1–104.9	29	5.0
100	106	18.4
95.0–99.9	220	38.3
90.0–94.9	80	13.9
85.0–89.9	50	8.7
80.0–84.9	26	4.5
75.0–79.9	12	2.1
70.0–74.9	9	1.6
65.0–69.9	8	1.4
60.0–64.9	6	1.0
Below 60	12	2.1
Total	575	99.9*

* Due to rounding

all the Committee's decisions are reductions of more than 5 per cent. Occasionally, as the frequency distribution shows, the size of the budget reductions is of crippling proportions — the more so if it is applied to the agency's base as well as to its plans for the future. Surely the sizable number of reductions greater even than 10 per cent is warning enough to the agencies that a Committee decision may hurt them very badly indeed. In one case during the 16 years, the Committee recommended no money at all for a bureau.[1] Every once in a while, on the other hand, the Committee forsakes its budget-cutting pattern to recommend appropriations greater than requested — though not of the same order of magnitude as the deepest cuts. For the agency that finds favor with the Committee, therefore, Committee decisions can also be very consequential. Whether the dominant pattern of budget reduction or the secondary patterns of decision-making are being examined, Committee decisions are primarily incremental ones. These kinds of decisions represent the logical outcome of the incrementalism which appears both in the agency's expectations about Committee action and in the Committee's perceptions of agency budgets.

[1] The Division (now Bureau) of Labor Standards in 1947 (see pp. 385–386.)

354

The description of Committee decisions according to the second measure — the relation of this year's Committee decision to last year's final appropriation figure — accents another angle of Committee decision-making. From this perspective, the great bulk of Committee decisions involve increases over the previous year's appropriation. See Table 8.3.

TABLE 8.3

APPROPRIATIONS AS RELATED TO PREVIOUS YEAR'S APPROPRIATION: HOUSE APPROPRIATIONS COMMITTEE DECISION, 36 BUREAUS, 1947 TO 1962

Committee Decision	Number of Decisions	Percentage of Decisions
1. Increase over last year's appropriation	398	69.2
2. Same as last year's appropriation	22	3.8
3. Decrease below last year's appropriation	155	27.0
Totals	575	100

The Appropriations Committee reduces agency budgets each year; but from one year to the next they grant the agency increased appropriations. The Committee's dilemma — caught as it is between expectations (its own and others) emphasizing support for programs and expectations emphasizing economy — has been described. In the pattern of its decisions can be found, perhaps, the basic solution. On the whole, the Committee supports programs and effects economies — *both at the same time.* Agency appropriations are allowed to grow, but at a slower rate than the agencies themselves desire.

The dominant pattern of allowing increases over the previous year ought not to obscure, however, the sizable minority of cases (over 25 per cent) in which the previous year's appropriation was cut back. In a great many of these instances, cutbacks mean reductions in the agency's base. And the frequency with which such drastic action does occur helps underline the possible consequences of Committee action for the executive agency.

A frequency distribution of Committee decisions relative to the previous year's appropriation reveals, again, a basic incrementalism. See Table 8.4.

The year-to-year expansion of the agencies is kept marginal by the Committee's action. A majority of the Committee's decisions (53 per cent) involve no more than a 10 per cent change over the previous year's appropriation. If one takes changes of 20 per cent as the cutoff point, three-quarters of all the cases are included. At each 10 per cent interval the number of cases drops, until a few extreme examples of growth or retardation remain at either end of the scale.

355

TABLE 8.4

APPROPRIATIONS AS RELATED TO PREVIOUS YEAR'S APPROPRIATION:
HOUSE APPROPRIATIONS COMMITTEE DECISIONS, 36 BUREAUS,
1947 TO 1962

	Number of Decisions	Percentage of Decisions
Percentage Increase		
Over 100.1	10	1.7
90.1–100.0	0	0
80.1–90.0	2	0.3
70.1–80.0	1	0.2
60.1–70.0	6	1.0
50.1–60.0	10	1.7
40.1–50.0	11	1.9
30.1–40.0	16	2.8
20.1–30.0	46	8.0
10.1–20.0	98	17.0
0.1–10.0	198	34.4
Same		
0	22	3.8
Percentage Decrease		
− 0.1− −10.0	86	15.0
−10.1− −20.0	28	4.9
−20.1− −30.0	16	2.8
Over 30.1	25	4.3
Total	575	99.8*

* Due to rounding

It is impossible to know what the consequences of an increase or a decrease over last year's appropriation will be unless one also knows what an agency's expectations are in each case. A decrease from last year's appropriation may not hurt the agency if, in fact, the agency had planned for and requested such a cutback. Conversely, an increase granted by the Committee may hurt an agency badly if, in fact, the agency had planned for and requested a much larger increase. The pattern of Committee decisions just described must be related to the pattern of agency expectations as described in Chapter 6. The contours of that relationship are revealed in Table 8.5.

The Appropriations Committee grants a great majority of agency requests for a dollars and cents increase over the previous appropriation. But, of the increases granted, the overwhelming number are for less than the agency requested. Some estimate of the order of magnitude of these reductions can be gleaned from Table 8.2. In most cases the difference between the estimate and the appropriation is a moderate one. The modal pattern is for an agency to request an increase and for the Committee to grant it a smaller in-

TABLE 8.5

HOUSE APPROPRIATIONS COMMITTEE DECISIONS IN RELATION TO
AGENCY REQUESTS: 36 BUREAUS, 1947 TO 1962

COMMITTEE DECISION (In Relation to Last Year's Appropriation)	AGENCY REQUEST (In Relation to Last Year's Appropriation)	
	Increase	Decrease
Increase Larger Than Requested by Agency	32[a] (7.0%)	—
Increase Same As Requested by Agency	72 (15.8%)	—
Increase Smaller Than Requested by Agency	287 (63.1%)	—
Decrease	64 (14.1%)	—
Decrease Smaller Than Requested by Agency	—	9 (9.9%)
Decrease Same As Requested by Agency	—	21 (23.1%)
Decrease Larger Than Requested by Agency	—	54 (59.3%)
Increase	—	7 (7.7%)
Total	455 (100%)	91 (100%)

[a] The figures refer to number of cases. Twenty-nine cases were omitted where bureau either requested (20) or received, though requesting an increase (9), the *same* appropriation as last year.

crease than requested. The Committee thereby cuts the budget but permits a conservative growth.

Table 8.5 sheds light on the sizable minority of decisions forcing cutbacks in agency appropriations. Slightly more of these cutbacks are in line with agency requests than are in opposition to them. That is to say, in 84 instances the agency requested and received a decreased appropriation, whereas in only 64 cases did the agency request an increase and receive a decrease. If, however, one combines the cases in which the agency asked for an increase and received a decrease (64) with those cases in which the agency asked for a decrease and got a bigger decrease (54), it is clear that most Committee decisions to cut back appropriations are more serious than the agencies expect. Once again, therefore, the capacity of the Committee to hurt the agency is made manifest and the seriousness with which the agencies view Committee activity is seen to be well justified. If the agency asks for an increase, it is most likely to get an increase. If it asks for the same amount as last year, it is most likely (13 out of 20 times) to get the same amount. If it asks for a decrease, it is most likely to get a decrease. But, within these broad categories, the agency may still receive a decision which it deems highly unfavorable. Its increases are most likely to be less than it wants, and, interestingly, if it asks for a decrease, it is more likely than not to receive an even greater decrease than it requested.

APPROPRIATIONS PATTERNS AND SOME ENVIRONMENTAL VARIABLES

The decision patterns presented thus far summarize 16 years of Committee activity with regard to 36 bureaus. A breakdown of the decisions into annual patterns reveals important differences from year to year. These differences point to the existence of at least three important and interrelated environmental variables. One such variable is the complexion of party control of Congress and the Presidency. A second variable is the existence or the nonexistence of an economy mood. Since these are usually triggered by some discrete set of circumstances, their effects show up in year-to-year comparisons. A third related variable is the direction imparted by the executive branch, which, after all, holds the initiative in drawing up the budget.

Considering the appropriations decision as a percentage of agency estimates (the first measure used earlier), the average of the 36 individual bureau averages was computed for each of the 16 years. The yearly variations are presented in Figure 8.1.

The years where the average percentage is low represent the years in which the Committee did the most severe budget-cutting. The years in which the average percentage is high represent the years of greatest Committee leniency in keeping appropriations close to estimates. In view of the dominantly incremental characteristic of Committee decisions, it is not surprising that the range between the Committee's most parsimonious year (1947) and its most profligate year (1960) is not great. Still the difference does seem significant. That is to say, it seems quite clear that decision patterns in 1947, 1948, and 1953 were substantially different from those of 1958, 1959, and 1960.

The most obvious contextual similarity linking 1947, 1948, and 1953 is the partisan complexion of Congress and the White House. The circumstances of 1947 have been mentioned in Chapter Five. The Republican party captured the Congress for the first time in 14 years and went to work reducing the budget of a Democratic President. The effect of their drive

FIGURE 8.1

YEARLY AVERAGES, APPROPRIATIONS AS A PERCENTAGE OF ESTIMATES:
HOUSE APPROPRIATIONS COMMITTEE DECISIONS, 36 BUREAUS,
1947 TO 1962*

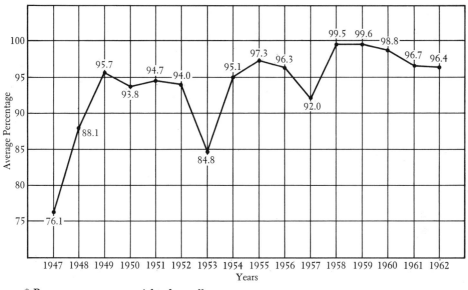

* Bureau averages are weighted equally

against further bureaucratic expansion and in favor of economy is reflected in the results. It hit a peak in the first year of the 80th Congress and subsided slightly in 1948. In 1953, after a hiatus of 4 years, the Republicans again took control of Congress and again confronted the executive budget. This time, the President was also a Republican — but in 1953, the budget was essentially that of the outgoing Democratic President. It was not, therefore, until 1954 that the Republicans in Congress faced the budget of a Republican President, and they acted with far greater leniency than in the previous year. Conditions for reducing budget estimates would seem to be optimal from a partisan point of view when a Republican Congress acts on a Democratic President's budget.

When party control was reversed, from 1955–1961, with the Democrats in control of Congress and the Presidency (budget-making) in the hands of a Republican, no unusual pattern of budget reduction (except in 1957) appeared. During those 6 years the Committee decisions which we have examined averaged 97.3 per cent of the budget estimates, whereas in the 3 years of Republican Congresses and Democratic budgets, 1947, 1948, 1953, the average Committee decision was 83.0 per cent of the budget estimates. Other things being equal, the partisan conditions most conducive to the smallest reductions in budget estimates exist when the Democrats control the

Congress and the Republicans control the Presidency. The years when the executive most nearly received what it asked for were 1958, 1959, and 1960. Democratic-controlled Congresses, it appears, were more lenient with the budgets of President Eisenhower than they were with those of Presidents Truman and Kennedy.

In understanding these patterns, however, it is necessary to know what the patterns of expectations looked like, as they were expressed in the President's budget across the years. And it is also necessary to know whether, despite reductions in budget estimates, dollars and cents appropriations were increasing or decreasing. These two additional factors are presented by years in Figure 8.2.

FIGURE 8.2

RELATION OF BUREAU REQUESTS TO HOUSE COMMITTEE DECISIONS: FOR BUREAUS REQUESTING THE SAME OR LESS MONEY THAN PREVIOUS YEAR, 1947 TO 1962

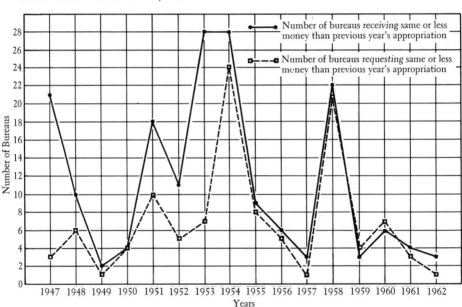

The broken line records the number of bureaus in each year which requested the same or less than their previous year's appropriation. The solid line records the number of bureaus that actually received, by Committee decision, the same or less money. To put it another way, the broken line reflects the budget-making pattern as guided by the President, and the solid line represents the Committee's response to the President's budget. And the gap between the two in any given year is a measure of conflicting expectations between the Committee and the budget-makers in the executive branch.

360

From the perspective of Figure 8.2, the yearly variations discussed earlier become clearer and some new ones appear. The antagonisms of divided party control in 1947 and 1953 are more firmly established. In both cases, Democratic Presidents (the 1953 budget was essentially the Truman budget) presented budgets with a "normal" number of requests for cutting back or holding the line on appropriations. But the Republican-controlled Committee proceeded to reduce or hold steady large numbers of bureau appropriations. In 1948, the other year of large average reductions, the same tendency appears but not strongly. After the first year of combat, the participants seem to have brought their expectations about expansion into closer proximity. Still, however, the Congress made severe reductions in budget requests.

The circumstances of 1951, 1954, and 1958 reveal decision patterns which were obscured in the previous analyses. In these years, Committee decisions were fairly normal when considered in relation to budget estimates. Yet what happened was that the executive and the Congress agreed on the necessity for slowing down or cutting back the growth of agency appropriations. Party factors would seem to account for the agreement on cutbacks evident in 1954. This was the first time in 23 years that a Republican President had made up a budget to be considered by a Republican House Committee. Their agreement on what should be done is recorded in Figure 8.2. This one case suggests the hypothesis that the optimum conditions for slowing down the dollars and cents expansion of executive agencies (as opposed to the reduction of budget estimates) occur when the Republican Party controls both ends of Pennsylvania Avenue.

The cutback years of 1951 and 1958, however, cannot be accounted for by unified party control. Their patterns can most reasonably be accounted for by the existence of external circumstances. The Korean War began in 1950, and the reaction of both executive and Committee was to hold domestic appropriations at prewar levels. Since the budget was drawn up in 1950, the executive concern does not register quite as strongly as that of the Committee, which was making its decisions with hostilities well under way.

The 1958 pattern seems to have been a product of the ardent budget-cutting campaign waged in 1957 by President Eisenhower, Secretary of the Treasury George Humphrey ("hair curling depression"), and conservative economy-minded groups in the country. It was the size of the 1957 budget which alarmed Eisenhower, and he sought to reduce appropriations in the next budget. The 1958 budget was being made out at the time of the economy drive, and executive concern was expressed in the 21 proposals for holding down appropriations. The Committee, still responding to the economy emphasis, met the expectations of the executive. In 1957, however, the executive branch had not acted to hold agency budgets at or below the previous year's levels. Neither had the Committee. Caught between

361

the budget estimates and Eisenhower's own statement that they should be cut, the Committee made a larger than average reduction of 8 per cent in the estimates. (See Figure 8.1.) Members of the House, though, caught the economy mood of 1957 even more strongly and made a number of further reductions on the floor. (See Table 1.1 and pages 478 ff.) By 1958, the country was experiencing a slight recession, but the Committee proceeded to hold down spending in accordance with the expectations of an executive budget prepared in 1957. The recession of 1958 does account for the upswing in Figure 8.1 from 1957 to 1958. And, by 1959 and 1960, both the agencies and the Committee were responding to the recession in terms of lenient treatment of budget estimates and the allowance of appropriations increases.

A larger question raised by the 1957–1958–1959 sequence involves the degree to which Committee decisions influence the obvious fluctuations in the level of appropriations. Does the Committee follow the general direction charted by the executive, or does the executive act in accordance with what it thinks Committee preferences are? As shown in Figure 8.2, the levels of estimates and levels of appropriations — considered in relation to the previous year's appropriation — change in harmony with one another. Since the budgetary initiative rests with the agencies, it seems reasonable to assume that the Committee follows the general trend established by the executive branch. Given the evanescence of congressional economy moods, it seems unlikely that agencies can make budgets in anticipation of them. But it seems probable that, over a period of time, so long as dramatic external events do not intervene, the agencies and the Committee do communicate and that in the context of their constant communication the Committee does indicate what levels of appropriations it deems acceptable. Again, 1947 and 1953, and to some degree 1951, appear as exceptions — as cases in which the congressional influence on the level of appropriations was independent of agency expectations. Judging solely by the small number of years involved, it would appear that overall appropriations trends are set by the agencies. They are set, furthermore, in the light of many considerations of which anticipated Committee response is only one. Under certain conditions of party control and in the presence of unusual external events, however, the Committee may independently influence overall increases or decreases in appropriations.

DEPARTMENTAL APPROPRIATIONS PATTERNS

Earlier in the chapter, we examined the gross patterns of Committee decisions. Three of the contextual variables affecting these patterns are revealed in year-by-year analysis. They are: the complexion of the party's controlling Congress and the Presidency, the inducement and the relaxation of economy moods by events external to both President and Congress, and the initiative of the executive branch. These conditions help to sort out the circumstances under which harsh and lenient treatment of the agencies (as measured in two ways) occur. A fourth rather obvious variable can also be isolated for its impact on Committee decision patterns. This factor is the type of agency involved. It is reasonable to ask whether all kinds of agencies receive the same treatment at the hands of the Committee. And it is reasonable to assume that they do not. If they do not, their differential treatments will reveal sub-patterns of decision in addition to those revealed in yearly variations.

Most obviously, the 36 bureaus fall into 7 departmental clusters. And the question arises as to whether different patterns of decision appear among these clusters. In general, the answer is that they do. But, in advance, it should be understood that any generalization made about departmental patterns must be extremely tentative. The 36 bureaus were not selected randomly from the departments involved. The main criterion for their selection was that they had maintained their organizational integrity throughout the period. For some departments the bureaus are neither a good sample nor do their appropriations totals constitute a majority of the departmental budget. Since they are often the most controversial, expensive programs are apt to undergo the most frequent organizational changes. Still, some departmental patterns emerge and are suggestive enough to merit description.

When appropriations are viewed in relation to budget estimates, it seems clear that the gross patterns observed earlier have some distinct departmental origins. See Table 8.6.

All departments, as would be expected, received budget cuts far more frequently than any other type of Committee decision. But beyond this general similarity, differences appear. Two departments, Agriculture and Health, Education, and Welfare accounted for the great bulk of the Committee decisions which granted the agencies more than they requested. Of the 17 cases in which agencies were granted an appropriation of 105 per cent or more of their estimate (see Table 8.2), 16 were agencies in these 2 departments. Similarly, 2 departments — Commerce and Interior — accounted for a disproportionate share of reductions in budget estimates. Of the 123 cases in which budget reductions of 10 per cent or more were made (see Table 8.2), well over half (67) involved agencies in these two departments. The difference between these two pairs of departments seems significant enough to warrant the statement that, according to this measure, the Departments of Agriculture and Health, Education, and Welfare received more favorable treatment at the hands of the House Appropriations Committee than did the Departments of Commerce and Interior. The decision pattern for each of the other 3 departments fell somewhere in between these extremes.

When the Committee's decisions are viewed in relation to the previous year's appropriation, departmental patterns are somewhat less clear. See Table

TABLE 8.6

HOUSE APPROPRIATIONS COMMITTEE DECISIONS AS RELATED TO BUDGET REQUESTS: BY DEPARTMENTS, 36 BUREAUS, 1947 TO 1962

COMMITTEE DECISION ON BUDGET ESTIMATE	DEPARTMENTS Agriculture (5 Bureaus)	Commerce (5 Bureaus)	HEW (5 Bureaus)	Interior (8 Bureaus)	Justice (3 Bureaus)	Labor (4 Bureaus)	Treasury (6 Bureaus)
Increase	17 (21.5%)	1 (1.2%)	18 (22.5%)	7 (5.5%)	1 (2.1%)	1 (1.6%)	1 (1.0%)
Same	15 (19.0%)	6 (7.5%)	10 (12.5%)	13 (10.1%)	15 (31.2%)	21 (32.8%)	26 (27.1%)
Decrease	47 (59.5%)	73 (91.3%)	52 (65.0%)	108 (84.4%)	32 (66.7%)	42 (65.6%)	69 (71.9%)
Total	79 (100%)	80 (100%)	80 (100%)	128 (100%)	48 (100%)	64 (100%)	96 (100%)

TABLE 8.7

HOUSE COMMITTEE DECISIONS AS RELATED TO PREVIOUS YEAR'S APPROPRIATION: BY DEPARTMENT, 36 BUREAUS, 1947 TO 1962

APPROPRIATION IN RELATION TO PREVIOUS YEAR'S APPROPRIATION	DEPARTMENTS Agriculture (5 Bureaus)	Commerce (5 Bureaus)	HEW (5 Bureaus)	Interior (8 Bureaus)	Justice (3 Bureaus)	Labor (4 Bureaus)	Treasury (6 Bureaus)
Increase	59 (74.7%)	54 (67.5%)	59 (73.8%)	81 (63.3%)	41 (85.4%)	41 (64.1%)	63 (65.6%)
Same	4 (5.1%)	4 (5.0%)	1 (1.2%)	2 (1.6%)	0 (0%)	4 (6.2%)	7 (7.3%)
Decrease	16 (20.2%)	22 (27.5%)	20 (25.0%)	45 (35.1%)	7 (14.6%)	19 (29.7%)	26 (27.1%)
Total	79 (100%)	80 (100%)	80 (100%)	128 (100%)	48 (100%)	64 (100%)	96 (100%)

8.7. All departments did receive increases over their previous appropriation more frequently than a decrease or the same appropriation. Differences among them on this score are not appreciable enough to give solid support to generalization about decision patterns. In terms of consistency in year-to-year increases, the Department of Justice fared better than the others. (One cannot, of course, judge anything about the size of increase from Table 8.7.) And, again, Agriculture and Health, Education, and Welfare fared better than do Commerce and Interior — but not by so substantial a margin. By this measure too, Labor was among the departments whose expansion was less consistent. It would appear that, in general, all departments experienced a steady growth in their appropriations. It also seems likely that when one of the contextual variables discussed earlier led to cutbacks in appropriations no department remained immune from the impact.

Where significant differences between departmental clusters appeared — such as those which separated the performance of the Interior Department bureaus from those of the Department of Health, Education, and Welfare — it seems likely that both external and internal factors were operative. The demand for expanded educational and welfare programs in recent years has been nationwide, and is felt by all members of the House. But the incidence of Interior Department programs falls in the West. The number of House members from the West, where population is relatively sparse, has been small. Correspondingly, they have enjoyed less success than education- and welfare-oriented groups in negotiating for support for their programs in the House. Surely this disparity in terms of base of support and access accounts for some of the difference in departmental success. Less obviously, however, departmental differences reflect differences in the internal legislative processes by which their appropriations decisions are made. The two appropriations subcommittees dealing with the Interior Department, the Subcommittees on Interior and on Public Works, have been deliberately and successfully weighted with non-Westerners (pp. 142–143) to guard against the interest-sympathy-leniency syndrome. Neither subcommittee had a chairman or a majority of its members from west of the Mississippi River during the sixteen-year period. Furthermore, as we shall see in Chapter Ten, Senate membership as a whole and the Senate Appropriations Subcommittees on Interior and Public Works are weighted top-heavily in favor of Westerners. The House Committee's parsimony has developed partly as a hedge against the anticipated aggressiveness and openhandedness of the Senate on behalf of the Interior Department.

By contrast, and despite the efforts of both Chairman Cannon and John Taber (pp. 232–235), the subcommittee handling the Health, Education, and Welfare appropriation has been headed for twelve of the sixteen years by a man who has consistently prodded these bureaus to develop new programs and to spend even more money in the area than they have been inclined to do. Among the many subcommittee chairmen of the period, John Fogarty has been the one least touched by the Committee's goals of budget-cutting. His disposition to loosen rather than tighten the purse strings is reflected in the performance of the five Health, Education, and Welfare bureaus. Departmental patterns can be explained, therefore, in part by subcommittee patterns.

BUREAU APPROPRIATIONS PATTERNS

Any further refinement of decision patterns by departments will yield greatly diminished returns. By proliferating categories (as, for example, would occur if Table 8.5 were reproduced for departments) the results become fragmented to the extent that a single bureau may account for a "departmental" pattern. At this point, it becomes necessary to take individual bureaus themselves as the units of analysis and to see whether any bureau-level decision patterns exist. As Chapters Six and Seven made clear, the behavior of individual bureaus is a key variable in describing and explaining Committee appropriations decisions. Yet neither time nor space is available within the confines of this study to proceed with the kind of analysis in depth, bureau by bureau, year by year, which precision requires. Some summary measures of bureau performance are available, however, and can be used as the basis for suggestive, not definitive, descriptions and explanations of Appropriations Committee output.

Two descriptive measures of Committee output have been employed throughout the chapter and are available for bureau-level analysis. They are, of course, the relation of bureau appropriations to bureau estimates and the relation of bureau appropriations to the bureau's previous year's appropriation. When these relationships are calculated in percentage terms, some bureaus will appear as more successful than others in getting the money they ask for or in increasing their money over the previous year. (And, of course, what from one vantage point appears as a pattern of bureau success or failure constitutes from another vantage point a pattern of Appropriations Committee decisions.) On the basis of these overall rankings — from the most successful to the least successful — it may be possible to adduce some generalizations about Committee-bureau interaction and Committee decisions.

BUREAU DECISION PATTERNS: APPROPRIATIONS AS A PERCENTAGE OF ESTIMATES

For each of the two measures, a method of summarizing bureau performance for the entire 16-year period must be found. In the case of appropriations as they relate to budget estimates, the problem has been dealt with as follows:

For each bureau for each of the 16 years, the appropriation decision of the House Committee has been calculated as a percentage of the bureau's budget request. Each yearly figure represents in percentage terms the ability of the bureau to get what it asked for. These 16 separate yearly percentages were then combined and averaged to produce one mean percentage figure for each bureau. This summary figure allows us to differentiate among the bureaus according to their relative success in getting what they requested from the Committee. The rank ordering of bureaus along this single dimension is presented in Table 8.8.[2]

The overall picture presented in Table 8.8 supports some generalizations made earlier in the discussion. One is that most bureau estimates are reduced most of the time by the Committee. Only 2 bureaus have a 16-year record of getting more than they asked for. The rest, on the average, have received less than they requested. A second generalization made earlier concerns the incremental nature of Committee decision-making. The fact that 27 of the 34 bureaus averaged reductions of 10 per cent or less helps to confirm that generalization. Though these averages obviously conceal yearly fluctuations, they reveal no concerted, wholesale attempts either to decimate or overinflate any individual bureau. The least successful of the bureaus averaged nearly 80 per cent of its requests and the most successful averaged only 2 per cent more than it requested. Over all, therefore, Table 8.8 gives further evidence of the Committee's attempt to respond at one and the same time to demands for economy and demands for program support. It is the presence of these cross-cutting expectations and the attempts to respond to them that ensures the incremental nature of Committee decisions. At the bureau level as well as all other levels, therefore, the existence of support for federal programs outside the Committee puts severe limits on the scope of Committee activity.

From a somewhat different perspective, the rankings of Table 8.8 reveal the Committee's ability to hurt and to help executive agencies. Or, conversely, they reveal the differential success which executive agencies enjoy in dealing with the Committee. In terms of averages and differentials, a comparison between the performance of the Soil Conservation Service and the Federal Bureau of Investigation on the one hand and the performance of the Census Bureau and the Bureau of Labor Standards on the other is convincing. But differences among averages do not have to be that substantial in order to represent differential outcomes of the greatest consequence for the

---

[2] This computation produces an unweighted average, in the sense that it is an average of yearly percentages. In order to check the reliability of this measure, an unweighted average was also computed. That is, for each bureau the sum total of all the dollars requested over 16 years was divided by the sum total of all dollars received over the 16-year period. The correlation between the two rankings was high — having a coefficient of correlation of .84. And, with the exception of 3 bureaus, the rankings are practically identical.

TABLE 8.8

HOUSE COMMITTEE DECISIONS: APPROPRIATIONS AS A PERCENTAGE OF
ESTIMATES, BUREAU AVERAGES FOR THE PERIOD 1947 TO 1962

Ranking	Bureau	Department	16-Year Average
1	Soil Conservation Service	Agriculture	102.1[a]
2	Federal Bureau of Investigation	Justice	100.2
3	Food and Drug Administration	HEW	99.1
4	Bureau of Narcotics	Treasury	98.9
5	Patent Office	Commerce	98.8
6	Extension Service	Agriculture	98.5
7	Bureau of Customs	Treasury	98.1
8	Bureau of the Public Debt	Treasury	97.8
9	Immigration and Naturalization Service	Justice	97.7
10	Social Security Administration	HEW	97.5
11	Office of Education	HEW	97.2
12	Forest Service	Agriculture	96.9
13	Public Health Service	HEW	96.7
14	Women's Bureau	Labor	96.4
15	Secret Service	Treasury	96.1
16	Wage and Hour Division	Labor	95.6
17	Rural Electrification Administration	Agriculture	95.3
18	Internal Revenue Service	Treasury	94.87
19	Bureau of the Mint	Treasury	94.86
20	Weather Bureau	Commerce	94.75
21	Coast and Geodetic Survey	Commerce	94.3
22	Federal Prison System	Justice	94.13
23	Office of Vocational Rehabilitation	HEW	94.05
24	Farmers Home Administration	Agriculture	93.5
25	Fish and Wildlife Service	Interior	92.9
26	Bureau of Mines	Interior	92.6
27	National Park Service	Interior	91.8
28	Geological Survey	Interior	91.7
29	Bureau of Land Management	Interior	91.3
30	Bureau of Indian Affairs	Interior	89.5
31	Bureau of Labor Statistics	Labor	88.6
32	Bonneville Power Administration	Interior	87.5
33	National Bureau of Standards	Commerce	84.2
34	Bureau of Reclamation	Interior	83.9
35	Bureau of Labor Standards	Labor	82.3
36	Census Bureau	Commerce	78.1

[a] Soil Conservation Service figure summarizes only 15 years — see note, Table 8.1.

bureaus involved. Furthermore, of course, these 16-year averages conceal
yearly performances by the Committee that range as low as zero for the
hardest hit bureau and as high as 122 per cent of estimates for the most successful one.

The bureau ranking in Table 8.8 presents a continuum in which it is not possible to distinguish any given bureau or group of bureaus very sharply from those closest to it. Any differentiation between one cluster of bureaus and another cluster for the purposes of comparison, therefore, will have to be arbitrary. Clearly, however, the averages of the topmost bureaus in the ranking differ significantly from the averages of the bottommost bureaus in the ranking. And these output differences can reasonably be assumed to reflect different Committee-bureau relationships. Such differences invite comparison. Quite arbitrarily, therefore, the 36 bureaus will be divided into 3 groups of 12 each. The performance of the top-ranking 12 will be compared with the performance of the bottom-ranking 12; and some suggestions as to the determinants of the two patterns will be offered. In the absence of a great deal of objective data about these 24 bureaus, the comparison will have to be highly impressionistic. Any generalizations which emerge must be taken as extremely tentative and tenuous rather than solidly established.

A comparison between the two clusters of bureaus reveals, again, the influence of departmental factors on Committee output. Despite the fact that the agencies cannot be said to be a perfect sample of their departments, a few gross patterns stand out very clearly. The most obvious characteristic of the low-ranking cluster is that it contains all 8 of the agencies from the Interior Department. There would seem to be no question that this department was markedly less successful than any of the other 6 studied in terms of receiving what it requested from the House Committee. And this departmental weakness reflects itself across the board in terms of its various subunits. Another apparent department-based pattern is involved in the differential success of the Departments of Health, Education, and Welfare and Labor. The budget estimates of these two departments are considered by the same subcommittee; yet the results differ strikingly. For Health, Education, and Welfare, 3 of its agencies appear among the top 12 and none is in the bottom 12. For the Labor Department, 2 of its agencies rank in the bottom 12 and none of them appears in the top 12. Some departmentwide factor would seem to be operative which makes for better relations between the Appropriations Committee and the Health, Education, and Welfare Department than between the Committee and the Labor Department. In the cases of the other departments, their agencies are pretty well scattered throughout the rankings — thus confirming the necessity of doing bureau-level analysis. This need is especially obvious when one looks at the high-ranking cluster, in which are found bureaus from 5 different departments. Whereas one might go far toward explaining the low-ranking bureaus by examining departmental factors (relative to the Interior Department), a bureau-level, cross-departmental analysis is called for in adducing the common characteristics of the top cluster.

One characteristic which most of the top 12 bureaus share is that the nature and the scope of their functions have been settled and put beyond controversy. Among the interested public, House members, Committee members, and subcommittee members alike, the boundaries of their activities are well known and widely agreed upon. Some of them are described as "popular" bureaus whose services to the public are universally appreciated. Others are simply accepted as performing essential tasks. In either case, the Committee's discretion in reducing their budgets is sharply limited. A second characteristic is that most of these bureaus have a type of work load such that specific expenditures can be related directly and tangibly to the performance of their noncontroversial functions. Hence, they can bring in a "tight budget" — a reduction in which will measurably curtail valued, ongoing activity.

These two characteristics are especially noticeable with regard to the 5 law enforcement agencies which appear in the group: the Federal Bureau of Investigation, the Food and Drug Administration, the Bureau of Narcotics, the Immigration and Naturalization Service, and the Bureau of Customs. Their functions are well established and have long been deemed essential to the safety of individuals and the good order of the community. The bulk of their appropriations are allocated to personnel expenses, and any very sizable cutback will directly and demonstrably curtail their investigative and law enforcement services. Three of the other agencies — the Patent Office, the Bureau of Public Debt, and the Social Security Administration — possess similar characteristics. Though perhaps not as well known or as widely appreciated for their services, each performs a function the nature of which has been prescribed by law. And, in strict accordance with that law, each processes a routine work load and produces tangible results — be it patent and copyright applications, the calculations incident to managing the national debt, or social security payments. Indeed, the Committee has little if any discretion in determining the work load of the latter two agencies.[3]

The twin characteristics of noncontroversial functions and a well-defined work load appear to be less important factors in the success of the other four bureaus in the top 12 — if, indeed, they are applicable. The case of the Office of Education will be discussed later. But each of the 3 agencies of the Agriculture Department owes its appropriations success to the supporting activity of influential grass-roots clientele groups. Each of these organizations is highly decentralized, and this structural characteristic is well suited to the mobilization of support in the House by agency clientele. The

---

[3] It is not uncommon for the Committee to reduce Social Security Administration funds only to be forced to put them back in a supplemental bill to fund matching grants to the states.

370

Soil Conservation Service is organized according to local soil conservation districts, each with its own governing group; the Extension Service operates in every county of every state in close cooperation with both the land grant colleges and the American Farm Bureau Federation; the Forest Service operates national forests in 41 states. Each one performs constituency-oriented functions for a great number of congressmen, and the supporters of each agency inside and outside the House have been among the most successful at organizing and conveying their message of grass-roots support. The large number of witnesses at the Agriculture Department hearings (see Table 7.1) conveys something of this activity. The point is not that the functions of these agencies are not important. They are. The point is simply that these agencies and their supporters have demonstrated a superior skill at persuading House members on and off the Appropriations Committee of this fact.

The appropriations success of the top 12 bureaus would seem to be associated either with the combination of a noncontroversial function and a well-defined work load or with constituency-oriented clientele support. All of these factors, however, are external to the Appropriations Committee itself, and their effect depends upon the degree to which the perception and reactions of Committee members are favorable. As we have emphasized, Committee members do not operate with complete discretion in dealing with a given bureau. They are limited basically by the degree of support evident for the programs of the bureau, as that support is mandated by law, fixed by long-standing levels of activity, and communicated in the sentiments of House members. To a large degree, that is to say, Committee members respond like typical House members to the expectations of a given bureau. But the Committee members also react and perceive executive agencies in Committee-oriented ways. Within their area of discretion, it is their Committee-oriented response to external factors that counts. When Committee members themselves speak of differentials in bureau success they stress "the human element" and "the human equation." They talk of their "pet" and "sacred cows," of bureaus that are "popular" or "unpopular" with the Committee. They speak of developing "a college spirit" toward particular agencies. They say that, "Of course, your personal favorites do better." Or, "If it weren't for me, the ——— agency would be cut much more than it has been. I hate to think what would have happened if I hadn't been here." Conversely, "This appropriation has been cut 25 per cent in the last 2 years. I take the credit for having taken the leadership on that."[4] Certainly the preferences of key individuals help account for the differentials recorded in Table 8.8.

Agencies whose functions are well established and whose work routines

[4] 97 *Congressional Record*, p. 5210.

371

are fairly precisely related to those functions possess a special potential for eliciting favorable reactions from the Committee. They are exactly the kind of agencies on which Committee members can project their self-image. They are seen as reliable "old-line" agencies, proved performers carrying out the most basic tasks of government. They are not seen as projecting the government into new fields of activity and thus requiring ever greater expenditures. The law enforcement agencies are viewed, like the Committee itself, in negative terms — as protecting and preserving rather than promoting. Given their established work loads, these agencies have the best opportunity to portray themselves as knowledgeable, efficient administrators — the bureaucratic counterparts of the Appropriations Committee. In sum, agencies with the external characteristics we have discussed are the agencies with the greatest potential for winning the confidence of the Appropriations Subcommittee members with whom they must work.

The three agencies of the Treasury Department are cases in point. To begin with, the Department itself is one of the oldest and most reputable of all federal departments. From its very inception, its officials have sought close relations with the Congress. And, given its concern with financial matters, it has successfully appealed to the Appropriations Committee on the basis of a similarity in goal expectations. For example, Republican Secretary George Humphrey's appearances during the Eisenhower Administration before the Democratic-run full Appropriations Committee or its Treasury–Post Office Subcommittee were unmitigated love feasts. The Secretary would identify himself with the Committee:

> We as a group are pretty much in the same boat. We are the people who are supposed to look after the money. The attitude of people who are supposed to look after the money is quite different from the attitude of the people who are spending the money. . . . I want to make it just as hard to spend money and make them give just as many reasons as possible and check them in every possible way we can so that a money spender finds he has it harder all the time to spend money.[5]

The Secretary would praise the work of the Committee:

> I think cutting these budgets the way you have done over the past dozen years or more has been a splendid thing to do and has been a great holding down here of expenditures that time has proven did not need to be made. . . . Congress's judgment has proved to be best . . . better than the executive judgment over a period of years.[6]

[5] House Committee on Appropriations, *Hearings on Administration Plan to Improve Congressional Control of the Budget*, 85th Congress, 1st Session (Washington: U.S. Government Printing Office, 1957), p. 42.
  [6] *Ibid.*, p. 24.

He would praise the subcommittee for its competence:

> I am pleased to say that we have now and have had ever since I have been here, the fullest cooperation with your committee. They have been very helpful and they know an awful lot about our affairs. They study them and they know just about as much about a lot of our affairs as I do. They look on their own and they travel around and look things over with a lot of care and make some very helpful suggestions and they always have.[7]

No clutch of sentiments could more closely approximate the Committee's self-image or more surely elicit from it avowals of high regard and confidence. Committee members customarily vied with each other in praising the Secretary:

> PRESIDING FULL COMMITTEE MEMBER: You have exhibited a very fine and wholesome American spirit which I am glad to see in a Cabinet officer, and in a man who is Secretary of the Treasury. I have a great deal of admiration for your objectives and efforts, and sincerity and for your capability.
> TREASURY SUBCOMMITTEE CHAIRMAN: Mr. Chairman, I would like to join the Chairman in those remarks.
> SENIOR MAJORITY COMMITTEE MEMBER: May I do so as well.
> PRESIDING FULL COMMITTEE MEMBER: I think that is the sentiment of all the members of the Committee.
> SENIOR MINORITY COMMITTEE MEMBER: It is unanimous.
> PRESIDING FULL COMMITTEE MEMBER: It is unanimous; yes, sir.[8]

On another occasion, the full Committee Chairman commented, "I believe I expressed the opinion of every man on this Committee that we would consider your resignation as an unmitigated national disaster."[9] And, not to be outdone, the Treasury Subcommittee chairman followed by saying, "Mr. Secretary, I want to assure you that I entertain the same high regard for you that others have expressed here today. I want to say, moreover, that you have the most economically operated department in the entire government."[10] The roots of this affinity lie in a correspondence of expectations and self-images. The Committee's friendly attitude toward the Department antedated and has postdated this particular example of warm personal regard.

The overall departmental relationship furnishes a kind of foundation for all Treasury bureaus on which some in particular have constructed ex-

---

[7] House Committee on Appropriations, *Hearings on the 1958 Budget*, 85th Congress, 1st Session (Washington: U.S. Government Printing Office, 1957), p. 58.

[8] *Hearings on Administration Plan to Improve Congressional Control of the Budget, op. cit.*, pp. 41–42.

[9] *Hearings on the 1958 Budget, op. cit.*, p. 30.

[10] *Ibid.*, p. 51. See also *Congressional Record*, Daily Edition, March 4, 1958, p. 2988.

ceptional reputations with the subcommittee. A newcomer to the Treasury subcommittee described his first hearing this way:

> The members of the committee have their pets. It was nauseating for me to sit and hear these older men talk to some of the people telling them what a good job they were doing — almost apologizing for having them come there. . . . Over the years, they built up friendships, they travel around the world together, go to dinner together — a mutual admiration society.

As pets of the subcommittee, he mentioned the Customs Bureau, the Coast Guard, and the Bureau of Narcotics.

The Bureau of Narcotics can be considered briefly. A bureau official commented generally on its wide base of support. "We're an established old-line agency. We've been in business thirty years. And of course we have a very popular bureau. Everybody is against sin." To this general base, the leaders of the Treasury subcommittee add their increment of confidence. The subcommittee repeatedly expressed its complete confidence in Dr. Harry Anslinger, Chief of the Bureau until 1963. They looked upon him as a model public servant, the world's greatest expert in his subject, a man who always brought in a tight budget, a bureaucrat who never tried to "pour it on."[11] Anslinger's belief that the Bureau should be kept small and should do its work by cooperating with state and local authorities stamped him as a brother under the skin, the very antithesis of an empire builder. A veteran subcommittee leader said,

> We're tremendously impressed with their leadership. Anslinger is one of the finest men in government. I think they are even too modest in what they ask for. I think — I know — they could use a lot more money than they get right now.

In every year but three during the sixteen years, the subcommittee gave the Bureau every penny it requested.

The prototype of the successful noncontroversial bureau with a well-established work load is the Federal Bureau of Investigation. The FBI is probably the best known and the most popular — indeed, the most revered — of all federal agencies. Its exploits have become folk legends; its agents have been fabled in song and story, radio, and television; and its Director since 1924, J. Edgar Hoover, is an American hero. The fact that President-elect John Kennedy's first public act was to ask Hoover to remain as head of the FBI is sufficient testimony to his unsurpassed standing with the American

[11] See House Committee on Appropriations, *Hearings on the Treasury–Post Office Departments Appropriations for 1961*, 86th Congress, 2nd Session (Washington: U.S. Government Printing Office, 1960), p. 166; 99 *Congressional Record*, p. 4926; *Congressional Record*, Daily Edition, March 4, 1958, p. 2990.

public. Surely, the general reputation of the agency severely restricts the discretion of the Appropriations Committee. But the bond of confidence which links the Committee to the FBI and accounts for the Bureau's extraordinary budgetary success exceeds the national norm. So close, indeed, is the relationship that the House Appropriations Committee — or, the subcommittee dealing with the Justice Department — appears as the arch supporter of the FBI within the American political system.

The subcommittee will restore reductions in the Bureau's estimates should they be made by the Budget Bureau. The rationale for this pattern, in terms of the Bureau's functions, was stated in 1950 by one of the subcommittee's members:

> For three years, this subcommittee has restored various cuts of the Federal Bureau of Investigation. We have restored to that agency cuts made by the Bureau of the Budget and have given it the full request. I believe with all my heart that the greatest national defense this country has in this hour is the Federal Bureau of Investigation that can lay its hands on thousands of these dangerous people at a moment's notice.[12]

The close connection between function and work load for this kind of agency is well illustrated by the following exchange which took place at a subcommittee hearing in 1950:

> RANKING MINORITY SUBCOMMITTEE MEMBER: How much did you ask the Budget for when you appeared before them?
> MR. HOOVER: The request of the Bureau of the Budget was $52,585,141. They allowed $50,987,000, a reduction of $1,598,141.
> RANKING MINORITY SUBCOMMITTEE MEMBER: For what purpose were you going to use that extra money?
> MR. HOOVER: I was going to use that extra money, Mr. Stefan, to try to cut down on the delinquency in our investigative work . . . our backlog is increasing rather than decreasing.
> RANKING MINORITY SUBCOMMITTEE MEMBER: So with that work in the security field, with the work in the atomic energy field, and with your tremendous backlog in fingerprint identification work, and with the increase in crime, is this cut by the Bureau of the Budget going to handicap you?
> MR. HOOVER: Most certainly, it will. When I submitted my estimate to the Budget, Mr. Stefan, I trimmed it to the very lowest figure that I felt would permit us to discharge our obligations. Any cut that is effective will result in comparable curtailment of our activities.
> RANKING MINORITY SUBCOMMITTEE MEMBER: I am very much disturbed about it.[13]

[12] 96 *Congressional Record*, p. 5403.
[13] House Committee on Appropriations, *Hearings on Justice Department Appropriations for 1950*, 81st Congress, 1st Session (Washington: U.S. Government Printing Office, 1949), p. 241.

In markup, the subcommittee restored the amount and the Bureau ultimately received exactly what it had originally requested from the Budget Bureau.

The Committee's reception of Hoover's presentation in the hearings illustrates how agencies of this kind can capitalize on their potential for meeting the Committee's self-image. His presentation is factual and his manner of presentation breathes efficiency. He reads a large typed manuscript "in rapid fire style" and he "snaps out pictures at us." He "always comes in well prepared and lays it on the line." "He brings in only three men. And when you ask him a question they don't say, 'We'll find out. We'll get it for you tomorrow.' They have the answer right there." From these samplings, subcommittee members conclude that the agency is in good hands and forego the customary probe for soft spots:

> MINORITY SUBCOMMITTEE MEMBER: We know that you not only operate a very efficient investigative agency, but a very efficient administrative agency. For that reason, we have not found it necessary to go into a great many details that we have to do sometimes with other agencies.
> MR. HOOVER: Thank you very much indeed.
> SUBCOMMITTEE CHAIRMAN: I wish to thank you. I wish I knew of some other administrators just one-tenth as good as you are for some other jobs.[14]

There would seem to be no question but that the function and work load characteristics of the FBI make it easier for Hoover as an administrator and easier for subcommittee members to sustain these flattering judgments. In any event, the subcommittee expressed its sentiments fully in 1955 by successfully inserting in the appropriations act of that year a proviso raising the Director's salary to $20,000 (more than the Secretaries of the Army, Navy, and Air Force) "so long as the position is held by the present incumbent."[15]

The Committee and the Bureau have forged some other unique links which have cemented this alliance. The FBI, for its part, furnishes the Committee with the Director, the Assistant Directors, and the bulk of the members of its Surveys and Investigations staff. With FBI men helping to staff the Committee, it is no wonder that Committee members come to look upon the Bureau as having a special relationship. So close is the identification that the Chairman of the Committee typically defended his staff by identifying the FBI with the legislative rather than the executive branch. "Does the gentleman charge that an FBI man is a bureaucrat?" queried Chairman Can-

---

[14] House Committee on Appropriations, *Hearings on Justice Department Appropriations for 1954*, 83rd Congress, 1st Session (Washington: U.S. Government Printing Office, 1953), p. 147. On J. Edgar Hoover, see also Homer Bigart, "J. Edgar Hoover: 40 Years the No. 1 Policeman," *The New York Times*, May 10, 1964.

[15] See House Committee on Post Office and Civil Service, *Report on Federal Executive Pay Act of 1955*, H.R. No. 1474, 84th Congress, 1st Session (Washington: U.S. Government Printing Office, 1955), p. 15.

non incredulously. "Nobody has ever charged that the Director or any of the staff or any of his investigators are bureaucrats."[16] As a service to the members of its subcommittee, the Bureau has printed a booklet entitled *The Story of the FBI*. On the back of its cover page, it notes that the booklet was prepared "at the suggestion of the subcommittee" and then lists the members of the subcommittee. The item has proven very popular with subcommittee members who have taken a natural proprietary interest in it. At the 1948 hearings we find the following comments on it by subcommittee members to Mr. Hoover:

> MINORITY SUBCOMMITTEE MEMBER: I have distributed a great many of them to schools in my district and they have proved very popular . . . it is very popular in my district.
>
> . . . . .
>
> NEW SUBCOMMITTEE MEMBER: You might send me some.
>
> . . . . .
>
> SUBCOMMITTEE CHAIRMAN: I assume you will change some of that book before you make a new issue, because we have a new committee here now and we have new members of the Committee, to bring it up to date.[17]

These comments stand in sharp contrast to the generally suspicious attitude of the Committee toward the public relations activities of executive agencies as empire-building devices. Another special factor in smoothing relations between the two groups has doubtless been the fact that for many years the clerk of the subcommittee dealing with the FBI has been a man who was himself a former FBI agent.

The payoffs for the Bureau are obvious. A member of the subcommittee summed up the relationship by recalling his first experience with the FBI budget:

> I noticed this attitude when I first went on the Committee. We were going along in the markup session regularly making cuts till we came to the FBI and no cut was made. I discovered it was sacrosanct. Nobody ever says anything about it, but you can feel it.

On only one occasion in sixteen years did the subcommittee reduce the Bureau's estimates.

For the top-ranking bureaus of the Agriculture Department, just as for those of the Treasury and Justice Departments, budgetary success must be explained in terms of Appropriations Committee response to the special

[16] 97 *Congressional Record*, pp. 2804–2805.
[17] House Committee on Appropriations, *Hearings on Justice Department Appropriations for 1949*, 80th Congress, 2nd Session (Washington: U.S. Government Printing Office, 1948), p. 264.

characteristics of a bureau. What needs to be understood, therefore, is not just that these three bureaus are well organized to generate grass-roots pressure but that the subcommittee members are especially receptive to it. In this case, subcommittee receptivity is rooted in constituency concerns. Throughout the sixteen-year period, the Subcommittee on Agriculture has been dominated by men from agricultural districts who came to their work with a natural desire to help the farmer. The Democrat who was chairman of the subcommittee for twelve of the sixteen years and ranking minority member for two, Representative Jamie Whitten of Mississippi, commented typically, "I know the value of the various agricultural programs at first hand, for I was raised on a hill farm in an area where erosion was and is a serious problem."[18] And the Republican with whom he exchanged roles, Representative H. Carl Andersen, had a similar background: "The Seventh Congressional District of Minnesota, which I have had the honor to represent for nearly seventeen years, is one of the few strictly agricultural districts in America."[19] And again, "The Department of Agriculture . . . represents in the government my personal industry."[20] Another long-time subcommittee member, Representative Charles Plumley, said, "I have lived my life in Vermont. I am for Vermont. I do not have to prove it. I am for Vermont farmers and their welfare. I do not have to say so. I will try to see to it that their needs are met and cared for. They know it."[21]

The subcommittee's eagerness to get into the legislative picture brought them into more frequent conflict with the substantive legislative committee involved than any other subcommittee. During the Eisenhower years, the subcommittee was in constant disagreement with Secretary Benson who sought to cut back agricultural expenditures. Every subcommittee member is a self-proclaimed "true friend of the farmer." It was, it will be remembered, the Committee Chairman's perception of the interest-sympathy-leniency syndrome that led in large part to the appointment of Representative Santangelo (and later Representative Addabo) of New York City to the subcommittee. But, just as importantly, it will also be recalled how the agriculturalists on the subcommittee engineered the subtle conversion of the urban congressman. The subcommittee did not forswear budget-cutting. But its members were especially receptive to agricultural agencies so long as they met the more traditional performance criteria of the Committee.

It has been suggested that the decentralized organizational structure of the three most successful Agriculture bureaus contributed to their suc-

---

[18] 98 *Congressional Record*, p. 4758. See also Representative Whitten's speech to the National Limestone Institute in *Congressional Record*, Daily Edition, February 11, 1960, p. 2213.
[19] 101 *Congressional Record*, p. 3847.
[20] 93 *Congressional Record*, p. 5880.
[21] *Ibid.* See also 95 *Congressional Record*, p. 3914.

cess in organizing the clientele they served. Just as important, a decentralized organizational structure with a minimum of personnel located in Washington, D.C., is the type most suited to the taste of House and Committee members.[22] And this is especially true of the rural congressmen whose interest and expertise give them dominant influence in agricultural decisions. An official of the Soil Conservation Service acknowledged the solid congressional support for the agency's work:

> It's something the public wants and they tell their congressmen about it. The hearings don't have a thing to do with it [budgetary success]. It's the pressure back home. When they get interested they write, individuals and organizations both . . . you won't find any congressman who will stand up and make a public statement opposing soil conservation. It's like religion. They want to be for it even though they may not have any idea what it is about.

This extraordinary receptivity of Congress to the program is based, he continued, on the patently decentralized nature of the organization:

> It isn't just that it's soil conservation. It's because Congress likes the way we go about it. We don't do it here. But people in the local district do it. The Soil Conservation Service is the closest thing to the New England town meeting of the Northeast. It's grass-roots democracy at work. And it's the only thing like it in the government. It's quite different from these straight-line federal agencies that deliver a service directly to the consumer.

Similar characteristics help explain the budgetary success of the Extension Service. In the estimate of Chairman Cannon, who once served as the Chairman of the Subcommittee on Agriculture and who spoke of himself as "a dirt farmer," "This [Extension Service] is the most popular of all federal farm activities. It reaches directly into the home. It touches every farm family intimately."[23] The work of the Service and its county agents wins approval as "a partnership" and as "a cooperative service" between federal, state, and county authorities. One subcommittee veteran explained,

> That's a state and local program. Actually, federal contributions have been falling behind the state and local ones. If the state and local people are willing to contribute their money, it's a pretty good indication that the program is worthy of federal support.

The appeal of the Forest Service to congressmen is similar. Said one Forest Service official, "In our 185 million acres of timber, we cover lots of congressmen who have this problem in their district. . . . When a man gets hurt by something he writes to his congressman pretty darn quick. That

[22] See 93 *Congressional Record*, p. 5959; 97 *Congressional Record*, p. 5464.
[23] 94 *Congressional Record*, p. 3086. See *ibid.*, pp. 3081–3088.

379

helps." And a veteran member of the subcommittee described the Service as "more near to the heart of the average member of Congress than any other service."[24] In addition to a locally oriented structure, the Forest Service can make a direct appeal to Appropriations Committee economy expectations. Their timber-cutting operations bring revenue into the federal Treasury. Thus expenditures for forest roads and trails, say, to get to the ripe timber represent not a drain on the Treasury but a sound, profit-making investment.[25] To an Appropriations Committee member concerned with guarding the Treasury the argument is most congenial. Since 1955, the Forest Service budget has been considered by the Interior Subcommittee, and, if anything, its treatment by that group has been more favorable than what it received at the hands of the Agriculture Subcommittee. This fact is testimony to its widespread appeal to congressmen on the Appropriations Committee.

Agricultural agencies generally recognize that Congress is their point of special access in the American system. These 3, more than any other cluster of agencies in the 36, work assiduously to cultivate the support of key congressional units such as the Agriculture Subcommittee. An official of the Extension Service pointed out,

> When we get a new congressman on our committee, I make it my business to know everything there is to know about him, so that I will understand his questions. That's not politics — that's just good common sense. If we spent half as much time getting to know our Committee as we do trying to size up the top administration, we'd be better off.

Doubtless their inquiries turned up relevant personal information, such as the fact that the occupation of the father of one influential subcommittee member, Representative Fred Marshall, had been the first county agent (in the Extension Service) in the State of Minnesota.[26] In his study of agricultural politics, Charles Hardin concluded that the Soil Conservation Service was more effective in cultivating the Appropriations Subcommittee on Agriculture than any other agricultural agency.[27] Furthermore, the Service has always had as one of its most dedicated adherents Representative Ben Jensen, who rose to become ranking minority member of the full Committee. Jensen, whose district was described by agency officials as having "badly eroded slopes and gullies which produce a bad flood control problem," was a particularly devoted friend of Service Chief Dr. Hugh Bennett.[28] The Service has also

[24] 96 *Congressional Record*, p. 5917.
[25] See 98 *Congressional Record*, p. 4697; 100 *Congressional Record*, pp. 5008–5009.
[26] 102 *Congressional Record*, p. 8902.
[27] Charles M. Hardin, *The Politics of Agriculture* (Glencoe: The Free Press, 1952), pp. 88–89. See also Robert J. Morgan, "Pressure Politics and Resources Administration," *Journal of Politics* (February, 1956), pp. 39–60.
[28] See *Congressional Record*, Daily Edition, August 29, 1960, p. A6469.

been a special favorite of both veteran subcommittee chairman Jamie Whitten and full Committee Chairman Clarence Cannon.

All three agencies sell their program to Congress by encouraging first-hand observation of their work. The public relations reputation of the Forest Service (see p. 389–390) is legend. An official of the agency explained,

> We have a general rule here that if we can only get people — congressional staff, congressmen, budget people — out on the ground to see what our people are actually doing, it will be tremendously helpful . . . it isn't just integrity and honesty — every agency likes to think it has that — but it's the enthusiasm of the people who do the job. If we can get people out on the ground they will see the enthusiasm much better than we can convey it here.

Members of Congress have even made parachute jumps with Forest Rangers into forest fire areas. The impression the Service makes in this way is just what it intends — a sort of "Marine Corps of the agencies." A veteran subcommittee member summed up:

> They are proud of their work. They always have so much to show you especially if you are a member of Congress. They are dedicated men. They have the same kind of missionary spirit that a good minister has.

The Soil Conservation Service, the Extension Service, and the Forest Service display an unmistakably strong congressional orientation. With the Appropriations Committee, their payoffs have been great.

Some Determinants of Unfavorable Committee Decisions

The twelve relatively unsuccessful bureaus clustered at the bottom of the ranking display some objective characteristics which are just the reverse of those displayed by most of the top twelve. Thus, nearly all involve a controversial federal governmental activity — controversial in the sense that they have no clear cutoff point. As such they arouse the fears of those congressmen and Committee members who would resist the growth of the federal government and its influence. Consideration of the Bonneville Power Administration and Bureau of Reclamation estimates can engender the controversial issue of public power. The Census Bureau and the Bureau of Labor Statistics collect statistics, but their activities can be viewed as progressing to infinity if not checked. Similarly, the research activities of the Geological Survey and the National Bureau of Standards are of an open-ended character. The Bureau of Labor Standards engages in purely promotional activity, urging on behalf of the central government certain standards of wages, working conditions, and safety upon the states and private industries. The Bureau of Indian Affairs and the Bureau of Land Management can be seen as imposing

381

more and more rules of a federal bureaucracy on the life of the Indians and on those who earn their livelihood from the public domain. The Fish and Wildlife Service and the National Park Service are less controversial, but still their construction activities carry no self-imposed limitation. Nearly all these agencies can be viewed, therefore, as engaging in open-ended activities carrying an unlimited potential for growth in federal spending and federal influence.

The controversial nature of these bureaus resides in the tractable, non-routine nature of their work load. One who believes that their activities should be checked finds it easy to believe that they can be checked. And this is so even if he believes in a minimal performance of their functions. For example, the Constitution requires the Census Bureau to take a decennial census, but who is to say how many additional kinds of censuses shall be taken concomitantly and in intermediate years? Proposals for additional censuses can, it will be felt, be cut from the budget without hurting anything. Similar arguments can be used in trimming funds for any information-collecting (Bureau of Labor Statistics) or research (Geological Survey, National Bureau of Standards) or information-dispensing (Bureau of Labor Standards) organization. Curtailment of these functions will not be viewed as producing any tangible loss of a demonstrably necessary service. For all those agencies heavily engaged in construction activities (Fish and Wildlife Service, Bureau of Reclamation, National Park Service), budget reductions can be made by cutting back proposed constructions which will not appear to hurt any ongoing activity. Whereas the budgets of a goodly number of the agencies in the top twelve are heavily weighted with expenditures for personnel, an appreciable number of the bottommost twelve have budgets heavily weighted in nonpersonnel items. And nonpersonnel items are the more easily reducible or made subject to a policy of "no new starts." For these bureaus their work load as well as their functions are of a sort which remains subject to wide differences of opinion. The metes and bounds of their activity remain unsettled.

The difference in the controversial nature of the top twelve and the bottom twelve bureaus is revealed by comparing Committee decisions during the four years of Republican control with Committee decisions during the twelve years of Democratic control. If the controversial character of the twelve lowest ranking bureaus lies in the open-endedness of their functions and work loads, one would expect a Republican-dominated Committee to be significantly more parsimonious than a Democratic Committee. That is to say, to the extent that an appropriations decision involved a decision to curtail or foster federal activity, one would expect the Republicans to cut budgets more deeply than the Democrats. Of course, Committee decisions are the product of negotiations across party lines. But the negotiations are governed by the subcommittee chairman from the majority party, and the level at which subcommittee bargains are struck varies according to which party is taking the lead. In those cases, however, where bureau functions are deemed to be relatively noncontroversial, either by virtue of a general consensus or an intractable work load, or both, one would not expect the appropriations levels to differ significantly. The top twelve bureaus should be characterized by partisan agreement and a relatively stable level of appropriations under both Republicans and Democrats.

In Table 8.9, average appropriations-as-percentage-of-estimates figures have been calculated for each bureau for the 4 years of Republican control (1947–1948; 1953–1954) and for the 12 years of Democratic control (1949 to 1952; 1955 to 1962). These averages have been compared with one another and the difference between them taken as an index of partisan controversy over each bureau.

As expected, the 12 least successful bureaus have been the object of considerable partisan controversy, with the index ranging from a low of 8.9 per cent to a high of 47.3 per cent. And also, as expected, the low-ranking bureaus invariably sustained their deepest appropriations losses in the 4 years of Republican control. For each of these 12 bureaus Committee decisions in the Republican years were a good deal lower than the bureau's 16-year average. And Committee decisions in the 12 Democratic years were uniformly higher than the 16-year average for each bureau. By contrast, the 12 top-ranking bureaus (with the exception of the Office of Education and possibly the Food and Drug Administration) did not appear to be the objects of much partisan controversy. They received a relatively high percentage of their budget requests no matter which party was in power. Indeed, the Democrats occasionally appear as having cut the budget of these bureaus by as much as the Republicans did. For the low-ranking set of bureaus, the average of the differences between Republican and Democratic percentages is 22.5 per cent. For the high-ranking group, the corresponding figure is only 3.2 per cent. These summary figures provide convincing evidence that, considered as a whole, one set of bureaus was much more the object of partisan controversy than the other set.

Since the Democrats controlled the Committee for all of the last 8 years of the period, it is possible that the contrast between Republican and Democratic treatment of the bottommost bureaus reflects a secular trend as much as it does a party difference. That is to say, more favorable treatment by the Democrats may reflect simply a steady decrease in the controversial nature of these bureaus as the period progressed. These influences are difficult to separate from one another. One clue, however, is to be found by examining

383

TABLE 8.9

BUREAU RANKINGS AND PARTISAN CONTROVERSY

Ranking	Bureau	Estimates as Per Cent of Appropriations: Average 12 Democratic Years	Estimates as Per Cent of Appropriations: Average 4 Republican Years	Index of Partisan Controversy
	Twelve Top-Ranking Bureaus			
1	Soil Conservation Service	102.9	99.8	3.1
2	Federal Bureau of Investigation	100.2	100.0	0.2
3	Food and Drug Administration	101.0	93.6	7.4
4	Bureau of Narcotics	98.9	99.0	−0.1
5	Patent Office	99.9	95.6	4.3
6	Extension Service	99.0	97.2	1.8
7	Bureau of Customs	98.7	96.0	2.7
8	Bureau of the Public Debt	98.6	95.5	3.1
9	Immigration and Naturalization Service	98.5	95.3	3.2
10	Social Security Administration	97.5	97.6	−0.1
11	Office of Education	101.5	86.8	14.7
12	Forest Service	96.5	98.4	−1.9
	Twelve Low-Ranking Bureaus			
25	Fish and Wildlife Service	97.6	76.7	20.9
26	Bureau of Mines	98.0	76.6	21.4
27	National Park Service	95.5	80.4	15.1
28	Geological Survey	97.0	76.0	21.0
29	Bureau of Land Management	94.4	82.0	12.4
30	Bureau of Indian Affairs	91.7	82.8	8.9
31	Bureau of Labor Statistics	94.4	71.1	23.3
32	Bonneville Power Administration	95.3	64.4	30.9
33	National Bureau of Standards	87.0	75.9	11.1
34	Bureau of Reclamation	89.3	68.1	21.2
35	Bureau of Labor Standards	94.1	46.8	47.3
36	Bureau of the Census	88.2	50.3	37.9

the bureau's treatment during the first 8 years when party control was evenly divided. If a bureau's fortune rose and fell with changes in party control during the first 8 years, the force of secular change would appear to be minimal. If, on the other hand, both Republicans and Democrats reduced the budget by similar amounts in those years and the bureau then reached new highs in the last 8 years, some evidence of a secular trend would exist.

Two patterns obviously based on partisan controversy are those depicted in Figure 8.3 for the Bureau of Labor Standards and the Bonneville Power Administration. The fluctuations during the first 8-year period make it clear

FIGURE 8.3

PERCENTAGE OF ESTIMATES GRANTED BY HOUSE APPROPRIATIONS
COMMITTEE IN YEARS OF REPUBLICAN AND DEMOCRATIC CONTROL
OF THE COMMITTEE TO THE BONNEVILLE POWER ADMINISTRATION
AND THE BUREAU OF LABOR STANDARDS

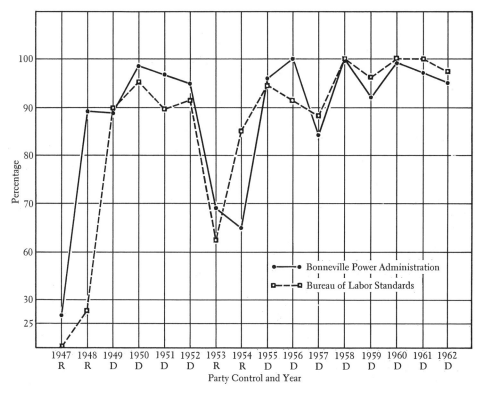

that these two bureaus owe their low ranking to the actions of the Republican-dominated Committee in the 80th and 83rd Congresses.

Given the differing centers of gravity of the parties generally, one would have expected sharp differences to have occurred over budgets involving the expansion of the Labor Department and of public power facilities. These subcommittees, it will be recalled, were especially riven by the atmosphere of partisanship in the 80th Congress.

The then Division of Labor Standards bore the heaviest brunt of the successful Republican effort to cut back the activity of the Labor Department. Representative Frank Keefe, chairman of the subcommittee handling Labor Department appropriations, was especially hostile to the Department. Under his leadership, the Committee cut every penny from the estimate of the Division in 1947. In discussing the action on the floor, he noted the special vulnerability of this agency since Congress had never expressed itself in terms of program support:

> Let me say to you, the Division of Labor Standards was created not by an act of Congress. It was a little division set up in the Department of Labor by Miss Perkins when she became Secretary of Labor by administrative order. . . . This outfit was not set up by an act of Congress. It is a mere administrative agency.[29]

A year later, the Committee granted the Division 39.4 per cent of its budget request. This time, the subcommittee chairman moved from a general antipathy toward the Department to an indictment of the open-ended nature of the Division's activities:

> At first, the committee was inclined to take away the entire appropriation for the Division of Labor Standards, but on reconsideration, we decided to give them a couple hundred thousand dollars. The man that is the head of it, Mr. Connally, is a fine fellow, but like everyone else he comes down here with a great deal of zeal to do a job. They are looking around for things to do. "What activity can we get into that we can make a showing and then start to build up?"[30]

When the Democrats have controlled the subcommittee, the chairman has been former union official, Representative John Fogarty. And, under his leadership, the Division has been treated more sympathetically.

Agency people agree that the Bureau (billed as "the promotional arm of the department") which collects information, conducts studies, and distributes information is especially vulnerable. Said a departmental official, "That's a hard one to hold because it's promotional. It doesn't have a tangible work load." A Republican subcommittee member echoed the sentiment. "They want to start a lot of new studies — getting into this and that. Whenever the policy is no new programs, they get cut." The policy of no new programs in the field of labor has been a Republican rather than a Democratic policy.

The Bonneville Power Administration is another agency whose activity stirred bitter partisan controversy. The effects of its presence on private power interests is real enough, but the prospect of an ever-growing public power facility that it poses is even more disturbing. Republican sentiment on the Committee was expressed by the man who was chairman of the Interior Subcommittee in the 83rd Congress and a ranking minority member for

[29] 93 *Congressional Record*, p. 2466. See also House Committee on Appropriations, *Hearings on Labor Department and Federal Security Administration Appropriations for 1948*, 80th Congress, 1st Session (Washington: U.S. Government Printing Office, 1947), pp. 27–28.
[30] 94 *Congressional Record*, p. 2341.

12 of the 16 years. Speaking in 1949 of the "Bonneville Power socialists," he charged,

> The Bonneville Power Administration is . . . very impatient with the legislative processes of Congress. It wants to be turned loose from any congressional controls, wants to be the complete and undisputed master of the Pacific Northwest region. That is why the Bonneville Power Administration, the Interior Department, and all the motley forces of Marxism are now centered on a thrust to reach this objective through a Columbia Valley Authority.[31]

When Committee members feel this way about an agency's functions, it is impossible for them to see the agency as they do so many of the top-ranking bureaus, in their own image. Where they see empire-building, they cannot see well-informed, efficient, thrifty administrators. A Republican subcommittee member defended his group action in giving Bonneville only 34 per cent of their request in 1947:

> In view of the fact that the Administrator of the Bonneville Power Administration when he appeared before our Committee . . . was a master of subterfuge, confusion, and evasion as to the conditions and facts pertaining to this situation — I think our subcommittee was most generous in what was allowed the Bonneville Power Administration to operate with in 1948.[32]

Under conditions of basic policy disagreement, subcommittee confidence is reluctantly given and precipitously withdrawn. An unstable budgetary situation results which is quite beyond the capacity of the administrator to allay. It is not his fault that he is not a Harry Anslinger or a J. Edgar Hoover.

For the Bureau of Land Management and the Bureau of Indian Affairs, their low rank among the bureaus can probably be explained as much by a secular trend as by partisan controversy. From 1947 to 1954, the Bureau of Indian Affairs suffered as much at the hands of a Democratic-controlled Committee as they did when the Republicans were in the majority. In the 4 years of Democratic control, it averaged 82.8 per cent of its estimates; in the 4 years of Republican control, it averaged 82.3 per cent. In the same period, the Bureau of Land Management appeared as the object of slightly more partisanship — averaging 87 per cent of estimates during the 4 Democratic years and 82 per cent of estimates during the Republican years. But in neither case do these differences of the first 8 years explain the high index of partisanship revealed in Table 8.9. That high index must be explained by what happened in the last 8 years — all of them with a Democratic majority in control of the Committee. The success of these two bureaus under the Democrats from 1955 to 1962 appears to be due to a secular improvement

[31] 95 *Congressional Record*, p. 3420.
[32] 93 *Congressional Record*, p. 4064.

in their appropriations fortunes rather than the diminution of some previously sharp partisan controversy.

Figure 8.4 illustrates that improvement.

FIGURE 8.4

PERCENTAGE OF ESTIMATES GRANTED BY HOUSE APPROPRIATIONS
COMMITTEE IN YEARS OF REPUBLICAN AND DEMOCRATIC CONTROL
OF THE COMMITTEE TO THE BUREAU OF LAND MANAGEMENT
AND THE BUREAU OF INDIAN AFFAIRS

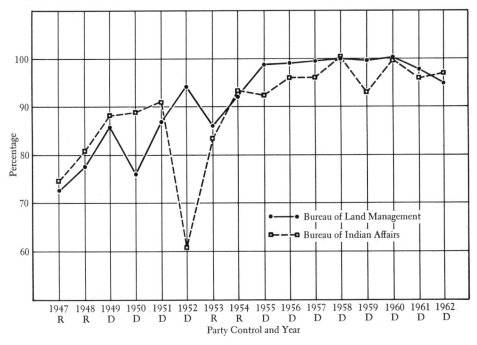

A comparison between Figures 8.3 and 8.4 helps to demonstrate that partisan controversy is less important and secular improvement more important to an understanding of Bureau of Land Management and Bureau of Indian Affairs appropriations than in the case of the Bureau of Labor Standards and the Bonneville Power Administration.

It would require a more intensive analysis than is possible here to determine what secular factors explain the change. In the case of the Bureau of Indian Affairs, a marked increase in Committee confidence certainly occurred. In the earlier period (1950) the Interior Subcommittee's expert on Indian affairs, Representative George Schwabe, declared, "The Bureau of Indian Affairs has been a stench in the nostrils of the government for many years." And he commented further, "The present Commissioner of Indian Affairs apparently did not know anything about any of the things he was questioned on."[33] In the later period (1957), however, with a new Commissioner, a long-time ranking Republican on the subcommittee, Representative Jensen, could say to him,

> After hearing you over the past years and knowing of your administration of Indian affairs and problems, I have quit worrying very much about the Indian Service. . . . It used to be a great worry to this Committee before you took over, Mr. Emmons, and before you proved to us that you were doing the worrying and a lot of deep thinking as well as your fine staff. . . . You have really given this problem — and it was a big problem — a lot of study, and you have handled it in the finest, business-like, common-sense, good, patriotic American way.[34]

The improved estate of the Bureau in Republican as well as Democratic eyes may be explainable in part by the greater confidence expressed in a new Commissioner.

In the case of the Bureau of Land Management, no explanation of its secular improvement is at hand. Two notes may be worth making. In the first place, that part of the Bureau which was formerly the Grazing Service was a focal point of controversy and was treated very unsympathetically by the eastern dominated Interior Subcommittee in the years preceding 1947.[34a] In the early years covered by this study there may have been a hangover of difficulty which was gradually eliminated. In the second place, in vivid contrast to the Forest Service whose programs (though not their locale) are very similar, the Bureau admits to a considerable inability to promote especially good rapport with the Appropriations Committee. With considerable self-deprecation and envy, a Bureau official compared his missionary efforts to those of the Forest Service:

> Frankly, I don't think we've done as much as we could do in getting our story across. My predecessor had one junket for some of the members of the Committee, but we haven't done that . . . I'm frank to say we could do more in this respect and we've talked about it. We have trouble, though, getting them to go. Most of them want to spend time in their districts [none of which are in the West where all the Bureau's work is located]. . . . We don't do public relations work like the Forest Service. They're real experts at it. . . . The Forest Service has camps and they can entertain the congressmen there. They just write and say, "Reserve so many rooms for

[33] 97 *Congressional Record*, pp. 4371–4372. On Schwabe's expertise, see 94 *Congressional Record*, p. 6599. See also Representative Taber's comment in 98 *Congressional Record*, p. 3060.

[34] House Committee on Appropriations, *Hearings on Interior Department Appropriations for 1958*, 85th Congress, 1st Session (Washington: U.S. Government Printing Office, 1957), p. 384.

[34a] See Philip O. Foss, *The Grazing Fee Dilemma* (Inter-University Case Program: University of Alabama Press, 1960).

Congressman X." And the congressmen can rough it in comfort there. They may have to take a shower instead of a tub or something; but they don't have to ladle water out of a cold stream. Why, they even run electric wires in there so that they can use their electric shavers. They are masters at glad handing. I was out there in ——— once, when a few of the foresters "just happened to drop in" for a friendly game of cards with some congressmen. Friendly game! Why, they had a generator already set up in the tent. If they can't give you a red carpet, they'll at least find some red maple leaves.

This confession of relative weakness may, indeed, have a relation to the real world of appropriations in which the Bureau seems to have had some difficulty in achieving a relationship of confidence with the Committee.

BUREAU DECISION PATTERNS: APPROPRIATIONS AS A PERCENTAGE OF THE PREVIOUS YEAR'S APPROPRIATION

As one analyzes the pattern of Committee decisions produced by one measure of bureau success, the question persists as to whether the same patterns would result if the alternative measure were applied. If bureau appropriations as a percentage of the previous year's appropriation were substituted for bureau appropriations as a percentage of estimates, would the rankings of bureaus remain the same or would they differ? The question arises because these two standards of success obviously measure somewhat different aspects of bureau performance. It is possible to conceive of a bureau receiving 100 per cent of its asking price each year for 16 years and yet not increasing its total dollar appropriation at all. Conversely, it is possible for a bureau to receive a huge increase in its appropriation each year while always receiving a low percentage of its asking price. Whether or not bureau rankings do vary when these different aspects of their performance are measured is an empirical question. It is a question which can be answered by ranking the 36 bureaus according to the second measure and by comparing the results with the earlier ranking presented in Table 8.8.

Statistically what needs to be done is to summarize for the 16-year period the yearly change in appropriations levels for each of the 36 bureaus. Since most bureaus (due to salary increases, inflated costs, etc.) would be expected to increase their overall appropriations from 1947 to 1962, the problem is to determine an average rate of growth for each bureau. This rate of growth can be used as a basis for ranking the 36 bureaus, and it will distinguish those whose appropriations increased most rapidly from those whose appropriations increased most slowly during the period. The average growth rate for each bureau has been computed according to the following procedure. For each bureau taken separately, the dollar amounts of its appropriations as granted by the House Committee were plotted against the years in which they occurred. A straight line was then drawn in such a way that it fit most closely to the array of 16 yearly points. Where a bureau's appropriation level increased markedly over the 16 years, the line (called a line of regression) slopes sharply upward. But when a bureau's appropriation level increased very slowly, the line has a small upward slope. For each of the 16 bureaus, one line of regression was produced. The slope or angle of each line was then determined, and that slope (the coefficient of regression) was taken as the basis for ranking the bureaus. A coefficient of regression of .230, for example, was converted to an average 16-year growth rate of 23.0 per cent per year. In this manner, a rank order of bureaus based on their relative ability to increase their appropriations from year to year has been produced. That ranking is presented in Table 8.10.[35]

How, then, does the ranking of Table 8.10 compare with the ranking of Table 8.8? Are the Committee's decision patterns or bureau patterns of success and failure the same no matter which measure is used, or do they vary? The statistical answer to that question can be found by correlating the two rank orders. If the two rankings are exactly the same, a perfect positive correlation will exist and a correlation coefficient of 1.0 will be found. If the rankings are exactly opposed to one another (the highest bureau in one ordering is the lowest in the other, etc.), a perfect negative correlation will exist and a correlation coefficient of −1.0 will be found. A correlation coefficient of zero would indicate that the two rank orderings had no relationship to one another. The actual correlation coefficient between the average appropriation as a per cent of estimates in Table 8.8 and the average growth rates in Table 8.10 is −0.033. It lies, therefore, very close to zero. It indicates that the two rankings are quite different and that they are virtually independent of one another. To put it another way, the fact that a bureau is successful according to one measure tells us nothing about whether or not it will be successful according to the other measure. For some individual bureaus, of course, it may, but as a general proposition it does not. If, therefore, one attempts to measure bureau success by one of these measures to the exclusion of the other, he will be neglecting a discrete dimension of bureau performance.

A more offhand comparison of the clusters of high- and low-ranking bureaus in the two orderings reveals the empirical basis for the −0.033

[35] The line of regression was calculated using the logarithm to the base e of the appropriations figures, and the result was then converted from logarithms to natural numbers. It should be noted, also, that these growth rates do not reflect the action of the House Committee only — even though the figures used are House Committee recommendations. Since each year's appropriation level bears a relation to the previous year's level, and since the Senate participated in setting the previous year's level, the growth rate to some degree reflects Senate action too.

TABLE 8.10

HOUSE COMMITTEE DECISIONS: APPROPRIATIONS GROWTH RATES,
BUREAU AVERAGES FOR THE PERIOD 1947 TO 1962

Ranking	Bureau	Department	Average Growth Rate (Per Cent per Year)
1	Office of Education	HEW	23.0
2	Bureau of Labor Standards	Labor	17.9
3	Bureau of Land Management	Interior	17.1
4	Public Health Service	HEW	15.3
5	National Park Service	Interior	14.9
6	Fish and Wildlife Service	Interior	13.0
7	Office of Vocational Rehabilitation	HEW	12.9
8	National Bureau of Standards	Commerce	12.9
9	Food and Drug Administration	HEW	12.7
10	Forest Service	Agriculture	11.5
11	Soil Conservation Service	Agriculture	11.0
12	Geological Survey	Interior	10.7
13	Weather Bureau	Commerce	9.5
14	Bureau of Labor Statistics	Labor	9.1
15	Bureau of Indian Affairs	Interior	9.0
16	Extension Service	Agriculture	9.0
17	Bureau of Narcotics	Treasury	8.7
18	Federal Bureau of Investigation	Justice	7.8
19	Social Security Administration	HEW	7.5
20	Wage and Hour Division	Labor	7.4
21	Patent Office	Commerce	7.4
22	Federal Prison System	Justice	6.9
23	Coast and Geodetic Survey	Commerce	6.4
24	Immigration and Naturalization Service	Justice	6.0
25	Secret Service	Treasury	5.9
26	Internal Revenue Service	Treasury	5.8
27	Women's Bureau	Labor	5.6
28	Rural Electrification Administration	Agriculture	4.7
29	Bureau of Mines	Interior	4.5
30	Census Bureau	Commerce	4.5[a]
31	Bureau of Reclamation	Interior	3.6[a]
32	Farmer's Home Administration	Agriculture	2.8
33	Bureau of Customs	Treasury	2.8
34	Bonneville Power Administration	Interior	2.8[a]
35	Bureau of the Mint	Treasury	.5[a]
36	Bureau of the Public Debt	Treasury	−.5

[a] The appropriations for these bureaus fluctuated so widely that the line of regression fit the various points rather poorly. The result was that the margin of error exceeded the growth rate itself. Hence these growth rates must be viewed as rather uncertain.

correlation coefficient. When both rankings are divided into clusters of 12, only 4 bureaus appear in the top one-third of both rankings and only 4 bureaus appear in the bottom one-third of both rankings. A total of 8 bureaus, moreover, appear in the top 12 in one ranking and in the bottom 12 of the other ranking. These facts make it doubly clear that no single measure of bureau influence will serve. Bureaus which receive the smallest reductions in their budget do not necessarily grow rapidly. And those that exhibit the most rapid growth may suffer substantial budget cuts. In very few cases, it would seem, will a single set of bureau level factors explain *both* a bureau's ability to get what it asks for *and* its ability to increase its appropriation from year to year.

An impressionistic glance at the dozen bureaus with the highest growth rate suggests that Appropriations Committee decisions are taken in response to the changing interests and enthusiasms of American society.[36] It sounds tautological to say that the bureaus that grow most rapidly in appropriations are those which administer policy areas where federal activity has been growing most rapidly. But the point is that the growth rates of bureaus are most strongly affected by external factors over which the Committee itself exercises no control. When Congress authorizes a new federal program or when the executive branch inaugurates the rapid expansion of an old program, it usually does so in response to strong demands generated inside and outside the government. When the Appropriations Committee votes to finance these programs at new levels, it usually does so in response to the same demands. The Appropriations Committee can assert an independent influence by accelerating or retarding the appropriations growth rate of a bureau. And in the short run its decisions can be especially helpful or harmful to the bureau involved. But the sharp expansion of bureaus whose programs have been given the highest priority by people outside the Committee could not be stopped by action inside the Committee. Nor could the Committee by its own action provide for the rapid expansion of a bureau whose activities were not commanding a commensurate increase in public support.

An observer of American life in the 1950's and 1960's will recognize within the top dozen bureaus the increased national concern for education, occupational safety, medical research, recreation in the national parks and national forests, rehabilitation of the physically handicapped, measurement in scientific research, control of drugs, conservation of the soil, and research in the field of strategically important natural resources. Bureaus implementing these programs display rising expectations accompanied by rising budget

[36] Short-run enthusiasms may, of course, be hidden by the cumulative data for 16 years. For example, the Centralia Coal Mine Disaster of 1947 had an immediate effect on the Bureau of Mines appropriation, and hurricanes Carol and Hazel of 1954 had a marked effect on the Weather Bureau appropriations in 1955. See 93 *Congressional Record*, p. 3970 and 101 *Congressional Record*, pp. 6918–6929, 8449.

estimates. To them Congress has given new statutory responsibilities or expanded existing programs under old statutes. Conversely, within the dozen bureaus having the slowest growth rates, the observer will recognize many which perform governmental functions that have remained essentially unchanged in recent years — taking the census, minting coins, managing the public debt, protecting the President, regulating traffic in and out of the country, and collecting taxes. In addition, one finds among the slow growth agencies some like the Bureau of Mines, which experienced a secular slowdown in pace with the coal industry, toward which much of its activity is directed. Others like the Rural Electrification Administration and the Farmer's Home Administration experienced an earlier period of expansion followed by a leveling off in activity. Also their external opponent, the private interests with whom they compete in making loans, may have gained in influence. It seems likely that these low-ranking bureaus will have stabilized their expectations and that these will be recorded in relatively stable budget estimates. If these gross characteristics of the most successful and the least successful of the bureaus in terms of their growth rates are at all accurate, Appropriations Committee decisions must be viewed basically as responses to policy priorities fixed by demands generated in the Committee's environment.

Confirmation of this argument can be found by examining the patterns of bureau estimates over a period of time. If the fastest growing bureaus are being pushed by forces outside the Committee, this fact should be reflected in rapidly increasing estimates. Not only should they be getting more money each year, but they should be *asking* for more each year. Since, as we have seen, a bureau's estimates are not cut too heavily percentagewise, at least not consistently, and since a bureau's estimates are rarely exceeded, only a bureau which asks for large increases over the previous year's appropriation will tend to receive fairly large increases. Table 8.11 ranks the 36 bureaus according to the average of their requested increases for the 16-year period. For each year, the budget estimate of a given bureau was expressed as a percentage increase over the previous year's appropriation. The 16 yearly percentages were then averaged to produce the totals in Table 8.11.

A comparison of the rankings in Table 8.11 and those in Table 8.10 indicates that, despite a few exceptions, the bureaus with the highest appropriations growth rates also have the biggest appropriations appetites.[37] Con-

---

[37] Among the important exceptions are some of the bureaus whose growth rates were most uncertain: the Census Bureau, Bonneville Power Administration, and Bureau of Reclamation. The appropriations levels for these 3 bureaus fluctuated a good deal more than did any of the others — the Census Bureau because its appropriations follow a 10-year cycle and the other 2 for less obvious reasons. It is this fluctuation that makes it difficult to fit a regression line to their appropriations performance. Their fluctuation also has the effect of exaggerating their average appetite. This exaggeration occurs because,

TABLE 8.11

BUREAU ESTIMATES AS A PERCENTAGE INCREASE OVER PREVIOUS
YEAR'S APPROPRIATIONS: BUREAU AVERAGES FOR THE PERIOD
1947 TO 1962

Ranking	Bureau	Department	16-Year Average
1	Office of Education	HEW	77.0
2	Bureau of the Census	Commerce	76.5
3	Bureau of Labor Standards	Labor	52.0
4	National Bureau of Standards	Commerce	41.0
5	Bonneville Power Administration	Interior	29.9
6	Bureau of Reclamation	Interior	26.5
7	National Park Service	Interior	24.2
8	Geological Survey	Interior	23.9
9	Bureau of Land Management	Interior	22.9
10	Office of Vocational Rehabilitation	HEW	20.9
11	Bureau of Labor Statistics	Labor	20.6
12	Bureau of Indian Affairs	Interior	19.4
13	Public Health Service	HEW	19.2
14	Fish and Wildlife Service	Interior	17.9
15	Coast and Geodetic Survey	Commerce	17.4
16	Weather Bureau	Commerce	15.9
17	Wage and Hour Division	Labor	14.7
18	Federal Prison System	Justice	14.3
19	Food and Drug Administration	HEW	14.1
20	Social Security Administration	HEW	12.7
21	Bureau of Mines	Interior	11.9
22	Soil Conservation Service	Agriculture	11.8
23	Women's Bureau	Labor	11.5
24	Federal Bureau of Investigation	Justice	10.0
25	Patent Office	Commerce	9.4
26	Immigration and Naturalization Service	Justice	9.2
27	Secret Service	Treasury	9.1
28	Bureau of Narcotics	Treasury	8.8
29	Farmer's Home Administration	Agriculture	8.84
30	Bureau of Customs	Treasury	8.79
31	Internal Revenue Service	Treasury	8.56
32	Rural Electrification Administration	Agriculture	8.28
33	Extension Service	Agriculture	7.30
34	Forest Service	Agriculture	7.30
35	Bureau of the Mint	Treasury	6.07
36	Bureau of the Public Debt	Treasury	.57

in calculating the mean, the impact of a sharp upswing is exaggerated and the impact of a sharp downswing is minimized. Hence, it seems likely that the high rankings of these bureaus in Table 8.12 is an artifact of the statistics. But, so too may their low rankings in Table 8.11 be an artifact of the statistics. Generalizations concerning these 3 bureaus should be taken, therefore, with an extra dose of skepticism. It might also be noted here that, since Tables 8.11 and 8.12 were calculated in a different manner, they cannot be compared arithmetically. Only the relation between the two rankings can be compared — not the 16-year averages.

versely, the bureaus which exhibit the slowest growth also tend to have the smallest appetites. In one sense, growth is a function of appetite. In order to grow, a bureau must ask for sizable increases. But, in a larger sense, both growth and appetite are a function of the same set of expectations. To a small degree, these expectations can be affected by aspiration levels generated from within the agency itself. But most important are the expectations emanating from the larger society to which agency, Appropriations Committee, and Congress respond.

A complete explanation of why the top dozen bureaus appear where they do would require detailed case histories of each one. A superficial and selective examination may, however, yield some explanatory clues. One way of trying to isolate the factors associated with growth is to look at those bureaus which rank near the top in terms of expansion but near the bottom in terms of getting what they asked for from the Committee. Four agencies of the Interior Department fall into this category. In terms of subject matter they (along with the two high-growth Agriculture Bureaus) reflect a growing concern with the development, conservation, and use of the land. Conflicting demands are expressed both within and across these agencies—as, for example, the conflict between the conservationists and the recreationists or between the conservationists and the cattlemen, sheep raisers, and miners who earn a living off the public land. No matter what the demands, however, the clientele group pressing them tends to be well organized, and most of them command widespread public support.

An official of the Fish and Wildlife Service said, typically,

> We have a lot of popular support. More people are interested in hunting and fishing than in anything else — except perhaps social security. It's a tradition in America and it's not controversial. It's like motherhood. Everybody is for it in principle and theory. It doesn't go to the heart of social or political reforms the way some programs do. Everybody is in favor of conservation. Of course when you close the duck season early, you find that a lot of "conservationists" just want to kill ducks. . . . What is it that Congressman Jensen always says, "Take your boy fishing and he won't land in reform school" . . . we feel that we have very strong organizational support. In fact, they think we don't ask for enough money and they try to push more money on us than we would have asked for.

The Appropriations Committee is expected to perceive these demands and respond to them. And they do. Interior Subcommittee Chairman Kirwan defended an increase in the Fish and Wildlife Service appropriation, saying,

> Twenty-six million people in the United States last year bought hunting and fishing licenses. There are only about twelve million who are members of fraternal organizations, but this is the biggest organization, larger than all fraternal organizations put together . . . twenty-six million people through-

out this nation are engaged in that pastime. I do not think there is a community in this country where you will not find during the hunting season men going out into the woods for this wonderful recreation. Yes, there are thousands of them. They are entitled to some consideration.[38]

Yet the average reduction in the Service's annual budget request was among the greatest of the bureaus studied. Strong external demands for expansion, it appears, bring a response in kind. Still, Committee suspicion of expansionist bureaus leads them to hold expanding budgets below bureau expectations. It may be, moreover, that it is precisely in the budgets of those bureaus that are expanding that the Committee can exercise the greatest discretion. And it may be that rapidly expanding budgets are the most difficult to defend against the Committee's suspicion that budgets are padded.

Committee decisions regarding the National Park Service produce a similar pattern of success and failure. In no one of the 16 years did the Park Service receive all that it requested; yet in 12 of the 16 years, the Committee voted to increase its appropriation. The relative neglect of the parks during wartime, the automobile affluence of postwar America, and the popularity of traveling vacations — especially camping — brought nationwide demands for improved park facilities in the 1950's and 1960's. The obvious inadequacy led to popular programs of acceleration, such as "Mission 66," which required sharp increases in funds. The Committee granted these increases, but at levels below the aspirations of the agency. Committee support for expansion was illustrated by the action it took on construction items in 1956. In the summer of 1955, subcommittee chairman Mike Kirwan (D., Ohio) took a 5,000-mile trip through the parks and discovered at firsthand severe over-crowding. In 1956 he reacted to his experience:

> When the Director of the Park Service appeared before us, I asked him, "Can you use $10 million for construction in the parks?" He did not want to answer, because his superior was present. But finally he admitted that he could. When I said, "I will double what the budget approves," somebody called the White House. They had a special meeting of the Cabinet. The Director of the agency appeared before the Cabinet, and they sent up a supplemental estimate for something like $8 or $9 million. The Committee, in its wisdom, never recognized that supplemental estimate. They had a job to do to help put those parks in proper condition. Every member of the Committee agreed to make the total $15 million for construction in the parks for the benefit of the people who visit the parks.[39]

In that year, the Committee voted the Park Service an increase of 50.3 per cent over its 1955 appropriation; yet still the 1956 appropriation fell a bit short of the 1956 estimate.

[38] 97 *Congressional Record*, p. 4735.
[39] 102 *Congressional Record*, p. 3046.

During the hearings in 1957, Chairman Kirwan referred back to the action of 1956 and asked Park Service Director Conrad Wirth,

> MR. KIRWAN: Are you satisfied with the action of this Committee in voting last year an amount which was not in the budget? There was no request from down the street, but this Committee on both sides — Republicans and Democrats — voted an increase from $5 million to $15 million for the parks and construction. Are you glad that this Committee did so?
>
> MR. WIRTH: Sir, we certainly were very very happy . . . the department officials and I are very happy, we appreciate the appropriation we got last year.
>
> . . . . .
>
> MR. KIRWAN: You are doing a good job. Not only does the Committee appreciate it but the people that are using the parks appreciate it.[40]

Again in 1957 the Committee increased the service's appropriation, by 14.1 per cent, but refused to grant its full asking price.

Park Service officials recognized that they had not allayed Committee suspicions. And beneath the public exchanges of solicitation, Park Service officials voiced private complaints. One of them expressed concern at the lack of sympathy which the long-time subcommittee twosome of Kirwan and Jensen had shown toward items classified as overhead expenses:

> Congress has been very restrictive on general administrative expenses. I don't know why, but they are down on this item and we can't get any expansion . . . Jensen and Kirwan think that our Washington operation is too big, but we can't run the agency with what we have now. I don't know what the solution will be. Something has to give. We can't go on this way . . . last year we had to be frank with Congress and tell them that we had to take money from other places and put it in G.A.E.

This official spoke also of unwise cuts in overhead items such as safety officers and field offices:

> Both Ben and Mike are down on regional offices for some reason or other. They don't think they are necessary. Frankly, I don't think Ben knows the function of a regional office. I hope some day I can get him out there to see how those fellows work.

Committee members, though responsive to external demands, retained their Committee-oriented suspicion of increased overhead expenses — in Washington or in the field. Furthermore, whereas the Committee could and did increase construction appropriations, by the same token it could exercise considerable discretion in reducing construction figures. Thus the Committee has acquiesced in, and at times accelerated, the rapid growth of the Park

---

[40] *Hearings on Interior Department Appropriations for 1958, op. cit.*, p. 223.

Service, yet the Service has not succeeded in convincing the Committee that its estimates represent its rock-bottom needs and cannot stand a greater than average reduction.

Another substantive characteristic of the cluster of twelve high-growth-rate bureaus would seem to be an emphasis on research. The National Bureau of Standards and the Geological Survey, both primarily research agencies, moved up dramatically from the bottom one-third to the top one-third when the second measure of agency success was used. The Public Health Service also rated high in terms of growth on the basis of increased appropriations for medical research. Indeed, all of the top dozen agencies in Table 8.11, save the Bureau of Labor Standards and the National Park Service, have substantial research components in their appropriations. A general emphasis on education and on research in certain high-priority areas was an obvious characteristic of the period in which these rankings were established.

In increasing federal expenditures for research, the Appropriations Committee responded to demands communicated to it from the larger political system. But the sources of these demands varied in terms of the breadth of interest involved. Neither the Geological Survey nor the National Bureau of Standards owes its growth to widespread public support. Indeed, both are virtually unknown. The head of one lumped the two together saying, "We have similar problems. We're both old established agencies — with well-established but much overlooked missions." Officials of both agencies worry about their lack of "glamor." The impetus for their expansion (save, perhaps, for the water surveys made by the Geological Survey) must be generated by the bureaus themselves with the help of specialized scientific groups. In the 1950's and 1960's the claim of scientific research on federal money was accepted by the Committee as self-evident, and it supported sharp increases in the activity of these two bureaus. But both bureaus remained conspicuously naive or reluctant about taking the initiative in improving their direct relations with the Committee. In this respect, they stand as the very antithesis of the agencies of the Agriculture Department discussed earlier.

Neither the Geological Survey nor the National Bureau of Standards lobbies for congressional support, and their Directors view such activity as irregular if not sinful — and in any case not appropriate for scientists. Said one, when asked about recruiting Committee support,

> That would involve you in a lobbying situation and I've never done that. I don't believe in it. Some agencies do, but in the long run it will turn against them and they'll pay for it.

Both confess to having considerable problems in terms of Committee rapport. Both find their hearings before the Budget Bureau "more penetrating and more satisfying" than their hearings before the Appropriations Committee. And both find Budget Bureau examiners more willing to visit their installations than are Committee members. Nonetheless, they are content to let the self-evident merits of scientific research carry the brunt of their case. The point of the discussion is that, whereas the obvious need for research has kept their appropriations expanding at a high rate, their failure to reach out for and gain a close relationship with the Committee[41] has cost them much in terms of relatively serious reductions in their estimates.

By way of contrast, the expanding research efforts of the Public Health Service have been based upon widespread public support. By increasing the appropriations of this agency, the Committee has responded to a popular demand, which has been spearheaded by a nationally prestigeful group — medical doctors and their leaders. "I do not believe there is a more popular program existing in our government,"[42] said veteran subcommittee chairman John Fogarty regarding medical research. In the plaintive acquiescence of Clarence Cannon, who fought hard to check the medical research explosion, we find a more graphic statement of the external support for the program. Said Cannon during a dispute in 1956,

> Every year we have increased this appropriation until today it has attained a percentage beyond that reached by any activity in any department of the government in a like time. . . . We are dealing here today with the most adroit and most effective lobby I have ever seen. Yesterday morning alone, between eight and twelve o'clock noon, over four thousand telegrams had come in, most of them demanding support of Mr. Fogarty.
> If Mr. Fogarty ever expects to run for President, now is the time. And if I . . . ever expect to run for President, now is the time to forget it. . . . You know in a superheated hysterically pressured atmosphere like this, nobody is going to vote against home and mother and free beer — nobody is going to vote in favor of cancer and heart disease. The answer to that is a foregone conclusion.[43]

Everyone is or can be made to be concerned about his health, and the medical advances made in the 1950's and 1960's carried general public interest in this field to a new height.

Unlike the research agencies discussed earlier, the Public Health Service has worked to maintain external support. They have encouraged a stable of highly respected witnesses — Paul Dudley White, for example, when he was attending President Eisenhower — to testify as to the need for and the pro-

---

[41] See House Appropriations Committee, *House Report No. 308*, 85th Congress, 1st Session (Washington: U.S. Government Printing Office, 1957), pp. 11–12.

[42] 96 *Congressional Record*, p. 5717.

[43] 102 *Congressional Record*, pp. 1126–1128.

spective gain from additional research funds. "I'm sure," said one Public Health Service official, "when these men come in here and testify as to what they think the needs are, they carry great weight." The Service has battled the Budget Bureau to retain a budgetary structure that would feature a large number of line items — one to a program — in the common belief that a program budget will draw external support and be harder to cut back:

> They [Budget Bureau] keep after us to reduce the number of line items in our budget. They want to [have] . . . the thing in large categories because they don't attract so much outside support. If you have a category called engineers, for instance, that doesn't mean much. But if you break them down by program, the air pollution people, the radiation people, the water pollution people all become interested and tell their congressmen. So we conduct a running battle with them on the structure of our budget.

The Service has actively sought to improve its relations with the Committee. Committee members regularly visit the National Institutes of Health in Bethesda where they can hardly help being impressed with the many very tangible results accomplished there. "There isn't a year that goes by that some members of the subcommittee or their staff don't visit some of our facilities." Committee members are urged to go abroad in the American delegation to the World Health Organization and to attend other professional conferences:

> Mel Laird [ranking subcommittee member from 1959 to the present] was new to this thing when I came in. But since then he has visited us and he has participated in the World Health Organization conference and in other conferences. He was very impressed with everything and it has made a great difference in his attitude on our appropriations.

The extra- and intra-Committee efforts of the Public Health Service resemble the efforts of the Agriculture Department agencies more than they do the behavior of sister research agencies like the Geological Survey or the National Bureau of Standards. And this resemblance characterizes their appropriations record as well. The Public Health Service ranked fourth in terms of growth and thirteenth in terms of getting what it asked for. If it were not for two 30 per cent reductions in its budget during the Republican budget-cutting years of 1947 and 1953, the Public Health Service would have been near the top in both rankings.

The Appropriations Committee response has not been tinged with the normal amount of suspicion. Quite to the contrary, the subcommittee, beginning with Chairman Frank Keefe in the 80th Congress and continuing with John Fogarty in the years since, has been among the nation's leaders in pushing for accelerated appropriations for medical research activity. In 1956, Fogarty commented regarding the Public Health Service,

> This Committee over the past ten years, to my knowledge, whenever it has been brought to our attention that we should appropriate funds for a specific thing, we have gone ahead and done so, whether there happened to be a budget request or not.[44]

Emboldened by this attitude on the part of the Committee, the Public Health Service has consistently sought more money than granted to it by the Budget Bureau; and, in contrast to the Geological Survey and the Bureau of Standards, its officials find their Committee relations far more satisfying than those with the executive branch. Some indication of the interaction among Budget Bureau, Bureau, and Committee can be gleaned from the exchange between subcommittee member Winfield Denton and Budget Director Percival Brundage:

> MR. DENTON: How much did the National Institutes of Health ask for and how much did you give them?
> MR. BRUNDAGE: They have always asked for more than we gave them. We gave them a substantial increase, but it was less than they asked for.
> MR. DENTON: You know that we gave them substantially more last year than you asked for or they asked for.
> MR. BRUNDAGE: That is right.
> MR. DENTON: I just wonder what you have done with that figure.
> MR. BRUNDAGE: They still came in for some more. We thought that we had given them a very generous increase last year and you added to it. I think that we have given them a very generous increase this year, but they are not satisfied.[45]

The Appropriations Committee has responded to external demands in this area more rapidly than has the executive branch. This differential response can probably be attributed in large part to the leadership of John Fogarty, who, despite the efforts of full Committee leaders to stack the Committee against him, has put his stamp on the appropriation. As a departmental official put it,

> John Fogarty has an obsession about the value of medical research. And he's become a real leader in the field. These outside groups — and you deal with plenty of them in this field — they love him. He's an idol of theirs.

By a recent count, this network of mutual admiration had gained Fogarty about 100 awards in the field of public health.[46]

[44] 102 *Congressional Record*, p. 3936. See also Fogarty's comments in 95 *Congressional Record*, pp. 2091–2092.
[45] *Hearings on the 1958 Budget, op. cit.*, p. 155.
[46] See *Congressional Record*, Daily Edition, May 10, 1962, pp. 7591–7592; February 28, 1964, pp. 3814–3815; July 18, 1962, pp. 13072–13073.

The characteristics of bureaus with high growth rates can be put in still sharper relief if we look briefly at the two bureaus which ranked in the top twelve in terms of low budget reduction, but which ranked in the bottom twelve in terms of growth rates. Committee decisions on these two bureaus — the Bureau of Customs and the Bureau of the Public Debt — are the exact reverse of decisions on such bureaus as the Fish and Wildlife Service, the National Park Service, the Geological Survey, and the National Bureau of Standards. And the bureaus involved do seem to display an opposite set of characteristics. Neither commands noteworthy public support either through nationwide recognition or through organized groups. Their functions are not expanding very rapidly. Their work is of such a routine sort that the Committee has relatively little discretion in cutting budgets. And, in the case of the Bureau of the Public Debt, the use of automatic equipment has steadily reduced the overall size and the "cuttable" elements of its budget. Yet the Committee relations of these two agencies are such as to inspire a maximum of confidence in their budget estimates. Commissioner Edwin L. Kilby of the Bureau of the Public Debt, for example, was considered by Treasury officials to be one of their star performers:

> He was one of the best witnesses in the department. He had been around a long time and knew all the legal ramifications of his program and they are plenty. You couldn't stump him. He picked the answers right off.

A Treasury official described Committee attitudes toward the Customs Bureau leadership, "They like Commissioner [Ralph] Kelly, but they have implicit confidence in Assistant Commissioner [David] Strubinger. He's a career man, and they believe what he tells them." The strength of these bureaus would seem to lie in their Committee relations — featured by a minimum of Committee suspicion. And this characteristic is reflected in their appropriations record.

As we have seen, Appropriations Committee members expressed a great deal of confidence in Treasury Department agencies, and as a group these agencies ranked high in terms of receiving what they requested. Yet every one of them slipped in the ranking produced by the measurement of growth rates. In the first ranking, three Treasury agencies appeared among the top one-third and none appeared in the bottom one-third. In the second ranking, no Treasury agencies appeared in the top one-third and five were found in the bottom one-third. These changes are significant, and they present an interesting contrast to the changes experienced by Interior Department agencies. Treasury agencies appear to be strong in their Committee relations but weak in terms of drawing external support. Some Interior agencies appear to be strong in commanding external support but weak in cementing Committee relations. These contrasts taken together with our previous descriptions furnish support for the following generalization: *High growth rates can be accounted for primarily by factors external to the Committee, whereas the ability to keep budget cuts to a minimum can be accounted for primarily by factors internal to the Committee-agency relationship.*

Even greater support for this generalization can be found by a final cursory examination of two categories of bureaus — those which rank high according to both measures of Committee decision and those which rank low according to both measures. If the generalization is accurate, one would expect that those bureaus with consistently high rankings would enjoy both external support and good committee relations and that those bureaus with consistently low rankings would enjoy neither. At the very superficial level of analysis essayed in this study, these predictions would seem to be borne out. The four consistently high-ranking agencies were the Office of Education, the Food and Drug Administration, the Soil Conservation Service, and the Forest Service. The appropriations success of the two Agricultural agencies discussed earlier provides ample evidence for the existence of support from both clientele groups and from the relevant Appropriations Subcommittee members. The same combination is present in the case of the two bureaus from the Department of Health, Education, and Welfare.

The rapid growth of the Office of Education surely reflects the high priority given to the improvement of and support for education by Americans outside and inside Congress in the 1950's and 1960's. Congress reflected this concern by passing legislation which gave new statutory responsibilities to the Office and by sharply increasing its budget. In 1950, and through subsequent renewals, the Congress gave the Office the responsibility for administering a program of grants to federally impacted areas. In the wake of the educational crisis illuminated by Sputnik, Congress passed the National Defense Education Act, and placed its implementation in the Office of Education. These programs are expressive of public concern and have commanded widespread external support. The aid to impacted areas program, which funnels federal money to the districts of over three hundred congressmen, has been particularly popular in the House. An older program for vocational education commands strong support from southern and rural congressmen and from all agricultural organizations; and it has been steadily expanded. The Office's appropriations growth rate was far and away the greatest of any agency studied.

The infusion of large amounts of money into the agency's budget has, relatively speaking, reduced the Committee's area of discretion. And, if a searching analysis were to be made of each bureau's budget to determine what percentage of it is subject to Appropriations Committee action, the Office might rank lower than it does in terms of getting what it asks for. But on the evidence collected, the Office ranks rather high in this regard. And there is no doubt but that its relations with the Fogarty subcommittee were excellent.

Here, as in the case of the Public Health Service, the Committee took the lead in pressing for appropriations increases and in holding down budget cuts. One subcommittee leader commented in 1959 that

> Education hasn't been getting anything up until the last four years. That's because we wrote in the report that they should come back and ask for more money. Now that's pretty unusual.

Just how unusual the interaction between the Office and the Committee became is convincingly displayed in this lengthy interchange between Commissioner of Education L. G. Derthick and Subcommittee Chairman Fogarty in 1957:

> MR. FOGARTY: You have been in the education field all of your life. Why is it that more interest has not been shown in the Department of Education here in Washington by educators and their organizations?
>
> MR. DERTHICK: Well, Mr. Chairman, in the last few years, organizations like mine, shall we say, if I may call it that at the moment, have been interested in the Office of Education; they have been greatly distressed that our Office of Education did not have more stature and that it did not have more resources to render services, and they have been passing resolutions for a good many years.
>
> MR. FOGARTY: And if that is all they did, that is why nothing was ever done. Just a resolution would never get you anything.
>
> MR. DERTHICK: You are right; it makes me happy to hear you say that. You are right.
>
> And yet, representatives of these organizations were talking to Presidents, they were talking to Secretaries, to Cabinet members, they were talking to members of Congress, urging something to be done to strengthen the Office of Education.
>
> MR. FOGARTY: I never heard much from them. Maybe they did not get down to this level.
>
> MR. DERTHICK: Maybe they did not get up to this level, as they should. But would you agree, Mr. Chairman, that the development that has given us our advantage in the last year or two has been the tremendous increase in public interest in education?
>
> MR. FOGARTY: No; I do not agree with that.
>
> MR. DERTHICK: Well, for whatever reason, of course, we are all encouraged, I would say.
>
> MR. FOGARTY: Well, I will tell you the reason there has been some pickup in your staff and in your appropriations, and I will read to you the report that this Committee issued two years ago. This report that I shall read was not written because of any outside interest that had been in to see me, or any of your national organizations that had spoken to this committee in support of higher appropriations for education.
>
> It was because of cuts that were made in your appropriations three or four years ago, and because of what we thought were attempts to change the status of the Office of Education. Because of these things, and strictly on our own initiative, this is what we said:

In the opinion of this Committee this spreading of activities and functions of the federal Government in the field of education can only lead to a further deterioration of the standing of the Office of Education in this country. The Committee feels very strongly that we ought to have an Office of Education that is effective and one that the education authorities all over the country would have pride in and would look to for leadership and for assistance in their problems. The Committee has therefore allowed no funds for the items of cooperative research on education and the National Advisory Committee on Education and has allowed $100,000 to complete the work of the White House Conference and has allowed increases over the budget request for salaries and expenses of the Office of Education.

Now, that was a direct invitation to the Office of Education to come up to Congress the following year with an increased budget, and that was the reason that the budget has been increased during the last couple of years and why you can have some hope, I think, that Congress really wants to keep your Office free of any outside interference and wants to see it grow for purposes of helping education all over the country.

MR. DERTHICK: Mr. Chairman, may I say this, that that is a very refreshing experience for me. I had not anticipated that from this Committee. I repeat that I have much to learn and I did not know that — strange as it may seem, being a schoolteacher, I did not know that — but it is very encouraging to me to think that that impetus would come from this congressional committee to strengthen the Office of Education.

I knew the Committee was sympathetic and interested and one had only to see the budget to know that it was very fine and responsive over here, but I did not realize the degree of initiative that the Committee has taken.

MR. FOGARTY: The Committee has always been sympathetic, to my knowledge, Mr. Derthick, for 11 years, anyway; it has always been sympathetic with this Office.

But it has not always received the support of Congress that it should have, and the main reason, in my opinion, is that the people connected with education nationwide just did not pay much attention to it. They never made themselves felt in the Washington area. Do you know what I mean?

MR. DERTHICK: Yes, sir.

MR. FOGARTY: We have seen many other programs in the Government grow and grow and grow. One of the main reasons they have grown to such an extent is that they have had committees on a national level that were meeting regularly and did not think it was below them to come and talk to members of Congress and ask them to support federal appropriations, nor did they seem to fear federal control over their activity if they talked to members of Congress to increase their appropriation.

It seems to me, in talks I have had with some of our educators all over the country, that they just were reluctant to come to congressmen because — well, they thought it might be called politics. As you perhaps know, there is not much today that is not in politics, even in your own system back in Chattanooga, Tennessee, and this job you had in Bavaria — there is always a certain amount of politics, no matter what kind of outfit you are working for. They all have their own politics. I do not know anything of importance today where there is not some politics. Does that make sense to you?

．　．　．　．　．

The point I want to emphasize is that one of the reasons the Office of Education has not advanced along with others is because you never did have any real organization out in the field. You have got to be organized.

．　．　．　．　．

MR. DERTHICK: Well, never in my experience have I seen such interest in the Office of Education and I think people do expect us to move out and I am glad for the initiative that came from the Committee. I am sorry that we did not do more out in the field.[47]

This network of mutual support was strengthened, in this case at least, by the friendliest of personal relationships between the Commissioner and the subcommittee chairman.

The consistently high rankings of the Food and Drug Administration result from the Committee members' conviction that "the Food and Drug Administration always comes in with a tight budget," plus the development of broad public concern in more recent years over the control of drugs. Widely publicized investigations of the drug industry led by Senator Estes Kefauver and widely publicized incidents demonstrating the potential danger of faulty drugs (e.g., polio vaccine and thalidomide) have combined to precipitate a demand for a vastly increased corps of scientific and investigative personnel. Accordingly, the agency's appropriation was tripled between 1958 and 1962. Long before their appropriations rose so rapidly, however, the Food and Drug Administration had acquired a reputation with the Committee which was the very prototype of the favorable image. Committee members viewed it as a noncontroversial agency, performing a necessary function in the protection of public health, and characterized by a routine, tangible work load. They viewed the agency in their own self-image and expressed special confidence in the Administration's leadership and personnel. The following comment made by subcommittee chairman Frank Keefe at the height of the budget-cutting mood of 1947 is illustrative of countless others:

> I think it would be desirable before the Committee writes this bill up for the entire Committee actually to visit the Pure Food and Drug Administration laboratory, and to observe the self-effacing, self-sacrificing, efficient scientists and chemists and research men who are doing work day

[47] House Committee on Appropriations, *Hearings on Departments of Labor and HEW Appropriations for 1958*, 85th Congress, 1st Session (Washington: U.S. Government Printing Office, 1957), pp. 229–233.

by day . . . without any fanfare, without any bells ringing or sirens screeching, or front-page publicity; but doing work that makes it possible to live daily without fear of the contraction of disease from foods, etc. I think it is an amazing piece of work and, so far as I am concerned, it . . . is not a type of activity which falls within the sphere of the contemplated use of the broadax in reduction of appropriations in order that we may effect very needed and necessary economies. . . .

One of the reasons that this Committee has in the past, and I believe will in the future, be inclined to be more generous with this type of activity is that I am certain that the membership of the Committee and the membership of the Congress have implicit confidence in the men and women who are devoting themselves to this service.[48]

John Fogarty, too, has given them his complete support:

Every person when he gets an ache or pain will take a chance with any kind of drug. They are flocking to the drug stores, trying this or that to straighten themselves out. If we do not have an agency like this, you are taking a chance and I am taking a chance, and every living person is taking a chance.[49]

The Committee's perception of the Administration has been the same as its perception of other law enforcement agencies. And this favorable image has kept Administration budget reductions minimal. At the same time, they have benefited by an external demand for greatly expanded activities. This outside support accounts for the fact that the Food and Drug Administration is the only one among the five law enforcement agencies which ranks so high in Committee confidence (Table 8.9) to experience also an exceptional degree of growth.

If the Office of Education, the Food and Drug Administration, the Soil Conservation Service, and the Forest Service had the best of all appropriations worlds from 1947 to 1962, the worst befell the Bureau of Mines, the Bonneville Power Administration, the Bureau of Reclamation, and the Census Bureau during that same period. The consistently low ranking of the latter four bureaus would seem to result from a combination of weakness in support from inside and from outside the Appropriations Committee. The controversial nature of the Bonneville and Reclamation agencies which robbed them of their bipartisan Committee confidence has already been discussed. The fact that their operations are surrounded by the public power issue probably has kept their external support contained within certain regions. On the other hand, these bureaus face standing external opposition. It is one thing for a bureau to be hit by a fleeting economy mood. But it is more damaging for a

[48] Hearings on Labor Department and Federal Security Administration Appropriations for 1948, op. cit., pp. 9–10. See also Representative Keefe's comment in 94 Congressional Record, p. 2343.

[49] 99 Congressional Record, p. 5380.

bureau to have to contend, year in and year out, with permanent, organized opposition. As far as the Bonneville Power Administration is concerned, its major expansion was completed during the period. The weakness of clientele support for the Bureau of Reclamation, when compared to the external support for the Army Corps of Engineers, both of which do similar work, has been the subject of intensive political analysis. The emphasis on flood control activities of the Corps as distinguished from the multipurpose interests of Reclamation, the national scope of one as opposed to another, and the Corps' intensive cultivation of grass-roots support have all been cited as basic reasons for this discrepancy. The Corps has retained a degree of support locally and in Congress that has been conspicuously denied to the Bureau of Reclamation.[50]

The Bureau of Mines and the Census Bureau each suffered, too, from the lack of intensive demand beyond the Committee. The Bureau of Mines experienced a secular decline in the importance of coal-mining. And, in addition, it experienced a serious loss of confidence on the part of the Committee midway in the period discussed. Representative Ivor Fenton, for whom the Bureau was a subcommittee specialty (See pp. 161–162), spoke out in justification of budget reduction saying,

> For the past two or three years, your subcommittee through investigations, etc., has become concerned of an apparent apathy on the part of the Bureau of Mines and the Interior Department to disregard requests for information needed to intelligently mark up the appropriation bill. Therefore, if some of the items appear to be reduced too much, I can only say that it is because we do not have the proper information in their so-called justifications.[51]

Since other subcommittee members followed Fenton's lead with regard to this bureau, his displeasure was probably significant.

Another example of an agency relatively short on appropriations "clout" is the Census Bureau. Occasionally, support wells up for a specialized census, but, ordinarily, the Bureau carries out a constitutional mandate which Americans accept but for which they generate no particular enthusiasm. Indeed, its activities draw an extra quantity of suspicion — suspicion reflected by Commerce Subcommittee members in such comments as: "Are you becoming a classical, horrible example of professional bureaucrats?" "Are you the world's number one snooper?" "Between you and Dr. Kinsey there are not going to be any more secrets left in this country."[52] It is perhaps somewhat unfair to describe the Bureau as having a low growth rate, since it must expand and

[50] See Arthur Maass, *Muddy Waters* (Cambridge: Harvard University Press, 1951).
[51] 100 *Congressional Record*, pp. 4617–4618.
[52] House Committee on Appropriations, *Hearings on Commerce Department Appropriations for 1958*, 85th Congress, 1st Session (Washington: U.S. Government Printing Office, 1957), pp. 679, 706.

contract in a rhythm governed by the prescribed ten-year cycle. Nonetheless, Bureau attempts to expand its census-gathering activities were repeatedly thwarted by the Committee in the period studied. Given its cyclical appropriations pattern, the case of the Census Bureau surely invites further attention. But it certainly appears at first blush to owe its consistently low ranking to a lack of positive support both externally and on the Committee.

SOME CONCLUSIONS

The foregoing bureau level analysis of House Appropriations Committee decisions is admittedly superficial. It represents only a crude first attempt to identify some patterns of Committee output and some determinants of those patterns. But the analysis does add supporting evidence for some of the generalizations about output made earlier in the chapter. And, because the units of analysis are more refined, bureau level explorations add new dimensions to those earlier generalizations.

From the outset, the basic point has been made that the Committee is subject to two sets of expectations — one holding that the Committee should supply money for programs authorized by Congress and one holding that the Committee should fund these programs in as economical a manner as possible. People outside the Committee and Committee members alike hold to both sets of expectations, but the potential conflict between them is obvious. Because of their different goals and perspectives, groups outside the Committee (e.g., House members and executive agencies) tend to emphasize the positive expectation of financial support, whereas Committee members tend to place special emphasis on the more negative expectations of economy and budget reduction. If Appropriations Committee decisions are to meet the expectations of House members and executive agencies, they must be generous in response to external demands for ever-increasing funds. If Committee decisions are to meet the dominant expectations of Committee members, they must prevent the unnecessary expenditure of funds. Committee decisions, then, can be viewed as efforts to satisfy both groups — either of which could, by taking certain actions, cause radical changes in Committee activity.

In terms of an overall summary of their decisions, it appears that the Committee meets both sets of expectations. Its dominant response to bureau requests is to grant an increase over the previous year's appropriation but, at the same time, to reduce their estimates. Furthermore, in an overall sense, the Committee meets both expectations by avoiding drastic action of any kind in any direction. Its decisions are mostly marginal or incremental — whether measured by the relation of budget estimates to appropriations or by the relation of appropriations to last year's appropriation — and they tend to sustain existing relationships. These incremental responses do not come

410

about simply as a matter of Committee choice, for the Committee acts within a set of historical, institutional, and informational restraints which circumscribe its area of discretion. Still, the Committee acts as an independent and significant influence on appropriations decisions. Viewed in the broadest perspective, Appropriations Committee decisions fall into a pattern which can be described as a balanced, conservative, incremental response to conflicting expectations.

An examination of Committee decisions bureau by bureau provides some further evidence of this balanced response. That is to say, over the sixteen-year period almost all bureaus received all types of decisions at the hands of the Committee, and, for the most part, these decisions were of an incremental kind. To put it another way, every bureau has a reason for its existence, every bureau commands some support from outside the Committee, and every bureau operates with some degree of economy. These facts set parameters within which the Committee must operate and which ensure a degree of balance in Committee decisions. Beyond these observations, however, a bureau level analysis highlights the presence of imbalance or differential treatment of individual bureaus. It highlights individual exceptions to overall decision patterns and invites an explanation of them.

Types of Committee responses do not occur randomly. Some kinds of bureaus account for a significantly larger proportion of some kinds of Committee decisions than do other types of bureaus. The Committee, that is to say, may respond to one set of expectations when it emanates from one kind of executive agency and to the other set of expectations when it comes from another kind of agency. Indeed, in terms of the bureaus affected, their seems to be no relation between Committee decisions which stress budget reduction and Committee decisions which stress increased appropriations. Working only with these two independent kinds of Committee decisions and ranking the bureaus in terms of their success, four possible patterns exist. Any given bureau may receive favorable treatment in both respects, unfavorable treatment in both respects, or favorable treatment in one respect and unfavorable treatment in the other (two combinations). When the bureaus are ranked and classified according to these four possible patterns, those bureaus that can be said with some confidence to fall into one of the four categories are listed in Table 8.12.[53]

The usefulness of the classification in Table 8.12 is not that it establishes any particular list of successful and unsuccessful bureaus. At best, this classification holds only for the conditions of the period 1947 to 1962. And, one suspects, a slice of this same period might even have yielded quite a different

[53] The least confidence can be had in the classification of the Census Bureau, Bonneville Power Administration, and Bureau of Reclamation. See Footnote No. 37 in this chapter.

TABLE 8.12

BUREAU LEVEL PATTERNS OF APPROPRIATIONS COMMITTEE DECISIONS

BUREAU RANKINGS — APPROPRIATIONS AS PERCENTAGE OF PREVIOUS YEAR'S APPROPRIATIONS	BUREAU RANKINGS — APPROPRIATIONS AS PERCENTAGE OF ESTIMATES	
	From the Twelve Highest-Ranking Bureaus	*From the Twelve Lowest-Ranking Bureaus*
From the Twelve Highest-Ranking Bureaus	Bureaus with strong support from the Committee and strong external support: Food and Drug Administration Forest Service Office of Education Soil Conservation Service	Bureaus with weak support from the Committee but strong external support: Bureau of Labor Standards Bureau of Land Management Fish and Wildlife Service Geological Survey National Bureau of Standards National Park Service
From the Twelve Lowest-Ranking Bureaus	Bureaus with strong support from the Committee but weak external support: Bureau of Customs Bureau of the Public Debt	Bureaus with weak support from the Committee and weak external support: Census Bureau Bonneville Power Administration Bureau of Mines Bureau of Reclamation

set of names. The usefulness of the classification in Table 8.12 is simply to relate types of Committee decisions to types of bureaus. A superficial effort of this sort indicates that bureau success in terms of obtaining its requests depends primarily on factors internal to the bureau, to the Committee, and to the bureau-Committee relationship. Such factors would be the perceived controversial character of the bureau, the nature of the work load, the background of subcommittee personnel, Committee perceptions of the bureau and its leadership, the ratio of Committee confidence to Committee suspicion of the bureau, and stability of Committee and agency personnel. On the other hand, bureau success in increasing its appropriations year by year depends primarily on the strength of the demands made in support of the bureau by people outside the Committee. Such factors would be widespread congressional recognition of the need for expanded federal activity in an urgent problem area and organized efforts by clientele groups served by the bureau, both of which might be abetted by the bureau itself. Bureaus that aspire to rapidly expanding appropriations will need a special increment of external support for their demands if these demands are to be met. In this way the bureau can tip the balance of Committee decisions toward the satisfaction of external expectations. Bureaus that aspire to obtain their requests will require a special increment of support from inside the Committee. In this way the bureau can tip the balance of Committee decisions away from budget reduction. Bureaus that achieve good internal relations and small budgetary reductions will be the most likely to have their maintenance expectations of certainty and predictability met by the Committee.

A bureau level analysis of Committee decisions makes it abundantly clear that the Committee operates within a network of restraints — restraints of the larger political system which direct its activity and contain its area of discretion. To an important degree, the Committee adapts to the demands of the society because a representative institution can scarcely do otherwise. Yet the great variety of decision patterns makes it clear, once again, that the Committee is an independent force in the total political system. On the whole, its influence is negative. The Committee acts as a restraining force on the level of federal expenditure and on the expansionist aspirations of the federal bureaucracy. But it also has taken a bold lead in selected policy areas and pushed the executive branch to expand its horizons — in the fields of soil conservation, medical research, and educational planning, for example. Just as the designs for the expenditure of money are manifold, so, too, are the Appropriations Committee's responses to them. Any final decision as to whether the Committee acts wisely and knowledgeably within its area of discretion will depend primarily on one's own estimation of America's needs. This study offers neither estimation nor judgment. But the evidence of this chapter would seem to indicate that the judgment cannot be easily or lightly made.

CHAPTER NINE

The House Committee's Decisions
II: Action on the House Floor

THE FLOOR: A NEW CONTEXT

An Appropriations Committee decision, whatever it may be and however it may have been arrived at, is not an authoritative decision of the House of Representatives. It is but a recommendation submitted to members of the parent chamber for their approval. Only the House, acting as a body and in accordance with certain prescribed procedures, can pass an appropriation bill and send that bill on to the Senate. Once the Committee has made its recommendations, therefore, its members must turn to the task of winning support for these decisions among their House colleagues. It is, of course, no new concern for Committee members. They know that House member support is, for the most part, won or lost well in advance of any debate and decision on the floor. And they remain continuously attentive and responsive to Member expectations and images throughout their deliberations. Still, decision-making on the House floor is not the same as decision-making inside the Appropriations Committee. And no matter how much advance consideration may have been given to the desires of "the House," anticipation is not the same as a direct confrontation. The House floor is a special context. Holding and winning House member support there requires special kinds of Committee behavior. It represents the acid test of the Committee's ability to adapt to its parent chamber.

One of the more obvious differences between decision-making on the floor and in the Committee is that the rules and procedures which govern floor action provide the opportunity for House members who are neither on the Committee nor agree with it to exert a direct influence on the proceedings. Inside the Committee, the number of influential participants is small — of subcommittee size — and the number of formal decision-makers is only 50. On the floor, the number of influential participants increases several times over, and the number of formal decision-makers rises to 435. If an increase in the number of participants does not bring wholly new interests to bear on decision-making, it is quite likely to produce old interests in new proportions. And, where this occurs, the conflicting claims for budgetary increases and budgetary decreases may be weighted differently than by the Committee. The existence of an economy mood among the membership generally, the presence of a floor coalition in support of some clientele interest, the active resentment of a legislative committee, the popularity of an individual member — all these can and may have an influence on the floor which they could not or did not have inside the Committee.

Not only can more people or different people become involved in floor decision-making, but they can involve themselves on the basis of information which they were previously unable to obtain. The Appropriations Committee holds its hearings and makes its decisions in secret executive sessions. During their deliberations, Committee members (i.e., subcommittee members) exercise a near-monopoly over the flow of appropriations information from executives to the House. When an appropriation bill leaves the Committee, however, the hearings and the Committee report are made public and are disseminated to all interested parties, in and out of the House. House members who could not know before what the Committee was doing now know at least what has been done. Members may decide to confront the Committee on the floor with a challenge the group neither contemplated nor dealt with in arriving at its own decision.

Of all the interests which utilize these increased opportunities and resources to participate more directly in floor activity, the most important are the House parties. Party leaders do not normally exercise much influence during Committee decision-making. And, as we have seen, Committee-based norms far more than party-based norms govern the behavior of members inside the Committee. On the floor, however, party leaders exercise some procedural and substantive guidance, and party affiliation becomes the most accurate indicator of how a House member will behave. The increased influence of party is not just a matter of some House members standing together under a party banner to oppose Appropriations Committee recommendations. It is also a matter of party influences becoming increasingly relevant for Committee members themselves during floor action. Said one of the Committee's young Northern liberals, "When you get outside the Committee room and get back with your own group, you flop back into your spending ways." It is one thing to compromise on a decision within a well-insulated,

415

well-integrated Appropriations subcommittee. It is quite another thing to stand up in the partisan atmosphere of the chamber and go on permanent public record against the majority of one's party. Changes in the importance of partisan considerations also change the context of decision-making.

These three contextual changes — in participation, in the distribution of information, and in partisanship — are among the most important in differentiating the processes of decision-making on the floor from those inside the Committee. Taken individually and in combination these changes have one major consequence. They loosen Appropriations Committee control over decision-making. To put it somewhat differently, on the floor external, environmental influences on decision-making become more important relative to internal Committee-oriented influences. From one decision-making context to another, it appears, the overall House-Committee relationship changes. During decision-making on the floor, the Committee stands in a less autonomous, more dependent relationship to the House. In all the cases where House and Committee expectations are in conflict, the loosening of Committee control puts its recommendations in danger on the floor. Indeed, House-Committee tensions are more likely to come to the surface during floor action than at any other time. And, in any confrontation, the Committee may be the loser. At the most, of course, Committee decisions may be reversed, but at the very least — and this is more to the point in terms of Committee behavior — its members cannot know in advance what the outcome of floor action will be.

Appropriations Committee members attach enormous importance to success on the House floor. For the Committee collectively, for its members individually, and for its leaders especially, their influence in the chamber depends upon the degree to which their recommendations carry on the floor. "When you get rolled," said one subcommittee chairman, "it lowers your prestige. It takes the wind out of your sails." In the House, those who win legislative battles acquire reputations as winners; and those who acquire such reputations find that it helps them to win more legislative battles. "You can't beat a strong subcommittee chairman on the floor," it is said in the House. But subcommittee chairmen achieve strength in large part by winning on the floor. In the accumulation of House prestige and influence, nothing succeeds like success, and nothing is so damaging as egregious or repeated failure. Committee members know that the fulfillment of their personal expectations hinges on floor success. They are powerful if their Committee is powerful. But their Committee will be powerful only so long as it can make independent judgments and then win House support for them. Every confrontation with the House tests anew the prestige and the influence of the Committee on Appropriations.

416

The Committee works in two ways to gain House acceptance of its decisions. In the first place, Committee members try to meet House expectations through the content of their recommendations. By the time the Committee has reported its bills to the floor, it hopes that all the potential points of conflict between itself and "the House" will have been settled and acceptance will be readily forthcoming. On the evidence (much of it to be presented later in this chapter), it appears that the Committee does win the bulk of its House support in this fashion — by making substantive decisions that meet House expectations. In the second place, however, the Committee does everything it can to promote the contextual conditions most congenial to House acceptance of its decisions. When the Committee has gone as far as it can to meet House expectations via the substance of its decisions, it then acts so as to bring about a set of floor conditions that are most conducive to the acceptance of its recommendations. The floor context contains hazards for the Appropriations Committee. When contests do take place there, the Committee will want to have them occur under the most favorable conditions. On numerous occasions, in spite of all its preliminary efforts, the Committee fails to meet House expectations and is overturned on the floor. This chapter discusses the Committee's efforts to preclude such an outcome and the conditions under which it succeeds and fails.

GETTING APPROPRIATION BILLS TO THE FLOOR

Timing

Before any Committee recommendation can be acted upon by the House, it must be brought to the floor in accordance with prescribed procedures. House rules designate reports from the Appropriations Committee as privileged matters. They do not require a special rule from the Rules Committee to clear them for floor action. They have precedence over most other kinds of business, and they can be taken up on the floor whenever the Committee desires.[1] All of this means that the Committee itself exercises a high degree of control over the movements of its bills to the House floor. One impediment to uncontrolled Committee discretion does exist. Rule 21, paragraph 6, a product of the Legislative Reorganization Act of 1946, prescribes "No general appropriation bill shall be considered in the House until printed Committee hearings and a Committee report thereon have been available for the Members of the House for at least three calendar days." This provision is interpreted, however, in a manner which makes possible a minimum

[1] Clarence Cannon, *Cannon's Procedure in the House of Representatives* (Washington: U.S. Government Printing Office, 1963), pp. 224–225, 256–258.

417

of delay. The day on which the report is filed may be counted as one day, *or* the day on which the bill is taken up on the floor may be counted as one day. Thus, a bill reported at midnight Monday could be taken up at noon on Thursday. Of course, if need be, all of these provisions can be dispensed with by unanimous consent of House members.

The more quickly the Committee can move its bills to the floor, the fewer contextual changes it is likely to confront. And the fewer the contextual changes, the less will Committee control be weakened. Most important, a speedy trip to the floor inhibits the dissemination of information. The more time that elapses between the publication of the reports and floor action, the smaller becomes the Committee's information advantage and the more resources become available with which to organize an opposition force in the chamber. For most of the period under study, the Committee utilized its prerogative to the maximum in keeping the elapsed time fairly close to the minimum.

Table 9.1 lists, for each original appropriation bill 1951 to 1963, the number of days which elapsed between the release of the Committee's reports and the passage of the bill. In nearly all cases less than a week transpired; and in the great preponderance of cases (63 per cent) there was a hiatus of only three, four, or five days. It must be remembered, moreover, that many of these figures (probably one half) include days of floor debate. Thus, the length of time actually available to House members to organize for action is exaggerated by Table 9.1. The information problem which faces even the most knowledgeable of House members is formidable. "I am just wondering,"

TABLE 9.1

ELAPSED TIME BETWEEN COMMITTEE REPORT AND HOUSE PASSAGE OF ORIGINAL APPROPRIATION BILLS: 1951 TO 1963

Number of Days[a]	Number of Bills
Same Day	2
1	5
2	13
3	25
4	34
5	44
6	15
7	12
8 or more	14
	164

[a] "Number of days" was arrived at by subtracting the date of the report from the date of passage. Thus a 2-day interval on this chart is considered by the Committee as 3 calendar days.

418

went a typical inquiry from one of the House's veteran leaders, Representative Howard Smith, "when we are presented with the final report this morning and expected to approve it in a day or two how the gentlemen's committee expects members of the House to vote intelligently on this enormous bill with as little information as we have."[2] Even if scraps of information have leaked out of the Committee — as may occasionally happen — the time between markup decisions and full Committee meetings is short. Of course, counterattacks can be launched against the Committee's recommendations; and we shall discuss some of them later. But success requires a concentrated expenditure of time, effort, and influence — more than most Members can regularly afford or will regularly produce.

The Committee helps preserve its information advantages by choosing the most propitious day on which to file its report. Until 1965, that day was Friday, a day on which 49 per cent of the reports in Table 9.1 were made public. If the Committee files on Friday, it can bring the bill up on Monday. As for its filing time, the Committee has until midnight on Friday. Thus it commonly asks and is granted "unanimous consent that the Committee on Appropriations may have until midnight Friday of this week to file a report."[3] Normally, the Committee does not wait until this late hour, but it can file at 11:59 P.M. and still get credit for a Friday filing. The modal pattern in recent years has been for the full Committee to meet on Friday morning, for the report to be released early that afternoon, for the bill to come to the floor on Tuesday, and for it to be passed either Tuesday or Wednesday. When Chairman Cannon published his appropriations schedule early in 1964 (see Table 9.2), this pattern was projected for every bill of that year. A Committee member discussed the consequences of the Friday-Tuesday pattern:

> No other member of the House can know what's in the bill. We usually report out our bills on Friday and bring them up on Tuesday. So you've got Saturday, Sunday, and Monday to read the hearings and the report. With all the work they have, not many members are going to spend Saturday, Sunday, and Monday trying to understand those documents.

Indeed, a great many House members ordinarily leave Washington Thursday evening and remain in their districts until the following Tuesday. Since most of these "Tuesday-Thursday Club" Members come from urban, Eastern areas and since those Members tend to be inclined toward more rather than less federal spending, Committee timing appears to handicap one group of Members who constitute a potential threat to their budget-cutting recommendations. Since 1965, the Committee has reported out its bills on Thursday and taken them up on Tuesday.

[2] 98 *Congressional Record*, pp. 3634–3635.
[3] This request is made so that the Committee can file its report when the House is not in session.

Committee control over the movement of its bills to the floor gives its leaders a capacity to fix the sequence and the spacing of appropriations legislation. With appropriation bills the question never is whether a bill will come to the floor; the question is always when and under what circumstances. The Committee can use these scheduling opportunities to its own advantage in winning House support. In recent years the sequence of bills has been determined mostly by the number of annually authorized programs. Typically, appropriation bills requiring no annual authorizations, e.g., Treasury–Post Office, Interior, Labor-HEW, are scheduled for action first. Appropriations which must await prior action by authorizing committees, e.g., military construction, foreign aid, independent office (NASA), are scheduled later in the session. Chairman Cannon's announced schedule for 1964, listed in Table 9.2, prescribed a sequence which has been followed more or less since the subcommittee reorganization of 1955.

TABLE 9.2

SCHEDULE FOR APPROPRIATION BILLS IN 1964,
AS ANNOUNCED BY CHAIRMAN CANNON, JANUARY 21, 1964

Appropriation Bill	Date of Committee Report	Date of Floor Action
District of Columbia	Friday, February 28	Tuesday, March 3
Interior	Friday, March 13	Tuesday, March 17
Treasury–Post Office	Friday, March 20	Tuesday, March 24
Labor-HEW	Friday, April 10	Tuesday, April 14
Defense	Friday, April 24	Tuesday, April 28
State-Justice-Commerce	Friday, May 1	Tuesday, May 5
Agriculture	Friday, May 8	Tuesday, May 12
Independent Offices	Friday, May 15	Tuesday, May 19
Military Construction	Friday, May 22	Tuesday, May 26
Public Works–AEC	Friday, May 29	Tuesday, June 2
Foreign Aid	Friday, June 5	Tuesday, June 9

Since 1955 the public works bill has been one of the last bills to reach the floor. Some of the projects do require authorization, but the Committee holds back the public works bill longer than is warranted in order to conserve a bit of leverage with the Members. The public works bill, containing as it does appropriations for the Corps of Engineers and the Bureau of Reclamation, among others, contains more pet projects than any other bill. A House member who is kept in suspense over the fate of his project may, it is felt, remain more amenable to pleas that he support the earlier Committee recommendations.

It will be noted that the 1964 schedule called for the last of the twelve bills to reach the floor on June 9th. This schedule was carried out almost to the letter, and the foreign aid bill was passed on July 1st.[4] Chairman Cannon's schedule was his response to heightened external criticism of a protracted appropriations stretch-out which had occurred in 1963.[5] In that year, the first appropriation bill was reported out on March 28 and the last one was passed on December 16. There were many interlocking reasons for the appropriations lag of 1963 — delaying action by strategically placed Southerners, so as to slow down the progress of civil rights legislation, and tardy authorizations, to mention only two — but the speed of 1964 makes it clear that the 1963 delay was deliberate. From the Committee's-eye view generally, the delay was a device for the achievement of its goals of Treasury guardianship. For governmental agencies, the fiscal year begins on July 1. If no appropriation bill has been passed by that date, the practice is for Congress to provide a "continuing resolution."[6] Under this resolution, agencies are allowed to spend at the previous year's rate or, if only the House has passed the appropriation bill, at whichever rate is lower, or, if both Senate and House have passed the bill, at whichever of those two rates is lower. The net effect is to hold spending at a rate below which it would surely be if the steadily rising appropriation bills were passed on time. Chairman Cannon was in no hurry to hasten Committee action in 1963. "The longer these bills are delayed," he said, "the more the possibilities of further reducing them and, in consequence, the less the drain on the Treasury."[7] It seemed likely, too, that the later in the session the bills came to the floor the greater would be the general jam-up of legislation, the less time could be given to organizing any action against the Committee recommendations, and the greater would be the disposition of the membership to ratify Committee recommendations as quickly as possible and go home.[8] The 1963 tactic constituted too great a violation of House expectations to be used regularly. But there seems little doubt that the Committee's scheduling powers give it some control not only over the fate of its own bills but over the flow of House legislation generally.[9]

With regard to the problem of timing, it should be noted that random external events may change the context of decision-making between the day a bill is reported out and the day it reaches the floor. Such events represent a condition over which the Committee has no control and to which it

[4] In only 4 other years from 1947 to 1964 did the Committee complete action on the regular appropriation bills by this date.

[5] See *Congressional Quarterly*, October 18, 1963; December 6, 1963; *Washington Post*, September 15, 16, 17, 1963.

[6] See, for example, the 1964 resolution in *Congressional Record*, Daily Edition, June 25, 1964, p. 14460.

[7] *Congressional Quarterly*, December 6, 1963, p. 2133.

[8] In every Congress during the period studied, the final appropriation bill cleared the House earlier in the second session than it did in the first session — which is indicative of the pressure to adjourn, go home, and campaign in an election year.

[9] Committee control over floor proceedings was a major complaint in 1885. See Chapter 2.

may have to adjust. Ordinarily, the Committee will not entertain amendments to the budget once its hearings have been closed and subcommittee markup is underway. Changes in estimates made by the executive at that late date must be put in a supplemental request to the Senate or in a regular supplemental appropriation bill. But should a critical external event intervene, the Committee may respond by offering to change its own recommendation on the floor.

Waiving Points of Order

In order for the Committee to follow its schedule of 1964, it became necessary to pass several appropriation bills before the authorizations had been duly enacted. Since these bills were clearly out of order, procedural steps had to be taken to prevent a floor challenge. Whenever the Committee legislates on a general appropriation bill (as above), the provision can be struck out by any Member who makes a point of order against it. On the military construction and foreign aid bills, therefore, the Committee asked for and received a special rule from the Rules Committee waiving all points of order against them.[10] A waiver of points of order can be viewed, in general, as a device whereby the Appropriations Committee seeks to protect some of its decisions from reversal on the floor. For, when granted, the waiver places certain decisions beyond the legitimate scope of House action. The device is used rather sparingly. From 1939 to 1954, for instance, the Committee requested an average of two waiver rules per year on original appropriation bills.[11] Each time the request was granted. Nonetheless, Rules Committee members grumble and House members express their unhappiness about surrendering their floor prerogatives.[12]

An illustrative conflict over the use of the waiver device occurred when the State-Justice Appropriation Bill reached the floor in 1956. A rule waiving all points of order against that bill had been granted, and it was protecting a legislative provision changing the civil service classification (and hence raising the salaries) of three employees of the Immigration and Naturalization Service. Members of the Post Office and Civil Service Committee rose in protest against the invasion of their jurisdiction. The Appropriations Subcommittee Chairman contended that what was involved was just "three inconsequential increases in grade," "a little matter of $3,600 increase in the salaries of these men," "this little thing which would cost the taxpayers in the neighborhood of $3,600."[13] He tried to treat the problem as strictly an

---

[10] *Congressional Record*, Daily Edition, May 26, 1964, pp. 11562–11564. They did not grant such rules, however, for the Independent Offices (i.e., NASA) appropriation. *Congressional Record*, Daily Edition, May 21, 1964, p. 11278 ff.

[11] These figures have been supplied by James Robinson.

[12] 102 *Congressional Record*, pp. 6970–6971, 6997.

[13] *Ibid.*, p. 6996.

appropriation problem, but the members of the legislative committee sought to superimpose a larger issue upon it. "The question before this Committee now is," they argued, "do you want to sustain the legislative committee of this House, or do you want to circumvent the legislative committee of this House?" "If the House wants to go across the board let us do it not by invading one committee, then another. Just abolish the legislative committees and let it go at that."[14]

The struggle was clearly one for control of the context of decision-making. The Appropriations Committee tried to restrict the scope of conflict to what it had been inside the Committee, and the legislative committee sought to bring the interests of all legislative committees to bear on the outcome:

> APPROPRIATIONS SUBCOMMITTEE CHAIRMAN: I telephoned the gentleman, did I not, and I telephoned the ranking minority member and said, "Look, I have been asked by the Commissioner of Immigration and Naturalization to do thus and so. It amounts to only so much." I tried to be fair about it. I never expected we would have such a hassle as this over it.
>
> POST OFFICE AND CIVIL SERVICE COMMITTEE CHAIRMAN: The gentleman did call me, and I want to cooperate with him.
>
> APPROPRIATIONS SUBCOMMITTEE CHAIRMAN: The gentleman could cooperate fully if he would not make any remarks here on the floor with regard to this matter.
>
> POST OFFICE AND CIVIL SERVICE COMMITTEE CHAIRMAN: However, as Chairman of the Committee on Post Office and Civil Service, I must protect the rights and authority of my own committee. As the gentleman knows, this is clearly an infringement and usurpation of the rights of the Committee on Post Office and Civil Service.
>
> APPROPRIATIONS SUBCOMMITTEE CHAIRMAN: I think it is an infringement, yes. I could not say that it was not. However, it is so slight that it is hardly worthwhile talking about.[15]

The rule was sustained by a voice vote, and the Chairman of the Post Office and Civil Service Committee subsequently offered an amendment striking the disputed provision from the bill. On a roll call, the amendment failed by a narrow margin, 179–184. Members of the Post Office and Civil Service Committee voted 23 to 1 to reverse the Appropriations Committee decision, but members of the Appropriations Committee voted 38 to 4 in support of it. The very fact that such a row and such a close vote occurred over such a small matter helps explain why rules waiving points of order are used sparingly. By prohibiting the free play of external influences on the floor, they operate to preserve the Committee context of decision-making on

[14] *Ibid.*, pp. 6997–6998.
[15] *Ibid.*, pp. 6982–6983. Another interesting contest will be found at 93 *Congressional Record*, p. 3949 ff.

the House floor. Every such application constitutes a request to House members to come to the floor at an obvious disadvantage.

On the other hand, House members customarily grant waiver rules because it is in their interest to do so. Legislative provisions carried in appropriation bills are not usually inserted just for the benefit of the Appropriations Committee. They enable House members generally to circumvent "the regular order" to accomplish ends with which they are in general agreement. When, on a supplemental bill in 1955, the Committee on Rules refused to grant a rule waiving points of order, Chairman Cannon decided to pound this point home to the House. He and another Committee leader stood on the floor and offered objections to every item carrying legislation, and every one to which they objected was thrown out on a point of order. The bill which was reported to the House carrying $1.2 billion on July 12 carried only $224 million when it was passed two days later. The anguish and consternation of House members were prodigious.[16] But the lesson was clear. Waiver rules help the Appropriations Committee; but they may help House members as well.

Appropriations Committee–Party Leadership Relations

As its bills move out to the House floor, the Appropriations Committee uses a number of prerogatives and techniques to maintain a maximum of autonomy. At some point in this process, however, the Committee normally begins to share control over the proceedings with the party leaders.[17] Whenever this intersection of activity occurs, it symbolizes more than anything else the changed context of decision-making. For the leadership of both parties, their major tasks revolve around scheduling and superintending the flow of legislative business on the House floor. Naturally, the movement to the floor of fifteen or so appropriation bills during every session is a matter of great concern, not only because these bills are substantively important but because their timing and success may well affect the course of legislation generally.[18] In the pursuit of their tasks, party leaders will need to communicate with and cooperate with those Appropriations Committee members (primarily the Chairman but also the subcommittee chairmen) who control procedural matters inside the Committee.

[16] The episode will be found in 101 *Congressional Record*, pp. 10604–10625. The sequel to it, equally illuminating in terms of Rules Committee attitudes, will be found in *ibid.*, pp. 10944–11059 passim.

[17] As used in this section, "party leader" refers to the Speaker, majority floor leader, majority whip, minority floor leader, and minority whip. One of the few discussions of this pivotal party leader-committee relationship will be found in David Truman, *The Congressional Party* (New York: John Wiley, 1959), esp. pp. 285–289.

[18] See the speech by majority leader Representative Albert in *Congressional Record*, Daily Edition, January 20, 1964, p. 563.

From the standpoint of the party leaders — of both parties since "the leadership" of the minority has the same problems of superintendence and since it consults with the majority party over scheduling — the earlier in the Committee's decision-making process communication and cooperation begin the better. The Committee, however, takes a different view: that the achievement of their goals requires party influence to be kept outside the Committee rooms. From this point of view, the later in the processes of decision-making communication and cooperation begin the better. This difference in attitude (or, really, in maintenance expectations) will, of course, prevent cooperation entirely when a Committee majority and the majority party leaders are at loggerheads, as, for example, they frequently were in the 1950's and 1960's over the foreign aid appropriation bill. Ordinarily, however, party leader–Committee leader cooperation does begin at some point in the scheduling process because it is to their mutual advantage to do so. Party leaders are, after all, in the business of recruiting support on the floor, and that is precisely what the Appropriations Committee wants.

A minority party leader discussed the mutual benefits of cooperation:

> I've got plenty to do. I can't keep track of what's going on and all the details in each of those little subcommittees. I expect from all the committees a measure of cooperation with the leadership. They have to carry the ball. But when they get out on the floor, then they need help. The Appropriations boys can't carry the weight by themselves there.

From his perspective a subcommittee chairman came to the same conclusions:

> As long as my subcommittee follows me — and usually they do — I could hold things back and mess things up good for the leadership. By the same token, when my bill comes to the floor, I need the help of the leadership to get it passed. I have delayed bringing my bill out when the boys are too hot about something. The leadership tells me that and helps me in that way. On some of my other subcommittees, there are a lot of things the leadership may want done. I try to cooperate with them in those particular areas where they need help; and they cooperate with me when I need their help.

Ordinarily, of course, the Committee does not have to contend with leadership influence as it is reflected on the Rules Committee. But whenever the Appropriations Committee does seek a rule waiving points of order it cannot succeed without the backing of leadership-oriented members of that strategically located group.

Party leader–Committee leader cooperation begins earliest in the decision-making process under conditions of greatest partisanship inside the Committee. During the 80th Congress, for example, Speaker Joe Martin and Chairman John Taber worked together setting targets for appropriations re-

425

ductions.[19] During the early days of 1963, when the Bow Task Force began to agitate the Committee, party leaders worked closely with their respective contingents on the Committee. The Republican leadership (and the Policy Committee, too) helped to set up the Task Force, recruit its staff, and organize its meetings. As soon as the Task Force published its target of a $15 billion budget reduction, the Democratic leadership compiled a prorated list of cuts in constituency-oriented projects and circulated it as a warning to individual Members.[20] Then they worked to protect the decision of the Democratic-dominated Committee against further reductions on the floor.

A few days before the first bill of 1963, the Interior bill, was slated to hit the House floor, a GOP leader described a relationship with the Committee which began even before subcommittee markup:

> Of course, I can't go into their meetings when they mark up the bill. And they take testimony in secret. So except for what they choose to tell me, I don't know what they're doing. But I know what's going on. I know what the preliminary markup figures are in the Interior Appropriation Bill. I've seen them and I've made a few suggestions. So I'd say as we're presently constituted, the leadership has a good deal of influence on the appropriations process.

The next day, a Democratic party leader discussed efforts to help his side of the Committee:

> On a day-to-day, dollars and cents basis for each department we don't get involved. When you get to the floor and the Republicans are going to cut the appropriation bill, we have to do everything we can to help. Next Tuesday, the Interior bill will come in and the Republicans will be in there chopping away at the recommendations. So we're sending a message to all Democrats to be there. Our job is to get them there and keep them there and defend the Committee.

In this particular instance the norm of minimal partisanship was being threatened within the Committee. It seems likely that party groups inside the Committee had, therefore, issued an abnormally early call for party intervention and assistance. Under more normal conditions of internal Committee integration, however, it seems reasonable to assume that the Committee works to keep party leader involvement both minimal and late.

Though Republicans and Democrats on the Committee are especially jealous of their independence, relations between party and Committee leaders have been more harmonious on the Republican than on the Democratic side during the period under study. The differential influence of Committee leaders in the selection process is evidence of this and has already been dis-

[19] 93 *Congressional Record*, pp. 5895, 6013.
[20] *Congressional Record*, Daily Edition, April 2, 1963, pp. 5181–5197. For the Republican floor leaders' efforts, see *ibid.*, p. 5172.

cussed. The reasons for this are several: the fact that the Committee's goals and expectations agree more closely with Republican than with Democratic ideology; the fact that the Democrats controlled the Committee and had charge of preserving its independence for most of the period; and the contrasting personalities of Clarence Cannon and John Taber. What follows describes primarily the majority party relationship in years of Democratic control of Congress.

Chairman Cannon stated his expectations as to what the normal pattern of cooperation should be:

> The leadership is supposed under ordinary circumstances to collaborate with the committees. After a committee has studied a bill, held hearings, processed a bill, and has spent months bringing in a report — other things being equal — the committees are entitled to the support of the leadership of the House.[21]

On another occasion, he phrased these expectations more bluntly. "The leadership is supposed to carry out the edict of the standing committees. The committees are the governing force, the power in their special fields." As Cannon saw it, procedural "collaboration" was primarily the responsibility of the leadership. The Committee's responsibility was to perform substantive tasks. And the performance of those tasks required a minimum of interference in its decision-making processes by any and all extra-Committee interests whatsoever. "Someone has to protect the Treasury. That will not be done [here] on the floor. It can be done only in Committee."[22] He supported and took advantage of all those traditions, rules, and procedures which would promote the autonomy of his Committee.

In the matter of scheduling, for example, the Committee's view has been that the party leadership should acquiesce in its desires — which it normally does. In cases of conflict, however, the Committee has often asserted its procedural controls to promote its own interest rather than that of the leadership. The following 1961 colloquy illustrates the capacity of the Committee and its Chairman to stand against the scheduling wishes of the leaders of both parties:

> HOUSE MEMBER: Can the gentleman tell me why the public works appropriation bill was put over until next Tuesday and the vote carried over until next Wednesday, when it was announced and programmed we were going to have it appear tomorrow? Now we are to get it next week.
> MINORITY FLOOR LEADER: Mr. Speaker, will the gentleman yield?
> HOUSE MEMBER: I yield to the gentleman from Indiana.
> MINORITY FLOOR LEADER: I have tried all day to get that bill up tomorrow. I might say in my conversation with the majority leadership, if they had

[21] *Congressional Record,* Daily Edition, October 13, 1962, p. 22206.
[22] 91 *Congressional Record,* p. 11260.

427

their way I think the bill would be scheduled for tomorrow. As to why it was not scheduled I do not know, although I have my suspicions about that. As I said earlier in the day, and I say it again, if we did get that bill up and over to the other body we would be well on the way to a sine die adjournment, and that is what we want.

HOUSE MEMBER: I agree with the gentleman one hundred per cent. I wonder if the gentleman from Oklahoma can tell us why that bill was carried over?

MAJORITY FLOOR LEADER: The only thing I can say to the gentleman is that the matter of calling up bills from the Committee on Appropriations is within the discretion of the Chairman of the Committee on Appropriations. The Speaker of the House has no authority to call up an appropriation bill. The chairman of the Committee or the Member responsible for the handling of the bill can call the bill up, if he so desires . . . the leadership has nothing to do with it.

HOUSE MEMBER: If the leadership has nothing to do with it, who is running this House?

MAJORITY FLOOR LEADER: The Chairman of the Committee on Appropriations is the one who has made the decision not to call up this bill tomorrow.

MINORITY WHIP: Mr. Speaker, if the gentleman will yield to me, I suggest he get together with his colleague from Missouri and take him to the woodshed tomorrow and find out what is the matter.[23]

In 1962, when the Committee was disputing with the Senate Appropriations Committee and refused to schedule conference committee sessions, the Committee stood fast against the wishes of the leadership. Cannon complained bitterly,

In that battle we did not have the support of the leadership. Daily we were importuned by the Speaker to yield to the Senate, to surrender the prerogatives of the House, to agree on any terms. The Committee on Appropriations under heavy criticism maintained its position but it was in spite of the leadership of the House when it should have been supporting us.[24]

In the closing hours of the 1962 session when the leadership failed to support his position on an appropriations item, Cannon killed one of his own bills by preventing it from going to conference. At that point communication and cooperation between Appropriations Committee leader and Democratic party leaders had reached an all-time low. "I have sat under ten Speakers," charged Cannon, "but I have never seen such biased, inept leadership."[25]

A year later, two of the leaders excoriated by Cannon recalled the incident:

The present leadership doesn't have much influence with Clarence Cannon . . . he fought with Rayburn, too, but he was afraid of Rayburn or at least

---

[23] *Congressional Record*, Daily Edition, September 6, 1961, pp. 17152–17153.
[24] *Congressional Record*, Daily Edition, October 13, 1962, p. 22206.
[25] *Ibid.*

I think he was. Rayburn had more seniority than he did. But the Speaker has less seniority and the new leadership, too. I think this is why Cannon staged his sit-down strike last year.

"There's a feeling," said a second leader, "that Clarence Cannon is getting old and cantankerous and pretty arbitrary sometimes. And there's some justification for it." A Committee member who is close to the leadership described the pattern of cooperation as it existed in 1964 as follows:

> There's not much rapport with the leadership. They respect Mr. Cannon, but they don't consider him a good Democrat. He's not a party man. He's not reliable. They don't feel they can trust him.

Another Committee Democrat agreed, "They ignore him and he ignores them, I think." It seems highly doubtful that this relationship was anything brand-new, nor, indeed, that Cannon himself would have dissented from this description.[26] The point is that his Committee-mindedness and his personal persistence in promoting its independence of all external interests prevented, except on his terms, any high degree of harmony with the party leadership.

Given the differing emphases in their expectations, substantive conflicts over Committee decisions are most likely to occur when the Committee reports out a lower figure than the party leaders deem necessary. Said one Democratic leader, "The leadership hopes that the Committee will do the best it can in meeting the administration requests. Sometimes, if the Committee cuts too much we may have to fight them on the floor." The organization of a floor fight, however, requires time and information — two resources over which the Committee retains as much control as it can. Without these resources it is nearly impossible to organize a whip poll, find out who the persuasible Members are, convince them, and mobilize outside interests.[27] "They work in secrecy," complained one party leader,

> I can't get any information. You can't find out anything until they get to the floor. And it's hard to lick 'em at that stage. They're a closed corporation. When they stick together, you can't lick 'em on the floor.

So, on matters like foreign aid and public works, which have produced the most regular substantive conflicts, the party leaders operate at a considerable

[26] For a description of the Rayburn-Cannon relationship, see *Time*, February 2, 1959, p. 14.

[27] Committee control of timing may make it difficult for the party leaders to conduct a thorough-going whip poll on appropriation bills. See Lewis A. Froman and Randall B. Ripley, "Conditions for Party Leadership: The Case of the House Democrats," *American Political Science Review* (March, 1965). On the one occasion when all the appropriation bills came to the floor at once, under the omnibus bill of 1950, the Democratic whip organization seems to have been very effective. See the comments of Representative Jensen, 96 *Congressional Record*, p. 6938.

disadvantage. With such scraps of information as they can pick up here and there, they work in makeshift patterns to bring their influence to bear as early as possible on Committee decision-making.

A member of the Committee described leadership activity during Committee deliberations:

> On things like foreign aid where the leadership is really concerned, Cannon won't pay any attention to them anyway. So there's no rapport there. The contact is all on an individual basis. The leadership will get in touch with individual members — mostly with regard to special projects. McCormack will call individual members of the Committee regarding public works projects that some Members have spoken to him about. On spending in general, the leadership doesn't put any pressure on the Committee. Oh, maybe on foreign aid — they do try to talk with individual members on that. But they can't do much there. That's a tough committee to deal with.

Party leaders sought to work around Cannon and to deal with more cooperative members individually. In view of their predicament, it is small wonder that Democratic leaders stress cooperativeness and responsiveness to party leadership as a prime criterion for selecting new Committee members. And it is understandable why, after the contretemps of 1962, the leadership chose five new Committee members without even informing Cannon. Still, finding cooperative individuals once they are on the Committee and have been subjected to its integrative norms is easier stated than accomplished — as the episode on page 38 makes clear. One Democratic party leader commented, "The members of the Appropriations Committee have respect for the wishes of the leadership . . . [but] the present leadership doesn't have much influence with Clarence Cannon. And he controls that Committee. He can make or break those subcommittee chairmen." This relationship as it existed between Cannon and Chairman Otto Passman rendered the foreign aid subcommittee an especially "tough committee to deal with." And, as a protection against House pressure, Cannon took the chairmanship of the Public Works Subcommittee for himself.

Party leaders understand the internal structure of the Committee, and they perceive the subcommittees as relatively independent entities whose chairmen, if they can be reached, may help build cooperative relationships. Accordingly, their image of the Committee is very largely one of subcommittees, and among the subcommittees they differentiate among their chairmen. "It all depends on the chairmen you have to work with," said one leader. "If the chairman is the kind you can deal with, the leadership has no trouble . . . we've got some good people like George Mahon on Defense Appropriations." And, in 1963, another leader revealed what surely was one of his innermost desires as he discussed various subcommittee chairmen:

430

They work very hard at their jobs, most of them. Men like George Mahon — he knows as much about the Defense Department as Vinson, maybe more. And Albert Thomas — these are very capable men. George Mahon would make an excellent Chairman of that committee.

When the leaders' daydream did come to pass in 1964, Chairman George Mahon had already been singled out by the leadership as a cooperative member of the Committee. Clarence Cannon had been shrewdly aware of this fact and had used Mahon as the Committee's spokesman when he (Cannon) was seeking favors from the leadership. And the new Committee leader–party leader relationship was tested almost immediately in the foreign aid fight of that year. In this instance, Chairman Mahon reversed the entire pattern of collaboration which had existed under Cannon. He fought against instead of with his subcommittee chairman; he invited leadership assistance in persuading individual members of his Committee to vote for the higher rather than the lower aid figure; and, working in closest harmony, the Chairman of the Appropriations Committee and the Democratic party leaders (in Congress and, it must be stressed, in the White House) won a spirited battle in subcommittee, in full Committee, and on the floor. Party leaders interpreted the events as auguring a new, more cooperative relationship between Committee and party. Committee members themselves were more cautious. They viewed the outcome as a personal victory for the Chairman over a particularly headstrong subcommittee chairman under the most favorable of circumstances. They also expressed the belief that any Chairman of the Committee must act so as to preserve a degree of autonomy for the group. For the long run, so their logic ran, this concern would lead Mr. Mahon, as it did Mr. Cannon, to keep party leader involvement to a minimum.

Only the passage of time will tell whether the events of the foreign aid fight of 1964 were an aberration or the forerunner of a new pattern. A short-run assessment would acknowledge evidence in support of both positions. Without doubt, the switch from Cannon to Mahon brought about change in Committee–leadership relations. Without doubt, too, this change was the most important external consequence of the succession. In matters such as scheduling, cooperation visibly increased. In announcing the Committee's plans for 1966, Chairman Mahon, in language quite uncharacteristic of his predecessor said: "We will shortly develop, *harmonious to the plans of the leadership*, a schedule of hearings and floor debate for the appropriation bills."[27a] This does not mean that party leaders become any more privy to internal Committee activity. Nor does it mean that Committee decision patterns were altered. But, clearly, the lines of communication were open to a degree that they had not been under Cannon.

[27a] *Congressional Record*, Daily Edition, January 24, 1966, p. 871.

House leaders continued to complain, in January of 1966, about the excessive autonomy of the Committee. "You may get an inkling of what they are doing, but never the whole picture," said one House spokesman. But he went on to stress the improvement in his relations with the Committee. "Cannon and Mahon are the same in their devotion to economy. But the whole atmosphere is different now. You can talk to George Mahon. Chairman Mahon took the same view. "There is still some degree of a gulf," he said in mid-1965, "but it has narrowed a lot. The leadership has no difficulty talking to George Mahon, and I don't have any difficulty talking to them." The root sources of Committee–leader conflict remained; but the probability that such conflict could be kept under control had been markedly increased. At the very least, the maintenance expectations of Democratic party leaders were better satisfied. And that being so, party leaders could feel (especially with the foreign aid contest as an example) that they even had a fighting chance to achieve their more cherished goal expectations.

An increase in communication produced a reduction of Committee–leadership tensions. This change — whether one thinks of it as a matter of degree or a matter of kind — may have had the effect of decreasing Committee independence in the short run while preserving it in the long run. In the 89th Congress, under the aegis of a new Joint Committee on the Organization of Congress, questions of internal reform were again being agitated. As always, many of these reforms were focused on the appropriations process; and most of them seemed likely to reduce the influence and the autonomy of the House Committee. In any decision to adopt internal reforms, the attitude of the majority party leadership is, perhaps, most determinative. And the decision of the leadership in the area of appropriations would be conditioned by the existing state of Appropriations Committee–party leader relations. These relations, formal and informal, had deteriorated under Chairman Cannon; they improved markedly under Chairman Mahon. Accordingly, Democratic party leaders may not feel the need or the desire, in 1966, to support alterations in the appropriations process which they might have been persuaded to support in 1963. Such thoughts are highly speculative. But it can be asserted, surely, that the probability of long-run Committee survival increased as a result of the death of Clarence Cannon and the succession of George Mahon.

GUIDING ACTION ON THE FLOOR

Rules and Procedures

Whether or not the Committee bill is shepherded to the floor with the cooperation of the party leadership, it is dealt with on the floor in accordance with the rules of the House. Since appropriation bills do not require a rule (which ordinarily would fix the terms of debate), the majority and minority leaders on the Committee agree on the length of time for debate and ask unanimous consent of the House that their time limit be accepted — with the proviso that one-half of the time will be at the disposal of the subcommittee chairman and one-half at the disposal of the subcommittee's ranking minority member. The standard consent request which the subcommittee chairman makes to start debate provides for the division of time. And the standard motion provides that House members sit as a Committee of the Whole House when considering appropriation bills:

> Mr. Speaker, I move that the House resolve itself into the Committee of the Whole House on the State of the Union for the consideration of the bill [HR ———] making appropriations for the Department of ——— and related agencies for the fiscal year ending June 30, ———, and for other purposes; and pending that motion, Mr. Speaker, I ask unanimous consent that general debate be limited to not to exceed ——— [usually 2, 3, or 4] hours, the time to be equally divided and controlled by the gentleman from ——— [state of the ranking minority subcommittee member] and myself.

The rules which obtain in the Committee of the Whole differ from those which obtain in the House. Several of these rules are especially helpful to the Committee in gaining support during floor action. In the Committee of the Whole a quorum consists of only 100 members instead of the majority as required under the United States Constitution. Under circumstances where no great controversy has been aroused, a 50-man Committee or any sizable portion thereof can dominate floor proceedings. Committee members agree that "if you have 50 men and have them well situated, you can always do pretty well on the floor." "If the Appropriations Committee stuck together and each member exercised the power he has over two or three friends — and that's a lot of power — the Appropriations Committee would never be beaten on the floor." The sheer size of the Committee is an asset on the floor. And the smaller the number required to do business, the greater the advantage which accrues to the Committee — so long as its members are united and present.

When general debate ends, the bill is read for amendment under a five-minute rule. Each Member may speak for five minutes on each amendment. Methods exist for temporarily circumventing this limitation. By submitting a pro forma amendment to strike out the last word of the previous amendment, for example, a Member may gain five extra minutes. But the five-minute limitation makes it certain that every Committee recommendation will be acted upon in one way or another and prevents endless debate from being used as a weapon against Committee proposals.

Most advantageous to the Appropriations Committee are the rules for voting in the Committee of the Whole. Three kinds of votes can be taken in

433

the Committee of the Whole: a voice vote, a division vote (for which Members stand to be counted), and a teller vote (for which Members walk up the center aisle to be counted). Since none of these votes is publicly recorded, Committee influence on fellow Members is likely to be at a maximum relative to extra-House influences.

Voting rules and related procedures give to the Committee still another strategic advantage. Amendments, i.e., changes in Committee recommendations, which are defeated in the Committee of the Whole, cannot be put to separate roll-call votes when the Committee concludes its business and the full House reconvenes to take final action. When the Committee of the Whole has completed its deliberations, the subcommittee chairman moves that "the Committee do now rise and report the bill back to the House with the recommendation that the bill (or, the bill as amended) do pass." The Speaker returns to the chair and final action is taken by the House. All amendments that passed in the Committee of the Whole are automatically reported back to the House, and any Member can call for a separate roll-call vote on any one of them. It is at this point that the Committee has a chance to ask for a vote to uphold its original recommendation. Amendments that have been rejected in the Committee of the Whole, however, are not automatically reported, and a special motion must be made if they are to be reconsidered. They are not so reconsidered because as soon as the amendments passed have been dealt with, the Speaker always recognizes the subcommittee chairman first; he, in turn, always says, "Mr. Speaker, I move the previous question on the bill to final passage." This motion shuts off debate at that point. The bill is then ordered engrossed and "read a third time." After this reading, the final question is put on the passage of the bill. At this stage, one motion to recommit the bill (send it back to the Appropriations Committee) is in order, and this motion can be made "with instructions" which will be binding on the Committee. Here is the only time, then, when an amendment rejected in the Committee of the Whole can receive a second vote — if it is made a part of the "instructions" accompanying a recommittal motion. Sometimes this strategy is tried, but it rarely succeeds. A recommittal motion which sends a bill back to Committee and gives the Committee another chance to consider the entire bill is a blunderbuss weapon. Since it is usually used to kill bills altogether, it is neither a very useful nor a very popular device for defeating selected, solitary items in an appropriation bill.

Practically, therefore, the situation is this. If the Committee can fight off an amendment in the Committee of the Whole, where conditions are relatively more favorable to it, it cannot be challenged again on a roll-call vote. On the other hand, if an amendment is passed which changes the Committee's recommendation, the Committee leadership can call for a roll-call vote. The Committee gets two formal opportunities to protect its recommendations, while the Committee's opponents get only one.[28] Should the Committee be defending what it believes is the popular cause, it may use the very threat of a public roll-call vote to prevail in the Committee of the Whole. These rules bestow a potential advantage on every House committee. But those committees which, like the Appropriations Committee, stress and maintain internal unity will be best able to realize that potential.

Floor action generally and the Committee's floor strategy especially are guided by the subcommittee chairman and ranking minority member. Each sits on his side of the House floor behind a table provided for the use of those managing bills on the floor. The subcommittee leaders typically sit on the aisle, from which position they can rise to one of the tables' microphones, walk to the well of the House, or move easily around the chamber for consultations. Again, subcommittee autonomy is manifest. The two subcommittee leaders are flanked at the table by their party's members on the subcommittee. The subcommittee clerk sits at the right hand of the chairman with the full public record spread out on the table before him for quick reference. Neither full Committee leaders nor other Committee members sit at these tables. Typically, the full Committee leaders move in and out of the chamber, keeping a watchful eye on the proceedings but participating only when their interests are especially involved or on very controversial questions. Clarence Cannon would not be heard at all during most appropriations debates. John Taber spoke more frequently during the discussion of amendments, but never enough to convey the slightest indication that his subcommittee leader was not in charge. Other Committee members are less likely to be in attendance, but are usually nearby if they are needed for a vote.

The subcommittee chairman and ranking minority member open general debate with summaries of the bill and explanations of its "high points." After they have led off, they allocate speaking time to subcommittee members and then to full Committee and House members. When the bill is being read for amendment, subcommittee members continue to dominate action. If the Committee is unified and is under attack, subcommittee leaders carry the brunt of the rebuttal with reinforcements from subcommittee colleagues. If the subcommittee is itself split, then the subcommittee antagonists are likely to be the main contestants in the debate. Except where key votes are at hand, attendance on the floor will be spotty. And even those Members who are physically present may not be very attentive to the proceedings. Or, even if they are concerned, they may find it difficult to keep up as the bill is being read for amendment.[29]

[28] Two examples of how these rules benefit the Committee will be found in the amendment reducing the Agriculture Conservation Program on June 6, 1961, and the amendment increasing Coast Guard funds on March 24, 1964.

[29] See remarks of Representative Jones, *Congressional Record*, Daily Edition, July 12, 1961, p. 11535.

Some indication of subcommittee dominance of floor proceedings can be gleaned from the examination of participation rates on all the money amendments offered to eight departmental and related agency appropriation bills (all but Defense and Post Office) and to public works appropriation bills during the period 1947 to 1962. Table 9.3 lists the total number of speakers on each of the 547 amendments offered. From this it can be seen that over half of all amendments attracted no more than 3 speakers, and that in 90 per cent of the cases there were 10 or less participants. Some member of the subcommittee participated in most of the debates. For example, the subcommittee chairmen spoke on 358 (65 per cent) of the 547 occasions, and the ranking minority member spoke on 184 (34 per cent) of the amendments. By contrast the full Committee Chairman and ranking full Committee majority member declared themselves only 29 and 81 times, respectively, on those bills where they held no position of subcommittee leadership. In some cases, obviously, House member interest and participation was high. But participation did not reach the level of 10 speakers as frequently as 1 amendment per bill in the period 1947 to 1962.

TABLE 9.3

NUMBER OF FLOOR PARTICIPANTS PER AMENDMENT:
9 DEPARTMENTAL AND PUBLIC WORKS BILLS 1947 TO 1962

Number of Participants	Number of Amendments on Which This Number Participated	Per Cent of All Amendments	Number of Participants	Number of Amendments on Which This Number Participated	Per Cent of All Amendments
1	40	7.3	9	12	2.2
2	148	27.1	10	13	2.4
3	98	17.9	11 to 15	25	4.6
4	62	11.3	16 to 20	13	2.4
5	44	8.0	21 to 25	9	1.6
6	35	6.4	26 +	7	1.3
7	25	4.6		—	—
8	16	2.9	Total	547	100

These participation rates can also be read as evidence of considerable Committee success in meeting House expectations. The great bulk of the 148, 2-speaker amendments consisted of a House member proposing an amendment, a subcommittee member (usually the chairman) objecting to it, and no one rising to defend the sponsor of the amendment. Similarly, the large number of amendments having a handful of speakers reflected occasions when little or no support was forthcoming for some proposed change in a Committee recommendation. Another indication of modest House participa-

436

tion and of Committee success is the fact that, of the 547 amendments, 264 were disposed of by a perfunctory voice vote. A total of 174 needed only a standing vote, 73 a teller vote, and only 36 were pushed to a roll-call decision. Since the bells in the House do not even ring to call Members to the floor for the first two kinds of votes, the great bulk of amendments were in fact disposed of under conditions of Committee dominance and under conditions of little serious opposition.

The Committee's All-Purpose Floor Defenses

If it is assumed, as is normally the case, that the Committee's integrative mechanisms are functioning and that the full Committee comes to the floor united in defense of its recommendation, the subcommittee's task is to protect that recommendation. Various recommendations may be protected with visibly different degrees of intensity. And, while normally the Committee earnestly tries to hold the line, there are occasions when it may not. These should be acknowledged at the outset. In the first place, the subcommittee chairman may, on behalf of the Committee, actually sponsor a few amendments (24 out of the 547 studied from 1947 to 1962), usually on the basis of events which have transpired between the subcommittee markup and action on the floor.[30] In the second place, subcommittee chairmen may willingly accept some amendments offered by others — 30 times, in fact, in the 547 cases studied. This usually occurs when, in order to avoid a prolonged struggle with its cost in terms of increased antagonism toward the Committee, a chairman gives in in the face of what he recognizes as overwhelming, inevitable defeat. In other cases, his defense of Committee recommendations will be transparently half-hearted:

> The position I have taken here today objecting to amendments falls to my lot because of the position I hold in the Committee on Appropriations, responsible for carrying this legislation through the House, and not because of any principle involved.[31]

Or, "I find my resistance weak in seeking to refute this amendment . . . I shall not resist too sternly."[32] The Committee does not defend all of its recommendations, nor does it defend with equal enthusiasm.

Normally the Committee does go to the floor with a fairly well-patterned line of defense encased in a fairly standardized rhetoric. Pre-eminently the argument and the rhetoric are designed to increase House member confidence in the work of the Appropriations Committee. As we have already noted, in

[30] Other subcommittee members may also offer such amendments and did so in 17 cases. Their reasons, however, are not clear, and one cannot make assumptions about them.
[31] 96 *Congressional Record*, p. 6837.
[32] 94 *Congressional Record*, p. 3095. See also 100 *Congressional Record*, p. 4719.

the 576 bureau case histories examined, 8 of every 10 Committee recommendations carried in the chamber. And we have discussed a number of explanations for this success: the congruence of goals, the Committee's adaptation to House expectations, and the strategic advantages of the Committee in cases of conflict. Still, in view of the patent uncertainty and guesswork of Committee decision-making and remembering the Committee's own self-doubt, the degree to which the House accepts these decisions remains a matter of some wonderment. An additional explanation can be found in the Committee's extraordinary efforts on the floor to promote a sense of identification and a relationship of confidence between itself and the House.

At the most general level, the Committee relies for its defense on the underlying House norm which states that, all other things being equal, members should support their committees. "Generally speaking and in the absence of convictions to the contrary," wrote Clarence Cannon in his *Procedure in the House of Representatives*, "members are justified in voting with the committee."[33] But this norm states at best a predisposition which each committee must turn into actual support. Appropriations Committee members go one step further, therefore, and plead for House support on the grounds that the Committee has acted in accordance with overall House expectations. With regard to maintenance expectations, they refer to themselves often as "your subcommittee" and profess allegiance to "the will of the House." One subcommittee chairman reminded his listeners, for instance, "We are all here and we want you to know we are your servants. We work for you. You tell us what to do."[34] Or, varying the same theme, Members may be assured that Committee members have come from the House and that they have all the qualifications for the job House members have assigned to them. Chairman Cannon introduced the omnibus bill of 1950 with these words of reassurance:

> The men who wrote this bill, the chairmen of the subcommittees, are all able and experienced men. They have served here for many years. They have been very carefully screened before they were assigned to the Appropriations Committee and the Committee screened them even more carefully. I think you cannot find in the House men better prepared and better qualified to write this bill.[35]

On these general grounds the Committee seeks support for its recommendations.

[33] Clarence Cannon, *Cannon's Procedure in the House of Representatives* (Washington: U.S. Government Printing Office, 1963), p. 213. It should be noted, perhaps, that Cannon compiled his precedents as a result of his former service as Parliamentarian of the House — not as a result of his Chairmanship.

[34] *Congressional Record*, Daily Edition, October 10, 1963, p. 18260.

[35] 95 *Congressional Record*, p. 4616.

Committee members also defend their recommendations as having met the goal expectations of the House. Since these expectations waver between those which stress adequate financing for programs and those which emphasize economy, the Committee finds itself making and seeking support for both patterns of decisions. In either case, the plea is made that the Committee's recommendation meets House expectations and that changes in one direction or another would not. Under normal conditions, the Committee finds itself defending mostly against floor pleas for increased funds.

In language less shrill and less colorful than the example to follow — but with the identical message — subcommittee chairmen will defend their recommendations as congruent with the House's desire to achieve economy:

> Remember these boys are asking for something for themselves. The Committee has no personal interest. The only thing the Committee has to gain by this is ill will and unpopularity for being a "wet blanket." But surely somebody has to protect the taxpayers' money . . . they are as redoubtable a gang of pirates as ever sailed the Spanish Main . . . millions of dollars were plundered by Captain Kidd and John Silver, but the amount of money Kidd and Silver took pales into insignificance compared to the money these highwaymen have taken from the U.S. Treasury here this morning. . . . They come in here after being denied by an impartial Committee and try their case here on the floor . . . why have a committee if you are going to support these rebels against legitimate authority like other Caribbean freebooters in Central and South American principalities?[36]

When the House is in an economy mood, the Committee may have to defend its recommendations against proposals for further reductions. Under these conditions they will emphasize that they have achieved all the economy that is possible and that the amount of money they have voted is necessary to fund the programs instituted by Congress:

> We took a very hard look at this bill and we have cut it right down to the bone and we think it should not be cut any lower. We think we have done a good job.[37]

> Some of the Members who voted for its passage are now complaining about the cost involved. We cannot blame the people down the street for this. This is the result of action on the floor of Congress. The Congress passed this bill.[38]

The Committee hopes that House members will accept these vague and outright assertions that their expectations have been met — and, having

[36] *Congressional Record*, Daily Edition, October 13, 1962, p. 22205.
[37] *Congressional Record*, Daily Edition, February 9, 1960, p. 2158.
[38] *Congressional Record*, Daily Edition, April 2, 1963, p. 5133.

accepted them, will tender the Committee a sufficient measure of confidence.

On a slightly less general level, the subcommittee uses three additional arguments to hold and to win House confidence. In both their opening speeches and during the debate on amendments, subcommittee speakers tirelessly reiterate that they have worked hard, that they have the facts, and that they are in agreement across party lines. Though it is impossible to factor out the influence of these arguments, their appearance at every turn of every debate is sufficient indication that Committee members placed heavy reliance upon them. Furthermore, as we have already seen, the norms of hard work, specialization, and bipartisanship are House norms, and House members readily admit their respect for the Committee on just these grounds. To the degree that the House does give weight to these arguments, the Committee's rhetoric serves a two-edged function: It aids in promoting success on the floor, and, since adherence to these norms promotes internal integration, any evidence that they pay off in terms of floor success also serves to strengthen the Committee's internal structure.

Typically, therefore, subcommittee chairmen open debate by reminding House members of the subcommittee's fidelity to the House norm of hard work:

> I do not believe there is a committee in the House of Representatives, whether it be a legislative committee or another subcommittee on appropriations, that has been more diligent or more sincere in its deliberations than has this particular subcommittee during the past two months . . . we held hearings for about five weeks, sitting continuously. . . . We did not miss one day of hearings from the time we started until we finished. The attendance of the various subcommittee members was practically one hundred per cent.[39]

> I want to tell you they have worked on this bill. I am rapidly acquiring the title around here of slave driver and I am afraid that it is not without some cause, because I do urge the members to work hard and, at times, for long hours. My only defense is that I work along with them, however hard or long the task. This committee held hearings for one solid month.[40]

In the House, hard work is a virtue in and of itself. It requires no qualification. But the implication is that hard work has produced an expertise to which other members should defer. And this, of course, is the argument underlying the general injunction that, other things being equal, one should "follow the committee."

Subcommittee spokesmen defend their recommendations on the grounds that the subcommittee specialists have a more informed understanding of

[39] 97 *Congressional Record*, p. 4008.
[40] *Congressional Record*, Daily Edition, April 4, 1963, pp. 5444–5445.

the subject matter than anyone else. On this basis, they appeal for a vote of confidence from their fellow Members. The following excerpts from a subcommittee chairman's opening speech contain the full complement of arguments:

> I ask for your sympathetic understanding and your support. I ask you to realize that it would have been impossible for one man to have gotten this bill past a twelve-man subcommittee and a fifty-man full Committee without being well fortified with the facts . . . I do try to know something about my bill. We have brought you a good bill. Will you not indicate that you have some confidence in your subcommittee and that you have some confidence in your full Committee. Over seven long years, not one time have I misled you . . . so, if I may be repetitious for thirty seconds, support the Committee. I spend 360 days a year on this bill. I think I know a little something about it because I have traveled and traveled and traveled. We have studied the requests. And we have the facts to back us up.[41]

In cases where chairmen themselves are somewhat less modest, other subcommittee members will extoll the hard work and knowledge of their leader with the same end in view. For example,

> [The subcommittee chairman] knows the workings of these important government agencies perhaps better than any single man in this House. His vast storehouse of information is unequaled. While dealing with the various agencies considered in his bill, [he] often demonstrated that he knew more about the workings, the activities, and the budgetary needs of the various agencies than many of the agency's heads themselves. He has a tremendously keen mind, a great insight, and a great capacity for dealing firmly and wisely with those appearing before his committee.[42]

> I hope the members will read the hearings; I hope they will observe the careful, painstaking, exhaustive manner in which he [the subcommittee chairman] works day after day digging out the facts, sometimes from reluctant witnesses, about the conduct of the agencies of government for which this subcommittee must appropriate. You can be sure that he keeps a very close check on expenditures.[43]

Not only is specialized knowledge a key norm of the House, but appropriations subcommittee chairmen are frequently found among those Members with the most outstanding House reputations for expertise. George Mahon, John Fogarty, and Albert Thomas are examples. Where this is true, their reputation constitutes a strategic asset which can be manipulated on the floor.

A basic tenet guiding all Committee behavior is the belief that its chances of winning acceptance on the floor depend on the internal unity it

---

41 *Congressional Record*, Daily Edition, September 5, 1961, pp. 16996–16999.
42 *Congressional Record*, Daily Edition, October 10, 1963, p. 18266.
43 *Congressional Record*, Daily Edition, June 1, 1961, p. 8717. See also, 99 *Congressional Record*, pp. 5530 ff.; *Congressional Record*, Daily Edition, August 10, 1959, p. 14033.

can muster in support of its recommendations. Whenever Committee members have achieved subcommittee unity, therefore, they seek to capitalize this asset by talking about it on the floor. House members expect the Committee to aid in the House task of consensus-building. When the Committee brings in its recommendations, its members assure the House that the procedural requisites of consensus-building have been observed — that the subcommittee chairman was scrupulously "fair" in giving every outside group a chance to be heard and in assuring the minority members a chance to participate fully. Said one ranking minority member, typically,

> I do not believe any chairman could have been any fairer to any member of the minority party, nor do I believe there was a witness who appeared before our Committee in the two months or so of hearings who can say he did not get all the time he needed to explain his case.[44]

Said another in the same vein, "You would never know, Mr. Speaker, as to who were Republicans and who were Democrats if you were to study the four volumes of hearings this spring."[45]

Subcommittee members go on to assure the House not only that minority interests were heard but that the minority participated in decision-making. In the commonly heard words of one subcommittee chairman, and one ranking minority member,

> I also want it understood at this time that this bill represents the thinking of every member of this subcommittee from both sides of the aisle. Some of us on the subcommittee with regard to some of the items thought they should be lower. But this bill represents an agreement patiently arrived at between all members of the subcommittee with regard to every item contained therein.[46]

> I want to say it was a nonpartisan effort on the part of our Committee in making those reductions, an effort supported by the minority members of the subcommittee, because if we had not made the cuts, and I am happy the majority members of the committee went along, you would have had a minority report on that bill, because I would have filed one myself. But because they were open-minded and very fine people and believed there should be cuts and they were justified, we came in with a unanimous report. And that is the way it should be.[47]

In view of the fact that Committee hearings and markup deliberations are held in secret, Committee members take special pains to convince the House

[44] 99 *Congressional Record*, p. 5331.
[45] 100 *Congressional Record*, p. 8764.
[46] 101 *Congressional Record*, p. 4460.
[47] *Congressional Record*, Daily Edition, April 3, 1963, p. 5254.

that a genuine attempt at consensus-building took place and that a viable consensus has been reached.

The heart of the subcommittee message is that the essential legislative processes of compromise and of give and take have been observed. Each member supports the bill with the statement that, though it does not meet all of his personal preferences, it is a composite judgment and it is as good a composite as can be attained. The appeal for support based on the House norm of compromise is a rhetorical staple of appropriations speeches. A minority subcommittee member made these exemplary remarks:

> If I have learned anything during the eight years I have served in this body, it is that no individual can have his own way all of the time. Legislation is necessarily the result of compromise and adjustment of views to the realities of the existing situation. The bill before you for consideration today therefore is the product of compromise and adjustment of the individual views of seven of your colleagues. It is the result of many hours of discussion, deliberation, and consideration of conflicting viewpoints and the result represents the collective judgment of the subcommittee on the question of how much money should be appropriated to run a multitude of important activities. If I had been writing this bill alone, I would have made deeper cuts in some areas than did the subcommittee and I confess that in other areas I would have provided more funds than are provided in the bill. Nevertheless, I support the action of the subcommittee, as approved by the full Committee, because I believe it represents the best judgment of the members.[48]

As we have already seen, subcommittees strive hard for internal unity during their internal deliberations; and it is a mark of accomplishment for the chairman when he can announce to the chamber — as he very frequently does — that his subcommittee (and the full Committee) have brought in a "unanimous" report. Committee members hope that the implications of "unanimity" will be clear. If all subcommittee members support the recommendations, surely any reasonable Member can feel justified in agreeing. And, lest the point be lost, Committee members will often be quite explicit. A subcommittee member can begin by subtly reminding his listeners that

> This bill is not often, in fact, it is very rarely, amended to any marked degree for obvious reasons. The reason is that we do our fighting back of closed doors and when the bill finally comes out of Committee after the markup it comes to the floor by unanimous consent, with full agreement by every member.[49]

Unanimity, of course, has its own special meaning in the argot of the Appropriations Committee. For it often masks those disagreements that have

48 *Congressional Record,* Daily Edition, April 19, 1960, p. 7635.
49 *Congressional Record,* Daily Edition, February 16, 1960, p. 2456.

been registered by the technique of "reserving." Normally, those who have reserved sit quietly by when claims of "unanimity" or "complete agreement" or "full support" are entered in the *Congressional Record*. Their posture, for example, may be of this sort: "I have reserved the right to vote for a few amendments if they should be offered."[50] The terminology must be handled with care. Overly aggressive assertions may bring some Committee member to his feet with the reminder that he entered "reservations" and that his position was being misrepresented.[51] Where that happens, the impact of the entire line of argument could be weakened.

In general debate, the Committee's arguments in terms of hard work, expertise, and unity function to maintain House confidence and to discourage any subsequent support for amendments. In the event, however, that amendments are proposed, the Committee then employs the same trio of all-purpose arguments in its defense. Should Members be put under pressure by clientele groups to support an amendment, the subcommittee can counterattack by stressing hard work and the resulting expertise:

> I know practically every member of this House has been bombarded with telegrams. I have a few of them here in my hand now. They come from my district. They come from men who know absolutely nothing whatever about this bill. Our committee has been studying this bill day after day, week after week, from 10 o'clock in the morning until 5 o'clock in the afternoon and we have heard witnesses from every division of the departments involved. We have gone into every item of the appropriation and we have presented to you our report. Here we have telegrams that come from men who have never seen the bill, who have no idea what is in it, and yet they try to influence your vote on the bill.[52]

Should a member of the full Committee support an amendment, he can be chastised by his fellows for a violation of an internal Committee norm at the same time that he is being held up before the chamber as lacking in knowledge. Thus did a subcommittee chairman defend his product against a fellow Appropriations Committee member:

> I know my friend from Florida is motivated by the highest intent in offering this amendment, but have you noticed how aware he is of things that happen in the military? It is because he sits on that committee and listens to it. When he brings his bill here, I am going to listen to him, because he will know what he is talking about. But when he comes here on the floor on another matter, behind which is just as much detailed testimony and evidence with which he is not familiar, I think he should listen to us.[53]

50 95 *Congressional Record*, p. 3426.
51 101 *Congressional Record*, p. 3832.
52 103 *Congressional Record*, p. 2251.
53 97 *Congressional Record*, p. 5210.

Should the relevant legislative committee question Appropriations Committee decisions, the Committee will argue that its judgment is as good as, if not superior to, that of others. And this, it argues, is all the more true in view of the uncertainty surrounding appropriations decision-making. In one such confrontation a Committee leader practically demanded the confidence of the House:

> I am getting just a little bit provoked at some of the performances we see here on the floor when we in hearings before the Committee on Appropriations for weeks and weeks have been doing our level best to have a meeting of the minds and to appropriate what we feel deep down in our hearts is adequate for every agency of government, then come to the floor of the House and have someone talk Tweedledee and Tweedledum when no one is sure whether it is enough or way too much.[54]

Because appropriations decisions are a matter of human judgment and because the Committee normally produces a unanimous collective judgment, its internal unity becomes an important bulwark against proposed amendments:

> I want to tell you something you should bear in mind, that this was a unanimous report of the subcommittee and a unanimous report of the Appropriations Committee. Everybody present voted for it. Now, you can kick and buck and haul as much as you want to, but you are sunk.[55]

Sometimes, as we have mentioned, when put under pressure from the floor, the Committee's united front collapses. If it is clear the Committee will be overwhelmed, a subcommittee chairman may rise to say that "the Committee is under no disillusion [sic] as to the attitude and the temper of the House, and without objection the Committee will accept the amendment."[56] Or, when an amendment is offered by someone else, a subcommittee member may choose to cash in on his "reservation." "Mr. Chairman, I rise in support of the amendment. Mr. Chairman, this is one of four reservations that I made when we were writing up the bill."[57] A flat assertion of unanimity is a formidable weapon when brandished by the subcommittee chairmen, but on occasion it may misfire or jam when he is forced to pull the trigger.

In guiding action on the floor the Committee tries to secure House approval for its recommendations by making external capital out of its

[54] *Congressional Record*, Daily Edition, August 19, 1959, p. 15035. See also, 96 *Congressional Record*, pp. 6310–6311.

[55] 93 *Congressional Record*, p. 5548.

[56] *Congressional Record*, Daily Edition, March 7, 1961, p. 3155. See also, *ibid.*, p. 3161.

[57] 94 *Congressional Record*, pp. 3096–3097. See also, 96 *Congressional Record*, pp. 5546, 5924.

445

internal norms of hard work, expertise, and unity. The fact the Committee members believe in the external effectiveness of these arguments strengthens the acceptance of these norms inside the Committee. And the fact that the norms help hold the internal system together makes it even more likely that they will be used in defense of the Committee externally. Internal and external behavior patterns, therefore, are mutually reinforcing.

In attempting to guide floor actions so as to protect its recommendations, the Committee employs a few other general lines of defense — arguments, again, which can be made without reference to the specifics of a proposal. Whenever possible, for instance, the Committee will utilize a procedural argument to fend off an amendment. Legislators typically act to convert substantive disagreement into a procedural one, thereby appealing to a general rule and softening whatever specific conflict is involved. If an amendment is offered on an item which has not gone before the Budget Bureau or on which the Committee has not held hearings, subcommittee leaders will most likely oppose it on those grounds:

> I want to say, Mr. Chairman, it does not give me a bit of pleasure to oppose this amendment, but I am compelled to do so because of the fact that . . . we have had no budget request. I think this item would have been approved if it had come to the Committee in the regular manner. But if we were to approve this item, we would have to approve many others of like nature.[58]

> I ask that this amendment be rejected because with all due respect, and I like the gentleman who presented this amendment, he did not appear before our committee. . . . If a Member does not come before the Committee, he should not try to offer an amendment on the floor of the House.[59]

Often, as in one of the cases above, Committee members will ask a colleague not to push his amendment in return for a promise to give the item their attention either next year or in a supplemental bill or in conference committee should the item find its way into the Senate bill. For example:

> HOUSE MEMBER: I wonder if the gentleman from Georgia would give consideration to my offering an amendment to provide $150,000 for these furnishings.
> SUBCOMMITTEE CHAIRMAN: Because of my great affection for the gentleman from New York, I would be prompted to answer that question in the affirmative, but in view of the long-established policy of the Committee, I must be reasonably consistent and insist upon a hearing on a budget request rather than coming to the floor and arbitrarily putting $150,000 in the bill. It would be a bad precedent for the Committee to adopt.
> HOUSE MEMBER: It is not without precedent, however; is it?

[58] 94 *Congressional Record*, p. 6626.
[59] 104 *Congressional Record*, p. 2311; See also, 93 *Congressional Record*, p. 5358.

SUBCOMMITTEE CHAIRMAN: Oh, no, the House, of course, can work its will on these bills regardless of whether there is a budget request or not. But I think, generally speaking, we all like to follow the established budgetary procedure rather than trying to write appropriation bills on the floor of the House.

HOUSE MEMBER: I'm inclined to agree with the gentleman. I, too, am one who is devoted to pursuing the regular order. But this seems to me to be a type of unusual situation that might call for unusual consideration. I trust that further thought will be given to this matter, and I appreciate the gentleman yielding to me at this time.

. . . . .

SUBCOMMITTEE CHAIRMAN: May I suggest that the more orderly way to approach this problem would be for the gentleman to establish all the pertinent information and present it to the Senate subcommittee which will be holding hearings shortly.

HOUSE MEMBER: And I assume that if the other body does give consideration to the item that you, too, will give fair and favorable consideration to it?

SUBCOMMITTEE CHAIRMAN: Well, we will give fair consideration to it.[60]

Committee members operate on the assumption that by "proceduralizing" their differences with House members they can dampen any antagonisms between them. As part of this dampening effort, the Committee also seeks to "depersonalize" conflicts. Opposition to proposed changes is always accompanied (as it was in each of the instances just cited) by protestations of personal affection for the individual who is being rebuffed:

> Mr. Chairman, I will have to object to this amendment offered by my good friend from North Carolina. He is one of God's noblemen in my book; but there are times when you just have to take issue with your good friends and this is one of those times . . . I hope the gentleman will not feel too bad if his amendment is defeated.[61]

In recent years, every subcommittee chairman has known that when his bill reaches the floor, he will have to joust with gadfly Representative H. R. Gross (R., Iowa). Gross, self-appointed watchdog of the watchdog, reads the hearings and comes to the floor to prick the Committee with minute inquiries or challenge it with amendments. In some cases (e.g., on representation or entertainment allowances for State Department officials abroad) his objections are predictable, in others not. And surely Committee members would just as soon not have to "go through our paces with him." But in the interests of depersonalizing all conflict, they treat his sallies with good humor

[60] *Congressional Record*, Daily Edition, February 9, 1960, p. 2147. See also, 102 *Congressional Record*, pp. 3048, 3053–3054; *Congressional Record*, Daily Edition, April 18, 1962, p. 6363; July 24, 1962, p. 13609.
[61] 100 *Congressional Record*, pp. 4724–4725.

447

and laud him as a hard-working, conscientious, and helpful member of the House.[62] By proceduralizing and depersonalizing floor debate, Committee members seek to keep the omnipresent House-Committee tensions from erupting into open warfare.

The Committee's basic strategy of defense is to avoid any and all head-on floor conflicts over its recommendations. Committee integration internally is directed toward this end and so is Committee behavior in bringing its bills to the floor and in guiding them through. The Committee's floor efforts which have been described — to prevent changes in the context of decision-making, to manipulate those procedural advantages given to it under the rules, to promote a sense of identification between it and the House, and to win the confidence of the membership — all these efforts win floor support for Committee decisions with a minimum of open disagreement. Obviously, this consensus type of strategy is not always successful. The Committee does have to engage in floor fights to protect its recommendations. In such cases, the Committee can use all of these all-purpose arguments. But it will supplement them with arguments and with coalition-building efforts appropriate to the specific decision under attack. Some illustrative cases of floor conflict will be discussed shortly. What needs to be done now, however, is to sketch out empirically the contours of Committee success and failure on the floor. We know how the Committee tries to guide floor action. The question is, does it succeed and under what conditions does it or does it not succeed?

PATTERNS OF FLOOR ACTION

Two arrays of evidence have been used to examine the patterns of floor action on Appropriations Committee decisions. First, there are the decisions taken on the floor with regard to the appropriations of the 36 bureaus discussed in the previous chapter. That is to say, these 576 case histories have been extended beyond the Committee decision-making stage and on through final floor decision. Here, then, is one summary picture of floor activity. In order to provide a broader base for empirical generalization, a second array of data has been collected. Data have been gathered for every money amendment offered to the appropriation bills for the departments of Agriculture, Commerce, Health, Education, and Welfare, Justice, Interior, Labor, State, and Treasury, and for public works for the sixteen-year period 1947 to 1962. This collection project has yielded data on 547 amendments which can be used to broaden and deepen our analysis of floor action.

[62] See "Gross Keeping Watch on Frills in House Bills," *Washington Star*, April 25, 1960, as reprinted in *Congressional Record*, Daily Edition, April 26, 1960, p. 8057; *Congressional Record*, Daily Edition, May 26, 1959, p. 8225.

Enough has been said in Chapter Eight about the limitations inherent in the data on the 36 bureaus. But a series of similar reservations should also be entered concerning the generality and the reliability of the data for the 547 amendments. As in the case of the 36 bureaus, certain policy areas are not covered. The data come only from original appropriation bills. They exclude language amendments which may limit the uses of funds. Just as budget estimates and Committee decisions for the 36 bureaus were taken at face value, so have the actions on amendments been taken at face value. That is to say, in aggregating the data on amendments, it has not been possible to divine which ones among them were put forward for purely tactical purposes and which ones were put forward with the genuine expectation that they should (or would) succeed. These kinds of concessions are even more serious when they involve the relative fluidity of floor maneuver than they are when they involve the more fixed budget estimates and Committee decisions. Furthermore, it must be recognized when reading the generalizations that the 547 amendments have been given equal weight. Obviously, however, they vary considerably in their significance.

In attempting to determine who did and who did not support any given amendment, total reliance has been placed on the written word in the *Congressional Record*. It is possible that the written word deviates from the spoken word (not to mention the possibility that a position has been declared for purely tactical purposes), but if a man says he supports an amendment, he has been recorded as supporting it. In defense of the method used, it should be said that it is not possible to do much better if one wants to put aside (for the moment at least) case histories in favor of a sufficiently large body of data on which to base generalizations. There are some roll calls on appropriations amendments for which more accurate support patterns are available. And these will be examined. The analysis which follows, then, is admittedly exploratory and tentative rather than definitive. And the data have been used in such a way as to suggest only the broadest kinds of relationships rather than more refined ones.

Committee Success and House Satisfaction

The use of amendments to generalize about Committee success in meeting House expectations contains a built-in deficiency which should be noted at the outset. The problem is that the best measure of Committee success lies in the very absence of floor amendments. Since, however, we have no way of knowing how many amendments might conceivably be proposed to any given Committee recommendation, we cannot draw any absolute kinds of conclusions from the fact that no amendments are offered. And, when they are, we cannot know what percentage of all possible amendments are represented. We do not know how many "amendable" segments each overall recommendation may have. Though, in a technical sense, the number of possible amendments may approach infinity, in a realistic sense the number is probably rather limited. Still, we have no way of estimating how many that might be. By the same token, we cannot get an accurate measure of House satisfaction or dissatisfaction by examining amendments. We can record the number of amendments that were in fact proposed and the number that were in fact voted on favorably, but we have no way of knowing how many Members would have offered amendments in any given situation if they thought they had a chance of success. Nonetheless, the examination of amendments does have some usefulness. While it cannot give us absolute measures of Committee floor success and of House satisfaction, it can provide us with some relative measurements which suggest the conditions under which Committee success and House satisfaction do or do not exist.

The best evidence of overall Committee success on the House floor is the fact that 90 per cent of its dollars and cents recommendations for the 36 bureaus were accepted without change by the membership. See Table 9.4. This record of success furnishes presumptive evidence that the Committee had met House expectations. At most, it reflects positive approval of Committee action; at least, it indicates that Members were insufficiently dissatisfied to take the time and effort and to endure the possible costs of failure involved in a public contest with the Committee. House satisfaction is both positive and negative, but, in either case, Committee success results.

TABLE 9.4

HOUSE ACTION ON APPROPRIATIONS COMMITTEE
RECOMMENDATIONS: 36 BUREAUS, 1947 TO 1962

House Action	Number of Decisions	Percentage of Decisions
Accept Committee Recommendations	517	89.9
Decrease Committee Recommendations	30	5.2
Increase Committee Recommendations	28	4.9
Total	575[a]	100.0

[a] Soil Conservation Service figures for 1957 not available; see Table 8.1.

Additional evidence of House satisfaction can be drawn from the number of amendments proposed and passed. Though flat statements cannot be made, it does not seem that a very great number of amendments were proposed and passed — in view of the tens of thousands of recommendations that might be challenged and the equally large number of individual demands for appropriations that surely must go unmet. In the case of the 36 bureaus, as shown in Table 9.5, 187 amendments were proposed during the 16-year period. And, as shown in Table 9.6, these proposals resulted in the passage of only 74 of them — *at the rate, that is, of about 1 amendment per every 8 bureaus per year.* (The disparity between the 58 changes recorded in Table 9.4 and the 74 changes recorded in Table 9.6 results from the fact that sometimes several floor changes were made in the appropriation for a single bureau). Considering the larger universe of amendments offered to the 8 departmental and public works bills during the same period (a universe which contains the 36 bureaus), the total of amendments proposed is 547 — of which 163 (30 per cent) passed. This is at the rate of *1 amendment passed for each departmental or public works appropriation bill submitted by the Committee.* When one considers, furthermore, that some of these were in fact proposed by the Appropriations Committee itself (and perfunctorily passed) to compensate for oversights and for quickly changing requirements, the sheer quantity of floor amendments proposed and passed does not seem very large. In this quantitative sense, the Committee's recommendations met

TABLE 9.5

PROPOSED FLOOR AMENDMENTS TO HOUSE APPROPRIATIONS COMMITTEE DECISIONS: INCREASES AND DECREASES BY YEARS 1947 TO 1962

Year	TO AMEND DECISIONS FOR 36 BUREAUS ONLY			TO AMEND DECISIONS FOR 8 DEPARTMENTS AND PUBLIC WORKS		
	Number of Proposed Amendments	Proposed Increases	Proposed Decreases	Number of Proposed Amendments	Proposed Increases	Proposed Decreases
1947	34	31	3	66	58	8
1948	10	10	0	26	21	5
1949	11	9	2	35	29	6
1950	13	4	9	51	33	18
1951	24	3	21	67	23	44
1952	19	4	15	58	18	40
1953	21	20	1	55	50	5
1954	21	21	0	39	33	6
1955	7	6	1	25	22	3
1956	2	2	0	15	13	2
1957	16	2	14	44	4	40
1958	3	3	0	16	15	1
1959	2	2	0	21	11	10
1960	2	2	0	11	5	6
1961	1	1	0	12	3	9
1962	1	1	0	6	2	4
Total	187	121	66	547	340	207

TABLE 9.6

SUCCESSFUL FLOOR AMENDMENTS TO HOUSE APPROPRIATIONS
COMMITTEE DECISIONS: INCREASES AND DECREASES BY YEARS
1947 TO 1962

	AMENDMENTS TO DECISIONS FOR 36 BUREAUS ONLY			AMENDMENTS TO DECISIONS FOR 8 DEPARTMENTS AND PUBLIC WORKS		
Year	Number of Amendments Passed	Increases Passed	Decreases Passed	Number of Amendments Passed	Increases Passed	Decreases Passed
1947	9	7	2	15	12	3
1948	4	4	0	7	6	1
1949	1	1	0	4	4	0
1950	2	2	0	6	4	2
1951	16	0	16	32	1	31
1952	9	0	9	20	1	19
1953	7	7	0	13	13	0
1954	11	11	0	19	19	0
1955	4	3	1	14	13	1
1956	1	1	0	4	4	0
1957	5	0	5	13	0	13
1958	2	2	0	8	8	0
1959	2	2	0	3	3	0
1960	0	0	0	1	0	1
1961	1	1	0	3	3	0
1962	0	0	0	1	0	1
Total	74	41	33	163	91	72

House expectations as the Committee hoped they would. And, as the Committee hoped, there was not a great deal of conflict on the floor.

Further examination of Table 9.5 reveals that the Committee faced more demands for increases than for decreases on the House floor. The explanation for this disparity lies in the large number of random complaints of individual Members whose pet projects had been neglected. Out of the 547 money amendments, 164 can be characterized as being wholly or primarily designed to benefit, through increased appropriations, the district represented by the sponsor. Many of these were simply grandstand plays for the benefit of those constituents who may be following the proceedings, and 142 (87 per cent) of the 164 constituency-oriented amendments were defeated. Though they are not so easy to identify, it is clear that a sizable (though smaller) number of grandstand economy amendments also were offered on the floor.

Whatever the ratio of proposed increases to decreases, both were more likely to be rejected than passed — and the likelihood was about the same for one type as another. Out of the 547 amendments (and assuming, for the moment, that the Committee opposed all of them), a total of 384 (70 per cent) were defeated. And the proportion of proposed increases defeated (73 per cent) was about the same as the proposed number of decreases (65 per cent) defeated. In raw figures, approximately the same number of increases (91) were passed as decreases (72). Committee success and House satisfaction seemed fairly equally balanced between increases and decreases.

Some discount must be made in the figures just cited, however, since the Committee could be said to have supported some amendments though with varying degrees of enthusiasm. The position of the subcommittee chairmen provides the most reliable indicator of such instances. The subcommittee chairmen actually sponsored 24 amendments, 21 calling for increases and 3 for decreases. And of these, all the increases and all but one of the decreases were passed by the House. Furthermore, the subcommittee chairmen were recorded as favorable to 30 other amendments, 28 of which ultimately passed. Of these 30, 24 were for increases and 6 for decreases. If these 54 cases are subtracted from the total of 547, the record of Committee success changes somewhat but not significantly. What they show is that the Committee was successful in defeating 381 of the 493 amendments to which it was opposed — for an improved record of 77 per cent. Since the Committee supported more increases than decreases on the floor, a revised record shows that they defeated 84 per cent of the increases they opposed on the floor and 68 per cent of the decreases they opposed. And finally, the raw numbers of increases and decreases balance out even more closely than before, with a total of 49 increases and 63 decreases being voted by the House in opposition to the Committee.

By either count, the Committee's floor record indicates success in defending its recommendations. On the other hand, it is clear that opportunities do exist for House members to seek redress and levy sanctions on the Committee. Since many unmet expectations are in fact met via amendment, the likelihood is increased that House member antagonism toward the Committee can be channeled largely within the bounds of the amending process. Furthermore, judging by the similarity in the number of floor increases and decreases actually passed, the Committee appeared over the sixteen-year period to have met the program expectations and the economy expectations of House members about equally well. In these various respects, then, the Committee's floor record helps explain why, despite obvious tensions, the overall House-Committee relationship remained stable in the period under study.

External Variables: Party Control and House Mood

The long-run sixteen-year totals obscure the short-run patterns of Committee success and failure and, hence, the conditions under which these outcomes occurred. Prime among the short-run factors are those changing external conditions (largely beyond the control of the Committee) which generate economy or permissive moods in the chamber. The traces of these short-run external conditions show up most sharply in a yearly breakdown of floor action. Tables 9.5 and 9.6 present a yearly summary of proposed and successful amendments, decisions involving the 36 bureaus only and decisions involving the larger universe of executive agencies. Obviously some of these amendments were of vastly more significance than others. Generalization cannot be carried very far, therefore, on the basis of this crude count. But the tabulations do make amply evident two differing patterns of proposal and disposal. No matter what the relative significance of the individual amendments involved, it is clear that the pattern of floor activity for 1947, 1948, 1953, and 1954 varied sharply from the pattern revealed for 1951, 1952, and 1957. Here, at least, are two patterns sufficiently distinct and different to require some explanation. Before attempting to explain the differences, it should be noted that these two clusters of years share two characteristics which distinguish them as a group, say, from the years 1960, 1961, and 1962. In each of the first two clusters of years there were a relatively large number of amendments proposed and passed. Furthermore, the proposals and the "disposals" went lopsidedly in one direction — either toward increases or decreases. In 1960, 1961, and 1962, on the other hand, few amendments were proposed or passed. Hence no marked consistency of increases or decreases could be observed. If one assumes that these differential rates of floor activity reflected changing levels of House member interest, then it is clear that member interest in appropriations matters fluctuated from year to year.

Table 9.7 accentuates the fact of changing interest levels by listing the number of pages of debate for the bills examined during each of the sixteen years. Here is additional evidence of the fluctuations from year to year. Again, the years 1959, 1960, and 1961 appear as years of low interest as compared either to the 1947, 1948, 1953, 1954 cluster or to the 1951, 1952, 1957 cluster. And, furthermore, it is evident that the focus of House attention changed from one subject matter to another through a period of time. In 1951, according to Table 9.7, prime interest was focused on Interior; in 1955, the main emphasis was on public works; and in 1957, the focus had shifted to Labor-HEW.

Table 9.7 helps to remind us, too, of the crucial fact that appropriation bills are not the only thing on which House members expend their energies. Vast quantities of legislation (not to mention other duties) compete for the time, attention, and interest of House members. Under some conditions, appropriation bills compete favorably, and under other conditions they do not. House members cannot and do not sustain a constant surveillance over Committee activities. In general, they have too much else to do. At any point in time, their attention will be held by just a few major policy questions — many of which do not turn on matters of appropriations at all. Relative to other

454

TABLE 9.7

PAGES OF HOUSE FLOOR ACTION ON APPROPRIATION BILLS: CONGRESSIONAL RECORD, 1947 TO 1962

APPROPRIATION BILL	PAGES PER YEAR																Totals
	1947	1948	1949	1950	1951	1952	1953	1954	1955	1956	1957	1958	1959	1960	1961	1962	
Agriculture	111	54	40		112	103	62	65	53	24	58	47	41	30	37	42	879
Interior	117	43	46		136	64	50	46	14	9	11	19	10	12	13	12	602
Labor–HEW	56	18	13	Omnibus Appropriation Bill	40	26	111	83	16	8	187	21	31	40	36	29	715
Public Works	62	35	59		54	59	74	28	103	46	53	33	55	27	32	29	749
State, Justice, and Commerce[a]	95	70	33		113	57	31	49	45	35	47	16	23	22	22	27	685
Commerce									22	18	14	8	21	9			92
Treasury–Post Office	37	27	12		51	36	24	15	14	11	32	19	17	22	17	19	353
Totals	478	247	203		506	345	352	286	267	151	402	163	198	162	157	158	4075

a Commerce bill included 1947 to 1954; 1961–1962.

concerns, therefore, House interest in appropriations waxes and wanes. And, within the field of appropriations, House interest shifts from one area to another. These simple facts of "salutary House neglect" are of significance in understanding the stability of the Appropriations Committee as a political system.

In 1947, 1948, 1953, and 1954, floor activity was characterized by the fact that amendments (considering the full list of 547) seeking increases in the Committee's money decisions far outnumbered those seeking decreases — by a combined total of 162 to 24. Furthermore, those that passed, though far fewer, were even more lopsidedly skewed in favor of increases — by a combined total of 50 to 4. In 1951, 1952, and 1957, a diametrically opposite pattern can be observed. In these years, proposed floor decreases exceeded increases by a combined total of 124 to 45. Decreases were similarly preponderant among the amendments which carried — by a combined total of 63 to 2.

The more significant of these contrasting sets of figures are precisely those which are most divergent — the figures on increases and decreases actually passed by "the House" in two sets of years. What these figures show is that, in those years when the House made the greatest number of increases in Committee recommendations, it made almost no decreases at all; and when it made the most decreases it allowed virtually no increases. From year to year, then, floor changes flowed in one direction or the other, almost never both at the same time. It would appear that floor action on appropriation bills is influenced by certain overall contextual variables that manifest themselves on a temporal basis. And, it appears further, that these are the same kinds of external variables which, as we saw in Chapter Eight, produce different patterns of decision-making inside the Committee itself. Figure 8.2 lists, for each year, the number of bureaus which received either the same as or less than the previous year at the hands of the Appropriations Committee. The seven years in which the number of such bureaus was the greatest coincide very closely with the years of greatest activity on the floor. The Committee and the House are moved to the same peaks of interest in appropriations matters (if not to the same kinds of decisions) by factors external to them both.

What links the years 1947, 1948, 1953, and 1954 most obviously is the fact that these were the four years in which the Republicans controlled the Appropriations Committee. In three of those years, they acted on a Democratic President's budget. In those years, as we have seen, the Committee tended to make greater budget reductions than under any other circumstances. Since, under these conditions, the Committee places an even greater than average emphasis on economy, House members need not and do not do so. In each of these years, floor proposals for change were many but called

456

lopsidedly for compensatory increases in appropriations. The great bulk of them were made by Democrats; but those that passed obviously required some Republican as well as Democratic support. The successful amendments — about one quarter of those proposed — pertained primarily to the kinds of executive agencies which were characterized in Chapter Eight as having strong external support. This is not surprising since the House would be subject to the same external pressures for increased appropriations as would the Committee. A comparison of Table 9.6 with Figure 8.1 supports the generalization that in Republican years extraordinary budget-cutting by the Committee will produce an extraordinary number of floor amendments seeking to counteract these cuts. Under these conditions, a few such increases, but almost no decreases, will pass.

In 1951, 1952, and 1957, the key external variable appeared to be not partisan control but the existence of an economy mood in the chamber. As demonstrated particularly by Figure 8.2 the Committee shared this mood. For in those three years they acted strenuously to hold down a large number of agencies to the same or to a lower appropriations level. But Committee action was not sufficient. On the floor, the Committee faced a flood of proposals for further reductions, and a sizable proportion of these passed. Whereas a Republican-controlled Committee can convince economy-minded House members that no further economies are possible, a Democratic-controlled Committee operates with no such advantage. In 1951, 1952, and 1957, their relatively economical recommendations were further decreased by House majorities composed of Republicans and Southern Democrats. The agencies and programs which suffered most were of the kind described in Chapter Eight as being involved in especially controversial policy areas.

External Variables: Program Area

Another contextual variable which cuts across partisan control and House moods and which affects the proposal and disposal of amendments is the type of executive agency or program involved. The number of amendments related to any given agency or program is too small to permit generalizations. But, at the departmental level, some patterns can be observed. That is to say, some departments attracted many more amendments than others, and some departments attracted more floor support for "their" amendments than others. Table 9.8 presents summary data for the 8 departmental and the public works appropriation bills.

The public works program stands by itself both in terms of the sheer quantity of amendments offered and the preponderance of proposed increases over decreases. Obviously, this program accounted for the greatest proportion of those proposed increases which flowed from random individual dissatisfactions over the treatment of their constituency-oriented pet projects. Most

457

TABLE 9.8

FLOOR AMENDMENTS TO HOUSE APPROPRIATIONS COMMITTEE
DECISIONS: INCREASES AND DECREASES BY DEPARTMENTS
PLUS PUBLIC WORKS 1947 TO 1962

Department	AMENDMENTS PROPOSED			AMENDMENTS PASSED		
	Number of Amendments Proposed	Increases Proposed	Decreases Proposed	Number of Amendments Passed	Increases Passed	Decreases Passed
Public Works	159	143	16	23	22	1
Interior	96	61	35	40	22	18
Agriculture	73	37	36	25	17	8
State	53	6	47	10	0	10
HEW	52	32	20	19	11	8
Labor	36	20	16	13	3	10
Commerce	30	25	5	10	8	2
Treasury	20	6	14	15	4	11
Justice	8	3	5	3	1	2
Other[a]	20	7	13	5	3	2
Total	547	340	207	163	91	72

[a] Amendments which covered several departments at once and could not be allocated to one department were left in this residual category.

of these were defeated. But, where support could be negotiated on the floor, some did pass.

The Interior Department attracted the next highest number of amendments, and many of these were also constituency-oriented. From 1947 to 1954, the Bureau of Reclamation appropriation was considered in the Interior Department bill, from which it was transferred to the public works bill in 1955. The presence of this constituency- and regionally-oriented bureau helped swell the number of proposed amendments. We have already noted that other Interior bureaus have a good deal of external clientele support, which one would expect to produce floor amendments. And this is all the more true since, as we have also noted, the Appropriations Committee treated the department more penuriously than any other. But we have seen, too, that a number of Interior bureaus attracted a good deal of controversy, of the sort that would produce proposals to decrease appropriations. This constellation of factors may account for the high rate of floor activity involving the Department. It attracted more amendments than any other department. It attracted twice as many proposals for increases as decreases; yet it still attracted about as many proposals for decreases as any other department except the State Department. Finally, in raw totals, more increases and more decreases were passed which involved the Interior than involved any other department.

The agencies and programs of the Departments of Agriculture, Health,

Education, and Welfare, and Labor also have a mixture of friends and enemies in the House, which resulted in a fairly even balance between proposed increases and increases. But in terms of the relative strength of their friends and enemies — as determined by the proportion of increases and decreases actually passed — they varied. Agriculture's friends clearly dominated on the floor, as they did inside the Committee. The same was true, though less so, of HEW. Indeed, these two subcommittees, more than any other, might be found tacitly or openly supporting some of the proposed floor increases. In the case of the Labor Department, however, its enemies would appear to have been more powerful than its friends on the floor of the House.

The Departments of Commerce, State, and Treasury appear to have attracted not a mixture of enemies and friends on the floor but a lopsided concentration of one or the other. Commerce Department appropriations did not draw a great deal of interest. But, such as there was, it was a friendly interest — as reflected in the high proportion of increases proposed and passed. The exact reverse was true of the Treasury Department. And this is not surprising in view of the characteristically weak external support for these agencies which has been revealed in Chapter Eight. And, though we have not examined the State Department previously, it would seem that its lack of external constituency or clientele support accounts for the floor record on its appropriations.[63] On that record, it had far more enemies than friends, and its enemies were more influential than its friends. However, another aspect of the State Department's floor record also needs to be emphasized. A smaller proportion of proposed decreases actually passed than for any other department save Agriculture. That is to say, the State Department subcommittee was more successful in protecting its recommendations against further reductions than any other subcommittee save that on agriculture. But, whereas the Agriculture Subcommittee had many friends to help it on the floor, the State Department Subcommittee had few. It seems reasonable to conclude that the long-time subcommittee chairman, John Rooney, was largely responsible for this record. And, since State Department officials have for so long tended to view Representative Rooney as their enemy, it ought to be pointed out to them that he may be in one sense the very best friend they have in the House.[64]

[63] State Department totals in Table 9.8 include appropriations for one especially weak agency, the United States Information Agency. See John W. Kingdon, "A House Appropriations Subcommittee: Influences on Budgetary Decisions," unpublished manuscript (University of Wisconsin, 1965).

[64] Cf. this comment by a House member. "The gentleman from New York, Congressman Rooney, truly represents the membership's composite ideal of a true Congressman's Congressman. . . . The Congress knows that when the gentleman from New York, Congressman Rooney, handles the committee bill on the floor, that the previous work of the committee . . . [has] culled out and eliminated within human error every major objection to its enactment." *Congressional Record*, Daily Edition, September 14, 1962, p. 18401.

The preceding discussion points up an important observation concerning the Committee's floor activity and an equally important conclusion about the overall function of the Appropriations Committee. Insofar as the Committee's task is to win support for its recommendations, it will do what it can to protect those recommendations against floor demands for decreases as well as increases. The Committee's tasks are not the same on the House floor as they are in the Committee. Inside the Committee, the dominant task is to protect the Treasury via budget-cutting. But on the floor, the dominant task is to protect its decision against change — whatever that change may be. As Committee members sometimes say, "Once we go on the floor, we are the advocates of the agencies' position." Depending on the floor context, then, the Committee may act as the major force *on behalf of* budget reduction or as the great bulwark *against* budget reduction. Whether it acts as one or the other will depend on the contextual variables we have discussed: on partisan control, on House moods, and on the agency or program under discussion. The Committee, we have concluded, is a conservative force in the appropriations process. As applied to its internal decision-making as examined in Chapter Eight, the term conservative refers to the Committee's tendency to reduce budget estimates and to keep the growth of appropriations at moderate, incremental rates. But, in reference to its floor activity, we must conclude that the Committee is conservative in a larger sense. By seeking to protect all of its incremental decisions, reductions and increases alike, the Committee acts as a brake against any and all extreme and sudden changes in the appropriations levels of federal agencies.

Internal Variables: Committee Unity

The fourth major variable affecting appropriations floor activity is the degree of Committee unity mustered in defense of its recommendations. Together with the three external contextual variables just discussed, this internal Committee-centered variable helps to explain the largest portion of what occurs on the floor. Every section of the book has revealed the Committee's own conviction that its floor success depends on its ability to present a united front in its confrontations with "the House." And floor success, we have repeatedly noted, is important to the Committee members because it enhances Committee influence and individual prestige. Unity is the one key variable over which Committee members can exercise some control, and they bend every effort to do so. Their internal structures for decision-making and for integration are shaped to this end. The reward for the elaboration of the Committee's integrative norms and for the operation of its sanctioning mechanisms is Committee unity and floor success. It is unlikely that Committee members themselves would place such emphasis on this linkage unless they had unimpeachable evidence that Committee unity did yield results on the floor.

The frequency with which they go to the floor gives them ample opportunity for feedback.

In view of the fact that partisanship is the most divisive force inside the Committee and inside the House generally, the analysis of Committee unity and the analysis of Committee partisanship must proceed together. Characteristically, analyses of Committee and party action on the floor of the House have drawn their empirical evidence from roll-call votes. The advantage of the roll call is that most Members' decisions are recorded in unequivocal "yes or no" fashion. And roll calls usually decide important controversies. One limitation of an exclusive reliance on roll-call voting is that a great number of floor decisions cannot be examined. Decisions which do not involve a roll call — such as a close teller vote on which the Appropriations Committee prevails in the Committee of the Whole — may be just as significant as decisions which result in yea and nay votes.

Another limitation arises from the fact that a roll-call vote is a special kind of decision which occurs in a special context. It is at once the most public and the most over-simplified decision taken in the appropriations process. It forces participation as no other decision does. Most House members will remain silent on amendments which do not come to a roll call. So will most Appropriations Committee members. Silence protects Committee unity and dampens partisanship. On a roll call, however, publicity, participation, and partisanship increase. Predictably the roll-call vote is the point at which any conflict, if there is one, between Committee unity and party loyalty will be most acute. To put it another way, one would expect that Committee unity would be less evident and Committee partisanship more evident on a roll-call vote than on any other floor decision. To the degree that this is so, the evidence on unity and partisanship which one gets from roll-call vote analysis is of limited usefulness.

Supplementary evidence of any sort is hard to come by — and none of it is as reliable as a roll-call vote. What has been done, however, is to record all the support and all the opposition to each of the 547 money amendments as revealed by speeches recorded in the *Congressional Record*. Some of the hazards of such an undertaking have been mentioned, among them the incompleteness and possible falsity of the printed word. On all non-roll-call amendments, Committee unity and disunity must be inferred from that written record. For example, where one Committee member speaks in opposition to an amendment and the rest of the members remain silent, the Committee will be described as united in opposition to the amendment in question. And, should two members be in open disagreement, the Committee will be described as split. These are long inferential leaps. But they can be rationalized, quite apart from the simple argument that we must make the best of what data are available. When Committee members feel strongly

461

about an amendment, they normally speak up. And their silence usually does connote acquiescence in the position being taken by the Committee spokesman. Though their position might be different if they were forced to a roll-call vote, most members are willing to support their leadership during the less public aspects of floor action. Admittedly, we are dealing with rather crude and "soft" data, and from it, therefore, we shall draw appropriately crude and "soft" generalizations.

The relationship of Committee unity to floor success can never be fully plumbed. For, again, floor success consists in part of discouraging amendments, and it is impossible to know what effect Committee unity might have had on the flow of amendments in the first place. Some tests, however, can be made of the Committee's notion that its unity promotes floor success. Taking the 547 amendments considered in the Committee of the Whole, an Appropriations Committee position was recorded on 515 of them. On 316 (61 per cent) of the amendments, the Committee was united. In 199 (39 per cent) of the cases, the Committee was split. Table 9.9 provides a breakdown of the various ways in which unity was recorded and relates them to the passage or failure of floor amendments. As seen in Table 9.9, Committee unity was registered by spokesmen of both parties (bipartisan unity) or by spokesmen for a single party (one-party unity). In both these ways, the Committee went on record either in support of or in opposition to an amendment. When the Appropriations Committee was united (Columns 1 through 6 in Table 9.9), it carried its position in 270 (85 per cent) of the 316 cases. Evidence exists, therefore, to support the contention that the Committee will win on the floor if it can remain publicly united.

Table 9.9 also suggests that a publicly bipartisan expression of unity creates the optimum conditions for Committee success. In the 89 cases where spokesmen for both parties took the same position, the Committee carried that position in 83 (93 per cent) of them. On the 227 occasions when members of a single party spoke for the Committee, its position carried 82 per cent (186 cases) of the time. It seems to make little difference to Committee success whether it was united in support of or in opposition to an amendment. In either case, it won about 85 per cent of the time. When, however, party spokesmen openly opposed one another, neither party was as successful as when it acted in unity. The Committee split along party lines on 114 amendments. In those cases, the majority party view carried 85 (75 per cent) times, and the minority view carried on 29 (25 per cent) occasions. The Committee's majority party was stronger on the floor with either the open or tacit support of the Committee's minority party than it was in opposition to them. And the statement is doubly true for the Committee's minority party. Other varieties of internal disunity do not lend themselves to easy classification and have been lumped in a residual category. Committee

TABLE 9.9

APPROPRIATIONS COMMITTEE UNITY AND PASSAGE OF AMENDMENTS IN THE COMMITTEE OF THE WHOLE HOUSE: 8 DEPARTMENTS AND PUBLIC WORKS, 1947 TO 1962

Outcome	Bipartisan Support	Bipartisan Opposition	One-Party Support: Majority	One-Party Opposition: Majority	One-Party Support: Minority	One-Party Opposition: Minority	Majority Party Support, Minority Party Opposition	Minority Party Support, Majority Party Opposition	Other and Not Recorded
Pass	23	6	39	29	1	0	7	26	31
Reject	0	60	4	140	7	7	3	78	86

unity does seem to be associated, as the members believe it is, with their success on the floor.

Additional evidence relating Committee unity to Committee success can be discovered by analyzing roll-call data. Of the 547 money amendments studied, 162 passed in the Committee of the Whole House. Of those that passed, roll-call votes were held on 36. There were also 8 motions to recommit which included "instructions" to increase or decrease funds as called for in amendments that had been rejected in the Committee of the Whole. All of these 8 were defeated, largely for reasons mentioned earlier, and they will not be considered further at this point. For the other 36, however, an index of Committee cohesion has been calculated arithmetically by subtracting the percentage of the Committee on one side of the vote from the percentage of the Committee voting the other way. Thus, a 50–50 split on the Committee will yield a cohesion index of 0, while a lopsided vote in which 100 per cent of the Committee voted one way will produce a cohesion index of 100. From this kind of calculation, some rough idea can be obtained as to how well the Committee held together under roll-call conditions.

Table 9.10 presents a frequency distribution of the 36 indices of cohesion. On over half the roll calls the Committee was split 60 per cent on one side and 40 per cent on the other — the split necessary to produce a cohesion index of 20. And in 30 of the 36 cases, the Committee split was no less than 70–30. If the 36 indices are combined, the average cohesion index of the Committee was 22.5 — reflecting an average split which found about 61 per cent of the Committee on one side of an issue and 39 per cent on the other.

Without going any further than this, it appears that Committee unity on roll-call votes involving amendments is not very great. Since the subcommittee might be expected to be the most cohesive unit of the Committee, it

TABLE 9.10

FREQUENCY DISTRIBUTION OF INDICES OF COHESION FOR APPROPRIATIONS COMMITTEE: 36 ROLL CALLS 1947 TO 1962

Index of Cohesion	
90–100	
80– 89	
70– 79	1
60– 69	1
50– 59	1
40– 49	3
30– 39	8
20– 29	3
10– 19	6
0– 9	13

is significant that the subcommittee was also noticeably disunited on roll-call votes. In the 34 cases when both the subcommittee chairman and the ranking subcommittee member voted, they went on record as opposed to one another in 26 cases and united in only 8 instances. Both Committee and subcommittee exhibited a markedly low degree of unity on roll-call votes.

When the Committee is split, it is hard to know whether to describe an amendment which passes as a victory or a defeat for the Committee. If, however, we take the subcommittee chairman as speaking for "the Committee," the record shows that he won in 14 and lost in 21 of the 35 cases in which he was recorded. In 10 of those 14 cases, an amendment passed over his objections in the Committee of the Whole House, he called for a yea and nay vote under procedures discussed earlier and the amendment was then rejected. On nearly a third of all roll calls, therefore, the subcommittee chairman was able to press the advantage given to him under the rules and reverse an earlier defeat. On the other 4 occasions where he won, the subcommittee chairman supported an amendment and it passed — and these were the only occasions when he did support an amendment. In each of the 21 cases where the subcommittee chairman lost, he opposed an amendment which passed in the Committee of the Whole, and passed again when forced to a roll-call vote. On the 8 votes where the subcommittee chairman and the ranking subcommittee member were united, they were victorious in 5 cases and lost in 3.

These figures are compared in Table 9.11 with the subcommittee chairman's success on floor amendments. The subcommittee chairman is always more successful when he supports amendments than when he opposes them. In the Committee of the Whole, however, he wins more often than he loses when he opposes amendments. This is not true on roll-call voting. When his support and opposition are combined and related to his success, therefore, the subcommittee chairman carries his position 79 per cent of the time (284 out of 358 times) in the Committee of the Whole House but

TABLE 9.11

SUBCOMMITTEE CHAIRMAN'S POSITION AND PASSAGE OF
AMENDMENTS IN THE COMMITTEE OF THE WHOLE HOUSE (COWH)
COMPARED WITH ROLL-CALL VOTES

Subcommittee Chairman's Position	Amendments Passed	Amendments Defeated
Support in COWH	51	3
Opposition in COWH	71	233
Support on Roll Call	4	0
Opposition on Roll Call	21	10

only 40 per cent (14 out of 35 times) on roll calls. In the light of the marked disunity of the Committee in roll-call voting on amendments, these figures would seem to add significant evidence to support the Committee-held proposition that the greater its disunity the less likely it is to be able to defend its recommendations and the greater is the likelihood of its defeat on the floor.

Two explanations for the low degree of Committee unity on roll calls come to mind. One is that the special context of roll-call voting brings new kinds of pressures to bear on Committee members — pressures that are highly disruptive of the Committee's internal unity. This *external pressures model* assumes that unity is achieved within the subcommittee and that a somewhat looser unity is maintained in the full Committee. In the context of floor action, for all the reasons previously discussed, Committee unity becomes more difficult to maintain. Oftentimes, the Committee sticks together on the floor only because some of its members remain silent. When, however, Committee members are pushed to a public yes or no type of decision, they respond to extra-Committee pressures — from party leaders, constituency groups, or House colleagues. At that point, the Committee is about as unified or as disunified as any other party or sectional or informal grouping in the chamber. According to this model, at each stage of appropriations decision-making — subcommittee, full Committee, Committee of the Whole, roll call — the context changes. And with each change it becomes increasingly difficult to maintain Committee unity. It is most easily maintained in the well-integrated subcommittee, and it is put under severest strain in roll-call voting. Hence, evidence of Committee disunity during roll-call voting should come as no surprise. Indeed, the wonder may be that the Committee continues to display as much cohesion as it does.

A second, quite different line of argument also explains the same roll-call results. According to this *internal disunity model,* roll-call disunity results from and reflects a degree of Committee disunity that has existed throughout the process. The assumption here is that the subcommittee involved found itself unable to resolve certain conflicts, and that its controversy was perpetuated in the full Committee and carried onto the floor. The conditions most conducive to this pattern would appear to be those which produce partisanship in the subcommittee. In such cases, the majority party would most likely impose its decision on the minority inside the Committee instead of bargaining to a consensus. The minority would then resist at every stage. It would propose amendments to help its cause in the full Committee and on the House floor. Then, should the minority and its allies carry their amendments on the floor, the majority side of the Committee might press for a public recording of votes in the hopes of reversing the verdict. The roll call which resulted would then show considerable disunity, but it would have been precisely that disunity — originating in the subcommittee — which had precipitated the roll calls.

Evidence exists in support of each of these explanatory models. Judging solely on the basis of Table 9.9, for example, patterns of party-based disunity and patterns of Committee unity can be seen to exist in the Committee of the Whole. And each of these patterns helps to support one of the lines of argument just advanced. An analysis of the 36 roll calls themselves provides additional evidence that both explanations have empirical validity. Some roll calls, that is to say, follow one pattern and some the other.

Nineteen of the 36 roll calls are accounted for by 2 concerted floor attacks — one on the Interior Appropriation Bill of 1951 and the other on the Labor-HEW Bill in 1957. Taken as a group, the 19 amendments and the 2 floor fights involved follow the internal disunity pattern. An unresolvable conflict originated in the subcommittee, persisted throughout the process, and culminated in a series of roll-call contests. For each of those roll calls, an attempt was made to measure the partisan disunity of the Committee. For this purpose an index of partisanship (which measures disagreement across parties) was used instead of the index of cohesion (which measures disagreement within any single group). An index of partisanship was calculated for the subcommittee, for the members of the Appropriations Committee not on the subcommittee, and for the members of the House not on the Appropriations Committee. Arithmetically, the index is produced by subtracting the percentage of the minority party in favor from the percentage of the majority party in favor of any particular measure. If all members of both parties vote together, the index is, therefore, 100 per cent minus 100 per cent, or 0. Should one party's members all vote one way and the other party's members all vote the other way, the index is 100 per cent minus 0 per cent, or 100.

For each of the 19 roll calls, the pattern of unity and of partisanship was almost the same. In every case, partisanship was greatest within the subcommittee. And in 16 of the 19 instances, partisanship was greater among the members of the Committee than it was among House members not on the Committee. Partisanship, in other words, decreased as one moved from the subcommittee to the full Committee and to the House membership. This relationship is presented by way of an average index of partisanship for each of the three groupings in Table 9.12. Perhaps the most striking fact about this pattern is the almost pure partisan conflict that registered among subcommittee members. On 16 of the 19 roll calls, the index of subcommittee partisanship was one hundred — which indicates that a united majority party group had deadlocked with an equally united minority party group inside the subcommittee. The average index of subcommittee partisanship is 96, which means that on the average 98 per cent of the majority party and

TABLE 9.12

TWO PATTERNS OF PARTISANSHIP

House Grouping	Average Index of Partisanship, 19 Roll Calls	Average Index of Partisanship, 13 Roll Calls
Subcommittee	96	35
Remainder of Appropriations Committee	49	52
All Other House Members	44	57

only 2 per cent of the minority party voted together on these roll calls. We cannot make inferences about what happened at other stages of the process from these positions taken at one point in time. Still, the evidence suggests that the 19 roll calls involved conflicts that the two subcommittees could not solve through their normal consensus-building processes; and it suggests that the party groups in the subcommittee continued as the main antagonists throughout the process. In general, each subcommittee group picked up support from its fellow party members in the full Committee and in the House, but these members did not display as much partisanship as the subcommittee. In sum, these roll-call data present a profile which points to the existence of the internal disunity pattern.

Of the 36 roll calls, 17 remain as rather isolated, scattered attacks on Committee decisions. They occurred in 9 different years — no more than 3 in any one year — and in no year did more than a single amendment apply to the same policy area. Three of these followed the pattern just described and 1 more was a blanket rider to the omnibus bill of 1950. A cluster of 13 remains — 5 of which involved increases for constituency-oriented pet projects of individual Members. The other 7 had a broader focus on one agency or on a program area. Though they do not all conform in each respect, these 13 do suggest that the external pressures pattern set forth earlier did in fact occur. That is to say, these 13 roll calls do not appear to have resulted from any serious division, partisan or otherwise, inside the subcommittee. Rather they seem to have been precipitated by contests which arose and split the Committee at some later point in the decision-making process.

In some cases, the subcommittee stood united to the end in opposition while their fellow Committee members split off in all directions. In other cases, majority or minority members of the subcommittee decided to support the amendment once it was offered. In other cases, voting patterns followed neither rhyme nor reason, in terms of their Committee-oriented or party-oriented aspects. In aggregating a number of roll calls such as this, the danger of losing more information than can be gained is very great. Nonetheless, the profile presented by the average indices of partisanship for various groups is strikingly different for these 13 roll calls than it was for the 19 examined previously. Table 9.12 presents the contrast.

The evidence seems to indicate that, though the Committee usually voted in considerable disarray on the 13 roll calls, it was not a disunity rooted in subcommittee disagreement. And it is the alignment in the subcommittee which is the key indicator as to which pattern is involved. Subcommittee partisanship was markedly lower than that of the other Appropriations Committee members. And their partisanship, in turn, was less than that of other House members. This profile is the exact reverse of that on the 19 roll calls. Though, again, firm inferences about a dynamic process cannot be drawn from a static analysis of roll calls, the contrasting profiles drawn from roll-call votes provide evidence to support the existence of the two patterns of floor action. Further elaboration of the external pressures and the internal disunity patterns — using some of the roll calls involved — can and will be undertaken by way of case studies shortly.

Other Variables: Party Leaders and Legislative Committees

As Appropriations Committee recommendations move to an authoritative House decision either in the Committee of the Whole or by roll call, two other variables may have an effect on the outcome. These variables are the position of the party leadership and the position of the members of the legislative committee in whose field the appropriation bill falls. Tension exists between the Appropriations Committee and both these groups of House members. Yet the Committee for all its assertions of autonomy does not and cannot risk the open opposition of either group on the floor. The party leaders influence a large bloc of votes; and each legislative committee can command considerable support if it unites in opposition to an Appropriations Committee recommendation. Powerful House norms support member allegiance to both groups. Conversely, the assistance of party leaders or legislative committee leaders may give the Committee the increments of support it needs when under attack. The impact of these variables is all the more relevant when the Committee is split into factions, and when these factions are casting about for allies on the floor. If, as seems to be the case, Committee cohesion does not count for a great deal on appropriations roll calls, one would expect party leadership and legislative committee activity to be among the important factors which do.

The majority leader or the majority whip or both spoke on the floor with reference to only 27 of the 547 amendments studied. They left the job of floor management to the Committee leadership. When they did speak, they usually supported the Committee's recommendations. And their support seems to have been helpful. Twenty-one times they supported the Committee against attack, and 19 times the Committee won. Six times the leader-

469

ship supported an amendment, and 4 times the amendment carried. In all, the majority party leaders carried their position in 23 of the 27 instances in which they chose to speak. There are, of course, many other ways in which party leaders communicate to others in the chamber, but a speech on the floor is surely one way. These speeches, coupled no doubt with other appropriate actions behind the scenes, appear to have been both successful and, on balance, helpful to the Committee.

The minority party leaders went on record in the case of 26 amendments. As might be expected, they opposed the Committee recommendations somewhat more often than they supported them — 15 to 11. And, as might also be expected, their record was not quite as successful as that of the majority leadership. When they supported the Committee, their position carried 8 times and lost only 3; when they opposed the Committee, however, their position lost 11 times and carried 4. It seems clear enough that the Committee benefited by the support of either the majority or minority leadership — though the majority leadership was the more useful of the two.

On a roll-call vote, the party leaders like every other Member — and even more so than most — are forced to declare themselves. In the 36 roll calls, the majority leadership went on record largely in support of the Appropriations Committee — that is, in support of the subcommittee chairman who was acting as spokesman for the group. On 31 occasions out of 35 (with one unrecorded), the majority floor leader and the subcommittee chairman agreed on roll-call votes. On 12 occasions they won, and on 19 occasions they lost. And, when they disagreed, each carried his position half the time. Similarly, the minority floor leader backed the ranking subcommittee member on 25 of 33 votes where they were recorded. They won 18 times and lost 7 — which contrasts with the success of the majority leader and the subcommittee chairman. What this contrast reflects is the success of the Republican minority in 1951 and 1957 in reducing the Committee's recommendations on the floor. In the 8 cases where they disagreed, the minority leader carried his position 5 times. The high frequency of agreements between the majority floor leader and the subcommittee chairman on the one hand and between the minority floor leader and the ranking subcommittee Committee leader on the other indicates that the leadership normally supported its party contingent on the Committee. And, since Committee unity on roll calls was generally low, most roll calls (27 of 34 recorded) found the two party leaders in opposition to one another. Again, we have evidence of the heavy impact of partisanship at the roll-call stage of decision-making.

The final variable to be discussed involves the attitude of the affected legislative committee. By way of aggregate data, we have the record of support or opposition of these relevant committees to each of the 547 amendments where some member of the Committee spoke and where the relevant

TABLE 9.13

LEGISLATIVE COMMITTEE SUPPORT OF AMENDMENTS AND PASSAGE

Outcome of Amendment	Bipartisan Support of Amendment	Bipartisan Opposition to Amendment	One-Party Support of Amendment	One-Party Opposition to Amendment	Other and not Recorded
Pass	13	3	30	5	111
Reject	5	11	58	27	284

committee could be easily ascertained. Where only one legislative committee member spoke, his position was recorded as the position of the committee. The weaknesses of this procedure have been discussed, but, again, no other evidence was available in the record. Table 9.13 presents some of the results in a pattern similar to Table 9.9. The simple fact that some member of the affected legislative committee spoke out on 163 occasions gives ample evidence of their interest. Furthermore, when the legislative committee spoke in a bipartisan voice it was able to carry its position in 24 out of 32 cases, or 75 per cent of the time. And, by such a concerted effort, the members were as able to defeat the Committee as they were to assist it to victory. Where members of only one party spoke for their committee, their position carried in only 57 of 120 cases, or 48 per cent of the time. Moreover, the one-party position was far more successful with the committee in opposition to an amendment than when it went against the committee in support of an amendment. Intervention by committee members of a single party may have been of some help to the Appropriations Committee, but it appears that a bipartisan effort by members of the legislative committee had the greatest independent effect on the appropriations outcomes. An example or two of this effect will be discussed in the case studies which follow.

RELATIONS AMONG VARIABLES:
SOME EXAMPLES

Some patterns of floor action have been described, and a number of variables affecting floor activity have been identified and related to outcomes. Variables such as Committee strategies, rules and procedures, partisan conditions, the mood of the House, the nature of the program, the unity of the Committee, the position of the party leadership, and the position of relevant legislative committees have been discussed — for the most part separately — as they enter into and affect patterns of floor action. But they have not been interrelated in any systematic way. And, given the disparity among available data, it is hard to see how they can be. Some suggestion of the variety and complexity of these interrelationships can be conveyed through illustrative examples. In addition to providing some prototypes, these examples will convey something of the flavor of floor contests which have up to this point been treated in a more statistical fashion.

1951: Economy Mood

From the figures presented earlier, 1951 was one of the best examples of a year in which an economy mood pervaded the chamber and exerted an across-the-board effect on appropriation bills. The key external event which produced the mood was the onset of the Korean War. With defense expenditures rising rapidly, the demand that nondefense spending be cut to a minimum began to be articulated in the House. And it was expressed by a coalition of Republicans and Southern Democrats which had been buttressed by Democratic losses in the off-year election of 1950. In terms of the economy mood of 1951, this coalition was "the House." Indications of the mood appeared as soon as the first appropriation bill (Treasury–Post Office) cleared the Committee and reached the floor. Minority Whip Leslie Arends rose immediately, urged all Republicans to be present to vote for the "economy amendments" that were to come, and delivered the following invocation for the proceedings. "May this be the beginning of a great economy drive. May we have a good attendance when each appropriation bill comes up and may we have votes for economy."[65] The leader of the Southern Democrats, Representative Eugene Cox, intoned in reply, "The importance of what we are doing here this afternoon is that it should help the bureaucrats downtown to realize that the honeymoon of the new order is over, and that the day of the fuzzy-minded, do-gooder is over."[66] Rules Committee Chairman, Representative Adolph Sabath, commented with regard to the Arends-Cox axis, "It does not make sense when the Republicans wean over a few reactionary Democrats and control nearly every proposition that is brought into this House. We are helpless. The Democratic majority is helpless now, due to the coalition that exists."[67] Coalition forces opened with five consecutive amendments reducing various Committee recommendations, and each amendment passed easily. The Treasury–Post Office Subcommittee, probably the least partisan of all subcommittees, and led by a Southern Democrat, remained unified in defense of a Department with which it enjoyed notably good relations.[68]

[65] 97 *Congressional Record*, p. 2694.
[66] *Ibid.*, p. 2704.
[67] *Ibid.*, p. 5136.
[68] When subcommittee members claimed they were being victimized by bringing out the first bill of the year, they assured that all others would be treated similarly. *Ibid.*, p. 2795.

Indicative of the temper of that debate was the following exchange which began with a typical all-purpose defense by veteran Committee member Louis Rabaut (D., Mich.) and which drew comments from Representative Cox and from Speaker Sam Rayburn:

> MR. RABAUT: What is going on here today is just a blunderbuss cut any place where anybody happens to strike regardless of the justice and regardless of the efforts and regardless of the opinion of the Members who are familiar with and have devoted themselves to the proposition. Further, over and above that, this bill has run the gauntlet of the full Committee. Downstairs there was no attempt made to cut this bill. To come here on the floor and have different Members nick it here and nick it there just for the purpose of politics is something which should not be tolerated.
>
> . . . . .
>
> MR. COX: Mr. Chairman, if the little nicking here and the little nicking there spoken of by the gentleman from Michigan has so disturbed him as he has evidenced here on the floor, then when he sees "the nicking here and the nicking there" that is going to take place on these later bills it will be enough to drive him crazy. . . . As I stated, what we are doing here this morning is but an indication of what is to follow. . . .
>
> . . . . .
>
> MR. RAYBURN: Mr. Chairman, my beloved friend from Georgia yesterday, as I understand it . . . spoke something about a honeymoon being ended. When I note the crossing of the aisle here and the conferences that are being held, it is my opinion that the honeymoon has just begun. I trust that in your temporary enjoyment, you are happy and contented.[69]

The fact that a united subcommittee backed by the party leadership acting in one of the least controversial program areas (Treasury) could not prevail against the economy mood in "the House," suggests the decisiveness of the mood variable when it is operative.

After 5 straight reductions had been carried overwhelmingly,[70] however, a $2 million cut in the Bureau of Internal Revenue's funds was defeated. The apparent reason for this turn of fate was the intervention for the first time in the debate of members of the relevant legislative committee. The Ways and Means Committee is the most prestigious committee in the chamber, and when 4 of its members (3 Democrats, including the Chairman, and 1 Republican) rose in defense of this one Appropriations Committee recommendation, they were victorious.[71] Indeed, in the debate on this

---

[69] *Ibid.*, p. 2795.

[70] It is of interest in terms of the categorization of the Customs Bureau as having strong internal but weak external support that every member of the subcommittee spoke against a reduction in this agency — but that they could not protect it against a cut.

[71] *Ibid.*, p. 2800. The same thing occurred again in 1952. 98 *Congressional Record*, p. 1775.

amendment, the Appropriations Committee left the task of upholding the decision almost entirely to the legislative committee. Since these Ways and Means Committee members were silent during most of the debate, their single intervention would seem to have been a strategic decision. The Committee might be expected to have an interest in protecting all of the Treasury appropriations, but they may have felt that they could save only one. It may be that when an economy mood is present and when "the House" is so bent on reducing Committee recommendations, the Committee's most important floor allies will be a representative cross section of the relevant legislative committee.

With House expectations being so unequivocally communicated on this first bill, the other subcommittee chairmen did what they could to build backfires with greater than average reductions during subcommittee deliberations. And when they came to the floor, each defended his bill with the claim that it had been cut as much as possible. This defense did not help the Labor–Federal Security Administration subcommittee to defend itself against 5 reductions. And it worked least of all for the Subcommittee on Interior, which brought the third appropriation bill to the floor.

Subcommittee chairman Michael Kirwan defended his recommendations with an argument tailored to the mood of the House:

> I am being very serious when I say to you: Do not cut this bill any further. The Committee has already cut it as deeply as we feel it should be cut and deeper than I personally feel it should have been cut . . . so I plead with you here this afternoon to try and see your way clear not to cut it further. When the bill is read tomorrow under the five-minute rule, stop, think, and listen, and look if you will, before you do any more cutting on this bill.[72]

When the ranking minority member of the subcommittee, Representative Ben Jensen rose to speak in general debate, however, it was clear that the subcommittee had been unable to compromise all of its differences. Said Jensen, "There are times, of course, when the Chairman and I do not agree on the amounts. We finally came to an agreement on many items in this bill, but there are many other items which should have been reduced."[73] These differences, it turned out, centered on the controversial program area of public power. And it was mainly on public power issues that Chairman Kirwan suffered defeat on 15 consecutive amendments, some of them money reductions and some of them language changes. These defeats were unrelieved by a single Committee victory — even on the one occasion involving a cut in Geological Survey funds when Representatives Kirwan and Jensen stood united in support of the Committee's recommendations.

[72] 97 *Congressional Record*, pp. 4192–4193.
[73] *Ibid.*, p. 4196.

The subcommittee chairman tried to reverse 5 of the cuts sustained in the Committee of the Whole by demanding roll-call votes. These 5 roll calls made up the 1951 contribution to the set of 19 roll calls discussed earlier, on which high subcommittee partisanship was reported. Four of the 5 centered on problems of public power, and 2 of these involved agencies about which some comments were made in Chapter Eight — namely, the Bonneville Power Administration and the Bureau of Reclamation. We observed then that these two agencies were among the least successful of the 36 studied in terms of their dealings with the Appropriations Committee. We related their lack of success to their immersion in partisan controversy.

Table 9.14 presents the indices of partisanship for 3 groupings in the chamber for the 5 roll calls. Partisanship ran high on these Interior Department amendments throughout the chamber. Partisanship ran highest, however, among subcommittee members. The profile conforms to the pattern we have already described, one which begins with the inability of a subcommittee to compromise its way to a decision internally. Now that these 5 roll calls have been placed in some context, however, some of the conditions of subcommittee disagreements become clear — as they had not been earlier. In these cases, high subcommittee partisanship developed out of attempts to reduce highly controversial and partisan programs in a year when the chamber was in an economy mood. Where serious subcommittee disunity exists, it will very likely be the product of external conditions such as these.

The chairman of the Agriculture Subcommittee faced a similar barrage of amendments when his bill reached the floor. In support of his subcommittee recommendations, he argued that the House was fulfilling economy expectations at the expense of its program expectations. Said Representative Jamie Whitten,

> In this day when it is popular to offer amendments to whatever hits the floor, it is a little difficult to get up here and speak in each instance against the amendment . . . you leave us where we do not know what to do. If, without regard to why the money is here, it is just a case of cutting each item that comes up, you are going to do a lot of damage to the program of this department.[74]

The Agriculture Subcommittee came to the floor unified, but with the ranking minority member having "reserved" on every single item in the bill. Though this equivocal posture annoyed the subcommittee chairman — especially when the ranking minority member offered an amendment — he was able to tell the House, "You are taking something where the Committee in its best judgment has reduced as much as we think we justifiably can, [and] I am talking about the joint judgment of the Committee."[75] Ex-

[74] *Ibid.*, p. 5221.
[75] *Ibid.*, pp. 5203–5204.

TABLE 9.14

PARTISANSHIP ON INTERIOR APPROPRIATIONS ROLL CALLS, 1951

| HOUSE GROUPING | INDEX OF PARTISANSHIP | | | | | |
	Reduce Southeastern Power Appropriation	Reduce Southwestern Power Appropriation	Reduce Bonneville Power Appropriation	Reduce Bureau of Reclamation Appropriation	Reduce Bureau of Land Management Appropriation	Average
Subcommittee	75	75	100	100	100	90
Remainder of Appropriations Committee	55	65	67	61	57	61
All Other House Members	53	68	61	49	46	55

pressions of subcommittee unity may have helped the chairman to fight off all but 5 of the 15 proposed amendments, making his the best record of any subcommittee to that point.

The contrast between the success of Agriculture agencies and the difficulty of Interior agencies before the Appropriations Committee and on the floor has already been noted in this and in the previous chapter. Their differential floor success in 1951 can probably be attributed to the broader support existing for agricultural programs in the House. And of particular importance is the bipartisan nature of that support. On several amendments, especially those involving proposed reductions in the size of allotment payments for soil conservation, the members of the substantive Committee on Agriculture spoke out in support of the Appropriations Committee. Representative Clifford Hope, ranking Republican member of that Committee and a highly respected member of the House, fought especially hard to turn back the economy bloc. He spoke three times, and every time he did the Appropriations Committee's position was sustained. So close was the rapport between Hope and the subcommittee leaders that when Hope protested against too large a subcommittee recommendation in one item, they suggested he take his grievance to the Senate and promised to reconsider it in conference. Consider this open bargain struck amidst the flow of amenities between Representatives Whitten and Hope:

> MR. WHITTEN: I want to say that sometimes in the heat of discussion we frequently overlook some things, but I want to say that there is no abler man in the House of Representatives than the gentleman from Kansas [Mr. Hope], and there is no man in the Congress that I know who knows more about the operation of agriculture and who gives a fairer approach to the subject than the gentleman from Kansas . . . certainly there is no prejudice on the part of the Committee. If the amount is cut too severe, we will be glad to reconsider it. In view of the very fine attitude and the confidence I have in the gentleman from Kansas, I wanted to explain our position and say that we would be glad at any time to go into the matter with anyone who may have a different idea about it.
>
> MR. HOPE: I thank the gentleman from Mississippi most sincerely for his kind references. I appreciate them, especially coming from him . . . let me report that because I have such great confidence in this subcommittee, which has brought in a splendid bill, I am simply calling attention to this situation with the thought that the cooperative organizations which are interested in this service will appear before the Senate Subcommittee on Agriculture Appropriations. I believe they can make a strong case for an increase above the amount carried in the House bill. In the event that the item is increased by the Senate, I feel certain that the distinguished Chairman and the other members of the House subcommittee will give the matter due and proper consideration.[76]

[76] *Ibid.*, pp. 5461–5462.

The Senate did increase the item, and the House conferees kept the higher figure in the bill — just as they had said they would.

When their recommendations are put under serious challenge, the Appropriations Committee obviously needs potent allies on the floor. During economy moods, the Appropriations Committee functions as a conservative defender of agency budgets against further reduction. Members of the relevant substantive committees (many of whom sought their committee assignments because of their interest in the program area) can be expected to have similarly sympathetic, protective instincts toward executive agencies working in their policy area. If their experts, their leaders on both sides of the aisle, will speak out on the floor, they can give the Committee an occasional victory. The point is that virtually no department, no agency, no program area can consider itself wholly immune from attack on the floor during an economy mood such as occurred in 1951. Many will suffer reductions; a scattered few will be able to dig in and resist. The optimum conditions for resistance appear to be a stout defense by a unified subcommittee with an assist from influential members of the substantive committee involved.

1957: Economy Mood

The economy mood of 1957 was domestically induced. President Eisenhower sent Congress the largest peacetime budget to that date. He publicly declared his own shock at its size; so did his Secretary and Undersecretary of the Treasury; so did the Chamber of Commerce, the National Association of Manufacturers, and other conservative groups; so did the Republican Policy Committee in the House; and so did many Southern Democratic congressmen. The President's equivocal defense of his own budget opened the door, and the refurbished coalition of 1951 re-asserted itself on the floor.[77] But, in this case, unlike 1951, the economy drive struck and spent itself in one concentrated floor assault on the Labor-HEW appropriation bill. It opened on March 26 and, after a record-breaking 8-day debate, was climaxed by 14 consecutive roll calls on April 4 — more than Speaker Rayburn could remember having occurred on a single day. In all, 27 reductions were proposed via amendment — 14 by Republican and 13 by Southern Democratic members of the coalition. Twelve of these carried and 15 were defeated. The Interior bill, which had come up a month earlier, had been passed in a little over an hour's time and without a single amendment being offered. The Commerce bill, which came to the floor only 5 days after the Labor-HEW bill had been dealt with, had but a single amendment offered to it and passed after half an afternoon of debate.

[77] On the President's equivocation, see Richard Neustadt, *Presidential Power* (New York: John Wiley, 1962), Chapter 6. For a subcommittee view of the President's activity, see 103 *Congressional Record*, p. 4924.

It is clear that external conditions were conducive to some sort of attack on Appropriations Committee recommendations, but the question arises as to why the economy drive took the form it did. As subcommittee chairman Fogarty asked plaintively when he found himself under fire, "In the Interior bill that was up here last week, there was no demand to cut it back . . . why start the pattern with the Department of Labor?"[78] There are three inter-related answers. In the first place, the subject matter of the bill made it an eminently acceptable target for a Republican–Southern Democratic coalition. That coalition had been cemented by opposition to many of the pro-labor, social welfare programs supported by the money in the Labor-HEW Appro-priation Bill. A Republican–Southern Democratic economy coalition could, therefore, maintain a unity against portions of this bill that they could not (and had not) maintained against, say, an agricultural appropriation bill. "I know," admitted Fogarty, "the Department of Labor is a popular place to cut because it is the Department of Labor; it has the word 'labor' in it."[79]

However attractive the target might have been, nevertheless, a highly con-centrated attack of this sort required leadership — and herein lay the second answer to Representative Fogarty's question. The leadership, the strategy, and force behind this economy drive came from within a badly divided Appro-priations Committee itself, specifically from Chairman Clarence Cannon and ranking minority member John Taber. The unusual degree of support which subcommittee chairman Fogarty had given to the programs under his aegis has been mentioned several times. So, too, has the grave concern with which Cannon and Taber viewed spiraling budgets in this area. And the various manipulations of Cannon and Taber to outvote Fogarty in his own sub-committee have also been described. One of these maneuvers brought Taber to the position of ranking minority member of the subcommittee in 1957. The battle had, therefore, been joined in the subcommittee, and, in markup, Taber, Representative Melvin Laird (R., Wisc.) and Cannon (ex officio) held Fogarty and his two Democratic allies to a tie vote. This sent Fogarty's recommendations to the full Committee, where he was also victorious. But the bill came to the floor in 1957 with the subcommittee totally split along partisan lines and with the full Committee Chairman opposing the recom-mendations of his subcommittee chairman. Taber and Cannon took advan-tage of the conditions of 1957 to pursue their long-smoldering internal Committee battle on the House floor.

The third factor which precipitated the economy drive was the timing of this particular bill. It came to the floor just after House members had returned from their mid-March Easter recess. While in their constituencies, many of them had felt the first touch of the conservative group pressure which

[78] 103 *Congressional Record*, p. 4427.
[79] *Ibid.*, p. 4427.

had been building up slowly, spearheaded by the Chamber of Commerce's city-to-city economy aircade. A leader of the Labor-HEW Subcommittee recalled, "We came up at a bad time that year. Between the time the previous bill and ours came up, there was a big campaign for economy. I don't remember whether it was the NAM or the Chamber of Commerce or what. But the Republicans and Southern Democrats got together, held a meeting, and decided on the amendments they thought they could carry." In 1957, Chairman Cannon urged his colleagues to respond to the national mood. "These protests, letters, telegrams, and telephone messages are coming in from every state in the union. They are coming in from large taxpayers and small taxpayers. The situation represents what amounts to a national uprising."[80] On the heels of their trip back to the district, many congressmen perceived that such a national uprising was in the making. And, insofar as they perceived that it was so, economy sentiment was strengthened in the chamber. Two months earlier or two months later, House members did not feel the same urgency about economy as they did in late March and early April.

It is not clear whether, when Representative Fogarty opened debate in the Committee of the Whole, he was fully aware of what was coming. In any event he began by looking up to the dais and making a prophesy. "Mr. Chairman, I'm very pleased to see in the chair, presiding . . . the other half of the Rhode Island delegation, my colleague Aime Forand. I am sure, with the gentleman from Rhode Island in the chair, this bill will pass without too much difficulty."[81] Though he did not proclaim Committee unity, he began with the customary round of mutual self-congratulation that is the hallmark on the floor of the well-integrated Committee. Representative Taber, however, quickly dispelled whatever hopes Fogarty might have had for a smooth passage:

> This bill has come before you with the Appropriations Committee divided . . . there are many items in this bill which, in my opinion, should be reduced further. I hope when these items are reached that those Members interested in economy will offer amendments to reduce the bill.[82]

Opening speeches of this sort by ranking subcommittee members are rare. Taber not only openly solicited amendments to Committee recommendations, but he also laid down a standard on which he and Cannon had agreed. They would support, he implied, reductions which contained agency personnel at existing levels. "The Committee has done something toward reducing the number of persons involved, but in my opinion I believe in a great many cases we could have done a great deal more and at least brought them back to the

[80] *Ibid.*, p. 4414. See also *Congressional Quarterly*, March 22, 1957.
[81] *Ibid.*, p. 4404.
[82] *Ibid.*, p. 4410–4411.

current year's figure."[83] The economy bloc took Taber's cue, and from the very first amendment most of them used the 1956 appropriation bill as the goal of reductions. The man who succeeded Eugene Cox as unofficial leader of the House's Southern conservatives rose to pledge support to the drive. Said Representative Howard Smith (D., Va.), "Personally I think there is not a bill that comes before this House that could not be cut ten per cent without hurting the essential functions of government."[84] But he, too, followed Taber's lead in setting 1956 as a standard, and he urged his Southern colleagues to stay on the floor and vote for all coming amendments.

Appropriations Committee member Hamer Budge (R., Idaho) assumed leadership of the coalition when the bill was read for amendment. On March 26, he proposed 4 straight reductions, and every one carried without difficulty. Beginning on March 27, the sponsorship of amendments was distributed among other Members — in order to spread the credit for economizing. Representative Fogarty resisted every amendment stubbornly. To one of his subcommittee colleagues, Representative Henderson Lanham (D., Ga.), an especially popular House member, fell the task of speaking to the Southerners. Lanham began his major speech by invoking the memory of a beneficent Southerner, moved through the Committee's standard repertoire, and ended with an appeal to stay the economy hand until the unpopular foreign aid bill came to the floor. His speech was a classic example of the all-purpose Appropriations Committee defense given a special twist to appeal to a particular audience:

> Mr. Chairman, when I was a member of the Committee on Public Works, Mr. Will Whittington was chairman of that committee and I used to marvel at the man's knowledge of every little dam in this country, every river and every creek, he knew exactly what the engineers were doing in every state of the union. I marveled that one brain could hold all he knew. John Fogarty is like that on this Committee. I have never seen a man with so much knowledge in the field of labor, health, education, and welfare. John Fogarty is as anxious as any one of you to cut the budget where it can be done . . . your Appropriations Committee has a sense of responsibility to the House. You voted for these programs, and the Appropriations Committee feels that it should make these programs work at the lowest possible cost. In making up this budget that is exactly what your subcommitttee did. Of course, we are not infallible, neither is any committee. But it does seem to me that as far as possible in our effort to cut the budget we ought to be very careful in what we do and put some confidence in your Committee. And we ought to listen to this man who above all others knows what he is talking about in this most important field . . . let me tell you, my friends, I am also on [the foreign aid sub-

[83] *Ibid.*
[84] *Ibid.*, p. 4423. On the Cannon-Taber-Smith agreement, see their comments, *ibid.*, pp. 4411, 4415, 4423.

committee] . . . and when we come to that appropriation, we will save you some money . . . let us try to be reasonable and sensible as we go ahead with the consideration of this bill, and I will guarantee you that we are going to cut a nice slice out of the foreign aid bill. [85]

The economy tide of those two weeks followed a pattern of flow and ebb. On the first day of debate, the coalition carried 4 of its 5 proposed reductions. They achieved the identical record on the second day. On the third day they were victorious on all 3 of their proposed cuts. But on the fourth and fifth days of debate, the tide turned. On each of these days the debate centered on a single proposal, and in each case the debate ended in defeat for the economy forces. Thereafter, the contending groups broke even with 4 victories each in the Committee of the Whole. The reversal of form coincided with the shift of focus from the Labor to the HEW portion of the bill. Against the recommendations for the Labor Department which were considered first, the coalition was victorious in 10 cases out of 12. Against the HEW appropiations, the coalition was victorious in only 5 out of 12 attempts. These shreds of evidence fit the patterns revealed in Chapter Eight, showing greater support for HEW programs than for Labor Department programs both inside the Committee and out.

Specifically, the ebb of the tide began when the coalition sought to reduce two programs with widespread House support — one on aid to rural libraries and one on aid to federal impacted areas. In both cases and on successive days, members from the Committee which passed the authorizing legislation, the Committee on Education and Labor, rose to help the Appropriations Committee majority defend its recommendations. The fight over rural library funds was the first solid defeat for the coalition. In that contest, 17 Members rose to defend the program; 4 were from the Appropriations Committee (3 from the subcommittee) and 8 were from the Committee on Education and Labor. The chairman of that committee, Representative Graham Barden (D., N.C.), a conservative Southerner, succeeded in splitting the coalition with the following frank appeal to its rural members on both sides of the aisle:

If you will just stop and think of the millions and millions of dollars in this bill that relate to urban people, the people in the towns and in the cities. . . . Here is a little bookmobile that goes out to every rural district, the country roads, the highways, and the byways — these bookmobiles carrying books to kids and grownups who would never see those books if they were not brought out there to them, as some live 30 miles or more from any kind of library. . . . I think the past history of this country shows that the rural people have been a pretty substantial people, and loyal. There is not a group of people on the face of this earth more loyal to this

[85] *Ibid.*, p. 4669.

nation and more patriotic than rural people; Commies and pinks do not dwell among them, and that the record will disclose through all time. Jefferson was not so far wrong when he said that so long as the balance of power remains in the hands of the rural people, democracy will be safe. But I am not so sure that they will be able to defend themselves against the isms and so forth, if one segment of our population is permitted to rise, while the rural people stand stationary intellectually or otherwise.[86]

Basically, the problem for the coalition member in such circumstances is to weigh his economy expectations against his program expectations. Programs that have the strong support of some key elements in the economy coalition — in this case, most likely, rural Southerners — these programs, obviously, are most likely to survive. And, again, the leadership of House substantive Committee members representing the key element of the coalition would seem to be of critical importance. The same lesson could be drawn in 1957 from the other coalition defeats on items such as aid to impacted areas, hospital construction, and the Public Health Service. Additional credit for the turn of the tide should be given to the stiffening of attitudes which occurred midway in the debate on the part of the President. But, in the end, it was the degree of external support for particular programs in the House that split and contained the economy forces.

Encouraged by the slow reversal of his fortunes, subcommittee chairman Fogarty decided to ask for roll-call votes on 14 of these reductions which had carried in the Committee of the Whole. On these public votes, he succeeded in reversing the earlier decision on 5 of the 14, thereby retaining the original Committee recommendation. As might be expected, his 5 victories involved programs for which external support could most easily be mobilized — veterans re-employment, Office of Education, Food and Drug Administration, Women's Bureau, and municipal sewage plant construction. Still, the overall result was a heavy and unusual defeat for the Appropriations Committee majority. The voting reveals what appears to be a necessary condition of this kind of defeat — a disunified Committee and, particularly, a split subcommittee. On the 14 roll calls (which make up the bulk of the set of 19 "internal disunity" roll calls described earlier), the average subcommittee index of partisanship was 98. And this is the key to the pattern of partisanship which, though considerably diminished because of Southern Democratic defection, carried through the Committee and to the floor. A majority of Democrats opposed a majority of Republicans on 12 of the roll calls; and the majority and minority leaders opposed one another on 10 of the 14 votes. In a showdown vote, if the "experts" of the subcommittee are divided, House members will tend to line up behind the experts of their own party.

[86] *Ibid.*, p. 4806. Another example of House support for vocational education will be found in 100 *Congressional Record*, pp. 7946 ff.

At no other time in the 16 years studied did the Committee members cast so many roll-call votes at one point in time. A closer look at the pattern of Committee voting provides us with a profile of the Committee at a point when its internal unity is at a minimum and its susceptibility to non-Committee pressures is at a maximum. What that profile reveals is that, with a few exceptions traceable to internal Committee considerations, Appropriations Committee members voted in response to the same broad set of conditions to which all other House members responded. That is to say, members of the Committee voted as one would predict if he knew everything about them *except* their Committee assignment. Democrats voted like Democrats; Republicans voted like Republicans; conservatives voted like conservatives; liberals voted like liberals; Southern Democrats voted like Southern Democrats; urban liberal Republicans voted like urban liberal Republicans, etc. This profile not only supports our generalizations about the special properties of a roll-call vote, but it also gives evidence of the conditions under which the external, non-Committee demands on its members outweigh integrative internal Committee demands. That is to say, it indicates the conditions under which the Committee loses its identification as a discrete subsystem.

Table 9.15, then, is a picture of Appropriations Committee behavior under conditions of great stress. The members are arranged in clusters and ranked according to the number of times they supported the recommendations of the Committee majority — that is, how often they voted, "No," on the 14 roll calls. The impression is strong that, on the whole, the voting pattern of Committee members mirrored that of non-Committee members who shared their party or constituency characteristics. One would have expected the most sizable defections from the core of Democratic votes to have occurred among the Southerners, and they did, just as much inside the Committee as in the House. Similarly one would have expected the most sizable defections from the Republicans to have occurred, as they did, among Representatives Canfield, Fenton, and Horan — long the three most liberal, least economy-minded Republicans on the Committee.

The most startling aberrations from these patterns are the positions of Representatives Cannon, Preston, and Passman. Chairman Cannon's special desire to cut this bill has already been mentioned, and it can be laid to conditions internal to the Committee. Similarly, the atypical record of the two Southern Democrats can probably be explained by internal considerations. It seems likely that Representative Preston was persuaded to go along by his friend and fellow Georgian, Representative Lanham, who was loyally supporting his subcommittee recommendations. It seems likely too, in view of his speech reported earlier, that Representative Lanham (also a member of the foreign aid subcommittee) had struck a bargain with the chairman of that subcommittee, Representative Otto Passman, to support him on for-

484

TABLE 9.15

APPROPRIATIONS COMMITTEE MEMBER SUPPORT OF COMMITTEE
RECOMMENDATIONS: 14 ROLL CALLS, 1957 — NUMBER OF
VOTES SUPPORTING THE COMMITTEE (PRO) COMPARED WITH
THE NUMBER OF VOTES OPPOSING THE COMMITTEE (VS).

Pro	Vs
14	0

Fogarty (D., R.I.)
  (Subcommittee Chairman)
Lanham (D., Ga.)
  (Subcommittee Member)
Flood (D., Pa.)
Natcher (D., Ky.)
Passman (D., La.)
Preston (D., Ga.)
Rabaut (D., Mich.)
Rooney (D., N.Y.)
Shelley (D., Calif.)

Pro	Vs
13	1

Denton (D., Ind.)
  (Subcommittee Member)
Marshall (D., Minn.)

Pro	Vs
12	2

Canfield (R., N.J.)
Kirwan (D., Ohio)
Sheppard (D., Calif.)

Pro	Vs
11	3

Boland (D., Mass.)
Fenton (R., Pa.)
Magnuson (D., Wash.)
Yates (D., Ill.)

Pro	Vs
10	4

Steed (D., Okla.)

Pro	Vs
8	6

Horan (R., Wash.)
Norrell (D., Ark.)
Riley (D., S.C.)

Pro	Vs
5	9

Evins (D., Tenn.)

Pro	Vs
4	10

Coudert (R., N.Y.)
Sikes (D., Fla.)
Wigglesworth (R., Mass.)

Pro	Vs
3	10

Whitten (D., Miss.)

Pro	Vs
2	11

Andrews (D., Ala.)

Pro	Vs
2	12

Alexander (D., N.C.)
Ford (R., Mich.)
Mahon (D., Texas)
Miller (R., Md.)
Ostertag (R., N.Y.)

Pro	Vs
1	13

Gary (D., Va.)
Thomas (D., Texas)

Pro	Vs
0	13

James (R., Pa.)

Pro	Vs
0	14

Taber (R., N.Y.)
  (Ranking Member of Subcommittee)
Laird (R., Wisc.)
  (Subcommittee Member)
Cannon (D., Mo.)
  (Committee Chairman)
Andersen (R., Minn.)
Bow (R., Ohio)
Budge (R., Idaho)
Clevenger (R., Ohio)
Jensen (R., Iowa)
Jonas (R., N.C.)
Scrivener (R., Kansas)
Vursell (R., Ill.)
Wilson (R., Ind.)

eign aid in return for Passman's support on this occasion. With these exceptions, internal Committee considerations do not seem to have been an important factor in Committee member voting.

The economy mood lingered in the chamber, but its floor manifestations began to disappear after the 14 roll calls. Primarily, this was the result of the Committee's adaptation to the mood in the chamber. At the close of the Labor-HEW debate, one Committee member noted that the floor fight had been having important consequences on the subcommittee markup sessions then in progress:

> I would like to state, Mr. Speaker, that the effect of the House action in the Committee of the Whole in carefully analyzing the appropriations line by line contained in this appropriation bill has been tremendous. Since this bill has been on the floor for action three other appropriation bills have been marked up by subcommittees of the House Appropriations Committee. These markups have brought about substantial reductions . . . requests for additional new personnel have been severely trimmed due to the manifestation on the part of the House in the last seven days that it is truly interested in holding down the number of new employees provided for in the President's budget.[87]

When the Committee brought its next bill, Commerce, to the floor the subcommittee chairman stressed Committee responsiveness to House expectations:

> Mr. Chairman, the subcommittee . . . has brought a bill to the House today which I think is in keeping with the temperament of the Congress and the people of this country. When I say "temperament" I mean the desire to reduce government expenditures to a more reasonable level.[88]

The comments by the ranking subcommittee member involved indicated that it was "business as usual" again inside the Committee. "It has been one of the pleasantest experiences of my nineteen years in the House. This bill has been put together without any partisanship politics."[89]

Similarly, the Agriculture Subcommittee chairman announced that his group had taken the cue from the Labor-HEW debate and accepted the Taber-Cannon-Smith standard. "Recognizing the need for economy," he began, "the Committee has held the appropriations for the regular programs of the department at the 1957 level."[90] The economy forces did attempt one more modest attack — on the recommendations for the State Department. But all 8 of their proposed reductions were rejected. The Committee had adjusted its thinking downward during and after the debate on the Labor-

[87] 103 *Congressional Record*, p. 5171.
[88] *Ibid.*, p. 5358.
[89] *Ibid.*, p. 5359.
[90] *Ibid.*, p. 6867.

HEW bill, and the House seemed satisfied with the results. In any case, it is doubtful whether, to the exclusion of other legislative matters, "the House" could or would organize itself to press another such attack in the same session. House surveillance is, as we have said several times, sporadic. But when exercised, as in 1957, it can and does serve to keep Committee decisions in line with House expectations.

Permissive Moods

In those years when an economy mood pervades the House, it is practically impossible (as Table 9.6 shows) for anyone to secure an increase over Committee recommendations on the floor. For those who desire more rather than less money for a program, their problem is to hold the Committee figure against threatened reductions. But there are other years (as Table 9.6 also shows) in which the "temper of the House" or the "climate on the floor" is favorable to proposed increases. Probably it is too strong to speak of a spending mood — permissive seems more accurate. That is to say, "the House" never seeks to raise Committee recommendations in the same across-the-board manner as it occasionally does when it seeks reductions. In years like 1951 or 1957, the House mood is so strong that the burden of proof is placed on those who would defend the Committee recommendations. But in the more permissive years, the House mood is less dominant, and the burden of proof is placed on those who would change the Committee decision. Given a favorable climate, however, a fair number of House members will prove their case for an increase on the floor. Different clusters of Members may trade votes in those years and thereby carry a series of related amendments. But amendments to increase appropriations are proposed and are carried selectively, not as the result of such tides as brought decreases in 1951 and 1957. The years of the permissive mood are identified in Table 9.6. Special attention has already been called to the fact that in several of those years a Republican-controlled Committee made larger than average budget cuts, and this action brought counteraction on the floor. It should be added that economic conditions, or House member readings thereof, influence the permissive mood. In 1954 and 1958, for example, each of which shows some increases and no decreases, "the House" (in this case its less conservative Members) may have been responding to the onset of a recession with a willingness to increase spending.

Three program areas in which the greatest number of proposals for floor increases were made and succeeded were (as shown in Table 9.8) Public Works, Interior, and Agriculture. The characteristic which these policy areas share is the large number of programs which are directly constituency-oriented. For most of the items in these appropriation bills, there is a House member or a cluster of House members whose constituents are its direct and

487

certain beneficiaries. And it is this fact that explains the high incidence of increases in the areas of Public Works, Interior, and Agriculture.

Since the push for increases comes selectively rather than as the result of some spending tide, increases tend to be proposed by Members with very tangible constituency-oriented projects — projects that are usually believed to be important to re-election. Since Members think it important to demonstrate that they are on the job, they will submit many an increase amendment that they know will fail. But since Members also want to be able to show their ability to deliver on their campaign promises, they may key all their legislative activities to winning a single project. Ideally, they will work through the Committee. But if the stakes are high and they fail here, they may expend a great deal of their time, energy, and their credits with other Members to build a majority on the floor. The same can be said for certain clusters of Members who share a special interest in a program area — Members from areas served by Agriculture or Interior Department programs.

1954: Agriculture

To call attention to specific instances of floor increases in these areas is to illustrate the variety of ways in which constituency-oriented members can win over enough allies to bring about floor success. Several examples will be discussed briefly. The first involves the series of amendments which increased research funds in the Agriculture Appropriation Bill in 1954.[91]

In that year, the Agriculture Subcommittee brought in a bill which gave the Department the amount it requested. But within the total amount of money, the subcommittee had taken sums away from research projects and given them to other programs which it deemed of higher priority. At bottom, its quarrel with the budget allocations was a quarrel with Agriculture Secretary Benson's priorities in agriculture. Subcommittee recommendations represented a compromise between its desire to boost certain programs while still keeping the total in line with the budgetary ceiling. This compromise was supported by all members of the subcommittee, and it carried despite attempts to raise the research items in full Committee meetings. Apparently, the subcommittee's zeal for staying within the budget represented a misreading of the mood of the House, the commitment of the administration, and the concern of the farm organizations. In 1954, the House mood was permissive; the Republican leadership was more strongly committed to a research and marketing approach than to a budget ceiling; and the farm groups, which had testified in favor of the full research amount, moved in to take the lead in overthrowing the Committee. The bill was reported out of Committee on Friday, and the debate opened on Monday. Over the weekend, however, the

[91] The sequence of events will be found in 100 *Congressional Record*, pp. 5038 ff. and 5154 ff.

Farm Bureau Federation, the Cotton Council, the National Grange, the Republican House leadership, key congressmen, and administration spokesmen met and agreed to seek increases. On Monday, lists were distributed on the floor showing each Member what his state stood to gain by the proposed increases. Since agricultural research laboratories and extension services are widely distributed across all the states, and since they are based in identifiable locations throughout each state, constituency-oriented appeals were most effective. The move apparently caught the subcommittee by surprise. The subcommittee chairman, Representative H. Carl Andersen (R., Minn.), dug in against the first amendment to increase research funds:

> I am disturbed at the evident pressure for spending money brought upon this Congress by farm groups and others in regard to the pending and other suggested amendments . . . are you going to succumb to such pressure? I personally am not. My committee has brought a good bill to the floor, not one dime over the budget and I intend to stand by it.

The ranking subcommittee member, Representative Whitten, heaped lavish praise on his colleague and supported his stand — leaving the clear impression, however, that he did so out of subcommittee loyalty rather than personal conviction:

> There is no finer friend of American agriculture than the chairman of the subcommittee Mr. H. Carl Andersen. He has stood up like a man and has helped to work out these programs. It was demanded of him that he hold his bill within the overall budget. He did that, I would guess, against his personal desires. I would be least appreciative if I did not stand here and say I thought he had done a wonderful job of trying to balance these things out in view of all his problems . . . I have my problem of supporting the majority of the Committee which has tried to do a good job. I think I should stand up and be counted. I do not know how to get so many things solved and then shift position.

Each man who supported the amendment spoke in glowing terms of the work of the subcommittee chairman and tried to soften the blow by indicating that nothing personal was involved. A veteran Appropriations Committee member said, for example,

> I rise not in repudiation of the subcommittee. If I should try to select the subcommittee of Congress with which I am most generally in accord, I think I would select the subcommittee headed by the able gentleman from Minnesota . . . while I hesitate to support an amendment which does not completely meet with the approval of the subcommittee, I cannot in good conscience do otherwise at this time.

Majority leader, Representative Charles Halleck (R., Ind.), said, "May I say that I recognize the magnificent work done by the gentleman from Minnesota and members of his Committee and it is with great reluctance that I find it necessary to take the position I do." When the amendment carried on a division vote, the Committee of the Whole rose, and the bill went over until Wednesday.

During the hiatus, meetings were held (one of them at the White House), support for floor increases was consolidated, and on Wednesday the same amendment carried overwhelmingly on a teller vote. The subcommittee chairman accused the party leadership of perfidy. He accused the administration of usurping congressional authority. And he upbraided House members generally for what he chose to construe as a vote of no confidence in his subcommittee. In Representative Andersen's long speech (in which he abandoned any further defense of his subcommittee recommendations) one can sense the personal trauma involved when a subcommittee chairman faces a total reversal of all the normal patterns of floor activity and the prospect of overwhelming defeat:

> Farm groups, dissatisfied with our allocation of funds in this bill appealed to the White House for aid — yes, and evidently these groups were sustained in their pleadings because seemingly suggestions were relayed to my leadership here to agree today to considerable increases in this bill. Remember, our bill had been approved almost unanimously by my subcommittee and by the full Appropriations Committee and yet my leadership deserted me in my efforts to bring a well-balanced, well-studied bill before you, within the budget overall limitation.
>
> I am not here going to be put in the position of fighting worthwhile programs in agriculture such as research, extension, and experiment stations. No, Mr, Chairman, if the White House, if the Secretary of Agriculture, if the Farm Bureau and the National Grange, if the leadership on my side in this House have determined that the lid shall be off on this bill, if they have determined as they evidently have, looking at the stack of amendments pending on the desk, that increases in the bill can be made, that there is no reason for too great a degree of fiscal responsibility, why there is nothing that I can do but accept gracefully . . . I need not worry too much in the future about holding adequate and painstaking hearings on all the various items in our bill, because here you have disregarded our judgment, gained from careful study . . . by your lack of confidence today in my subcommittee, who know these programs, and by following the dictates of our leadership here, whose knowledge of these programs is necessarily not as deep, you have injured for years to come the great Department of Agriculture.

When Andersen sat down, the members of his subcommittee from both sides of the aisle rose to pledge him their fealty and to disclaim any part in the floor revolt. Nonetheless, before the uprising ran its course, nine more increases were tacked on to the Committee's recommendations. And, to make his abdication complete, Representative Andersen sponsored one of the increases himself on the theory that if "the lid was off" he would give added protection to the program he favored.

What happened to Andersen is precisely what every subcommittee chairman dreads — being "rolled" on the floor. And he took it very hard. An official of the Extension Service recalled,

> All the farm organizations were united. . . . They went to work politicking and button-holing. They saw every favorable Republican and Democrat and knew they had the votes. So they fought it on the floor and they spanked the Committee. The Appropriations Committee had never taken a licking like that before. H. Carl fought it bitterly. Some of the things H. Carl said — before he revised it for the *Record* — couldn't be put in the *Record*. He fought bitterly and hasn't forgotten it. Whitten, who is a little sharper and quicker with his political footwork, retreated while he had a few bridges left. But H. Carl burned all of his. We were terribly sorry to see it happen, because he's never forgotten it.

In this case the subcommittee chairman had been defeated in a constituency-oriented policy area by the well-organized efforts of agricultural groups (whose influence has already been mentioned), the leadership of his party, and the administration's agricultural officials. This is one coalition of external interests, surely, against which a united subcommittee is not likely to be sufficient.

1954: Fish and Wildlife

In the same year, 1954, an amendment to the Interior bill carried under circumstances that illustrate even more graphically the kind of Member interest which produces increases. The amendment involved the Fish and Wildlife Service, but it could as easily have been the Bureau of Reclamation or the National Parks Service or the Bureau of Mines — all of which received more than one floor increase during this period. The amendment as proposed requested over half a million dollars for investigation into the problems of the fishing industry.[92] It was offered by Representative William Bates (R., Mass.), who represented the Massachusetts seacoast area including the fishing port of Gloucester. Support for the amendment began emanating from the four corners of the chamber. The delegates from Hawaii spoke of the "development of the fishing resources of the Pacific." A California congressman said, "I represent the tuna industry in Southern California. The tuna industry has been very hard hit." A Mississippi Member added, "The shrimp industry has been corresponding with me now for several months about getting some additional funds." A Washington Member spoke of his interest in the seals on the Pribilof Islands, of salmon, and of halibut. Members from seacoast

[92] The sequence of events will be found in 100 *Congressional Record*, pp. 4729–4737.

491

Connecticut and Massachusetts echoed their interests. So quick was the welling up of support that a bystanding Member observed,

> There is a coalition here today and there is evidently groundwork laid because of the response that was made when the gentleman arose to speak. Everyone wanted to get on the bandwagon as being for the amendment, the gentleman from Massachusetts was unable to say a word to explain his amendment.

At this juncture, five Members from the Great Lakes area mentioned the need for eradicating the lamprey eel and proposed earmarking funds for this purpose. A hassle ensued between those who favored earmarking and those who did not. The representative from Cape Cod suggested that if eel studies were to be earmarked, studies should also be earmarked for starfish, oysters, quahogs, and soft-shelled clams. The original sponsor argued frankly for the lump-sum, grab-bag approach in terms of attracting the largest body of support:

> Mr. Chairman, the thing I fail to understand is why we should set aside any amount of money for a specific cause. Coming from New England, and with Gloucester in my district, I should be primarily interested in ground fishing, but I do not think that would be fair to those along the Atlantic Coast, in Alaska, or on the Pacific Coast; so I offered an amendment in a lump sum so everybody might get what they needed.

The subcommittee chairman, bowing to the inevitable, agreed to accept the amendment — either version of it — but warned that if the logrollers could not settle their differences he might withdraw his support. When the imbroglio continued, Committee Chairman John Taber stepped in and played a decisive role. Said Taber,

> We have been at it over an hour, and if we are ever going to get through, we ought to get at it and kind of calm ourselves down and work it out . . . we are in a mess and we have only a minute to get out of it. If you do not do business while we are up against it, we will have to oppose all of it.

Even after agreement had been reached and the debate had expired, Members struggled to play at least a "walk-on" bit in the constituent-oriented drama. Representative Edith Nourse Rogers (R., Mass.) addressed the chair:

> MRS. ROGERS: Is there any way that I can get time at the present time?
> CHAIRMAN: All time has expired.
> MRS. ROGERS: I want to express my great interest in the fishing industry and the Bates amendment.
> CHAIRMAN: All time has expired.

The congressmen who supported the increase could see the direct benefit to their constituencies and to themselves. The amendment, moreover, was pur-

492

posely drawn to distribute these benefits among as many constituencies as possible.

1955: Public Works

A third example of selective coalition formation on behalf of floor increases comes from the area of public works. In 1955, floor increases totaling $86.3 million were carried over the objections of the subcommittee.[93] This was essentially an attempt to restore the amount by which the subcommittee had reduced the original budget estimates. The device by which the increases were secured was a caucus of Members hurt by the cuts, held after the Committee report became public. The leader of the group was Representative Overton Brooks (D., La.), who was also serving a term as President of the Rivers and Harbors Congress, the most influential pressure group in the field. When the bill reached the floor, Brooks explained what had transpired:

> Yesterday I think it was — perhaps the day before — we had a meeting of all Members of Congress who wished to be present in the caucus room of the Old House Office Building and went over the matter of restoring funds to the extent of the budget estimates for reclamation and for flood control and for river and harbor improvements . . . we agreed at that time to support this amendment and asked for support from everybody in the Congress for an amendment that would simply put back the funds taken from those recommended by the Budget Bureau. We are not against the Committee. The subcommittee did a grand job and they are all my friends, but we are for this program of improving our own country.

Not only did Brooks have the support of the affected Members, but he also had the backing of the majority party leadership.

A member of the Democratic leadership recalled his involvement:

> The President sent down a public works budget and they cut it by about $78 million. But they cut more projects of Democrats than Republicans. Here was the Republican President sending down a budget for projects in Democratic districts and a Democratic-controlled Congress cutting them. There were a few Republicans, but not many. Most of the cuts were on Democrats. The money was in the budget and the projects had been authorized, but the Committee refused to appropriate $78 million. That was terrible, and the Members were upset. They came in here and yacked, yacked, and yacked. I said to them, "What's the matter with you? Are you afraid of the Appropriations Committee? You are elected Members of Congress aren't you? Why don't you go out and round up some support? Get all these Democrats that have been hurt, and suck the Republicans in, too. There are some of them. Get yourselves a coalition. I'll be helping you." So I went around and said to people, "Isn't it terrible what the Committee is doing? Just think, a Republican President sends down a budget

[93] The sequence of events will be found in 101 Congressional Record, pp. 8500 ff.

493

with money — not new money either — for projects that have already been authorized, and here the Democratic-controlled Committee cuts it. If that were my district, I'd be humiliated. I don't know how I would explain it to my people." We had a vote on it and I voted against the Committee. I marched right through the tellers and voted against them. . . . That was a party matter. But even the Republicans joined us.

The Appropriations Committee had not been caught napping. Subcommittee Chairman Cannon knew all about the caucus, and he knew his subcommittee would most likely be overturned. A Committee clerk explained, "We knew what was coming. They even caucused. We got rolled and we knew we would. But the Chairman wanted to make the fight. He knew he would lose but he wanted to fight it out for the shock effect." The man whom Cannon customarily asked to manage the bill on the floor, Representative Louis Rabaut (D., Mich.) and ranking subcommittee member Representative Glenn Davis (R., Wisc.) fought back. "This is a perfect example of you rub my back and I will scratch yours," complained Rabaut. And Davis replied,

Exactly . . . we have had the Appropriations Committee completely shoved aside in favor of the deliberations — if that word might be used to describe what is going on here today — of a rump caucus which met in one of the office buildings the day before this bill came before us for consideration. . . . Well I submit that all these things that have been said of logrolling and pork-barreling and other things are pretty true so far as what has occurred here on the floor of the House today.

The Committee, however, was swept aside. As Chairman Cannon said later,

The boys held a little caucus over in the caucus room in the Old House Office Building. Both sides of the aisle got together and they agreed, "You scratch my back and I'll scratch yours," and they came over here and ran over us like a bunch of wild steers."[94]

For Rabaut, the wisdom of allowing himself to be run over was not altogether self-evident. Said one of the leaders of the stampede,

The fellow who was handling the bill, Louis Rabaut, was a nice fellow and a good friend of mine. I said to him, "Don't get caught like that again." And he said, "I never will let Cannon get me into that position again, never."

Isolated individuals may find it difficult to overthrow the Committee on a public works project. Hence the small percentage of requests for increases which succeed. On the other hand, a sizable coalition cemented by mutual constituency interests represents the formula for success. When the majority

[94] 102 *Congressional Record*, pp. 8699–8700.

party leadership joins the coalition — as they did in this case and in the case of the agriculture increases — the Committee faces the almost impossible task of combating party and constituency appeals at the same time. This is difficult to do.

Individual Member Activity in Winning Increases

Despite the odds against them, individual Members may feel strongly enough about their pet projects to challenge the Committee on the floor. Representative Clem Miller writes, however,

> To tackle the Appropriations Committee on the floor of the House is a major decision, frequently the most important decision a member will make that term of Congress. Here is the choice. If he is silent, perhaps the Senate will restore the item to the bill. If he speaks up, and is beaten, he will *never* get it back. And the chances of winning are better than 500 to 1 against. These odds mean silence to most congressmen. . . .[95]

Some, however, do try to gain support on the floor, and a few win. Representative Miller proceeds to discuss the case of Representative Billy Matthews, who, in 1960, challenged and beat the Committee on the floor.[96] At stake was money to build an agricultural research laboratory in his district. Matthews' path to victory will not be retraced here; but its lesson is to underscore the importance of interpersonal relations in such a victory. Matthews' success is attributed (by Representative Miller) to his personal popularity among his colleagues on both sides of the aisle and to his skill at capitalizing his assets during debate. In this particular joust, the subcommittee chairman offered to give Matthews what he wanted if he would only wait until the next bill came along. Matthews gently and whimsically persisted. In the end, the subcommittee chairman had no stomach for a protracted contest, and he did not even challenge the simple voice vote by which Matthews' amendment carried. A member of the Public Works Subcommittee put the proposition this way, "If a man's got a pet project and is well liked and makes a good case for it on the floor, they'll put in some money."

An illustration of the importance of interpersonal relations to the passage of a floor increase occurred on a pair of public works amendments which came to a vote on the same day in 1959. One was a pet project of veteran Appropriations Committee member Representative Otto Passman to eradicate water hyacinths in Southern streams. The other, sponsored by Representative Lester Johnson (D., Wisc.) involved planning money for a rivers and harbors project in his district. Both increases were forced to a

---

[95] Clem Miller, *Member of the House* (New York: Scribners, 1962), p. 39.

[96] *Ibid.*, pp. 39–41. The episode can be found in *Congressional Record*, Daily Edition, June 23, 1960, pp. 13043–13047. Matthews' successful attempts to steer his amendment through conference can be viewed in *ibid.*, July 2, 1960, pp. 14628, 14651.

roll-call vote after they had passed in the Committee of the Whole. Passman's amendment carried 199 to 198. Minutes later Johnson's amendment failed 192 to 205. The interesting thing about the roll calls is the fact that, exclusive of the vote of Appropriations Committee members, the vote on the two measures was nearly identical. House members voted 188 to 164 for the Passman amendment. They voted 187 to 164 for the Johnson amendment. The stands taken by party leaders were identical. Members of the Appropriations Committee, however, voted 41 to 5 against Johnson and only 34 to 11 against Passman.[97] In both cases, the Committee remained highly unified in support of the subcommittee recommendations. But the difference in outcome was brought about by Passman's superior ability to win support among his fellow Committee members. Doubtless his appeals to these men (4 of whom were subcommittee colleagues of his) were based on grounds of personal friendship or the arrangement of some personal quid pro quo.

It is unusual that a member of the Committee should have to fight publicly for his projects. Passman's failure to secure his money during internal negotiations resulted from the fact that he had not come before the subcommittee to plead his case and had tried in full Committee meeting to get his money. Subcommittee Chairman Cannon disapproved of such a procedure. Passman's success does not diminish the validity of the proposition that it is much easier for a Committee member to get money for his pet projects than it is for a non-Committee member. Indeed, this is one of the lures to service on the Committee. The Passman episode demonstrates, perhaps, that the proposition is as true for a roll-call decision as it is for a Committee decision itself.

In order for a House member not on the Committee to win a showdown fight with an appropriations subcommittee he needs some very influential allies. Such is the conclusion to be drawn from the successful overthrow of a Committee recommendation in 1959 which had denied funds for a new maximum security prison.[98] The prospective site lay in the district of Representative Kenneth Gray (D., Ill.). But Gray's pet project was stymied by the fact that his constituency interests came into direct conflict with those of Clarence Cannon. The Federal Prison System had chosen five acceptable

---

[97] The vote will be found in *Congressional Record*, Daily Edition, June 9, 1959, pp. 9323–9324.

[98] The sequence of events will be found in 105 *Congressional Record*, pp. 9027–9028, 9125–9127, 9182–9183. On the part played by O'Brien, see Tom Littlewood, "How Powerful Uncle Tom O'Brien Landed Prison for Illinois," *Chicago Sun-Times*, July 26, 1959, as reprinted in *Congressional Record*, Daily Edition, July 28, 1959, p. A6529. On O'Brien's relationship with James Bennett, Director of U.S. Prison System, see Committee on Appropriations, *Hearings of Department of Justice Appropriations for 1948* (Washington: U.S. Government Printing Office, 1947), p. 298. For an attempt to pass the same amendment which failed for lack of support, see 102 *Congressional Record*, pp. 6988–7001.

sites, one of which was in Gray's district and two of which were in Cannon's district. It had given top priority to the southern Illinois area, but had not made any final decision. Chairman Cannon, whose constituents could not unite in support of one site in the district, asked Representative Rooney, the subcommittee chairman, not to allow any money for construction — at least not until the Prison Service formally announced the location of the prison. Prison Service officials, on the other hand, did not want to make a move that would jeopardize the project. One of them recalled a meeting with Cannon:

> I told him if he wanted it in his district, just give me the word and we'd put it there. I didn't care where we put the prison, so long as we got it. But I showed him the figures — that it would cost five hundred thousand dollars more to put it in his district than to put it in Illinois. He said, "I'm not going to question or oppose your judgment." That's what he said to me. He looked me right in the face and told me. Then he went and told Rooney not to appropriate any money for the prison — period.

Apparently, Cannon was playing for time, hoping either that his constituents would get together or that the Prison Service would do something to help him. Representative Gray, meanwhile, was pushing his advantage through Representative Thomas O'Brien, dean of the Illinois Democrats. O'Brien was a long-time friend of Speaker Rayburn and, incidentally, a staunch supporter of the Prison Service. When O'Brien took the Illinois group to see Cannon, the Committee Chairman said, "How can I refuse my old friend Tommy?" O'Brien, like the Prison Service, thought Cannon had relented; but both learned that he didn't mean what they thought he said. When the subcommittee denied the money, said another Prison Service official, "We gave up. We thought we were licked. But we reckoned without Congressman Gray, who wanted to get it for his district." Accusing Cannon of "welching" (a cardinal violation of House norms), O'Brien and Gray sought the help of the Speaker and of Democratic party leaders generally. O'Brien's high standing, together with their perception of Cannon's high-handedness, probably encouraged the leadership to challenge the Committee on the floor.

One member of the leadership recalled,

> Cannon sent word down not to include any estimates for it. That would give him time to work on it. He was using his power — sending down the word, don't you see. It was an injustice, and I don't like injustice. It so happened that the prison fell in the district of Kenneth Gray. He happened to be a Democrat, but I would have felt the same way if it had been a Republican. Cannon was using his power. He's an able man, a very able man. He works in secret down here, out of the limelight, and he has great power. Gray came to see me, and I said, "Go get your Illinois delegation, Tommy O'Brien and the rest. I'll help you." And I did. When it came to

497

the floor, Gray offered a motion to put in $2 million. The subcommittee chairman who was handling the bill opposed it. Cannon wasn't on the floor at the time. I was going around saying, "Isn't it terrible what they're doing to poor Ken Gray," trying to stiffen up Tom O'Brien and the rest. We had a standing vote; and I voted against the Committee, right down there in front where everybody could see me.

After losing the division vote, the subcommittee chairman called for a roll call, on which the subcommittee was decisively beaten 266–133. Some evidence of the influence of the party leadership can be gleaned from the 238–22 vote among Democratic members. Of the 22 dissidents, 13 were members of the Appropriations Committee loyal to the interests of their Chairman.

RECOMMITTAL AND FINAL PASSAGE

When the yea and nay votes called for on any amendments have been taken, the only possible votes remaining are those on recommittal and final passage. Neither are very frequent. In the period 1947 to 1964, in the 8 departmental areas plus public works, only 10 recommittal votes and only 16 final passage votes were recorded. Usually final passage is by voice vote. A few recommittal motions, too, are made and are perfunctorily rejected by voice vote. Nearly all of the important floor decisions are made in the Committee of the Whole and on the few roll calls that are forced on amendments that pass there over the objections of the Appropriations Committee. Characteristically, the recommittal votes are close, but just as characteristically they fail. Of the 10 recorded, only 3 carried, and each of these involved a language change rather than a change in appropriations levels. No recommittal motion calling for an increase or decrease carried during the period studied. Votes on final passage, on the other hand, are customarily lopsided. And this motion invariably carries. An average of only 37 votes were recorded against final passage on the 16 roll calls.

These final votes would seem to be invested with a ritual quality. On recommittal, the Members go through the formal motions of a contest the outcome of which is known in advance. On final passage, the vast majority of Members, whatever their votes heretofore, hasten to get on the record as favoring the programs funded in the bill. At the same time, a minority of Members can record their opposition to federal spending — secure in the knowledge that the funds to keep the government going will be voted anyway. Recommittal motions are decided primarily by party line votes. Majority party Members may support the bill as it stands even if they are not enthusiastic about it. The reasoning here is that they have done all they can to shape the bill to their liking and the problem now is to move the business to completion. That job, they reason, is pre-eminently the job of the majority party. Minority party members take a different view. They are less concerned with the flow of legislative business than with making a record or, perhaps, embarrassing the majority party. So, for either reason, its Members will usually vote for recommittal. But the paucity of such votes — less than one per year — is testimony to the sense of futility which the minority has about such matters.

TABLE 9.16

PARTISANSHIP ON RECOMMITTAL AND FINAL PASSAGE VOTES

| | AVERAGE INDEX OF PARTISANSHIP | |
HOUSE GROUPING	10 Recommittal Votes	16 Final Passage Votes
Subcommittee Members	75	25
Appropriations Committee Members Not on Subcommittee	85	19
Other House Members	76	17

Table 9.16 confirms the difference between the two votes and conveys something of the party basis of that difference. It contrasts partisanship on final passage for several groupings of Members. In every grouping, partisanship is much higher on recommittal than it is on passage. On the votes where some party leader (floor leader or whip) was recorded, their behavior supports the picture above. Party leaders opposed each other on 9 of the 10 recommittal motions. They were in opposition to one another on only 3 of the 16 final passage votes. With final passage every appropriation bill moves from its place of origination in the House of Representatives across the Capitol to the Senate.

CONCLUSION

The House floor is a distinctive decision-making context. The participants are more varied, information is more widely distributed, and party influences are stronger than is the case when the Committee makes its decisions internally. Moreover, floor action takes place at a different point in time. From the Committee's perspective, the House floor presents a test of the viability of Committee decisions. And the ability of the Committee to win acceptance of its decisions there becomes an acid test of the Committee's ability to solve its more general problem of adaptation to its environment. On the record, the Committee's decisions are viable, and the Committee does succeed in winning House acceptance of the great bulk of the recommendations it brings to the floor. In a minority of cases, however, the House can and does alter Committee decisions. This combination of overall House satisfaction plus the opportunity given to the House to assuage its dissatisfaction helps account for the stability of Committee-House relations.

Committee success can be explained by a number of factors whose weight may differ depending on the situation. In the first place, the Committee can manipulate the floor context to its advantage by controlling the flow of its bills to the floor, by restricting the spread of information, by minimizing the influence of party leaders, and by dominating floor participation. In the second place, the Committee operates under favorable conditions in the Committee of the Whole House. The rules making provision for a quorum and those specifying amending and voting procedures bestow advantages on the Committee. The Committee also benefits from the inability and the unwillingness of House members to devote their scarce resources of time, energy, and legislative credit to a consistent or concentrated or conflict-producing consideration of appropriations legislation. A great deal of crucial activity proceeds in the Committee of the Whole under these conditions. Floor action is not wholly, or even primarily, action on roll-call votes — where conditions are least advantageous to the Committee.

In the third place, the Committee commands a substantial measure of respect and confidence among House members. It uses the floor as a forum in which to remind House colleagues of the bases for their respect and confidence. Committee members emphasize their desire and their accomplishments in meeting House expectations. They identify themselves with the House and attempt to soothe antagonisms both institutional and personal. They play up their hard work, their fact-gathering, their expertise, and their internal consensus-building. On the basis of their obedience to these House norms, they lay claim to a deserved leadership in their prescribed area of operation. Their claim is bolstered by the more general House norm which says that when a committee behaves in accordance with these particular norms, the House should follow it.

Finally, and most important, the Committee succeeds on the House floor because it usually maintains a high degree of unity. But for its cohesiveness, the Committee could not manipulate the floor context, could not avail itself of favorable conditions in the Committee of the Whole, and could not hold House member respect and confidence. On the evidence, Committee unity (which is the floor manifestation of successful internal integration) does seem to be the key underlying variable — just as Committee members believe it is. The extraordinary effort at internal integration, especially at minimizing partisanship, brings success on the floor. Success on the floor results in Committee influence, and Committee influence determines Com-

500

mittee member influence. Of all the actions which promote success on the floor, the Committee takes the most important when it creates and maintains an internal structure for integrating its decision-making elements. Provided only that the context of its decisions does not constitute a gross violation of House (and, in addition, executive agency and clientele group) expectations, Committee unity in defense of its recommendations is the necessary condition of victory on the House floor.

The fact that the Appropriations Committee seeks to win House acceptance of all its decisions on the floor plus the fact that it is normally found unified in that effort reveals an important aspect of the Committee's contribution to the congressional appropriations process. The Committee defends its recommendations against proposed increases *and* proposed decreases. Since its recommendations tend to be of an incremental character, Committee defense of them acts as a brake against less moderate increases and less moderate decreases. Over all, the Committee faces more proposals for increases than decreases when it comes to the floor. Hence, the Committee more often than not appears as a conservative influence holding the line against increased spending. But, under certain conditions, the Committee faces just the opposite kind of barrage from the House. In such cases, the Committee acts as a conservative influence holding the line against greater reductions in spending. In general, therefore, Committee behavior on the House floor functions as a balance wheel to keep the appropriations levels of most agencies and most spending programs from rising or falling precipitously from year to year.

Committee recommendations do not always carry on the floor. Indeed, it is important in terms of tempering Committee-House conflict that the parent chamber's capacity to overturn the Committee be demonstrated often enough to keep Committee member and House member mindful of the fact. Challenges to Committee recommendations vary in volume (from year to year), in content (increases or decreases), and in scope (from one program area to another). During certain periods of time, the Committee confronts a large volume of proposals for change — at other times, none at all. When the intensity of House interest is greatest, floor proposals tend to run either to increases or decreases but not to a mixture of both. Partisan sentiment and House moods seem to be the most important conditions controlling the volume of floor proposals. The greatest outpourings of floor increases (both proposed and successful) were associated with Republican control of the Committee — and abetted by the existence of a permissive mood. And the greatest number of floor decreases were proposed and passed when the House was in an externally induced economy mood — abetted by Democratic control of the Committee.

Challenges to House decisions come more often in some program areas than in others, though the focus on particular programs varies from one point in time to another. The nature of the challenge (increases or decreases) differs from one program area to another; and the ease with which Committee decisions are overturned varies according to the content of the program involved. Committee success, when under fire, will also be affected by the stand being taken by such influential sources of voting loyalties as interested legislative committee leaders and party floor leaders. And, finally, the Committee's ability to win on the floor depends on its ability to come to the floor unified and to maintain unity in the face of divisive influences of every sort.

CHAPTER

TEN

The Senate Committee
I: *The Senate, The Committee,*
and The Committee's Structure

Once an appropriation bill has been passed in the House, it moves to the Senate, where a second decision to appropriate must be made. The following two chapters describe appropriations politics in the Senate. They attempt to examine the same range and kinds of relationships for the Senate and its Committee on Appropriations as have been described thus far for the House of Representatives and its Committee on Appropriations. An analysis which consumed nine chapters in the case of one chamber cannot be duplicated in the space of two chapters for the second chamber. But this book, as stated earlier, does not purport to give equal treatment to equal legislative bodies. It gives lopsided emphasis to the House Committee on the assumption that this group dominates appropriations politics in Congress. Except in the formal stipulations of bicameralism, the two chambers are not equal — not, that is, in terms of their influence in the area of appropriations. Some of the evidence on which this judgment is based will be presented in the next two chapters. But this is not to say that the Senate exerts no independent influence on appropriations decisions. It certainly does. And this assumption underlies the decision to treat the Senate and the Senate Appropriations Committee as political systems and to utilize the same framework for analysis as the previous chapters. What follows, then, is an encapsulated but not truncated description of Senate appropriations behavior. It concentrates on illuminating the ways in which Senate appropriations relationships differ from those of the House.

503

THE SENATE COMMITTEE AND THE SENATE

In the Senate, as in the House, most appropriations decisions are made in committee. And we must first examine — as we did for the House — the relationships between that committee, the Senate Committee on Appropriations, and the larger system of which it is a part, "the Senate." House-Senate differences in system-subsystem relationships — of expectations, images, satisfactions, and sanctions — underlie many of the important differences in the appropriations activity of the two chambers.

Senate Goal Expectations

Like its counterpart in the House, the Senate Appropriations Committee was established (in 1867) to aid the parent chamber in meeting its major tasks — of lawmaking, of representation, and of oversight — in the area of appropriations. In terms of formal expectations, the Rules of the Senate give to the Committee jurisdiction over "all proposed legislation, messages, petitions, memorials and other matters relating to the appropriation of the revenue for the support of the Government."[1] Less formally but more specifically, however, the twin charges given to the Committee are to finance programs as authorized and to finance them in as economical manner as possible. Senators do not state their goal expectations as often as House members do, for the simple reason that system-subsystem disagreements are less frequent. But, on occasion, the expectations of program support and economy are articulated. And there is every reason to believe that these potentially conflicting goal expectations are identical for the two chambers.

Senators have policy commitments, of both a general and a constituency-oriented sort, which impel them to argue in favor of increased appropriations. They are also mindful of the economy sentiment which exists in the country at large. And they press both demands upon their Committee on Appropriations. The balance of senatorial expectations, however, is tilted more toward program support than toward economy. On purely impressionistic grounds, the reader of the *Congressional Record* is struck by the relative paucity of economy talk in the Senate. Such as there is emanates more often from an isolated crusader than from any appreciable bloc of legislators. Senator Paul Douglas in the 1950's and Senator William Proxmire in the 1960's (hardly the blood relations of any House economizers) preached economy and frequently proposed amendments to reduce appropriations in very selective areas. But their preachments went unheeded, and their amendments were nearly always defeated. Senator Douglas, for example, quixotically focused his attacks on

[1] U.S. Senate, *Senate Manual* (Washington: U.S. Government Printing Office, 1963), pp. 27–28.

the rivers and harbors and reclamation bills.[2] His crusades hardly reflected the sentiment of "the Senate."

Somewhat more solid evidence can be gleaned by examining the kinds of changes made by the Senate in the Committee's recommendations for the 36 executive agencies used earlier in the period 1947 to 1962. Of course, action taken on the floor is only one way in which Senate expectations can be measured. Still, the evidence indicates a dominance of program over economy expectations. Out of a total of 66 alterations made on the floor, 51 (77 per cent) were increases and only 15 (23 per cent) were decreases. (See Table 11.12, p. 597.) The normal Senate pattern has been to vote several increases over Committee recommendations annually while voting no decreases. Doubtless, economy expectations are expressed at other points in the process. But only during the years of the Korean War did the Senate register any marked concern for economy on the floor.[3] Furthermore, the differences in the patterns of expectations between the Senate and the House run consistently in one direction. It will be recalled from Table 9.4 that out of a total of 58 changes made in House Committee recommendations on the House floor, 30 (52 per cent) were for decreases and 28 (48 per cent) were for increases. These differences indicate a balance of Senate expectations which tends more toward program support and less toward economy than that in the House. The proportion of increases to decreases is significantly greater in the Senate; and the Senate increases its Committee's recommendations more consistently than does the House.

The Korean War brought overwhelming pressure to bear on both chambers to reduce their Appropriations Committees' recommendations. If, however, an explanation be sought for the slight differences in House and Senate patterns of expectations in all other years, the analysis should begin by noting the differences in Senate and House member constituencies. To the degree that chamber expectations are a reflection of constituent expectations, it seems logical that Senate expectations should be tipped more toward program support than those of the House. Many but not all members of the House represent fairly homogeneous constituencies. In some of them — mostly rural ones — the ideology of minimal government, small budgets, and frugality remains strong. And, in any event, the more homogeneous a con-

---

[2] The story of one of his unsuccessful campaigns against the rivers and harbors appropriation is told in Stephen K. Bailey and Howard D. Samuel, *Congress At Work* (New York: Henry Holt, 1952), Chapter 7, especially pp. 188–192. Examples of Senator Douglas' run-ins with the Committee will be found in 96 *Congressional Record*, pp. 10071 ff., 10853, 11472–11482; 97 *Congressional Record*, 6294–6496 passim; 98 *Congressional Record*, pp. 4449–4450, 7983 ff.; 101 *Congressional Record*, p. 10396.

[3] The Bridges-Byrd amendment to the omnibus bill of 1950 was an important economy measure which does not show up in the bureau totals used here and reported in Table 11.13. The amendment is in 96 *Congressional Record*, pp. 11818–11820.

stituency the fewer the number of interests which must be represented. The demands for increased funds, therefore, will be concentrated on relatively few programs, and economy expectations can safely be voiced on all the others. Hence, there has existed in the House — more or less permanently — a minority group of economy advocates. By turns, they support and prod the House Committee toward budget reduction and they provide a nucleus around which a majority of House members can — as in 1957 — coagulate.

Senators, on the other hand, have larger and less homogeneous constituencies than do House members. Most Senators represent a near-microcosm of the nation as a whole. Nearly all represent some urban interests, for example, as well as rural ones. Though economy sentiment exists in each state, it cannot be said to dominate any of them to the degree that it may dominate some House districts. Every Senator faces demands that he support not a few but many federal programs all of which require federal spending. There are few programs on which any given Senator can talk economy without turning a deaf ear to some group of constituents. There are few programs, therefore, on which he will not be asked to make a plea for adequate funding, if not expansion. These differences surely help explain why no economy drive was mounted in the Senate to match the 1957 drive which took root in the House. And, in terms of constituency-oriented pet projects, each Senator will be pushing for a far greater number of them than will his counterpart in the House. Appropriations decision-making is not simply a matter of translating constituency demands into legislation. But, if one knew nothing about House and Senate except the constituency differences just mentioned, one would predict that the two patterns in Figure 11.12 would differ in the way that they in fact do.

Senate Maintenance Expectations

Even more significant differences between the two chambers involve Senate maintenance expectations — that is, views as to the proper relationship between the chamber and the Senate Appropriations Committee. Maintenance expectations center on the sharpness of the differentiation between system and subsystem and the degree of independence of one from the other. House members state a basic expectation that their Committee should be a dependent, subordinate system. But they differentiate the Committee fairly sharply as a subsystem and willingly grant to it a high degree of operating autonomy. The result, when compounded with the expectations of the House Committee members themselves, is to create a relationship in which an undercurrent of tension persists and periodically breaks out into open conflict — even though it is a relationship of marked stability.

Senate members, too, prescribe for their Committee a basically dependent status within the larger system. That is to say, the Senate as a whole

506

clearly reserves the right to have the last word on all appropriations matters. But they differentiate only minimally between "the Senate" on the one hand and "the Senate Appropriations Committee" on the other. And they do not expect the Committee to exercise a great deal of operating autonomy. The result is that very little tension exists between the Committee and "the Senate" and head-to-head conflict is a rarity. Rather than act on behalf of the Senate, the Committee is expected to act *as the Senate*. Some distinction between system and subsystem is, of course, maintained. Not every Senator is a member of the Committee. The Committee cannot legislate on an appropriation bill. The information and communications prescription of the 1946 Act applies to the Senate Committee as well as to the House Committee. But Senate maintenance expectations blur system-subsystem boundaries to such an extent that in operational terms it is nearly impossible to differentiate one from the other.

The critical maintenance expectations of the Senate are those involving committee memberships. In the first place, Senate rules prescribe a sizable number of members. With 27 members, the Senate Appropriations Committee is the largest in the chamber and contains, to begin with, over one quarter of the entire membership of the body. The House Committee, by contrast, contains only one ninth of the membership of that chamber. Proportions alone, therefore, make the Senate Committee less exclusive of and less distinguishable from "the Senate" than the House Committee is from "the House."

More important, however, Rule 25, Section 4, provides that "Each Senator shall serve on two and no more of the following standing committees" — one of which is the Appropriations Committee. This means that every member of the Committee participates actively in the work of a substantive Senate committee. Quite apart from any effect this dual (or in many cases triple) membership may have on his attitudes, in terms of sheer communication every one of them is in constant contact with a group of Senators outside the Appropriations Committee. Collectively, Appropriations Committee members are expected to participate in the activities of nearly every other Senate committee. They did in all cases except Finance and Public Works in the 88th Congress. Multiple membership makes possible a constant interchange of views, not across Committee boundaries but through committees that are effectively interlocked. In some cases, indeed, the splice is nearly complete since senior Appropriations Committee members sit also as the chairmen of important substantive committees. In 1963, eight Appropriations Committee members were also chairmen of other Senate committees. With so great an overlapping in the memberships and the leadership of the Appropriations Committee and other substantive committees, it is hard to speak about Appropriations Committee autonomy.

507

Rule 16, Section 6, blurs the distinction between Committee and chamber even further. It prescribes that in the case of eight appropriations bills, three members of the substantive committee involved shall serve ex officio on the Appropriations Committee.[4] It provides further that one of those three shall be a member of the relevant Appropriations Conference Committee. These provisions of Rule 16 sustain a dual membership which is the reverse of that prescribed by Rule 25. Not only do some Appropriations Committee members participate in the internal deliberations of the various substantive committees, but some substantive committee members participate in the internal deliberations of the Appropriations Committee. Customarily, the two senior majority members and the ranking minority member of eight substantive committees sit as voting members with the Appropriations Committee. And the senior majority member will be a Senate conferee. Ex officio members have the same voting rights as the regular Appropriations Committee members. In 1964, the net effect of Rule 16 was to bring seventeen additional Senators into Appropriations Committee decision-making. Added to the regular members, this meant that in 1964 a grand total of 44 out of 100 Senators were engaged in helping to make the decisions of the Appropriations Committee. Among these Senators were 37 of the 50 most senior men in the chamber. House maintenance expectations countenance a considerable amount of Appropriations Committee–substantive committee conflicts. Senate maintenance expectations do not.

Still another feature of Appropriations Committee membership blurs the system-subsystem differentiation. Normally, some leaders from both parties — floor leaders or whips — sit on the Appropriations Committee. Nowhere is this close interlocking of Committee and party prescribed in the rules, but its occurrence is frequent enough so that it does seem to be an important informal maintenance expectation. In some cases, Committee membership preceded party leadership, and in some cases party leaders have sought membership on the Committee. From the 84th through the 88th Congress, either the Democratic floor leader (four years) or the Democratic whip (four years) or both these party leaders (two years) have sat on the Appropriations Committee. On the Republican side of the aisle, there was not a single year between 1947 and 1964 when either their floor leader and their whip (seven years) or their whip alone (eleven years) has not sat on the Appropriations Committee. In addition, it might be noted that, from 1949 through 1964, the Chairman of the Appropriations Committee has also served as President Pro Tem of the Senate. On the Democratic side, Com-

---

[4] The committees involved are: Agriculture and Forestry, Post Office and Civil Service, Armed Services, District of Columbia, Public Works, Foreign Relations, Joint Committee on Atomic Energy, Aeronautical and Space Sciences.

mittee members constituted (in 1963) a majority (9 of 15) of the Steering Committee, which makes Committee assignments. And they also constituted a majority (7 of 9) of the Policy Committee which decides on the scheduling of legislation. On the counterpart Republican policy organs, Appropriations Committee members did not make up a majority, but nearly all of them served on one group or another.

In accordance with Senate maintenance expectations, the Appropriations Committee, the substantive committees, and the party leadership of the Senate are joined together in a system of interlocking memberships. Table 10.1 lists the members of the Committee at the beginning of the 88th Congress, together with their substantive committee memberships and their membership on important party organs. It conveys in concrete terms the extent to which Senate maintenance expectations prescribe a lack of differentiation between the Committee and "the Senate" — its substantive committees and its party structures.

The interlocking directorate pictured in Table 10.1 demonstrates vividly the congruence between the Appropriations Committee and "the Senate." If, as William S. White has insisted, there is an inner club in the Senate, surely the Senate Appropriations Committee must be its formal embodiment. Yet an "inner club" of 27 members which permits 17 other members to participate in its internal deliberations at one point or another hardly seems like a very exclusive club — hardly seems, that is to say, worth talking about in terms of its exclusivity. More to the point than the notion of an exclusive inner club is the idea that *the Senate appears to do business via the maximum participation of a maximum number of its members.* The key norm is, as Matthews puts it, "reciprocity" among as many Senators as have an interest in a decision and who are willing to abide by that norm in decisions affecting others. Expectations involving the membership of the Appropriations Committee thus shed some light on decision-making patterns in the Senate as a whole.[5]

Surely when one contrasts the membership expectations of the Senate with those of the House it becomes apparent that the House, not the Senate, is the oligarchically organized chamber. If, for example, the same maintenance expectations obtained in the House as in the Senate in 1963, the House Committee on Appropriations would have counted among its *regular Democratic members* the following men: John McCormack, Carl Albert, Carl Vinson, Harold Cooley, Adam Clayton Powell, William Dawson,

[5] A similar criticism of White is argued in Nelson Polsby, *Congress and the Presidency* (New York: Prentice Hall, 1964) pp. 32 ff. Cf. William S. White, *Citadel* (New York: Harpers, 1956), Chapter 7. Donald R. Matthews, *U.S. Senators and Their World* (Chapel Hill: University of North Carolina Press, 1960), Chapter 5.

Wright Patman, Oren Harris, Chet Holifield, John McMillan, Wilbur Mills, and a majority of the Democrats on the Ways and Means Committee! Moreover, several other committee chairmen and senior members would have been serving ex officio on certain appropriation bills. As it is now, each of these men functions within a substantive committee or a party group separated from his colleagues within or across structures. Throughout most of the

TABLE 10.1

THE SENATE APPROPRIATIONS COMMITTEE AS THE SENATE — 1963

Democratic Members	Other Committees	Party Position
Carl Hayden	Interior and Insular Affairs	Member, Steering Committee
(Chairman)	Rules and Administration	Member, Policy Committee
Richard B. Russell	Armed Services, *Chairman*	Member, Steering Committee
	Joint Committee on Atomic Energy	Member, Policy Committee
	Aeronautical and Space Sciences	
Allen J. Ellender	Agriculture and Forestry, *Chairman*	Member, Steering Committee
Lister Hill	Labor and Public Welfare, *Chairman*	Member, Policy Committee
John L. McClellan	Government Operations, *Chairman*	Member, Steering Committee
	Judiciary	
A. Willis Robertson	Banking and Currency, *Chairman*	Member, Steering Committee
Warren G. Magnuson	Commerce, *Chairman*	Member, Policy Committee
	Aeronautical and Space Sciences	
Spessard L. Holland	Agriculture and Forestry	Member, Steering Committee
	Aeronautical and Space Sciences	
John Stennis	Armed Services	
	Aeronautical and Space Sciences	
John O. Pastore	Joint Committee on Atomic Energy, *Chairman*	Member, Policy Committee
	Commerce	
A. S. Mike Monroney	Commerce	
	Post Office and Civil Service	
Alan Bible	District of Columbia, *Chairman*	Member, Steering Committee
	Interior and Insular Affairs	
Robert C. Byrd	Armed Services	
	Rules and Administration	
Gale W. McGee	Post Office and Civil Service	
	Commerce	
Hubert Humphrey	Foreign Relations	Majority Whip
	Government Operations	Member, Steering Committee
Mike Mansfield	Foreign Relations	Majority Leader
		Chairman, Steering Committee
		Chairman, Policy Committee
E. E. Bartlett	Commerce	
William Proxmire	Banking and Currency	

510

Republican Members	Other Committees	Party Position
Leverett Saltonstall	Armed Services, ranking minority member	Member, Policy Committee
Milton R. Young	Agriculture	Member, Policy Committee
Karl E. Mundt	Foreign Relations	Member, Committee on Committees
	Government Operations, ranking minority member	
Margaret Chase Smith	Aeronautical and Space Sciences, ranking minority member	Member, Policy Committee
	Armed Services	
Thomas Kuchel	Interior and Insular Affairs, ranking minority member	Minority Whip
		Member, Policy Committee
Roman Hruska	Judiciary	Member, Policy Committee
Gordon Allott	Interior and Insular Affairs	Member, Committee on Committees
Norris Cotton	Commerce, ranking minority member	Member, Policy Committee
Clifford Case	Aeronautical and Space Sciences	
	Armed Services	

Democratic Ex Officio Members	Substantive Committee Involved in Appropriation Bill
Clinton P. Anderson	Aeronautical and Space Sciences, *Chairman*
	Joint Committee on Atomic Energy
Harry M. Byrd	Armed Services
J. W. Fulbright	Foreign Relations, *Chairman*
Albert Gore	Joint Committee on Atomic Energy
Olin D. Johnston	Post Office and Civil Service, *Chairman*
	Agriculture and Forestry
Thomas J. McIntyre	District of Columbia
Pat McNamara	Public Works, *Chairman*
Jennings Randolph	Public Works
John Sparkman	Foreign Relations
Stuart Symington	Aeronautical and Space Sciences
	Armed Services
Ralph Yarborough	Post Office and Civil Service

Republican Ex Officio Members	Substantive Committee Involved in Appropriation Bill
George D. Aiken	Agriculture and Forestry
J. Glenn Beall	District of Columbia
Frank Carlson	Post Office and Civil Service
John Sherman Cooper	Public Works
Barry M. Goldwater	Armed Services
Bourke B. Hickenlooper	Foreign Relations
	Joint Committee on Atomic Energy

decision-making process, they are as cut off from the Appropriations Committee as the Committee is cut off from them. The norms of compromise and reciprocity obtain, but they operate across differentiated structures more than within one relatively undifferentiated, interlocking decision-making structure.

House Committee members are not expected to have close formal working relationships with other committees or with the party leadership. Their communications pattern is not expected to run outward into the chamber so much as it is expected to run inward to fellow Committee members. In sum, the Senate Committee is not expected to be such an independent decision-making entity in the Senate as its counterpart is in the House. Consequently the Senate Committee confronts an easy problem of adaptation to the parent body.

Senate Images and Satisfactions

Senate perceptions of and attitudes toward their Appropriations Committee are not easy to come by. It is possible, therefore, that a more intensive analysis would disclose a very different distribution of Senate images than the one about to be reported. On the available evidence, however, unfavorable images of the Committee are fewer in number and are held by fewer Senators than is the case in the House. In largest part, this conclusion is deduced from the fact that the record reveals very few conflicts between "the Senate" and the Committee. And such conflicts as do break the surface seem to be precipitated by a relatively small band of Senators. A survey of Senators' attitudes might uncover tensions that take no public form. But interviews with 20 members of the Committee itself failed to turn up any opinions to the effect that unfavorable images were either deep-seated or widespread. For the moment, therefore, we conclude that though Senate-Committee tensions do exist, they are not as consequential for the appropriations process as those which exist in the House.

Evidence that the Committee meets Senate goal expectations can be gleaned from the fact that the Senate usually accepts its recommendations on the floor. Of the 576 separate recommendations brought in by the Committee for the 36 executive bureaus from 1947 to 1962, the Senate accepted 88.5 per cent (510) of them without a change. This high acceptance rate is very similar to the one (89.9 per cent) which held for the House. And the combined acceptance rate of 89.2 per cent — that is, of 1027 acceptances out of 1151 recommendations — gives striking evidence of the importance of the two appropriations committees in appropriations decision-making.

To the extent that the Senate Appropriations Committee fails to meet Senate goal expectations, it is more likely to appropriate too little rather than too much money. As we have seen, when the Senate did make changes on the floor, increases predominated by a margin of three to one. Some Senators whose devotion to fairly expensive government programs is strongest may, therefore, tend to perceive the Committee as a conservative force. And that perception may become the source of some unfavorable attitudes toward the

512

Committee as being insufficiently liberal. Such an image was voiced by Senator Paul Douglas when he argued in favor of Treasury borrowing and against the appropriations process as a way of financing his depressed areas bill in 1961. Said Douglas,

> Now I have to say something [about] . . . the bipartisan, unholy alliance which exists in this body . . . between the conservative Republicans and the conservative Democrats of the South . . . the members of the alliance are stronger in the Appropriations Committee than they are on the floor of the Senate . . . the Appropriations Committee is one of the strongholds of the alliance; it is one of their castles; and they are saying, "Put the fair maiden into this secret recess, separate her from the light of day and let murder or worse things be committed upon her."[6]

Where new programs are at stake, as in this case, a majority of Senators may view the Committee as more conservative than the Senate as a whole and hence prefer to use Treasury financing. In this case, the Senate voted 49 to 45 in support of Treasury financing. It is quite likely that, although Douglas was the only Senator who expressed an unfavorable image of the Appropriations Committee, others shared his view.[7] The Committee, moreover, gave this view some credence by voting against Treasury financing by a margin of 15 to 10. Still, it should be noted that some members of the Committee fought hard in favor of Treasury financing, that 40 per cent of the Committee voted for it, and that this constituted a majority (by 10 to 7) of the Committee's Democrats. Under such conditions, it is probably hard to sustain an image of "the Appropriations Committee" as excessively conservative, to sustain Senate dissatisfaction with the Committee, or to maintain any very persistent conflicts between the two because of the Committee's failure to meet Senate goal expectations.

Sporadic, idiosyncratic dissatisfactions with Committee decisions inevitably exist — usually because the pet project of an individual Senator has been denied. But these are random dissatisfactions, are usually accepted as part of the game, and do not cumulate so as to produce serious tension. One of the Committee's most vocal critics, however, has been Senator Wayne Morse of Oregon, who has charged the Committee with systematically discriminating against his pet projects. In 1964, when he was denied money to build a high school for Indian children, Morse said that "this rejection is the straw that broke the camel's back." And he launched into a two-hour attack on "what I consider to be unfair discriminatory policies which have

[6] *Congressional Record*, Daily Edition, March 14, 1961, p. 3638. See also, *ibid.*, p. 3640.

[7] Senator Douglas' own image of the Committee is not a consistently conservative one. On flood control projects, he has long criticized the Committee for its liberality. See note 2 supra.

developed in the Senate Appropriations Committee against deserved projects in the State of Oregon." "My state has been raided," he protested,

> My critics in Oregon charge that I have permitted my state to be economically raped by the State of Washington and the State of California particularly time and time again. My state has received the least consideration from the Senate Appropriations Committee . . . of any Western State.

The image he portrayed in that speech was one of a Committee which met the expectations of its own members far more often than the expectations of other Senators. "Oregon," he said, "has no Senator who is a member of that Committee . . . I have no doubt what the result would be if someone from Oregon were on the Appropriations Committee."[8] Perhaps other Senators harbor the same image, but there is no public record to support such an assumption. The Committee appears to be successful in meeting the goal expectations of most Senators most of the time.

With regard to maintenance expectations, it should be noted at the outset that non-Committee members perceive the Committee as powerful within the Senate. Senator Russell Long spoke for many of his colleagues when he said that

> The Committee on Appropriations is usually regarded as one of the most powerful committees. Most of us regard the Committee as the most powerful committee in the Senate. It has 27 members, far more than the average committee. Usually those members are among the most senior and the most powerful in this body.[9]

Given this image of the Committee, Senators, like House members, do not relish the idea of open combat. During his attack on the Committee, for example, Senator Morse said, "I have no illusions about the power of the Senate Appropriations Committee. I have not been in the Senate for twenty years without having learned that when one takes on the Senate Appropriations Committee one takes on a group with a powerful leverage in the Senate."[10] On another occasion, Senator Douglas referred to the Committee's floor influence in this way:

> We are already pretty much in its hands now; because its members always stick together and the chairmen of all the other committees — the union of chairmen so to speak — pitch in and help them. So on any move to amend — that nucleus is almost impossible to beat.[11]

This image of a powerful committee is widespread.

[8] Senator Morse's comments will be found in *Congressional Record*, Daily Edition, June 22, 1964, pp. 14119–14133.
[9] *Congressional Record*, Daily Edition, August 21, 1961, p. 15397.
[10] *Congressional Record*, Daily Edition, June 22, 1964, p. 14132.
[11] *Congressional Record*, Daily Edition, June 17, 1959, p. 10105.

Senate maintenance expectations do not countenance, however, an Appropriations Committee that wields its great power autonomously. They prescribe, instead, a Committee so interconnected with other Senate structures that when it acts it does so on behalf of a senatorial consensus. Such expectations would seem to have been met, since there exists no large body of Senate opinion to the effect that the Committee is "too powerful" — that is, too autonomous. Again, Senator Morse is one of the few who voices such a view:

> I shall continue to oppose the idea which seems to be developing in the Senate that when the Committee on Appropriations reports a bill God has reported to the Senate and no one ought to raise any question as to what the Appropriations Committee proposes. The Appropriations Committee is a child of the Senate and it is the duty of the Senate to correct its erring ways when it is wrong.[12]

As to Morse's second sentence, setting forth orthodox maintenance expectations, all Senators would agree. But his first sentence was one — as Morse himself implies — to which most of his colleagues would not subscribe. It is a comment more typical of a House member than of a Senator.

Probably the greatest degree of Senate dissatisfaction springs from the image that the Appropriations Committee invades the territory of substantive committees. The Senate, like the House, has written a series of rules prescribing jurisdictional boundaries between legislation and appropriations.[13] Senators protest against "further encroachment on the part of the Appropriations Committee on the jurisdiction of the respective legislative committees."[14] "The Committee on Appropriations is taking the power of legislation into their own hands and defying a law which was passed by the Congress of the United States and they are doing it times without number."[15] But even this kind of complaint is kept to a minimum and well below the level reached in the House, by the fact of overlapping memberships. When the chairmen of eight substantive committees sit on the Appropriations Committee, it is more likely that substantive committee–Appropriations Committee conflicts will be resolved privately. Of course, this overlap may encourage more rather than less legislation on an appropriation bill (though no quantitative comparison is available), since the same Senator may effectively govern both authorization and appropriations decisions. But substantive committees are not as often ranged against the Appropriations Committee, and the image

[12] 100 *Congressional Record*, p. 7501.
[13] *Senate Manual, op. cit.*, pp. 17–20.
[14] 95 *Congressional Record*, p. 11909.
[15] 93 *Congressional Record*, p. 7976. See also 94 *Congressional Record*, pp. 7571–7576; 99 *Congressional Record*, pp. 7349–7351; *Congressional Record*, Daily Edition, July 31, 1961, p. 13127.

of an imperialistic Appropriations Committee is not widespread in the Senate.

Given Senate maintenance expectations regarding interlocking memberships, it comes as no surprise to find very little Senate dissatisfaction on the grounds that the Committee monopolizes the flow of information from the executive branch to the chamber. The Committee's communications network ties into that of the substantive committees and the party leadership. Significantly, too, the Senate Committee holds most of its hearings in open, public sessions which any Senator (or, more likely, a member of his staff) is free to attend. This simple fact eliminates the image so galling to House members of the "star chamber" or the "closed corporation." The Senate Committee appears, once again, as less sharply differentiated from the Senate and less subject to criticism as "a club" or "a clan" which keeps non-members ignorant of its proceedings. A great deal of information is available to any Senator at any stage in the process. A substantial amount of House dissatisfaction and House-Committee tension stems from the fact that so large a proportion of House members generally and so many important House members particularly feel left out of the appropriations process. Neither the fact nor the image of exclusiveness prevails in the Senate.

But, if the image does not prevail, neither is it wholly absent. Some Senators do perceive the Senate Committee as both "too autonomous" and "too exclusive." Some Senators do feel very much shut out of the process. On the evidence, this is but a small handful of Senators — though the handful may in fact be somewhat larger than the number who speak out for the record. It is striking that over ninety per cent of the unfavorable public statements about the Committee seem to emanate from Senators Paul Douglas, Wayne Morse, and Joseph Clark. These are, as one might predict, the kinds of Senators whom Ralph Huitt describes as "outsiders" in the Senate.[16] They have quite deliberately chosen not to become influential inside the Senate. They are less concerned about observing what Donald Matthews calls "the folkways of the Senate" than they are in publicizing for the world outside the Senate the liberal causes in which they believe. They have knowingly sacrificed influence inside the Senate by attacking the ground rules of the legislative system of which they are a part. Because it does not favor the causes in which they believe, these Senators are opposed to the existing influence structure in the Senate. Hence, it is natural that they should focus heavy fire on the Senate Appropriations Committee — not because it is so easily differentiated, but precisely because it is so nearly coterminous with "the Senate." "I call the

[16] Ralph K. Huitt, "The Outsider in the Senate: An Alternative Role," *American Political Science Review* (September, 1961), pp. 566–575. The article is about Senator William Proxmire, who had several run-ins with the Committee, was rejected for membership on the Committee in 1963, but became a member a year later.

attention of the Senate and of the country," says Senator Clark in his attack on "The Senate Establishment," "to the close analogy between the members of the Senate establishment and the members of the Appropriations Committee."[17] Conversely, Senate Committee members have interpreted Clark's attacks on them as attacks on "the Senate." When Clark chastised the Committee for the appropriations lag of 1963, Committee veterans painted Clark not as anti-Committee, but as anti-Senate. Senator John McClellan blasted Clark for "this harangue about the way the Senate conducts its affairs."[18] And Senator Spessard Holland retaliated in stronger language against

> all this child's play in the Senate in which the good faith of the Senate is being attacked. I shall not permit it to be attacked in my presence any more. I have listened to the Senator from Pennsylvania hour after hour in this session. Apparently he wishes to tear down the temple in which he lives. I do not share that feeling.[19]

Formally, Senators Douglas, Morse, and Clark are not linked to Committee decision-making, and, informally, they do not cooperate closely or easily with most Committee members. It is probably the case that neither their goal nor their maintenance expectations have been particularly well met. Their dissatisfactions, therefore, constitute the main source of Senate-Committee tension. Should they ever recruit a large number of allies, they could produce major changes in Senate appropriations politics. For the moment, however, they cannot do so. Though their behavior wins support from people outside the Senate, the role they have chosen to play makes the recruitment of allies inside the system very difficult. At present, therefore, their behavior may result paradoxically in their continued isolation. Pinprick criticisms serve to alert the Committee without endangering it; hence, they encourage the Committee to maintain the close relationship with the rest of "the Senate" which now exists.

Senate Sanctions

Everything that has been said thus far points to easier adaptation or less system-subsystem conflict than exists in the House and, therefore, to less need for the application of sanctions. And such is the case. Still, it should be pointed out that the Senate has the same range of sanctions available to it as does the House.

1. The Senate can and has altered the jurisdiction of the Committee. But it has not done so because its expectations have been unmet. It has acted in this regard only after the House had taken action. All indications are that

---

[17] *Congressional Record*, Daily Edition, February 26, 1964, p. 3637.
[18] *Congressional Record*, Daily Edition, November 27, 1963, p. 21814.
[19] *Ibid.*, p. 21811.

the Senate would have been perfectly content with the status quo in 1865 and in 1885, and that they simply followed the example of the House in both cases. The Senate Committee was established, for example, two years after the House Committee, in 1867. In 1921, after the House returned jurisdiction over all appropriations to the Appropriations Committee, the Senate again followed suit.[20] Members of the substantive committees protested the diminution of their influence, however, and it was in response to their objections that the Senate adopted the rule in 1922 regarding ex officio Committee members. It is interesting to note the different methods by which substantive committee objections were met in the two chambers at this time. In the House, a number of objectors were put on the Appropriations Committee; in the Senate, a number of objectors were given ex officio status. In the short run, the sting was withdrawn from substantive committee members to an equal degree. But, in the long run, the House solution made possible an exclusive, differentiated Appropriations Committee, whereas the Senate solution perpetuated a direct substantive committee influence in the appropriations process.

2. The Senate can and has altered Committee jurisdiction by making provisions for financing via methods that bypass the Appropriations Committee. The case of the depressed areas bill has already been mentioned. And all of the other instances mentioned in Chapter 2 are relevant for the Senate as well as for the House. Indeed, the Senate has used this sanction more frequently and more successfully than the House. On such matters as depressed areas, Export-Import Bank, and housing, the Senate has repeatedly provided for backdoor spending, whereas the House has objected. But the Senate position had usually been taken with large-scale Committee acquiescence. In the Senate, therefore, bypassing the Committee is more frequent than it is in the House. However, such action represents far less of a sanction than it does in the House. The Senate Appropriations Committee is usually willing to be bypassed. The conflict between Senate and Committee is rarely as sharp as it was even on the depressed areas bill discussed earlier. Always, a large number of Committee members have been among the staunchest advocates of backdoor spending.

The one area where the Committee has dug in as a group and opposed Treasury financing involves the foreign aid program. A vote taken on this matter in 1959 represents the equivalent in the Senate of the vote on the Thomas amendment (pp. 47 ff.) voted on in the House that same year. At stake was a proposal from the Foreign Relations Committee recommending a five-year development loan program to be financed by Treasury borrowing at the rate of $1 billion per year. On the floor a point of order was made that

[20] See the Committee's unofficial 7-page memorandum entitled, "From: The Senate Committee on Appropriations, The Capitol, Washington D.C.," pp. 4–7.

518

the proposal was an appropriation on an authorization bill. The point of order was overruled; a motion was made to appeal the ruling of the chair; and a motion was made to kill this appeal by laying it on the table. This last motion was defeated by the narrow margin of 48 to 42, and the proposal for Treasury borrowing was subsequently dropped. At that time, no member of the Foreign Relations Committee was a regular member of the Appropriations Committee, and so overlapping membership could not soften the conflict. On the key vote, Appropriations Committee members declared themselves 22 to 5 against Treasury financing in the foreign aid field, and the Foreign Relations Committee members went on record 11 to 4 in favor of it. The conflict between the Appropriations Committee and one of the substantive committees was unusually clear. And the conflict can be described as an attempt by the Senate to control Appropriations Committee behavior.

For the Appropriations Committee, Senator Richard Russell claimed that the proposal

> can lead to a serious impairment of the power at the purse and control of the purse that has resided in parliamentary bodies since the dawn of at least English parliamentary history . . . this provision of the bill collides squarely with Rule 16 of the Senate which provides that appropriations shall be considered by the Committee on Appropriations.[21]

Chairman J. W. Fulbright of the Foreign Relations Committee replied,

> I do not criticize the Committee on Appropriations. I suppose if I were a member of that Committee, having confidence in my own judgment and opinions, I would seek the power to control such programs. So I do not criticize that Committee at all. They are among the ablest members of this body, some of them are senior members . . . I have been treated very generously by the Appropriations Committee; it has always been very generous with many items in which I have been interested. But if we place all the authority in the hands of the Appropriations Committee, the rest of the members of the Senate will have very little to do except play golf and take vacations.[22]

Even here, when the Senate was clearly trying to take away from the Appropriations Committee authority which the Committee did not want to surrender, the tone of the contest was different from that in the House.

Indeed, Senator Fulbright argued that the proposal was really a sanction against the House Committee and not aimed at the Senate Committee at all. "It is only human nature," he said, "that members of the Appropriations Committee like all other human beings like to get all the power they can. This is especially true of the House Committee. The record shows that the

---

[21] *Congressional Record*, Daily Edition, July 1, 1959, p. 11331. The debate will be found in *ibid.*, pp. 11312–11348.

[22] *Ibid.*, pp. 11338–11339.

519

Senate Committee has been extremely cooperative in carrying out the policy determined by the Congress as a whole; but in several instances the House has not been."[23] In most debates over backdoor spending, "the Senate" views the House Committee rather than the Senate Committee as the real opponent. They consider victory in the Senate as providing momentum for the really difficult companion assault against "the House." In this view, the Senate Committee often concurs. Despite the rhetoric of Senator Fulbright, the Senate Committee perceived the foreign aid proposal as a direct threat to its influence, and it resisted.

3. The Senate can and has voted in favor of increasing the number of annual authorizations — the effect of which is to dilute Appropriations Committee influence by forcing it to share its look at the budget with substantive committees. But, as in the case of Treasury borrowing, there has been little sense of conflict on this matter. Hence, annual authorizations can hardly be described as a sanction employed against a recalcitrant Committee. On the matter of annual authorization for military procurement, for example, the impetus came from Senator Richard Russell — a member of the Appropriations Committee who doubles as Chairman of the Armed Services Committee. Annual authorization in the Senate, therefore, often means two looks by many of the *same* people — not, as in the House, two looks by two discrete committees. And, in any case, the point is that the Senate Appropriations Committee is expected to and already does share its decision-making influence with substantive committee members. To let them in on the process a little more does not constitute a significant change — let alone a significant sanction.

4. The Senate can and does change Committee recommendations on the floor, and this kind of sanction clearly does get used. Of the 576 recommendations detailed, 11.5 per cent were changed. They will be discussed in Chapter Eleven.

5. Individual Senators have the same sanction as House members in making a point of order under Senate Rule 16, which forbids legislation on an appropriation bill. And, since so much Senate business is conducted by unanimous consent, an individual Senator has more opportunity to levy small sanctions against the Committee than does his House counterpart. A Committee staff member said, "You can do a lot of things in the House that you can't do in the Senate. If you get up to speak on appropriations there, they can shout you down. But over here, you got to listen to what a Senator has to say no matter who he is. If you don't, he'll filibuster you and hold up an appropriation bill for three days."

[23] *Ibid.*, p. 11333. A "Short History of Proposals for Borrowing Authority for Development Loans" will be found in *Congressional Record*, Daily Edition, August 7, pp. 13803 ff.

In 1964, for example, Senator Joseph Clark objected to the customary unanimous consent resolution granted perfunctorily at the beginning of each year, which permits the Committee to sit while the Senate is in session. Clark disliked the fact that the Appropriations Committee was singled out as the "one specially favored committee" and felt it was an "invidious discrimination against other standing committees of the Senate."[24] His action was a minor irritant to Committee members in that it forced them to hold hearings earlier in the morning than they might have preferred. It had few other consequences. But it illustrates the possibilities of harassment that lie in the hands of every Senator in a system where liberal rules of debate require constant unanimous consent agreements in order to transact business.

6. As a sanction to curb an errant Appropriations Committee, the Senate can prescribe new budgetary procedures. But, here again, the evidence indicates little need or desire to do so. Such budgetary reforms that are proposed find the Committee and the Senate united in pursuit of the same goals — usually increased influence for the Senate in the overall appropriations process. For example, Senator John McClellan's perennial project, a Joint Committee on the Budget, regularly gets 60 to 70 co-sponsors and has passed the Senate in at least five different Congresses.[25] It has commanded the support of members ranging from Senator Hubert Humphrey to Senator Styles Bridges on the Committee and from Senator Harry Byrd to Senator Jacob Javits off the Committee. But the Joint Committee, whose members would be 7 House and 7 Senate Appropriations Committee members, has been opposed by the House Committee and has never been voted on in that chamber. Senate-House interplay on these matters will be discussed in Chapter Twelve. Still, it should be noted that yet another potential Senate sanction against its Appropriations Committee is in fact more likely to be used by the Senate and its Appropriations Committee jointly to affect the appropriations activity of the House Committee. For now, however, the main point is, once again, that sanctions are seldom used because the Committee seems to be well under the everyday control of "the Senate."

7. In the House, the most important sanction — surely the one most frequently used — over the Appropriations Committee lies in the recruitment and selection of its members. As Table 10.2 indicates, the same opportunity is regularly available to "the Senate." And "the Senate," too, regulates the size of the group and its party ratios.

Committee selection is an important mechanism for ensuring Committee responsiveness to chamber expectations. The fact that the Senate keeps the party ratios on the Committee proportionate to those in the chamber is

[24] *Congressional Record*, Daily Edition, February 26, 1964, p. 3636.
[25] *Congressional Record*, Daily Edition, January 23, 1961, pp. 1033–1035.

521

TABLE 10.2

SENATE APPROPRIATIONS COMMITTEE: PARTY COMPOSITION
AND VACANCIES FILLED BY EACH PARTY DURING
EACH CONGRESS, 80TH TO 88TH CONGRESSES

Congress	Committee Membership by Party	Vacancies Filled by Each Party	Vacancies Filled with Freshman Senators	Total Membership
80th (1947–1948)	9D — 12R	0D — 4R	1R	21
81st (1949–1950)	13D — 8R	5D — 0R	0	21
82nd (1951–1952)	11D — 10R	0D — 2R	0	21
83rd (1953–1954)	11D — 12R	1D — 4R	0	23
84th (1955–1956)	12D — 11R	3D — 1R	0	23
85th (1957–1958)	12D — 11R	2D — 0R	0	23
86th (1959–1960)	18D — 9R	6D — 3R	3D	27
87th (1961–1962)	17D — 10R	1D — 2R	0	27
88th (1963–1964)	18D — 9R	3D — 1R	0	27
89th (1965–1966)	18D — 9R	1D — 0R	0	27

evidence of this concern. In the House, party ratios on the Appropriations Committee remained (until 1965) constant regardless of changing party ratios in the chamber. Here again, therefore, the Senate has ensured the responsiveness of its Appropriations Committee in a manner which the House has not customarily observed.

On the Democratic side in the Senate, committee selection is decided by majority vote of the Steering Committee, the chairman and leading figure of which is the party leader. In recent years, he and a majority of the members of the Steering Committee have also been members of the Appropriations Committee (see Table 10.1). It is hard to conceive of the relationship as one involving sanctions, when the Steering Committee members are the very ones who choose the members of the group. Still, there are always more applicants than vacancies, and the party leader and Steering Committee do make estimates involving an individual's responsiveness when they decide among the applicants.

On the Republican side, a Committee on Committees assigns committee memberships. But the Committee on Committees usually allocates assignments on the basis of the seniority of the applicants. In most cases, therefore, it exercises no discretion and, hence, does not use its authority as a sanction against anyone. Insofar as Senate committee-makers overlap with Appropriations Committee members (as they do in the case of the Democrats) and insofar as Senate committee-makers enjoy little leeway in making their selections (as they do in the case of the Republicans), the committee selection process becomes less consequential for appropriations politics in the Senate than it is for the House.

A fairly superficial investigation of the selection process and its results indicates that the qualifications for membership on the Senate Committee are very similar to those existing in the House. Considerations of Senate experience, geographical representation, and legislative style appear to be most important. Table 10.3 portrays the extent to which prior experience in the Senate operates as a requisite for Committee membership.

TABLE 10.3

LENGTH OF SENATE SERVICE BEFORE APPOINTMENT TO
APPROPRIATIONS COMMITTEE — 58 MEMBERS, 1947 TO 1964

Number of Years in Senate Before Appointment	0	1	2	3	4	5	6	7	8	9	10	11	12
Number of Men	13	1	8	2	12	1	4	4	6	0	2	2	3

The 58 men who served on the Committee during the years 1947 to 1964 waited an average of 4.4 years before winning membership on the Committee. Most Committee members mention seniority considerations in describing their road to membership. "I waited 8 years to get on and I didn't mind. I figured that was par for the course." "I had to wait 6 or 7 years; and I was seasoned for the job." "I was on the waiting list. I had to get into the top third of the Democrats in seniority before I could get on the Committee." "No member who just came gets on this Committee . . . [it] is a prize committee. You have to wait to get on it." As Tables 10.2 and 10.3 indicate, freshmen do not ordinarily get assigned to the Committee. Of the 13 freshmen listed in Table 10.3, only 4 (as shown in Table 10.2) were put on the Committee in the 18-year period 1947 to 1964. The other 9 are members who served during the period but were put on the Committee as freshmen sometime between 1933 and 1946.

Of some note, however, is the fact that, in 1953, Steering Committee Chairman Lyndon Johnson promulgated the Johnson rule: that every freshman Democrat should be given one major committee assignment. In 1959, three newcomers were placed on the Appropriations Committee. Committee veterans were happy about the rule, but were surprised to find it applied to their particular committee. "I didn't think he'd find places on the Appropriations Committee for them," said one. "With all due deference to them," said another, "they don't have the running knowledge of the workings of government." These appointments were, in part, a function of the fact that the Democrats had six vacancies to fill in 1959. Majority leader Mike Mansfield, with fewer positions to fill in 1961 and 1963, did not apply the Johnson rule to the Appropriations Committee. To the degree that 1959 has set a precedent, however, the Senate Committee may enhance its responsiveness to the chamber by keeping in communication with the ideas of the newest generation of Senators.

Table 10.4 lists the man-years of service on the Committee by region and party for the years 1947 to 1964. Each member who served on the Committee from 1947 to 1964 was credited with his total years of service during that period. Thus, 18 man-years of service would be the maximum for any one Senator; Committee service prior to 1947 was not counted.

Committee Democrats come overwhelmingly from the South and Far West. The Southerners themselves constitute nearly a majority, and, with the Far Westerners, they constitute four fifths of the Democrats. Conversely, Eastern and Midwestern Democrats combined represented only a tiny minority during the period. On the Republican side, Midwesterners dominate in terms of numbers with sizable minorities of Eastern and Far Western Republicans also achieving membership. To some degree these regional distributions reflect the operation of the prior-experience criterion. That is, Republican and Democratic Committee members tend to come in largest absolute numbers from those regions where their party is strongest, their seats the safest, and their seniority the greatest. Southern dominance on the Democratic side and Midwestern dominance on the Republican side reflect in part Senate longevity. Conversely, Eastern Democrats and Border State Republicans have found it relatively difficult to win successive elections and thus increase their eligibility via seniority.

Seniority is obviously not the only factor governing Committee assignments. If it were, geographical representation would be different than it is. Some attempt is made, for example, to achieve a minimal geographical representation, and this works to mitigate purely seniority considerations. A veteran committee-maker said,

> We try to keep a regional representation. Sometimes, it gets a little unbalanced, but we try to have at least someone from each region. I remember once when Senator Green decided to go off the Committee and go on Foreign Relations. I looked around to find someone from the same general region. I had to go as far as Kilgore of West Virginia to find someone who wanted to go on. I asked him if he'd like to go on the Committee and he thanked me and said he'd never thought of it.

Republican committee-makers can achieve the same effect by encouraging a man with high seniority to "run" for a position on the Committee. The point is that committee-makers do exert an independent influence — and if they influence it on behalf of minimum geographical representation they can do it on behalf of lopsided geographical representation or any other nonseniority consideration as well.

524

TABLE 10.4

REGIONAL DISTRIBUTION OF COMMITTEE MEMBERS — MAN-YEARS OF SERVICE AND AVERAGE SERVICE PER MAN: 58 MEMBERS, 1947 TO 1964

REGION[a]	MAN-YEARS OF SERVICE			AVERAGE YEARS OF SERVICE PER MAN		
	Democrats	*Republicans*	*Total*	*Democrats*	*Republicans*	*Total*
East	19 (8%)	55 (30%)	74 (17%)	6.3 (3 men)	9.2 (6 men)	8.2 (9 men)
South	122 (49%)	0	122 (28%)	10.2 (12 men)	0	10.2 (12 men)
Border	27 (11%)	0	27 (6%)	4.5 (6 men)	0	4.5 (6 men)
Midwest	5 (2%)	86 (46%)	91 (21%)	2.5 (2 men)	6.1 (14 men)	5.7 (16 men)
Far West	75 (30%)	44 (24%)	119 (28%)	8.3 (9 men)	7.3 (6 men)	7.9 (15 men)
Total	248 (100%)	185 (100%)	433 (100%)	7.8 (32 men)	7.1 (26 men)	7.5 (58 men)

[a] For states in various regions, see Table 2.6.

The story of the Green-Kilgore switch points up an important complication, however, in any discussion of committee-maker influence. Regional distributions of members may be the result simply of regional preferences for Appropriations Committee membership. Eastern and Midwestern Democrats did not average between them as many as two Committee members in the period. From 1947 to 1961, not a single Midwestern Democrat sat on the Committee; and for most of the eighteen years, Senator John Pastore (see Table 10.1) was the only Eastern Democrat on the group. But these figures may be a reflection of their preferences rather than a reflection of any discrimination on the part of committee-makers.

The legislative assistant of an Eastern Democratic member complained,

> One of the troubles with the liberals down here is that none of them ever gets on the Appropriations Committee. That's one reason why they are the most ineffective group down here. They gravitate to committees like Foreign Relations where they can't do any good, in my opinion. Almost every major conservative in the Senate is on the Committee — on both sides.

The interests of Democrats from the large industrial states of the East and Midwest may be more important than their seniority in keeping them off the Committee. Democratic Senators from the small Western states, given the relative importance of federal projects to their economy, covet Appropriations Committee membership as the most advantageous place from which to influence the financing of those federal projects.

One such Democrat with low seniority explained that the senior Senator from his state advised him and had worked to get him a Committee membership:

> I was advised, Senator ———— advised me to go on Appropriations. My main interest is foreign relations, but I was told it wouldn't do me any good back home . . . all matters come before this [Appropriations] Committee. It's the master committee . . . the main reason I got on was because my senior colleague went to bat for me. He turned the screws on a lot of the older leaders in the Senate who were indebted to him for favors done during service in the Senate. He turned the screws and called in a lot of old political debts. He was most helpful. He used the argument that there was an historic role for our state to play on the Appropriations Committee.

These comments reflect a degree of desire and diligence which may account for the fact that the Far Western states have been represented by an average of four Senators per year among Committee Democrats. It may also account for the sizable minority of Republican members from the Far West and for the fact that of all regions the Far West has the best balanced two-party representation on the Committee.

526

To some degree the Democratic regional distribution figures simply reflect the composition of the Democratic Steering Committee. Southerners and Westerners — for the most part the very same Southerners and Westerners — dominate the membership of both groups. To the degree, therefore, that committee-makers use their discretion in making appointments (as they surely do), it is not surprising that they would favor Senators from their own area. But just why Southerners and Westerners would prefer other Southerners and Westerners to Easterners and Midwesterners is not a self-evident matter. And it is here that the criterion of legislative style comes into play. Insofar as they have a choice, Senate committee-makers would prefer to bring onto this important Committee Senators whom they believe are devoted to the Senate as an institution, to the protection of its influence, and to the preservation of its basic rules of the game. They want, in a word, the same kind of "responsible legislator" that House committee-makers seek. They want an institutional insider rather than an outsider. And they want him for the same reasons — to ensure that the powerful Appropriations Committee, a citadel of institutional influence, be kept responsive to the other centers of influence in the chamber.

Senators who possess the desired legislative style are most likely to be Southerners and Westerners. And this is so because the Senate as an institution is more important to them than it is to Eastern and Midwestern Senators. The Senate has long been a place of special Southern influence in the American political system — "Old Southern Home," "The South's revenge for Appomatox," says William S. White. It is also the institution which gives the small, sparsely populated States of the Union — particularly the concentration of them in the Far West — their most disproportionate representation and influence in the national system. Southerners and Westerners care about the Senate, use the Senate, and are protected by the Senate more than members from any other region. It is natural that this common interest should produce a common desire to gain the major offices of institutional influence and observe the traditional rules of the game.[26]

In 1959, when Senator Johnson chose three freshmen for the Committee, he picked one old friend (Senator Thomas Dodd of Connecticut, who did not want the position and left it two years later) and two small-state Senators (Senator Gale McGee of Wyoming and Senator Robert Byrd of West Virginia). Johnson had campaigned for each of them, felt they would be amen-

[26] On the power of Western Senators on the Committee, see Neal Maxwell, "The Conference of Western Senators," *Western Political Quarterly* (December, 1957). On the paucity of Easterners, see the comment of Senator John Williams (R., Del.). "As an Easterner, I have never been able to crash the sacred precincts of the Appropriations Committee . . . I am looking forward to the day when some of us from the East can crash the sacred precincts of the Appropriations Committee and be on the inside. . . ." 97 *Congressional Record*, pp. 8130–8131.

able to the party leadership, and, in general, would devote themselves to the work of the Senate. In 1961, the Steering Committee faced a choice among ten Senators for two seats. Majority leader Mansfield, who also had top seniority, was given one seat. The second went to a small-state Westerner, Senator E. L. Bartlett of Alaska. Bartlett was given preference over two men who had more seniority, Senators Ralph Yarborough of Texas and William Proxmire of Wisconsin, and over two others with equal seniority, Senators Clair Engle of California and Philip Hart of Michigan.[27] As Senator Joseph Clark points out in his attack on "the Senate Establishment," Bartlett was the only one of the five who voted against a change in the cloture rule.[28] Doubtless he did so not because he wanted the appropriations assignment nor because he was opposed to civil rights, but because he saw the Senate rule on debate as a bulwark of the Senate's and hence his small state's influence. In this and other procedural matters, Southerners and Westerners have a community of interest. And along with seniority and interest it counts for a great deal in Steering Committee decisions.

A comparison of Table 10.4 with Table 2.6 reveals somewhat different regional distributions on the Senate and House Appropriations Committees.

Considering the two-party regional totals for the two committees, the representation for the Southern, Border, and Midwestern regions is approximately the same in both houses. Far Western representation is appreciably greater, however, on the Senate Committee than on the House Committee. And Eastern representation is significantly greater on the House than on the Senate Committee. Both these differences are reflections on the relative importance of certain regions in the chambers generally and in the committee-making bodies particularly. Moreover, both of the differences are traceable to the Democratic rather than to the Republican side of the aisle. Far Westerners have proportionately greater representation in the Senate than in the House; they also have held proportionately greater influence on such bodies as the Democratic Steering Committee in the Senate than they have in the "leadership" or on the Democratic side of the Ways and Means Committee in the House. Far Westerners in the Senate are especially well-attuned to the norms of the Senate and hence well-entrenched in its informal influence structures. For this reason, they work in a more natural harmony with the Southern legislators in organizational matters than do their counterparts in the House. On the other hand, the power of large-state delegations in the House committee-making process helps Eastern Democrats (and large-state

---

[27] Joseph Clark, *The Senate Establishment* (New York: Hill and Wang, 1963), pp. 47, 50. Senator Proxmire secured membership in 1964, Senator Yarborough in 1965. The lesson seems to be that, sooner or later, seniority triumphs over all.

[28] *Ibid.*, p. 100.

Midwestern Democrats) gain more representation on the House than on the Senate Committee. It may not be that Eastern and Midwestern Democrats in the House are attracted to the Appropriations Committee much more than their Senate counterparts. We have already seen that a number of them were coopted. But it is likely that large-state delegations in the House value a place on the Appropriations Committee more highly than do large-state Senators and that they work accordingly on behalf of some member of their delegation.

These differences in regional representation reflect, therefore, different constellations of influence in committee-making. The Senate and the House, to which their respective Appropriations Committees are expected to be responsive, are different political systems. And, ultimately, one would predict that differing committee memberships will produce different patterns of appropriations decisions. However, before any such determination can be made, more of the factors involved in Senate Committee behavior must be discussed.

COMMITTEE EXPECTATIONS AND ADAPTATIONS

Individual Senator Expectations and Satisfactions

Senate Appropriations Committee behavior must be viewed in part as a response to the expectations of the Senate and in part as a response to the expectations of its own members. When asked why they sought membership on the Committee, every one of the Senators interviewed gave the same broad answer — power. They are attracted to it because they see it as a powerful committee. "It's the top committee and everybody aspires to the top." "It's the most important and powerful committee in the Senate. It's the ambition of every Senator I know — or 99 44/100 per cent of them, like Ivory Soap."

> Appropriations and Foreign Relations are the most powerful ones in the Senate in the sense of being sought after. I wouldn't say all the Senators want to get on it, but eighty to ninety per cent of them do. Do you want to know how to confirm it? Just count em. There are ten men who have been here longer than I have and six of them are on Appropriations.[29]

Obviously the source of Committee power is its control over money. And members believe that the ability to grant or withhold money from others

[29] The prestige ranking of Senate Committees as developed by Matthews confirms this estimate. Donald Matthews, *U.S. Senators and Their World, op. cit.*, p. 149.

529

gives each of them more influence over more people more frequently than any other committee would. In the words of a Southern Democrat,

> Appropriations are the main arteries of government. They give you the best chance to influence the course of government every year. Maybe on some other committee, like Public Works, you get a good chance to do something one year, but not consistently.

And a Midwestern Republican echoed the idea when he said, "[I concluded that Appropriations] was the most powerful committee as far as the influence of a single person was concerned. Everything came to that committee . . . it's the place where one person can have the most influence on the trend of government." Committee members believe that membership on Appropriations gives them, as individuals, influence of unusual weight and scope.

Given senatorial expectations that Appropriations Committee decision-making should be closely intertwined with senatorial decision-making generally, it is not surprising to find Committee members stressing the fact that their position makes them influential as individuals in Senate decision-making generally. Descriptions of their quest for influence shade imperceptibly into general descriptions of Senate decision-making. One Republican member discussed his reasons for seeking membership:

> Coming from a small state, I needed a pry in order to make myself heard . . . I needed a national committee to make myself felt; so I went on Appropriations . . . This is a peculiar place. On the surface there is courtesy, geniality, cordiality, but underneath it's the worst dog-eat-dog place in the world. You're expected to use a pry or to use pressure or whatever you want to call it around here. If you don't, they think you're a sap. I don't like to use a pry, so some people think I'm soft. If you don't wedge a fellow over and make him move, he just isn't going to move, that's all. That's the way it is in the greatest governing body in the world. They expect it of you.

A Southern Democrat described his relations with his fellow Senators.

> I'm nice to them and they're nice to me . . . I don't mean to be boastful, but there's a kind of attraction when you're on the Appropriations Committee. I wouldn't say they are envious or anything like that, but they look up to a person when he's on the Appropriations Committee. There seems to be that respect that they have.

A freshman Senator and member of the Committee noted that his position gave him influence with other Senators which he otherwise would not have. "It's a magical title, a badge of distinction to be on Appropriations. Even though you're at the bottom of the Committee, you are respected. They're not interested in you — it's just that you're on the Appropriations Committee. It's a back-scratching operation." Senate decision-making is viewed as a bar-

530

gaining process among individuals. No matter whom you are bargaining with and no matter what the subject, Appropriations Committee membership is a dependable source of influence.

So, too, is it a source of influence with the bureaucracy. A veteran Southern Democrat recalled,

> It's a funny reaction. When I first came down here, I had to go around to the agencies here and there to get what I wanted done. Now that I'm here, on Appropriations, they come to me. Instead of me having to bow and scrape, they have to bow and scrape. It's just natural for people to be nice to you when they know you have the power to give them what they want.

What the bureaucrats want, of course, is money. What the legislators want from the bureaucrats is, of course, something more tangible than respect and deference. They want favorable consideration of specific projects in which they are interested. Such consideration may come through inclusion in the budget for Committee approval or through the allocation of an appropriation after it has been voted by the Committee. Committee members, therefore, value not only the capacity to influence other Senators but the capacity to influence executives as well.

In talking about their expectations, Committee members specify their interest in two kinds of projects. One expectation is that membership on the Committee would bring influence with people who could help them get appropriations needed in their home state. "It's a power committee," said one senior Southerner, "there's a lot of development going on in our state. I know I can get more for my state on this Committee than on any other committee in the Senate." And a Senator representing a small, Far Western state exclaimed,

> On Appropriations you can, just by the flick of the hand or by a personal endorsement, get things for your state that you couldn't get otherwise. Last spring, I was able to get one million dollars for ———, one million for ——— and tens of thousands for ——— [all in his state]. I got it because I made a personal appeal in the subcommittee and being a member of the Committee I was honored. None of them was even in the House bill. I ask you, can you beat that?

Senators, of course, hasten to report their successes to their constituents.[30]

Other members stressed their concern for the financing of programs which they nurtured in their substantive committees. Having spent time developing substantive programs, they decided to move over to the Appropriations

[30] For an example, see the comments of Senator Robert Byrd, *Congressional Record*, Daily Edition, November 2, 1962, pp. A8040–8042.

Committee to see that these programs received adequate funding. When asked why he sought membership on the Committee, one Senator replied,

> It was the best place in which to follow through on the things I was interested in and was prepared for. I was the author of the bill to authorize the ——— and on Appropriations I was in a position to see that through. On agricultural matters, too, I had several things I was interested in and I could follow through on them.

A Southern Democrat who had authorized programs in his capacity as the chairman of a legislative committee, described the advantages of sitting on two committees.

> The longer I was in the Senate, the more I saw that everything sooner or later funnels down into this proposition of funds. You can authorize anything you want, but that doesn't take money out of the Treasury. Unless you get an appropriation bill to provide the money, the authorization doesn't mean a thing. I saw how powerful this Committee was . . . [my two committees] dovetail very nicely. You've got to have an appropriation. One is no good without the other. I'm in a strategic position to influence both sides. I get two cracks at it.

For Senators who develop strong program interests, the Senate system of interlocking committees gives them a chance to influence that program at every stage of Senate decision-making. In these cases, an Appropriations Committee member wields greater program influence than his counterparts on the House Committee.

Individual Senators seek the satisfaction of certain personal expectations through Appropriations Committee membership. These expectations center almost exclusively on increased power or the respect and deference which result from increased power. They talked very little about the desire to get information so as to feel a part of things — a desire that was expressed by many House Committee members. Even less did Senators talk about seeking or deriving personal satisfaction from any distinctive committee style. For House members, hard work is a source of considerable individual pride and satisfaction; and it is important to individual Committee members because it gives the group identity, cohesiveness, and morale. It is believed to differentiate Appropriations Committee members on the one hand from Members of the House on the other. Senate Committee members, significantly, do not speak in terms of a distinctive Committee style and do not mention the intangible satisfactions of group esprit. They do not, that is to say, distinguish between themselves and other Senators on any dimension other than the increase in influence which accrues to them as individuals. In speaking of their personal satisfactions, they express little if any emotional attachment for the Committee as a group. Just as the Senate does not differentiate between themselves and the Committee in terms of expectations, neither do Committee members for their part develop a sense of group identity which sets them off from "the Senate." Decision-making in the Senate is very much a process involving individuals; decision-making in the House is seen as a process involving collectivities.

In talking to Senate Committee members, one basic element of personal style does impress itself indelibly on the interviewer. It is that the Senators feel themselves perpetually short of time and forced to act in great haste on many problems at once:

> The only thing we don't have around here is time. We never have enough. I got up this morning and had a meeting downtown. Then I had two Appropriations Committee markup meetings. Now I've just come back to the office and I haven't done anything yet. Here it is Friday, too; and I have a campaign this year so I try to fly back home as many weekends as I can. I don't know how to solve the problem. If you did Appropriations thoroughly, there would be absolutely no time for anything else.

> We're busy. We sit on many subcommittees . . . I have to sit on five [Appropriations] subcommittees. And I sit on two legislative committees. Sometimes in the morning I have four meetings scheduled at ten o'clock. I go to one for an hour and then pick out another one to go to for an hour.

> I'm entitled to several subcommittee chairmanships by seniority, but I've declined them. I've been on other committee work for three years and its taken two-thirds of my time. I just don't have the time to devote to Appropriations Committee work. There's a limit to how much one man can do. So I've declined several chairmanships.

For every House Committee member who speaks about how hard he works digging out the facts behind closed doors, there is a Senate Committee member who describes his daily routine as a frenzied rush from one meeting to another without adequate time to devote to any one of them.

One kind of style has just as significant a set of consequences for appropriations decision-making as the other. But the crucial difference is this: Whereas the House Committee's style is Committee-oriented and is used to differentiate the Committee (the hardest working committee in Congress) from the parent chamber, the Senate Committee style is a chamber-oriented style and is used to characterize all Senators. All Senators, that is, have at least two committee assignments, several subcommittee assignments and, usually, much larger constituencies to tend than do House members. Senate Appropriations Committee members do not claim that they are any busier than other Senators. They do not use their style as a badge of distinction. The style which Committee members express most often, therefore, is one which blurs rather than sharpens the boundaries between the Senate and its Committee on Appropriations.

Committee Goal Expectations and Adaptation

If it is to survive, the Committee must satisfy to a substantial degree the goal expectations of the Senate. And, of course, it must also satisfy the goal expectations of its individual members. Both sets of expectations, however, prescribe general goals. They do not prescribe a set of goals specific enough to guide day-to-day Committee decision-making. In attempting, therefore, to meet the goal expectations of the Senate and all its individual members, the Committee develops for itself a more specific version of its goals. It is this self-defined notion of its tasks, along with the perceptions and attitudes which support it, that guides the Committee in its day-to-day deliberations.

The Committee's idea of its goals derives most importantly from the structural arrangement whereby the Senate always makes its formal appropriations decisions after the House has acted. Furthermore, the perceptions and attitudes which surround the Committee's version of its goals take their shape from the basic facts of the appropriations sequence. As Senate Committee members view it, their primary goal is to listen to and act on appeals brought to them by people who are dissatisfied with the appropriation bill passed by the House. These people normally include executive agencies, clientele groups supporting such agencies, members of the House, and members of the Senate. Committee members describe themselves variously as a "court of appeals," "appellate court," "appeals court," and "court of last resort."

Two Committee veterans, the first a Democrat and the second a Republican, discussed their tasks similarly:

> The House gets the bill first. They get the first shot at it and they work hard on it. It's an advantage to deal with a thing first, and get your own house in order. What's that old story about Washington and cooling a cup of tea in a saucer? You have to make the tea before you can cool it. That's what its like . . . we take the bill up like an appellate court.

> The Senate always gets the bill after the House has dealt with it. Every group or interest in the community that feels aggrieved comes over here and asks us to put the money back in. We get all these appeals because we are the court of last resort.

Among Senate Committee members the idea is basic that since the Senate position in the appropriations sequence differs from that of the House, the circumstances in which the Senate Committee acts will differ from those in which the House Committee has acted. Consequently, they believe that their self-defined goals are bound to be different from those of their counterpart in the House. For both House and Senate Committees, however, it is their

534

position in the appropriations sequence which leads them to define their goals as they do. The House Committee's budget-cutting task derives in larger part from the fact that it always gets "the first crack at the budget." The Senate Committee's appeals court task derives in large part from the fact that it is always the second chamber to act.

Objectively, a court of appeals can be instituted to hear all kinds of cases. But Senators believe that the nature of prior House action is such that only one kind of case normally gets on their kind of docket — a plea for the restoration of money cut by the House:

> I do not recall ever having heard a witness appearing before the Senate Appropriations Committee in connection with one of these items tell us that we have allowed too much. We do not have representatives of the general public coming before us and saying, "This department can be run for so much money." We have representatives of the government agency, after its request has been disallowed in the House, saying, "We want more money."[31]

> A lot of congressmen will come over here, too, and ask us to help them out. We'll say to the congressman, "Did you try to get it over in the House?" He'll say, "Yes, but I didn't get a roll call on it because I was afraid it would prejudice our Committee against it. Can you get it in over here?"

The Senate Committee receives a lopsided proportion of requests for increases precisely because the House normally reduces budget estimates.

These demands for restoration are not only one-sided, but concentrated and intense. Since the House Committee takes testimony and makes its decisions in secret, no one outside the group can know what the Committee's decisions are until shortly before the bill comes to the floor. Time is often too short in which to launch a counterattack there — but time does remain in which to muster support in Congress and out for a counterattack in the Senate. When they come before the Senate Committee, therefore, the executive agencies and their supporters are primed to concentrate their efforts, as they could not in the House, on a few selected items which they wish to have increased.[32] On the heels of a House cut, agencies may (though they consider it a last resort) send out discharge notices to their employees, thus stimulating instant pressure on the Senate to restore money and jobs.[33] The Senate, of course, does not have to yield, but the fact is that such pressure is

[31] 95 *Congressional Record*, pp. 5217–5218.

[32] See the comments of Rep. Michener in Joint Committee on the Organization of Congress, *Hearings on the Organization of Congress*, 79th Congress, 1st Session (Washington: U.S. Government Printing Office, 1945), p. 213. An example can be found in 99 *Congressional Record*, p. 5888.

[33] See, for example, Senate Committee on Appropriations, *Hearings on Agricultural Appropriations for 1948*, 80th Congress, 1st Session (Washington: U.S. Government Printing Office, 1947), p. 379.

probably more intense, more concentrated, and more publicized than that faced by the House Committee.

If areas other than those reduced most heavily in the House are to be reopened for consideration in the Senate, it is the Senators and not the agency people who must do it. The agencies will be content to leave well enough alone in those areas where their demands were relatively well satisfied by House action. If the Senate Committee were to view its goal as the inspection de novo of every budget request, it might disregard House action completely and treat every area of appropriations equally. But it does not. In the words of its members,

> In appropriating moneys for any department we have a one-sided proposition generally speaking. What are the mechanics? We get the bill from the House. Every item that has not been cut by the House is forgotten. We take it as a matter of course. Then we receive evidence only from those who want appropriations increased.[34]

> The Senate Committee on Appropriations does not go into the millions and billions of dollars in expenditures which the House has approved. I do not think I have ever known of a bill in connection with which we have gone into an investigation in the way the House does, of the billions of dollars that are called for . . . what do we go into? We go into the items the agencies want increased or that private citizens back home want increased.[35]

The Senate defines its tasks, then, as dealing primarily with those intense and one-sided appeals that come to them as a consequence of House action. As one Senator summed up, "In actual practice the function of the Senate Appropriations Committee is like that of an appeals board in passing upon reductions made by the House."[36]

To the degree that the Senate takes as its task the granting or denying of appeals for more funds, it is obvious that the main thrust of Senate decisions will be toward increasing rather than decreasing appropriations figures. Though they sometimes express an uneasiness about it, most Committee members accept this outcome as the logical consequence of their self-defined goals. "As a general rule . . . it is expected that the Senate will restore cuts made by the House."[37] "They call us the 'upper body' because we 'up' appropriations, and it's true. We cut some but usually we raise appropriations."

Transparently, the Senate Committee's goals differ from those of the House Committee. Nothing makes the contrast clearer than the comments of a Senate Committee member who had served earlier as a member of the

[34] 95 *Congressional Record*, pp. 5217–5218.
[35] *Ibid.*
[36] 94 *Congressional Record*, p. 4287.
[37] 97 *Congressional Record*, p. 6336.

House Committee. He did not approve of the Senate Committee's self-defined goals and was having trouble adjusting to them after his House experience:

> Is the House more thorough, more conscientious, and more discerning? Very, very, very, very much more so. I learned from old John Taber and some of those old-timers. When we'd come to a bureau, they'd say, "I see you are asking for fifty new positions this year. Why do you need these positions?" Here, they don't give a damn about such things. They let 'em go right by. Unfortunately, the Senate has come to be an appeals body. They look at the items the House has cut and see whether some of them should be restored. But they don't look at items the House didn't touch but which they could cut. Why shouldn't we look at places the House left and cut them a hundred thousand dollars or two hundred thousand dollars? But they don't. They assume that if the House didn't catch it, it's all right . . . you can cuss old Taber and Chairman Cannon over there but they stood up for balanced budgets and cutting spending. Nobody over here gives a damn.

A second Senator who had also served on both Appropriations Committees viewed the difference in tasks more dispassionately, as a useful division of labor. "Appropriations bills are more thoroughly and carefully processed in the House. And we depend upon it over here. I've found that out. We depend on them to do it."

Senators display some sensitivity to the notion that they are nothing but an appeals court. One subcommittee chairman lectured a new agency head who had come to appeal a House cut in his budget:

> Well, now, this is your first appearance here, and I want to suggest something. This is not just an appeal committee. We may cut the House too. So you just tell us what you have to say. Talking about appeals, we might cut the House, which we do on occasion, but everybody comes over here as if we are going to accept the House figure and then they appeal for something else.[38]

Senate Committee members buttress their version of their goals with a set of supporting images of others and of themselves. These images help to justify their goals and to assuage any doubts they may have about the adequacy of their performance in pursuit of these goals. The great bulk of Senate Committee members' images centers around contrast between themselves and the House. And in this they differ from and yet follow the pattern of the House Committee. Just as each committee is led to a definition of its goals by its position in the appropriations sequence, so do the sharpest supporting images held by each committee pertain to that group which acts

[38] Senate Committee on Appropriations, *Hearings on Independent Offices Appropriations for 1963*, 87th Congress, 2nd Session (Washington: U.S. Government Printing Office, 1962), pp. 151–152.

immediately prior to it in the sequence. The House Committee supports its budget-cutting task with images about the profligacy of executive agencies. The Senate Committee supports its appeals court task with images about the parsimony of the House.

The dominant image which Senate Committee members have of the House is that the House deliberately reduces budget estimates below what it knows is reasonable in order to get the credit for economy action. It then expects and allows the Senate to restore funds to a reasonable level. "The House gets every bill first, so they can afford to cut an item to twenty-five million when they know darn well it'll take fifty million to do the job. They know the Senate will have to raise it and then they scream that the Senate are the big spenders." "We're not as tough over here. They know that. So they wrap up an economy record and expect us to get them off the hook." On the Senate floor, this image of the House is useful in explaining why the Committee's recommendations are slanted more in favor of the program expectations than the economy expectations of the Senate:

> We on the Appropriations Committee are placed in an embarrassing position. We believe in economy. We are trying to bring about economy. Yet we are receiving bills from the House with exceedingly large cuts. The argument is made, "Do not worry about that. The Senate will take care of it."[39]

Then in the words of a Committee member's legislative assistant, "We have 40 House members every year who come over here and say, 'We couldn't get it in over in the House. Can't you fit it in over here?' They come over and beg us and plead with us." So long as Committee members hold to the view that House reductions are more tactical than final, they can justify their appeals function as well as such increases in appropriations as may result.

Committee members harbor another set of images which help them to feel comfortable about the goals they have adopted. In the first place, Senators believe they simply do not have enough time to examine agency budgets de novo. "Over there [in the House] you have a large fifty-man committee broken down into subcommittees. These fifty men work together as long as they get elected and they have one department they specialize in. They work hard at it and do a good job. Over here, we are much busier." In the second place, Senators believe that their statewide constituencies compel them to take a broader view of national needs and hence a more lenient view toward agency budgets than House members whose district interests are narrower:

> The House is half right when they say we're the upper body that ups appropriations. House members only have one district to please. They may have

[39] 98 *Congressional Record*, pp. 4455.

one interest they have to cater to. They can get elected by looking after one thing, and they just say the hell with everything else. You've got some pretty mean and ornery fellows over there. You ask the agencies and they'll tell you that we're much more lenient over here. A Senator has a whole state to look after.

As a corollary to the view that "we've got a much larger picture to deal with over here," Senators consider that their six-year term gives them more freedom to act in keeping with their own judgment than a House member has. The belief is that since economy moods are evanescent, they are more likely to be felt by House members campaigning at two-year intervals than by Senators campaigning every six years:

> Those Members have to run for office every two years. When the public gets hot on their tail to cut spending or reduce expenditures, they cut it out and hope the Senate will put it back in. They can tell the folks back home that they cut and the Senate raised it. Usually we do, but sometimes we don't and then they are miserable.

These perceptions and attitudes about the House help Senate Committee members to rationalize the obvious differences between their goals and those of the House Committee.

The Senate Committee's self-defined goals would seem to be well adapted to the goal expectations of Senate members generally. The Senate's high rate of acceptance is one piece of evidence to this effect. If anything, moreover, Senate goal expectations are slanted toward program support and increased spending rather than toward economy. Such criticism as is voiced paints the Committee as too conservative. The appeals board function, the willingness to consider mostly those items reduced by the House, and the increases over the House figures which are likely to result from such a process — all these are well attuned to the Senate's predominantly liberal goal expectations. Most Senators are likely to agree, too, with those images of the House which Senate Committee members evoke in support of their choice of goals. As for the capacity of Committee goals to satisfy individual Committee member expectations, the low rate of departure from the group to other committees is fairly conclusive. Between 1947 and 1964, only four men left the Committee voluntarily. Three went to the Foreign Relations Committee, and one, Minority Leader Everett Dirksen, left in order to preserve Republican harmony by making his seat available to another Senator. The individual Committee member's influence and his reputation for influence depends on his ability to grant or withhold money. The fact that he grants it more often than he withholds it does not alter his influence and hence his personal satisfaction at all.

539

Senate maintenance expectations prescribe the barest minimum of Committee autonomy. What is more, these expectations are institutionalized in the structure of interlocking Committee memberships. Only if the Committee members banded together to assert a greater autonomy than the rules prescribe would a conflict over maintenance relationships result. Committee members do not do this. They perceive of Senate bargaining as proceeding among individuals rather than among committees. Their Appropriations Committee membership gives each of them an important source of influence in this process. Membership alone, therefore, meets their expectation. They develop no strong sense of group self-consciousness, no sharp distinctions between "we" and "they," because they do not need these to satisfy their individual expectations. They approve of the arrangements which allow them to sit on other committees and which allow members of other committees to sit with them. They do not aspire to greater autonomy and influence as a committee. If they did, they would hardly define their main task as that of an appeals court. Senate maintenance expectations, therefore, are easily and willingly satisfied by the Senate Committee.

The lack of conflict in system-subsystem maintenance relationships contrasts sharply with the situation in the House. Members of the House Committee seek to maintain a high degree of autonomy for themselves, are aware of the resentment of House members, and must tread a tension-filled course between the two conflicting sets of expectations. Relations between the Senate and the Senate Committee, on the other hand, are characterized by a notable lack of tension and by the easiest of communication between them. "I've never seen any resentment or jealousy. Why should there be?" declared one veteran Committee member. There should be no resentment, Committee members believe, because the appropriations process is freely open to nearly every Senator who wishes to press his demands. In making this point, they contrast the Senate decision-making style with that of the House. A Senator who served in both houses said,

> The Appropriations Committee isn't nearly as important over here as it is in the House. Over there it's life or death for a Member. He has to get his project approved by the Appropriations Committee and they're very tough. Over here it's much looser. It's much easier for the individual Senator to get his project in the bill.

An administrative assistant who had served one Senate Committee member in both House and Senate agreed. "The Senate is more courteous than the House. You've got some pretty independent boys on the House Appropriations Committee and if they don't like you they may say so and that's that.

What they say goes. Over here, it's more clubby and chummy." Another Senator made the same contrast. "Over there you serve on one committee and Appropriations lords it over the others. You have to get in to see them. They deny an awful lot of projects. You don't get that over here." "It's pretty rugged over in the House," agreed a third Senator. "I don't want to be quoted, but the House members feel that the Appropriations Committee keeps a pretty tight rein on them." The Appropriations Committee is a more important, more autonomous, and more self-conscious unit in House decision-making than it is in the Senate.

In discussing maintenance relations in the House, special attention was given to the sensitive problem of Appropriations Committee–substantive committee relationships. Since so much of the conflict in the House centers here, it is instructive to take particular note of the different situation that exists in the Senate. Two Senate Committee members, both of whom had served in the House, discussed the difference.

> There's a feeling on the part of the members of the House, and I can attest to this from my own experience, that the Appropriations Committee may infringe on the rights, privileges, prerogatives, and jurisdictions of the legislative committees. There isn't that feeling in the Senate — or if there is, it's nowhere near as strong — that there is in the House. Once in a while, we may appropriate without authorization, but not very often.

> They got 'em tied down pretty tight in the House. You sit on one committee, and everything has to go through the Appropriations Committee. You can't legislate on an appropriation bill. Any legislation can be knocked out on a point of order. But the House Appropriations Committee does it. The members of the other committees don't like it; and you'll hear them rise time and time again. They'll knock out legislation right and left on a point of order. That's why I felt the way I did as a member of the House. We felt that if the Appropriations Committee were going to appropriate all the money and make policy too, the rest of us might just as well go home. I've never felt that jealousy over here. I think it's because we sit on other committees. I'm on Agriculture and Appropriations. If there's something I want, I get two shots at it. If I can't get something in Agriculture, maybe I can weasel something in the appropriation bill. Of course legislation on an appropriation bill is against the rules over here, but here the rules don't mean as much as they do in the House.

Interlocking Committee memberships, again, are seen as preventing the kinds of inter-Committee friction which characterizes House maintenance relations. If this pattern of conflict is lacking, one would not expect to find the consequences of it in Senate appropriations politics. Harmonious maintenance relationships will have, however, particular consequences for appropriations decision-making. And it is to the description of decision-making patterns inside the Senate Committee that we now turn.

541

STRUCTURE FOR DECISION-MAKING

The decision-making structure of the Senate Committee cannot be described with the same degree of precision as that of the House group. For one thing, interviews with Senators tended to be less intensive than those with House members. Less evidence, therefore, pertaining to roles and role behavior was accumulated. It has been virtually impossible to separate them from one another, and thus what was a partial inadequacy in the description of the House Committee structure becomes a total inadequacy in the treatment of the Senate Committee. Even more important, though, the weight of the evidence that has been collected suggests that the Senate Committee's internal structure simply is not as elaborate or well defined as that of the House Committee. If this is so, then the accumulation of more evidence, for example, on Committee members' expectations surrounding certain positions would not enable us to say much more about an internal structure than what follows. The validity of the conclusion is supported by everything said thus far about the lack of differentiation between the Senate and the Senate Committee. The greater its interconnections with other elements of the Senate and the less its own sense of group identity, the less likely is the Committee to develop an elaborate and distinctive internal structure of its own. Nonetheless, pending the actual accumulation of additional evidence, the sketchy description of the decision-making structure which follows must be considered tentative.

Formally the Senate Committee processes the same work load as its counterpart in the House. As an appeals court, however, it processes something less than that. Still, its work load is so great that it, too, has divided tasks and positions among subcommittees. These subcommittees constitute the basic elements of the Committee's decision-making structure. In the 84th Congress they reported holding a total of 330 separate sessions (300 public and 30 executive), a total of 900 hours for the purpose of taking testimony on appropriations. These figures do not include subcommittee markup sessions or full Committee meetings on the bill.[40]

The number of subcommittees varies. In 1963 there were twelve. Technically, of course, the number of subcommittees and their jurisdiction are decisions to be made inside the Committee — presumably by the Chairman. In practice, however, the subcommittee structure of the Senate Committee is in largest part determined by the Chairman of the House Committee. Since the House always processes appropriation bills first, it is free to package agencies in any combination it may desire and to create subcommittees to

---

[40] Senate Committee on Government Operations, *Activities of the United States Senate*, Report No. 96, 85th Congress, 1st Session (Washington: U.S. Government Printing Office, 1957), pp. 6–7.

542

deal with these packages. Thus, the number of subcommittees, their jurisdiction, and the contents of each appropriation bill are decided upon by the House Committee — usually by its Chairman. When the Senate receives an appropriation bill, it has little choice but to create a subcommittee to study the bill as packaged in the House. Hence, for the most part, the Senate subcommittee structure parallels that of the House, and changes in that structure occur in lock step with changes made in the House. When the House subcommittees and their jurisdictions were reorganized in 1955, for example, the Senate followed suit. In the case of foreign aid appropriations, however, the Senate has simply not created a subcommittee at all, and this bill is considered by the full Committee. (And, it should be noted, this means that some party leaders usually participate in foreign aid deliberations from the outset — in sharpest contrast to the separation of party leaders from foreign aid appropriations activity in the House.) The inability to manipulate subcommittees removes a potent source of influence from the hands of the Senate Committee Chairman. It probably diminishes, also, the amount of attention which Committee members generally pay to matters of subcommittee structure — and, hence, any disposition they might have to say much about it.

Though there are about half as many members of the Senate Committee (27) as there are members of the House Committee (50), subcommittees in the Senate are twice as large. While the average size of the 13 House subcommittees in 1963 (excluding ex officio members) was 6 men, the average size of Senate subcommittees (exclusive of ex officio members and including the full Committee as the foreign aid subcommittee) was 14 men. And, whereas the average House member sat on 2 subcommittees, the average Senate Committee member sat on 7. All Committee members including the Chairman, who formally fixes the size, want it this way. Subcommittee membership provides the best position from which each individual can influence appropriations decisions. The more subcommittees each sits on the more opportunity there is for exerting his influence. Member expectations, therefore, are best met by bulky subcommittees. "They want to be able to vote in subcommittee on all these matters," said a staffer, "even though they don't attend the hearings." And a Committee member explained, "If you're a member of a subcommittee, you can get preferential treatment. If there's a $10 million appropriation for something, I can usually work with the clerk and get some of it for my state. They trade a lot more over here [than they do in the House Committee]." Inside the Committee, as in the Senate, decisions are made in such a way as to give a large number of people some share in them. And, having such a generous number of opportunities to exercise influence, Senate Committee members do not complain about their subcommittee assignments, do not see the subcommittee system as limiting their activities, and do not, therefore, define a range of expectations concerning subcommittee activity to the degree that House Committee members do.

With subcommittee memberships as plentiful commodities, the process of allocation is not as consequential in the Senate as it is in the House. It is not an important point of leverage for the Chairman and ranking minority member, and it is not a decision that is likely to thwart the expectations of the individual member. Not all, of course, receive each of their preferences; but, by the same token, no Senate careers are made or broken (as they can be in the House) by virtue of the decision. On the Democratic side, said a Committee newcomer, "You put in for your preferences and you may not get them all, but you get some. I got two of mine." Those who are on the subcommittee remain, and the vacancies are filled as they occur. The allocation is made by the Chairman, in consultation with his subcommittee chairmen. "They tell us what they want and we give it to them if we can," said one of the Committee's elders. "If we can't, we fit them in here and there." No one appears to be upset by the outcome.

The Republican method of allocating seats stresses seniority. One member explained,

> At the beginning of each year we hold a meeting, and we go down the line by seniority. Styles Bridges has the most seniority and he says he wants to be ranking member of some subcommittee — I've forgotten what. Then Leverett Saltonstall, and he takes Armed Services, and so on. Then we [go down the line again and] say which subcommittee we want to be on next. It depends on what you're specially interested in.

Each Republican ends up as ranking minority member of one subcommittee. Who picks what in the process of going around the table may depend on prior negotiations, with the result that a man having little seniority may get on subcommittees he otherwise could not. A member with service on both Appropriations Committees contrasted the selection processes:

> Over in the House the leadership counts for more. Mr. Taber would take the list of Committee members and assign them on the basis of experience or lack of experience and so on to the various subcommittees. Mr. Bridges listens to the members. There are a lot fewer people so that we can visit among ourselves on it.

Neither the Chairman nor the ranking minority member exercises much intra-Committee influence via the selection process. And Committee Republicans, too, seem satisfied with the results.

The most important consequence of the subcommittee allocation process — in contrast to that of the House — is that Senate subcommittees are populated by individuals who have a positive preference for that subcommittee. As one of the Republicans put it earlier, "It depends on what you're

544

specially interested in." In the House, the Chairman and ranking minority member use their control over subcommittee memberships to strike a balance between interested and disinterested members. They do so in the hopes of minimizing the interest-sympathy-leniency syndrome and hence maximizing their goal of budget-cutting. The Senate Committee, however, does not define its primary goal as budget-cutting, and its subcommittee selection processes positively *encourage* the interest-sympathy-leniency pattern of activity. The apotheosis of the syndrome occurs when the chairman of an Appropriations subcommittee sits as the Chairman of the substantive committee making decisions in the same field. Subcommittee chairmenships and ranking minority status go to the most senior man on the subcommittee — with the informal proviso that no man sit as chairman or ranking minority member of more than one subcommittee. Senior Senators, therefore, who have a special interest in a policy area advance on the substantive committees and on the Appropriations subcommittees dealing with that area at the same time.

In 1964, one Senator held *both* positions of influence in the policy areas of defense, regulatory agencies, labor, and education. Sometimes the same result is achieved when the substantive committee splits up into subcommittees as is the case where one man sat as chairman of the Armed Services Subcommittee on Military Construction and chairman of the Appropriations Subcommittee on Military Construction. In addition, some subcommittees divide the work so as to give especially interested Senators the opportunity to make decisions on programs they are interested in. The subcommittee on public works gives Senator Hayden of Arizona charge of the reclamation and power appropriations and Senator Hill of Alabama charge of the TVA and Atomic Energy appropriations.[41] When individuals come to the Appropriations Committee to promote programs they are interested in, as many do, the process of distributing them to subcommittees guarantees that soon they will sit on the appropriate subcommittee and may, eventually, chair it.

It is obvious from the discussion of the allocative process involving subcommittees that the Chairman of the Senate Committee is no match for his counterpart in the House in terms of intra-Committee influence. He simply cannot wield the kinds of sanctions that the House Chairman is expected to use. The Senate Committee, like the Senate itself, is managed more by consensus than by the directives of its leader. Given the fact that so many Committee members are influential individuals in their own right as Senators, as chairmen of substantive committees, and as party leaders, an autocratic method of internal Committee management would be difficult to sustain. The Chairman is the single most influential man on the Committee, and he is expected to be. He is expected to and does take the lead in all procedural

[41] *Congressional Record*, Daily Edition, August 7, 1964, pp. 17895–17896.

matters connected with Committee management — hiring, firing, and over-seeing the Committee staff, scheduling meetings, supervising the flow of subcommittee business, arranging for conferences with the House, and representing the Committee to the external world generally. He is expected to and does observe the norms of fairness, of compromise, and of consultation that apply to his House counterpart. He is expected to have a loyalty to the Senate as an institution. And such influence as he exercises is based primarily on his observance of these norms. The point is, however, that the potentialities of his role are not as great as those of the House Chairman. Two staff members discussed Chairman Carl Hayden and his influence:

> He runs the Committee in an efficient orderly way . . . he's the elder states-man of the Senate, more respected and loved than any other man. He knows everything that goes on in this Committee and in this body. Why, you see him over here on Sunday — just checking up on things. He attends one hundred per cent of the subcommittee markups of the Committee — all except when he's sick. The Senate is his whole life . . . he never makes a speech; he never talks on the floor. He just knows the mechanics and the processes of legislation. He's a tremendous man and an influential man. Anything he wants on this Committee, he gets — just like that.

> Hayden is a very popular old gent — President Pro Tem, senior man in the Senate, and Chairman of the Committee. Whatever he wants he gets. I've never seen that to fail in my years here. He doesn't ask for much — he doesn't abuse his power. But when he does, he gets it. Just let him intimate that he wants something and thirteen guys will try to outrace each other to give it to him.

The thrust of these comments is that Hayden's influence can be measured by his ability to "get what he wants," to extract benefits from the process for his state, for the programs in which he is interested, and for the Senators he wishes to help.[42] Thus he may be described as more successful than any other Committee member in fulfilling his individual expectations for influence. But, to this end, neither the Chairman nor any other Committee member requires a concentration of influence at the top of a hierarchically run Committee.

If the Committee Chairman plays the role of first among equals, it should come as no surprise to find Committee newcomers among the "equals." Veteran members do have the feeling that newcomers should "be on the job," "be diligent and attend as many meetings as you can," "know your business," etc. And newcomers are conscious of their ignorance of Committee procedures. "I haven't been on the Committee very long and I don't know the intricacies. I'm pretty ignorant about a lot of it; and I have to take

---

[42] On Senator Hayden, see the collection of articles and remarks in *Congressional Record*, Daily Edition, February 19, 1962, pp. 2185 ff.

it on faith." But there is no expectation that the newcomer should observe an apprenticeship. A veteran Southerner said, "Even though he's junior and sits way down at the end of the table, he has the same right to speak and to oppose as anyone else."

A first-year member acknowledged the importance of seniority, but without any sense of his own impotence as a member:

> Seniority is just one of the facts of life. The further you rise, the more influence you have. It's a matter of association. People get to know you. If you're a crazy spender they get to know that pretty fast. And they learn whether you know what you're talking about. I talked my subcommittee chairman up $7 million for ———, because I knew my lesson on that and he accepted it. That's pretty good for a new member.

Another freshman said, "The older members do get irritated at the younger ones sometimes. But you know what you can do about that. You get the facts. If you do the work and get the facts, and they don't have them, there isn't very much they can do about it is there?" Senate newcomers are not as influential as senior members. But they do not share the feeling of House newcomers that they are shut out of the decision-making process or that they have a special role to play. They do not feel separated by social distance from their senior colleagues. And they do not have the misperception that House Committee newcomers display concerning the influence and the bases of influence of their Committee elders. The absence of a restrictive apprenticeship role eliminates from the Senate Committee a structural element that underlies a good deal of conflict inside the House Committee.

In a decision-making process structured to give a large number of participants some share, it is natural that influence would extend across party lines and be exercised by minority as well as majority party members. The norm of minimal partisanship seems to apply as strongly to the Senate Committee as it does to the House group. Republican Committee members were unanimously of the opinion that very little partisan conflict existed in the Committee. They said, "You sit on the Committee as Republicans and Democrats, but you don't vote that way. On Appropriations, partisanship plays a very little part." "I've never really thought about it in partisan terms." "You got very little partisanship, almost never . . . usually we compromise and then go along with the Committee." "Come to think of it, you don't get many [minority reports]. It's not done very much on this Committee. A fellow may disagree in Committee, but he won't write a minority report about it. He'll just take it to the floor."

The minority members do have some staff assistance, and they will occasionally meet by themselves to see if they can arrive at a consensus on some controversial items. But for the most part they work in an open relationship

547

with their opposite numbers. The following exchange between a ranking sub-committee member and a subcommittee chairman is a prototype of the exchanges so often (much more often) injected into House appropriations debates:

RANKING MINORITY SUBCOMMITTEE MEMBER: Even if the Republicans were in control in the Senate I should be perfectly happy to have the Senator continue to be chairman of the subcommittee. He has made a great record. No one in the Congress renders better service in handling this appropriation, not only with respect to taking care of the needs of agriculture but also with regard to keeping the appropriations within bounds.

SUBCOMMITTEE CHAIRMAN: Let me sincerely thank my distinguished friend. I will say that no observer from outside the Congress could sit in the Committee room and detect the party membership of any member of the sub-committee. I have never seen the slightest effect of partisan influence or any reference to partisan predilections on the part of any member of this subcommittee.[43]

In view of the lack of structural differentiation between the Senate and the Committee, one would expect the Committee to partake of as much partisanship as exists in the chamber. To the degree, however, that minimal partisanship is observed, the Senate Committee exhibits a special property that sets it off from the Senate. Committee Republicans explain that it is the subject matter of the Committee that underwrites their special lack of partisanship. "It's a pretty down to earth Committee. There is not much philosophizing here. It's a matter of dollars and cents." A minority staff member agreed:

There's a lot less partisanship on the Appropriations Committee — much less than on other committees. You're not legislating on policy, you're dealing with money. You can't cut a policy in half, but you can cut money that way. If one fellow wants one million and another wants two million, you can settle on a million and a half. But you can't do that on a policy — either you do it or you don't.

A veteran Committee Republican felt that this was the major reason, but he also felt that the influence of the Southern Democrats and of Chairman Hayden also helped to explain the Committee's low partisanship:

Of all the committees I've served on, Appropriations is the least partisan. That's because we're not a policy committee. Oh, once in a while there may be a difference but I don't think in all my years on the Committee there has been a straight line party vote in the Committee or in any subcom-mittee. Perhaps the Democrats are more willing to spend money than the Republicans. But you've got the Southern Democrats who are as con-servative as a rural Republican from the North when it comes to appropria-

[43] *Congressional Record*, Daily Edition, August 25, 1962, p. 16500.

tions. You've got fellows like Spessard Holland, Stennis, and Willis Robertson — why, they might be less willing to spend money than I am . . . you might have more partisanship, too, if you had a different chairman than Carl Hayden. He's a very nonpartisan guy. And so are all the subcommittee chairmen that I've served with.

Whatever its explanation, minimal partisanship is a norm and a characteristic of the Senate Committee just as it is for the House Committee. As such, it operates to promote and preserve the internal unity of the Committee.

In the Senate as in the House, the key decision-making units are its subcommittees, and the most influential subcommittee members are its chairmen. Each subcommittee operates autonomously — though not to the degree that exists in the House. In the first place, their hearings are public. In the second place, the membership of no less than seven subcommittees consists of over half the members of the full Committee. In the third place, subcommittee barriers are not so impermeable for non-subcommittee members. A Committee newcomer said,

> I raised hell with some things in another subcommittee for one or two years. The chairman said to me, "Why don't you come and participate in our hearings?" I said, "I can't come. I'm not a member of your subcommittee and I'm not allowed to come." He said, "We invite you to come. We invite you." So I went to their hearing and I got what I wanted.

Attendance at another subcommittee's markup session is more strongly proscribed. The legislative assistant of a freshman member recalled, "One time my Senator went into a subcommittee markup that wasn't his. They let him stay, but afterward Carl Hayden came over and said, 'I didn't want to embarrass you but we don't attend other peoples' subcommittees.' " It is inconceivable, however, that any Committee member would even contemplate such an action in the House, and it is certain that if he had, his violation of a sacred norm would not have been treated so gently. Still, a minimum of autonomy does exist; and it is in subcommittee markup sessions that most Senate appropriations decisions are effectively made.

The steps leading to a subcommittee markup do not differ much from one chamber to the other. The agencies send their justification books to the subcommittee — occasionally with a revised budget estimate. Subcommittee members and Committee staff people study them, and hearings are held by the subcommittee. The chairmen, the clerks, and sometimes the ranking minority member of the subcommittee then prepare an agenda together with suggestions for the markup session. Throughout, the subcommittee leans heavily on its clerk. The chairman is expected to dominate the proceedings; but he is also expected to achieve subcommittee consensus. As a means to this end, his relations with the ranking subcommittee member do not receive

549

the special emphasis which they do in the House Committee. Rather, the chairman is expected to reach a consensus by considering the desires of all members of his subcommittee. In the more oligarchically organized House Committee, chairman–ranking minority member agreement is usually sufficient to produce subcommittee agreement. Not so in the Senate, where the expectation is that every Senator should be given some influence over those decisions that interest him. It is in anticipation of this influence that Committee members insist upon keeping the subcommittees so large and insist on sitting on so many of them. Subcommittee decision-making has two features therefore. One is the leadership of the chairman; the other is the special influence which each subcommittee member has over the disposition of those projects which affect or interest him. A freshman member summed up. "Subcommittee chairman pretty much railroad the thing through — with this exception, that with things that are of particular interest to your region or to you as a matter of principle, you will have a chance to have your say."

The main sources of influence for the subcommittee chairman are the same in the Senate as in the House. He works harder, spends more time on the job, accumulates more experience, and possesses more subject matter information than other members. These resources are not reinforced in the Senate through the elaboration of an apprenticeship role for junior members. But they do not need to be in order for the subcommittee chairman to be the dominant figure. One long-time subcommittee chairman explained his behavior:

> We hold our hearings first, of course; and not all the members can attend the hearings. I attend all of them, where I'm the chairman of the subcommittee. I try to see that everybody on the subcommittee has a copy of the hearings before markup. You don't know what's going on unless you know the hearings. But then when you get to markup, some of them still haven't read them; so somebody has to take the leadership. But it's done on a completely nonpolitical, nonpartisan basis.

When asked about his influence, a second veteran subcommittee chairman answered,

> You want to know the truth on that? They [his subcommittee members] don't question a thing I do. They've got that much faith in me. I sit there in hearings, sometimes for two and a half months, and I know everything that's in the bill. When we have a markup, I say, "Here's what I've done," and it goes right through. Sometimes, they will ask me why did I leave this out or put that in and I'll have to be ready to justify it and explain why. Once in a while a person will want to add something that isn't in the bill, for political reasons. But to tell the truth, I can't think of a single thing since I have been chairman of the subcommittee that has been taken out

550

of the bill. A few have been added, but not one has been taken out after I've put it in. That's because I do the best job I can to balance up things . . . the members know that I do that and they have faith in me because I try to do the best job I can.

Nearly all senatorial comments about the lack of time refer to subcommittee work. Moreover, their time problem is accentuated by the fact that they must await House action. Thus the Senate Committee's peak work load strikes late in the session when all other legislation is likely to be piling up. "The bills don't get to us until late in the session and we always get into a log jam there. I've seen the Appropriations Committee sit day and night for several days trying to get through." By contrast, the legislative calendar is kinder to the House Committee. Given their lack of time, subcommittee members willingly follow the lead of the chairman on all matters save those of particular consequence to them. Four men, all subcommittee chairmen, put it this way. "A Senator is so busy. He sits on two or three committees and he has lots of subcommittees. I have five on Appropriations. If I know what's going on in those five, that's all I can do — so I have to take the other fellow's word on his work." "Unless a member is particularly interested in something, I'd say he's disposed to go along with the chairman." "The practice is and it has grown up by custom and by understanding that the subcommittee chairman's word carries the greatest weight. He's the best informed member on that particular matter." "On agricultural matters, Senator Russell and I are so close that I'm willing to take his figures almost blindly — except, of course, in areas where I have some special knowledge." Most Senators view the chairman's dominance as welcome relief from a decision-making burden that they otherwise could not manage. For this reason, if for no other, a subcommittee chairman's dominance is not so likely to be resented as it is in the House Committee.

Another important reason for acquiescence in the subcommittee chairman's leadership is simply that subcommittee members do not feel shut out of the process. No Senator can, of course, keep in touch with the flow of appropriations business through the House and through the Senate subcommittees. What each Senator usually does is to assign a member of his personal office staff to keep him apprised of all those appropriations items about which he already is or should be concerned. The staff man who works on appropriations matters is expected to tell the Senator when and where to jump into the process to make his case — especially at the critical markup time. Members of senatorial staffs are allowed to attend markup sessions, from which they can report back to their Senator, send out messages to get into the meeting at the appropriate juncture, or persuade some Senator who is present to intervene on his behalf.

551

A freshman Committee member explained his monitoring system:

> I have a member in my office riding on every appropriation bill to see that anything in there that is of interest to me is brought to my attention. Others do it too, because I have copied their system. Members of my staff learn from their opposite numbers on the staffs of others, and that's how I learned to ride herd on five appropriation bills. I also have a member of the Committee's staff doing the same thing. He knows what I'm interested in and he alerts me when something is coming up that I want to know about. With that many checks we don't miss much. On those things, I speak up in subcommittee.

From his angle, the legislative assistant of another new committee member said,

> I'll tell you frankly, I know a lot more about it than he does. His participation in subcommittee hearings is very scanty. He attends very few of them, so he has almost no personal experience with the presentation of the witnesses. I have to keep reminding him what subcommittees he's on. He doesn't know as much about it as he should, but he just doesn't have the time. . . . He relies on me to tell him through memos what's in the bill that affects our state. Then he usually goes to the Committee . . . he has a chance to put in a word there.

A similar description plus an explanation were offered by a Committee newcomer.

> Many Senators will not or cannot get to the subcommittee hearings. Those who are there can get what they want in the bill. Some can do it by not even being there. They come to subcommittee markup after never having been to the hearings and say, "I want more money for a hospital in my state. We need it." And the chairman will say, "O.K." and the Senator leaves. If I attend the hearings and attend the markup, I can get most anything I want. I know what's in the bill and I know what other Senators want from the bill. If they oppose me, I know what their pets are and I can discuss those. So they will give me what I want.

Subcommittee members observe the norm of reciprocity at markup time, to the end that each more fully satisfies the kind of expectations that led him to the Committee in the first place. The widespread acceptance of subcommittee trading keeps the behavior (and the image) of the subcommittee chairman relatively benign.

By all accounts, the markup sessions proceed much as they do in the House. They are informal; the chairman runs the meeting; the subcommittee clerk does a great deal of the preparatory work; and decisions are usually reached by consensus. If anything, Senate markup sessions are more informal than markups in the House — members from various Senators' office staffs being in attendance, the constant movement of Senators in and out of the room, and less than the full subcommittee in attendance. Three descriptions of markup proceedings, the first by a subcommittee chairman and the others by two ranking minority members, paint a composite picture with which all informants agreed:

> We have three figures before us: What the actual appropriation was last year, what the budget request was for this year, and what the House has recommended in its bill. Then we have a blank space for our recommended figure. Some member will have a proposal and that will start the discussion. The chairman has the right, though, to make the first proposal. Someone may say, "This outfit has not been functioning well." Or someone may say, "This program is really paying off and should be expanded." So we'll kick it back and forth, around and around; and people will propose that we cut five per cent or ten per cent, or raise. Then we'll finally agree on a figure. That's how a markup goes.

> It's very informal. On this, we work very closely with the staff. It's a professional, nonpartisan staff. Their relations with the agencies downtown are very amicable. They have the list of items prepared that we are going to act on. Usually, the subcommittee chairman and the ranking minority member meet before the markup and decide on a figure and present it to the subcommittee. We have some rousing, rattling debates, too. It's a give and take. We air our differences. We usually don't have a roll-call vote. Usually it's just a voice vote or a show of hands since there are only seven or nine people in the room.

> It's very informal. Maybe there are only three or four members there and sometimes even two. We'll sit around and I'll say, "I didn't think much of that guy. What do you think?" Or, "They don't seem to me like they're using that money well. Let's cut 'em off." And we will. Then we'll take it to full Committee and the subcommittee chairman will say the same thing. "We didn't think they were doing such a good job with the money, and we recommend such and such." Usually it goes right through.

Since markups proceed in executive session, it is not possible to be much more specific about what occurs. But it is certain that, in the Senate, as in the House, the fact that subcommittee decisions are in the first instance money decisions eases the internal process of bargaining and facilitates subcommittee agreement.

Decision-making in the full Appropriations Committee has all of the characteristics of the process in subcommittee. All Senators agree, furthermore, that the full Committee normally ratifies the decisions of the subcommittee. They approve, said one subcommittee chairman, "almost invariably. I can't think of but one or two times when they haven't. Once in a great while we have a split in the subcommittee and we refer it to the full Committee. But that has happened only once or twice in all the years that I have been subcommittee chairman." The full Committee meeting also gives

Senators not on the subcommittee an opportunity, if they had not pressed their case earlier with subcommittee members, to seek an amendment in which they are interested. The decision on its acceptance will rest in the hands of the subcommittee leaders. Minor adjustments will usually be allowed. One member concluded,

> The full Committee follows the subcommittee 98 per cent of the time. The only changes are to raise the appropriations when some Senators who are on the full Committee, but not on the subcommittee, ask to have projects put in. They are almost always granted. Sometimes they are not; but if the subcommittee chairman and ranking minority members of the subcommittee agree, it goes in just like that without any fuss.

An observer of one full Committee meeting on a defense appropriation bill described the sequence of events as follows. Subcommittee recommendations were assumed to be accepted unless amended, and the floor was open to amendments. A minority Senator rose to ask for inclusion of money for an item to be built in his state. He argued that it had been in the bill before, that it had lost in conference, that it would probably lose again in conference, but that it would help him to have it included in the bill. The subcommittee chairman accepted the amendment with the comment, "To say that it won't be accepted in conference is the understatement of the year." An ex officio member then made a formal speech (the only one in the meeting) asking for more money for an Army modernization plan. The subcommittee chairman said he had been thinking it over and could agree to one half of the proposal but not to the other half. The ex officio member accepted the subcommittee chairman's proffered figure. A third Senator then asked that certain language, already in the House bill, be put in the Senate bill also. The subcommittee chairman said he did not want the language in the bill, but he agreed not to oppose the House on the matter during conference proceedings. His assurances were gratefully acknowledged. A fourth Senator, one not on the subcommittee, rose asking for money for something that had always been in the bill but had been left out in this particular year. The subcommittee chairman agreed to put it in. The same Senator then asked for some very explicit language on the use of the money. The subcommittee chairman replied, "No. Five minutes ago I gave you a banana. Now you want the whole bunch." The Senator making the request sat down.

A fifth Senator then said that he would support all the increases voted on by the subcommittee and the full Committee if Committee members would agree then and there not to support any further increases on the floor. The subcommittee chairman replied that he did not think it necessary to extract any such pledge from the members. At this point, the full Committee Chairman intervened for the very first time. "Are all the amendments in and can we close the meeting?" An ex officio member then proposed that a sizable amount be appropriated to continue a program eliminated by the subcommittee. This proposal produced the only debate of the meeting, with the subcommittee chairman defending the action of the subcommittee and two or three other Senators, majority and minority, presenting their views. The ex officio member pressed for a formal vote. The full Committee Chairman inquired, "Are the Senators ready to vote?" A vote was taken and a subcommittee was upheld by a margin of 17 to 4. The ex officio member announced he was going to push for the increase on the floor. The meeting was adjourned. The observer commented, "That was it. They disposed of a $41 billion bill in an hour and a half."

The importance of the subcommittee recommendations and the influence of the subcommittee chairman are obvious in this synopsis. So, too, is the willingness to help individual Senators with matters of special interest to them. Anticipation of upcoming floor action and of the conference may be a bit more acute at this point than it is at prior stages. There was, for instance, the attempt to get agreement to stick together on the floor. With regard to the ex officio member's statement that he was going to press for a floor amendment, a very senior Committee member commented the next day:

> We have an understanding in the Committee that the members will support the Committee — unless a member says in advance that he's opposed to something. Just yesterday, two members said they didn't think we were spending enough for defense, and they were going to speak on the floor. That's perfectly all right. That's legitimate — just so as they tell you in advance. It's not kosher just to get up and speak out. You can't be a lone wolf. You just can't do it that way.

The Committee has, it seems, a norm of unity. But it does not seem to be as self-consciously discussed as it is in the House group. The subcommittee chairman, in the instance described, preferred not to make the kind of formal statement or exhortation that is frequently made in the House Committee. The decision-making process in the Senate is itself the major unifying influence operative on the Committee. One of the Committee's junior members commented,

> They talk about unity, but I don't pay any attention to it. I just say, "I'm going to oppose this on the floor." And I do. Usually, it's the people who are in favor of something who talk about binding ourselves. And those who are against it do as they please. Why should anyone bind himself to anything? That's ridiculous.

To the degree that all Senators are satisfied, they will support the Committee. To the degree they remain disgruntled, a pledge of unity is not likely to stop them from speaking out on the floor.

The influence of the ex officio subcommittee members on decision-making varies depending on the interest and the expertise of the Senators involved. On the whole, they are not as influential as regular Committee members. "They have the same rights and the same vote as any other member," said one subcommittee chairman. "But the practice is that they don't speak as much." Another subcommittee chairman explained:

> I don't want to discredit any of those people, but their opinions don't change the result very much. We're a lot more apt to listen to the regular members of the Committee and take their advice. . . . If they're also members of the legislative committee, it gives them a little extra advantage over the rest. I'm on the Armed Services Committee and Appropriations. On defense matters we pay special attention to those members of Appropriations who are also on the legislative committee involved. . . . One of the Senators said to me just the other day about an ex officio member, "Why, hell, he only has this one bill to worry about. But we have the responsibility for all the appropriation bills." You see, he was discounting that fellow's opinion. We have the collective responsibility for all appropriation bills, so we rely mostly on our regular members.

"But," speaking of the minority ex officio member on his particular subcommittee, this Senator continued, "I always ask ———— to come over here and sit in even though he's ex officio. He's got a fine mind on these things."

A Republican member made the same generalization but with an exception:

> They don't come around very much. One exception may be Bob Kerr, chairman of the legislative committee on public works. He's very conscientious, and sits through a lot of the testimony on appropriations. But most of them don't do much. Maybe they don't have time, or maybe they feel funny edging their way into the Appropriations Committee. In theory, it's a good idea. But in practice, I'd say the ex officio idea hasn't worked.

Another subcommittee chairman, however, said that his ex officio member wielded considerable influence in subcommittee decision-making:

> He's Chairman of the ———— Committee. He attends all our subcommittee hearings, markups, and full Committee meetings. He's very much interested and he works to see that he gets what he wants. Of course, the chairman and the ranking minority member of every committee are part of the Appropriations Committee for that particular subject. So when they want something, they work with the members of their legislative committee and they all work with the Appropriations Committee.

Finally, an Appropriations Committee member recalled the extent to which he as a member of the legislative committee and the chairman of that committee ex officio were involved in making all the decisions on a key program:

We wanted to restore some money the House had cut out of the program. He came over to the subcommittee markup, and I was there. The chairman of the subcommittee said, "I don't know nuthin about nuthin on this, so why don't you two boys decide." We did, and were able to get the money restored. We understood the program and the others didn't.

The access of the ex officio member is more consequential than his actual influence on the Appropriations Committee.

The 30 members of the Committee's professional staff play the same role in their subsystem as House staff members do in theirs. And, while measures of relative influence are not available, it seems likely that Senate "clerks" are at least as influential as those attached to the House group. That is to say, they are very influential. "The Senators like to call us clerks. We 'clerk' the bill as they say. It's not a very exalted title, but it's a very important position," said one. It is important because there is not a stage in the formal process when the clerk is not present — in observing agency activity, in the hearings, in subcommittee markup, writing the report, in full Committee, on the floor, and in conference. "I do everything," exclaimed one staff member in reference to the scope of his activity. The clerk is important, too, because he works especially closely with the chairman of the subcommittee to which he is attached. "You get so you say 'I' and 'we' as if you were the Senator," said another staff member. "You live their lives with them after a while." Proximity to the key decision-maker obviously gives the clerk an opportunity to be more than his title implies.

There is no need to spell out the staff member's role in detail. It differs little from the staff member role described in Chapter Four. Perhaps the only variation involves the wider range of contacts which the Senate clerks appear to maintain within and outside of the Committee. A staff member described his job:

> I work for the United States Senate. I see the subcommittee chairman more during the hearings and do more chores for him on the side. But I hear from all members of the subcommittee and from other Senators too. They call me about the same things every year, the same projects. The members of the Appropriations staff get more calls from other Senators than the staff of any other committee.

Another staff member, viewing the decision-making from his perspective, described it thus:

> I have Senators call me up and ask me questions all the time . . . [or] they may ask me to drop by their office and give them the facts. So I do . . . it's not like the House. Over there they keep the process locked up tight. Nobody knows what they are doing while they're running the show.

557

These descriptions illustrate another consequence which flows from the relatively low degree of Committee autonomy. Since the Appropriations Committee is linked to other decision-making structures of the chamber at the level of its members, it is not surprising that similar linkages are maintained by the staff. And the converse holds true in the House. Given the greater autonomy of the Appropriations Committee there, its staff members have less interaction with other decision-makers in the chamber.

It is tempting to draw the conclusion that from their wide range of communications Senate staff members are more influential than their House counterparts. The fact that Senate Committee members have less time to devote to appropriations matters would tend to reinforce such a conclusion. That is, the dependence of Senators on a staff member's information would seem to be especially great. But the relatively easy access which Senators on and off the Committee have to its decision-making structure tends to reduce the weight of staff member influence in the overall picture. These two characteristics of Senate Committee decision-making produce opposite consequences for the staff member. One seems to point to greater influence for him than for his House counterpart; but the other seems to point to less. A closer analysis than has been undertaken here will have to be made before conclusions about relative influence can be drawn.

The fact that the staff man's contacts are wide-ranging should not be allowed to obscure the fact that he is most closely attached to the subcommittee chairman. One minority member described his somewhat attenuated relationships to the subcommittee clerk in the hearings:

> When the Secretary of Agriculture begins his testimony, that's the first inkling I have of what he's going to say. I have no advance notice whatsoever. So, I have to play it by ear. I'm cold. I try to pick up what I can out of the hearings and ask questions. But you're at a great disadvantage. Now, you ask, "Doesn't the clerk know what's coming? Has he read the House testimony and the House report?" Yes he has. He has more information than anyone else. And he may have spotted something and written out some questions. But he hands them to the chairman and works through him. He doesn't pay a damn bit of attention to me. I'm on my own. Oh, if I call him over and ask, he's very cooperative and will tell me all he knows. But ordinarily he works through the chairman.

It was in recognition of this de facto association that the Committee minority asked for and received money to hire three minority staff members. One of them explained why he was hired:

> They felt they were so outnumbered that they wanted to have somebody around of their own stripe to advise them. Some of the subcommittee clerks work very closely with the subcommittee chairmen and some are beholden to them so to speak. They aren't consciously partisan but they tend to take

on the coloration of the subcommittee chairman. After all, the Democrats have been around for so long. If the minority wants an investigation made without tipping their hand to the Committee clerk, I'll get that information up.

Partisanship is low on the Committee, and the subcommittee clerks do work well with ranking minority members. But when partisanship does enter in, the minority has some staff assistants to work exclusively for them.

For the Senate as well as for the House the most important generalization one can make regarding staff member influence is that it depends primarily on the staff member's relationship with the subcommittee chairman — the man, that is, with whom he works most closely and who is himself (usually) the most influential Senator in a given subject matter area. The possibilities of the relationship are pretty well bracketed by this pair of comments by staff members:

> Here's the way I look at my responsibilities and I think it's the way [the subcommittee chairman] looks at them, too. He wants the facts. He's got the opinions and he wants the facts. When I first came here, I caught myself saying, "I think," and, "My opinion is," and I thought I saw his eyebrows twitch a little. I don't do that now. I used to sit in Committee markup and I had to keep preaching to myself, "Sit on your hands. You don't vote." They'd be talking and I'd want to say, "Don't go that way." You get a proprietary interest in a bill. But I say to myself now, "When that report goes out it says Senator ———— for the Appropriations Committee reports the following." It's his bill. It's not like the downtown system where a staff member passes a recommendation to his superior. Oh, there are times when I can see that I influence him a little bit, but not as much as in an administrative agency. He wants the facts.

> You don't expect me to tell you the clerks put things in the bill, do you? We do, but you can't say it. We just do what the Senators tell us to do. Of course a clerk can put things in a bill. I put language in the bill that I don't think anybody else knows is there except myself and the other clerk. But you can only do that in places where the Senator isn't interested. The things he's interested in I just take orders. If he's for it, I'm for it; if he's against it, I'm against it. That's the way you work. In places where he doesn't care one way or another, I'll say to him, "We ought to do this," or, "We ought to do that," and he'll let it go in. I've taken a special interest in a few things. Last year on this ———— item, we increased it two and a half million. I kept telling him to do it and finally he said, "Who wants this put in there?" I said, "I do." I've taken an interest in it and he has confidence in me. I've worked with him for many years and he knows I'm not going to do anything wrong or anything that will hurt him.

The first man has described a situation of minimal staff influence; the second man has described one of maximum influence. In both cases, the crucial factors are the desires and the confidence of subcommittee chairmen. In both cases, too, the staff member will have some effect, be it large or small, on the Committee's decisions.

THE COMMITTEE AS SYSTEM —
STRUCTURE FOR INTEGRATION

The internal integration of the Senate Appropriations Committee is not a problem for its members. They do not talk about it. They do not have any readily identifiable structure for maintaining or promoting it. Of course, the various elements of the Committee's decision-making structure just described are held in an harmonious relationship to one another. Conflict among them is minimized, and the internal disruption of the Committee does not threaten its survival. The Committee, that is to say, is an integrated system. But the Committee's integration does not appear to be the result of norms voiced within the Committee by Committee members with any special reference to Committee members. Nor does the Committee's integration appear to be maintained by internal processes that involve only Committee personnel. Senators are expected to behave like Senators on the Committee. And the socialization and sanctioning processes which help keep Committee member behavior in conformity with such norms are Senate-wide processes. In all of these respects, the Senate Committee stands in the sharpest contrast to the House Committee.

Students of political systems have long made the point that the differentiation of a system logically precedes its integration. This relationship holds on two levels. In the first place, since the House Committee is more clearly differentiated from its chamber than the Senate Committee is from its chamber, one would expect the House Committee to have the greater need to provide for internal integration. Only thus can it translate its autonomy into influence. The Senate Committee, on the other hand, since it is less autonomous and more closely attached to the parent chamber, has less need for a separate structure for its internal integration. Since the differentiation between them is not great, that structure which serves to hold the Senate together can serve the Committee just about as well. That is to say, the Senate norms by which the Committee is held in a harmonious relationship with the Senate as a whole will be applied in the same way inside the Committee. These norms which prescribe the interlocking of many structures of influence together with bargaining and reciprocity among them have already been discussed. They apply in the same way to the relationship of subcommittees inside the Committee as they do to Committee-Senate relationships externally.

In the second place, to the degree that the Committee is not differentiated from the Senate, it is less likely to develop a differentiated structure internally. And to the degree that roles are not differentiated internally, no structure of integration will be required. Such appears to be the case in the Senate Committee — where roles such as subcommittee member, apprentice, ranking minority member are not as clearly differentiated as they are in the House. And, in every case, a potential source of disruption is minimized from the outset. The need for integration is correspondingly less.

The Senate Appropriations Committee, then, does not appear to have developed a discrete, elaborate, and, hence, a describable structure for integration. With more intensive interviewing, one could doubtless tease the outlines of such a structure from the responses of Committee members. In this sense, one difficulty in identifying the integrative structure lies in the fuzziness with which some Committee roles were adumbrated. Still, data on integration do not appear near the surface of any available materials, whereas data on decision-making clearly do. Hence one wonders whether any description of the Committee's structure for integration would be worth the extra effort involved in extracting it. In any case, no such effort has been expended for the purposes of this book. The dearth of evidence has been taken to reflect a minimum of structure. And the minimum of structure has been assumed to be another important consequence of the minimal structural differentiation existing between the Committee and "the Senate" and within the Committee itself.

CONCLUSION

As elements of the same national legislature, the Senate Committee on Appropriations and the House Committee on Appropriations perform similar decision-making tasks and follow similar rules of procedure. But they are different. Some of their differences flow from the divergent characteristics of the Senate and the House of Representatives. Others flow from the special characteristics of the appropriations process itself. Among the important differences are the following.

The Senate Committee's relationship to its parent chamber is characterized, at the level of expectations and behavior, by less structural differentiation and less conflict than the House Committee–House relationship. Maintenance expectations prescribe a Senate Committee which is formally linked, through a network of interlocking memberships, with the substantive committees and the party leaders of the Senate. And, in terms of behavior, the pattern of appropriations communication flows outward to the various elements of the Senate — to individual Senators, their staff assistants, substantive committee personnel, and party organs — as much as it does inward to fellow Committee members. The Senate Committee is not viewed as a "star chamber" or as a "closed corporation." Criticism exists, but it is concentrated among a relatively few Senators. Sanctions are exercised, but they are as likely to be exercised by the Senate and the Senate Committee *jointly* against a mutual antagonist, the House Committee on Appropriations, as they are by the Senate against the Senate Committee. The Senate Committee on Appropriations is expected to, and usually does, act *as the Senate*. It is, therefore, minimally troubled with problems of adaptation to the parent chamber.

The personal expectations and satisfactions of Senate Committee members emphasize the desire for individual influence. They do not involve — as they do in the case of House Committee members — the desire for special access to information, for a special group identity, or for a distinctive style of work. Senators view the decision-making processes of their chamber as processes in which a large number of Senators participate as individuals and not as parts of collectivities. Membership on the money-granting committee obviously increases one's individual influence. But it is thought neither necessary nor appropriate — as it is in the House — to develop the distinctiveness and the autonomy of the Committee as a collectivity in order to satisfy one's personal expectations. If Committee members have a recognizable style, it is one produced by an overriding lack of time. But this is a senatorial style which only serves further to identify the Committee with the Senate. The substance of the individual Committee member expectations, therefore, contributes to the minimum of structural differentiation between Committee and Senate.

The Senate Committee prescribes for itself the tasks of an appellate court, which makes decisions on the basis of agency appeals for the restoration of the incremental reductions made by the House Committee. This goal expectation — which contrasts with the House Committee's expectation of budget reduction — is primarily a result of the fixed appropriations sequence, in which the Senate invariably acts after the House decisions have been made. And, since the House usually acts to reduce budgets, the Senate will inevitably be subjected to one-sided and intensified appeals for increases. By prescribing an appeals court task for itself, the Senate Committee makes it very likely that it will, in fact, grant increases. In this light, the Committee's appeals court function is further sustained by two other factors. The Senate's goal expectations are weighted more in favor of increases than decreases, and the personal expectations of the Committee's members involve mostly a desire to gain influence so as to secure increases in appropriations. In addition, the Senate Committee lacks the time to investigate agency budgets de novo.

The Senate Committee's decision-making structure is characterized by a more widespread distribution of influence than that of the House Committee. The subcommittees remain as the key decision-making units, and their chairmen are the most influential decision-makers. But, as compared to the House group, the Senate Committee is smaller, its subcommittees are much larger, each Committee member serves on a greater number of subcommittees, and apprenticeship norms do not keep any member from influencing Committee action at any point on matters of special concern to him. Furthermore, Committee members serve on several if not all the subcommittees of their choice. The Chairman possesses and exercises fewer sanctions than his House counterpart. The Committee is at once less hierarchical and less oligarchical than the House group. This kind of internal decision-making structure in which a large percentage of individual members bargain to most decisions reflects the decision-making structure of the Senate itself. It is also precisely the kind of decision-making structure through which Committee members can most easily pursue their personal desires for individual influence. And, finally, by giving individuals who want increased appropriations access to all decision-making units and special access to the subcommittees of their choice, the internal structure is well adapted to the performance of its appellate court–budget increasing tasks.

Given the fact that structural differentiation is slight and given the fact that the internal Committee decision-making structure allows every member a great deal of influence, the need for an elaborate structure for internal integration is small. And no readily visible one exists. The Committee does, interestingly, observe minimal partisanship — a condition which members attribute to the easily compromised dollars and cents character of their decisions. In view of the fact that the Senate Committee makes no institutionalized effort at minimizing internal conflict, the similarity of the two appropriations committees in terms of low partisanship is striking. It suggests that the dollars and cents subject matter of appropriations may be the single most important factor in facilitating the internal integration of the House Committee. In any case, the Senate Committee does not need to guard its internal unity in order to do battle with the parent chamber; it does not need to teach its members distinctive norms; and it does not need internal control mechanisms to maintain a highly differentiated role structure inside the Committee. Integration may be a problem for the Senate as a whole, but it is not a special problem for the Committee.

The Senate Committee
II: *Executive Agencies, Committee*
Decisions, and Senate Floor Action

THE SENATE COMMITTEE AND
EXECUTIVE AGENCIES

Agency Expectations, Images, and Behavior

Executive agency officials perceive that the similarities in their relations with House and Senate Committees far outweigh the differences. The formal processes, the informal contacts, the incrementalism of substantive requests, the tribulations of the hearings, the kinds of factors influencing decisions — all these relationships are seen as being similar from chamber to chamber. There is no need to repeat the discussion of Chapter Six. The differences as viewed from the agency perspective are of interest to us here, and these can be dealt with briefly.

In the first place, experience has led most agencies to view the Senate Committee as an appeals court. Typically, they prepare a "reclama" for presentation to the Committee — an appeal to the Senate for the restoration of reductions made in the House Committee and carried on the House floor. For each item of the reclama, the agency explains what adverse effects the House cut will have on agency programs if it is allowed to stand. The Secretary of Commerce and the Secretary of State opened two of their regular appearances before the Senate Committee as follows:

> On the occasion of my appearance before the House Subcommittee on Appropriations, I outlined the major program considerations which form the basis for the budget of the organizational units of the Department.

Since that statement has been made available to the Committee, I will confine my remarks to and summarize the effects of the reductions made by the House.[1]

I come here to appeal with respect to $29,228,000 of the $47,331,000 which the House of Representatives would cut from the $227,714,000 appropriation that the President requested to enable the State Department to conduct our foreign relations during the coming year.[2]

The agency decides whether it wishes to put in a reclama for all or some or none of the House reduction. This may be a strategic decision of some importance. Once the agency has made that decision, however, it believes that its dialogue with the Committee will center on the segments being appealed. The agencies perceive Senate Committee concerns as incremental ones with the reclama specifying the outer limits of the increments.

Sometimes hearings before the Senate Committee will take place before the House has acted. Such is typically the case with agencies whose appropriations normally reach the House floor at the end of the fiscal year (or during the next one). Under such circumstances the Senate Committee proceeds with its hearings and the agency cannot present a reclama during the hearings. In such cases the reclama is made by written and oral communication as soon as the House decision is known. In 1956, for example, the Subcommittee on Agriculture opened its hearings prior to the passage of the House bill. The Department's Budget Officer set the tone for the hearings by saying, "Since we do not have a House bill, I do not have in mind any extended budgetary statements. After the House bill is available, we will, of course, submit additional statistics and comments on the House action."[3] After the passage of the House bill and after the Committee hearings were over, the Secretary of Agriculture wrote a letter to the subcommittee chairman. It began, "Pursuant to your informal request, we are sending you separately, amendments and notes in reference to the House Committee bill on Agricultural appropriations. The House Committee made a number of changes from the budget estimates which we recommend be restored."[4] There followed a reclama which, when appended to the hearings, consumed 37 pages of small type. The point is that when the schedule precludes a formal appeal in the hearings, the agencies make their appeal in other ways.

[1] Senate Committee on Appropriations, *Hearings on Department of Commerce Appropriations for 1960*, 86th Congress, 1st Session (Washington: U.S. Government Printing Office, 1959), p. 89.

[2] Senate Committee on Appropriations, *Hearings on State Department Appropriations for 1958*, 85th Congress, 1st Session (Washington: U.S. Government Printing Office, 1957), p. 44.

[3] Senate Committee on Appropriations, *Hearings on Agriculture Department Appropriations for 1957*, 84th Congress, 2nd Session (Washington: U.S. Government Printing Office, 1956), p. 1.

[4] *Ibid.*, p. 868. The reclama is on pp. 868–905.

But they always make such an appeal, and the Senate Appropriations Committee always has it in hand during its markup deliberations.

Should the agency have no losses to recoup or should it be content with House action there may be little or no reason to go before the Senate at all — formally in the hearings or informally. One rather affluent bureau chief noted that he rarely appeared before the Senate:

> The other night Edgar Hoover had a liaison party for all the enforcement agencies over at the Mayflower. I was talking to the clerk of the House Committee and the Senate clerk came over. He said, "We don't see much of you over on our side. We just give you whatever the House tells us."

A second agency head remarked that he goes before the Senate Committee only because the subcommittee involved wishes to preserve the fiction that it is considering every agency budget de novo. "It's strictly pro forma. It's — well I hate to use the term — it's ridiculous. They might just as well not have us come up. Last year I think I had forty-five seconds." These agencies are probably not typical, but they do help to illustrate the general proposition that, as the agencies see it, the Senate Committee concentrates its attention on a smaller segment of the budget estimates than does the House Committee.

To the degree that a Senate subcommittee operates as an appeals court — and of course sometimes it may not — its decisions will tend to increase agency appropriations. Agency officials are also aware that, by virtue of the appropriations sequence, they can generate more concentrated pressure on the Senate Committee than on the House group. For both reasons, agency officials see the Senate group as more liberal and less exercised about budget-cutting than the House group. But agency officials explain Senate liberality as an artifact of the appeals court function and the appropriations sequence. They do not express the view that Senate Committee increases spring from some intrinsic sympathy which Senators in general have for agencies in general. Moreover, despite the fact that the Senate Committee usually helps the agencies monetarily, considerable dissatisfaction with the relationship persists.

The single most widely held image of the Senate Committee is that it is less thorough and less interested in examining agency activity than is the House Committee. The contrast is expressed most commonly in regard to the hearings, which, after all, constitute the major confrontation of agency and Committee. Two departmental budget officers summed up their image this way:

> The hearings are pretty cursory. The Senators just don't have the time to devote to it. They serve on several subcommittees and other committees too. Oftentimes just one Senator will be there. Oh, one or two may come in and leave. They drift in and out, ask questions to show they were there,

and then go on to another subcommittee. You don't get the detailed informal discussion that you do sitting around the table in the House.

They aren't so concerned about doing their homework in reading the estimates as the House members. Everybody knows they haven't opened a book. Usually there's only one — or maybe two men — there; and others are walking in and out. One man will come in to ask a question that he's interested in, and it may not have anything to do with your estimates. But he's interested in it, and you'll talk about it and then he'll get up and go. That doesn't show in the record, but once you've got his answer in the record he leaves. Then maybe another one will come in and ask you the same question about his particular district. That's the way it goes.

These descriptions capture, from the agency perspective, something of the ways in which individual Senators pursue their special interests during subcommittee decision-making. Executive officials are virtually unanimous in describing Senate Committee hearings as being less well attended, less detailed, less intensive, less focused, and shorter than hearings before the House Committee.

Some agency officials emphasize, too, differences in the atmosphere of the hearings that make for less satisfactory and less thorough exchanges with the Senate than with the House group. In the first place, the public nature of Senate hearings is felt to have an inhibiting effect. Said one department budget officer,

I think making the Senate hearings public was a great mistake. A lot of things that they used to take up in the hearings they don't anymore. If there's a controversy, they won't take up the matter in hearings — they'll take it up after the hearings informally. If they come to something they want information on, they hesitate to bring it out in public so they'll call a private meeting some other time and we'll go around.

In the second place, Senate hearings are felt to be excessively formal and not conducive to helpful discussion. A bureau chief commented,

The House is much more informal. You sit around a small table in a small room and have a man-to-man discussion. But the Senate is the most exclusive club in the world. It's a little like walking into the Union League Club. The Senators sit up on a raised platform and talk down to you. You sit there and talk up to them. It's the difference between talking with your brother and your father.

And a department budget officer agreed:

[The House subcommittee chairman] puts everyone at ease and you talk back and forth. I don't mean that [the Senate subcommittee chairman] is anything but courteous and sympathetic. But in the Senate, you're sitting far away from them and you need a microphone to make yourself heard. People are coming in and out behind you and in front of you.

567

Agency officials complain at length about their inability to discuss their program before the House Committee. But much less can they discuss program on the other side of the Capitol.

The Senate Committee can be as helpful or as harmful to an executive agency as the House Committee, and officials know it. Still, they consider their relationship with the House Committee as the more consequential. House members are seen as devoting themselves single-mindedly to their appropriations tasks. And House members are seen as setting the basic framework of decision. The House Committee is the more likely to hurt them by its actions than is the Senate Committee. From the agency perspective, the House Committee remains *the* Appropriations Committee. The elements of that relationship as they have been described in Chapter Six are present in agency relations with both committees. But the relationship with the House is felt to be more important, more intimate, and even, one suspects, more satisfying than that with the Senate.

Committee Expectations, Images, and Behavior

Senatorial perceptions of the executive agencies come to a focus within the context of the hearings. And Senators put the hearings to the same uses as do House members. They make a public record and sample for information that will help in evaluating agency requests. The major difference is simply that they concentrate on a narrower segment of the agency budget. One subcommittee chairman set the frame of reference for his colleagues on the State Department Subcommittee this way:

> So that members of the Committee may get this picture clearly, the House cut out $10,725,000 of the approximately $228,000,000. The Department is asking for restoration of $9,205,000 of that cut; so they are asking for approximately nine and a quarter million dollars out of the ten and three-quarters million that were cut. They are here on appeal on the nine and one-quarter million. It may be that on review we will want to go over some of the action by the House, but the primary thing we are interested in is whether or not they can justify this $10,725,000 that the House cut out.[5]

Committee members will question agency witnesses within this framework.

The subcommittee chairman may say, typically, "We will insert your prepared statement in the record and you may explain to us briefly the details of this item and explain to us the effects of the House cut if sustained and the Bureau's reason for wanting the reduction restored."[6] And other

[5] Senate Committee on Appropriations, *Hearings on State Department Appropriations for 1960*, 86th Congress, 1st Session (Washington: U.S. Government Printing Office, 1959), p. 101.

[6] Senate Committee on Appropriations, *Hearings on Department of Health, Education, and Welfare Appropriations for 1956*, 84th Congress, 1st Session (Washington: U.S. Government Printing Office, 1955), p. 87.

Committee members will inquire, "What programs will have to be curtailed if the House reduction is allowed to stand?" As in the House, the approach in incremental. The difference is that the increment is smaller. Except as the random curiosity or interest of some Senator dictates, the Senate Committee does not cast its net the length and breadth of agency activity.

Whenever the House has completed action and agency requests for restoration are in hand, the Committee staff prepares a chart which lists, for each budget item, last year's appropriation, this year's budget request, House action, and the amount being appealed. Where the agency does not appeal a House cut, Committee members will take no further notice of it. The following exchange took place when the Commerce Department appealed only six out of many House cuts in 1957:

> SUBCOMMITTEE CHAIRMAN: Some of us are lawyers and we are accustomed to this philosophy, that when a party in court has an adverse decision going against him and does not appeal, that indicates to our mind that the party is accepting the decision gracefully and thinks that there is not any substantial reason for appealing . . . in other words we are not going to appeal for you.
> SECRETARY OF COMMERCE: Well I think you have drawn a correct deduction, Senator, but at the same time I assume you want the bureau heads to talk about their budgets as they came up in the first instance.
> SUBCOMMITTEE CHAIRMAN: We would be very happy to hear them.
> SECRETARY OF COMMERCE: You might conceivably gain a different opinion than perhaps they in the House did on various items.
> SUBCOMMITTEE CHAIRMAN: That is conceivable, but right now we are trying to get the opinion of the head of the Department and I want to make it very clear that if the head of the Department does not appeal in the other instances than the six, many of us, including this chairman of the subcommittee, will conclude that the cuts in all those other instances are acceptable, at least can be lived under, and do not require any complaint or appeal by the head of the Department.[7]

Whenever final House action remains pending, agency witnesses will be assured of another day in court:

> I think it is apparent to everyone present that we are beginning these hearings somewhat earlier than in the past . . . I want to make it clear that the Department of the Interior and the other agencies will be given an opportunity to comment on the bill as it passes the House of Representatives.[8]

The Senators' main concern is to create the opportunity for all agencies to register such appeals as they may choose. Senators do not operate as prose-

[7] Senate Committee on Appropriations, *Hearings on Department of Commerce Appropriations for 1958*, 85th Congress, 1st Session (Washington: U.S. Government Printing Office, 1957), pp. 10–11.

[8] Senate Committee on Appropriations, *Hearings on Department of Interior Appropriations for 1961*, 86th Congress, 2nd Session (Washington: U.S. Government Printing Office, 1960), p. 5.

cutors or with the same degree of suspicion that characterizes House Committee members.

One other slight variation which the Senate Committee displays in the use of hearings involves its preparation for the conference encounter with the House. At the point in the sequence when the Senate hearings are held, the House decisions may be a known quantity. In such cases, Senators can weigh alternative decisions in the light of the conference situation each would produce. And, in the hearings, they may look for the kind of information that will enable them to hold any given decision against the House. As one subcommittee chairman put it to an agency head,

> I have to go to the Senate and then I have to go to the conference. I may be a better advocate before [the House subcommittee chairman] and his group than you have been. You have come through that wringer over there, but I have to go back and face him and I have to sell him whatever I do and bring him into agreement with me. I am not a technical person and I am not well informed on this. I want a little indoctrination myself . . . last year, when I added $5 million more onto their allowance, I had a battle; and I still have in the conference room a little hide, hair, and blood that they took off of me.[9]

The task of the agency official is to supply information and reasoning that will strengthen the position of the Senate conferees.

Senators view their performance in the hearings just about the way agency officials do. They admit that their attendance at hearings and their knowledge of the agencies is not praiseworthy, but they plead, as always, the lack of time. Said one,

> Some morning, I'll have five appropriations subcommittee hearings to attend. What do you do then? Do you go to one hearing and stay all the way through? Or do you drop in to each one for half an hour to get the general idea? Or do you just attend the ones where you are ranking minority member so that you can follow one subcommittee through to the end and get to know all about it? I've watched the senior members to see how they handle it and there's just no pattern. One thing that some of them do is to attend only those meetings where something of special interest to their state is up. But somehow or other, it seems to me that my responsibility is greater than that. Time is the problem I've never solved.

From his vantage point, a subcommittee clerk concurred:

> Sometimes we're holding subcommittee hearings in two adjacent rooms and its like a floating crap game. A Senator will tell the clerk to let him know when a certain item comes up in the next room and the clerks will be giving them messages so they can float.

[9] Senate Committee on Appropriations, *Hearings on U.S. Information Agency Appropriations for 1958*, 85th Congress, 1st Session (Washington: U.S. Government Printing Office, 1957), p. 1147.

Senators get themselves on the record and then move on to other tasks, leaving the hearing in the charge of the subcommittee chairman, the subcommittee clerk, and, perhaps, the ranking minority subcommittee member.

These subcommittee leaders attend regularly. A subcommittee chairman explained that his attendance at hearings was the key to his influence:

> I'm always there. I have to be there. But sometimes there aren't too many others. . . . The others will follow the chairman. In addition to the prestige he gets by virtue of his position of subcommittee chairman, he has the additional advantage of having heard the testimony. Some fellow will get up and say, "I think they ought to be cut or raised so much." And if you've heard the testimony you can say, "That's not so. In the testimony, they showed thus and so."

In some cases, the subcommittee clerk helps to carry the burden. A ranking minority Committee member pointed up the importance of the clerk as the right-hand man of a subcommittee chairman who wants help:

> The chairmen of these subcommittees are powerful — very powerful. And that's one reason — they have the clerks working for them. Haven't you ever wondered why the chairman asks most of the questions at these hearings? They've got the clerks' questions, that's why. Old ———, God bless his soul, sits there and just reads off the clerk's questions. He asks seventy-five per cent of the questions, and most of them he doesn't care about but he gets them in the record. People who read the hearings probably say, "Doesn't he know a lot." Well, he does. He's had the experience or he wouldn't be subcommittee chairman. But he isn't that much smarter than all the rest of us. It's the clerks, too. You've got to understand about the clerks.

The Senators' picture of the hearings does not differ from that of the agencies. From both viewpoints, the subcommittee chairman (with or without the clerk) dominates the proceedings. Agency activity, however, is not scrutinized in the Senate as thoroughly as it is in the House.

Though one cannot compare their relative frequency or importance, informal communications between Senate Committee member and agency officials proceed along lines identical to those on the House side. Through inspection trips, telephone calls, and visitations on and off Capitol Hill, informal contacts compensate for the inadequacies of the public hearings and supply the most important kinds of information. Lest we should think that, somehow, the formality and remoteness of the Senators in the hearing room reflect a formality and remoteness outside the hearing room, the following comments of a subcommittee chairman and a ranking minority member are apposite:

> [My contact is] not so much with the agencies themselves but with the control group in the department — the Budget Director, the Assistant

571

Secretary for Administration, and the Secretary. When they run into some particular problem in their program, they come over here — even the Secretary himself comes over. I have frequent conferences with him during the year — I say frequent, maybe a half dozen or more if there is particularly rough going.

[The agencies] come in here and lobby about their program. That's what you'd call it — lobbying. We may call them in and ask them for information. It's a help to us and we want their opinion. We may say to them, "We're trying to arrive at a figure for the Forest Service. We think that Budget cut you down too much. What did you ask Budget for? Can you use some more money? And if so, how much?" They're under obligation to defend the budget, but they're also under obligation to answer our questions. So they may say, "Well, yes, we asked the Budget Bureau for $8 million and they only gave us $4 million. And we think we need all $8 million." That's a help to us. We don't want to go off into the ozone somewhere picking a figure . . . we get to know them pretty well and whether they need the money or not. After all, they have to come back here and deal with us every year. Sometimes we say to them informally that we'd like to have things done in a certain way. Maybe a letter from the Chairman will tell them that we want them to put more money into the field offices and less into the Washington offices. That doesn't have the force of law, but they've got to come back and face us next year. If they misrepresent their case or don't make some effort to comply, they'll get hurt.

Communication of this sort proceeds, too, through Committee clerks, through the personal staffs of Committee members, and through experienced liaison specialists in the departments. Of particular importance will be the informal communication of an agency reclama that has not been discussed in the hearings. A web of informal contacts, on all matters, is vital to the maintenance of stable relationships between the Committee and the executive agencies.

SENATE COMMITTEE DECISIONS

Overall Appropriations Patterns and Determinants

We have examined some of the expectations, perceptions, and attitudes concerning Senate Committee behavior, and the question now arises: How in fact does the Committee behave? Does the Committee's behavior meet the expectations of Senators, of Senate Committee members, and of agency officials? Do the kinds of decisions made by the Committee provide evidence that the perceptions which others have of the Committee are accurate? Do patterns of Committee decisions emerge which help to explain further the Senate Committee's contribution to the total appropriations process? These questions are not easily or thoroughly answered with dollars and cents decision data. All the limitations ascribed to these data in Chapter Eight apply here as well. Still, dollars and cents decisions do constitute a large and significant portion of the Senate Committee's output. By analyzing them we can enrich and solidify our knowledge about the Committee and the appropriations process.

Senate Committee decisions can be placed in broadest perspective by the application of the same measuring devices as used in Chapter Eight. Table 11.1 relates Committee action to the budget estimates as presented to the Committee by the agencies.[10] Table 11.2 categorizes Committee decisions as they relate to the final appropriation granted to the agency in the previous year's bill. The distributions of comparable House Committee decisions are placed in parentheses to facilitate comparison.

TABLE 11.1

APPROPRIATIONS AS RELATED TO ESTIMATES: DECISIONS OF
SENATE APPROPRIATIONS COMMITTEE, 36 BUREAUS, 1947 TO 1962

Committee Decisions	Number of Decisions	Percentage of Decisions
1. Increases Over Budget Estimates	109 (46)[a]	18.9 (8.0)
2. Same as Budget Estimates	106 (106)	18.4 (18.4)
3. Decreases Below Budget Estimates	361 (423)	62.7 (73.6)
Total	576	100

[a] Comparable House Committee figures, from Table 8.1, in parentheses.

TABLE 11.2

APPROPRIATIONS AS RELATED TO PREVIOUS YEAR'S APPROPRIATION:
DECISIONS OF SENATE APPROPRIATIONS COMMITTEE,
36 BUREAUS, 1947 TO 1962

Committee Decisions	Number of Decisions	Percentage of Decisions
1. Increases Over Previous Year's Appropriation	432 (398)[a]	75.2 (69.2)
2. Same as Previous Year's Appropriation	14 (22)	2.4 (3.8)
3. Decreases Below Previous Year's Appropriation	129 (155)	22.4 (27.0)

[a] Comparable House Committee figures, from Table 8.3, in parentheses.

[10] Estimates presented to the Senate Committee may not be exactly the same as those presented to the House group. The passage of time necessitated changes in 58 of the 576 estimates studied. Table 11.1 uses the original estimates in all cases.

Both distributions reveal broad similarities in the decision patterns of the two Appropriations Committees. The Senate Committee, like the House group, keeps most agency appropriations below the budget estimates. At the same time, it grants most agencies an increase over their previous year's appropriation. It would seem that the two committees meet conflicting expectations within their chambers with a similar mixture of decisions. Economy expectations are met by keeping appropriations below estimates; program expectations are met by allowing appropriations increases.

Given the perceptions of the participants that the Senate Committee maintains a looser hold on the purse strings, and given the lack of any budget-cutting ideology among its members, one might be surprised to find that the Senate group keeps such a high percentage of the agencies below their estimates. Table 11.1, therefore, helps to put Senate Committee liberality in perspective. They may well make more liberal decisions than the House group, but this does not mean that they engage in any wholesale raising above budget requests. Their actions in this regard reflect the fact that House and Senate Committee members alike are legislators and as such are interested in maintaining the coordinate status of the legislature. By keeping most appropriations below budget estimates, they avoid "rubber-stamping" executive requests and assert their legislative authority.

Despite these large similarities, however, Tables 11.1 and 11.2 reveal some differences in the decision patterns of the two committees. They do reveal the Senate group to be more willing to spend money than the House group. The Senate Committee appropriates sums higher than the budget estimates in 10 per cent more cases than does the House Committee. And the Senate group allows agency appropriations to exceed the previous year's figure in 6 per cent more cases than the House group. These differentials are not earth-shaking. But they do run in the direction that one would have predicted on the basis of earlier discussion. This fact is important. But, for the moment, the relatively small difference involved should be highlighted as calling attention to the fundamental similarities between the two groups and to the impingement of similar internal and environmental forces on them both.

Once put in perspective, Senate Committee liberality and House-Senate comparisons are most meaningfully described by relating Senate Committee decisions to prior House decisions. It is this relationship, after all, that Committee members stress when they make their decisions. They act after the House has acted, they know what the House has done, and they sit as an appellate court to hear agency appeals for restoration. Decisions taken in this context must be analyzed in this context.

Table 11.3 presents a distribution of Senate Committee actions relative to 575 separate decisions carried in the House appropriation bills. Viewed in

574

TABLE 11.3

DECISIONS OF THE SENATE COMMITTEE ON APPROPRIATIONS
AS COMPARED WITH FINAL HOUSE DECISIONS:
36 EXECUTIVE BUREAUS, 1947 TO 1962

Senate Committee Decision		Number of Decisions	Percentage of Decisions
1. Increases Over House Figure		323	56.2
2. Same As House Figure		193	33.6
3. Decreases Below House Figure		59	10.2
	Total	575[a]	100

[a] House figures for Soil Conservation Service unavailable for 1957.

this way, the liberality of the Senate Committee comes more clearly into focus. In a majority of cases, that is, the Committee does allow a larger appropriation than has been sent to it by the House. It is in this respect that the several forces making for Senate liberality have their most noticeable impact. And it is because of this pattern that the Senate group has been tagged as the "upper" body. The distribution of Table 11.3 reflects the fact that Senate expectations lean more toward program than House expectations. It reflects the fact that Committee member expectations run more to constituency gain in the Senate than in the House. It reflects the fact that appropriations and authorizing Committee personnel overlap in the Senate and that the Senate Committee's self-defined function is that of an appeals court whereas the House stresses budget-cutting. It reflects the fact that Senate subcommittees are made up of people with a special interest in the subject matter whereas House subcommittees are less so. It reflects the fact that more intensive external pressure — from agency, from clientele groups, and from legislators — can be brought to bear on the Senate group than on its counterpart in the House.

One-third of the time, the Senate Committee leaves the House figure untouched. Most of these cases occur when the House grants an agency everything, or nearly everything, it asks for and the agency involved decides not to make an appeal to the Senate. Thus the percentage of Senate Committee increases rises markedly — probably to something approximating 75 per cent — when one excludes cases in which the House figure is not appealed. In only one case out of ten does the Committee reduce the figure which comes to it as a result of prior appropriations action. This contrasts sharply with House Committee action (see Table 8.1) in reducing seven out of every ten appropriations figures which come to it as a result of prior appropriations decisions. Occasional Senate cuts in the House figure serve as reminders to the agencies of the authority which the Senate Committee

575

possesses. It reminds them that, even though the Committee functions as a relatively liberal appellate court, the Committee's favor cannot be taken for granted.

These patterns of Senate Committee action are related to the three possible kinds of final House decisions in Table 11.4. With the previous year's appropriation (that is, the figure carried in the final appropriation bill) as a standard, final House action and subsequent Senate Committee action are related to it. For instance, in the 400 cases where the final House figure was an increase of agency appropriations above the previous year, the Senate Committee raised the figure still further in 219 (54.8 per cent) of them. The Committee left the House figure untouched in 33.8 per cent (135) cases, and it reduced the agency figure below what the House had granted in 11.4 per cent (46) of the instances. In 40 of these 46 cases in which the Senate Committee cut the House figure, it should be noted that its decision still left the agency with more money than it had received in the previous year. Thus the Senate Committee reversed the general thrust of the House decision in only 6 of the 400 cases. That is, the House decided to grant agencies an increase over their previous year's appropriation in 400 cases, and the Senate Committee concurred in this broad decision in 394 of them. Though this generalization does not take into account the magnitude of the increments involved, it certainly supports the idea that the framework and the direction of appropriations decision-making are fixed in the House.

TABLE 11.4

SENATE COMMITTEE DECISIONS AS RELATED TO FINAL
HOUSE DECISIONS: 36 BUREAUS, 1947 TO 1962

| FINAL HOUSE APPROPRIATIONS DECISION | SENATE COMMITTEE APPROPRIATIONS DECISION | | | |
	Increase Over House Figure	Same As House Figure	Decrease Below House Figure	Total
Increase Over Previous Year's Appropriation	219 (54.8%)	135 (33.8%)	46 (11.4%)	400 (100%)
Same As Previous Year's Appropriation	8 (36.4%)	14 (63.6%)	0	22 (100%)
Decrease Below Previous Year's Appropriation	96 (62.7%)	44 (28.8%)	13 (8.5%)	153 (100%)
Total	323	193	59	575

When the House votes to cut an agency below what it received the previous year, the Senate usually concurs in the broad outline of this decision — though less enthusiastically than in the case of House increases. For instance, the Senate Committee does not normally follow up a House decrease by piling on still another decrease. It did this in only 13 (8.5 per cent) of the 153 cases when the opportunity presented itself. What the Senate Committee usually did when the House voted a decrease was to increase the appropriation above the House figure. This it did 62.7 per cent (96 cases) of the time. But, again, in 66 of those 96 cases, the Senate figure still put the agency at an appropriations level lower than the previous year. When the House Committee decides to keep an agency below its previous year's appropriation, the Senate usually — in 123 of 153 cases (80.4 per cent) — concurs.

One variable that has been left out of this analysis is, of course, the agency's own desires in the matter — as expressed via its estimates and its reclama strategy. If they were worked into the equation at this point, the results might be altered somewhat. But the information on agency appeals policy is not available, and the subject will not be pursued in this study. At the point where the analysis now stands, however, the evidence is quite convincing in support of the proposition that the broad outlines and the main thrust of appropriations decision-making in Congress are set in the House (which means the House Committee on Appropriations) and that the Senate's contributions are marginal.

To the degree that the Senate Committee accepts an appeals court function, it willingly prescribes for itself a marginal kind of influence over congressional appropriations decisions. With respect to the entire budgetary process as it reaches back into the executive branch, House action, too, is marginal. House Committee decisions are, as we have seen, incremental, leaving the largest part of most budgets untouched. But at the very least the House Committee focuses on a larger appropriations increment than does the Senate group. And at the very most the House group re-examines the agency's budgetary base. The appropriations increment involved in an agency's reclama is invariably smaller than that considered by the House. It directs Senate Committee members to consider the effect, seriatim, of each particular House reduction on a single agency program. And, though the Senate Committee may, and sometimes does, move into areas of the budget where House action is not being appealed or where no House action was taken at all, the idea of the appeals court (which in turn is heavily conditioned by the Senate's place in the appropriations sequence) militates against it.

Some impression of the Senate's incremental contribution to the process can be gained by considering the magnitude of the changes made by the

577

Senate in the House figure. As Table 11.1 shows, the Senate Committee altered the final House figure in 382 cases and left it untouched in 193. How large were these 382 changes? The Senate Committee changes arrayed in Table 11.5 have been calculated by comparing the percentage change over the previous year's appropriations voted by the House with the percentage change over the previous year's appropriations voted by the Senate Committee.

Table 11.5 reveals the incremental character of Senate decisions. In one third of the cases the Senate Committee made no change at all. And in 40 per cent of the remaining cases (or, in over 60 per cent of those cases where changes were made) the Senate Committee altered the final House figure by an amount equal to 6 per cent or less of the agency's previous year's appropriation. A superficial comparison between this distribution, indicative of the magnitude of Senate Committee changes in House totals, with

TABLE 11.5

MAGNITUDE OF SENATE COMMITTEE CHANGES IN FINAL HOUSE FIGURES: APPROPRIATIONS AS A PERCENTAGE OF PREVIOUS YEAR'S APPROPRIATIONS, 36 BUREAUS, 1947 TO 1962

Percentage of Increases		Number of Decisions	Percentage of Decisions
Over 30		18	3.1
27.0–29.9		3	0.5
24.0–26.9		5	0.9
21.0–23.9		5	0.9
18.0–20.9		7	1.2
15.0–17.9		11	1.9
12.0–14.9		12	2.1
9.0–11.9		36	6.3
6.0–8.9		38	6.6
3.0–5.9		67	11.7
0.1–2.9		121	21.0
	Total	323	
No Change		193	33.6
Decreases			
−0.1– −2.9		37	6.4
−3.0– −5.9		14	2.4
−6.0– −8.9		1	0.2
−9.0– −11.9		2	0.3
−12.0– −14.9		0	0
Over 15		5	0.9
	Total	59	100

Table 8.4, which is indicative of the magnitude of the original House Committee changes, makes it clear that increments of change as voted by the House Committee are larger than the increments of change voted by the Senate group. Of the 382 changes listed in Table 11.5, the change voted by the Senate Committee was smaller in percentage terms than the original change voted by the House in 284 (74.3 per cent) cases. In only 98 (25.7 per cent) cases was the Senate incremental change more sizable than the change originally voted on by the House. When one adds to this the fact that in 193 cases the Senate left House figures untouched, the lesser impact of the Senate Committee (and of the Senate) — or the dominance of the House Committee and the House — is more clearly established than ever. As appropriations decision-making proceeds in Congress, the area of discretion becomes progressively narrower, and the influence of decision-makers at the end of the sequence is less than the influence of those near the beginning.

Senate Committee changes in final House figures tend to run in the same direction as, and tend to be smaller than, the changes which the House makes in the figures presented to it. But this does not mean, obviously, that the Senate Committee has no independent impact on appropriations outcomes. At the very least, there is a minority of cases in which the Senate Committee makes substantial alterations in the House decision. And at the very most, even marginal changes may have important consequences for the agency involved. In general terms, the nature of the Senate Committee's impact has been revealed. It is to increase appropriations above the House figure — usually at a greater level than the previous year's appropriations, more often than not at a level below the budget estimate, but sometimes above the budget estimate. The question arises as to how Senate Committee actions are distributed in relation to some of the variables discussed in Chapter Eight — for instance, party control, external conditions, and type of program.

House and Senate appear to respond similarly to changing conditions of party control and to relevant external events. The impact of these variables, it will be recalled, is most easily isolated by observing yearly variations in appropriations decision patterns. Thus years of Republican control (1947, 1948, 1953) appear as the heaviest budget-cutting years. And the years when external events produced economy or permissive moods are reflected in appropriate decision patterns. Using appropriations as a percentage of budget estimates for a measure, we find that the yearly averages for the cluster of 36 bureaus present a picture of these variations. The yearly averages for the House Committee were charted in Figure 8.1. The yearly averages for the Senate Committee have been charted alongside the House Committee averages in Figure 11.1.

579

As Figure 11.1 demonstrates, the yearly pattern of Senate Committee decisions corresponds closely to that of the House Committee. In each year, as one would expect, the Senate Committee average is higher than that of the House group. But the yearly pattern is the same. The years of greatest and least budget-cutting are the same for both groups. The direction of change is similar from year to year. The only noteworthy deviation occurred in the shift from 1954 to 1955, when the House became more lenient and the Senate less so. The reason for this is that in 1954 the Senate increased one bureau's (the Census Bureau) appropriation by 211 per cent above the budget request. An increase so disproportionate and so much greater than any other during the 16 years has to skew that yearly average to an abnormal height. The marked similarity of pattern could be explained in terms of the Senate Committee following a response set by the House or in terms of both groups responding to the same set of external conditions. Probably both are involved — though the contribution of each will not be measured here. The important point is that variables such as party and mood do *not* seem to produce distinctive decision-making patterns on the part of the Senate Committee.

FIGURE 11.1

SENATE AND HOUSE COMMITTEE DECISIONS: APPROPRIATIONS
AS A PERCENTAGE OF ESTIMATES, YEARLY COMBINED
AVERAGES FOR 36 BUREAUS, 1947 TO 1962

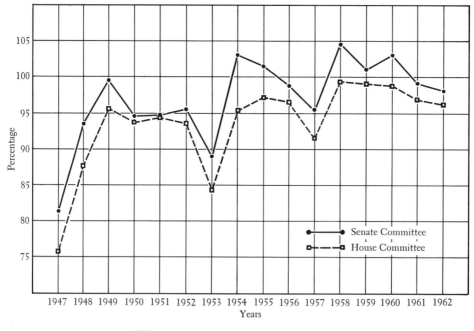

The Senate does register an independent impact on appropriations decision-making in terms of the type of program involved. In departmental and bureau level analyses, Senate decisions form patterns that diverge from those set by the House. Senate liberality is not distributed equally among all departments and bureaus. It is differentially distributed according to program areas and according to specific programs that command special support in the Senate Committee and in the Senate. Table 11.6 shows the allocation by departments of the changes made by the Senate Committee in the final House appropriations.

If Table 11.6 is compared with Tables 8.7 and 8.8, it becomes apparent that patterns of departmental support vary from committee to committee — and from House to Senate. The most striking finding of Table 11.6 is the fact that the Interior Department received the most favorable treatment from the Senate Committee whereas it received the least favorable treatment of all the departments at the hands of the House Committee. The reasons for this disparity are several, and most have already been mentioned. The Interior Department programs are heavily concentrated in the Western area of the country. The Western area sends proportionately more members to the Senate than it does to the House. Western Senators achieve a greater degree of representation on the Appropriations Committee than they have in the Senate. And, since Senate subcommittee assignments are made on the basis of interest, the Interior Subcommittee is almost wholly composed of Westerners. Furthermore, both the full Senate Committee and the Interior Subcommittee are led and have been led during most of the sixteen-year period by Senator Carl Hayden of Arizona. And Senator Hayden has devoted his senatorial career (the longest in American history) to the development and promotion of Western-oriented programs. Conversely, the House Subcommittee on Interior has been led and, for the most part, manned by non-Westerners. The point is that differences in system representation, in Committee selection, in internal Committee structure, and in Committee leadership do make a difference in congressional Committee output. And the case of the Interior Department is the most obvious example in the field of appropriations.

The Senate Committee treats the other departments with varying degrees of liberality and with varying shades of difference from the House Committee. Another noteworthy divergence from the House Committee's pattern involves the Commerce Department. This Department, which was treated unfavorably by the House Committee, fared relatively well at the hands of the Senate group. No explanation for this reversal of form is immediately apparent other than a recognition on the part of the Senate Committee that the department absorbs abnormal budgetary damage at the hands of the House.

581

TABLE 11.6

SENATE COMMITTEE CHANGES IN FINAL HOUSE APPROPRIATIONS:
BY DEPARTMENT, 36 BUREAUS, 1947 TO 1962

SENATE COMMITTEE DECISION	DEPARTMENT Agriculture (5 Bureaus)	Commerce (5 Bureaus)	HEW (5 Bureaus)	Interior (8 Bureaus)	Justice (3 Bureaus)	Labor (4 Bureaus)	Treasury (6 Bureaus)	
Increase Above House Figure	46 (58.2%)	47 (58.8%)	55 (68.8%)	105 (82.0%)	10 (20.8%)	28 (43.8%)	32 (33.3%)	323
Same As House Figure	26 (32.9%)	23 (28.7%)	14 (17.5%)	7 (5.5%)	29 (60.4%)	31 (48.4%)	63 (65.6%)	193
Decrease Below House Figure	7 (8.9%)	10 (12.5%)	11 (13.7%)	16 (12.5%)	9 (18.8%)	5 (7.8%)	1 (1.0%)	59
Total	79 (100%)	80 (100%)	80 (100%)	128 (100%)	48 (100%)	64 (100%)	96 (100%)	575

TABLE 11.7

MAGNITUDE OF INCREMENTAL INCREASES BY SENATE COMMITTEE OVER FINAL
HOUSE FIGURE: BY DEPARTMENTS, 36 BUREAUS, 1947 TO 1962

SIZE OF SENATE COMMITTEE INCREASE	NUMBER OF INCREASES PER DEPARTMENT Agriculture	Commerce	HEW	Interior	Justice	Labor	Treasury
0.1%–5.9%	31 (67.4%)	27 (57.4%)	35 (63.6%)	44 (41.9%)	9 (90%)	16 (57.1%)	26 (81.3%)
5.9% or more	15 (32.6%)	20 (42.6%)	20 (36.4%)	61 (58.1%)	1 (10%)	12 (42.9%)	6 (18.7%)
Total	46 (100%)	47 (100%)	55 (100%)	105 (100%)	10 (100%)	28 (100%)	32 (100%)

When departments which receive the most favorable treatment by the House Committee also receive relatively favorable treatment in the Senate, it is the mark of exceptionally widespread support for their program. Such is the case, obviously, with the Health, Education, and Welfare and Agriculture Departments. Little more need be said about their internal and external sources of support except that the conditions which obtain in the House obtain equally, if not more so, in the Senate. Senator Lister Hill, if anything, is a more unabashed partisan of HEW programs than Representative John Fogarty. And constituency factors make Senators, if anything, more concerned about agriculture than House members. In the words of Senator Richard Russell, former Chairman of the Agriculture Subcommittee,

> There is a considerable difference in the two houses of Congress with relation to activities of this kind. Every Senator has in his state agricultural activities, land grant colleges, experiment stations. When we consider the other body of Congress . . . we find that only about 25 per cent of the Members there have located within their districts any of those activities. . . .[11]

The Senate Committee's treatment of the other departments, can be briefly summarized. Its disposition toward Treasury and Justice seems dominated either by satisfaction with House action or lack of interest or both. The programs of these departments remain the least controversial throughout the entire appropriations process; and it seems likely that the high percentage of House decisions which go unchanged reflects an absence of appeals by the agencies involved. The Labor Department stands with the Senate Committee as it did with the House group — in the middle of the scale — overshadowed, one suspects, by interest in and concern for the appropriations of the Health, Education, and Welfare Department, with which it has traditionally been lumped in appropriation bills.

The Senate Committee's special support for the Interior Department can be illustrated by examining the magnitude of the changes made in House figures. Table 11.7 takes the incremental increases (based on final House and Senate Committee action relative to the previous year's appropriation) listed in Table 11.5, consolidates them into two quite arbitrary categories, and relates them to the seven departments.

The Committee increases Interior Department appropriations not only more frequently but also by larger percentages than it does for any other department. Interior appears as the only department the majority of whose incremental increases are 6 per cent or more. As one would expect, Treasury and Justice have the smallest increases. The other departments fall in between — with the proportion for Agriculture being somewhat smaller than one might guess and that for Labor being somewhat larger — based strictly on support

11 *Congressional Record*, Daily Edition, April 21, 1958, p. 6098.

for the two departments. However, it is likely that, in view of House action, the appeals presented by the Labor Department are more sizable than those from Agriculture.

Bureau Appropriations Patterns and Determinants

A brief examination of Senate Committee decisions at the bureau level makes possible the further specifications of similarities and differences between the appropriations actions of the two Committees — and, hence, of the two chambers. Table 11.8 duplicates, for the Senate Committee, the ranking of bureaus presented for the House in Table 8.8 — a ranking based on the sixteen-year averages of bureau appropriations considered as a percentage of estimates.[12] Comparable rankings and figures as produced by the House Committee appear in parentheses.

Over all, the bureau averages in Table 11.8 provide further evidence of the relative liberality of the Senate Committee. For 31 of the 36 bureaus, the Senate Committee was more generous than the House group in granting budget requests. In one case the two committees produced the same average; and in only four cases were the Senate Committee decisions less generous over the sixteen-year span than those of the House Committee. Given the incremental character of most Senate decisions, the differences between House and Senate Committee averages are modest — ranging from a low of 0.1 per cent to a high of 13.2 per cent and averaging 3.3 per cent. These differences are not enormous. But, in some cases, as always, they can be decisive in terms of program support. And, since the difference between Table 8.8 and 11.8 is substantial, it is obvious that the Senate Appropriations Committee distributes by its decisions, however marginal they may be, advantages and disadvantages in a somewhat different pattern than does the House Committee.

From the evidence of Table 11.8, it is possible to distinguish the bureaus whose fortunes were advanced most appreciably by the Senate Committee from those whose fortunes were advanced the least. In Table 11.9 House and Senate Committee averages are compared, and the bureaus are ranked according to the magnitude of the Senate increase.

The gradations at each interval in Table 11.9 are so small that the only meaningful comparisons that can be made are those which differentiate the most successful from the least successful bureaus. As in Chapter Eight, the top and the bottom one third of the bureaus have been selected arbitrarily for a rather unrefined and highly impressionistic analysis. The aim of the

---

[12] In the 58 cases where the Senate Committee acted on different budget estimates than the House Committee, Table 11.8 and, hence, Table 11.9 use the revised estimates as the basis for the calculation.

TABLE 11.8

SENATE COMMITTEE DECISIONS, APPROPRIATIONS AS A PERCENTAGE OF
ESTIMATES: BUREAU AVERAGES FOR THE PERIOD 1947 TO 1962

Ranking	Bureau	Department	16-Year Average	
1 (13)[a]	Public Health Service	HEW	107.7	(96.7) [a]
2 (12)	Forest Service	Agriculture	103.8	(96.9)
3 (1)	Soil Conservation Service	Agriculture	102.1	(102.1)
4 (6)	Extension Service	Agriculture	101.5	(98.5)
5 (5)	Patent Office	Commerce	100.7	(98.8)
6 (11)	Office of Education	HEW	100.1	(97.2)
7 (2)	Federal Bureau of Investigation	Justice	99.9	(100.2)
8 (4)	Bureau of Narcotics	Treasury	99.5	(98.9)
9 (25)	Fish and Wildlife Service	Interior	99.0	(92.9)
10 (3)	Food and Drug Administration	HEW	98.9	(99.1)
11 (7)	Bureau of Customs	Treasury	98.5	(98.1)
12 (8)	Bureau of the Public Debt	Treasury	98.13	(97.8)
13 (20)	Weather Bureau	Commerce	98.08	(94.75)
14 (26)	Bureau of Mines	Interior	97.8	(92.6)
15 (10)	Social Security Administration	HEW	97.6	(97.5)
16 (15)	Secret Service	Treasury	97.4	(96.1)
17 (9)	Immigration and Naturalization Service	Justice	97.2	(97.7)
18 (29)	Bureau of Land Management	Interior	96.97	(91.3)
19 (30)	Bureau of Indian Affairs	Interior	96.95	(89.5)
20 (14)	Women's Bureau	Labor	96.8	(96.4)
21 (23)	Office of Vocational Rehabilitation	HEW	96.6	(94.05)
22 (17)	Rural Electrification Administration	Agriculture	96.44	(95.3)
23 (19)	Bureau of the Mint	Treasury	96.37	(94.86)
24 (27)	National Park Service	Interior	96.3	(91.8)
25 (21)	Coast and Geodetic Survey	Commerce	95.9	(94.3)
26 (18)	Internal Revenue Service	Treasury	95.8	(94.87)
27 (24)	Farmers Home Administration	Agriculture	95.4	(93.5)
28 (16)	Wage and Hour Division	Labor	95.0	(95.6)
29 (22)	Federal Prison System	Justice	94.7	(94.13)
30 (28)	Geological Survey	Interior	93.0	(91.7)
31 (34)	Bureau of Reclamation	Interior	92.7	(83.9)
32 (32)	Bonneville Power Administration	Interior	92.6	(87.5)
33 (31)	Bureau of Labor Statistics	Labor	92.3	(88.6)
34 (35)	Bureau of Labor Standards	Labor	92.0	(82.3)
35 (36)	Census Bureau	Commerce	91.9	(78.1)
36 (33)	National Bureau of Standards	Commerce	87.2	(84.2)

[a] Rankings and averages by House Committee decisions taken from Table 8.8 are in parentheses.

585

TABLE 11.9

DIFFERENCE BETWEEN SENATE AND HOUSE 16-YEAR AVERAGES:
APPROPRIATIONS AS A PERCENTAGE OF
ESTIMATES: 36 BUREAUS, 1947 TO 1962

Ranking	Bureau	Department	Difference Between Senate and House 16-Year Averages
1 (36)[a]	Census Bureau	Commerce	13.8
2 (13)	Public Health Service	HEW	11.0
3 (35)	Bureau of Labor Standards	Labor	9.7
4 (34)	Bureau of Reclamation	Interior	8.8
5 (30)	Bureau of Indian Affairs	Interior	7.5
6 (12)	Forest Service	Agriculture	6.9
7 (25)	Fish and Wildlife Service	Interior	6.1
8 (29)	Bureau of Land Management	Interior	5.7
9 (26)	Bureau of Mines	Interior	5.2
10 (32)	Bonneville Power Administration	Interior	5.1
11 (27)	National Park Service	Interior	4.5
12 (31)	Bureau of Labor Statistics	Labor	3.7
13 (20)	Weather Bureau	Commerce	3.3
14 (6)	Extension Service	Agriculture	3.0
15 (33)	National Bureau of Standards	Commerce	3.0
16 (11)	Office of Education	HEW	2.9
17 (23)	Office of Vocational Rehabilitation	HEW	2.5
18 (5)	Patent Office	Commerce	1.9
19 (24)	Farmers Home Administration	Agriculture	1.9
20 (21)	Coast and Geodetic Survey	Commerce	1.7
21 (19)	Bureau of the Mint	Treasury	1.5
22 (28)	Geological Survey	Interior	1.3
23 (15)	Secret Service	Treasury	1.3
24 (17)	Rural Electrification Administration	Agriculture	1.1
25 (18)	Internal Revenue Service	Treasury	0.9
26 (4)	Bureau of Narcotics	Treasury	0.6
27 (22)	Federal Prison System	Justice	0.6
28 (7)	Bureau of Customs	Treasury	0.4
29 (14)	Women's Bureau	Labor	0.4
30 (8)	Bureau of the Public Debt	Treasury	0.3
31 (10)	Social Security Administration	HEW	0.1
32 (1)	Soil Conservation Service	Agriculture	0.0
33 (3)	Food and Drug Administration	HEW	−0.2
34 (2)	Federal Bureau of Investigation	Justice	−0.3
35 (9)	Immigration and Naturalization Service	Justice	−0.5
36 (16)	Wage and Hour Division	Labor	−0.6

[a] The rankings of these bureaus in terms of their success in obtaining their requests from the House Committee, from Table 8.8, are in parentheses.

analysis, however, is simply to see whether any gross differences appear between the clusters of bureaus.

The most striking fact about the top twelve bureaus is the very close correspondence of this list with the twelve least successful bureaus (by the same measure, of course) at the hands of the House Committee. Of the twelve lowest ranking bureaus according to House Committee decisions (as pictured in Table 8.8), ten of them appear among the bureaus most favorably treated by the Senate group. To put it bluntly, the bureaus which the Senate Committee helps the most are the ones which the House Committee hurts the most. To a lesser degree, the converse relationship also holds. That is, eight of the twelve highest ranking bureaus according to House decisions appear among the twelve lowest ranking bureaus according to Senate Committee action. Or, many of those bureaus helped the most by the House Committee are helped least by the Senate Committee.

These patterns are precisely what one would predict that an appeals court would produce. That is, it would receive most — and its largest — appeals from those bureaus which had suffered the severest cuts originally and would respond by restoring some funds. On the other hand, bureaus which had already received nearly everything they wanted would have no need to and would not appeal. The striking contrast which appears, then, between Tables 8.8 and 11.9 provides supporting evidence, at the bureau level, that the Senate Committee does in fact perform its self-defined appellate court function.

The twelve bureaus on which the Senate Committee makes the most sizable and most favorable impact appear to have another distinguishing characteristic. They are bureaus whose programs command an especially large degree of extra-Committee support. And this support from clientele groups and from non-Committee legislators can be brought to bear intensively on behalf of the agencies' reclama. Several factors have been mentioned in the study, all of which tend to make the Senate Committee more responsive to extra-Committee pressure than is the House group. Among these factors are the following: the lesser autonomy of the Senate Committee which gives non-Committee members a greater opportunity to influence appropriations decisions; the greater number of pressures for spending that play upon the Senate Committee member, given the heterogeneity of his constituency; the strong constituency orientation of Senate Committee members; the appropriations sequence which gives external groups more time and information when they deal with the Senate; and the appeals court function which narrows the scope and makes possible a greater concentration of effort.

The impression is strong that the top twelve bureaus — those from the Interior Department, Forest Service, and the Public Health Service, for

587

example — enjoy a degree of external support which enables them to exploit favorable Senate conditions. (The Census Bureau may be an exception here, but it was treated so badly by the House Committee that the most modest of restorations would account for its high ranking. Even so, the Senate responded to business pressure for a manufacturing census in 1953, whereas the House did not.) The impression is equally strong that the bottom twelve bureaus — those from the Treasury and Justice Departments, for example — rank among the bureaus which do not need (for appropriations purposes) or do not have especially strong extra-Committee support. (Obviously, the Soil Conservation Service is one glaring exception, but it usually comes to the Senate having already received more than it asked for from the House Committee.) It also seems likely that the Senate success of the Bureau of Labor Standards and the Bureau of Labor Statistics on the one hand and the Senate failure of the Wage and Hour Division on the other are due to the unity of labor and business in support of such things as occupational safety and the consumer price index and the disunity of these clientele groups regarding the enforcement of minimum wage and hour laws.

It is not easy to support these impressions as to relative degrees of extra-Committee support. All bureaus have some external support or they could not survive. But, given the appeals court function of the Senate Committee, some bureaus can surely muster a more compelling appeal than others. And extra-Committee support would be just as surely an important element in their persuasiveness. One rough indicator of this kind of support would be the number of non-Committee witnesses who asked to be heard in support of an agency's reclama. In 1962, for instance, the subcommittee hearing testimony on the Interior Department plus the Forest Service took oral testimony from nearly 75 spokesmen for state, local, and private organizations, 20 non-Committee Senators, and a handful of Representatives.[13] The Labor–Health, Education, and Welfare Subcommittee heard over 25 outside witnesses (mostly noted doctors) in support of the Public Health Service. The two subcommittees taking testimony on the Treasury and Justice Departments, on the other hand, heard no outside witnesses at all on these departmental budgets. Such differences, paralleling those in Table 7.1, are surely relevant to the comparative success of these bureaus with the Senate Committee.

Another factor which helps to explain some of the high rankings in Table 11.9 is the preference of important Appropriations Committee decision-makers. Chairman Carl Hayden's concern over half a century for the welfare of the Interior Department has already been mentioned. The impact

[13] See especially the comments of Senator Stennis, Senate Committee on Appropriations, *Hearings on Interior Department Appropriations for 1960*, 86th Congress, 1st Session (Washington: U.S. Government Printing Office, 1959), p. 736.

of individuals is noteworthy, also, on the two agencies which have combined high ranking at the hands of the House Committee with even higher rankings in their dealings with the Senate — the Public Health Service and the Forest Service. Clearly, these agencies rank, in the period under study, as the two most popular with the Senate Committee on Appropriations — and with the Senate. Every Committee hearing and every floor debate support that conclusion. And in terms of the factors which separate these spectacularly successful agencies from the merely successful ones, prime recognition must be given to a few individuals who have made these agencies their special object of concern. Senator Lister Hill, since 1955 the chairman of the subcommittee appropriating for the Public Health Service, has been nothing less than a special guardian of that agency and its programs, especially in such areas as medical research and hospital construction. Likewise, the Forest Service, influential enough on its own, has benefited from the special devotion to its program shown by two men who chaired its appropriations subcommittees, Senator Richard Russell and Senator Carl Hayden, and by another Committee member who has become a Senate specialist in forestry research, Senator John Stennis. These Senators have actively promoted the programs of the two agencies, have consistently urged more money upon them than the agencies have been able to wring from the Budget Bureau, and have smoothed the legislative path of these agencies through the closest of informal contacts. Hill's lifelong interest stems probably from the fact that his father was a doctor. Russell's, Hayden's, and Stennis' interest took root in constituency concerns. All illustrate the potential impact of a sympathetic, well-placed individual on the appropriations fortunes of an agency.[14]

One final question arises from the bureau level comparisons between House Committee and Senate Committee appropriations decisions. To what degree is the pattern a function of the perceptions which the two groups have of one another rather than a product of the differential impact of other forces upon them? That is to say, does the House Committee cut Interior Department agencies because it knows the Senate will restore them? And, if this is so, how can one explain the greater success of Interior Department agencies in the Senate in terms of Senate-related factors? This problem of

[14] On Senator Hayden, see Chapter 10, note 43. On Senator Hill, see Senate Committee on Appropriations, *Hearings on Health, Education, and Welfare Department Appropriations for 1960*, 86th Congress, 1st Session (Washington: U.S. Government Printing Office, 1959), p. 178; 102 *Congressional Record*, pp. 9526–9531; *Congressional Record*, Daily Edition, June 12, 1957, pp. 7969–7985. On Senator Russell, see the comments of Forest Service Chief Richard McArdle, Senate Committee on Appropriations, *Hearings on Interior Department Appropriations for 1963*, 87th Congress, 2nd Session (Washington: U.S. Government Printing Office, 1962), p. 1023; 95 *Congressional Record*, p. 6416; *Congressional Record*, Daily Edition, June 6, 1961, p. 8861. On Senator Stennis, see *Congressional Record*, Daily Edition, April 30, 1958, p. 6917; February 8, 1960, pp. 1989–1994; January 31, 1961, pp. 1445–1459.

anticipated reaction confronts us at every turn in the appropriations process, where repeated interactions between units lead to accurate predictions about behavior and to patterns of interactions which regularly fulfill prior predictions.

At the level of analysis being pursued in this study, only an ambiguous answer can be given. An agency's success with the House Committee is not independent of its success with the Senate Committee. A single appropriations process produces a single interrelated pattern of decisions. Nevertheless, the pattern forms as it does because the House and Senate Committees are distinct, each reacting differently to various agencies. The House Committee knows, therefore, when it reduces the agency requests of the Interior Department that the Senate will vote to restore them. And that may encourage the House Committee to cut a bit deeper than it otherwise would. On the other hand, the Senate Committee is, for all the reasons cited, more sympathetic to Interior Department programs than is the House Committee. The fact that the Committees may base their strategy on this difference does not make it any less real. And it is this objective difference in sympathy which provides the primary explanation for changes in bureau appropriations patterns from one stage in the process to another.

Insofar as the House and Senate Committees do not respond with equal favor to the demands of all executive agencies, the agencies may benefit from the consequences of bicameralism. An agency which cannot get what it wants from one group can seek it from the other. And the existence of these alternatives is likely to be a source of stability in the appropriations process — in mitigating dissatisfaction with the process on the part of executive agencies and their clientele groups. By itself, neither Appropriations Committee might satisfy the executive agencies; but combined in a single process they can do so by offering each agency two distinct opportunities to get what it wants. Some people (Senators included) have advocated devices which would, in effect, tend to merge the two Committees into one joint committee. In view of the benefits of having two separate channels of access, many executive agencies might view unification with some skepticism.

ACTION ON THE SENATE FLOOR

Guiding Action on the Floor

Every Senate Committee decision must be ratified by majority vote on the floor before it becomes an authoritative decision of the Senate. Due to the lack of sharp Committee-Senate structural differentiation the contextual differences between the Committee and the floor are not as striking or as important in the Senate as they are in the House. To be sure, contextual changes do take place. Committee control over decision-making is loosened; Senate-Committee conflict, such as there is, will show up on the floor. Nevertheless, the number of participants, the diffusion of information, and the impact of party leadership do not change as radically from one stage to another as they do in the House. The goal of the Senate Committee on the floor remains the same — to win and hold support for its recommendations. And the Senate prestige of Committee leaders is certainly affected by floor performance. But Senate Committee members do not convey the feeling (as their House counterparts do) that Armageddon awaits them on the floor. Rather, the floor is viewed more as an extension of the Committee context than as a new and different arena of activity.

A Senate Committee bill, once reported out of Committee, is placed automatically on the Senate Calendar, from whence it will move to the Senate chamber. Timing is decided by informal consultation between the majority and minority floor leaders on the one hand and the Committee chairman and ranking minority member together with the subcommittee leaders on the other. Since all Senate agenda-making follows similar unanimous consent procedure and since the Senate Committee is so minimally differentiated from the Senate, there appear to be no permanent strains in this relationship. Should an individual Senator be planning extensive amendments to the bill, however, he may be upset by the fact that once the agreement between party and Committee leaders has been reached, the bill often moves precipitously to the floor.[15]

The length of time allotted to appropriations debate is also a matter to be decided by informal consultation and agreed to by unanimous consent. Senate rules in debate are so loose compared with the restrictions operative in the House that a Senator can cause considerable delay by dilatory tactics — and could even escalate his objections into a filibuster if others joined him. The Senate does not use the Committee of the Whole device with its accompanying restrictions on the length of debate. Roll-call votes are more easily obtained and more frequently held than in the House. Each Senator can talk for as long as he wishes on an appropriation bill, and time is allowed for every Senator to speak. Any limitations which exist are self-imposed.

In view of the very great freedom of debate, it is interesting to note that the Senate generally spends much less time debating appropriation bills than does the House. On the basis of a flat page count for 6 bills over 15 years, the Senate floor debates consumed an average of 192 pages per year while House debates averaged 272 pages per year. Table 11.10 breaks these figures down by bills and can be compared with Table 9.7.

[15] *Congressional Record*, Daily Edition, April 24, 1963, p. 6583, and June 7, 1961, pp. 1061 ff.

TABLE 11.10

PAGES OF SENATE FLOOR ACTION ON APPROPRIATION BILLS CONGRESSIONAL RECORD, 1947 TO 1962

APPROPRIATION BILL	PAGES PER YEAR																Totals[a]
	1947	1948	1949	1950	1951	1952	1953	1954	1955	1956	1957	1958	1959	1960	1961	1962	
Agriculture	7	37	50		94	43	29	36	13	12	41	11	55	28	12	18	486 (879)
Interior	12	14	163		144	33	21	27	6	9	20	16	10	10	26	62	573 (602)
Labor-HEW	45	2	60	Omnibus Appropriation Bill	134	9	37	12	14	16	13	8	22	8	68	76	524 (715)
Public Works	18	47	28		62	28	26	15	21	21	15	18	14	22	18	56	409 (749)
State, Justice, and Commerce	28	4	31		58	33	102	35	3	11	32	3	15	10	111	21	497 (685)
Commerce									50	12	14	5	29	41			151 (92)
Treasury– Post Office	5	8	51		27	18	17	19	4	2	25	3	13	6	7	30	235 (353)
Totals[a]	115 (478)	112 (247)	383 (203)		519 (506)	164 (345)	232 (352)	144 (286)	111 (267)	83 (151)	160 (402)	64 (163)	158 (198)	125 (162)	242 (157)	263 (158)	2875 (4075)

[a] Comparable House totals in parentheses. For more detailed comparisons, see Table 9.7.

The technique of counting pages as they are listed in the *Congressional Record* Index has many obvious pitfalls; and the number of pages of actual talk may differ quite widely from the pages in the Index. Only the gross and relative differences are being noted here, however. And they indicate that a greater interest in appropriations matters is registered on the House floor than on the Senate floor — a pattern which is the more striking in view of the Senate's freedom of debate and the House's restrictions.

Several possible explanations for the disparity come to mind. Most important, probably, is that for the House Committee member, this stage represents the one major occasion when he is expected to and does take an active part in floor proceedings. Therefore, on his subcommittee's bills, he tends to make the kind of long, detailed speech which consumes the greater part of the time on the House floor. The bill is his one major legislative "baby." For the Senator, sitting on several other committees with access to the floor at any time, this stage assumes a great deal less importance. For him, the appropriation bill is one among many legislative "babies." Senators do not customarily make long introductory speeches, but very quickly get down to the business of reading the bill for amendment.

A second, related explanation may be that since the Senate Committee concentrates on a smaller segment of the budget than does the House Committee, debate declines in similar proportion. That is to say, House Committee members make more extensive introductory speeches because their Committee deliberations have been more extensive. It may also be relevant, third, that many non-Committee Senators will have already participated in Committee deliberations by the time the bill reaches the Senate floor whereas non-Committee members in the House will have been shut out. Hence there may be less need for non-Committee members in the Senate than in the House to use the floor as a place to communicate.

Whatever the explanation of the relative paucity of Senate debate, it is clear that the rules governing floor action bestow no such advantage on the Senate Committee as they do on the House group. The Senate Committee does, however, possess several other advantages, the most important of which is the disposition of Senators to accept the recommendations of their committees. Unlike their House counterparts, Senate subcommittee leaders do not, as a rule, throw up an oratorical defense of their diligence and judgment before they face a specific amendment. But once they come under attack they will rely heavily on the division of labor–specialization type of appeal. In the words of two of its Chairmen,

> I hope very much that as long as we have Appropriations Committees and subcommittees which do long, tedious, hard, conscientious work, the Senate will back up Committee action.[16]

[16] 93 *Congressional Record*, p. 7982.

The bill was reported after the most careful investigation and after extensive proof and after careful consultation both in the subcommittee and in the full Committee. Is it not reasonable to suppose that what was done in the subcommittee and in the full Committee is a better way of legislating than simply to take the offhand opinion of one of our own members on the floor?[17]

For most Committee recommendations, this argument is sufficient. And most of the time, it is not even necessary to utter it.

The idea of "support your Committee" has procedural as well as substantive connotations. Not only does a specialized Committee possess knowledge but the process of Committee hearings and Committee deliberations is deemed to be necessary before a legislative decision is acceptable. Should an amendment be offered on the floor which has not even been considered by the Committee, and for which there is no budget estimate, it can frequently be turned back with a general argument:

The Secretary has never made a request to me that we avoid the regular procedures of the Senate. No human being asked me until I heard the amendment read. It is an amendment to the State Department appropriation bill and it has no business there. The Secretary did not ask for it. The minority leader did not ask for it. The clerk of the Committee did not know about it. The Chairman of the Committee did not discuss it with me. Why all the rush to get this item in the State Department appropriation bill?[18]

When a subcommittee chairman can make a rejoinder of this sort to an amendment, the predisposition of the Senate to follow orderly procedure stands in his favor.

Given the predilection of Senators to support any committee, a committee composed of especially respected and influential individuals will be even more likely to have its recommendations accepted. One veteran Committee member explained:

When the Appropriations Committee has heard the testimony, made up its mind, and reported out a bill, they won't be upset very often. Most of the members will defer to the Committee. They don't know what's in the bill and they haven't heard the testimony. They look around and there's Hayden on one side and Bridges on the other and Russell and Johnson and some of the most powerful men in the Senate. They're going to take their word rather than that of some outsider who doesn't know what's going on.

A staff member concurred, "When they agree and go out on the floor with a bill you can't beat this crowd. They've got a following." Should the Committee run into opposition on the floor, it can remind Senators to "pay

[17] 96 *Congressional Record*, p. 10392.
[18] *Congressional Record*, Daily Edition, June 30, 1960, p. 14077.

attention to the Senators who are members of the Committee, many of whom have been members of the Committee for a great number of years. Some of the members of the Committee have been members of the Senate for more than a quarter of a century."[19] Committee members freely admit that most of their decisions involve matters of judgment. "Upon the proof before them, they exercise their best judgment."[20] When questions on the floor become those of trusting another's judgment, the elite nature of the Committee's membership is an obvious source of its strength.

Ordinarily, the Committee members go to the floor united in support of their recommendations, and their unity helps them to capitalize on their standing as a committee and as individuals. If the very open process of intra-Committee bargaining has been successful, unity will be a natural result. Furthermore, the norm that the Committee should bargain to a decision and then stick together on the floor is sometimes voiced by the members. A senior Republican said,

> I think we get fewer amendments on our bills than any other committee. Well, maybe Finance has fewer . . . but we stick together pretty well. Sometimes the Chairman will say after we've compromised on a figure, "They're going to attack us on it and I want you fellows to get out there and support me on this position." Sometimes, of course, a person will have a project from his district and he'll disagree and he'll say, "I'm going to have a shot at this on the floor." That's all right. There's no rule against it. But you don't get many amendments adopted on the floor.

Occasionally, Committee members will remind each other of their "loyalty" pledge during floor debate on an amendment. Or, more frequently, evidence of the norm of unity comes from members who declare with varying degrees of enthusiasm that whatever their personal views might be they feel constrained to support the final recommendations from the Committee. Said the Chairman, for instance, "The Chairman of the Committee must support the recommendations of the Committee. Although the Committee's recommendation is for a somewhat larger amount than I felt necessary, nevertheless I feel that the recommendation of the Committee can be justified."[21] "I wish I could go along with this amendment," explained a subcommittee chairman. "Although it nearly breaks my heart to do so, I feel duty bound to stay with the Committee's recommendation."[22] And an ordinary Committee member may say, "I made my fight in the Committee and, as I say, we received some valuable concessions and I feel honor bound to stand by the Committee in what it has done."[23] Committee members and

19 96 *Congressional Record*, pp. 1178–1179.
20 *Ibid.*, p. 10508.
21 99 *Congressional Record*, p. 5970.
22 96 *Congressional Record*, p. 11659.
23 95 *Congressional Record*, p. 7345.

other ex officio Senators see Committee unity as a source of their strength on the floor — especially so since they can, if they remain united, make up more than half of a constitutional majority and a considerably larger portion on most actual votes.

Though the norm of unity is obviously invoked by the Committee, it is by no means as widely held nor as frequently applied on the Senate as on the House side. Aggressive assertions of individual rights seem to be an important part of the senatorial self-image. And, though Senators may bind themselves to a Committee decision on an ad hoc basis, they shy away from the statement of the norm of unity. "If I'm opposed to something, I'll vote against it on Appropriations or any other committee." "On some things, I go against the Committee every year. I knock them down on the floor year after year. I do that." "A vote in favor of reporting a bill to the floor of the Senate does not preclude any member of the Committee . . . from voting against it or offering an amendment which will either decrease or increase the amount in the appropriation bill."[24]

A Committee member who had served in the House interpreted the weakness of the unity norm as a senatorial characteristic:

> Sometimes out on the floor you have just the chairman of the subcommittee fighting the bill through all by himself. In the House, the whole Committee is out there supporting the bill. We don't have that kind of esprit that the House Committee does, of standing together to knock down all amendments. If we had that esprit, and the whole Committee stood together, there wouldn't be as many amendments as there are on the floor. But that's the same on all committees in the Senate, not just Appropriations.

A more senior member — one who is strongly attached to the norm of unity — attributed such Committee disunity as exists to the new members on the Committee:

> We stick together, but not as much as we should. We used to stick together a lot better than we do now. I think that's because we've got so many new members on the Committee who haven't — well — who don't feel their responsibilities as Appropriations Committee members. We had a case yesterday. A lot of the younger people on the Committee didn't stand with the Committee. I thought it was pretty loose . . . if they don't, we could be in some real trouble.

Whatever their enthusiasm for the norm of unity, Committee members agree that it is rather loosely espoused and sporadically followed. But they would agree that the Committee is more often unified than not and that this degree of unity constitutes a source of its influence on the floor.

[24] *Congressional Record*, Daily Edition, August 1, 1961, pp. 13243–13244.

596

No attempt will be made to duplicate the analysis of floor decisions which was undertaken for the House Committee. But some indication of the Senate Committee's floor success and of Senate satisfaction with its work can be found by examining the fate of its 576 recommendations for the 36 executive bureaus. Table 11.11 shows the same high proportion of acceptance of Committee recommendations as obtained in the House.

TABLE 11.11

SENATE ACTION ON SENATE APPROPRIATIONS COMMITTEE
RECOMMENDATIONS: 36 BUREAUS, 1947 TO 1962[a]

Senate Action	Number of Decisions	Percentage of Decisions
Accept Committee Recommendations	510 (517)	88.5 (89.9)
Decrease Committee Recommendations	15 (30)	2.6 (5.2)
Increase Committee Recommendations	51 (28)	8.9 (4.9)
Total	576 575	100 100

[a] Comparable House figures, from Table 9.4 in parentheses.

As evidence of the slightly more liberal expectations of the Senate, the floor changes are slanted in favor of increases — as compared with a 50–50 distribution of increases and decreases on the House floor. These gross totals would seem to indicate overall Senate satisfaction (or at least the absence of substantial dissatisfaction) with the work of the Committee. They also suggest the absence of any persistently strong Senate-Committee conflict.

On the basis of very partial analysis, the number of amendments proposed on the Senate floor appears to be — as in the case of the House — relatively few. In the first three Congresses studied (1947 to 1952), for example, only 74 amendments were proposed to the 216 separate recommendations made for the 36 bureaus. These figures, of course, support the conclusion that Committee recommendations do seem to meet Senate expectations. On the basis of the variations in degree of structural differentiations between House and House Committee on the one hand and Senate and Senate Committee on the other, we would predict two mutually offsetting patterns in terms of the frequency of Senate floor amendments. To the degree that the internal decision-making processes of the Senate Committee are more open to other members of the parent body than is the case in the House, we would predict that more accommodation would go forward inside the

Committee and hence fewer amendments would be offered on the Senate than on the House floor. On the other hand, to the degree that the floor context is not perceived as being markedly different from the Committee's context of decision-making, Senators would view floor activity as a simple extension of one long bargaining process and would be less reluctant or inhibited about proposing changes on the floor than would House members. The dominance of one or the other pattern of behavior has not been tested here. The strong impression, however, is that either tendency can be anticipated at a given point in time and that in the long run they balance each other out. That is to say, over a period of time we will not find any very significant differences between the number of appropriations amendments offered on the House and Senate floors.[25]

Table 11.12 reports the pattern of actual floor changes by years, in an effort, again, to relate floor decisions to external factors which vary over time.

TABLE 11.12

SUCCESSFUL FLOOR AMENDMENTS TO SENATE APPROPRIATIONS COMMITTEE DECISIONS: INCREASES AND DECREASES BY YEARS AND BY BUREAUS, 36 BUREAUS, 1947 TO 1962

Year	Number of Amendments Passed	Increases Passed	Decreases Passed
1947	1 (4)[a]	1 (2)[a]	0 (2)
1948	0 (4)	0 (4)	0 (0)
1949	5 (1)	5 (1)	0 (0)
1950	4 (1)	4 (1)	0 (0)
1951	13 (13)	0 (0)	13 (13)
1952	6 (9)	4 (0)	2 (9)
1953	8 (4)	8 (4)	0 (0)
1954	6 (8)	6 (8)	0 (0)
1955	4 (3)	4 (2)	0 (1)
1956	3 (1)	3 (1)	0 (0)
1957	1 (5)	1 (0)	0 (5)
1958	3 (2)	3 (2)	0 (0)
1959	1 (2)	1 (2)	0 (0)
1960	4 (0)	4 (0)	0 (0)
1961	3 (1)	3 (1)	0 (0)
1962	4 (0)	4 (0)	0 (0)
Total	66 (58)	51 (28)	15 (30)

[a] House totals by Bureaus (not, as in Table 9.6, by individual amendments).

[25] The comparable figures for the first three Congresses, for example, are 74 proposed amendments in the Senate and 111 in the House; for the last three Congresses, however, the House totals (see Table 9.5) are only 25, and one suspects the Senate totals would be higher. This impression remains to be confirmed, however.

Of particular interest is the fact that whereas floor increases distribute themselves fairly regularly through the years, floor decreases are concentrated in only two years.[26] Since the same pattern existed in the House, it suggests by way of generalization that members of both chambers expect their Appropriations Committee to undertake the budget-reduction task on behalf of the parent body and to do whatever budget-cutting needs to be done. Non-committee legislators do not, in other words, perceive themselves as performing the task of budget-cutting. They normally look upon the Committee recommendation as the minimum amount of money to be appropriated. This normal posture of the majority in both chambers can only be changed by the broadly based pressure of some external event to which, as representatives, they feel compelled to respond. It is for this reason that floor decreases come infrequently and in bunches. The national mood of economy in nondefense matters, produced by the onset of the Korean War, affected Senators just as it did House members. The largest number of floor decreases in both chambers occurred in 1951 and the second largest in 1952. In those years, neither Representatives nor Senators were prepared to perceive Committee recommendations as minimal — no matter what the Committee's actions had been.

The economy mood which prevailed in the Senate in 1951 differed very little from that in the House. "As a matter of moral right, we ought to cut,"[27] said one Senator. And another exclaimed, "Many of us took a solemn vow that we would try to do something for economy."[28] The mood was articulated by a coalition of Republicans and Southern Democrats. It provoked serious disagreements inside as well as outside the Committee. And it struck with particularly heavy force at the first appropriation bill reported out. As soon as the Committee recommendations for the Labor Department and the Federal Security Administration reached the floor, none other than Committee Chairman Kenneth McKellar rose to plead that "in this time of emergency, in this time when we need money to provide for the defense of this great country and the defense of our way of life, I appeal to Senators to reduce the amount appropriated in this bill."[29]

The coalition forces inside the Committee, led by McKellar and Republican Homer Ferguson, had agreed on a target of a 10 per cent cut in the budget estimates for "personal services" of every bureau. The subcom-

[26] Really three years (as explained in note 3, Chapter Ten), since an across-the-board cut was attached to the omnibus bill of 1950. But, since it was not applied to specific bureaus, it has been left out of the calculation here — just as a similar across-the-board cut, the Thomas-Taber amendment of the same year, has not been included in House calculations. In terms of comparison, therefore, they cancel each other out.

[27] 97 *Congressional Record*, p. 6355.

[28] *Ibid.*, p. 8029.

[29] *Ibid.*, p. 6308.

mittee involved had produced only a 5 per cent cut in these items. Said McKellar,

> I pleaded with the [full] Committee — I did not simply ask the Committee — but I pleaded with the Committee, with all the fervor at my command, "For heaven's sake let us cut down the appropriations carried in this bill" . . . it is exceedingly embarrassing to me as Chairman of the Committee as Senators may realize to be voted down so often, though by a close vote. But I was voted down. My friends on the Committee voted me down.[30]

On behalf of the minority of the badly split Committee, Senator Ferguson offered an amendment cutting each appropriation by an amount equal to 5 per cent of its estimate for "personal services." Despite a stout defense by the subcommittee chairman, the Ferguson amendment passed 58 to 24 — supported by 36 Republicans, 17 Southern Democrats, and 5 other Democrats. This action accounts for 9 of the floor reductions recorded in Table 11.12 for 1951.[31] Once the Ferguson amendment had carried, the Committee reformed its ranks and helped defeat 6 more amendments carrying reductions sponsored by Senator Paul Douglas.

The Committee read the vote on the Ferguson amendment as a statement of Senate expectations, and it abided by those expectations by making a 10 per cent cut in "personal services" items in the next two appropriation bills — Independent Offices and Interior. When the Interior bill reached the floor, Senator Ferguson sought further cuts. But the division inside the Committee had been largely repaired:

> CHAIRMAN MC KELLAR: I never saw anyone make a more determined and vigorous fight in Committee on a bill than was made by my distinguished friend from Michigan. He did everything in the world which was possible for the Senator to do to reduce government expenditures. . . .
> SENATOR FERGUSON: I appreciate the Senator's kind words, but I must disagree as to my success. I am not so enthusiastic about the success of my effort as the distinguished Senator from Tennessee is.
> CHAIRMAN MC KELLAR: The Senator from Michigan had greater success in connection with this bill than he ever had before in his life, in connection with any other appropriation bill . . . I had hoped, as I told the Senator yesterday, that the Senate would pass the bill in ten minutes.[32]

The problem of balancing one's expectations as a member of the Appropriations Committee with what one perceives to be important external expectations is nicely illustrated in the comments by Republican Committee

---

[30] *Ibid.*, p. 6309.
[31] For the effects of the amendment, see *ibid.*, pp. 6553–6554.
[32] *Ibid.*, p. 7621.

member William Knowland in support of the Committee recommendations and by Senator Ferguson in support of his proposed cut:

> SENATOR KNOWLAND: I would say that, of course, no member of the Appropriations Committee believes that the bill is not subject to scrutiny by the Senate or subject to such amendments as the Senate itself may desire to write into it, because this is a legislative process. But I will say . . . that I believe great weight should be given to the recommendations of the Appropriations Committee of the Senate. I am a member of that Committee, and I do not know of a committee of the Senate which spends longer hours or does more work than does the Committee on Appropriations and I have served on other committees which have been hard-working. . . .
> SENATOR FERGUSON: As far as the Senate Committee on Appropriations is concerned, I agree with the Senator from California. It is a hard-working committee. I am a member of that committee. I know something about the amount of work we are required to do. . . . [But] when an appropriation bill comes to the floor each Senator is responsible to his constituents back home as well as to all the people of the United States. We should look at this question in the light of the economy of the United States.[33]

The debate on the Interior bill consumed nearly two weeks. In the end, Senator Ferguson carried one of his three proposed decreases (for the Bureau of Indian Affairs), and Senator Paul Douglas failed to carry a set of proposed reductions voted upon en bloc.

The Committee's success in defending its Interior Department recommendations is attributable to the Committee's bipartisan responsiveness to external expectations — not to the subsidence of the expectations themselves. When the Treasury–Post Office bill reached the floor, conditions inside the Committee had reverted to an earlier state of disagreement, and its recommendations suffered accordingly. Senator Ferguson offered an amendment, explaining, "The Committee has breached the 10 per cent rule and this amendment proposes to restore it." Subcommittee Chairman Harley Kilgore protested that and said,

> I did not nor do I believe now that because a 10 per cent cut was made on Labor–Federal Security Administration appropriations, members of the Senate who vote against a cut of 10 per cent in other appropriation bills should be hung, drawn, and quartered. I will say to my friend he is consistent. In fact he gets me all stuck up with consistency.[34]

Once again, "the Ferguson amendment," bringing each cut in "personal services" to 10 per cent of original estimates (some of which were already at that level) passed easily 43 to 23.

[33] *Ibid.*, p. 8035.
[34] *Ibid.*, p. 9019.

Senator Richard Russell brought the Agriculture Department bill to the floor without rigid observance of the 10 per cent rule, but, nonetheless, with considerable bipartisan support on and off the Committee. In addition, he made an unusually long (by Senate standards) opening presentation in which he detailed, with charts and graphs, a picture of secular retrenchment and a steady "downward trend in the appropriations for the Department of Agriculture." He argued that because of this record the Department should be put "in a somewhat special category" as far as proposed floor reductions were concerned. He further contended, "There can be little question that the Agriculture Appropriation Bill during a period like the present, is a defense measure."[35] These backfires helped contain the economy drive — not because of the rhetoric, but because a sufficient number of Senators agreed with Russell's assessment. Of 11 proposed reductions, Russell succeeded in fending off all but 1 — and in a couple of cases he defeated the Farm Bureau Federation's official position in so doing.[36] Again, the strength of agricultural programs on the floor of Congress together with the special skill and prestige of Senator Russell are evident. Indeed, the two subcommittee chairmen who had the most success on the floor in 1951 were the two most respected: Senators Hayden (Interior) and Russell.

By the time the State, Justice, and Commerce Department Bill reached the floor in late August (nearly 3 months after the first attack on the Labor–Federal Security Administration Bill) the economy mood had clearly subsided. On that bill, the first floor increase of 1951 was voted, for the Voice of America program — a boost of $22 million. Minutes later, Senator Douglas proposed the last of his economy amendments for 1951 — a cut in the State Department's entertainment allowance. He lost (as usual), but the mood was recognizably one of relaxed good humor rather than of messianic economy as in early June:

SENATOR DOUGLAS: Mr. President, I again address the distinguished chairman of the subcommittee. I see his eyes shining with humanity, and I throw myself on his mercy. I know that he will want to enable the State Department and its guests to lead a more simple life. So I hope very much that he will consent to this reduction of $175 thousand in the so-called representation allowance which is primarily the provision for "booze." . . .

SENATOR MC CARRAN: However my heart swells for the effort of the able Senator from Illinois and however much I agree with him in trying to cut down at all times, I am following his example set by his vote which was cast just a few minutes ago when he voted to increase the appropriation [of the Voice of America] from $63 million to $85 million. I cannot go along with the Senator in his amendment. . . .

SENATOR DOUGLAS: I simply asked the Senate not to confuse the Voice of

35 *Ibid.*, p. 8708.
36 *Ibid.*, pp. 8812–8816 passim.

602

America with the breath of America [laughter]. We want a strong Voice of America; but I do not think the same requirement applies to the breath of America; I think we can diminish with profit the strength of the breath of America and increase the strength of the Voice of America [laughter].[37]

On closer inspection, the factors which produced the Senate pattern of floor decreases were similar to those in the House. Figure 11.1 shows, for example, that House and Senate Committee actions were pushed to their closest proximity in 1951. In the presence of strong external expectations for economy, the Committee must respond to them and must stand fairly solidly behind its response in order to protect its recommendations against floor sentiment for further decreases. The importance of these generalizations is heightened by the fact that, in the period under study at any rate, economy coalitions are bipartisan in nature. The first bills out on the floor are more likely to bear the brunt of the economy drive than the later ones. For one thing, subcommittee chairmen whose turn will come later can profit by watching the fate of their colleagues. For another thing, all economy drives have a tendency to spend themselves over a period of time as legislative attention shifts to other matters of higher priority. The difficulty in sustaining an economy drive over an entire legislative session may help to account for the fact that the Senate did not respond as vigorously with floor decreases in 1957 as did the House. The Senate felt the Eisenhower-induced economy drive of that year but, unlike 1951, it reacted by holding down increases (only 1 increase involving the 36 bureaus was approved) rather than voting additional decreases.[38] Whereas the House devoted 630 pages of debates to all appropriations matters in that year, the Senate used only 289. One suspects that senatorial time and attention were directed at other more pressing matters.

Whereas floor decreases appear to require broadly based external pressure, more limited, highly concentrated activity — external or internal — can bring about specific increases. An examination of the 66 floor increases and decreases by departments indicates that the program area is one important variable affecting floor increases. Table 11.13 confirms what we have already observed — the strong support present in the chamber for the programs of the Interior and Health, Education, and Welfare Departments. With the possible exception of the Labor and Treasury Departments, floor increases are more likely than decreases for all departments. In terms of absolute numbers, Interior and Health, Education, and Welfare, followed by Agriculture and Commerce, again appear to have special increments of support in the Senate — on the floor as well as inside the Committee.

[37] *Ibid.*, p. 10657.
[38] See the comments of Senator Russell, *Congressional Record*, Daily Edition, June 11, 1957, p. 7910.

603

TABLE 11.13

FLOOR AMENDMENTS TO SENATE APPROPRIATIONS COMMITTEE DECISIONS: INCREASES AND DECREASES BY DEPARTMENTS, 36 BUREAUS, 1947 TO 1962

FLOOR ACTION	DEPARTMENT Agriculture	Commerce	HEW	Interior	Justice	Labor	Treasury
Increases Above Committee Recommendation	7 (8.8%)	6 (7.5%)	18 (22.5%)	15 (11.7%)	0	4 (6.3%)	1 (1.1%)
Decreases Below Committee Recommendation	1 (1.2%)	0	5 (6.3%)	2 (1.6%)	0	4 (6.3%)	3 (3.1%)
Acceptance of Committee Recommendation	72 (90.0%)	74 (92.5%)	57 (71.2%)	111 (86.7%)	48 (100%)	56 (87.5%)	92 (95.8%)
Total	80 (100%)	80 (100%)	80 (100%)	128 (100%)	48 (100%)	64 (100%)	96 (100%)

Five of the floor increases in HEW programs centered on the Public Health Service. The solidity of congressional support for medical research has already been detailed. Little more needs to be added by way of explanation except to repeat that the National Institutes of Health have been the special favorites of the two relevant appropriations subcommittees and their leaders: Representative John Fogarty in the House and Senator Lister Hill in the Senate. These two men, their subcommittees, the full Appropriations Committees and the members of both houses take pride in the fact that it is the Congress rather than the executive branch that has seized leadership in this field. "We have had leadership in the Senate that has earned for this body a decent reputation for foresight and statesmanship," exclaimed Senator Hubert Humphrey. "Would that America had it every time on every subject. There is not a Senator present who is not proud of his service in the Senate because of what we have done in the field of health."[39]

Furthermore, the field itself is one which asserts an unusual emotional tug — especially on a body of men whose average age is between 55 and 60 and for whom their health and that of their friends is of immediate and deep concern. "All I can say to Senator Lister Hill is: Thank you very much for helping to save my life," said a Senator recently cured of cancer. "I say to you, Senator Hill, that whatever I may do in my future and in my career, you are partly responsible for it, because if it were not for you and for the medical research which was made possible by your leadership I would not be here."[40] It is hard to overestimate the emotional force of such face-to-face testimony. "Let me remind Senators," said Senator Hubert Humphrey in defending the Public Health Service budget,

> that since I have been in this body one Senator after another has been stricken with cancer or heart disease. I remember when the late and beloved Senator from Nebraska, Ken Wherry, sat here. I remember when the late beloved Senator from Ohio, Bob Taft sat here. I remember when the late and beloved Brian McMahon and the late and beloved Matthew Neely were in this chamber. I cannot call the entire roll.[41]

In recent years the Appropriations Committee has brought in a sufficiently generous recommendation for the Public Health Service so as to discourage any flood of additional increases. But those that are proposed usually get through, and, barring economy moods, any attempts to cut them (such as were made by Senator William Proxmire in the early 1960's) regularly fail.[42]

[39] *Congressional Record*, Daily Edition, August 1, 1961, p. 13229.
[40] *Congressional Record*, Daily Edition, June 24, 1959, p. 10652.
[41] *Congressional Record*, Daily Edition, August 1, 1961, p. 13229.
[42] On the Proxmire failures, see *Congressional Record* for August 1, 1961, and July 6, 1962.

The formula which guarantees the success of Interior Department programs in the Senate has already been spelled out. It need only be added that the ingredients which operate in favor of these Western-oriented programs inside the Committee operate also on the floor — especially the over-representation of the Western states and the leadership of Senator Hayden. In 1952, for instance, an illuminating contrast in floor activity was presented when the House and the Senate considered the Interior Department bill. The economy mood of the Korean War was distinctly present though considerably modified in force from 1951. On the House floor, nine separate reductions were proposed. Subcommittee Chairman Michael Kirwan objected strenuously to every one. Four of them passed over his protests, reducing funds for the Bureaus of Land Management, Reclamation, and Mines as well as Geological Survey. On the Senate floor, three decreases were proposed. Senator Hayden opposed all, and all were defeated. Three increases were also proposed; Senator Hayden agreed to each of them and they passed[43] Only under the most unusual circumstances is it possible to reduce an Interior Department program on the floor of the United States Senate. Thus the difference in House and Senate treatment of the Interior Department follows the same pattern from Appropriations subcommittee to final action on the floor.

Economy mood and program area affect floor action. But they are largely external to the situation on the floor. In Chapter Nine, some investigation was made into the effects of factors more closely related to the operation of the chamber. Committee unity, legislative Committee support, and partisan alignments were discussed as they affected the course of floor amendments. There is no reason to believe that these factors do not operate in the Senate as well as in the House. But they have only been touched upon tangentially in this chapter. Due to constraints of time, the quantification of these kinds of data has not been undertaken for the Senate. The research remains, therefore, still to be done. A guess might be hazarded that the three factors mentioned will prove to be slightly less relevant to a discussion of floor action in the Senate than in the House. Committee unity on the floor may become less important where the sense of identification with the parent body is as close as it is in the Senate. Committee members certainly do value unity, but not to the degree that House Committee members do. Legislative committee support may be less obvious on the floor simply because so many opportunities for securing it are available at the Committee stage. Finally, partisanship may increase as appropriations reach the roll-call stage — but the tendency of the Senate to record so many of its decisions by roll call may at the same time keep patterns of partisanship obscure. At any rate,

43 98 *Congressional Record*, pp. 2963 ff. and 7964 ff.

roll-call analysis of Senate appropriations decisions remains a task for the future.

Bargaining on the Senate Floor

Influence in the making of appropriations decisions is more widely shared in the Senate than it is in the House. Evidence for this basic generalization can be found on the floor as well as inside the Committee. More bargaining among individual Senators occurs on the floor of the Senate than among House members on the floor of that chamber. The fact that the floor constitutes yet another bargaining arena for Senators helps account for the predominance of increases over decreases. A majority of the increases voted via amendment involve pet projects or pet programs in which one Senator has taken a special interest and for which he makes a special plea on the floor. Senate Committee members hold to the basic idea that one cannot write an appropriation bill on the floor. But the senatorial habit of doing favors on a face-to-face, personal basis produces considerable sympathy for the floor pleadings of a colleague for some modest increase. At the most, the supplicant may get all he wants. More likely he will get a part of it. And, at the very least, he will get some assurance of friendly consideration in the near future.

When asked why they willingly accepted increases proposed from the floor, two subcommittee chairmen replied,

> To avoid a fight or to avoid getting more put in. After all there's such a thing as logrolling and if you get twelve Senators each with a project of his own and each one helping the other . . . or sometimes we'll accept it to help a fellow get elected. It's political in that way. But I can count on the fingers of one hand the number of times that a project has been added to the bill on the floor in my eight years as a subcommittee chairman.

> I won't accept anything unless I know my committee agrees to it. I can't just stand up and agree to things. Sometimes I'll say, "That looks all right to me and if you can get a vote on it I'll accept it." I like to have a vote on it. Of course, if it's something I know the committee understands and wants . . . I may let it go right along. But you can't have people get up and pop off and load the bill up that way. It has to go through committee first.

Subcommittee leaders freely admit the pattern exists and legitimately so. At the same time, they do not wish to give their endorsement to it as an accepted regular procedure. If, for example, the Committee does not wish to accept an amendment, it may use as an excuse the failure of the Senator involved to come before the Committee and urge him to testify next year. Or, when the executive agency in question has not appealed a given item in the hearings and a Senator asks on the floor that the item be included, the Committee may reaffirm its appellate function and refuse to accept

607

the amendment.[44] Whenever it refuses an amendment offered on the floor, it will do so on procedural grounds if at all possible, thus allaying interpersonal tensions. Similarly, the attention to the wishes of other Committee members noted in the comments just given reflects the Committee's preference for regularized procedure.

In the case of a plea on the floor, personal relationships bulk large. A staff member explained a condition of subcommittee acceptance of an amendment:

> It all depends who the person is — personal friendship comes into it. If he is a nice guy, someone you like, someone who's a member of the club, why, you'll take his project and help him out. But if it's some guy who'll never do things for others and who won't help you out, then you won't do it. A fellow like ———, he won't do favors for you. If he's got the floor he won't give it to you. He obstructs you and degrades you on the floor. ——— is the same way; he won't help. They may not get a project . . . you're not going to take a project of a guy who will gouge you. It's the human element.

It would of course be next to impossible to demonstrate the effects of personal factors, but observers have no doubt they are important. It might be noted, in this regard, that Senators like Wayne Morse and Paul Douglas who have been most vocal in their attacks on the Committee have not fared especially well at the hands of the Committee.

It is a characteristic of the appropriations process that decision-makers at each stage make decisions that are to some degree based on their prediction of events at the next succeeding stage. The position of the Senate Appropriations Committee near the very end of the long appropriations sequence gives it an advantage in establishing the framework for the conference committee proceedings. If there is to be a difference between final House and Senate decisions, it lies within the capacity of the Senate to determine the substance and the magnitude of that difference. When the Senate Committee fixes upon its recommendations, it makes educated guesses about the potential effect of its decision on the course of the conference. Assuming that the Senate seeks a conference result as close to its own desires as possible, it will want to recommend to the Senate a figure that will give its conferees the best possible bargaining situation when they meet with the House.

The concern of Committee leaders for the conference situation becomes most acute at the floor stage. As conferees they may, for example, wish to retain maximum room for maneuver. Hence the following suggestion by the Committee Chairman to a Senator requesting money for airport construction in his district:

[44] See, for example, *Congressional Record*, Daily Edition, May 15, 1957, pp. 6058–6059, pp. 6385 ff.

This matter will go to conference between the Senate and the House. The House figure is $1 million; the amount proposed by the Senator from Indiana [$950 thousand] would bring the figure to an amount which would allow the conference very little latitude in which to negotiate. If the Senator would consider modifying his amendment to bring the amount about halfway between the Senate and House figures, for example, to the sum of $750 thousand, so that there would be latitude for study and negotiation by the committee of conference, I, as one member of the Senate Committee which has handled the bill, shall be glad to accept it.[45]

The same concern for maneuver may lead the Committee to resist an amendment on the grounds that it will overload its bill to the point of provoking an unfavorable reaction by House conferees. Said one subcommittee chairman to a Senator requesting funds for a reclamation project,

The Senator, by asking the Committee to add funds to the bill at this time, places the Senate conferees in a most difficult position, because the bill as reported now crowds the budget limit . . . the question is whether we are to load down a bill with projects which will not be approved in the end and with which we will have difficulty in conference. The trouble is that by insisting on such projects, we run the risk of losing some other very important ones.[46]

Or, Committee leaders may simply suggest to a Senator that if he were to modify his amendment, the conferees might be better able to hold it in conference. The following comment was addressed to a Senator seeking additional money for the Soil Conservation Service:

I had hoped that the Senator would be willing to modify his amendments so as to provide for an appropriation of $500 thousand. I suggest that if the item were to go to conference with the enthusiastic approval of the Committee it might fare much better than if a larger figure were placed in the bill with no enthusiasm on the part of the conferees.[47]

Strategic considerations such as these affect the fate of floor amendments in the Senate.

The interplay of procedural and strategic factors sometimes determines whether or not a roll call will be taken on any given amendment. Should the Committee wish to retain maximum flexibility in the conference, it may not wish to have the preferences of the parent body clearly recorded in yea and nay form. Without such a record vote, the conferees will be the only voice through which "the Senate" speaks to "the House" in conference. If the Senate has spoken on a roll call, the Senate conferees may lose bargaining

[45] 99 *Congressional Record*, pp. 5895–5896.
[46] 100 *Congressional Record*, pp. 7713 ff.
[47] *Ibid.*, p. 7513. Other examples will be found in *Congressional Record*, Daily Edition, June 11, 1957, pp. 7889–7890, and June 17, 1959, pp. 10087–10088.

room.[48] Conversely, if the Committee wants to be able to dig in and hold a given item, it may seek the recorded support of the Senate on behalf of its position. Thus the Committee may deliberately bind itself inflexibly to a set position in order to strengthen its case in conference.[49] For non-Committee Senators, the device of forcing a roll-call vote can be employed as a sanction to ensure the compliance of the conferees with "Senate" expectations. Senator Douglas, for one, has voiced his desire on more than one occasion for a roll-call vote to ensure Committee responsiveness:

> I have been in this body long enough to beware of the chairman of a committee who says in an enticing voice, "Let me take the amendment to conference," because I think that is frequently the parliamentary equivalent of saying "Let me take the child into the tower and I will strangle him to death."[50]

Committee members regard the idea of binding them when they do not wish to be bound as a reflection on their integrity if not their ability. "No Senator should think that he is the only honest member of this body," replied a Committee member to Senator Douglas. "If we do not have faith in the integrity of each other — faith in the integrity of all members of this body — there is no use in our proceeding further."[51] Clearly it is considered improper to imply that the members of the Appropriations Committee are unsenatorial. Such an implication, it might be added, does fly in the face of a good deal of evidence to the contrary.

The decision of the Appropriations Committee's leaders on whether and how to "take the amendment to conference" is compounded of procedural, personal, and strategic factors. A small increment proposed by a highly respected Senator in an area where the Committee already stands in some disagreement may represent an optimum set of conditions:

> SENATOR HAYDEN: I suggest that the amendment increasing the item $400 thousand be agreed to, which will restore the $110 thousand cut made by the Committee of both Houses. If the amendment is taken to conference and a compromise is reached on a figure between $110 thousand and $400 thousand the Senator from Arizona will be satisfied. . . .
> SUBCOMMITTEE CHAIRMAN: I must call to the Senator's attention the fact that the $400 thousand increase which the Senator proposes is $290 thousand above the Budget Bureau's recommendation in the first place. That would make it exceedingly difficult for me, as subcommittee chairman,

---

[48] See, for example, *Congressional Record*, Daily Edition, March 29, 1960, pp. 6254–6255.

[49] See, for example, *Congressional Record*, Daily Edition, June 7, 1961, p. 9042.

[50] 97 *Congressional Record*, p. 6483. See also, *Congressional Record*, Daily Edition, March 29, 1960, pp. 6254–6255.

[51] 97 *Congressional Record*, p. 6483. See also the comments by Senator Chavez, 96 *Congressional Record*, p. 10075; 98 *Congressional Record*, p. 4550.

to take such a sum to conference. I should be perfectly satisfied and agreeable if the Senator from Arizona would modify his amendment so that the increase would be in the amount recommended by the Budget Bureau, $110 thousand, because, as I have frankly stated, I had a question mark on this item when I carried it from the subcommittee to the full Committee. I felt that the subcommittee had been too conservative. However, for me to state that I would be willing to take to conference an item which is $290 thousand above the recommendations of the Budget Bureau would be inconsistent with a subcommittee chairman's responsibility to the full Committee.

SENATOR HAYDEN: If the Senator from Minnesota [Senator Thye] feels that way about it, I modify my amendment by proposing to increase the amount $110 thousand instead of $400 thousand.

SUBCOMMITTEE CHAIRMAN: Mr. President, I shall be very happy to take the item to conference with that increase.[52]

If the Committee leader managing the bill has the confidence of other Committee members, and if the supplicant happens to be on good personal terms with him, the conditions may be present for the passage of a more sizable amendment with a minimum of concern for procedural delicacies. Committee Chairman Styles Bridges revealed something of his own area of operating freedom on the floor in striking the following bargain with his friend Senator Andrew Schoeppel:

SENATOR BRIDGES: Mr. President, as to the first amendment I will say to the Senator from Kansas that, in view of his expression of interest and in view of the fact that many Senators are unavailable at the moment, and also because I do not wish to delay action on the bill, I should be willing to take to conference a figure of $3.5 million instead of $3 million if the Senator from Kansas will agree to that. I may say frankly that I am speaking on my own authority, without concurrence or approval of other members of the Committee; I wish to make that very clear. I am willing to split the difference and take to conference the sum of $3.5 million instead of $3 million. That would place the subject in conference where the fact could be determined and any later information or evidence that might become available could be offered before the conference committee.

SENATOR SCHOEPPEL: Mr. President I should like to see the subject go to conference on that basis . . . let me ask the distinguished Chairman of the Committee what he would be willing to do as to the second item of $2,613,000. I think that is a very important matter.

SENATOR BRIDGES: With respect to that item, if we could reach an agreement, I would be willing to take to conference a similar split. The Senator from Kansas is asking for $2,613,000. I am willing to take to conference a figure of $2,306,500, which represents a similar split with respect to this item.

SENATOR SCHOEPPEL: I had hoped that the distinguished Senator might be a little more generous with respect to the second item. I had hoped he

[52] 100 *Congressional Record*, pp. 8932–8933.

might be willing to take to conference the figure of $2.4 million. This item represents a very important program in the electronic field.

SENATOR BRIDGES: I know the Senator from Kansas is a distinguished Midwestern trader. I think it is a fine thing to be a good trader. However, I am a New Englander, and have roots in the soil as far as trading is concerned. I think if I go halfway with the Senator that is about as good a trade as anyone could make.

SENATOR SCHOEPPEL: I am willing to have the distinguished Senator take the items to conference on the basis suggested.[53]

Committee leaders exercise considerable discretion in arranging constellations of procedural, personal, and strategic factors to suit their purposes on the floor. Contrast, for instance, Chairman Bridges' behavior above with his behavior in the following case as he dealt with a plea from a Senator closely allied with the Committee's severest critics:

SENATOR BRIDGES: It is possible that there might be some justification for increasing an item somewhat because of a particular Senator's interest in some particular phase of a problem. But when it is proposed to double the amount of an appropriation, such action completely changes the policy . . .

SENATOR LEHMAN: Will the Senator from New Hampshire who, I think, has already acknowledged that there are weaknesses in the system, agree to support an amendment providing for an amount less than $6 million? . . . I should like to ask the Senator from New Hampshire whether he would agree to take to the conference an amendment providing for an increase of $3 million [for the Immigration and Naturalization Service]?

SENATOR BRIDGES: My answer to that question is, "No." I shall not change my position or that taken by the Committee until we have further evidence to justify the Senator's statement on the situation. I do not believe we can legislate in this way on the floor of the Senate without a record being made.[54]

Though the difference in the amount of money requested, $1.6 million as opposed to $3 million may have been an important factor, Senator Bridges does seem to have placed more rigid procedural requirements in the path of one Senator than he did in the path of the other.

Necessarily, many a senatorial blandishment will be resisted by the Appropriations Committee. Typically, however, the Committee tenders its refusal "regretfully," "with the greatest of reluctance," and with sympathetic "assurances" for the future — all of which places the abruptness of Chairman Bridges' reply to Senator Lehman in perspective. The following exchanges typify the resolution of floor bargaining in cases where Appropriations Committee leaders decide not to "take it to conference":

[53] 99 *Congressional Record*, pp. 6056–6057.
[54] 100 *Congressional Record*, pp. 8127 ff.

612

SUBCOMMITTEE CHAIRMAN: I hope the Senator will not press the amendment.

SENATOR: In view of the fact that the Committee is against it and I can see that the amendment will not prevail, I shall graciously withdraw it.

SUBCOMMITTEE CHAIRMAN: I thank the distinguished Senator. I deeply appreciate his action. If the project in his state does not get along this year, we shall see that it gets along next year.[55]

. . . . .

SUBCOMMITTEE CHAIRMAN: I hope very much our distinguished colleague will realize the situation in which the Committee was placed and in which the Senate is now placed and take my assurance that next year if there is any chance for a recommendation of this matter, the project for the customs stations in Montana will be very fully considered.

SENATOR: Mr. President, on the basis of the assurances given by the distinguished Senator from Virginia I will withdraw my amendment.[56]

. . . . .

SUBCOMMITTEE CHAIRMAN: The Senator from Wyoming is so appealing that it really hurts me not to go along with his request, but I could not do it because of the responsibility which I have to other members of the subcommittee and the full Committee. I will say that the Senator from Wyoming has made a persuasive case, and I hope he will make it if and when a supplemental bill comes before the Senate. I assure him of a special invitation to appear before our Committee. . . .

SENATOR: The Senator from Florida has been gracious enough to say that he will welcome the Senator from Wyoming and other members of the committee on the judiciary with open arms if a supplemental bill is offered. . . . I shall take full advantage of the Senator's kind offer.[57]

Committee leaders normally make their decisions on the floor with the same degree of concern for the wishes of other Senators which characterizes their internal decision-making relationships. Not only do they listen receptively to pleas for floor increases, but if they feel constrained to refuse, they ordinarily do so in such a way as to ensure the continuance of the smoothest Committee-Senate relationships — present as well as future.

On the Senate floor, the Appropriations Committee maintains the same degree of control that it maintains throughout the process of decision-making in that body. It is a looser control and a more diluted influence than is exerted over appropriations activities in the House. The Committee shares its influence more willingly with other Senators and, withal, exhibits less anxiety about its relationship with the parent body than does its counterpart in the

---

[55] 94 Congressional Record, pp. 8106–8107.
[56] Congressional Record, Daily Edition, May 13, 1957, pp. 6058–6059.
[57] Ibid., May 17, 1957, pp. 6387–6388.

613

House. These characteristics are evident on the floor as well as inside the Committee. Yet it is clear from a sketchy examination of the floor activity that the Committee dominates action there just as it dominates activity at the Committee stage. Overwhelmingly, the recommendations of the Committee are approved on the floor. Some of their decisions are adjusted there — occasionally and incrementally. When they are, the Committee retains the greatest share of influence in shaping floor adjustments. In behavior as well as expectations the Committee remains closely coterminous with "the Senate." But the lack of sharp differentiation between the two does not alter the fact that the Committee clearly dominates all aspects of appropriations politics in the chamber. The Senate Appropriations Committee, as we have repeatedly stressed in contrasting it with the House Committee, *is* the Senate. Equally to the point, in appropriations matters, is that the Senate *is* the Senate Appropriations Committee. To describe the relationship in this way is to call attention to similarities between House and Senate. The centrality of both Committees cannot be better illustrated than by the fact that it is their representatives who go to the conference table to prepare the final form of every appropriation bill.

CONCLUSION

Not only is the Senate Appropriations Committee structured differently from the House Committee, it behaves differently from the House Committee. In terms of direction and magnitude, Senate Committee decisions have a less consequential impact on the appropriations process than House Committee decisions. Still, the Committee's decisions do have an independent influence on congressional appropriations patterns. Since the Committee's recommendations are normally accepted by the parent chamber, these generalizations about the Senate Committee apply equally to the appropriations activity of the Senate.

The Senate Committee's (and the Senate's) consideration of agency requests is less extensive, less thorough, and less time-consuming than is the same range of relationships for the House Committee. The Senate Committee, acting as an appeals court, focuses on a smaller increment of the budget than does the House group. The Committee makes smaller adjustments in the appropriations figures which come to it from the House than the House group does on the figures which come to it from the agencies. In comparison with the previous year's appropriations figures, Senate Committee decisions run in the same direction (toward increasing or decreasing appropriations levels) as that of the House Committee. These differences of style, of task, and of output are powerfully influenced by the intractable appropriations sequence, in which the House acts first and the Senate last.

All these differences provide support for the assumption that the House Committee is the more dominant — and hence the most dominant — force in congressional appropriations politics.

The appropriations sequence contributes, also, to the kind of independent impact that the Senate Committee has on appropriations. For it is the sequence which promotes the self-prescribed appellate court function. And the appellate court function promotes the distinctive liberality of the Committee. Generally speaking, the main characteristic of Senate Committee decisions is the tendency to increase most appropriations most of the time to a dollars and cents figure higher than that allowed by the House. If increases are not voted, the House figure is usually left untouched. This tendency to "up" appropriations results, of course, from a number of other differences between House and Senate and between their respective appropriations committees described in Chapter Ten.

The Senate Committee's tendency to increase appropriations is not uniform over time nor across all program areas. The influences of party or of mood alter the pattern of increases from time to time, and a special senatorial concern for certain programs results in more favorable treatment for some than for others. In contrast to House Committee decisions, the Senate has its most substantial and most distinctive impact on the appropriations for Interior Department programs. The Senate also gives especially favorable treatment to some Agriculture and Health, Education, and Welfare Department bureaus. In view of the fact that these same departments and bureaus tended to be relatively well treated by the House Committee, they can be viewed as the executive agencies most favored by the entire Congress.

The Senate's position in the appropriations sequence gives it a special source of influence over conference proceedings. Its decisions determine the items that will go to conference, and, if one is to be held, the Senate decision will determine the magnitude of the difference and the range within which the conference committee decision will fall. Bargaining inside the Committee and on the Senate floor is affected by a lively concern for the prospective conference situation.

CHAPTER TWELVE

The House
and The Senate:
The Conference Committee

Whenever an appropriation decision of the Senate differs from that of the House, representatives of the two chambers meet to write one bill acceptable to both chambers. Only when they have produced a single bill can the congressional product move to the President's desk for his action. The institutional device for settling money or language differences is the conference committee. Appropriations Committee and subcommittee leaders become the conferees, or managers, on behalf of their respective chambers. Every agreement they make must, of course, be ratified by the membership of both houses. Since, however, ratification is rarely denied, and since the President almost never vetoes an appropriation bill, the conference is the final stage in the annual appropriations process in Congress.

For each of the two Appropriations Committees, the conference represents a test of its capacity to adapt to the elements of its environment. House and Senate conferees face a dual test. Each must adapt to the actions of the other conferees, and each must adapt simultaneously to the actions of its parent chamber. Each set of conferees faces the problem, that is, of reaching agreement with the representatives of "the other body" while, at the same time, meeting such expectations as emanate from its own chamber. To adapt to each other, the two groups establish and maintain a decision-making structure and operate with a degree of independence from forces external to the conference. In order to adapt to their respective chambers, however, each set of conferees operates with a degree of dependence on external forces.

616

Conference committee activity can be described in terms of these twin problems of adaptation and the balance of independent and dependent behavior which arises from attempts to solve them.

SHARED GOAL EXPECTATIONS: HOUSE AND SENATE

Among members of the House and Senate and among members of the two Appropriations Committees there exists general agreement on what the broad goals of the conferees and of the conference committee should be. The consensus on goal expectations establishes some outer boundaries for conference activity and promotes the survival of the conference committee device for transforming two bills into one.

Two such goal expectations are of basic importance. One holds that the task of each group of conferees is to fight and win. House members expect House managers to represent the House's viewpoint and to fight for the House's version of the bill in dispute. Senators fix for their representatives the task of winning a conference victory on behalf of the Senate's bill. The managers themselves share this view of their tasks. A second expectation holds that the conference committee must produce a bill — a bill that will win majority approval in both chambers. All concerned prefer some bill — any bill — to no bill at all. Without money, all federal government activity would cease, and neither the members of the two chambers nor those of the Appropriations Committees desire such an outcome. Since differences exist, only the methods of compromise will bring about a bill. In combination, then, the two key goal expectations express the belief that the conferees should conflict with one another and should eventually compromise. Each side should try to win, but at the same time neither side should act so as to preclude the passage of a bill.

The expectation that conferees should fight to win is expressed when members of the Appropriations Committees stress the representative aspect of their conference task. Managers on both sides of the Capitol see it as their duty to defend their chamber's bill regardless of what personal reservations they may hold. Said a House subcommittee chairman, "Despite what personal feelings they may have, I have always held the position that the managers on the part of the House represent the majority of the House and not their own views as individuals."[1] And a ranking minority subcommittee member agreed. "All we can do as members of the House Committee is to go to conference and try our very best to bring back a bill as close to the House figure as we possibly can."[2] A veteran Senate subcommittee chairman reflected his

[1] *Congressional Record*, Daily Edition, September 11, 1961, pp. 17675–17676.
[2] *Congressional Record*, Daily Edition, October 12, 1962, p. 22100.

expectations and those of his fellow Senators in stating his view that "the Senate conferees are the servants of the Senate. They serve as agents in conferring with the representatives of the other body."[3] "When I go into a conference as a representative of the Senate, I represent the Senate viewpoint as vigorously as possible, even though it might not be in accord with the vote or votes I cast on the floor of the Senate. I conceive that to be my duty as a conferee."[4] To the degree that the two sets of managers do act in a strictly representative capacity, they will fight as hard as possible for dissimilar points of view.

When the conferees report the results of the conference to their respective chambers, they again give voice to the expectation that they should fight to win. In the first place, they give assurances that they struggled as hard as humanly possible in defense of their position. If they yielded somewhat, it was not for want of a valiant battle against a totally adamant and obstinate opponent:

> Those Members who have criticized the conferees for yielding on $101 million over and above the House bill, I am sure, have no idea how long we were in conference on this bill and how hard we worked to present the position of the House . . . this bill was in conference for four weeks. We had many meetings, [but] the conferees on the part of the Senate were adamant in their position by insisting on the inclusion of the full . . . figure which the Senate approved . . . every effort was made to forcefully present the position of the House of Representatives. I believe that your House conferees did the best possible job they could do under the circumstances on this particular bill.[5]

> Mr. President, I have participated in conferences on appropriation bills for many years; but never yet have I attended a conference which has given the Senate conferees more trouble than we had on yesterday. The five men who were as adamant as any men could possibly be gathered together, downstairs, and discussed this measure. We tried our best and argued practically all the afternoon, in order to sustain the position of the Senate. But when they said, "No," they meant, "No."[6]

The two sets of managers talked this way precisely because they were expected to fight and to win.

In the second place, the returning conferees seek support of their conference agreement with the argument that they have, on balance, won a victory in the conference:

[3] *Congressional Record,* Daily Edition, September 24, 1962, p. 19316.
[4] *Congressional Record,* Daily Edition, August 26, 1960, p. 16599.
[5] *Congressional Record,* Daily Edition, July 30, 1959, p. 13469.
[6] *Congressional Record,* Daily Edition, August 19, 1959, p. 15005.

Let me assure you that the best interests of the House were well preserved . . . we held our own and came back to the House with the biggest number of SR's — Senate Recisions — that this or any other subcommittee will bring back here.[7]

Every effort that could possibly be made was made in conference. We really thought we did pretty well. If the Senator will examine the entire conference report, he will see . . . we actually got the House conferees to agree with us in two-thirds of the disagreements.[8]

Each group of managers wants to be able to go back to his chamber and claim not a total victory but a limited one. Just what constitutes such a victory is most difficult to determine, since normally a great many items of varying value to the respective chambers must be processed. But for purposes of describing expectations, it is only necessary to note that assertions of victory in conference are used as justifications for chamber support.

The expectation that an appropriations bill must be passed is expressed most frequently, too, when the conferees are seeking ratification of the conference report. They defend their handiwork from criticism with the argument that compromise was necessary in order to produce a bill. And they use the argument precisely because of its congruence with chamber expectations. "If the Senate conferees at every conference took the position," explained one subcommittee chairman to his fellow Senators, "that everything the Senate did was one hundred per cent right and that we would not yield for one moment on anything, we would not get one appropriations bill enacted into law. We must give due deference to the views of the other body."[9] Other Senate conferees echoed this expectation: "When one is in conference after all he has an obligation to reach an agreement sometime."[10] "If the two houses sit at arm's length and neither house yields, we would jeopardize the entire bill itself."[11]

House managers make similar statements to their colleagues, stressing the practical impossibility of total victory and the necessity of compromise if there is to be a bill — and assuming that House members do want a bill. "Your conferees did not desert the House bill," explained one of them. "It was necessary to compromise our position with the Senate to get any bill at all."[12] In a similar vein, one finds House managers seeking support with these words: "This was not exactly what I wanted, but what in the Congress

[7] 95 *Congressional Record*, p. 9510.
[8] *Congressional Record*, Daily Edition, June 6, 1960, p. 11020.
[9] *Ibid.*
[10] 99 *Congressional Record*, p. 9934.
[11] 94 *Congressional Record*, p. 7571.
[12] *Congressional Record*, Daily Edition, July 30, 1959, p. 13471.

satisfies everyone to every degree? It was, I feel, the best agreement the Senate would accept and I do not think the compromise was unreasonable."[13] "Personally I think this bill carries too much money . . . but a conference is a conference and you must have a meeting of the minds."[14] The road to agreement may be tortuous and exhausting — often it is. And we shall view the complexity of the process shortly. But in the simplest terms, the two sets of conferees eventually reach agreement because they are expected to do so. And this basic expectation sets some outer limits to all conference committee activity.

SHARED MAINTENANCE EXPECTATIONS: HOUSE AND SENATE

Faced with the twin prescriptions that they win and that they write a bill, the conferees can only achieve these goals by compromising their differences. In the broadest sense, then, the maintenance expectations of both chambers and of the managers themselves prescribe a bargaining process in which each team of negotiators should yield something of its position to the other side. Every House-Senate conference is expected to proceed via the methods of "give and take," "trading back and forth," "pulling and hauling," "horse-trading and compromise," "splitting the difference," etc.:

> A conference report is not expected to be completely satisfactory to both sides, but merely acceptable to both sides. If the report is a reasonable compromise, one which takes into account and properly weighs the judgments of both sides it is a good report. If it rides roughshod over the views of one or the other, it is a bad report.[15]

The basic prescriptions concerning conference procedure stress the desirability of bargaining and compromise.

Supplementing and complementing, however, the most general maintenance expectations is a body of more specific rules — formal and informal — which govern appropriations conference activity. The House and Senate are normally in agreement as to how appropriations conferences should be convened, how they should be conducted, and how their results should be disposed of. The substance of their procedural agreements shapes the structure and the output of the conference.

Because the appropriations sequence remains the same, conference committee proceedings also follow a regular course. When the House originally passes its bill, an engrossed copy is sent to the Senate. If the Senate makes changes, a Senate appropriation bill takes the form of amendments

13 *Congressional Record*, Daily Edition, December 30, 1963, p. A7848.
14 93 *Congressional Record*, p. 9615.
15 103 *Congressional Record*, p. 7590.

to the House bill. When, therefore, the Senate passes the bill, and if it has altered the House bill, the Senate formally requests the House for a conference. The rules governing conference procedure prescribe that the house in possession of the "papers" (in this case the engrossed copy of the House bill and the engrossed copy of Senate amendments) asks for the conference. Thus the subcommittee chairman managing the Senate bill typically says, "I move that the Senate insist upon its amendments, request a conference thereon with the House, and that the Chair appoint the conferees on the part of the Senate." Formally, Senate conferees are appointed by the Presiding Officer (which would always be, if he desired it, the Vice President). But the informal rule holds that the floor manager suggest the list of conferees in accordance with arrangements worked out within the Appropriations Committee. The only formal proviso, stated in Rule 16, prescribes that for each bill where ex officio substantive committee members sit with the Appropriations Committee, one representative of the substantive committee (usually one of the ex officio members) must be appointed as a conferee.

When the Senate has voted to ask for a conference and its managers have been announced, the "papers" (now including the Senate request) are sent or "messaged" to the House, where they are placed "on the Speaker's table" — actually, locked in a drawer at the reader's desk. It is then in order for the House to disagree with the Senate amendments and agree to the proposed conference. Or, the House may, by unanimous consent, concur in the Senate amendments. When the House Committee assents to a conference — and it may, for strategic reasons, delay its agreement — the subcommittee chairman rises to say, "I ask unanimous consent to take from the Speaker's table the bill (H.R. ——) making appropriations for the Department of ——, with Senate amendments thereto, disagree to the Senate amendments, and agree to the conference asked by the Senate." And, if he hears no objection, the Speaker then appoints the managers on the part of the House.[16] Formally, the power to select conferees belongs to the Speaker. But, informally, he appoints those conferees designated by the Committee chairman in keeping with intra-Committee traditions.[17] In both chambers, the relinquishment of this appointment authority constitutes a basic chamber-Committee accommodation. It is an especially noteworthy concession by the party leadership to the Appropriations Committee in the House, where Appropriations Committee–chamber tension exists and where House leaders are more likely to feel the need for an extra sanction to curb Committee autonomy.

[16] For an objection, see 107 *Congressional Record*, p. 14546. A rules change in 1965 makes it in order to accomplish this by a motion, but unanimous consent remains the typical method.

[17] From 1865 to 1875, the Speaker appointed one member of the appropriate substantive committee to appropriations conferences. See the remarks of Representative Cannon, 17 *Congressional Record*, p. 208.

The House informs the Senate that it has agreed to a conference by "messaging" the conference papers (now including House formal agreement) back to the Senate. By informal agreement, a time and place will be set for the conference. Sometimes, one or the other group will stall in making these arrangements in order to win tactical advantages in the upcoming conference.[18] All subsequent deliberations go forward in secret executive sessions subject to procedures agreed upon by the conferees. The only rule thrust upon them from without provides that, "Conference reports must be signed by a majority of the managers on the part of each house."[19] The Senate conferees bring the papers to conference. If a successful conference has been concluded, a conference report is prepared by the staff people involved, the conferees sign the report, and the papers (now including the conference report) are handed over to the House conferees. Pursuant to House Rule 28, the House conferees prepare a "statement of the managers on the part of the House" which explains the various provisions of the report. It is important to know which chamber is in possession of the conference papers at each point because only the house in possession of the papers can take action. Typically, the House conferees take the papers back to their chamber, and the House acts on the conference report first.

Since the House nearly always considers the conference report first it is left with two options. It can adopt the conference report or it can recommit the bill to the conference. The latter step is possible because technically the conference committee still exists. If, however, the House adopts the report, its conferees are automatically discharged and the conference committee no longer exists. When, therefore, the Senate takes up the conference report, it does not have the alternative of recommittal to conference for the purpose of ironing out the particular matter involved. The Senate, therefore, is under greater pressure at this point to adopt the report. If it does not, the situation reverts to what it was before the conference, a new conference must be called for, new conferees appointed, and the process must begin all over again. Few Senators would relish this prospect. As one Senate subcommittee chairman said in just such a situation, "Mr. President, we cannot afford to send the report back to conference and thereby hold the Senate of the United States and the Congress for God knows how long, because if the bill goes back to conference, it goes back with every item in dispute and where shall we be then?"[20] By giving the House more appealing options in dealing with conference reports, the sequence bestows some ad-

18 An example is discussed in *The New York Times*, September 24, 1961.
19 *U.S. Senate Manual* (Washington: U.S. Government Printing Office, 1963), p. 148.
20 97 *Congressional Record*, p. 13080. See also, 99 *Congressional Record*, pp. 9947–9948.

vantage on that chamber.[21] On the other hand, as we have seen in Chapter Eleven, the Senate gains an advantage from its position as the last chamber to act prior to the conference.

The conference report takes the form of a list of recommendations from each set of managers to their chamber colleagues for each of the various Senate amendments. Only those items that were the subject of Senate amendments can be dealt with by the conference. That is, the conferees cannot add an item that did not appear in either bill, and it cannot change an item agreed upon in both bills. Indeed, "Where the differences involve numbers, conferees are limited to the range between the highest figure proposed by one house and the lowest proposed by the other."[22] Thus the conferees will report on each item and only each item for which the Senate decision differs from the House decision. And the recommendations of the report will suggest that one or the other house recede from its position entirely or agree to the Senate amendment with a further amendment. The conferees often report that some items are still in disagreement. Where such is the case, the items reported as settled can be acted upon and adopted, leaving the rest for further action. A conference report must be voted up or voted down or (in the case of the House) recommitted in its entirety. It cannot be taken apart by the House or Senate and dealt with piecemeal. Therefore, the managers of a bill seek agreement to the conference report first and then go back to work on the few items which remain. Many of these are technical matters which are kept out of the conference report because they could be subjected to a point of order. If they were included in the report and a point of order were lodged against them, the entire report would be rejected. In such a case or when a disagreement has been ironed out subsequent to the conference, the subcommittee chairman will simply recommend that his chamber "recede and concur" in the position taken by the other chamber.

Occasionally the conferees will be in genuine disagreement. In such cases, the House managers usually move to "insist" on their rejection of the Senate amendment involved and will, if adopted, so inform the Senate. The Senate has the option of receding and concurring in the House position or it can "insist" on its disagreement and ask for another conference. At this point, both chambers appoint conferees and the process begins anew, but, if the conference report has been approved, only those items still in disagreement will be considered. Occasionally, where a single item is in question, one chamber will say nothing and wait, hoping that the other house, which wants

[21] See *Congressional Record*, Daily Edition, December 19, 1963, p. 24059.
[22] Clarence Cannon, *Cannon's Procedure in the House of Representatives* (Washington: U.S. Government Printing Office, 1963), p. 132.

623

the bill, will capitulate.[23] Theoretically a ritual dance of disagreement could continue till the end of the session. But, unless there is agreement on or deletion of the item, there will be no bill. Invariably, the items involved are of sufficient importance to both chambers that they come to agreement. At the close of the 1961 session, however, the House used its strategic advantage on a supplemental appropriation bill by adopting the conference report, insisting on its position on all items reported in disagreement, and then adjourning sine die. The Senate was left with the option of receding and concurring on all items or having no bill at all. Enraged, it nonetheless opted for the first alternative.[24]

The body of maintenance expectations prescribes considerable autonomy for the conference committee. The method of selecting conferees, the conduct of business in executive session, and the provision that a conference report must be voted up or down in its entirety — all these procedures work to promote conference committee independence from external influence. A countervailing procedure, however, allows the parent chambers to "instruct" their respective managers. When passed by the House or Senate, a motion to instruct will bind the conferees of that house strongly to the position set forth in the motion. It is possible to give instructions to a group of conferees immediately before their names are actually announced and prior, therefore, to the opening of the conference. Such a move is rarely made. More likely, though still infrequently, the House will vote to "recommit with instructions" when it is being asked to vote on the conference report. The Senate, similarly, is more likely to instruct its conferees when it asks for a new conference. Such moves are seldom taken, yet they constitute a standing sanction which the parent chambers hold over the conference committee. More important, this provision gives formal underpinning to a variety of less authoritative yet persuasive methods — from statements on the floor to roll-call votes — whereby the House or Senate expresses its sentiments to the managers and thereby influences the outcome of the conference.

SHARED PERCEPTIONS AND ATTITUDES: HOUSE AND SENATE

The Appropriations conference committee is a viable institution in part because House and Senate members, together with their conference representatives, share some basic expectations about what the conference should accomplish and what rules of the game should be observed. It is viable, also, because those who share goal and maintenance expectations share some very general perceptions and attitudes regarding the conference. When asked,

[23] *Congressional Record*, Daily Edition, May 18, 1961, p. 7782.
[24] *Congressional Record*, Daily Edition, September 27, 1961.

for example, to describe what happens in a conference, House and Senate participants report the same basic perceptions. Both see the conference as a struggle which inevitably culminates in a negotiated settlement of some sort. A veteran Appropriations Committee Senator conveyed this perception when he said,

> Basically it's a matter of settling a difference of opinion between two bills. Its a knockdown drag out affair until you get agreement. It's a lot of fun if you like that sort of thing. You get in there and pinko pinko back and forth . . . a conference on an appropriation bill is just horse-trading. You've got a horse you want to trade and I've got a pony I want to trade. And you know you've got to have a bill.

In somewhat more strenuous terms, a senior House Committee member voiced the same perception:

> It's psychology, being stubborn, being boisterous — even walking out if something is important. I've seen a conference last for days — weeks. You sit around and no one will give in and someone will say, "Well, I guess we had better adjourn." And you come back the next day. Usually you get through an Appropriations conference in one day. Sometimes, though, both sides are so adamant you think you'll never come to a compromise. But eventually you do.

A Senator summed up the major ingredients when he said, "You start a conference like diplomats. There's a lot of hand-shaking and back-slapping. If you have a bad conference, a real ugly one, you end it just before there is a general fight." In analogies ranging from those of twentieth-century politics ("It's a psychological cold war") to those of the nineteenth-century frontier ("It's just thievery and horse trading"), a conference is uniformly perceived as meeting those expectations which prescribe both conflict and compromise.

In terms of their most general attitudes toward what they see, most participants seem to be satisfied that, given a bicameral legislature, the conference committee is, at the very least, necessary. If they do not agree with one Senator's estimate of the conference as a "knockdown drag out legislative fight with a lot of wisdom in it," they certainly do concur with the statement of another that "nothing was ever accomplished in Congress without compromise, and that's the principle you have to work on." The existing consensus on expectations and images concerning the Appropriations conference committees indicates the existence of a fairly stable pattern of activity — so long as one thinks of this pattern in general terms. House and Senate members want the conference to accomplish certain things in certain ways. They perceive the conference as meeting these expectations. They support continued conference activity of that type.

DIFFERENT PERCEPTIONS AND ATTITUDES: HOUSE AND SENATE CONFEREES

The existence of a consensus sufficient to underwrite the continuance of an institution and to stabilize a very general pattern of activity should not be taken to mean that conference committee activity is not the object of disagreement. Far from it. Some members of the House, for example, see conference committee autonomy as additional evidence in support of their contention that the House Committee enjoys excessive independence. And, certainly, some members of both chambers will find themselves in disagreement with any given item of a conference report. More significant, however, than any external sources of conflict are those which arise from differences associated with the two groups of people who meet at the conference table.

The House and Senate Appropriations Committees do not share all the same perspectives on the conference committee. And this fact accounts for much short-term conflict both in and about the conference committee. Of course, the two Committees fight with one another in conference; that is what they are expected to do. But their contests over specific dollars and cents amounts or over specific words in an appropriation bill are heightened by differences between the two Appropriations Committees as political units and between the two parent chambers as political units. The self-image of the two groups differs, and so does the image which each group has of the other. These differences generate additional sources of antagonism. Throughout 1962, for example, the two Appropriations Committees became embroiled in a conflict which brought all conference committee activity to a halt, thus disrupting normal patterns of activity in the larger political system. A necessary condition for this kind of conflict might be that the two Committees (and the two chambers) favor different bills. But a sufficient condition is the existence of added dissimilarities between the two Committees (and the two chambers) as political systems. From these institutional differences flow perceptions and attitudes that can affect specific conference decisions and overall conference relationships. The views which House and Senate groups have of one another have been mentioned previously. But it is useful to describe more fully some of those images which are especially relevant for understanding conference committee action.

House Conferees: Their Images

The managers on behalf of the House approach the conference table with an image of themselves as the responsible guardians of the federal Treasury and with an image of their Senate counterparts as being excessively profligate with the public money. "If the fiscal integrity of this government is to be defended and kept intact, it will be done in the House of Representatives and in no other place in the government,"[25] exclaimed one subcommittee chairman upon his return from conference. The perception of the Senate as the "upper" house dominates House thinking — the more so because it is cast in relief against the House Committee's self-image of economy-mindedness. House members frequently allude to the assumption of the founding fathers that the Senate would be the more conservative of the two chambers. "If ever there was a bad prediction, it was that one." "The House, not the Senate, is the more conservative body." And, of course, "the House" means the Appropriations Committee.

According to House Committee perceptions, a guiding principle of the behavior of Senate Appropriations Committee members is their willingness to vote appropriations for their fellow Senators on a personal basis. House conferees view the Senate as "a mutual admiration society," "a club," and "a small body where trading is easy." Instead of acting as a brake on the reciprocal passing of favors, the Appropriations Committee performs an active brokerage function. "There's an unwritten rule over there that when a Senator from a state wants something put in a bill over and above the House, there are no questions asked." As House conferees see it, the Senate "throws anything in over there." The Committee "piles everything on earth in these bills," "throws everything in but the kitchen sink," and "piles stuff into these bills no end."[26] To some degree, House managers believe, Senate bills are "loaded for compromise." Many items go into the bill so that a few can be taken out in conference. Thus House conferees do go to the bargaining table expecting the Senate to yield fairly easily on some of these items.

Still, House Committee members disapprove of senatorial back-scratching. "We are tired," said one subcommittee chairman publicly, "of the courtesy which Senators show each other."[27] They believe that this general pattern of behavior is a major cause of Senate appropriations increases and a major source, therefore, of conference room conflict. Said one subcommittee chairman,

> We go over there and I say, "This item is not authorized. The Corps of Engineers hasn't agreed. It's ridiculous and I'm not going to vote for it." And they say, "Oh, that's Senator so and so's project; oh, that's Senator such and such's project. We can't touch that." They have a system over there where any Senator can get anything in a bill he wants — a gentleman's agreement.

[25] 93 Congressional Record, p. 9298. See also comments about the Senate Committee in 94 Congressional Record, p. 8187, and 101 Congressional Record, p. 11058.

[26] Time, February 2, 1959, p. 14; Congressional Record, Daily Edition, August 19, 1959, p. 15033; 102 Congressional Record, p. 11122.

[27] Quoted in Earle Wallace, "The Politics of River Basin Appropriations: A Case Study of the Roanoke River Basin," unpublished manuscript (University of North Carolina, 1959), p. 193.

A ranking minority member of another subcommittee complained similarly:

> Someone on the other side will say, "Senator so and so wants this project or Senator so and so is interested in this item." That Senator isn't even on the Committee and hasn't attended the hearings, but he wants something and the rest look out for him. He isn't physically in the conference room but he's in there just the same. It's a club and they are trying to help him out. Maybe he just spoke to the chairman or the clerk and said, "I want this in," and they'll fight for him in conference.

With these comments (see also Chapter One), House members display an accurate perception of the minimal structural differentiation which characterizes Senate–Senate Appropriations Committee relationships, and, insofar as they find it different from their own situation, they also emphasize two patterns of system-subsystem relations. Of course, House members do not generalize in this manner. But House conferees find in this perceived difference both an explanation for Senate openhandedness and a source of annoyance and frustration in conference.

The irritation which House conferees feel concerning Senate Committee behavior is compounded by the House members' perception that they know much more about the subject matter than the men who sit on the other side of the conference table. The House Committee members' style of hard work and their specialized knowledge are prime sources of pride, self-satisfaction, and influence. Nowhere is the information gap perceived to be greater than between themselves and Senate Committee members. "I'm not saying this as a House lover," shouted one subcommittee chairman, "but all the work is done in the House." A ranking minority subcommittee member spoke for the unanimous judgment of his colleagues when he said, "The thing I notice most about conference is that the House is much better prepared than the Senate. We spend more time on it than they do and have more information." Senators are perceived as leaning heavily on their clerks during conference: "They have to look over to their staff to get the answers." In view of such obvious superiority, even the necessity of compromise becomes something of an irritant to House conferees. "That's the thing that gripes me," said one. "We do all the work and they always beef it up . . . then we have to bargain with them." Nonetheless, once bargaining begins, House managers believe that their superiority in information gives them one important advantage over their opponents.

In large measure, the comparisons which House conferees make between themselves and their Senate counterparts come down to this: The House Committee takes its appropriations tasks more seriously than does the Senate Committee. If this is true, then it follows that the House Committee and the House deserve a position of pre-eminence in exercising Congress' power of the purse. To the degree that House Committee members believe they now enjoy pre-eminence, they will oppose changes in the appropriations process which they perceive as increasing the relative influence of the Senate. And they weigh every proposed budgetary reform in exactly these terms. For example, some of them see Treasury borrowing as "this silly backdoor shenanigans put in by the Senate"[28] or as "a Senate scheme for getting around the law and originating appropriations over there." Some view the increase in annual appropriations as partly an attempt by the Senate to reduce the influence of the House Committee. And, when the legislative budget was prescribed in the Reorganization Act of 1946 (setting up a joint House-Senate committee to estimate revenue and fix appropriations ceilings), it was the House Appropriations Committee with the support of the Ways and Means Committee which protested against it in the first year and thereafter refused to participate.[29]

A member of the Senate Appropriations Committee recalls what happened:

> One of the best things in the Legislative Reorganization Act was the legislative budget — [but] old Clarence Cannon and old John Taber decided the Senate had no business getting in on appropriations this way and they threw it out. Over in the Senate we can pass a bill to put it through. But if it goes over to the House it will die there. They won't even take it up. One thing that runs all through the process, and I didn't realize it until I got close to appropriations, and that is the House feeling of primary responsibility over appropriations.

Since the demise of the legislative budget, Senators on and off the Appropriations Committee have proposed a Joint Committee on the Budget, consisting of several members of the two Appropriations Committees plus a staff. Six times the bill, usually sponsored by Appropriations Committee member Senator John McClellan, has passed the Senate unanimously.[30] And there is some support for it in the House — but very little on the Appropriations Committee, whose members see it as an attempt to increase Senate and Senate Committee influence in the appropriations process. "I don't support that," said one House Committee member, "because I don't have any confidence in the Senate on appropriations." Prevailing sentiment was expressed more bluntly by a Committee clerk when he stated, "Whenever you let the Senate in on appropriations, you're sunk." "Every key provision of the bill embracing the [Joint Committee on the Budget] is, in my judgment, either unsound, unworkable, or unnecessary," testified Chairman Mahon to the Joint Committee on the Organization of Congress in 1965. He defended the

---

[28] *Congressional Record*, Daily Edition, April 26, 1961, p. 6299.

[29] See the Report of the Committee as reprinted in *Congressional Record*, Daily Edition, February 5, 1953, pp. 1754–1756.

[30] *Congressional Record*, Daily Edition, January 25, 1963, pp. 1036 ff., and May 20, 1963, pp. 8505 ff.

positive value of "two co-equal but independent branches contentiously juxtaposed." And, in response to senatorial inquiries, he argued that the Joint Committee would "tend towards a unicameral type of legislature without the checks and balances we now have [and] . . . would further downgrade Congress and upgrade the executive."[31] When pressed in the House to explain their opposition, Committee members have tried to impress upon their colleagues that appropriations pre-eminence is the House's greatest source of influence within the American political system and that the House itself, therefore, would be the institutional loser in any such change.

Curiously, perhaps, the Committee's argument in the House has not been simply that the Joint Committee would give the Senate parity. It has been that the Senate would dominate any Joint Committee. In the words of a Committee leader,

> It [Joint Committee Bill] provides for a joint setup of research people which would be simply a duplication of effort and I am afraid that it would be controlled by the other body, so that we would get nowhere and have no information that could possibly be used successfully by us. It would permit increases in appropriations by the other body to be promoted beyond endurance.[32]

Calling the Joint Committee a "super duper conference committee," another Committee member agreed:

> I am sure that if any of you have served on a conference committee on appropriations with members of another body . . . I am referring to the upper house so called because of the fact that it ups most of the appropriations made in the House . . . there is no question but if the Committee is established, the upper body to which I refer would dominate.[33]

These defenses rest, at bottom, on the House Committee's perception of its own greater sense of fiscal responsibility. But it betrays, also, an interesting lack of confidence on the part of House Committee members in their ability to dominate face-to-face House-Senate relationships.

The apprehension of House Committee members that the Senate might dominate a Joint Committee on the Budget derives primarily from their feeling that in the areas of prestige and public relations, Representatives are no match for the "prima donnas" in the Senate. A Senate Committee member, formerly in the House, stated the problem this way. "A good House

---

[31] Joint Committee on the Organization of the Congress, *Hearings on the Organization of Congress*, 89th Congress, 1st Session (Washington: U.S. Government Printing Office, 1965), pp. 1652, 1654, 1751. One veteran Committee member, Representative Ben Jensen, gave the plan lukewarm support in 1963. Senate Committee on Government Operations, *Hearings on S 537 to Create a Joint Committee on the Budget*, 88th Congress, 1st Session (Washington: U.S. Government Printing Office, 1963), pp. 22 ff.

[32] 103 *Congressional Record*, p. 4416.

[33] *Ibid.*, p. 3908.

member is like a good lineman on a football team; he works like hell, gets banged around, and only the experts know what he's doing. The Senators are like backfield men — they grab the ball and the glory."[34] With particular reference to an appropriations conference, a senior House member said,

> I know that the members of the other body are more highly evaluated in some quarters, possibly, because they, like gold, are fewer in number and possibly have a better press. But I am not ready to confess any such inferiority complex so far as I am concerned as a member of this body. I cannot understand the thing that we are confronted with so many times in the House. "Well, we did the best we could, but the other body overwhelmed us."[35]

As members of the House, Appropriations Committee members certainly share this sentiment. But, as conferees, they perceive that prestige advantages accrue to their Senate opponents. Accordingly, they believe that they need every formal institutional advantage they possess if they are to overcome these prestige superiorities of the Senate.

House Committee members believe that they take their appropriations job more seriously and act more responsibly than do Senators. Yet Appropriations Committee Senators enjoy prestige and publicity advantages quite unrelated to performance on appropriations matters. This combination of perceptions breeds a resentment among House managers, which may increase antagonism in the conference room. On the merits, House conferees feel they deserve to win. Yet they may not. This state of affairs is the more aggravating to them because House Appropriations Committee members have a much greater psychological investment or ego involvement in the handiwork of their one committee than Senators do in the work of what is for them one of a multiplicity of interests. For most House Committee members, their one conference each year is a matter of paramount concern. It is probably incorrect to speak of an inferiority complex, but it is probably accurate to say that elements of resentment and suspicion exist toward what Chairman Cannon called "the House of Lords." This complex of psychological elements may help account for the aggressive, even belligerent, attitude that House members say they sometimes must take in their dealings with the Senate. Here, for example, are the image of and the response to the Senate's conferees as voiced by one House subcommittee chairman:

> The Senate members usually come in about fifteen minutes late. Half of them aren't there. They come in with a holier than thou or a higher than thou attitude. There is that attitude on their part. [Until 1962] we had to go over there to meet. We met on their territory. They have six years to wait

[34] Quoted in David S. Broder, " 'The Other Body' — Not 'the Upper House,' " *New York Times Magazine*, May 20, 1962, p. 23.
[35] 103 *Congressional Record*, p. 3915.

before coming to any agreement. We have only two. They take the attitude that they can't understand why we won't agree to the higher figures — and they're always higher. They say, "Senator so and so won't stand for this cut." Everything is done on a personal basis there. . . . I'm happy to say that it doesn't happen with the subcommittees I'm on. We really put their feet to the fire and teach them the facts of life. We just sit there — sometimes it takes us days to let them know we mean business.

By their own admission, and by agreement of the Senate, House conferees talk and act tougher than Senators. "We don't have to go to conference if we don't want to. If we don't agree, there won't be a conference. Sometimes we make them wait." House members often make this assertion — even though it is equally true for the Senate and even though the conference is always held. It seems as if it were a source of satisfaction to House Committee members that it is the Senate that must ask them for a conference — that it is the Senate, not the House, who is put in the position of petitioner. Perhaps "talking tough" or "putting their feet to the fire" are ways of compensating for the frustrations and giving vent to the resentments of House conferees. Whether such speculation is correct or not, the point is that intangible sources of House-Senate antagonism exist and may trigger or exacerbate more tangible conflicts.

Senate Conferees: Their Images

Senatorial images of the Appropriations conference take shape as reactions to the House conferees, much as Senate decisions come as reactions to House decisions. Senate Committee members perceive the House Committee, first of all, as "a very conservative group."[36] And Senators freely concede their own relative liberality — even their tendency to proceed on a personal basis. "Sometimes we say, 'This man wants this. He's a nice fellow,' and we'll help him out. But they do that in the House too." Senators believe, however (as indicated earlier), that the House Committee secretly approves — even while it publicly protests — some Senate openhandedness. "They're more money conscious over in the House than we are," said one senior Democrat. "More parsimonious — they say economical. They make a lot of cuts and expect us to put them back in." And a veteran Republican agreed:

> Over in the House it's a great thing to economize. They cut out a lot of things because they know very well that when the bill comes over here, we will restore the money. I know — I was in the House. I used to vote to cut all these funds and then come over here and ask my Senators to be sure that the money got back in. We get plenty of that around here.

[36] 98 *Congressional Record*, p. 4464.

"The worst thing that could happen to the House Appropriations Committee," says a veteran Senate Committee clerk, "would be for the Senate to pass the bill they send over. They'd be heartbroken." When the Senate Committee members fight in conference for the higher appropriations figure, they believe all the while that part of the House's protest is a sham. Hence, they believe that the House conferees, despite their talk of economy, are quite willing and prepared to yield part of their position without any real contest. Both sets of conferees go to the bargaining table, therefore, convinced that some segment of the other's bill is freely negotiable. This mutuality of perceptions helps lubricate the bargaining process.

On the matter of information, too, Senate conferees agree that the men across the table are better informed. "They know the bill much better than we do." Senate leaders are quick to praise their opposite numbers in the House, but they are equally quick to add that House members have more time to devote to appropriations. "We can't specialize like the members of the House Committee do. You take Al Thomas on Independent Offices. He knows that bill backward and forward and he does a good job. But he's been over the same bill for twenty years and that's all he does." A Senate subcommittee chairman spoke about the House subcommittee chairman with whom he meets regularly in conference:

I have a great deal of respect for him. He does a real fine job. He's had a lot of experience and he knows all about it. But it's a one-barreled shotgun for him. It's all he does. And I'm mixed up in all this other business around here. He starts in December and on into January and all down through until the bill is finally passed. He digs into the bill in great detail. I'm usually more liberal than he is and we knock it around. But I keep in the back of my mind that he's had a lot of experience and knows the bill pretty thoroughly.

Committee members do not admit that their information deficiencies hamper them in conference. But several staff men did voice that opinion. "The Senators are much weaker in conference," said one. "Every House member has one committee assignment and he specializes in one subcommittee. Every man knows one aspect of the bill. But over here a man sits on five subcommittees. Sometimes he doesn't know whether he's coming or going." Another agreed, "The House is a little stronger argumentatively. . . . I've seen the House carry its point by a flow of words and information which couldn't be matched on the Senate side. They're better informed." Of course, the clerks can help. Indeed, they view their task in conference as one of "out-informationing the House." Given their perspective, Senate staff men are more likely to emphasize information problems than are the Senators themselves. It seems fair to assume, though, that Senate conferees perceive

633

their relative lack of specialization and detailed knowledge as a handicap which must be overcome by their own negotiating skills in the conference room.

In the eyes of Senate Committee members, the style of the House managers engenders additional heat in conference committee meetings. They describe the House conferees variously as "stubborn and bullheaded," "rigid and thick-skinned," and as akin to "the chiseled faces on Mount Rushmore."[37] This conference room manner derives, Senators believe, from House protectiveness concerning its appropriations prerogatives. Senate conferees, by contrast, see their own bargaining style as more relaxed. A senior Senator gave voice to the consensus of his colleagues when he said,

> Some of the conferences can be pretty rough. You've got some fellows over in the House who are really hard-boiled about it. They pride themselves on just being tough . . . they feel that we don't have any business dealing with appropriations, and sometimes they can be downright insulting. Fellows like Cannon — when he leads a delegation over here, which he often does. Many times he speaks for the conferees instead of the subcommittee chairman. Usually a subcommittee chairman speaks for the conferees, but sometimes he just sits there and Cannon takes over. He says, "I'll do this and I'll do that. I'll give you this or I won't give you anything on this. Where did you ever get such an outlandish idea, anyway?" That's not true over here. The subcommittee chairman sometimes polls the conferees right there and everybody speaks up.

From the senatorial standpoint, the most serious consequence of House assertiveness is not that it presages a House victory in conference. It does not. But it may provoke an equal and opposite reaction from Senate conferees, thus aggravating whatever antagonisms already exist. "Sometimes you get a chairman over in the House," said one Senate veteran, "and he says that he's it, that he won't give you this. Well you tell him that you won't give it up either and that you won't have a bill." Another experienced Senator voiced a sharper reaction in detailing his image of the House conferees:

> The House attitude is reared in stubbornness and confusion . . . their attitude is little less than arrogant. And you have to be damned charitable to say less than arrogant. They come over here and say, "This is what you'll get and if you don't take it, we're going home and you won't get anything." I'm getting sick and tired of it. One of these days, when I get in a position to do it, I'm going to say, "All right, you bastards, go on home and we'll see you next year." It's an unwarranted arrogance — based on their power to initiate appropriations. Now there's another thing. Each man over there sits on only one committee. They go into it much deeper than we do. And they should. It's their primary responsibility. But that's no excuse for this unseemly arrogance. They have too much control over appropriations. I wouldn't say complete control, but too much control. For three years, we

[37] 99 *Congressional Record*, p. 9943.

fought them in the ———— bill, and last year we just went in there and said, "We want this." And we stood there until they gave it to us.

Senate Committee members know that their appeals court function leaves them with less influence than the House over the total appropriations product. They remain sensitive to this fact, and House assertiveness may heighten their touchiness on the point. One Senate Committee member complained to House Chairman Mahon:

> We have come to be derided by our colleagues in the House because we raise the appropriations and never do anything on our own . . . never cut them. This is somewhat degrading it seems to me, for an equal body . . . our function is a very minor one . . . a kind of review of only those items which the administration does not accept your action on, and this is what it is, George, this is what it is. . . . It is almost useless for the Senate to add anything, for example, that is not in the budget. The House Appropriations Committee just says as a rule that "we will not take any Senate action on such nonsense as this. If we want to add something that is not in the budget, that is up to us. But you guys will sit here until hell freezes over and you will get nothing." . . . The Appropriations Committee in the House and the Appropriations Committee in the Senate have very different functions in practice and it is a big thing over there and a little thing over here.[38]

Once again, the perceptions and attitudes of one group about the other can be seen as important sources of conflict — sources which affect individual conference committee outcomes and which could even produce structural alterations in the conference committee.

Senatorial images of the House conferees coincide almost completely with the House member's self-image. And the Senator's self-image agrees to a substantial degree with what the House member says about him. Taken together, therefore, the images which the two sets of conferees have of themselves and of one another are remarkably congruent and remarkably accurate. It would appear that, due to the frequency and duration of interaction, neither misconceptions nor mutually exclusive perceptions survive. Differences in attitude, of course, persist; but at least each knows what it has to contend with, and it can work out, over time, ways of dealing with the other side. The congruence and accuracy of House-Senate images act as a source of stability in conference committee relations — even though the substance of the images may be a source of conflict.

The Conflict of 1962

Conference committee activity must be understood in terms of a conflict between two on-going political subsystems whose permanent differences are more deeply rooted than any single dollars and cents controversy. The com-

[38] Hearings on the Organization of Congress, *op. cit.*, pp. 1750–1752.

635

parisons of Chapters Ten and Eleven elucidated many of these system types of differences. And some of them have been elaborated further in the preceding sections. Given the fact that the main point of interaction between the two Appropriations Committees (and hence the two chambers) in this field is the conference committee, it is natural that their differences should be most prominently displayed at the conference table. And it is likely that they will, whether they involve disputes over prerogatives or prestige, affect conference committee behavior. In 1962, House-Senate appropriations differences came into public view in a dispute over the procedures of the conference committee itself. It is worth recalling briefly because, in the course of a six-month confrontation, a large proportion of the permanent, system-based sources of conference committee conflict were activated and developed.[39]

For as long as anyone could remember, and perhaps since 1865, appropriations conferences had been held on the Senate side of the Capitol, and the Senate subcommittee chairman had presided over the meeting. The arrangement was part of the larger consensus on maintenance expectations providing a framework for conference committee action. In January of 1962, the House Committee unanimously passed a resolution that one half of all conferences should be held on the House side of the Capitol — carrying also, apparently, the unexpressed implication that meetings held on the House side should be chaired by the House subcommittee chairman managing the bill. Minor though the suggested change may have seemed, it threatened to upset traditional rules of the game, to alter the delicate balance of prestige between the two chambers, and, perhaps, to change the pattern of conference committee decisions. The Senate Committee read the proposal as a very substantial threat to the status quo. It reacted with a proposition that would have, if accepted, brought about the most radical and drastic changes imaginable in appropriations politics. The Senate proposed, as a quid pro quo, that the Senate should originate one half of all appropriation bills each year. The House rejected the idea out of hand and resubmitted its original proposal. From that moment in early February until July 20, only one conference committee session was held, not a single appropriation bill was passed, and some federal agencies very nearly ran out of money.

The question as to what triggered the House proposal in January of 1962 cannot be very satisfactorily answered. Almost surely, despite his pro-

---

[39] The sources for this account are interviews with several House participants; James C. Kirby, Jr., "The House-Senate Appropriations Dispute in the 87th Congress," *American Bar Association Journal* (December, 1962), as reprinted in *Congressional Record*, Daily Edition, January 28, 1963, pp. 1155–1157, July 9, 1962, pp. 12010–12030, July 16, 1962, pp. 12762–12763; *Congressional Quarterly*, June 22, 1962, pp. 1061–1062; *Washington Post*, April 24, May 15, 17, 29, June 17, 20, 1962; *The New York Times*, July 16, 19, 1962.

testations, Chairman Cannon precipitated the move. But he never advanced any persuasive answer to the question of proximate cause. One close observer recalls that Cannon first mentioned the plan in December of 1961 in the context, presumably, of the abrupt House adjournment after passing the supplemental appropriation bill of that year. At the time they adjourned, leaving the Senate with a conference report and no option but to pass it, House-Senate conferees had been stalemated on two propositions about which Cannon held passionate convictions — backdoor spending and the liberal use of franked mail. He saved his position on both issues with the adjournment maneuver. But the battle may have been the event which triggered his decision to make some small anti-Senate move. No other immediate cause suggests itself, other than the newspaper explanation which spotlighted the personality quirks of an eighty-three-year-old man. For all of his forty years in the House, however, Cannon had been a fearless and independent curmudgeon, and for most of these years he freely and frequently criticized the Senate for its appropriations behavior. Since Cannon was anything but senile in 1962, the "octogenarian" explanation begs the question, "Why this year?"

Once Cannon decided to initiate an anti-Senate maneuver, the proposal to change the meeting place was a natural. In the first place, it seemed very minor. But, more important, the prevailing practice had long been a sore point with House Committee members. In 1960, a senior Republican complained in an interview, "The House members have to walk over to the Senate side. We don't like that at all. We've asked the Senators, 'Why don't you come over here once in a while?' but they won't. They're the appeals court over there and we don't like having to walk over." Not only did the Senate seem like enemy territory, but the fact that they, not the Senators, took the long walk reinforced the House image of Senate prestige and activated their resentment of it. To House members the arrangement was at the least "inconvenient" and at the most "galling." Cannon himself cited the basic inconvenience of the arrangement as the reason for the House proposal:

> We meet, of course, when the houses are in session. When the bells rang for a quorum call, the Senators ran out the door, slipped into the elevator, answered to their names, and came back. But we were two blocks away from the House and sometimes we couldn't get back in time to answer to our names. It took us so long that we would have to cancel the conference altogether.

There is no doubt but that the House managers did accommodate the Senate managers under this system. And there is little doubt that House . Committee members preferred a new procedure. On a somewhat more general level, the proposal can be explained as an attempt to increase House prestige in the appropriations process. A senior House subcommittee chairman said,

> There had been grumbling among some of the boys for quite a while about the conditions of the conference and how impossible it was to have a reasonable conference. In the first meeting of the full Committee someone made a motion that we hold half of the conferences on the House side and half of the conferences be chaired by a House member. The resolution was passed and we were all bound by it. These people were interested in prestige. Prestige plays a very important part around here and some of the boys get very worked up about it.

It was at this level, certainly, that the Senate members reacted, since their prestige would have been diminished. Not only would it have been altered by the substance of the proposal, but even more by acquiescence in a peremptory House demand. Insofar as the desire for an added increment of prestige caused the House Committee to initiate the demand, it reflects fundamental attitudes on the part of the House group. It reflects their feeling of necessary and deserved pre-eminence in the appropriations process and their desire to fortify that pre-eminence in every possible way.

One additional explanation for the House move was the idea that by rotating chairmanships the pattern of conference committee decisions might be changed to the benefit of the House. It is not entirely clear at what point the issue of the chairmanships was joined. Cannon appears to have assumed it was involved from the beginning, but the Senators do not agree. In any case it did become an open issue sometime in June. And, when it did, Cannon took the view that if conference sessions were chaired by House members, more economical decisions would result. Thus, contended Cannon, the large question of economy versus spending was at stake in the controversy. Conference committees inevitably compromise, he said. And he added, "The chairman frequently decides what the compromise will be and that puts us at a great disadvantage." The proposal, as he elaborated it, rested on the familiar House complaint that the Senate makes additions to a bill on a courtesy basis, thus bloating the appropriations figures. "Every bill we have passed for years has been increased by the Senate. They put in everything they can think of just because some Senator wants it for his state," said Cannon. "If we could preside at conferences half the time, maybe we could cut out half of these increases."[40] Most available evidence indicates, as we shall see, that the conference chairman exercises no such substantial control over conference outcomes. It seems more likely that this part of the proposal was another gambit to gain additional prestigeful emoluments

[40] Quoted in *Congressional Record*, Daily Edition, January 28, 1963, p. 1156.

for the House. But it afforded Cannon and other House members in support of him a launching pad for their long-standing criticism of the Senate as excessively liberal.

At one point in the controversy the House Committee passed a resolution stating flatly that, "During the past 10 years, the Senate has raised appropriations bills above the amount passed by the House by approximately $32 billion."[41] And it went on to label the Senate as "the body consistently advocating larger appropriations, increased spending, and corresponding deficits."[42] Surely this fundamental element in the House Committee's image of the Senate was one of the deep-running sources of the 1962 conflict. Though it was not the proximate cause, it was an underlying one. And, once the battle was joined, House members wasted no time in bringing it to the surface.

When the initial House Committee move came in January, the Senate was still smarting from the "take it or leave it" adjournment of the previous September. On that occasion, Majority Leader Mansfield had cried out, "We have taken a 'shellacking' and I think it is outrageous . . . it is a poor sign of the comity which should exist between the two bodies." And Minority Leader Dirksen echoed, "An outrage is being perpetrated on the Senate, I agree . . . are we a coordinate branch of the legislative establishment or are we not?"[43] It was in exactly this spirit that the Senate Committee interpreted the new controversy — as a threat to its coordinate status in the legislature. In a July resolution, it accused the House of trying to upset an "established and time tested procedure," and declared itself as "unwilling to accept unilateral alterations in the procedures which have always existed in considering appropriation bills." House-Senate differences, said the Senators, are "not the minor question of the location of the room where conferences shall be held or the individual to preside, but involve the question of whether the Senate Committee is coequal with the House Committee in the consideration of appropriation bills." The House proposals were reviewed ominously as "unreasonable demands for the surrender of the Senate to the will of the other body."[44] And, the challenge having been so defined, the prestige of the Senate became just as much involved as the prestige of the House.

From the Senate standpoint the controversy brought to the surface latent resentments at the House's procedural dominance of the appropriations process. The Senate counterproposal went, therefore, right to the heart of the matter. As the Senate viewed the situation, it is the custom

---

41 *Congressional Record*, Daily Edition, July 9, 1962, p. 12010.
42 *Ibid.*
43 *Congressional Record*, Daily Edition, September 26, 1961, p. 20192.
44 *Congressional Record*, Daily Edition, July 9, 1962, pp. 12010–12011. See also the statement of Senator Mansfield in *ibid.*, June 23, 1962, p. 10624.

whereby the House originates all appropriation bills that distributes the significant advantages and disadvantages in the process. On pain of disrupting existing arrangements, the Senate has accepted this crucial House prerogative. When provoked, however, it will reassert its constitutional right to originate appropriations and in so doing call attention to what is, from its perspective, the sorest point of Senate-House relations. To the very end of the sessions, and long after the dispute over meeting place and chairmanships had been settled, the Senate continued to push its side of the argument. The conferees on the agriculture bill remained deadlocked into October over a move by the Senate to add to the bill a group of projects that had not been considered by the House Committee. The House Committee chose to interpret the Senate action as an attempt to initiate appropriations and refused to discuss the items in conference. Senate subcommittee chairman Russell construed the House refusal as a test of the Senate's power to amend and originate appropriation bills. "If the Senate has one ounce of self-respect it will stay in session till Christmas . . . to establish our position as a coequal body in every respect."[45] Eventually the House yielded. But on the day the Senate adjourned, it fired off a last resolution stating that its willingness to let the House originate appropriation bills "cannot change the clear language of the Constitution nor affect the Senate coequal power to originate any bill not expressly raising revenue."[46] This resolution, too, was introduced by Senator Russell, who (rather than the other "octogenarian" featured in the newspapers, Chairman Carl Hayden) led the Senate forces in their defense of senatorial prerogatives.

Apart from the question of relative power and prestige, the House statements which drew the greatest senatorial ire were those which labeled them as spendthrifts. The House Committee resolution blaming the Senate for adding $32 billion to appropriations bills in 10 years was called by Senate Committee elder Willis Robertson "the most insulting document that one body has ever sent to another." Mindful of Senate goal expectations, Robertson assailed "the tricky compilation of what the House says it has saved and what it says the Senate has wasted,"[47] and argued that the Senate had by no means been as liberal as House figures implied. On the other hand, he explained at length some reasons (discussed in Chapter Ten) why the Senate normally added to House bills. He stressed especially the increased pressure for spending which came in the form of agency reclamas and restoration

[45] *Congressional Record,* Daily Edition, October 8, 1962, p. 21551.

[46] The Senate buttressed its position with a 50-page documented study published in April 1963. Senate Committee on Government Operations, *The Authority of the Senate to Originate Appropriation Bills,* Senate Document No. 17, 88th Congress, 1st Session (Washington: U.S. Government Printing Office, 1963).

[47] *Congressional Record,* Daily Edition, July 9, 1962, p. 12012.

pleas from members of the House who learned, only too late, what the House Committee had decided.

To settle the controversy, two five-man negotiating teams, one from each Committee, finally met on "neutral ground" in the Old Supreme Court Chamber midway between the Senate and the House. At first, they agreed to hold all conferences in that room; subsequently, they moved to another room, which straddles the center line of the building in the newly constructed East Front of the Capitol. Some time later, the negotiators agreed that each conference should choose its own chairman by some mutually agreeable method. When the first conference was held, the chairmanship was decided by a flip of the coin. Some conferences have followed this procedure, others have rotated, and still others have permitted the Senate subcommittee chairmen to preside. The negotiators then agreed to set up a committee to solve their differences permanently. That committee has never met and no one expects that it ever will. Thus, through conference committee methods, the dispute over the conference committee was settled.

While it lasted, however, the dispute brought to the surface underlying sources of conflict between the two chambers — or, perhaps more realistically, between the House Committee on Appropriations and the United States Senate. For, as we have seen, the Senate and its Appropriations Committee are closely interrelated — a relationship confirmed when the House Committee demand was translated as an attack on the Senate itself. The settlement of July, 1962, by no means exorcised or laid to rest the basic differences between the two units involved. The eruption of 1962 brought about some very minor structural changes (mostly psychological) in appropriations conference committee activity. But the differences still exist and are of sufficient magnitude to cause far more radical changes than they have up to now. If they should, it will come as no surprise. On the other hand, so long as they do not, a comprehension of them will aid us in understanding the current dynamics of the conference.

THE CONFERENCE COMMITTEE: INDEPENDENCE AND DEPENDENCE

The literature of political science stresses the independence of conference committees. Typically, a conference is described as a device whereby a handful of senior legislators meet behind closed doors to work their independent wills on the two pieces of legislation before them — frequently producing a result that is more their own creation than that of the two chambers involved. Certainly, evidence exists in support of this conception. For example, conferees are customarily self-selected without interference from the parent chamber. They establish their own working rules and relationships. Since conference committee meetings are held in executive session and since no public record of their proceedings exists, direct observation of decision-making is impossible. From the bits of evidence that are available, however, it seems clear that the conferees do arrive at many decisions on the basis of internal negotiation relatively free from external influences. We will refer to this pattern as the independent decision-making pattern. It is not a pure type but an empirically observable one taking several forms. The pattern conforms more or less to the common view of the conference committee as an autonomous political entity whose members act on the basis of intraconference considerations. The pattern is made necessary, furthermore, because each group of conferees must solve the problem of adapting directly to the other.

Each group of conferees also faces the problem of adapting to its environment — especially to the wishes of its parent chamber. One cannot, therefore, understand the behavior of a conference committee without perceiving it as an institution dependent upon and responsive to external influences. House and Senate rules, for example, hold conference activity within specified limits, particularly where monetary amounts are at issue. Both chambers can, furthermore, "instruct" their conferees to act in a prescribed manner. Some decisions do seem to be influenced more by factors external than internal to the conference. We shall speak of this alternative pattern as the dependent decision-making pattern. It must not be thought that internal influences are wholly absent from this pattern any more than are external influences from the other pattern. The difference is a qualitative one. But it is a difference which is upheld by evidence and which lends critical support to the notion that the conference committee must be understood in terms of a two-sided problem of adaptation.

THE CONFERENCE AS INDEPENDENT DECISION-MAKER

The basic structural feature of a conference committee is two groups whose individual members have stronger ties to their own committee than to the conference as a whole. It was precisely because of the relative weakness of their conference committee ties that the two groups feuded for so long and so hotly over the smallest of internal procedural changes in 1962. A small intraconference matter assumed such large proportions because, loyal to their respective committees and chambers, the two sets of conferees transformed the issue from one of internal mechanisms into one of external prestige. Viewed as an independent institution, therefore, an appropriation conference committee appears badly split and constantly on the brink of an internal breakup. But the institution survives, as we have explained, because its tasks are both very necessary and very limited, because members of Congress agree on what these tasks are, and because members of Congress also agree on some basic rules of the game for carrying them out. The conference committee also survives because members of Congress share similar perceptions of and attitudes about it. And, finally, it survives because though there are serious differences between the two sets of conferees, they possess congruent and accurate images of one another and have stabilized their intergroup conflicts into fairly predictable patterns.

The fact that chamber leaders allow the two Appropriations Committees to pick their own managers is a source of conference committee autonomy. In the first instance, of course, it is the two committees themselves that are strengthened by this procedure — especially in the House, where the leadership is more likely to want to sanction Appropriations Committee activity. Leaving the decisions in the hands of the two committees has, for the conference committee, the principal effect of promoting membership stability. From year to year most of the same senior subcommittee leaders return to the conference table. They establish procedural routines, adjust to one another's personal idiosyncrasies, anticipate one another's desires, become friendly enemies, and, in general, develop an important degree of institutional stability. In any given year one side may temper its demands and desist from disruptive behavior because its members know it is highly likely that they will meet again next year. As one Senator put it in explaining why he finally receded on a House demand, "We will have to do business with the House of Representatives in the future. This is not a one-day stand or a one-day battle."[48] Personnel stability promotes a view of the conference as a continuing institution and, hence, as an autonomous one.

Typically the House Committee sends a 5-man delegation to the conference room. It consists of the subcommittee chairman, the next ranking majority subcommittee member, and the full Committee Chairman plus the ranking minority subcommittee member and the ranking minority member of the full Committee. The presence of the ranking minority Committee member on every conference team began about 1951 when Chairman Cannon agreed to make John Taber an ex officio member of each subcommittee. The arrangement continued until 1963, when Cannon declined to extend ex officio prerogatives to Taber's successor, Ben Jensen. Chairman George Mahon reverted to the former practice with Frank Bow, Jensen's successor. In addition to Bow, Mahon began in the 89th Congress to take all subcom-

---

[48] 99 *Congressional Record*, pp. 11025–11026.

mittee members to conference. During the Cannon-Taber era, however, these two men made up two fifths of every 5-man team of managers. In the 87th Congress, for example (Taber's last Congress), all 19 separate conferences were attended by 5 House managers. This small number accents, again, the importance of the subcommittees in House appropriations decision-making. So long as the subcommittee members remained unified, they could carry the House position in conference — even over the opposition of Cannon and Taber. But, since the norms surrounding the Chairman–ranking minority member roles call for them to support their subcommittee leaders, divisions did not frequently occur.

In keeping with all their previous appropriations decision-making patterns, the Senate sends a large number of interested Senators to the conference table. For them, the conference committee is yet another extension of the bargaining arena which begins in subcommittee, grows to the full Committee, and expands onto the floor — and at each point a large number of Senators participate in the making of appropriations decisions. In the 87th Congress, in contrast to the 5-man teams from the House, the Senate Committee sent an average of 9 men to the 29 conferences. The number of Senate conferees ranged from a low of 5 to a high of 14. Chairman Carl Hayden attended 21 of the 29 conferences, and Committee veteran Richard Russell attended 14 of the 29. One ex officio member from the substantive committee involved sat on 10 of the 29 conferences. This arrangement brought such influential (nonmember) Senators as Robert Kerr (4 conferences), Harry Byrd (4 conferences), and J. W. Fulbright (2 conferences) to the appropriations conference table. It is an expectation of both the Senate and of individual Senate Committee members that the appropriations process should be relatively open to them at all stages. The conference committee is no exception.

House conferees frequently gather before going to conference to work out a united front. "I try to get our conferees together beforehand," said one subcommittee chairman, "to see how far we are willing to go on the different items and then we go in and bargain." Several subcommittees follow this pattern. On another subcommittee, said its clerk, "It's common practice for our conferees to get together after we've had one meeting with the Senate. After we've had one go-around to feel them out and find out how strongly they feel about things, we can pretty much tell what the results will be." On one subcommittee, the practice is for the majority party members to get together prior to conference and decide where and where not to yield. And on still another, preconference agreements are hammered out when specially controversial items are expected. But, for all subcommittees, the clerk will prepare "conference notes" for the conferees, explaining the items in dispute between Senate and House, recalling salient arguments, and, perhaps, at the suggestion of the subcommittee chairman, a recommendation on strategy. In all cases, the subcommittee clerk meets with the chairman prior to conference, and depending on the relationship between them, they may or may not work out a "battle plan." In sum, the House conferees prepare extensively and carefully, stressing the familiar practice of internal unity, before they go to conference.

On the Senate side, the clerks work just as hard gathering information. Indeed, they customarily prepare much more voluminous conference notes than do House clerks. But the Senators themselves prepare less thoroughly (which is the reason why the staff prepares such large folios for the meetings) and with less self-consciousness about their own internal unity. They assume, perhaps, that every Senator will support every other Senator. Their individualistic approach to the conference is a source of despair to some committee staff people. "We never get together prior to a conference," said one. "Senators don't have that opportunity. They are too busy. Normally the House members meet before a conference, and it puts them at a great advantage. Sometimes, I wish we could take just a minute or two to get together. It would help." A second clerk lamented,

> The House conferees hold a meeting and decide which way they are going to jump on every item. When they come over here, they know what they're going to do. But not over here. To my mind we don't have enough sense to do that. It's a matter of contention over here whether a Senator ought to uphold the Committee in conference or just put his own projects in . . . you never know what they're going to do. We may start the conference with 8 men and they may stay for an hour. Then you're down to 4 and by the time it's over, nearly everyone is gone and you have to hunt all over creation to find your signers. They're all too busy.[49]

The Senate's polyarchal decision-making style continues unchanged into the conference room.

At all stages in the appropriations process, House decision-making follows a more hierarchical pattern than it does in the Senate. Thus a newcomer to the ranks of House managers will most likely observe an apprenticeship there too. Said one,

> It was my first conference. I sat there like a bump on a log. I was a duck out of water. But it was fascinating to watch two men like ——— and ———. You know your man is going to give in, but he won't — not at the first nibble. Or you've agreed to stick to a position and you see one of your guys begin to waver.

[49] In some cases, a Senator's assistant or another Senator may initial a report on behalf of an absent colleague. See *Congressional Record*, Daily Edition, June 29, 1959, p. 11010.

A House Committee clerk contrasted the two patterns of decision-making revealed at the conference table:

> The House conferees are truly the agents of the House, much more than the Senate conferees. That's a real club over there and they put things in just because some Senator wants it there. Sometimes that's the only reason they give for an item being in there. And each Senate conferee has his own interests. The House conferees are in there to defend a House position, but the Senators more often are defending personal positions. Sometimes we get the feeling that we are arguing against seven different Committees instead of one Committee.

The point is not that one of these styles is more advantageous than the other. The point is that they are distinctive — as distinctive in face-to-face encounters as in their separate chambers.

Conference committees operate in accordance with one basic norm — one which follows logically from the two-headed nature of the institution. That norm prescribes that a conference decision must be a joint decision of the two groups of managers, with a majority vote of each group determining its decision. Each group remains free, therefore, to pursue its own distinctive style of decision-making and to observe its own internal norms. For example, it is a norm of the House Committee that the subcommittee chairman should manage his bill throughout the appropriations process and, hence, lead the House managers on the bill. As leader of the House managers he traditionally occupies (when a Senator is presiding) the chair to the immediate left or right of the conference chairman. He sits next to the chairman, "so that they can whisper together and negotiate on the side if that becomes necessary." His fellow managers then arrange themselves — first the majority members of the subcommittee, then the full Committee Chairman, then the minority members — down one side of the long conference table.

At one conference a few years ago, when the House subcommittee chairman entered the room, he found Chairman Cannon already occupying the chair at the top of the table — the chair traditionally reserved for the spokesman of the House group. The subcommittee chairman took an empty seat midway down the table. When the conference began, and the first item was broached, Chairman Cannon spoke up and outlined the House position. Whereupon the House subcommittee chairman said, "If the Chairman is going to run the conference while I have been the one to sit in the hearings all these weeks, I am going to leave." He got up and left the conference room. The other majority subcommittee member then said, "If my subcommittee chairman is going to leave, I will too." And he left. The two majority members walked over to the House restaurant for coffee. The conference meeting immediately adjourned, and Chairman Cannon called on his subcommittee chairman and admitted his mistake. The conference resumed the next day with everyone in his customary seat playing his customary role. The episode illustrates the limitations placed on the power of the Appropriations Committee Chairman by informal norms — especially those which delineate his relations with his subcommittee chairmen. The episode also illustrates the degree to which the two committees persist as independent units within the loose framework of the conference committee. The autonomy of the conference committee depends, paradoxically, on the autonomy of its two basic structural units.

Such norms as the conference committee develops on its own — other than its voting procedure — are those which pertain to the role of the chairman. They make him the presiding officer and the preserver of standard parliamentary procedure. But, despite Clarence Cannon's arguments in the dispute of 1962, they do not prescribe for him much substantive influence. One senior House conferee went as far as any of his colleagues would go when he said, "It makes some difference — psychologically if in no other way. He bangs the gavel. You have to address him in order to be recognized. He's the major domo in there. But it doesn't make a difference to the extent that the chairmanship of a standing committee does." A House subcommittee chairman said, "I can raise more hell outside the chairmanship. It makes no difference to me." And a ranking minority subcommittee member asserted, "What the hell. I don't see that it makes any difference who's chairman. You can be just as stubborn without being chairman as you can if you are. To me it's a hollow honor." The chairman may "keep order" and "guide things a little" but he lacks special influence because he is but the leader of one of two coequal teams of negotiators.

Under no circumstances is the conference chairman expected to play a leadership role with regard to the managers of the other house. A senior Senator recalled one occasion when the slightest of moves in this direction precipitated a near riot:

> I remember one time when McKellar was Chairman of Senate Appropriations, and we were having a conference — on civil appropriations. The thing went on for about six or eight weeks. We'd come back every two weeks, disagree, and come back again. Cannon was saying, "I'll do this," and, "I'll do that." Of course he had met with his conferees before, but he was doing all the talking. McKellar finally said, "How do the other House conferees feel about it?" And McKellar started to poll the House conferees! Cannon got so mad they almost had a fight — and they would have, too. McKellar was going to hit him with a cane. Oh, those conferences can get tough sometimes.

Another Chairman of the Senate Committee kept his contacts with Mr. Cannon within the bounds of key norms. "We talk over the telephone about the mechanics of the bill. 'What are you going to do and when are you going to do it?' I don't try to influence him on how to vote and he doesn't try to influence me." The conference committee will survive so long as the basic norm of two distinct voting units is preserved. The chairman's role plainly is to preserve the identity of two units, not to fuse them.

One form of independent decision-making occurs when the House and Senate subcommittee chairmen have established harmonious working relationships and can iron out their differences prior to the formal conference meeting. In such cases, the two leaders hold a preconference meeting in company with their clerks to see if a compromise can be negotiated. A veteran Senator described how it works:

> I don't want to be conceited, but last year on the bill I got up a package — Senate recede on so many items, House recede on so many items. I showed it to ————, who is the chairman on the House subcommittee. I know him very well and we got together confidentially to work the thing out. He changed the ante a little and came back with a compromise to my compromise. On the basis of those two plans the thing was finally worked out. But it took a hell of a lot of time — three days and I'd say about thirty hours.

The clerk of another House subcommittee crossed his fingers to describe a similar relationship between his boss and the Senate subcommittee chairman:

> They're just like that. They have great respect for each other and work well together. They are in touch with each other all through the year. They are personal friends. When we get to conference we have a real conference. We have the reputation here on the Hill for having one of the finest conferences on appropriations.

The implication in both of these cases is clear that if the subcommittee leaders are able to reach agreement between themselves, the conferees will follow their lead in decision-making.

Sometimes the same kind of personal relationship develops between the two staff men involved and makes possible preconference conversation — once again, smoothing the path to agreement. The clerk of still a third House subcommittee explained the procedure followed by him and his Senate counterpart:

> We do staff work before conference. I'll ask him, "What are the Senators really interested in?" And, "How do they feel about this?" The idea is to make the conference run better. After all, there's no sense arguing for $30 million on item X if what they really want is item Y. Sometimes I'll write out a statement to use and give it to him just to make sure we're both talking about the same thing. And it usually turns out we agree all the time on something we were arguing over. We're very close — it varies de-

pending on personalities. Next year, there will be a new man in there and it will take ten years to build up the relationship of confidence with him that I have now.

A relationship of this sort is only possible where both staff men operate as the alter egos of their subcommittee chairmen. To the degree they influence decision-making in the conference — and surely they do — their influence is a distinctly internal one.

Perhaps it should be mentioned that some House-Senate staff men remain aloof from one another and exert no joint influence on conference proceedings. "I know him," said one House clerk in reference to his opposite number in the Senate. "But the idea of a conference is for the House conferees and the Senate conferees to have a full and free discussion. I work with the House conferees and he works with the Senate conferees. It would be presumptuous for us to get together and decide things." The clerk who spoke works, as one might expect, for a subcommittee chairman who likes to keep all decision-making arrangements in his own hands. As the working habits of subcommittee chairman vary, so do staff relationships — between the extremes of close and influential collaboration on the one hand and strictly formal procedural contacts on the other.

Conference decisions made on the basis of superior information, subject matter knowledge, and careful preparation on the part of one set of conferees make up another form of independent decision-making. There is no way of knowing how frequently such a case occurs, but they do. A House clerk recalled with great relish a conference in which his subcommittee faced both a new Senate subcommittee chairman and a new Senate clerk in conference:

> The Senate was totally unprepared. They had put back every reclama asked for by the department, and the only arguments they had were those given to them by the department. Our men were well briefed and had all the information. We had a meeting of the conferees beforehand as we usually do. We had decided what we would do and what we would not do. And I had prepared the regular notes for the conferees which they had before them. It was ridiculous. The House completely dominated the conference. Except for a couple of political items we let them keep in there, we completely ran it. It was just ridiculous.

It is, of course, a favorite House member generalization that superior information gives them a great advantage in conference. Apparently it did in this case where they faced unseasoned opponents. Occasionally, the Senate conferees will have to admit to the Senate that they were simply out-informationed by the House:

> FIRST SENATE CONFEREE: On the conference committee, we were confronted with statistical data we could not refute.
> SECOND SENATE CONFEREE: In short, out of the blue came pages of statistics

. . . I suspect — though I cannot prove — that the amount of money involved is small . . . however, we had no figures. The House conferees had a great many statistics.[50]

Decisions which turn on such matters as superior preparation by one side or the other fall within the category of independent decision-making.

Similarly, decision-making which is affected by a dominant personality on one side or another is governed by an internal factor. When asked what factors influence conference outcomes, members of both Committees sometimes mention a personal quality. "A conference committee is the greatest forum for advocacy in the congressional service. A strong advocate of his position can be very effective." "I have seldom seen a case where the sheer weight of the argument had such an effect on the members of the conference as did the argument of the Senator from Idaho," reported a conferee to the Senate. "He led the fight; and by sheer weight of the argument and discussion in the committee, I saw . . . a change in the position of the House conferees on this item."[51]

It is said also that "the man who excels in conference is the man with a genius for compromise." Stubbornness, frequently cited as a House member characteristic, is still another personal attribute which may win a case. "I've never lost a conference," exclaimed one veteran House subcommittee chairman:

Never lost anything I think is important. If I think something has got to go out, I'll sit there 'til Christmas. I'm in no hurry to go home. I'll sit there 'til Christmas. My wife is not here; she's back home in the district, and I'm in no hurry to go home!

A House Republican leader revealed some assorted tricks of the trade — all designed to win points in conference:

It's like all things between men. Many times I stand up and talk and pound the table and try to make them take notice or get mad. Once in a while I get under their skin a little and they see things better. It gets to be a kind of game. If the Senate is too stubborn, sometimes we just get up and leave. The Chairman gets up and we follow him out. Oh, I've walked out of many conference committees in my seventeen years. Old John Taber and I, we tell them we won't be back till they are ready to be reasonable. They'll call up the next day and say they are ready for another session and we'll say, "Well, we aren't. We don't think you've had enough time to think it over."

Interpersonal skills — of advocacy, compromise, stubbornness, bluster, and threat — may influence decision-making in the conference. They, too, can be classified as influences making for relatively independent decision-making.

50 101 *Congressional Record*, pp. 9721–9722.
51 103 *Congressional Record*, p. 14560.

A classic form of independent decision-making occurs when the conferees, faced with opposing monetary amounts, decide to "split the difference" and agree on a figure midway between the high and the low figure. This is one obvious solution for two groups of conferees who are free to strike any bargain they choose. It satisfies each and deprives no one unduly. No one (or everyone) "wins." All are comfortable. In the absence of factors tending strongly to promote some other particular solution, the midpoint is what Thomas Schelling calls a "clue for coordinating behavior" — a conspicuous or obvious focal point on which people trying to solve a problem can base their solution.[52] "Usually when there's a difference," generalizes one experienced House conferee, "it's split down the middle. If you give him five dollars and I give him ten dollars, he usually gets seven dollars fifty cents. How else are hard-headed men, when you have your honest opinion and I have my honest opinion, going to get together?" Thus a pair of House subcommittee chairmen reported back to the House:

> In the Solicitor's office the House cut out $500 thousand and the Senate restored $200 thousand. So we had a long amiable visit over how many lawyers are required in the Department of Agriculture. Finally we took the $200 thousand restoration and we cut it in half. So they gained $100 thousand and we gained $100 thousand.[53]

> The conferees spend about as much time on the National Institutes of Health as all of the other items in the bill combined, and we finally agreed on a fifty-fifty split.[54]

As the analysis of the 36 bureaus reveals, the pattern of splitting the difference is a common, though not the dominant, one. It has the feature of keeping the conference "amiable" and allowing it to rely on its own internal devices for a solution.

One internal factor which affects conference decision-making but which may be tied to an external factor is the unity of the conferees. Other things being equal, a team of managers that is united will be more likely to carry its version of the decision than a team of managers that is divided. Disunity among a set of conferees, however, often reflects disunity on their committee. A Senate clerk described how such a situation may affect conference deliberations:

> The House will make up a package and they'll say, "We'll recede on items 3, 5, and 6 if you'll recede on items 1, 2, and 4." Then you'll get the jocular remark, "That's just like trading a rabbit for a horse. You're

[52] Thomas C. Schelling, *The Strategy of Conflict* (Cambridge: Harvard University Press, 1960), Chapter 3.
[53] 93 *Congressional Record*, p. 9298.
[54] 107 *Congressional Record*, p. 18818. See also, 106 *Congressional Record*, p. 9236.

giving up $10 million and we have to give up $15 million." . . . But maybe you had a split in the subcommittee or committee on one of the items. Maybe it got through by a slim margin and the conferees are really split four to three on it even though they are supporting one position. After a while one of them may say, "Oh, let's give up on this. That's a pretty good proposition they made us."

A Senator recalled a specific example involving the approval by the full Senate Committee by the narrow margin of 14 to 12 of a $40 million increase over the House bill:

> That was almost a fifty-fifty vote in Committee. When we went to conference, the House wouldn't take a cent — not a cent. The closeness of that vote very definitely affected the Senate conferees. If it had been a unanimous vote in the Committee, the Senate would have put up a stronger fight. But they were mindful of the fact that it was a 14 to 12 vote, and the House won.[55]

Whether a division among conferees involves primarily them or primarily the full Committee would be a matter for empirical determination. Probably both situations do occur — the one falling into the category of independently made decisions, the other falling into the category of decisions primarily influenced by environmental factors.

THE CONFERENCE AS DEPENDENT DECISION-MAKER

No matter how autonomously a given conference decision may seem to have been taken, a closer inspection would surely turn up the existence of environmental influences. Indeed, for many decisions, internal and external factors will be too tightly interlinked to permit any kind of classification on these grounds. For now, the main point is simply that there are two kinds of factors at work in conference decisions, and that some decisions can be classified in accordance with the dominance of one type or the other. A single conference may, in fact, change classification while in progress. One senatorial description of such a change highlights the subtle yet distinctive difference between the independent and the dependent patterns of decision-making:

> The conference is the most interesting thing that happens on Capitol Hill. The managers on the part of the two houses sit at the head of the table and the others straggle on down the sides. Most of the conversation goes on between these two — the chairman and the vice chairman of the conference. Each will poll their delegations. There's a lot of jockeying around

[55] For another good example, see *Congressional Record*, Daily Edition, May 4, 1960, p. 8701.

— "I'll give you this if you'll give me that." . . . If you can't agree, you go back to your houses for a vote. And that puts pressure on you. They'll say, "If you don't agree to this, we'll take it back to the House and get a vote insisting on our position. Then we won't be able to compromise with you — so you'd better take what we give you now." Then, of course, if both houses get votes insisting on their position you have to hold another conference and see how you can compromise.

A House Committee member remembered an example in which House strategy involved just such a threat to change the pattern of decision-making.

Last year there was a difference of about $400 million between the House and Senate versions of the foreign aid appropriation. The chairman of the House delegation in the conference took a very firm position that we had to end up with slightly less than 50 per cent of the difference as a matter of prestige. It was the day we were to adjourn. We were in conference until about 10:30 P.M., and the Senate wouldn't give in. I think the difference between conferees was only five or ten million dollars. The Senate was fighting for its prestige and our chairman for his. At 10:30 he started to close his book and got up saying he would get instructions from the House. All the rest of our conferees did the same. That prospect was too much for the Senators. They capitulated.[56]

When the conferees cannot come to a decision without first taking their disagreement back to the House and Senate for help or instructions, they become engaged in a new pattern of decision-making. The nature of the game changes from one in which the conferees were free to bargain subject to their own intergroup relationships to one in which the conferees become bound to positions fixed outside the conference room. In the latter case, we have the prototype of dependent decision-making in conference committee.

Several elements of the external environment are capable of influencing appropriations conferees. One is the full Committee (of which we have spoken briefly), another is the executive branch, and a third is the parent chamber. Of the three, the most important is the parent chamber. Sometimes, from the very outset of a conference, one group or the other recognizes that the weakness or strength of its position is directly bound up with attitudes prevalent in the parent chamber. When conferees threaten to change the pattern of decision-making, it is the sanctions of their parent chamber they invoke. For purposes, then, of illustrating the dependent decision-making pattern, the relation of conferees to their parent chambers will be employed.

On some items at issue between the Senate and the House, the conferees will bargain autonomously simply because no one outside the confer-

[56] As quoted in Charles L. Clapp, *The Congressman: His Job As He Sees It* (Washington: The Brookings Institution, 1963), p. 249.

ence speaks to them on the subject one way or another. No attempt has been made here to determine how frequently this occurs. But we can tell from the public record (which is surely just the peak of the iceberg) that many gradations of chamber pressure are focused on the conferees. Perhaps the mildest form of external influence comes by way of a general exhortation conveying to the conferees the dominant mood of the chamber. "I hope that the members of the Appropriations Subcommittees of the House will . . . fight until the snow comes if necessary to maintain the position of the House in effecting reductions in their bills."[57] Slightly stronger are the rhetorical pleas made by individuals for items in which they have a special interest. "It is my hope that the Committee and the conferees will stand firmly on the matter when it goes to conference and that we shall prevail in connection with this item."[58] Doubtless for every public appeal of this nature there are fifty private appeals directed to individual conferees. Sometimes a private commitment will be made which will bind the conferee involved. "I had promised the gentleman from Washington that if the Senate looked with favor on restoring the amount submitted by the Budget for this particular idea, I would agree to it in conference."[59]

More likely, however, most private conversations follow the path of this public one:

> HOUSE MEMBER: I note [my] amendment has been stricken from the bill by the other body. I would hope that the managers on the part of the House would exercise their power and put that amendment back in the bill.
> SUBCOMMITTEE CHAIRMAN: As the gentleman knows I did not oppose the gentleman's amendment at the time. ·
> HOUSE MEMBER: The gentleman did not oppose it at the time and therefore acquiesced in the amendment.
> SUBCOMMITTEE CHAIRMAN: It was accepted by a practically unanimous vote of the House at that time. Offhand I would be constrained to stay with the House's position on it. Of course, I would not want to tie the hands of all the conferees.
> HOUSE MEMBER: . . . My objective has been to make legislative history.[60]

Ordinarily, conferees will wish to retain some room for maneuver in conference. And each side comes to the conference table, as we have seen, holding that assumption about the other — that they are willing and free to negotiate, at least on some items.

Members of the chamber, however, may try to restrict the maneuvering room of their conferees by making "legislative history" — that is, by ex-

---

[57] 95 *Congressional Record*, p. 8688.
[58] *Congressional Record*, Daily Edition, June 1, 1961, p. 8643.
[59] 100 *Congressional Record*, p. 5167.
[60] *Congressional Record*, Daily Edition, September 23, 1964, p. 16748. See also, *ibid.*, May 15, 1963, p. 8183.

tracting some kind of pledge out of the conference leaders. But binding pledges come hard.

> SENATOR: I ask the distinguished Senator from Georgia whether it is the intention that the amount for these research items shall by all means be given preferential status in the event the Senate conferees may have to recede on certain items . . .
> SUBCOMMITTEE CHAIRMAN: . . . I can assure the Senator from Kansas that a determined effort will be conducted as the Senator has indicated it should be.
>
> . . . . . .
>
> SENATOR: I very much hope that the distinguished chairman of the subcommittee . . . will not take it to conference in order to abandon the baby and let it die of suffocation inside the conference committee room, but that he will struggle with all the ability he has . . .
> SUBCOMMMMITTEE CHAIRMAN: I assure the Senator from Illinois that I shall bring to the attention of the conferees the very strong statement which he has made with respect to this item, and I will express it as the view of the Senate.[61]

Even the following empathetic colloquy does not commit the conferee involved to specific actions.

> HOUSE MEMBER: It is my hope that the conferees will go to conference and sit if necessary until the snow flies before they give away any substantial part of the figure as was passed by the House of Representatives. . . .
> SUBCOMMITTEE CHAIRMAN: I, myself, would say not just until the snow flies, but until it has flown and melted away.[62]

Whether a public exchange places any more restraints on conferees than a private conversation is questionable. On the one hand, the conferee does place himself on record; on the other hand, he does so in the vaguest possible way. And, indeed, he might be more willing to make an informal pledge than a public one. In any case, these public exchanges should be read as illustrative of informal activity as well.

A significant escalation in external influence occurs when the position of the chamber is stated via a roll-call vote. In the Senate it is recognized, for example, that when a subcommittee chairman agrees on the floor to "take the amendment to conference," that amendment (voted on by voice vote) will not have the degree of support from the conferees that it would have had if a roll call had been held. Said a senior Appropriations Committee member,

> Mr. President, I think there is a real difference between adopting an amendment and simply taking it to conference. If the Senate adopts an

[61] 97 *Congressional Record*, pp. 8996–8997.
[62] *Congressional Record*, Daily Edition, October 3, 1962, p. 20654.

655

amendment, I think the conferees then are under instructions in regard to that amendment. On the other hand, if an amendment is just taken to conference, such instructions do not apply.[63]

To a group of conferees who had agreed to take an amendment to conference, one of its supporters argued for a roll call:

I have always felt that when one is moving to attack it is not enough to send a rifle squad up to the front, but that one should have a supporting detachment behind them. The best reinforcement we could give to the Senators would be a ringing yea and nay vote. I am confident the amendment would pass by an overwhelming vote. Then the Senators would not enter the conference chamber with empty hands, but would enter with the massed power of the Senate behind them.[64]

In this case, the speaker feared the conferees might negotiate away his position, and he wanted to bind them to it.

The essential proposition was stated by a veteran Senate subcommittee chairman:

In theory one set of conferees is no more powerful than the other. But you may have a practical situation in one chamber where you had a battle on something and a roll-call vote. That puts the conferees from that chamber under a compulsion to stand up for that proposition. That's just common sense. Because that stand was taken by their house after a hot battle and a yea and nay vote. They have to do that.

Inside the conference room, the conferees involved will point to the roll call and say that they have no choice. It strengthens their claim that they cannot yield their position. It makes credible any threat. It makes it very likely that the other side will be forced to give in even if the conferees are not in sympathy with the roll call. They are expected to act, as far as conference decision-making is concerned, as the agents of the parent chamber and hence to "dig in" particularly hard on that item.

Just as a "ringing roll call" in support of an amendment will have a powerful influence on the outcome of a conference, so, too, will a roll call in which an amendment is defeated. This proposition bulks large in floor strategy in the House. A person who supports an amendment to an appropriation bill on the floor may not wish to push his claim to a roll-call vote — or, indeed, to any vote for fear that he might lose. If he loses, the vote goes into the record; and if the Senate subsequently passes his amendment, the case for it will have been badly weakened in conference. That is, if the conferees have it on record that one chamber disapproves of the amendment, the amendment is not likely to survive. Hence, advocates on the House floor may

[63] 97 *Congressional Record*, p. 8937.
[64] *Congressional Record*, Daily Edition, March 29, 1960, p. 6254.

be chary of bringing their amendments to a vote, preferring to let the Senate act and hope that an unblemished record in the House will help in conference:

> I do not intend to try to amend the bill here on the House floor, because I am advised such an amendment would not be agreed to by the Committee and would be defeated. If the Senate increases the amount for the Food and Drug Administration, I would not want to have an adverse vote on record to be used against the higher figure in the conference committee.[65]

It is accepted by both sets of conferees that they must act as the agents of their parent chambers. If one chamber has spoken, its conferees are expected to stand for that position more strongly than would otherwise be the case.

A technique considered even more binding on the conferees than an ordinary roll-call vote is the practice of "instructing" the conferees to take a given position. An "instruction" is deemed to be as close as one can come to a totally binding resolution. Instructions may be given either just before the conferees have been appointed or when the conference committee reports back to the chamber that a given item is in disagreement. In *Cannon's Procedure in the House of Representatives*, it is said to be "unusual" to give instructions prior to the first conference. The reason, it seems clear, is that expectations in both chambers prescribe compromise, and compromise cannot be effected if the two sides come to the table bound hand, foot, and finger. No case of instructions given prior to conference was uncovered in the period under investigation. But at least one plea to do just that was made by Senator Javits as a method of strengthening the Senate position in the mutual aid conference committee:

> We make a battle for the Mutual Security appropriation in the Senate and then what happens? . . . The conferees split the difference. . . . This is absolute nonsense and the reason for it is that we have not stood up on our hind legs in the Senate and made our conferees do what we voted . . . Senators stand here and talk about being agents of the Senate. When? When have they fought for the Senate figure completely? . . . The only way we will get anything we wish . . . is to instruct our conferees before they walk out the door. Then the Senate will really be tough . . . someday I would like to see the Senate show it means what it says by instructing its conferees not to yield until they come back to the Senate for a vote.[66]

Should both sets of conferees ever be instructed in this fashion on all matters at issue, conference committee decision-making would be impossible. It is for this reason that conferees seek and the two chambers give "instructions" only after the conference committee has "winnowed out" or "sugared off" as

[65] 102 *Congressional Record*, pp. 3944–3945.
[66] *Congressional Record*, Daily Edition, August 26, 1960, p. 16607.

many items as it can and finds itself deadlocked on one or two items. Typically, when an item is reported back to the chamber in disagreement, that group of conferees most confident of its position will seek a vote which, according to the language, "instructs" the conferees to "insist" on their position. Should both chambers produce equally strong instructions with equally overwhelming votes (and the size of the vote will be a factor), the conferees must seek some other sources of internal persuasion or external pressure.

Inside the conference room, the threat of one group to seek instructions from the parent chamber is considered the ultimate weapon. The strategy is, of course, for the group to prove to the other side that it is inflexibly committed to a given position, that it cannot yield, and that it prefers no bill at all to a version other than its own. This externally based threat may be accompanied by the more personal threat to "sit 'til Christmas," "sit until doomsday," "stand hitched 'til Hell freezes over," "sit until the snow flies," which play a part in autonomous bargaining. In strictly internal bargaining, the only threat used is one designed so to inconvenience an opponent by prolonging the conference that he will eventually yield. It is a kind of endurance or stubbornness test, pure and simple. And in this form it does not carry the threat of seeking a vote from the parent chamber. In case of prolonged disagreement, the personal threat may be buttressed by the stronger external threat, and the two may be pressed simultaneously. "We just sit there — sometimes it takes days to let them know we mean business," said a House subcommittee chairman. "The one thing they don't like is when you finally threaten to take an item back to the House for instructions. They know the House will back you up. I don't know why that is but it's true."

In the conferences on the Labor–Health, Education, and Welfare appropriation bill during the late 1950's and early 1960's, the external threat was implicit from the very beginning. It was this House subcommittee, it will be recalled, under the leadership of John Fogarty, that most frequently violated internal Committee expectations of budget reduction. And it was the membership of this subcommittee that was manipulated by Messrs. Cannon and Taber so as to deliver voting control into their hands. In conference, Cannon, Taber, and the other Republicans could control the House vote. Fogarty's strength, however, lay in the fact that if he took a dispute back to the House floor he was likely to win. The Senate conferees, under the leadership of Lister Hill, typically supported a greatly increased Senate appropriation, with which Fogarty sympathized. Fogarty's strategy was to try to seek compromise on the high side by threatening implicitly and explicitly to return to the House for binding instructions. "A couple of times," he said, "I've brought it back to the House. If I can get to the floor of the House, I can usually win." Though they could outvote Fogarty, the other three House conferees were in a precarious position. Explained one of them,

Now you have to be careful on the HEW bill not to bring it back to the floor because you'll get rolled if you do. So you have to go slow there and it weakens you a whole lot in conference. Fogarty will usually go for the Senate figure, and if you make a strong stand and it comes back to the floor he will win. In Congress there is a lot of support for these programs and there's no telling how high you might go on the floor before enough people would stop.

As we shall see presently, the conferees usually agreed on a figure closer to the Senate's than to that of the House. The case provides a good illustration of the proposition that the conference committee — or, more accurately, each of its units — is dependent ultimately on the support of the chamber of which it is a part.

An original roll call in support of an item together with a second indication of sentiment when the item is reported back in disagreement binds the conferees involved and places the strongest kind of pressure on the other side to yield. Said one Senator in explaining why he conceded to the House,

> The amendment was voted into the bill in the first instance in the other body and, when the bill came to the Senate, it was stricken out after hearings by the Senate Committee. The bill went back to the House in disagreement and the House took a second vote on the matter. At that time an effort was made for a yea and nay vote in the other body, but the Senate amendment did not have sufficient strength in the House even to get a call of the yeas and nays. Even those who were in favor of the Senate position agreed that the decision of the House would be the same if the amendment went back for another vote. Therefore, it would have been futile for the Senate to attempt to maintain its position longer on that particular item.[67]

The proposition probably holds that the greater the number of similar expressions of sentiment which come from a given chamber the more binding the sentiment on that chamber's conferees.

Also of relevance to the strength of external sentiment is the matter of which legislators and how many take which position. When asked why he was forced to concede a strongly held position and split the difference when the conference reconvened after an item had been reported in disagreement, a House subcommittee chairman spoke as follows:

> HOUSE MEMBER: As one member of the Committee on Appropriations which felt when this bill went over that 1500 people was adequate, I would like something more than the statement that "we split the difference with the Senate" . . . I would like an explanation.
> SUBCOMMITTEE CHAIRMAN: Let me say to the gentleman from California . . . that they took a vote in the other body and the vote was 75–0 for 7,000 additional employees.

[67] 93 *Congressional Record*, p. 10323.

HOUSE MEMBER: I guess that is the explanation.

SUBCOMMITTEE CHAIRMAN: There was, however, a difference of opinion on the question on the floor of the House. The members will recall that when we brought back our conference report, there were several members of the House who urged additional employees over and above the number that the House had allowed . . . under these conditions we went into conference.[68]

In a situation where the Senate was unanimous and the House split, Senate conferees were strengthened and the House "had to" yield. Moreover, in the particular case cited above (involving the Bureau of Internal Revenue), the critical increments of Senate support and House nonsupport appear to have come from key chamber leaders — from the relevant legislative committees particularly and to a lesser degree from the party leaders. In the Senate, a bipartisan group including the Chairman and ranking minority member of the Finance Committee together with the Senate majority leader spoke strongly on the floor *in support of* their conferees.[69] In the House, on the other hand, the Chairman of the Ways and Means Committee spoke strongly *against* the position of the House conferees. He was joined by another senior member of his committee and by the majority floor leader.[70] On other occasions, conferees may cite as one reason for yielding, "This same legislation had been before the legislative committee in the other body and had been acted on unfavorably and that the legislative committee was very much adverse to this legislation and it would certainly oppose it."[71] From the first stages to the last, the legislative committee exercises on behalf of the parent chamber an important, albeit occasional, influence over appropriations decisions.

So, as we have seen, may the party leadership act on behalf of the parent chamber at the conference stage, lending increments of support or nonsupport to their conferees. Given its primary concern for scheduling and for moving the business of the Congress, the leadership becomes especially active trying to prod conference committees to speedy action near the end of each session. While the conferees themselves might prefer to wait each other out, the leadership reflects the pressure of the membership for a bill. That pressure grows intense as adjournment seems possible. In the early hours of the morning on December 21, 1963, the House foreign aid conferees reported that

In the interest of maintaining the position of the House, at 4:30 o'clock this afternoon we got up and walked out of the conference room without

[68] 98 *Congressional Record*, p. 8688.
[69] 95 *Congressional Record*, pp. 8114–8116.
[70] *Ibid.*, pp. 7742–7743.
[71] *Congressional Record*, Daily Edition, May 4, 1960, p. 8700. See also *ibid.*, July 1, 1960, pp. 14310–14311.

any agreement at all . . . we subsequently went back into the conference room at the urging of the Senate and upon the urging of the leadership of the House and finally reached an agreement.[72]

Annually, Speaker Rayburn importuned an embattled Clarence Cannon to yield his conference position for the sake of a year-end bill. And Cannon complained with feeling:

> We're sitting there and then Sam Rayburn calls up and says, "Clarence, let's get the hell out of here. Everybody wants to go home. Let's get away from here." It's like someone sticking a gun at your head and saying, "Stand and deliver."

The point is that Cannon had to "deliver" under external pressure of this sort. From general exhortations through telephone calls from the Speaker, the conferees are subjected to environmental influences and they do make decisions which are directly responsive to these influences.

CONFERENCE COMMITTEE DECISION PATTERNS

The appropriations case histories of the 36 bureaus provide data for the analysis of conference committee decisions. These data have serious limitations. Indeed, of all appropriations decisions, conference committee decisions may be the least amenable to examination by dollars and cents data. The central question of conference committee decision-making is, "Who wins?" It must be answered before the other important questions of "how" and "why" can be broached. Yet we cannot know what "winning" means unless we know the preferences of the two sides (and preferably those of each conferee) with regard to the various amendments at issue. If, for example, one group is willing to give up an item costing $50 million to get some especially valued item costing $10 million, dollars and cents measures will be inadequate to define "winning." Or, a key point at issue may be a matter of language providing for the distribution of money, in which case one side may yield entirely on the monetary amount in order to get the language provision it desires. Any empirical measure which uses only monetary data will miss the outcome of this bargain entirely. In short, the analysis of conference committee outcomes requires and invites a detailed analysis of the preferences of the conferees. This is the only approach that will yield definitive answers to the questions, "Who wins?" and "Why?" What follows represents, therefore, the most rudimentary kind of description and explanation.

As a very rough empirical measure of "winning," it was determined for each of the 576 instances whether the dollar outcome was closer to the figure

[72] Congressional Record, Daily Edition, December 21, 1963, p. 24220.

in the Senate bill or closer to the figure in the House bill. If a conference decision was closer to the House figure, the House was said to have "won." If the decision was closer to the Senate figure, the Senate was the "winner." No attempt was made (and this introduces another caveat) to take account of the magnitude of the victory — except in those cases where the conference decision gave one side or the other the exact figure recommended in its bill. If the decision fell midway between the two figures, the result was described as "splitting the difference." Quite arbitrarily, a $1000 margin on either side of the exact midpoint was allowed in designating cases of splitting the difference.

Only those cases were used where the Senate and House Committees began with identical budget estimates. Fifty-eight cases, where the budget estimate was changed between the time of House and Senate consideration, were eliminated on the grounds that such a change placed the conferees on an unequal footing. The 58 cases were not distributed randomly. Forty of the 58 were either in the Interior (26) or the HEW (14) Departments. What this seems to reflect is the fact that some agencies are more likely than others to revise their estimates between the time the House and the Senate deals with their budget — and usually this means a revision upward. The analysis which follows includes the remaining 518 cases. But in examining these 518, it should be kept in mind that a margin of error exists for the two departments mentioned above.

Before one asks or answers the question, "Who wins in conference?" the question itself needs to be put in some perspective. Of the 518 cases studied, 186 of them were decided without resort to conference at all. That is, in 36 per cent of the cases, House and Senate figures were identical. And they were identical because the Senate simply adopted the decision of the House. In this large group of cases, then, it is possible to say that the House won a victory. Its recommendation was accepted by the Senate and, indeed, it is possible that some informal intercommittee communications may have influenced those results. Whatever the reason (and executive branch satisfaction is probably the major one), the House goes to conference already having won Senate acceptance in a substantial number of cases. This situation reflects the general dominance of the House and of the House Committee in appropriations politics — a dominance which was noted in Chapters Ten and Eleven. Again, we see evidence in support of the proposition that, as the appropriations process proceeds through its several stages, the amount of money at issue becomes smaller and smaller. Decisions of the greatest magnitude and import are made in the House; Senate decisions involve smaller increments of money; in conference committee the range of discretion is smaller still. This does not mean that a conference conflict is any less difficult to resolve. It simply means that *dominance in the conference committee must never be confused with dominance in the appropriations process as a whole.*

With that admonitory note, the simplest answer to the question of who wins in conference appears to be: *the Senate.* Of the 331 cases in which a conflict was present, the Senate conferees won 187 times, the House conferees won 101 times, and in 43 cases the two groups split the difference. (See Table 12.1.) With respect to the latter pattern, the 43 cases give ample evidence of the existence of the kind of independent pattern described earlier. Given the method by which figures were collected, this category is probably somewhat smaller than it should be. Cases where the overall figures for a bureau were split show up here. But cases where a bureau's appropriation was subdivided into several line items, where these line items were packaged and split ("House recede on two items, Senate on two items"), were not captured in this total.

TABLE 12.1

DISTRIBUTION OF SENATE AND HOUSE CONFERENCE COMMITTEE VICTORIES, 331 CONTESTS

Conference Decision	Number of Decisions		Percentage of Decisions	
Senate Victories	187		56.5	
Same As Senate Bill		70		21.2
Less Than Senate Bill		102		30.8
More Than Senate Bill		15		4.5
House Victories	101		30.5	
Same As House Bill		28		8.5
More Than House Bill		61		18.4
Less Than House Bill		12		3.6
Split the Difference	43		13.0	13.0
Total	331		100.0	100.0

The difference between the number of Senate and House victories seems, despite the limitations of the data, to be a significant one. It is certainly not — especially if one includes the splits — overwhelming. Still, a Senate victory is the modal pattern, and it occurs in over a majority of the cases. And if one considers only the 288 cases where a victory was won, the Senate conferees defeated the House conferees by the significant margin of 65 per cent to 35 per cent, or nearly 2 to 1. The fact of the Senate's superiority is supported — indeed by the same ratio of 2 to 1 — by House Committee Chairman Clar-

663

ence Cannon's own calculations, which he presented during the feud of 1962. Said Cannon, "In the past ten years (1952 to 1961) the Senate conferees have been able to retain $22 billion out of the $32 billion in increases which the Senate added to House appropriations — a 2–1 ratio in favor of the [Senate]."[73] Even if one makes allowance for the fact that some of Cannon's differential is due to the fact that the Senate was confronted with some supplemental budget estimates which the House was never called to act upon (a factor which has been dropped from our calculations by the elimination of the 58 cases mentioned earlier), the public admission by the House Committee's life-long champion that the Committee was beaten 2 to 1 in conference must be regarded as strong corroborative evidence.

At the very least, the data failed to confirm Gilbert Steiner's conclusion (based on his study of five appropriation bills — one in 1928, two in 1929, one in 1933, and one in 1943) that "House influence was predominant" and "outweighed" that of the Senate in the area of appropriations.[74] At the very most, the data establish presumptive evidence that Senate, not House, conferees are the more influential in appropriations conferences. And certainly it is in order to seek explanations which account for Senate dominance.

Before embarking on an explanation for Senate dominance, it should be noted that, so far as one can tell from the output data we have, both goal expectations involving the conference committee are met. That is, the two sets of conferees do apparently fight for their respective bills, and they do reach agreement by compromise. Table 12.1 presents — for those 331 cases in which there was a conference contest — a breakdown of decisions.

Senate conferees were able to get exactly what their bill called for on 70 occasions; the House conferees received exactly what their bill called for 28 times. Assuming the conferees' fight to obtain this kind of a decision, complete victories came to one or the other group nearly 30 per cent of the time — and about two and one-half times more frequently for the Senate than for the House. This figure may, as we have mentioned, overestimate the number of total victories and underestimate the number of package-deal type splits. Most decisions — 70 per cent of them — fulfilled the expectation that they should be compromises. Typically, as one would expect, the decision was less than that called for in the Senate bill or more than that called for in the House bill. One of these two patterns occurred in 163 cases, or nearly 50 per cent of the time. In a small number of cases, the Senate ended up taking more than it originally wanted or the House less than called for in its bill.

In Table 12.2, the total of 331 contests are presented by departments, in an attempt to ascertain whether overall decision patterns could be explained

[73] *Congressional Record*, Daily Edition, July 9, 1962, p. 12012.
[74] Gilbert Y. Steiner, *The Congressional Conference Committee* (Urbana: University of Illinois Press, 1951), pp. 170–172.

TABLE 12.2

CONFERENCE COMMITTEE DECISIONS: BY DEPARTMENT, 331 CONTESTS

DEPARTMENT	OUTCOME Senate Wins	House Wins	Split	Total
Agriculture	29 (59.2%)	11 (22.4%)	9 (18.4%)	49
Commerce	27 (48.2%)	18 (32.1%)	11 (19.7%)	56
HEW	32 (59.25%)	17 (31.5%)	5 (9.25%)	54
Justice	10 (58.8%)	5 (29.4%)	2 (11.8%)	17
Interior	63 (66.3%)	29 (30.5%)	3 (3.2%)	95
Labor	15 (50.0%)	9 (30.0%)	6 (20.0%)	30
Treasury	11 (36.7%)	12 (40.0%)	7 (23.3%)	30
Total	187	101	43	331

by program area or by the relative strength of subcommittees. With the exception of the Treasury Department — which was a draw — the Senate conferees won more often than the House conferees in every program area studied. The fact that there were very few contests over Treasury Department bureaus to begin with (only 30 contests out of 96 possibilities) stems from the fact that the Senate accepts House figures most of the time in this area. Thus, the stronger House showing on the Treasury Department appropriation follows a well-established pattern. It will be recalled that feelings of high confidence and mutual respect characterize relations between this department and the House subcommittee on appropriations with which it deals. It will also be recalled that Treasury Department bureaus are especially noncontroversial, which may account for the fact that the conferees seem more disposed to split the difference for these bureaus than for any of the others. Certainly the contrast between Treasury on the one hand and Interior and HEW on the other, with regard to splitting the difference, is marked. It seems clear that conferences on the latter two bills are much more hotly contended than those on the Treasury bill.

Leaving aside the Treasury Department, the most general conclusion one can draw from Table 12.2 is that over a period of time (1947 to 1962) Senate conferees dominated all six departmental areas about equally strongly. Even though it does seem valid to say, for example, that the Senate was somewhat stronger relative to the House in Interior conferences than it was in Commerce Department conferences, the data do not support very firm generalization. All that can be said is that there are some suggestive differences which need further exploration. Such differences as do exist, however, support the generalization that the Senate will be strongest in conference in supporting those programs which it supports most strongly on the floor. The Interior Department — the one which the House Committee treated most harshly and the Senate Committee treated most sympathetically — is the major case in point. After watching the especially favorable treatment accorded the Interior Department throughout Senate appropriations decision-making, we would have predicted that the Senate would fight hardest to win in conference on this bill. The evidence in Table 12.2 confirms that prediction. Still, the difference between Interior conference outcomes and the outcome of HEW, Agriculture, and Justice conferences is not very substantial.[75] And while the Senate Committee and the Senate did give strong differential support in HEW programs, it did not support Agriculture bureaus especially strongly across the board, and it was noticeably unconcerned about Justice Department appropriations. It may well be, therefore, that special explanations can be found for each conference. The circumstances of the HEW conference, for instance, were discussed earlier. Or, perhaps, the similarities in Senate success across programs should be emphasized and some Senate-oriented explanation should be sought. The data of Table 12.2 would seem to call for such a search.

One explanation for Senate dominance — an explanation supported by arguments made elsewhere in this study — is this: It is not the Senate that wins in conference, but rather the chamber supporting the higher of the two appropriations figures wins in conference. The Senate wins, not because it is the Senate, but because it normally comes to conference supporting the higher appropriations figure. The argument here is merely an extension of an argument used to help explain the prevalence of Senate increases over House appropriations recommendations. The demands for increased appropriations become more concentrated and more intense as appropriations decision-making moves from stage to stage and as the controversial increment of the budget progressively narrows. Individuals and groups have more time to mobilize, have more information, and have fewer issues to contest at each succeeding stage — from House to Senate, from Senate to conference. Conversely, economy sentiment (unless maintained by extraordinary external events) tends to take the form of evanescent moods, to become progressively weaker with the passage of time and with the intrusion of new legislative events.

At the Senate stage, the most intensive demands for increases come from the executive agencies and their clientele, with additional assistance from interested Representatives and Senators. At the conference stage, however, the executive agencies become less important. Some of them maintain informal communication with the conferees and occasionally there is formal communication in the conference room. To the extent that they do intervene, however, it must be noted that they will do so in support of the Senate, thus adding to Senate strength. Neither the executive agencies nor their

[75] In the 26 missing Interior cases, the final figure was closer to the Senate appropriation in 21 cases.

interest group supporters are the major sources of demands on appropriations conferees. The most important external influence on the conferees, it has been stressed, comes from the two chambers. Thus the argument that the house supporting the higher figure wins in conference is grounded in the notion that members of the two chambers put the conferees under intensified pressure to support particularly valued programs or projects. This notion is supported by the unanimous feeling on the part of Senate Committee members that House Committee members really expect and hope that the Senate will restore a sizable amount of money to the bills and that they, the House conferees, come to the conference under pressure from the House members to act more liberally than they talk. In the words of a veteran sub-committee chairman,

> The House members want to take credit for economy. So they cut below what they expect to get. Then they come over here and agree to put it all back in. They get it coming and going. They make the record and then when the howl goes up, we put it back. Five years in a row they cut the ——— bureau and five times they agreed to put it all back in conference.

This general line of argument supports the idea that the Senate wins in conference because it is the "high house."

When one looks in this way at the 287 conference contests[76] in which the House or the Senate "won," it becomes apparent that another answer to the question, "Who wins in conference?" is "The 'high house.'" The conferees supporting the higher appropriations figure won 170 (59.2 per cent) times and the conferees supporting the lower appropriations figure won 117 (40.8 per cent) times. Furthermore, as one might expect, the conferees supporting the higher figure normally came from the Senate, and the conferees supporting the lower figure normally came from the House. The Senate was the high house 82.6 per cent of the time — or, in 237 out of 287 conferences. The Senate won and the high house won. The question arises as to whether Senate success occurred more by virtue of the fact that it was the high house or more by virtue of the fact that it was the Senate.

Table 12.3 indicates strongly that the Senate wins in conference because it is the Senate and not just because it is usually the high house. The Senate wins in conference just as often (66.0 per cent of the time) when it comes to conference supporting the *low* figure as it does (64.6 per cent of the time) when it comes to conference with a figure higher than that of the House. *The*

---

[76] This represents one less case than listed in Table 12.1. There was one bureau (Social Security Administration, 1953) for which the overall totals in House and Senate bills were identical, yet the components of the appropriation differed. Hence, there was, in fact, a contest and the Senate won. It was impossible, however, to make a determination as to which was the high house. There may have been other such cases, but no systematic effort was made to dig into the components of each bureau appropriation.

TABLE 12.3

SENATE CONFERENCE VICTORIES AS HIGH HOUSE AND AS LOW HOUSE

	Senate Victories	Senate Defeats	Total
Senate Figure Higher Than House Figure	153 (64.6%)	84 (35.4%)	237 (100.0%)
Senate Figure Lower Than House Figure	33 (66.0%)	17 (34.0%)	50 (100.0%)
Total	186	101	287

Senate wins in conference primarily because it is the Senate and not primarily because it is the high house. Senate conferees, in other words, would appear to have greater independent strength than House conferees. And, to the degree that this is true, it spurs a search for Senate-related explanations for Senate superiority at the conference table.

The dollars and cents data suggest no further explanation for independent Senate strength.[77] Furthermore, if we recall the discussion of the internal and external factors affecting conference decision-making, none seems very promising as an explanation for Senate success. Quite to the contrary, most of the factors would indicate that the House, not the Senate, should be the stronger in conference. By general agreement, the House conferees are better prepared, better organized, better informed, more single-minded in their interest, and employ a–more belligerent bargaining style. Indeed, because the House seems to possess so many resources, it may have come as quite a surprise to find all the data indicating that it loses more often than it wins. Of course, some part of the explanation has to do with its position as supporter of the low figure in a context where particularistic pressures to spend are stronger than pressures to economize. Even so, none of the data show the House to have as much independent strength as the Senate conferees. Why?

The answer to be given is a speculative one. But the speculation rests on the logic of system-subsystem analysis and on some empirical committee-chamber relationships described in this book. *The Senate is stronger in con-*

[77] Yearly variations in Senate and House victories, for example, do not seem very substantial. The Senate won more often than the House in 12 of the 16 years; and the years when the House won more often than the Senate (1952, 1954, 1956, 1959) suggest no apparent pattern. Furthermore, yearly variations in victories for the high and low houses indicate that the low house does somewhat better in the years of economy moods, in 1951 and 1952 for example, but this pattern does not hold consistently or strongly. Events beyond the chambers, that is, do not seem to have any discernible influence on the conference outcomes.

ference because the Senate Committee and its conferees draw more directly and more completely upon the support of their parent chamber than do the House Committee and its conferees. The importance of chamber support to conference outcomes has been demonstrated: The greater the chamber support, the more will the position of its conferees be strengthened. The greatest source of Senate support for its Appropriations Committee comes not from any single visible act or pronouncement. It flows from the close structural identity of the Senate and the Senate Appropriations Committee. When the Senate conferees go to the conference room, they not only represent the Senate — they are the Senate. The position they defend will have been worked out with a maximum of participation by Senate members and will enjoy a maximum of support in that body. The figures they defend may be higher because of the bargaining process, but they will be backed by a more durable consensus. And the bill will be defended in conference by men who are the leaders not just of the Committee, but of the Senate. Their style in conference may seem individualistic and disorganized, but the appearance is deceptive. What they are doing is continuing to solidify a Senate consensus and Senate support (for this conference and all future conferences) by the same methods as are used at every stage of decision-making in that body. When a conference contest comes down to a matter of demonstrating superior massed support in the parent chamber, the Senate conferees will normally command it. Indeed, they are simply its front echelon.

By contrast, the House conferees do not command any such sure or solid support. The structural differentiation between the House of Representatives and its Appropriations Committee is much greater than obtains in the Senate. Conflict between the House and the House Committee is common, albeit sporadic, and a number of clearly discernible points of tension exist between them. Decision-making inside the Committee is more hierarchically organized than is the case in the Senate, thus conferring considerable influence on a few individuals while leaving support for them among other House members problematical. The House Committee's stress on integration derives from its sense of special goals and special structural identity and from its desire to preserve those goals and that identity over and against the parent house. Its own high degree of integration acts as a deterrent to a higher degree of integration between it and the House. When the Committee's representatives come to conference, they are not in very close communication with the ranks of the House. And they do not come with such a dependable body of support from those ranks as does the Senate group. Their conference style, too, may be deceptive. Behavior which seems to indicate superiority may represent attempts to compensate for their deficiencies. The senatorial conference members' style is relaxed because they enjoy fairly solid backing. House conference style may be more strenuous because House chamber support is less predictable and the conferees' success depends more on their own resources. That is perhaps why they need to coordinate their position beforehand and why they resort more often to a kind of personal stubbornness. In a showdown depending on degrees of external support, the tentativeness of chamber support may be an important source of weakness for the House conferees.

The contrast once made ought not to be overdone. The idea is put forward as but a partial explanation for Senate strength in conference. To the degree that the Senate exhibits independent strength above and beyond its advantage as high house, however, this argument is advanced as the major explanation. In fact, just as the "high house" generalization can be used to explain away some of the Senate's victories, the idea just advanced concerning the Senate can be used to explain away some of the high house victories. That is, one source of conflict between the House conferees and House members may well be due to the fact that House members want increased expenditures and are supporting the Senate figure. An awareness of this fact among House conferees may contribute to their willingness to yield in key situations. In sum, explanations relevant both to the Senate as Senate and to the Senate as high house help us to answer the question why the Senate wins more often than the House. How well the generalization of Senate dominance holds up and, if it does, which explanation is more helpful — these questions must await more refined research on conferences than has been undertaken here.

It is worth noting, however, that the results of conference negotiations support the fear of House Committee members (voiced with regard to the joint budget committee, for example) that they will be bested in any combined endeavor. But it appears that House Committee members are right for the wrong reasons. It is not, as they believe, the Senate's superiority in glamor or prestige that accounts for their conference victories. Senate strength in any joint enterprise is likely to spring primarily from its greater success in adapting to the demands of its parent chamber.

HOUSE AND SENATE REACTION

House Reaction

Conference committee decision-making may take one hour or it may drag on for several weeks. But when the report has been agreed upon and House conferees take the "papers" from the conference room back to the House for action, the appropriations process is virtually completed. Compared with the area of controversy which existed when the House Committee first tackled the President's budget, the area of controversy remaining after the conference report has been written in miniscule. In the vast majority of cases, the conferees will be in complete accord. Sometimes, a few items will remain in genuine (as opposed to technical) disagreement between the conferees. Usually, they can be resolved without another conference. House members have a last opportunity to influence ultimate decisions, but under the most propitious of circumstances, they will be able to affect only one or two individual items. Circumstances, moreover, are not propitious.

In seeking House approval of the conference report, all the advantages lie with the Appropriations Committee. Debate is limited to one hour under House rules, and control of the time is completely in the hands of the subcommittee chairman who led the House conferees. Explained one frustrated House member,

> We get one hour of debate — all controlled by the majority, by the ranking majority member on the conference. We vote to approve the conference report first, and then take up the amendments. I don't like that. They ought to have thirty minutes controlled by those who oppose it. Usually, the conferees all support it and if you want to speak against it you've got to get them to yield to you for five minutes. But he doesn't have to if he doesn't want to. It's at the election of the majority. You can't move to strike out the last word or anything.

Committee control over procedure at this stage is illustrated by the following exchange:

> HOUSE MEMBER: Mr. Speaker, will the gentleman [subcommittee chairman] yield to me to offer an amendment to this section.
> SUBCOMMITTEE CHAIRMAN: I refuse to yield, Mr. Speaker.
> HOUSE MEMBER: Then I will offer the amendment. I think I have a right to offer it under the rules of the House.
> THE SPEAKER: Not unless the gentleman from Michigan yields for that purpose.
> HOUSE MEMBER: Would the gentleman yield me some time? I would like to rise in opposition to the amendment.
> THE SPEAKER: The gentleman from Michigan has full control of the time . . .
> SUBCOMMITTEE CHAIRMAN: No; I will not yield any time.[78]

The conference report must be voted on in its entirety. To get at any single provision on which the conferees have agreed requires that the entire report be recommitted with instructions.

What is more, any delay takes time, and time may be of the essence. The end of the fiscal year may be fast approaching or, indeed, so may the end of the session. One subcommittee chairman explained, for example, why there had not been time even to print the conference report. "May I say to

[78] 93 *Congressional Record*, p. 10485.

the gentleman that tomorrow is the last day of the fiscal year. Time is of the essence and the conference report is in complete agreement."[79] Or, "I do not intend to do so [move to recommit the conference report]. The Departments of State, Justice, and Commerce run out of money at midnight tonight."[80] The Committee is aided, too, by the widespread feeling that a bill which has come this far probably contains the best agreement that can be reached and should be disposed of. Usually there are other legislative matters — especially as adjournment nears — to command the attention of the Members. The House may confront a conference report under conditions of near chaos. A House member recalls,

> At 2:00 in the morning, we took up the conference report on the foreign aid bill. I tried to find out what was in it, but how could you? I doubt if even the ranking members of the Appropriations Committee knew all of what was in that bill. Everybody wanted to get out and go home. At 6:30 A.M., we adjourned.

On another occasion, the House conferees kept the House in session awaiting their report, while they ran back and forth across the Capitol negotiating final agreements.[81] Under conditions of this sort, time and a division of interest among Members will preclude the mobilization of support for some solitary items in a conference report. The feeling of the membership is well summed up by a House veteran when he said, "There is little that can be done after an agreement is made by a conference committee, especially the powerful Appropriations Committee."[82]

Once again, the dominance of the Appropriations Committee over House appropriations decision-making is manifest. Committee members have all the advantages at this point, but they rarely allude to them or press them. Confident that their recommendations will pass, they try to make the membership feel comfortable about the substantive goals secured and about the relationships of dependence maintained by the Committee. They use their time on the floor to promote — as they do during regular floor debates — a sense of identity between themselves and the chamber. It is on this occasion that the Committee leaders explain that they fought the good fight on behalf of the House version of the bill. On balance, they will try to claim a victory, and they will stress the necessity of compromise. The bill is not all that any of us wanted (and occasionally a conferee may "reserve" on a conference committee item),[83] they will say, but it is about the best result that can be obtained under the circumstances. House acceptance regularly follows.

[79] *Congressional Record*, Daily Edition, June 29, 1959, p. 11011.
[80] 100 *Congressional Record*, p. 9333.
[81] *Congressional Record*, Daily Edition, October 11, 1962, p. 23258.
[82] 102 *Congressional Record*, p. 10072.
[83] *Congressional Record*, Daily Edition, October 4, 1962, p. 21184.

An indication of the anticlimactic nature of action on the conference report and, hence, of the Appropriations Committee dominance can be gleaned from a look at some summary figures. Final debates on the conference reports were examined for 8 departments plus public works for the period 1947 to 1962.[84] Because several of the departments were combined in one bill, since in one case the combination was changed midway in the period, and since the omnibus report of 1950 was excluded, the total number of House floor actions examined was 97. For each of them, the number of pages of floor explanation and debate in the *Congressional Record* — actual floor talk — was calculated. These figures provide a crude measure of time, interest, and controversy which, in turn, provide a crude measure of House Committee control over decision-making at that stage.

Almost half of the 97 conference reports (42 of 97) were disposed of with 1 page of explanation and debate or less. A reasonable estimate would be that these reports were dispatched in 10 minutes time or less. When one sets a half-hour upper limit on the time (i.e., 3 pages of debate), it appears that two-thirds of the conference reports (67) fall in this category. Or, to put the matter another way, it took more than a half-hour to dispose of only 31 (or 32 per cent) of the conference reports examined over a 16-year period. The total number of pages of debate for the 97 separate floor actions was 316. The average length of floor consideration was, therefore, 3.2 pages — or a little over 30 minutes time. The greatest number of total pages for any one category of bills over the period was for the public works bills, which meant mostly that individuals were given time to complain for the record that their pet project had been left out.[85] As a regular matter, therefore, House influence at this stage is almost nonexistent.

Yet the House can wield influence over a few items if support can be mobilized. On 7 occasions — that is, on 7 per cent of the reports — a motion to recommit the report to conference was proposed. These motions gave specific instructions to the House conferees. Five of them were defeated by the conferees. Two of them passed, and on these two, the House position prevailed.[86] The recommittal motion would seem to be a kind of ultimate weapon more important as a stick behind the door than as any regular technique for forcing compliance by the House conferees. Once the report has been agreed to and the items remaining in disagreement are called up for decision, the House becomes slightly more active. On 9 different occasions, a roll call was held on a motion to recede and concur in the Senate amendment — that is, adopt the version in the Senate bill rather than that in the House bill. All

---

[84] The same departments as used for the extended analysis in Chapter 9.

[85] The number of pages per bill was: Public Works, 91 pages; Agriculture, 82; Labor-HEW, 42; State, Justice, and Commerce, 42; Interior, 38; Treasury–Post Office, 21.

[86] Both were "Jensen amendments."

of these motions were opposed by a majority of the appropriations conferees. Six of the motions failed and 3 passed. In the 3 cases where the motion passed, the conferees acquiesced in the demand of the House, and chamber influence was exerted. But it is worth noting, again, that the Committee won more than it lost on these showdown votes. A final kind of roll-call vote involved the motions offered by the conferees either to recede and concur in a Senate amendment with a further amendment or further to "insist" on the House version of an item in dispute. Five such motions were made. The Appropriations Committee conferees won 4 and lost 1.

In sum, a total of 21 controversial motions — i.e., controversial enough to get to a roll-call vote — were put forward at this final stage. (There were other occasions when the same motions were passed by another kind of vote, but they were not recorded.) On the 21 votes, the position of the Committee conferees (or a majority of them) was upheld in 15 cases and the House forced the Committee to do what it did not want to do in 6 cases. To the last, House sanctions over its Committee on Appropriations remain. But it is the autonomy rather than the dependence of the Committee which is most noteworthy during its final appearances on the floor.

Senate Reaction

The "papers" that are messaged over to the Senate carry House agreement to the conference reports (unless the report has been recommitted) together with a further statement of House position on any items that were in disagreement. The House may have decided to recede and concur in the Senate amendments with or without amendment, or it may have decided to insist on its disagreements. The Senate may accept or reject the conference reports; it may agree or not agree to any House amendment to its amendments; and it may recede and concur or continue to insist on those items where the House has "insisted." Except in a few cases, the Senate acts in the most expeditious manner. The press of time, a division of interests and attention, and the general feeling that the best possible result has been achieved — all these factors operate as much if not more so in the Senate than in the House. Senate approval is the last significant congressional step, and the pressure to get it over with is correspondingly great. Though the rules of debate do not give an advantage to the Committee in debate on the conference report, our description of Senate–Senate Committee relations would lead us to predict (quite apart from the press of circumstances) even less disagreement in the Senate than in the House. Such evidence as has been collected confirms that prediction.

Of the 97 conferences examined, over half (53) of the reports required less than 10 minutes of floor time — that is, 1 page or less of debate and explanation. Action on 73 of the 97 was completed in a half-hour or less — that is, consumed 3 pages or fewer in the *Record*. Over all, the Senate spent about one-quarter less time (239 pages)[87] dealing with the conference reports on the floor than did the House. Despite the fact, therefore, that no strict limitation on debate exists in the Senate, less time was spent dealing with conference reports than in the House. Though it is possible for a Senator to conduct a filibuster against a conference report, no such delaying action was discovered in the 97 cases studied.[88] The explanation probably lies in some combination of situational factors (time, interest, etc.) and the structural affinity of the Senate and its Committee.

The Senate can reject the conference report as it comes over from the House, thereby necessitating an entirely new conference. The disadvantages of such a move were mentioned earlier and are so obvious that only one serious attempt at rejection (i.e., that came to a roll-call vote) was tried in the 97 cases. It was rejected — and the following colloquy explains why:

> SENATOR: Mr. President, there is only one way in which the Senate can insist upon keeping amendment number 106 in the bill. That is by rejecting the conference report from which the amendment has been dropped.
> SUBCOMMITTEE CHAIRMAN: There were 108 items in dispute. All of them have been settled by the conferees except one item, with respect to which a majority of the conferees agreed. If the bill goes back to conference, all the items will be in dispute and no one can tell when or if the bill may come back to the House or Senate again.[89]

Eight other roll calls were called for in the cases examined. On 6 occasions, the Committee asked for a supporting vote and insisted on its amendment — in continued opposition to House insistence on its version of the bill. In each case, the Committee received Senate support. Once, the Senate tried to force the Committee to insist on an item, but the attempt failed. And, finally, on one occasion the Committee offered a motion to recede and concur in a House amendment, but was defeated. On the total, therefore, of 9 roll calls devoted to conference committee matters, the Committee carried its position on 8 of them. The House Committee faced 21 controversial roll calls and won 15 (71 per cent) of them. The Senate Committee faced only 9 controversial roll calls, and it won 8 (89 per cent) of them. The figures are not at all conclusive, but such differences as there are again support the generalization that, compared with the House Committee, the Senate Committee conflicts less with and is, therefore, stronger in its parent chamber.

[87] The number of pages per bill was: State, Justice, and Commerce, 60; Agriculture, 48; Public Works, 47; Interior, 32; Labor-HEW, 28; Treasury–Post Office, 24.
[88] For a threat which did not materialize, see 93 *Congressional Record*, pp. 9643 ff.
[89] 97 *Congressional Record*, p. 13082. See also, 94 *Congressional Record*, p. 8086.

When a conference report has been approved in both chambers, an authoritative congressional decision has been made, and the bill moves to the President's desk to be signed into law. Only a presidential veto can prevent this outcome. And, lacking an item veto, Presidents are reluctant to leave an entire area of governmental activity without money to operate in order to eliminate some aspect of the bill. One veto was cast on the bills studied — by President Eisenhower on the Public Works Appropriation Bill of 1959. His veto, on the grounds that the Committee had appropriated money for projects not approved by his Budget Bureau, was upheld by a single vote in the House. The House Appropriations Committee met, and, rather than withdraw any of the projects, it cut every project in the bill by 2½ per cent. It then reported the bill back to the House, where it was re-passed by a margin of 303–93; the Senate agreed by a vote of 73–15. The President again vetoed the bill. This time both chambers supported their Committee against the President and overrode the veto: 280–121 in the House and 72–23 in the Senate. Partisanship ran high. Democrats, thirsting for a victory over the President at that stage, voted almost unanimously to override. A large majority of Republicans supported the President, but a group of defectors — 20 in the House and 10 in the Senate — who wanted to protect their pet projects proved decisive.[90]

CONCLUSION

The representatives of the House and Senate who meet face to face around the conference table confront the problem of creating and maintaining an institution to perform the task of melding two appropriation bills into one. Each group must adapt sufficiently to the expectations, images, and behavior of the other to ensure the survival of the conference committee as an entity. This problem of adaptation has been successfully solved — though not always with ease, as the 1962 conflict attests. Members of both chambers and the managers from the two appropriations committees share the expectations that each side should fight to win, that there should be a bill, and that the result, therefore, should be a compromise. And all interested parties agree on certain basic procedural rules of the game. No uncertainty exists about the general nature of the outcome — it will be a negotiated settlement. And no uncertainty exists either about the behavior and the style of the two sets of conferees. Repeated contact has produced fairly congruent and accurate self-images and other-images among House and Senate conferees. Since these images of one another are not always favorable, they add elements of intergroup conflict to the conflict on appropriation bills. On the

[90] 105 *Congressional Record*, pp. 17752, 18564, 18593, 18924–18926, 18983.

other hand, the fact that the images are widely shared among the conferees introduces some predictability into the proceedings. Predictability, in turn, eases the problem of adaptation and helps stabilize the institution.

Within a framework of shared expectations and images, the two sets of conferees develop their own procedures and patterns of decision-making. Each group maintains its complete autonomy, and decisions are made only when a majority of House conferees agrees with a majority of Senate conferees. For the most part, each group of conferees follows its own norms and its distinctive style of decision-making. Hence, only the minimum by way of an internal structure can be produced; and even the minimum that does exist was, in 1962, the subject of long, bitter controversy. Still, the conferees develop and use their own devices to arrive at viable decisions. Decisions made by private negotiation of subcommittee leaders and clerks, by splitting the difference, by the weight of information and argument, or by a superiority of interpersonal skills — all these illustrate a pattern of independent decision-making.

A different, less independent pattern of conference decision-making is also evident. The conferees, that is, make decisions in direct response to influences external to the conference. Most important, their decisions are shaped by the distribution and the intensity of expectations in their respective parent chambers. An exhortation by chamber colleagues, a promise extracted from the conferees, a roll-call vote, formal "instructions," legislative committee interest, pressure from the party leadership — all these forms of external influence, singly or in combination, produce a dependent pattern of decision-making. House and Senate conferees respond to these external forces because each faces the problem of adaptation to its parent chamber. And it is out of a need to adapt to these environmental groups that each set of conferees maintains its autonomy at the conference table and contends as vigorously as it can on behalf of its chamber's version of the bill.

The question, "Who wins in conference?" can be answered only in the most unrefined terms and on the basis of the limited evidence collected for this study. If one includes, out of the 576 cases, only those involving conference contests (thus eliminating all instances where House decisions were accepted by the Senate), the answer is that the Senate wins more often than the House. One explanation for this is that the Senate wins because it usually is defending the higher appropriations figure. And the reasoning is simply that here, at the final stage of the appropriations sequence, expectations on behalf of the higher figure are much stronger than expectations on behalf of the lower figure. Members of House and Senate, executive branch agencies, clientele groups, and the Senate conferees stand in support of the higher figure, while only the House conferees and the House Committee on Appropriations stand foursquare in support of the lower appropriation.

677

Doubtless this explanation is appropriate. But it cannot explain the fact that the Senate wins just as frequently when it supports the lower figure as it does when it supports the higher one — though the total number of cases is, of course, smaller. A second explanation for Senate dominance emphasizes the close structural identity and harmony between the Senate Committee on Appropriations and the Senate, which provides the Senate conferees with dependable external support for their position. House conferees, on the other hand, stand in a more differentiated, more conflict-ridden relationship to their parent chamber, which weakens them at the conference table. The Senate Committee is more successful at solving the problem of adaptation to its parent chamber than is the House Committee. And this success is its vital source of strength at the conference table. To the degree that this explanation is valid, it confirms the necessity of underpinning the analysis of congressional committees with an investigation of their relationships with the parent chamber.

The preponderance of Senate victories in the conference room by no means signifies Senate dominance of the appropriations process in Congress. Throughout the book, we have noted the impact of the appropriations sequence upon appropriations decision-making. We have observed that with each successive step in that sequence, the amount of money at stake in the decision grows progressively smaller. In pure dollars and cents terms, the conferees make the least consequential decisions of all. Another, and even less consequential, decision can occur when the conference report is being ratified, but floor changes at that stage are rare. Indeed, conference decisions assume a special importance precisely because they are so final — and not because they are so consequential. Dominance in conference must not be confused with dominance of the larger process. In that respect, it is the House rather than the Senate which makes the more consequential appropriations decisions. The Senate makes no change at all in nearly one third of the House's decisions. And House dominance means — despite tensions — the dominance of the House Committee on Appropriations. This fact reminds us — as the final disposition of conference reports also reminds us — that the appropriations process in Congress is, in the end as in the beginning, a committee-centered process.

Conclusion

In the Introduction, three aims were set forth for this book — to describe appropriations politics in Congress, to demonstrate the value of committee-oriented studies of congressional activity, and to suggest the usefulness of certain elements of theory for the study of congressional committees and, hence, of Congress. If the preceding pages have failed to enlighten or convince, nothing written now by way of a conclusion is likely to achieve these aims. Throughout the book, primary emphasis has been placed upon the presentation of data about appropriations politics. It is, therefore, quite likely that in the eyes of most readers the first of the three aims, and only the first, has been fulfilled. However, it is hoped that this judgment has not been made by too many professional students of Congress. For it is the author's intention that the description of appropriations politics, the committee-centered approach to that description, and the elements of theory used in the committee-centered approach be considered as a single, interconnected attempt to improve our understanding of Congress. If the description of appropriations activity is deemed enlightening, a large share of the credit should go to the committee-centered approach to such activity. And if the committee orientation is considered rewarding, considerable credit should be given to its theoretical underpinnings. Such, at least, is the hope of the author.

With respect to this blend of aims it may be objected that because of the very great power of the appropriations committees, the appropriations process is a poor case with which to prove the general utility of committee-oriented analysis. It can only be replied that one case cannot prove the point either way and that conclusive proof awaits further research. Obviously, the generalizations of the preceding pages apply to only two committees. But the hope is that, by force of example, this study in the area of appropriations will encourage similar committee-centered research in other areas of congressional activity. Certainly it is reasonable to assume that other congressional committees do make decisions and do exercise some influence in their specified policy fields. An explanation for varying degrees of committee influence would, indeed, be a primary object of such research. It is the author's belief, in any case, that many more studies of congressional behavior focused on pairs of committees would be both feasible and enormously beneficial. More than that, the author is convinced that a dozen or so such studies are absolutely necessary if we are ever to understand our national legislature.

Some students may be persuaded to undertake analyses similar to this one because of the crying need for basic information about the internal workings of Congress and because committee-oriented research promises, at the very least, to generate such data. Others, however, are more likely to proceed if they can be convinced that committee-centered analysis holds some promise of producing important generalizations about congressional activity. For them, the burden of this book's example will be carried not by its array of facts but by the elements of theory used to guide the collection, interpretation, and presentation of those facts.[1] The word "guide" is used advisedly. As the Introduction made clear, only bits of theory have been employed in this study; and, as the succeeding chapters have made equally clear, these theoretical underpinnings have been granted a relatively inconspicuous and secondary status. They became most obtrusive, perhaps, in organizing the book (as revealed by the Table of Contents), but even here the appropriations sequence supplied some counterpoint.

In providing a structure for the book, these theoretical elements have focused attention on certain observable activities and suggested a number of variables which might help explain them. As befits their essential fragmentation, the bits of theory have not been used to formulate a series of interrelated and testable propositions. They have been used rather to help chart the terrain inside of Congress, to point up relevant kinds of relationships, and to suggest directions for further research. Indeed, the appeal of the political system as a central idea lies in the fact that it sensitizes the researcher to the broadest range of relationships. And it may be precisely this kind of capacious sensitivity that is most needed at the present juncture in congressional

---

[1] One element of theory used in this book — the idea of integration — was discussed in an earlier article on the House Committee. At least two students of Congress found that idea sufficiently worthwhile to use it as the theoretical basis for analyses of the House Agriculture Committee and the House Ways and Means Committee. See Richard F. Fenno, Jr., "The House Appropriations Committee as a Political System: The Problem of Integration," *American Political Science Review* (June, 1962), pp. 310–324; Charles O. Jones, "The Role of the Congressional Subcommittee," *Midwest Journal of Political Science* (November, 1962), pp. 327–344; John F. Manley, "The House Committee on Ways and Means: Conflict Management in a Congressional Committee," *American Political Science Review* (December, 1965), pp. 927–939.

research — as scholars turn away from the mapped and traveled paths which trace external (interest group, constituency, executive) pressures on Congress and plunge into the forest of internal congressional life. If the results of research guided by such theory be largely heuristic — identifying key relationships and suggesting propositions for further testing — they nonetheless constitute an essential step forward in congressional research. Since some of these heuristic results can properly be attributed to the use of specific bits of theory, a few of them will be reemphasized here in the hopes of encouraging similar research.

SYSTEM-ENVIRONMENT RELATIONS

One idea central to the organization of the book holds that a congressional committee, as a political system, exists in an environment and that committee behavior must be explained partly in terms of its interaction with elements of its environment. These elements include the parent chamber, clientele or constituency groups, the executive branch, and the other chamber. How and how much these various elements do influence a given committee or what kinds of problems each poses for the survival of a given committee become empirical questions. But the conceptualization of the system-environment relationship and the posing of the adaptation problem for the system do direct one's attention to important relationships and do suggest explanations for committee behavior.

In the preceding study the most important result of such conceptualization was the focusing of attention on the committee–parent chamber relationship — a relationship which has gone virtually unexamined by students of Congress. Aspects of the relationship such as the committee selection process have been treated, but they have been viewed as isolated interactions and not as aspects of a total committee–parent chamber relationship. In the case of the appropriations committees, the conceptualization of the committee–parent chamber relationship as a system-environment problem yielded several important and suggestive findings.

First, the appropriations committees are not so dominantly independent and autonomous as the time-honored, Wilson-based generalizations of political scientists have made them out to be. Members of the parent body hold identifiable sets of expectations and images concerning committee behavior, and can employ a range of sanctions to maintain the ultimate dependence of the committees. It is precisely because the committees have limited autonomy that the problem of adaptation is important for them — and for us.

Second, the appropriations committee–parent-chamber relationship is substantially different in the Senate from what it is in the House. An explora-

681

tion of committee–chamber interactions in terms of expectations, perceptions, attitudes, and behavior demonstrates that the two groups are far more sharply differentiated in the House than they are in the Senate. The committees are about equally limited in their independence, but the mechanisms for maintaining committee dependence differ. The Senate achieves control over its Appropriations Committee primarily by maintaining a close working relationship with it — by a kind of structural absorption. The House, on the other hand, curbs the autonomy of its Appropriations Committee more through the periodic exercise or threat of overt sanctions — by a kind of structural check and balance. (Mechanisms such as anticipated reactions and procedural restraints operate in both cases.) This difference in degree of structural (and psychological) separateness suggests, at least, that the Senate and the House have two very different decision-making structures. Committees, it appears, are more influential decision makers in the House than they are in the Senate. Conversely, decision-making influence is more widely distributed among the members of the Senate than among members of the House.

Third, differences in committee–parent-chamber differentiation may help explain other phenomena. The greater the degree of differentiation, the more difficult will be a committee's problem of adaptation or the more likely it is that tension and conflict will exist between committee and parent chamber. And such differences will have consequences. The consciousness which House Committee members have of their problem of adaptation may help explain that group's heavy emphasis (and the Senate Committee's corresponding lack of emphasis) on internal integration. Committee integration produces committee unity, and committee unity may be necessary to adapt to or get along with a somewhat antagonistic parent body. House Committee integration and unity, for instance, increase the likelihood of success in having Committee decisions upheld on the House floor. More generally, House Committee integration and unity will decrease the likelihood that the parent body will interfere with or alter the Committee's chosen ways of behaving.

As another example, it has been suggested that the relative lack of differentiation between the Senate Committee and the Senate and, hence, the relative ease of Committee adaptation helps explain Senate success in conference committee negotiations. The greater the support which a group of conferees can command in their parent chamber, the more likely they are to win in conference; and Senate conferees, by virtue of their close identification with the Senate, command chamber support more often than do their House counterparts. The finding that (in case of conflict) the Senate wins in appropriations conference more often than the House runs counter to previous studies and to the beliefs of most participants. Viewed in terms of

682

a system-environment kind of theory, the result seems perfectly logical and a nonobvious, reasonable explanation for it is contained within the analysis.

The idea of a system-environment relationship and the system's consequent problem of adaptation have been used, also, to organize the analysis of appropriations committee–executive branch interaction. An investigation of expectations, perceptions, and attitudes between the two sets of government officials indicates that this cross-branch relationship is characterized, more than any of the committees' other external relationships, by a pervasive uncertainty. Committee uncertainty centers on the adaptational problem of meeting executive demands by making informed and wise decisions. Executive branch uncertainty centers on its difficulty in achieving meaningful and effective communication with the legislature. Much of the behavior of the two sets of officials can be explained as attempts to reduce uncertainty or adjust to the presence of it.

It is recognized by both the committees and the executive branches that one necessary antidote for the uncertainty which they feel is the development of confidence in one another. Especially vital is the creation of committee confidence in the executive agency for which it appropriates. Where appropriations committee members can trust the information, the judgment, and the goals of an executive group, they can live more easily with the degree of informational uncertainty which they cannot radically change. Where executives can win and hold the confidence of the committee, they can live more comfortably with a degree of unpredictability which remains characteristic of committee behavior. The presence of informational uncertainty together with the need to cope with it by creating conditions of confidence help to explain appropriations committee behavior toward executive officials. Especially, they help explain the committee's efforts to sample — by assessing a budgetary increment, a personal experience with the agency, an incident involving a constituent, a specific non-programmatic expenditure, or an administrator's personality.

Committee members find it both necessary and desirable to sample in order to reason inductively toward somewhat broader policy judgments and in order to determine whether an agency merits their confidence. It is by judiciously combining information, experience, and confidence that the committee makes its decisions and thus adapts to the executive elements of its environment. Armed with some such perspective as this, political scientists might well undertake further research into the actualities and possibilities of appropriations committees oversight instead of railing, as they typically do, at the committees for meddling in details (i.e., sampling), invading administrative discretion (i.e., losing confidence), and making incremental rather than overall policy judgments (i.e., lacking certainty). The funda-

683

mental difficulty with this stereotyped "public administration" line of analysis is, very simply, its utter failure to consider the committees' problems from the committees' perspective. A committee-centered approach guided by theory about system-environment relations might serve as a valuable corrective.

INTERNAL SYSTEM RELATIONS

For the description and analysis of activity inside the appropriations committees, the central theoretical notion is the idea of a political system. The key elements of that system are a set of differentiated yet interrelated roles, defined by norms and maintained by various mechanisms of social control. The system faces at least two internal problems if it is to maintain itself — decision-making and integration. These problems serve as foci for describing and explaining behavior inside the committee. And these descriptions and explanations of internal activity, in turn, suggest explanations for committee behavior in adapting to its parent chamber and to the executive branch.

Of special importance in understanding the internal system is knowledge about expectations or desires of the individual members — why they became and why they remain members of the committee involved. Such knowledge is usually neglected in committee analyses, partly because it is difficult to obtain. The relationship is, of course, a circular one. Individuals are attracted to committees because of the kind of internal system the committee has, and this system is reinforced because of the desires which members bring to the committee. What seems worth summary notation, however, is the finding that the nature of member desires (wherever they come from) helps explain a committee's solution to its problems of decision-making and integration.

House Committee members want increased influence. In the presence of a marked structural differentiation of Committee and House, they believe that their influence as individuals depends on maintaining the influence of the Committee as a collectivity. This desire for influence as a committee helps explain why the group adheres to the goal of budget-cutting: it seems to them the only way of exerting corporate influence. The alternative — rubber stamping executive requests — does not look to them like a way of building committee influence, the more so because the Committee must act first on these requests. Similarly, adherence to a decentralized yet tightly integrated decision-making structure is explainable partly by the capacity of such an arrangement of roles to distribute discrete sources of influence (via subcommittees) among individual members while at the same time preserving (via integrative norms) the essential unity of the whole. Once on the Committee, members place a high value on the sense of social solidarity which their group identification brings them. And their desire to preserve the collectivity for these reasons helps, also, to explain their internal system.

684

Senators also seek membership on the Appropriations Committee in order to increase their influence. But what they seek is a special opportunity (in addition to the many opportunities Senators already have) to influence specific appropriations that interest them. And this expectation does not entail any emphasis on corporate power through committee unity. Similarly, this desire does not lead the individual to seek or to value membership as an important source of social solidarity. Committee membership is a more important source of satisfaction for individual legislators in the House than in the Senate, and this fact has consequences for internal structure.

An understanding of these senatorial goals helps explain why the Committee remains satisfied (given also the fact that it must act last) with an appeals court function. As an appellate court, the Senate Committee is not nearly as influential as the House group — as a group. But individual Senators have ample opportunity to exert the highly individualistic kind of influence which they seek. Similarly, personal senatorial desires help explain the persistence of a subcommittee structure in which Senators sit on many subcommittees and on the subcommittees of their choice and in which a large proportion of Committee members sit on each subcommittee. Given the absence of member desires (or needs) for corporate committee power, their relative lack of concern for internal integration also becomes more understandable. And, given such differences, we should not be surprised to find that the elaboration of distinctive committee norms and a distinctive committee work style to guide behavior in the House group is not duplicated in the Senate Committee.

Internal committee variables such as individual expectations, self-prescribed tasks, decision-making structure, and degree of integration are linked in a mutually explanatory way. And all are affected by such environmental relationships as degree of committee differentiation from the parent chamber. Internal system differences between pairs of committees such as the two appropriations committees seem to be affected, too, by the sequence in which they act. It is the merit, perhaps, of the idea of a political system that it helps to suggest linkages such as these. But more committee-centered research will be needed to turn them into verified causal statements.

DECISION PATTERNS

A political system produces decisions. And two of the most fundamental questions one can ask about a political system are, what kinds of decisions does it make, and why? It is a frequent weakness of research on Congress that elaborate descriptions of decision-making processes are not linked in any systematic way to the substantive output of those processes. Except in case studies, we are more skilled, too, at describing who wants what than we are at describing who gets what. One problem here — a problem which poses a key obstacle to committee research — is the difficulty in devising appropriate ways to measure policy output. Since, however, an important segment of all appropriations decisions is expressed in dollars-and-cents terms, a crude measure is available for this particular study. Given the possibility of describing and differentiating among kinds of decisions, the bits of theory used in this study do seem helpful in suggesting relationships between policy-making variables and policy output.

At the most general level, for example, committee decisions reflect an attempt to meet the external problem of adaptation to the environment while at the same time satisfying desires of the committee's members. Hence, House Committee decisions reduce agency budgets (which meets member desires) while allowing agency budgets to increase from year to year (which meets House and executive desires). Senate Committee decisions increase agency budgets above the amount voted by the House Committee (which action meets member, Senate, and executive desires). Other internal variables which help explain the same overall decision pattern are the self-defined goals of the committees (budget-cutting or accepting appeals) and their decision-making structures (as they encourage or discourage the interest-sympathy-leniency syndrome).

At the more specific level of individual departments and bureaus, *House* Committee decisions seem to be explainable largely in terms of two variables: the degree of external support (especially in the parent chamber) which an agency commands and the degree of confidence which the committee (i.e., subcommittee) has developed in the agency as a result of committee-agency interaction. The greater its external support, the more rapidly will an agency budget increase from year to year, and vice versa. The more confidence the committee has in an agency, the smaller will be the yearly reductions in its budget estimate, and vice versa. With a few noteworthy exceptions, it appears that agencies which enjoy a high degree of external support do not enjoy a high degree of committee confidence, and vice versa. Decision patterns involving them will vary accordingly. Senate Committee decisions may reflect these same variables, too; although reaction to House decisions would likely be a complicating factor on that side of the Capitol. No one recognizes more clearly than the author the tenuous nature of these post facto explanations. The obvious need is for intensive research into the appropriations record of each of the 36 bureaus used in the text. It is hoped that the suggestions of this study will help guide subsequent research.

The overall pattern of House and Senate floor decisions (i.e., acceptance of committee recommendations) reflects the success with which each committee adapts to its parent chamber. To some degree that success is due to factors common to the two chambers. There is a general unwillingness on the part of chamber members to make regular, heavy investments in the business of amending committee recommendations — especially since there are so many appropriation bills each year and since the policy implications of dollars-and-cents language are usually not clear enough to excite people. There is a general willingness, on the other hand, of party leaders to support the committees' recommendations. And both committees (especially the House Committee) have fixed advantages in terms of procedure and timing. Similarly, lack of floor success may reflect some variable common to both houses, such as the existence of an economy mood or the partisan composition of Presidency and Congress.

Since, however, the decision-making processes and the committee–parent-chamber relationship differ from House to Senate, committee success on the floor will be explainable in terms of committee related factors. Of special importance is the relationship between internal integration and floor success for the House Committee. The proposition suggested by this single study is that in cases where there is a marked structural differentiation between the parent chamber and a congressional committee, the more highly integrated the committee, the more likely it is to succeed (have its recommendations adopted) on the chamber floor. Where structural differentiation is less marked (as it is in the Senate), no distinctive committee characteristic may be necessary except a continued willingness to respond (as by floor bargaining in the Senate) to the expectations of the parent chamber.

It might be noted, in addition, that the two variables which seem determinative of executive agency success with the House Committee also affect Committee success on the House floor. The presence or absence of external support, from legislative committees or party leaders, will affect the capacity of the Committee to hold its decisions on the floor. So too will the existence or nonexistence of House member confidence in the Committee's expertise, judgment, and responsiveness affect Committee success. This same trio of variables — unity, external support, confidence — appears to affect appropriations decision at every stage, from subcommittees inside the two committees through to their confrontation in conference. Future committee-centered research into "who gets what, and why?" in other policy areas might pay them special heed.

Two other variables which give some basic contours to the pattern of appropriations decisions but which do not depend upon this book's theory for their interpretation, are subject matter and sequence. The subject matter of appropriations makes it necessary that a certain number of appropriations requests be processed and become law. The question "who gets what?" can never be answered "nobody gets anything," lest the operations of the government come to a standstill. Most appropriations decisions are resolved in terms of "more or less" rather than "something or nothing." This fact not only

687

facilitates compromise (as pointed out in the discussion of integration), it necessitates compromise — most strikingly in conference committee. The most vital decisions for some committees may involve whether a bill shall be reported out or stopped altogether. Appropriations committees are not, save in rare instances, allowed such a choice.

A second variable which sets some outer limits to appropriations decisions is the sequence in which the chambers act. The fact that the House always acts first is probably the single most important fact in explaining the dominance of the House of Representatives (i.e., the House Committee) in setting the overall direction and magnitude of appropriations decisions. It is impossible to know how the substance of committee decisions would change if the Senate were to act first. At the least, the Senate would come to dominate appropriations decision-making; and at the most, a decrease in the conservative bias of appropriations decisions would result. For the majority of other pairs of congressional committees, the decision-making sequence will not be fixed. But the nature of the sequence may, nonetheless, have an important effect on the pattern of decisions in the policy area involved.

STABILITY

The elements of theory used in this book lead inevitably to questions about stability — the stability of the committees as political systems and the stability of congressional behavior in the policy field being examined through these committees. Estimates concerning the stability of observed relationships have been made throughout the book. As we have said, committee stability depends on the committee's ability to solve the problems of adaptation, decision-making, and integration. The stability of congressional behavior in a policy area will depend on committee stability and on the stability of factors beyond the control of the committees (such as the sequence in the case of appropriations). To the degree that committees are influential in a policy area, to that degree will the stability of these committees underwrite a stable policy-making process. Such is the case in the field of appropriations.

It is sometimes said of the elements of theory used in this study (i.e., the idea of a system, for example) that by posing the questions of stability so insistently, the researcher may be blinded to questions of change. In studying an on-going system, the assumption is easily made that all observed activity is helping to solve one or another of the system's survival problems. Hence all activity is necessary, all activity fits together, and instability seems nowhere in sight. If a system seems to be surviving, it must be solving its problems of adaptation, decision-making, and integration. And since all solutions to these problems involve the reduction or elimination of conflict, this particular vehicle of change may disappear from the equation. These reservations about system-oriented kinds of theory have a certain validity — more in terms of actual performance, however, than in terms of logic.

In terms of performance, an overemphasis on stability may be the natural result of a "turning inward" of congressional research. For a long time, research on Congress centered on the clash of interest groups, on their problem of access to the legislature, and on the conflict between contending alliances of interest groups plus sympathetic legislators. This body of research emphasized the response of Congress to those external forces which called upon it for action (or inaction). Group conflict was viewed as the engine of change. Students of Congress became wise in the ways of conflict and sensitive to the problem of change. By contrast, perhaps, concern for the internal workings of Congress leads to a preoccupation with the degree to which internal elements harmonize, with the ways in which the Congress holds itself together as an institution, and with its capacity as an institution to minimize conflict. A special sensitivity to problems of adaptation, integration, and stability may be a necessary sequel to the earlier emphasis on problems of group conflict, access and change.

Logically, there would seem to be no reason why theoretical notions such as those employed in this study should prevent the analysis of change. Every estimate of stability involves a converse estimate of instability. Every generalization about success in the solution of a survival problem contains a generalization about the lack of success. Provided only that the researcher is prepared to entertain the possibility of instability and change, he will find that the kinds of theory used here will provide him, at the very least, with a specification of those relationships where the potential for change is greatest. It may well be that in a relatively stable institution such as Congress, change can be recognized, charted, and measured only with the advantage of a lengthy time perspective. But shorter range analysis can identify for any political system and for the policy process involving that system the places where change is most likely to occur. And such identification will be of assistance to those who wish to understand or predict.

In the preceding study, estimates of stability have often been made by comparing, for each external or internal committee relationship, the normative expectations, images, and behavior of the people involved. The idea here has been simply that the relationship involved can be viewed as fairly stable where participants express an idea of what they or someone else should do, where they perceive that their expectations are being met, where they are satisfied with what they perceive, and where the analysis of behavior gives evidence that expectations are in fact being met or that expectations can be brought into harmony with behavior. On the other hand, where there is lack of congruence or difficulty in producing congruence within or between these elements, the relationship can be viewed as potentially unstable. Behavior

689

may follow expectations or expectations may follow behavior. The point is that so long as the two remain in disharmony, the relationship involved is unstable. Change, of course, can come about by alterations in expectations, images, or behavior. On the whole, a description of the Appropriations Committee and the appropriations process presents a picture of marked stability. Still, the points can be located where tension and conflict exist and, hence, where the potential for change is the greatest. Since the House Committee dominates appropriations politics in Congress, it is not surprising to find that all of the important points of instability involve that group. Moreover, if present instability produces future change, the result will almost certainly be a reduction in the influence of the House Committee. A few comments on the prospects for such a change might demonstrate how the theory of this book can focus attention on the questions of stability and change.

In terms of the size of the gap between expectations and behavior and in terms of the monetary stakes affected by that gap, the most serious conflict is the one which exists between the House Committee and the agencies of the executive branch. However, this conflict is not the most likely source of change. Sharp dispute between the branches is accepted as perfectly legitimate and, in addition, both parties have developed techniques for dampening any face-to-face conflicts. Furthermore, the executive agencies which feel most aggrieved do have a safety value in the Senate. Though they might, on occasion, want to reduce the influence of the House Committee over their fiscal fortunes, there is very little the executive agencies can do, by themselves, to accomplish such a change. However, should the House Committee fail conspicuously to make wise and informed decisions, the supporters of executive agencies could bring about changes in the appropriations process by operating through the legislature itself.

The Senate is, of course, in a position to affect appropriations politics directly, and its conflict with the House Committee is perhaps the second most obvious point of tension in the process. Given the lack of structural differentiation, it is correct to view the antagonists here as the Senate as a body and the House Committee on Appropriations. The conflict of 1962, during which the extent of Senate–House Committee conflict was revealed, also revealed the inability of the Senate to bring about change. By striking at the appropriations sequence, they struck at the procedural foundation of House Committee power, but to little avail. Despite their resentments over the status quo and despite their perennial proposals for change, Senators have stabilized their relationships with the House Committee. The necessity of producing a bill and the relatively small monetary stakes involved have promoted mutual adaptation in the conference room. And, most important of all, the fixed sequence has served to stabilize their expectations, images, and behavior. The House Committee follows a decision pattern that regularly anticipates Senate Committee action; Senate Committee decisions regularly take the form of reactions to prior House decisions. Their self-prescribed goals, as budget cutter or appeals court, take into account the order in which they act relative to one another. And each develops images of itself and of the other group that support its consistent decision patterns and its self-defined goals. Doubtless, these habits produce inertia, if not a reluctance to spend Senate resources in pressing for changes. To the extent, however, that Senators do push for changes, they, too, can do very little by themselves.

The one group which could combine both the desire and the authority to alter significantly the activity and influence of the House Committee is the House of Representatives itself. And it is the House that holds the key to change in the appropriations process. If the dissatisfactions of executive agencies and their supporters or the dissatisfactions of the Senate are to find their way into changed appropriations relationships, the result will be brought about by action taken against the House Committee by the parent chamber. Some underlying tensions in Committee-House relations have been described. Despite the persistence of conflict, however, there are reasons why the House has refused (since 1920) to make drastic changes in Committee operations. Specific disagreements tend to be occasional and piecemeal rather than constant and cumulative. The Committee does make strenuous efforts to meet House expectations. The House can and does apply sanctions against the Committee when conflict becomes serious. Furthermore, the Committee system is the cornerstone of the House's internal structure. An ill-advised attack on one committee might put the entire system in jeopardy.

In the last analysis, House action will probably be influenced by institutional considerations. Specifically, the House will not reduce the influence of its Appropriations Committee so long as it believes that a powerful Appropriations Committee is a necessary condition for a powerful House of Representatives. House leaders can be expected to be protective of their institution's place in the American political system. And they know that their control over the public purse is the kernel of the House's power as an institution. If and when House leaders move to curb the Committee, they will first have to be convinced that they can do so without hurting the House in the process. And Appropriations Committee members will surely work to convince them otherwise.

A last potential source of instability and change is the membership of the Committee itself. It has been repeated often that Committee activity must meet the expectations of its members at the same time that it meets the expectations of the parent chamber. And, on the whole, the Committee has succeeded in doing this. It has succeeded by adopting a certain kind of decision-making structure and by making certain kinds of decisions. Most important, perhaps, it has maintained a highly integrated committee internally — a committee whose unity in defense of its judgments discourages attacks, commands respect and support in the chamber, and at the same time brings influence to its members. The Committee's integrative norms, the socialization and sanctioning mechanisms used to bring about obedience to those norms, and Committee resistance in the face of disintegrating influences have produced marked stability inside the Committee. And this internal stability is in turn a fundamental source of stability in the appropriations process. It may even be that, despite their sometime antagonism toward "the powerful Appropriations Committee," House leaders will refrain from attacking it so long as — but only so long as — the Committee retains its signally high degree of internal integration.

These few brief sentences on the problems of stability and change involving the House Committee on Appropriations do not sum up to a prediction. No more than the rest of this Conclusion do they really conclude anything. But like the rest of the final section, the remarks about stability and change point to the kinds of questions that do get posed by the kinds of theory used in the book. And they indicate something of the kinds of answers one might expect. Where this study of appropriations politics finds stability, similar studies centered on other committees may find instability; where this study finds one kind of system-environment relationship, other studies will find a different one — and so on. The suggestion is made, however, that questions like those highlighted in the last few pages are important questions and that they stem logically from certain theoretical underpinnings. The entire book can be read as support for a final suggestion — that the kinds of questions raised by the kinds of theory used are *researchable* questions. If the analytical scheme presented here lacks the virtue of completeness, it would seem to possess the virtue of having a close tie with the empirical world of politics. If such a link does exist, others may see in this scheme a basis for undertaking the kind of research that will eventually produce generalizations about committee and congressional behavior. And, while the research goes forward, the analytical scheme can be revised, modified, and, perhaps, made whole. If any such results occur, this piece of research will have achieved its ultimate objective — the production of more research.

Index

Information
flow from House Committee to House, 71
House Committee collection of, 321-324
Inner-circle recruitment, 65
"Instruction" of House and Senate conferees, 624, 657-658
Interior and Insular Affairs Committee (House), 86, 119-120, 143
Interior Department, 142, 363-366, 368-369, 455, 458, 581, 582, 583, 587, 588, 590, 592, 604, 606, 615, 665-666
In-term selection, 64
Internal Revenue Service, 368, 392, 395, 473-474, 585, 586, 660

Jensen, Ben, 56, 142n., 144, 147, 474, 630n., 643
and John Taber, 253-258, 474
and Clarence Cannon, 254-256
Jensen rider, 117
Johnson, Lester, 495-496
Johnson, Lyndon, 523, 527
Johnson rule, 523
Joint Committee on the Budget, 521, 629-630
Joint Committee on the Organization of Congress, 629
Jones, Charles, xvii, 680n.
Justice Department, 363-366, 368-369, 455, 458, 582, 583, 588, 592, 604, 665
"Justification books," 134, 135, 323

Keefe, Frank, 385-386, 401, 407
Kelley, Harold, xxin., 128n.
Kerr, Robert, 644
Key, V. O., 13
Kilgore, Harley, 601
Kingdom, John, 459
Kirby, James C., Jr., 636n.
Kirwan, Michael, 88, 89-90, 474, 606
Knapp, David, 118n.

Labor Department, 140, 363-366, 368-369, 455, 458, 478-486, 582, 583, 584, 603, 604, 665
Laird, Melvin, 89, 234, 479
Langen, Odin, 64
Lanham, Henderson, 481, 483
Legislation on appropriation bills, 21-23, 35, 74, 116-118, 122, 270-271
Legislative budget, 24, 122
Legislative committees. See Substantive committees.
Legislative Reorganization Act of 1946, 4, 5, 6, 10, 24, 122, 417, 629
Lehman, Herbert, 612
Liberalism
and opposition to House Committee, 47-50
ratings, 48
Lindblom, Charles, 266n.
Long, Russell, 514

Maass, Arthur, 72n., 409n.
Macmahon, Arthur, xiv, 273n.
McClellan, John, 517, 521, 629
McCormack, John, 49, 52, 76
McEachern, Alexander, xxin.
McGee, Gale, 527
McKellar, Kenneth, 599-600
Mahon, George, 56, 100, 118, 121, 122, 135, 142, 144, 146, 147, 155, 430-432, 629, 643
and Clarence Cannon, 259-262
Maintenance expectations
agencies, 273-274
House, 20-29, 112-113
House Committee, 81, 112-124, 189
Senate, 506-512
Senate Committee, 540-541
Manley, John, 680n.
Mansfield, Mike, 523, 528
Markup session, 134, 135, 157, 158, 164, 182, 185, 186
House subcommittee, 171-176
Senate subcommittee, 549, 552-553
Marvick, Dwaine, xiv, 179n.
Mason, Ward, xxin.
Masters, Nicholas, xvii, 25, 52n.
Matthews, Billy, 594
Matthews, Donald R., xvii, 509n., 516, 529n.
Maxwell, Neal, 527n.
Merriam, Robert, 257
Merton, Robert, xviiin.
Michener, Earl, 535n.
Miller, Clem, 32n., 495
Miller, Warren, 58n.
Minority reports, 203-204, 221
Money decisions, 194-195
Morgan, Robert, 118n., 380n.
Morrow, William, 117n.
Morse, Wayne, 513, 515, 516, 517, 608

National Aeronautics and Space Administration, 71, 72ff., 120
National Bureau of Standards, 368, 384, 392, 395, 399, 412, 585, 586
National Park Service, 368, 384, 392, 395, 397-399, 412, 585, 586
Neustadt, Richard, 478n.
Newcomb, Theodore M., 128n.
Norm, defined, xxi, 128

Obligational authority, 7
O'Brien, Thomas, 61, 94, 496-498
Office of Education, 368, 384, 392, 395, 404-407, 412, 585, 586
Office of Vocational Rehabilitation, 368, 392, 395, 585, 586
O'Neil, Thomas, 50-51
Opposition to House Committee
in 1885, 43-44
in 1920, 45-46
and liberalism, 47-50
Otten, Allen, 16n.

702